Visual Basic .NET Programming

Visual Basic® .NET Programming

Harold Davis

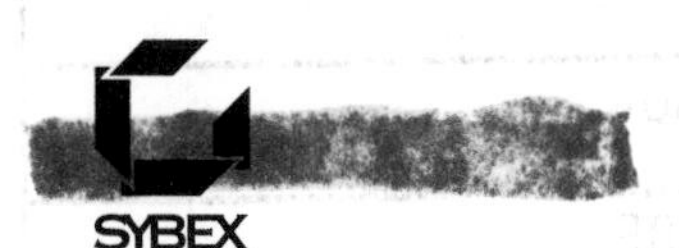

San Francisco · London

Associate Publisher: Richard Mills
Acquisitions and Developmental Editor: Denise Santoro Lincoln
Editor: Marilyn Smith
Production Editor: Mae Lum
Technical Editor: Scott Swigart
Graphic Illustrator: Tony Jonick
Electronic Publishing Specialist: Judy Fung
Proofreaders: Nancy Riddiough, Nelson Kim, David Nash, Nanette Duffy
Indexer: Jerilyn Sproston
Cover Designer: Caryl Gorska, Gorska Design
Cover Photographer: Jon Morgan/Photo Japan

Library of Congress Card Number: 2002101977

ISBN: 0-7821-4038-6

Manufactured in the United States of America

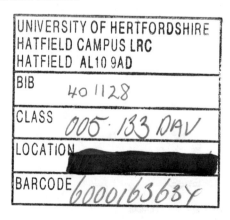

10 9 8 7 6 5 4 3 2 1

For my parents, Martin and Virginia

Acknowledgements

It takes a village, they say, to raise a child. Undoubtedly, it takes a team to create a book like this. Without the wonderful people at Sybex, this book wouldn't exist. Richard Mills and Denise Santoro Lincoln originated this project and brought me into it. Denise got the book off the ground and moved it from conception through toddlerhood. Mae Lum masterfully handled the logistics, as the book became a full-fledged project. Scott Swigart technically reviewed my manuscript with a great and rare attention to detail. His technical understanding of .NET has greatly enriched this book. Marilyn Smith copyedited this book and has substantially helped to make it something we can all be proud of.

I would also like to thank the Sybex production team, including graphic illustrator Tony Jonick; electronic publishing specialist Judy Fung; proofreaders Nancy Riddiough, Nelson Kim, David Nash, and Nanette Duffy; and indexer Jerilyn Sproston.

In addition to team Sybex, I would like to thank my friend and agent, Matt Wagner, and Bill Gladstone, both of Waterside Productions. Without them, this book wouldn't exist. John Kilcullen and Stephen Compagni Portis also indirectly contributed to this book's genesis.

Finally, I need to thank my wife, Phyllis Davis, who is once again a major contributor to a book of mine. Phyllis and my children, Julian and Nicholas, provided the inspiration, space, and motivation that made this book possible.

Contents at a Glance

Contents

Introduction

At first, .NET was no more than a distant echo in my consciousness. For a long time—it seems like years, and actually, it was years—I heard the distant beating of publicity drums regarding .NET, and I couldn't care less. My concern has always been to work with high-quality programming tools that are solid, rather than playing with the latest technology toy, and I am ever suspicious of publicity campaigns. Visual Basic 6 worked well enough for me, my consulting clients, and the readers of my books. Why should I bother taking the time to understand this .NET thing until it was tried-and-true technology?

What's the .NET Strategy?

Before we get to my "Aha!" moment—and I've had several epiphanies related to .NET and Visual Basic .NET—I would like to step back for a second and consider exactly what .NET is and what it is not. This is particularly confusing because some things that Microsoft calls .NET are a matter of "vision," some are marketing terms, and others—such as Visual Basic .NET—are grounded technologies that are here today. (I mean, what could be more grounded as a technology than a programming language?)

Pushing aside the clouds of confusion that swirl around the terminology, Microsoft's .NET strategy involves three related offerings:

- .NET Framework and Visual Studio .NET, a runtime platform and development environment that works with languages including Visual Basic .NET
- .NET Enterprise Servers, a set of enterprise server products such as Biztalk Server, Exchange Server, Mobile Information Server, and SQL Server, which happen to have been given the .NET moniker for marketing purposes
- .NET MyServices, also sometimes called Hailstorm, which is a vision for creating services, such as the Passport user authentication service, that can be drawn upon as utilities by myriad distributed applications

The domain of this book is the first of these: applications written in the Visual Basic .NET language, using the Visual Studio development environment, targeting the .NET Framework as a runtime platform. You can think of the runtime platform that .NET applications are written for as being analogous to the Java runtime "sandbox" that Java applications target, except that, at this point, the .NET Framework is primarily deployed on Microsoft Windows platforms.

What's Special about Visual Basic .NET?

So, what is so exciting about another programming language and another development environment, targeting another runtime? In some ways, the proof of this is "in the pudding"—you really need to take it for a test drive and find out for yourself. In the meantime, I would like to share with you a few of the features that made me sit up and take notice.

The first thing that I found extraordinary was that Windows applications could be run within Internet Explorer. (There are some caveats here, of course: The target system needs to have the .NET Framework and a recent version of Internet Explorer installed.) Every time you successfully run a program, such as a Windows application, within the Visual Studio .NET development environment, a compiled executable is created. If you open this executable file in Internet Explorer, the application will run, looking and behaving for all the world like a normal Windows application. This creates the possibility of easily producing distributed applications with an extraordinarily rich user interface, and the user doesn't need to do anything more than click a hyperlink (Microsoft terms this *no-touch deployment*).

My next epiphany was related to a slightly silly programming wish. It has always bugged me that application windows had to be rectangular. No more! In Chapter 6, "Working with Form Methods and Modules," I'll show you how to easily create an ovoid window. You may never create an application that uses a curvilinear interface, but what a relief to know that windows don't have to be square!

I also found it very exciting that Visual Basic .NET allows you to create web applications using an event-driven programming model (rather than a top-to-bottom linear HTML model). And rolling your own web services, complete with XML definition and discovery files, is a matter of clicking a few buttons. In Chapter 19, "Building ASP.NET Web Applications," I'll explain the mechanics of creating web applications and web services.

What Kind of Book Is This?

The features I've mentioned, and many more features that are explained in this book, sound glitzy. But this book has its two, solid, peasant feet firmly planted on the ground. It is not a "gee-golly-whizz, isn't this technology wonderful" book. It is a matter-of-fact, here's how you do it kind of book.

As author to reader, my pledge to you is that I do not tell you to do anything I haven't tried to do (and got to work). Every example, and every line of code, in this book is the result of my own (sometimes fluid and easy, sometimes desperate) attempts to get things to work. I believe this makes me a better guide for you than if I were some kind of programming superhero. It's not my job to show you that I know more than you do. It is my job to help you find your way. I am there with you, swerving to avoid the pitfalls, one step ahead, shining a flashlight in the dark. I know what you are likely to want to know, because I have been there, done that, and have been as blind as you. I know that everything in this book works, because I have made it work myself.

This book is not a book about how to transition from Visual Basic 6 to Visual Basic .NET, and it is not a book about the future. It is a book about the present. Visual Basic .NET is now, and this book is a pragmatic guide to working with it.

Who Should Read This Book?

This book does not assume any formal programming knowledge on the part of readers. I do assume that, as a minimum, you are the kind of power user who knows your way around Microsoft Windows, has a basic grasp of HTML, and may have written a script or two. If you are a professional or advanced-level programmer, this book will get you started with the fundamentals of .NET. If you are already experienced with .NET, this book may not be for you.

This book is intended for readers who answer affirmatively to any of these questions:

Have you always wanted to learn to program? If you want to learn to program, I believe that Visual Basic .NET is the best and easiest language to use. This book is here to help you learn in a step-by-step, painless, and fun fashion.

Are you curious about the latest "new, new thing" in programming, .NET? If you want to understand the nuts and bolts of programming using the .NET Framework, you'll find that information in this book.

Do you have some experience with an earlier version of Visual Basic, such as version 6? If so, this book will help you leverage your knowledge so that you can start creating powerful Visual Basic .NET applications right away.

Are you a beginning or intermediate-level developer looking for a focused, task-based reference guide to Visual Basic .NET? If so, this book is for you. You can use it to quickly achieve tasks by following the steps described in the book.

I am very, very excited about Visual Basic .NET as a beautiful and powerful programming environment. I hope that excitement is conveyed in this book, and that you find it interesting and useful, no matter what your programming level is.

How to Download the Code

Most of the code samples in this book are not very long, since they emphasize the principles of how to do something rather than full implementation details or production software. I encourage you to follow the examples in this book by re-creating the objects in the projects and by using your keyboard to enter the source code. You will learn the most by doing this!

Alternatively, you can download projects containing the source code used in this book. (One reason to do so is for comparison if the code you entered manually doesn't work.) Sybex has published all the code used in this book on their website at `http://www.sybex.com/`. Search for this book (using the title, author, or the ISBN number 4038), and click the Downloads button. Once you have accepted the license agreement, you'll be able to download any of the code listed in this book, organized in zipped projects by chapter.

How to Contact the Author

I've made every effort to make this book as useful and accurate as possible. Please let me know what you think. I would love to hear from you. I have set up a special e-mail address for this book: `vbnet@bearhome.com`. I would greatly appreciate any suggestions or information about problems that you have with the text.

I hope you enjoy this book. Visual Basic .NET is a wonderful, exciting, easy-to-use programming language. The goal of my book is to help you get up and running with it quickly and productively.

Chapter 1

Understanding Visual Basic .NET

- The .NET Framework
- The .NET languages
- Command-line compilation
- Visual Studio .NET requirements

This chapter explains important background material related to Visual Basic .NET (VB .NET). If you are the hasty type and want to dive right into programming, there's no need to start with this chapter. (Although you may want to check the "Visual Studio .NET Requirements" section at the end of the chapter, to make sure you have all the tools you need.) You can skip right over it and go on to Chapter 2, "Introducing Projects, Forms, and Buttons." (The sample project in the "For the Very First Time" section of Chapter 2 will get you up and running with a Windows program in the blink of an eye.) As you go on with VB .NET, understanding some of the concepts behind it will become important. You can then come back to this chapter for a dose of background information.

On the other hand, if you prefer to have your ducks in a row before you get to programming with VB .NET, you can start right here. Armed with the conceptual understanding provided in this chapter, you should be able to make good progress as a VB .NET programmer.

The chapter includes an important preliminary topic: command-line compilation. You would probably be pretty foolish to try to create Windows or web programs outside the world-class Visual Studio integrated development environment (IDE). But it's important to know that you can, and that Visual Studio, which is used throughout the rest of this book, is optional. You should clearly understand that VB .NET (the language) is complementary but not identical to Visual Studio .NET (the IDE).

What Is .NET?

The term *.NET* is somewhat confusing because it is commonly used in a variety of contexts. Some of these contexts are mostly marketing in nature, rather than the kind of precise language needed when attempting to understand technology. Here are some of the ways in which .NET has been used:

- To mean the .NET Framework, a runtime platform and programming framework largely consisting of class libraries
- To include Visual Studio .NET, a professional IDE optimized for working with .NET Framework languages, including VB .NET and C# .NET
- To refer to .NET Enterprise Servers, a set of enterprise server products such as Biztalk Server, Exchange Server, Mobile Information Server, and SQL Server, which have been given the .NET moniker for marketing purposes
- To describe .NET My Services, also sometimes called Hailstorm, which is a vision for creating services—such as lists, contacts, schedule information, and more—that can be accessed in a platform- and language-independent way

This book is mostly concerned with the first two of these meanings: the .NET Framework and Visual Studio .NET. The focus in this chapter is understanding the .NET Framework.

The .NET Framework

The .NET Framework consists of two main parts:

- The Common Language Runtime (CLR), which is a platform that manages code execution (discussed in detail in the next section)
- The .NET Framework class libraries

The relationship of the two parts of the .NET Framework to the operating platform and to Visual Studio .NET is shown in Figure 1.1.

FIGURE 1.1: The two parts of the .NET Framework have different functions: the Framework class libraries are used to build applications, and the CLR layers on top of the operating system manage execution of a program.

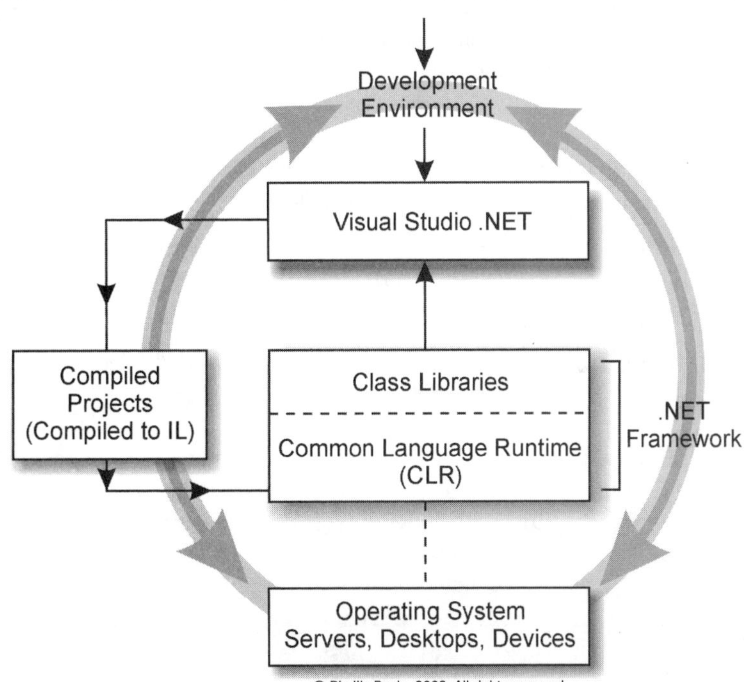

As you'll see in the "Using a Text Editor to Create VB .NET Programs" section later in this chapter, it's possible to create, compile, and run VB .NET programs without using Visual Studio .NET. However, as programs get more complex, this quickly becomes cumbersome. Except for the one example in this chapter, this book will show you how to create VB .NET applications using Visual Studio, because it's the simplest way to go most of the time. But it's important that you be aware that Visual Studio is not integral to the definition of the .NET Framework.

The .NET Framework Base Class Library is a large set of types, classes, and interfaces that form the basis, or blueprint, for objects that can be used programmatically to create applications, including Windows forms, web forms, and web services applications. The .NET Framework types form the basis for building .NET applications, components, and controls. .NET Framework types perform many functions, such as representing value types for variables, performing input-output (I/O) operations, and providing data access. An example of a value type that is probably familiar to most programmers is the Integer, which in the .NET Framework is called an Int32 and used to type values that contain a signed 32-bit integer number.

NOTE The .NET languages are interoperable, which means that one language can use class libraries in another. For example, a VB .NET program can use a class developed in C# .NET, or vice versa. To ensure this interoperability, the .NET Framework types are compliant with the Common Language Specification (CLS). They can be used by any language that conforms to the CLS.

The .NET Framework uses a dot operator (`.`) syntax to designate hierarchies. Related types are grouped into namespaces, so that they can be more easily found. (See the "Namespaces" section later in this chapter for more details.)

Reading left to right, the first part of a type, up to the first dot, is the namespace name. The last part of the name, to the right of the final period, is the type name. For example `System.Boolean` designates a Boolean value-type in the `System` namespace. `System.Windows.Forms.MessageBox` designates the MessageBox class with the `Forms` namespace, which is part of the `Windows` namespace, which is part of `System`.

TIP When you are referring to a member of the `System` namespace, you can usually leave off `System`. So, for example, the variable declaration `Dim IsEmployee As Boolean` is the equivalent of `Dim IsEmployee As System.Boolean`.

As these examples suggest, the `System` namespace is the root namespace for all types within the .NET Framework. All base data types used by all applications are included in the `System` namespace or the `Microsoft` namespace.

One of the most important types within the `System` namespace is `System.Object`. `System.Object`, also called the Object class. The Object class is the root of the .NET type hierarchy and the ultimate parent (or *superclass*) of all classes in the .NET Framework. This implies that the members of the Object class—such as `GetType()` and `ToString()`— are contained in all .NET classes.

NOTE Don't let this talk of objects, types, classes, and hierarchies throw you! It all works out in a fairly intuitive way once you start programming. But if you want to jump ahead, the Object Browser, the best tool for learning about class hierarchies, is explained in Chapter 14, "Using the Object Browser." Object-oriented programming concepts, including some of the terminology used in this section, are explained and further defined in Chapter 15, "Object-Oriented Programming in VB .NET."

The Common Language Runtime (CLR)

The CLR manages execution of compiled .NET programs. The role of the CLR is comparable to Sun's Java Virtual Machine (JVM) and the VB runtime library that shipped with older versions of VB.

The CLR is a runtime for all .NET languages. Its job is to execute and manage all code written in any language that has targeted the .NET platform.

When you write an application in .NET, you can choose from a number of languages. Primarily these are VB and C# (pronounced "see sharp"). You can also build .NET applications using languages such as COBOL, Eiffel, Pascal, and even Java. Each of these languages will include its own compiler, written by third parties. However, instead of compiling into machine code, as compilers typically do, the language-specific just-in-time (JIT) compiler translates the code (whether it is VB, C#, or any other language) into another language called Microsoft Intermediate Language (MSIL, or even just IL for short). The IL is what you actually deploy and execute.

Upon execution, the CLR uses another compiler to turn the IL into machine code that is specific to the platform where it's running. In other words, the CLR may compile the IL into one thing on a machine that runs on an AMD processor and into something else on a machine with a Pentium processor.

TIP Intermediate Language (IL) is, in fact, fairly easy to read and understand. You'll find that documentation for doing this is part of the .NET Framework Software Development Kit (SDK). In addition, you may find it interesting to know about a program named `ILDasm.exe`, which ships with the .NET framework. ILDasm is an Intermediate Language disassembler. You can run any .NET compiled program through ILDasm, including important parts of the .NET Framework itself. ILDasm will output the IL code that has been created, along with other information, including namespaces, types, and interfaces used.

The CLR handles, or manages, some other very important aspects of the life of a program:

Type, version, and dependency information .NET compilers produce not only IL, but also metadata that describes the types contained within an EXE or DLL and version and dependency information. This means that the CLR can resolve references between application files at runtime. In addition, the Windows system Registry is no longer needed for keeping track of programs and components. One way of thinking of the CLR is as an object-oriented replacement for the Win32 Application Programming Interface (API) and Component Object Model (COM, used for component interoperability). Placing the CLR as a kind of abstraction layer on top of Windows has neatly solved a great many of the technical problems with Windows programming. This approach has worked to the benefit of VB programmers, since much of the Win32 functionality was not available to us. All of the functionality of the CLR and its class libraries are exposed as objects and classes, whose methods can be used in your programs.

Garbage collection *Garbage collection* means that memory is automatically managed. You instantiate and use objects, but you do not explicitly destroy them. The CLR takes care of releasing the memory used by objects when they are no longer referenced or used. It is understandable that some programmers like to manage memory themselves, but this practice, particularly in large team projects, inevitably produces memory leaks. The CLR's automatic garbage collection solves the problem of memory leaks.

NOTE There is no way to determine when the CLR will release unused memory. In other words, you do not know when an object will be destroyed (also called *nondeterministic* finalization). To say the same thing in yet another way, just because there are no more in-scope references to an object, you cannot assume that it has been destroyed. Therefore, you cannot place code in an object's destructor and expect deterministic execution of the code.

Code verification Code verification is a process that takes place before a program is executed. It is designed to ensure that a program is safe to run and does not perform an illegal operation, such as dividing by zero or accessing an invalid memory location. If the program does include code that does something naughty, the CLR intercepts the flawed commands and throws an exception before any harm can be done.

Code-access security Code-access security lets you set very granular permissions for an application based on "evidence." For example, you can configure an application that is installed on the local machine to access local resources such as the filesystem, Registry, and so on. However, the same application, if run from the intranet, can be denied those permissions. If it tries to perform an operation for which it does not have permissions, the CLR will prevent the operation.

Managed Code

The first step in the managed-code process is to compile a .NET project to IL, which also generates the required metadata. At execution, a JIT compiler translates the IL code to native machine code. During this translation process, the code is also verified as safe. This verification process checks for the following:

- Any reference to a type is strictly compatible with the type.
- Only appropriately defined operations are performed on an object.
- Identities are what they claim to be.
- IL code is well-formed.
- Code can access memory locations and call methods only through properly defined types.

If a program fails this verification process, an exception is thrown and execution is halted. Otherwise, the CLR provides the infrastructure that actually executes the native code.

The managed-execution processes, and services provided by the CLR such as memory garbage collection, are collectively referred to as *managed code*.

Programming in the .NET Framework

Fundamentally, programming in the .NET Framework means making use of the classes, objects, and members exposed by the Framework, building your own classes on top of these, and manipulating the resulting objects using familiar programming language and syntax. (If you are unfamiliar with programming languages altogether, don't worry—starting in Chapter 2, each step will be explained as we go along.)

NOTE One of the goals of the .NET Framework is to make programming more standardized across languages. Thus, you can create and use objects based on the same classes, whether you are programming in VB .NET, C# .NET, or Managed C++.

This section explains some of the key building blocks and concepts of the .NET Framework that will be helpful for you to understand as you begin creating VB .NET programs: assemblies, namespaces, and objects.

Assemblies

Assemblies are the fundamental unit for deployment, version control, security, and more for a .NET application. Every time you build an executable (EXE) or a library (DLL) file in .NET, you are creating an assembly. An assembly contains the information about an application that used to be stored in a type library file in previous versions of VB, and you use the contents of assemblies and add references to them much as you would manage a type library.

The Assembly Manifest

When you start a new VB project, it is the basis of an assembly. Within each built assembly is a manifest, which is part of the executable or library. In VB .NET, some of the general manifest information is contained in a file that is part of the project named `AssemblyInfo.vb`. Figure 1.2 shows a small project in the Visual Studio Solution Explorer with `AssemblyInfo.vb` selected, and Figure 1.3 shows the contents of a sample `AssemblyInfo.vb` file when opened with the Visual Studio editor.

TIP To open the `AssemblyInfo.vb` module, double-click it within the Solution Explorer. Using the Solution Explorer is covered in Chapter 2.

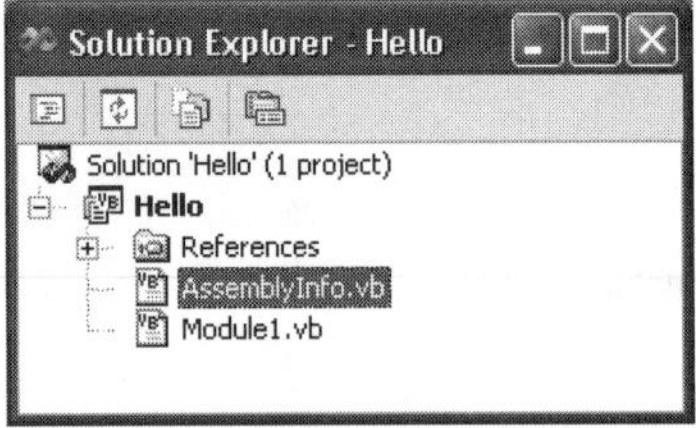

FIGURE 1.2: Each VB .NET project includes a file that is the assembly manifest.

FIGURE 1.3: The assembly manifest contains information about content, version, and dependencies, so that VB .NET applications do not depend on Registry values to function properly.

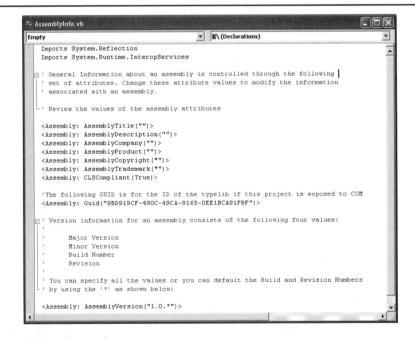

AssemblyInfo.vb

Empty | (Declarations)

```
Imports System.Reflection
Imports System.Runtime.InteropServices

' General Information about an assembly is controlled through the following
' set of attributes. Change these attribute values to modify the information
' associated with an assembly.

' Review the values of the assembly attributes

<Assembly: AssemblyTitle("")>
<Assembly: AssemblyDescription("")>
<Assembly: AssemblyCompany("")>
<Assembly: AssemblyProduct("")>
<Assembly: AssemblyCopyright("")>
<Assembly: AssemblyTrademark("")>
<Assembly: CLSCompliant(True)>

'The following GUID is for the ID of the typelib if this project is exposed to COM
<Assembly: Guid("9BD919CF-490C-49CA-9165-0EE1BCA91F8F")>

' Version information for an assembly consists of the following four values:
'
'      Major Version
'      Minor Version
'      Build Number
'      Revision
'
' You can specify all the values or you can default the Build and Revision Numbers
' by using the '*' as shown below:

<Assembly: AssemblyVersion("1.0.*")>
```

The assembly manifest can be thought of as a table of contents for an application. It includes the following information:

- The assembly's name and version number
- A file table listing and describing the files that make up the assembly
- An assembly reference list, which is a catalog of external dependencies

The external dependencies in the assembly reference list may be library files created by someone else, and likely some of them are part of the .NET Framework.

Assembly References

To use an assembly, or an object within an assembly, it must be referenced in your project. Depending on the type of project, you'll find that many of the assemblies that are part of the .NET Framework are referenced by default.

Different project types have different default references. The references that come "out-of-the-box" for a Windows forms project are not the same as those for a web forms project, although both do reference certain important .NET assemblies such as `System.dll`.

You can see which assemblies are already referenced in a project by expanding the References node in the Solution Explorer, as shown in Figure 1.4.

FIGURE 1.4: You can view the references in a project in the Solution Explorer.

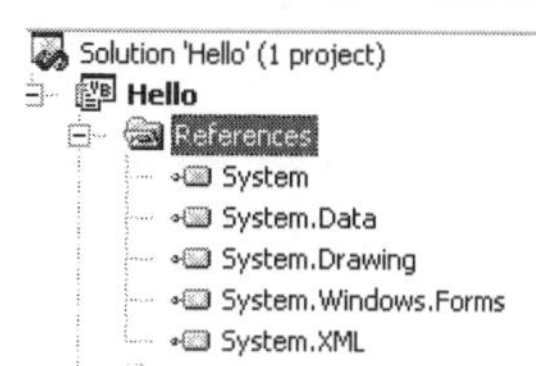

If you need to reference an assembly that is not already included in your project, follow these steps:

1. Open the Visual Studio Project menu and click Add Reference (select Project ➢ Add Reference). The Add Reference dialog will open, as shown in Figure 1.5.
2. Click the Browse button in the upper-right corner of the Add Reference dialog. The Select Component dialog will open.
3. Locate the assembly to be added and click Open. The assembly will be added to the Selected Components panel of the Add Reference dialog.
4. Click OK to add the reference to your project.

FIGURE 1.5:

The Add Reference dialog is used to add a reference to a project.

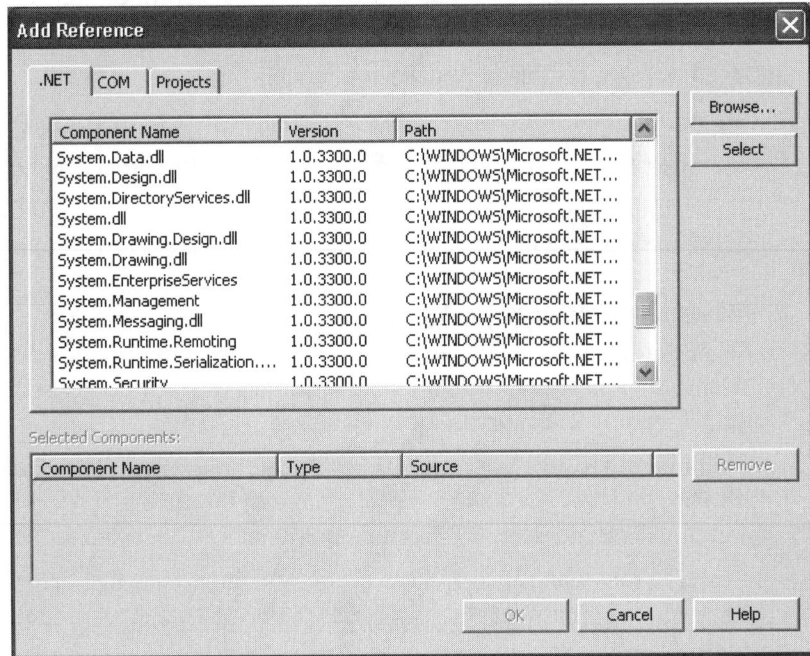

Once a reference to an assembly has been added to a project, you'll need to reference an item you want to use using the namespace it is in. You'll find more information about working with references in Chapter 15, "Object-Oriented Programming in VB .NET."

Namespaces

Namespaces are used to organize the objects (such as classes) within an assembly. Assemblies can contain many namespaces, which, in turn, can contain other namespaces. Namespaces are used to make it easier to refer to items, to avoid ambiguity, and to simplify references when large groups of objects are involved (for example, in a class library).

By default, every executable file you create in VB .NET contains a namespace with the same name as your project, although you can change this default name.

You should also know that namespaces can span multiple assemblies. In other words, if two assemblies both define classes within a namespace `myspace`, then the `myspace` namespace is treated as a single set of names.

Namespace References

There are several ways to refer to an item within a namespace once the assembly containing the item you are interested in has been referenced. You can use the *fully qualified* name of the item, as in this example:

```
Dim myBox As New System.Windows.Forms.TextBox
```

Alternatively, you can place an `Imports` statement at the beginning of a code module, as shown here:

```
Imports System.Windows.Forms
```

After you add an `Imports` statement, all of the names in the imported namespace can be used (provided they are unique to your project), like this:

```
Dim myBox As New TextBox
```

Important VB .NET Namespaces

Table 1.1 lists some of the namespaces that are important to VB .NET developers. For more information about creating and using namespaces, see Chapter 15.

TABLE 1.1: Selected .NET Framework Namespaces

Namespace	Description
`Microsoft.VisualBasic`	Contains the runtime used with the VB .NET language, as well as classes that support VB .NET compilation and code generation
`System`	Contains fundamental classes that define types, events, event handlers, interfaces, data-type conversion, mathematics, and much more
`System.Collections`	Includes a set of classes that lets you manage collections of objects
`System.Data`	Includes the classes that comprise the ADO.NET architecture
`System.Diagnostics`	Provides classes used for debugging, tracing, and interacting with system processes, event logs, and performance counters
`System.Drawing`	Provides access to GDI+ basic graphics functionality (namespaces hierarchically beneath `System.Drawing`—including `System.Drawing.Drawing2D` and `System.Drawing.Text`—provide more advanced and specific GDI+ graphics functionality)
`System.IO`	Contains types used for reading and writing to data streams and files
`System.Reflection`	Contains classes and interfaces that provide type inspection and the ability to dynamically bind objects
`System.Web`	Contains the classes that are used to facilitate browser-server communication and other web-related functionality
`System.Web.Services`	Contains the classes used to build and consume web services
`System.Windows.Forms`	Contains the classes for creating a Windows-based user interface
`System.XML`	Provides support for processing XML

Objects and Classes

It's important to understand the distinction between objects and classes. An *object* is a unit of code and data created using a *class* as its blueprint. Each object in VB .NET is defined by a class, which specifies the properties, methods, and events—collectively referred to as *members*—of the objects based on the class.

Objects, which can themselves contain other objects, are manipulated by the following:

- Setting and retrieving property values
- Invoking object methods
- Executing code when an object event has occurred

Once you have defined the class, you can create as many objects as you need based on the class. The process of creating an object based on a class is called *instantiation*.

A metaphor that is often used is that of cookie cutters and cookies. The cookie cutter is the class, and it defines the characteristics of the cookie, such as its size and shape. Each cookie is an object based on the cookie-cutter class.

Each object, which is called an *instance* of a class, is identical to other objects based on the same class when it is created. Once objects exist, they will likely be loaded with different values than other instances of the same class. The class might specify that each Employee object has Name and Salary properties. Once the Employee objects are instantiated, each will probably have a distinct name and may have a different salary.

The controls in the Toolbox in VB .NET are representations of classes. When a control is dragged from the Toolbox to a form, an object that is an instance of the control class is created. (See Chapter 2 and Chapter 7, "Working with Windows Form Controls," for information about working with the Toolbox.)

A form, which represents an application window that you work with at design time, is a class. When you run the project containing the form, VB .NET creates an instance of the form's class. (The following chapters explain the use of Windows forms in detail.)

When one class inherits from another class—which can be done in code using the `Inherits` keyword or, in some circumstances, by using visual inheritance—the blueprint for the members of the parent class is now transferred and becomes the blueprint for the members of the newly created child class. With this inherited blueprint as a starting place, the members of the class can be extended and changed, and new members can be added. As I mentioned earlier in this chapter, the `System.Object` class is the ancestor, or *superparent*, of almost all classes you will use in VB .NET.

Programming in VB .NET is an exercise in the use of objects and classes, so you will find information about them and how to work with them in every chapter of this book. For information about the theory and background of object-oriented programming, see Chapter 15.

The .NET Languages

Visual Studio .NET is specifically designed to help programmers develop applications in VB .NET, C# .NET, and C++. VB .NET and C++ are the next generation of languages that have been in use for years. C# .NET is an entirely new language developed for .NET. Since much of the .NET Framework is written in C#, it is in some sense the "native" language of .NET.

NOTE Programs written in VB .NET and C# .NET produce CLR-managed code. (An exception to this is if an old-style COM component is added to a project.) Programs written in C++ produce unmanaged code, unless the C++ Managed Extensions are used (by selecting a Managed C++ project type).

In addition to these three core development languages, it is expected that programmers will use Visual Studio for working with ancillary language tools, including the following:

HTML The ASP web forms editor provides excellent Hypertext Markup Language (HTML) support. See Chapter 19, "ASP.NET Web Applications" for details.

JScript JScript is essentially JavaScript and is used in web applications (see Chapter 19 for an example) and for some kinds of application customization.

SQL Structured Query Language (SQL) is used for interacting with databases. Visual Studio provides tools for automatically generating SQL, as explained in Chapter 17, "Working with Data and ADO.NET."

XML eXtensible Markup Language (XML) is used to describe structured data, and .NET uses XML as a primary technology for interoperability. See Chapter 18, "Working with XML in VB .NET," for details.

Upcoming .NET Languages

A number of third parties (companies other than Microsoft) are creating CLS-compliant versions of languages that target the CLR and the .NET platform. Time will tell whether any of these other languages—which range from research languages to products intended for commercial development—gain any traction. However, the very existence of these languages speaks to the scope of the ambition of the .NET platform. .NET languages in the works include the following:

- APL
- COBOL
- Eiffel#
- FORTRAN
- Mondrian

- Oberon
- Perl
- Python
- Smalltalk

From VB6 to VB .NET

Some VB users will feel that VB .NET is so different from Visual Basic version 6 (VB6) that it counts as an entirely new language. There is some truth to this, because many things have changed. But another way of looking at the transition to VB .NET is that you can go on writing VB code in very much the way you always have.

TIP In order to make it easier for VB6 programmers, Microsoft has provided a whole special set of classes in the `Microsoft.VisualBasic.Compatability.VB6` namespace.

Readers who are new to VB need not worry about how VB .NET differs from its predecessors. They will find an intuitive, easy-to-use, robust language that is fully object-oriented (as explained in Chapter 15). The language can be strongly typed, which is the best programming practice, or perform implicit type conversions, if you prefer. VB .NET is a true peer to the other .NET languages; there's really no reason to choose VB over C#, or vice versa, other than personal preference.

The CLR/.NET Framework is a comparable mechanism to the JVM, although undoubtedly, the extent to which .NET is deployed on platforms other than Windows will be limited by technology and industry politics.

If you are a VB6 programmer interested in migrating applications from VB6 to VB .NET, you'll find some useful information in Appendix B, "Migrating Applications from VB6 to VB .NET." You'll also find information about some of the language differences between VB6 and VB .NET in Appendix C, "Key Syntax Differences Between VB6 and VB .NET."

The History of Visual Basic

The BASIC (Beginner's All-Purpose Symbolic Instruction Code) programming language was invented in the early 1960s by two Dartmouth College professors, John G. Kemeny and Thomas Kurtz. They wanted to create a language that was good for teaching computer programming, and they succeeded wildly in meeting that goal.

From its earliest years, BASIC was very easy to understand because it is English-like and unstructured—meaning not too fussy about how you organize programs and how you type variables. (Of course, this is no longer true about VB .NET!)

Continued on next page

A trade-off for this ease of use was speed of execution. Early versions of BASIC were slow because they were interpreted (translated into machine code on the fly), rather than compiled (run as a stand-alone program that has already been converted to machine code). The current incarnation, VB .NET, is really "neither fish nor fowl" in this respect, since it is just-in-time compiled, but its performance characteristics are really quite good.

Microsoft has a long history of commitment to BASIC (and the languages that descended from BASIC). In the 1980s, Microsoft shipped various versions of the BASIC language, such as QuickBasic (shipped in 1982) and QBasic, part of the MS-DOS 6 product.

In the early 1990s, as Microsoft Windows appeared on the scene, a visual version of BASIC, Visual Basic 1.0, was created, leaning heavily on the concepts originated by interface designer Alan Cooper, who has been called the father of Visual Basic (VB). VB added an intuitive visual framework for creating an application's interface and a straightforward mechanism for responding to events to the easy-to-use, unfussy underlying BASIC language.

Possibly on the principle that "anything this easy can't really be good," VB got a reputation as the Rodney Dangerfield of languages—a toy development environment, not really suitable for serious work, and not worthy of respect. VB programmers responded by pointing out how much more productive they were using their "toy" language than their hardcore cousins.

By the late 1990s, millions of programmers were using VB, now VB6, more than any other language. However, its future had become murky. Java, a new language written from the ground up under the sponsorship of Sun Microsystems, was gaining currency as truly object-oriented and cross-platform (provided the platform had a Java Virtual Machine). And the relationship between C++ programmers and VB programmers had settled into a situation in which C++ programmers wrote the heavy-lifting components and VB coders wrote the user interfaces that connected to the C++ components. As the time lengthened since the last release of VB (VB6 came out at the end of 1997), the future of VB became uncertain. VB .NET is the answer to these concerns.

Using a Text Editor to Create VB .NET Programs

As I've mentioned earlier in this chapter, it's important to understand that the VB .NET language is distinct from the Visual Studio .NET development environment. Visual Studio happens to be by far the best and easiest way to create VB .NET programs. I can't really imagine anyone trying to develop a complex Windows application using Notepad, but, in theory, it could be done, and that is the point.

In this section, you'll see how to create a simple VB .NET application using Notepad. Before we get started, you should know about *console applications*. Console applications typically have no user interface other than printed text on the screen. They are run from a command line, with input and output information being exchanged between the command prompt and the running application.

TIP You can create a console application from within VB .NET by selecting Console Application as the project type from the New Project dialog.

As an example, we'll use Notepad to create a VB .NET program that prints "Hello, World!" to the screen and pauses. Next, we'll compile using the VB .NET command-line compiler, `vbc.exe`. Finally, we'll run the program in the console window.

Creating a VB .NET Program in Notepad

To create our sample program, open Notepad. Type in the program shown in Listing 1.1.

Listing 1.1 A "Hello, World!" Console Application

```
Module Module1
   Sub Main()
      System.Console.WriteLine("Hello, World! ")
      System.Console.Read()
   End Sub
End Module
```

When you're finished, save the file as `console.txt`, as shown in Figure 1.6.

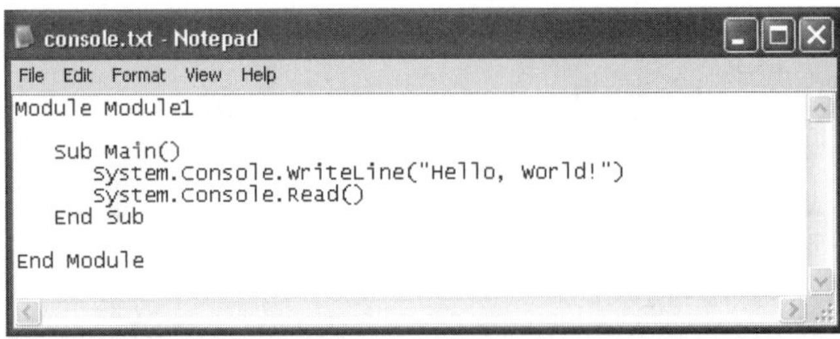

FIGURE 1.6: The code to be compiled is saved as a Notepad text file.

Let's take a look at some of the individual lines in Listing 1.1. The first line names the module:

```
Module Module1
```

The module is named `Module1`, but could instead be named anything you like.

The next line designates the subroutine:

```
Sub Main()
```

This is the procedure that is the program's entry point, or where it starts executing.

Following `Sub Main()` is the code to write the text:

```
System.Console.WriteLine("Hello, World!")
```

This line uses the `WriteLine()` method of the `System.Console` object to display a line of text on the screen.

The last line in the subroutine keeps the text on the screen:

```
System.Console.Read()
```

This uses the `Read` method of the object to pause things so that the text stays on the screen until you hit a key.

As you can see, you can't have a much simpler program in VB .NET—or in any other language!

Compiling the Program

To compile the program, open a command window. Depending on your system, you probably have a version of `cmd.exe` available in the `Windows\System32` folder. You'll probably also find a link that opens a command window on the Windows Program ➢ Accessories menu. In addition, Visual Studio provides a command prompt window, which you can open from the Windows programs menu by selecting Microsoft Visual Studio .NET ➢ Visual Studio .NET Tools ➢ Visual Studio .NET Command Prompt.

TIP If you use the Visual Studio .NET Command Prompt, `vbc.exe` will already be in your path, which means that you don't need to know its location or type in its full path to invoke it.

With a command window open, invoke the VB .NET compiler, `vbc.exe`, with **`console.txt`** as the argument, as shown in Figure 1.7. (You'll find `vbc.exe` in one of the folders beneath `Windows\Microsoft. net\framework`.) For example, the command line to compile `console .txt` might look like this:

```
c:\windows\Microsoft.net\framework\v1.0.3705\vbc console.txt
```

FIGURE 1.7: You can use vbc.exe, the command-line VB .NET compiler, to create executable programs.

Press Enter. A compiled executable named `console.exe`—the original filename without the suffix and with `.exe` added as the filename extension—will be created.

VB Compiler Switches

There are a number of command-line switches you can use with `vbc.exe`. The `/out:`*`filename`* option names the executable (as opposed to the default described in this example).

The `/target` option allows you to specify the type of the output file:

- `/target:exe` produces a console application executable.
- `/target:winexe` produces a Windows executable.
- `/target:library` creates a DLL.

For a full list of VB .NET command-line compiler switches, see the "Visual Basic Compiler Options" topic in online help.

Running the Application

Run the new application, `console.exe`, either from the command line or by double-clicking it in Windows Explorer. The text "Hello, World!" will be displayed in the console.

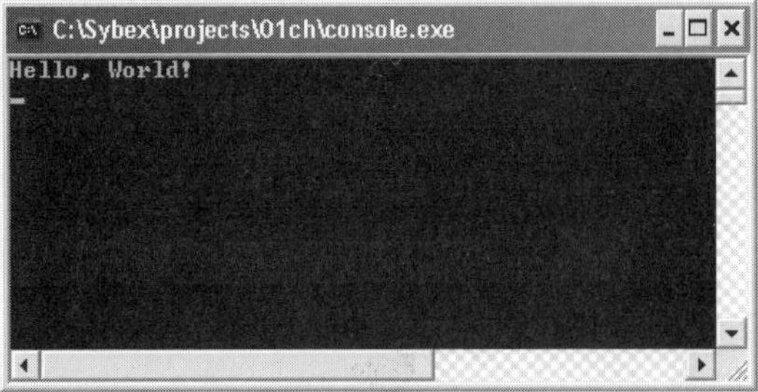

You've now successfully created, compiled, and run a VB .NET program without using Visual Studio. It's true that this program doesn't do much. It's also true that in the real world, you'll probably almost always use Visual Studio for creating and compiling your programs. But now you know, for once and for all, that the programming language is not the development environment—an important insight.

Visual Studio .NET Requirements

Since we'll be using Visual Studio .NET in the remainder of this book, you'll need to make sure that your system meets the requirements for running it. Let's review the software and hardware necessary for the projects covered in this book.

Software Requirements

Obviously, you'll need a copy of Microsoft's Visual Studio .NET, including the .NET Framework. You can purchase Visual Studio .NET online (and download the product) at `http://msdn.microsoft.com/vstudio/`.

Also, your computer should be running (in either their Professional, Server, or Advanced Server guises) Microsoft Windows NT 4.0 (with service pack 6A) or Windows 2000 or XP, with the latest service packs. Note that NT 4.0 Workstation is supported only for client-side development.

Finally, you will need a copy of Microsoft's web server, Internet Information Server (IIS) version 5.0 or later, and Internet Explorer 6.0 or later.

TIP If you don't have Internet Explorer 6.0, it will be installed when you install Visual Studio .NET.

Hardware Requirements

You will need a computer powerful enough to run your particular mix of software and operating system. Microsoft's minimum recommended specifications for Visual Studio .NET are a 450MHz Pentium II class processor or above, 64MB of RAM, and a 3GB of installation space available on the hard drive. Microsoft's recommended specifications are a 733MHz Pentium III class processor, 128MB of RAM, and a 3GB hard drive for the installation.

As a practical matter, Visual Studio .NET will run very poorly on a system that is as low in resources as even the Microsoft-recommended system. If at all possible, I suggest using a system with a 733MHz Pentium III processor, at least 256MB of RAM, and at least a 10GB hard drive.

Summary

Enough preliminaries! VB .NET is an exciting and elegant language. Familiar because of its antecedents, in this incarnation, VB really flies! The .NET Framework is a powerful and radical solution to many development problems.

This chapter has provided background information that will help you to learn the language faster and be a better VB .NET programmer. Now, let's get started building programs!

CHAPTER 2

Introducing Projects, Forms, and Buttons

- Understanding projects and solutions
- Starting and configuring Visual Studio .NET
- Configuring your project and environment
- Adding a Windows form
- Adding controls
- Running a project
- Introducing event handlers

In this chapter, you'll learn the basics of working with VB .NET solutions, projects, forms, and controls. Visual Studio .NET, the integrated development environment (IDE) for VB .NET, is powerful, flexible, almost infinitely configurable, and somewhat confusing. But there's no need to get bogged down in confusion! This chapter introduces the tools and processes that you need to get started.

Understanding Projects and Solutions

It's very important that you understand how to work with projects and solutions. These are the organizational groups that are used to create programs from VB source code files.

Projects are used to organize VB .NET programs. In other words, the source files, objects, and code contained in a VB .NET project become a program when the project is *built* and *deployed*. For example, the Windows forms in a VB .NET Windows Application project (described in the next section) become the windows of the completed program.

Solutions are used to organize related projects. Often, a VB .NET solution will contain only one project. Other times, a solution might contain multiple projects—for example, a number of class and control projects, together with several applications. Even if it contains only one project, you must have a solution in the VB .NET development environment. As Gertrude Stein might have said, while there are different kinds of projects, a solution is a solution is a solution. If you have multiple projects in a solution, the project set as the Startup project will run when the solution is executed.

You can *run* a project in the VB .NET development environment. This allows you to see what it will look like and how it will behave without going to the trouble of building and deploying the project. (You also get the benefit of the debugging tools provided by the development environment, as explained in Chapter 13, "Errors, Exceptions, and Debugging.")

Types of Projects

There are a number of different kinds of VB .NET projects, each using a template to lay the foundation for a different kind of program. These foundations include the following:

- Necessary empty files, ready for you to start work, such as a Windows Form file
- Assembly information, which is used for deployment
- Project references to appropriate .NET Framework namespaces

Table 2.1 describes the various types of VB .NET projects. Select a new project type by using the New Project dialog (see the "Starting a New Project" section later in this chapter). Once the project has been created, the files that make it up are shown in the Solution Explorer, along with any other projects that are part of the current solution (see the "Using the Solution Explorer" section later in this chapter).

TABLE 2.1: Types of VB .NET Projects

Project	Description
Windows Application	Used to create a traditional stand-alone Windows application
Class Library	Used to create a reusable class or component
Windows Control Library	Used to create a custom control for use on Windows forms
ASP.NET Web Application	Used to create a programmable ASP.NET web application
ASP.NET Web Service	Used to create web services
Web Control Library	Used to create custom controls for web forms
Console Application	Used to create a command-line application
Windows Service	Used to create a Windows service (a long-running system application with no user interface)

NOTE Depending on the version of VB .NET you are using, the projects available to you will vary. For example, Standard Edition users will not see all the project types shown in Table 2.1. For more information about the different versions of VB .NET and Visual Studio .NET, see Chapter 1, "Understanding Visual Basic .NET."

Windows Application and Web Application Projects

It's likely, at least at first, that you will be most interested in Windows Application and ASP.NET Web Application projects. (Windows Application projects correspond to good old Standard Exe projects in older versions of VB.) Once a Windows Application project has been built and deployed, it will look and behave like a standard Windows program. This will most likely (but not necessarily) involve displaying windows that the user can manipulate in the familiar way—by resizing, moving, clicking, and doing all the wonderful things with a mouse and windows to which users have become accustomed.

NOTE It is possible for a Windows Application project to have no forms, just running code modules without a user interface. For more information, see Chapter 6, "Working with Form Methods and Modules."

The focus of the first half of this book is Windows Application projects. When all is said and done, VB .NET will be used to create good, old-fashioned Windows executables more often than anything else. (It's worth considering that some of these programs might be used as rich front-end interfaces for web-based client/server applications.) Additionally, the same tools, tricks, and techniques that are used in Windows Application projects are also used in other kinds of projects.

ASP.NET Web Application projects bear the same relationship to ASP web applications that Windows Application projects do to Windows applications. VB .NET can help you easily create HTML-based interfaces, as opposed to Windows form-based interfaces, with web components that communicate using XML. For more information about creating ASP.NET Web Application projects, see Chapter 19, "Building ASP.NET Web Applications."

For the Very First Time...

VB .NET (and, more generally, Visual Studio .NET) has a very powerful, flexible, and fluid development environment interface. Frankly, at first this interface is also overwhelming and confusing. You should plan to spend at least a few hours playing with it to get to know the possibilities and to learn how you're most comfortable working with it.

TIP Each of the three development languages—VB, C#, and C++—use the same Visual Studio .NET development environment. You will see only the languages you have installed in Visual Studio. For example, if you have only VB installed, you will see only VB projects in the New Project dialog; if you have all three languages installed, you will see projects based on each of the languages.

The first time you start Visual Studio .NET, you will see an HTML-style Start page in the center of the development environment, as shown in Figure 2.1. The Start page lets you enter a profile (you should make sure that your profile lists you as a Visual Basic Developer), start a new project, open an existing project, download updates to VB .NET, and much more.

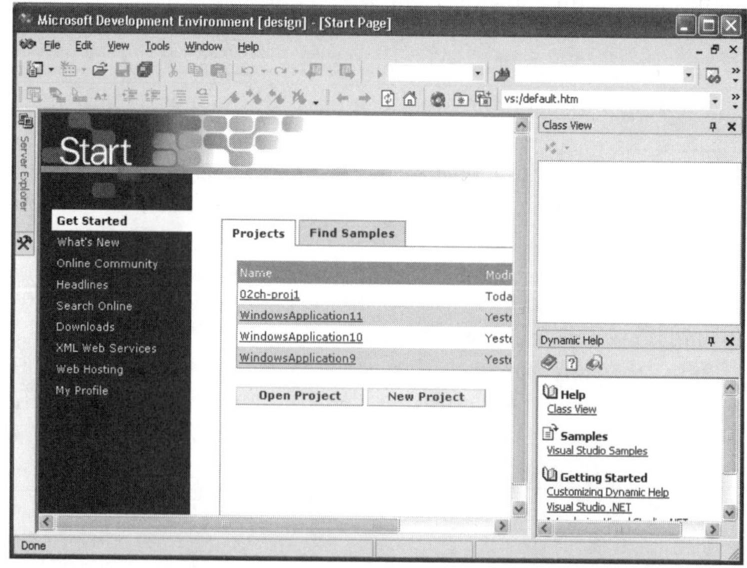

FIGURE 2.1: When you open Visual Studio .NET for the first time, by default, you will see a Start page featured in the development environment.

Setting Your Profile

Your profile controls some of the development environment options, including the keyboard scheme, the layout of the windows within Visual Studio, and—most important—the default way the Help system filters information. (For more information about using the Visual Studio Help System, see Appendix A, "Using VB .NET's Help System.")

You can change your profile settings by selecting My Profile from the Start page. Depending on how you have configured the environment, the Start page may appear each time you open a solution. If it does not, to display the Start page, select Show Start Page from the Help menu.

Configuring Your Startup Environment

After a while, you may wish to configure your startup environment differently. To change your startup options, select Options from the Tools menu (Tools ➢ Options). When the Options dialog opens, make sure that the General Environment page is selected, as shown in Figure 2.2.

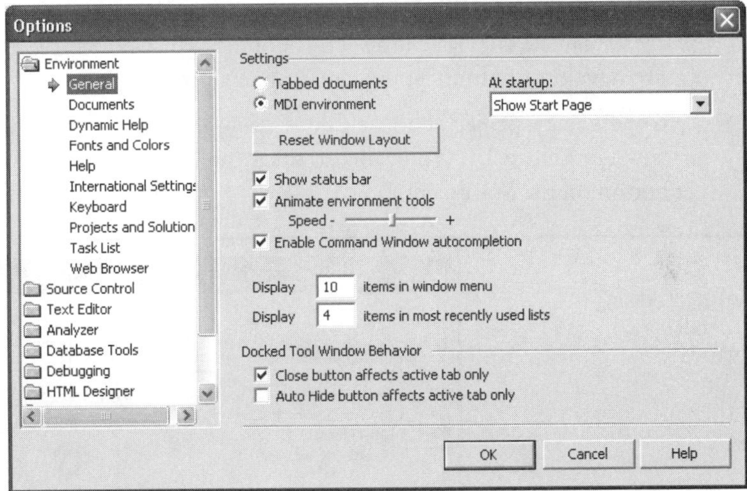

FIGURE 2.2: The At Startup drop-down list in the Environment Options dialog determines what you will see the next time you start Visual Studio.

There are a number of possible options for starting up, including the following:

- Show Start Page
- Load Last Loaded Solution
- Show Open Project Dialog
- Show New Project Dialog
- Show Empty Environment

There are also two general styles for the entire development environment you can select depending on your taste: Tabbed Documents or MDI Environment. Basically, the Tabbed Documents option docks windows along the perimeter of the environment, and the MDI (for Multiple Document Interface) Environment option places windows on top of each other. There is quite a difference between the appearance and behavior of these two options, so you should experiment to see which you like best. (Note that changes do not take effect until the next time you open Visual Studio.)

Since it is possible to get this development environment twisted out of shape like some warped Windows pretzel, you may be glad to know about the Reset Window Layout button. When clicked, this button restores the default layout for either the tabbed or MDI style environment, with the restoration taking effect the next time you open Visual Studio.

TIP Visual Studio .NET is sufficiently complicated, and has so many interface windows, that I do not recommend developing with it on a less than 21-inch monitor. Screen resolution should be set to at least 1024 × 768.

Starting a New Project

As I've explained, the basic unit of development in VB .NET is the project. Before you can start to develop anything, you need to open a project.

To open a new project, choose File ➢ New ➢ Project. The New Project dialog will open, as shown in Figure 2.3. (You can also open the New Project dialog by clicking the New Project button on the Start page.)

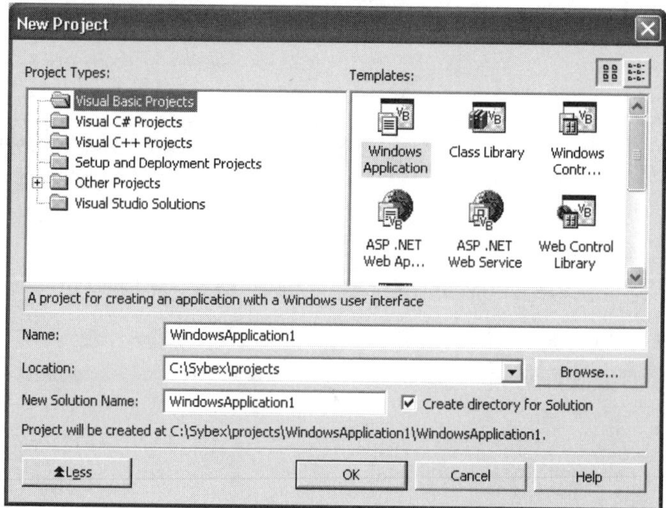

FIGURE 2.3: The New Project dialog lets you choose a project type.

The left pane of the New Project dialog lets you select the project type, or language, for your project. (If VB is the only language you have installed, then you will not see other languages.) The bottom of the dialog includes fields for naming the application, providing a location for the project files, and naming the solution that contains the project. (Often, in a one-project solution, the project and solution will share the same name.)

NOTE If a solution is already open, you are given the option of merging the new project into the existing solution or starting a new solution for it.

To create a standard Windows program, select Windows Application from the Templates pane and click OK. The new application will open in the Visual Studio .NET development environment, as shown in Figure 2.4.

FIGURE 2.4: You are now ready to get started working on your new VB .NET project.

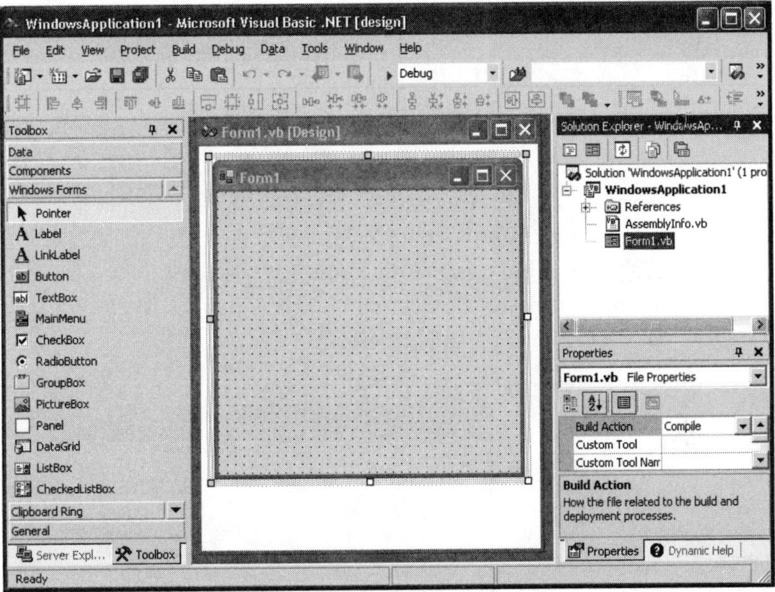

Configuring Your Project and Environment

Both the Visual Studio .NET environment and the properties of an individual project have settings that will have a big impact on the way your project behaves and how easy and efficient it is for you to work on it. You should take the time to get to know these settings and learn how to configure the environment and projects to suit your preferences.

Changing Environment Settings

Environment settings control the way all projects loaded in the Visual Studio .NET environment behave. Selecting Tools ➢ Options from the Visual Studio .NET menu opens the configuration dialogs that control these settings. Many aspects of the development environment are configurable, as you can see from the list in the left pane of the Options dialog.

One setting that's important is Build and Run Options, set in the Projects and Solutions dialog, shown in Figure 2.5. You should set this option to either the Save Changes to Open Documents setting or the Prompt to Save Changes to Open Documents setting (otherwise, you risk losing changes to your work).

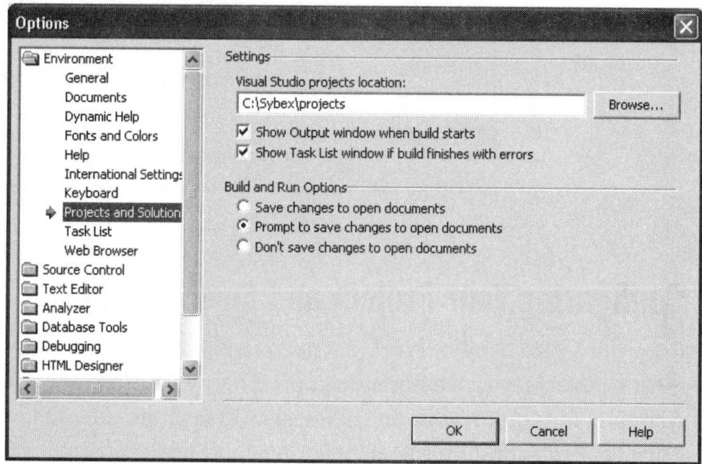

FIGURE 2.5: You should set the project Build and Run options to save changes to open documents.

You can set VB editing preferences in the Basic subsection of the Options dialog, which is found in the Text Editor section, as shown in Figure 2.6.

FIGURE 2.6:

Setting Basic-specific options for the text editor

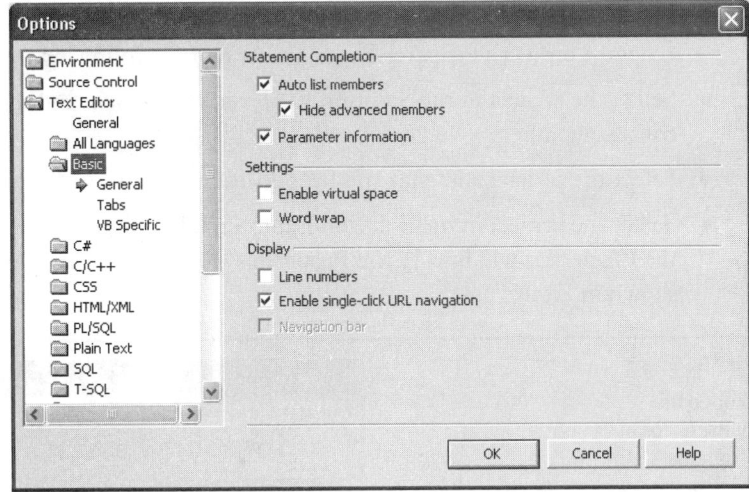

Using the Solution Explorer

The Solution Explorer is an important part of the Visual Studio .NET interface. Its most important function is to give you a hierarchical view of the objects that are part of a project, as shown in Figure 2.7. You can use the Solution Explorer to configure various aspects of a project, such as adding and removing objects from a project or setting the Startup project for a solution, using the context menus provided.

FIGURE 2.7:

The Solution Explorer shows you a hierarchical view of the objects that are part of a project.

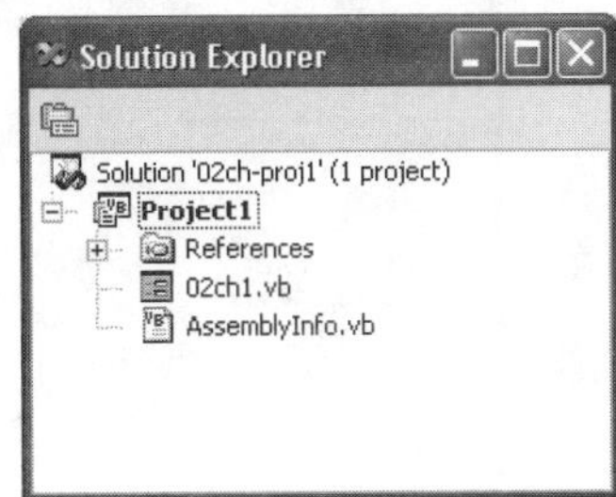

TIP To add a new project to an existing solution, with the solution open in Visual Studio, open the New Project dialog. Select the project type and name it. Make sure that the Add to Solution button is selected, and then click OK.

Using Project Property Pages

The Property Pages that allow you to configure preferences for a particular project can be opened from the Solution Explorer. There are several options that you'll need to set in these project Property Pages.

To open a project's Property Pages, use one of the following methods:

- Select the project in the Solution Explorer, right-click, and select Properties from the context menu.
- Select the project and click the Properties button on the Solution Explorer toolbar.
- Select the project in the Solution Explorer. The properties for the project will appear in the Properties window. In the Properties window, click the Property Pages button, as shown in Figure 2.8.

FIGURE 2.8:

You can open the Property Pages for a project from the Properties window.

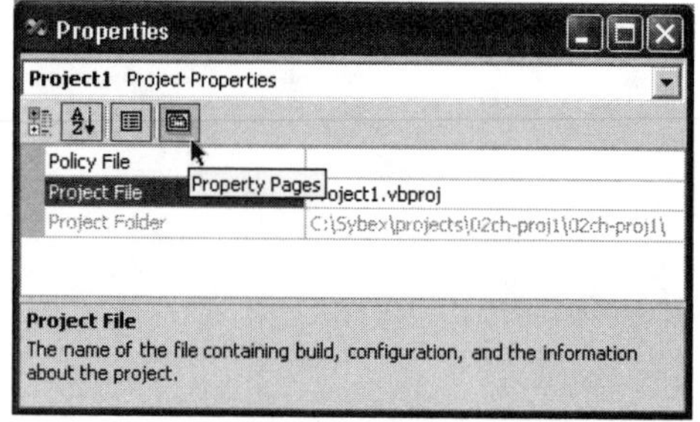

Once you have the project Property Pages open, you should start by making sure that Option Explicit is turned on. This option is on the Build page, as shown in Figure 2.9.

FIGURE 2.9:

You should make sure that explicit variable declaration is required.

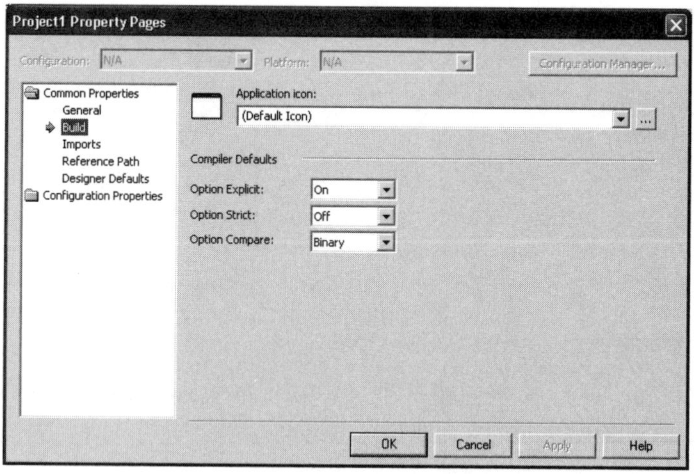

NOTE Turning on Option Explicit at the project level using the project's Property Pages is equivalent to adding an `Option Explicit` statement to the beginning of code in each module in a project.

Selecting the Option Explicit setting makes sure that using an undeclared variable causes a syntax error in the compiler. Forcing variable declaration imposes good programming habits. It also saves you time in the long run, because some of the most common programming bugs come from variable name confusion, which is avoided for the most part when strict declaration is required.

NOTE The Startup object, set on the project Property Pages, determines whether code or a form (and, if a form, which form) loads first when an application runs. See the "Running a Project" section later in this chapter for details.

Renaming a Project

The Solution Explorer is also used for a variety of housekeeping tasks related to projects and solutions. For example, you might not like the project name that Visual Studio has automatically supplied. To change the project name to something more to your taste, use the project's context menu within Solution Explorer and select Rename.

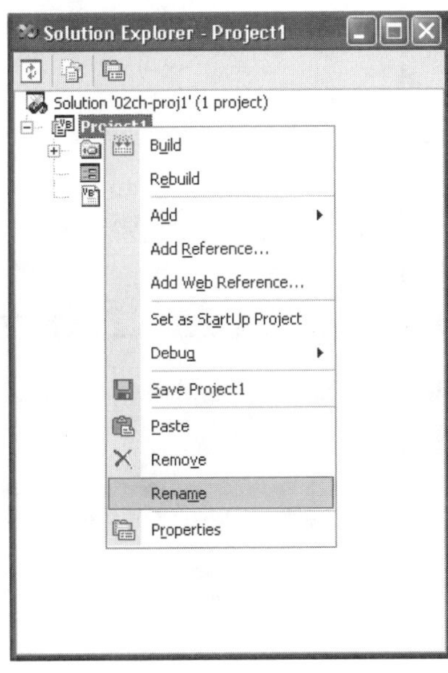

Adding a Windows Form

The Add New Item dialog is used to add a Windows form (or other object) to a project. To open the Add New Item dialog, select a project in the Solution Explorer, choose Add from the context menu, and then select Add New Item. Alternatively, selecting Project ➢ Add Windows Form in Visual Studio also opens the Add New Item dialog.

The Add New Item dialog, shown in Figure 2.10, lets you provide a *filename* for the Windows form you are about to add to your project. (See the "Naming a Form" section later in this chapter for an explanation of the difference between a filename and the internal name for an object.) By default, if you do not provide a name, the filename will be `Form1.vb`...`Formn.vb`, depending on the other modules in the project. (If there is no `Form1.vb`, the form's filename becomes `Form1.vb` by default; if there is a `Form1.vb`, it is named `Form2.vb`, and so on.) The default internal name is the same as the filename, without the suffix, for example, `Form2`.

FIGURE 2.10: The Add New Item dialog lets you add a new form to a project.

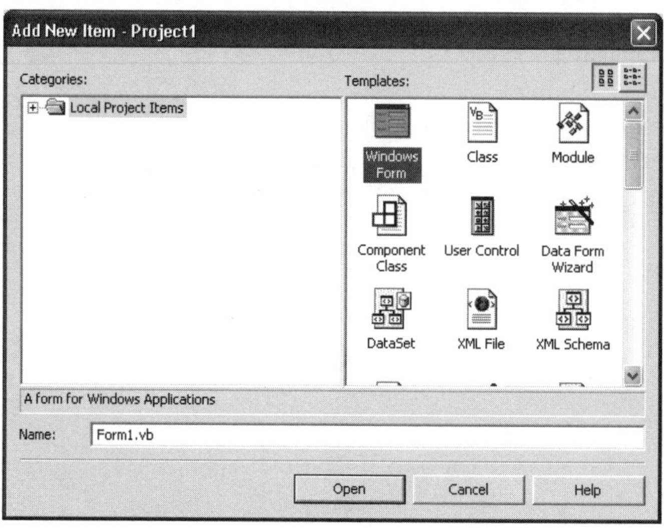

When the Windows form has been added to the project, it will appear in the Solution Explorer.

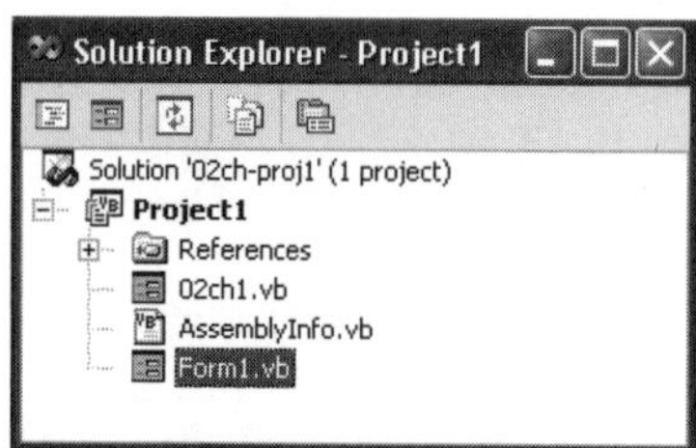

As you might expect, you can also manipulate Windows forms in various ways from within Solution Explorer. For example, you can delete a form by selecting Delete from the form's context menu.

Setting Windows Form Properties

There are many properties that you can set at design time that control a great deal about the behavior of a Windows form. Many of these properties can also be set dynamically while a program is running in code, in response to a system event or a user action. (I'll show you an example of this later in the chapter, in the "Introducing Event Handlers" section.) But before you get to manipulating forms in code, it is important that you take the time to run through the properties listed in the Properties window, so that you get a feeling for what they are and what they can do.

TIP The bottom pane of the Properties window provides a description of what each property does when the property is selected.

This section shows you how to set a few of the more common form properties, along with an exotic one that is new to VB .NET. This selection of form properties is meant to give you a taste of working with them. You'll find a great deal more material about working with form properties in Chapter 4, "Working with Windows Form Properties."

The properties of a form are often referred to using the dot operator, both in English and in code. Thus, `Form1.Text` means the Text property of `Form1`, which is distinguished from `Form2.Text`, the Text property of `Form2`.

File Properties versus Object Properties

Objects in Visual Studio have two kinds of properties:

- File properties, which relate to the physical storage of the object in the filesystem
- Object properties, which are the properties of the object internal to the .NET development environment and control many aspects of how the object behaves

The Properties window is used at design time to change both file properties and internal object properties for forms. However, only one set of properties is displayed in the Properties window at any time. (In previous versions of VB, the only properties were internal object properties.)

To open the Properties window for a form in file properties mode, select the form in the Solution Explorer. Next, choose Properties from the context menu. The file properties will be displayed in the Properties window, as shown in Figure 2.11.

FIGURE 2.11: The file properties for the form are shown in the Properties window.

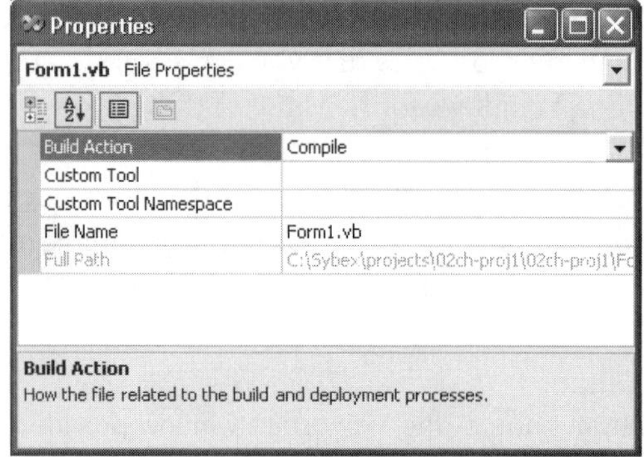

You'll find yourself doing much more work with internal object properties than with file properties. To open the Properties window with object properties for a form displayed, double-click the form in the Solution Explorer. Alternatively, open the form in a designer by selecting View ➢ View Designer from the Visual Studio menu. The Properties window will automatically show the object properties for the form that is open in the designer, as shown in Figure 2.12.

FIGURE 2.12: The internal object properties for the form are shown in the Properties window.

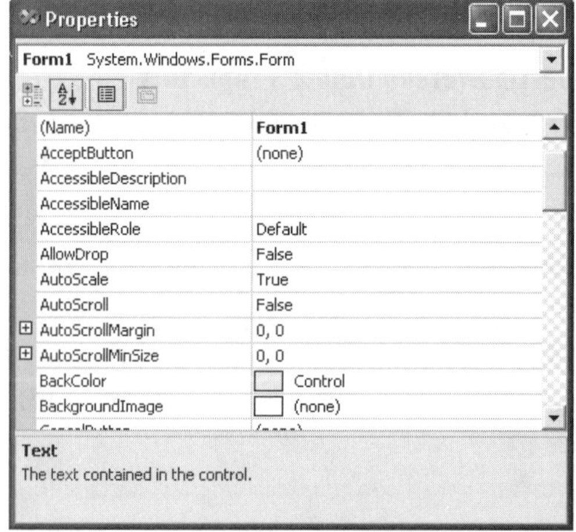

Naming a Form

By default, the internal name of an object is the same as its filename, without the suffix, so `Form1.vb` is internally named `Form1`. But you do not need to keep the default internal name. You can give the form with the filename `Form1.vb` any internal name you like—for example, `myForm`—and refer to it by that name inside your .NET program.

The property listed at the top of the Properties window, Name, is used to change the internal name of the form. To change the internal name, select Name in the left column and type the new name for the form in the right column, as shown here.

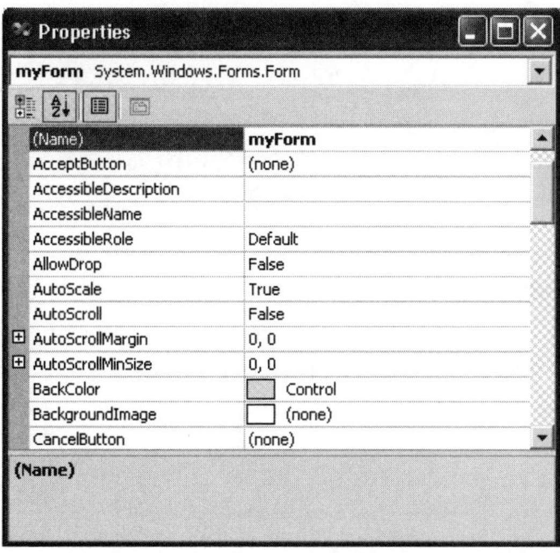

NOTE Name is the only property that doesn't appear in alphabetic order; instead, it is displayed at the top of the Properties window.

Centering a Form

The StartPosition property sets the initial position of a form when it launches. Choose CenterScreen from the drop-down menu to center a form in the screen when it first opens.

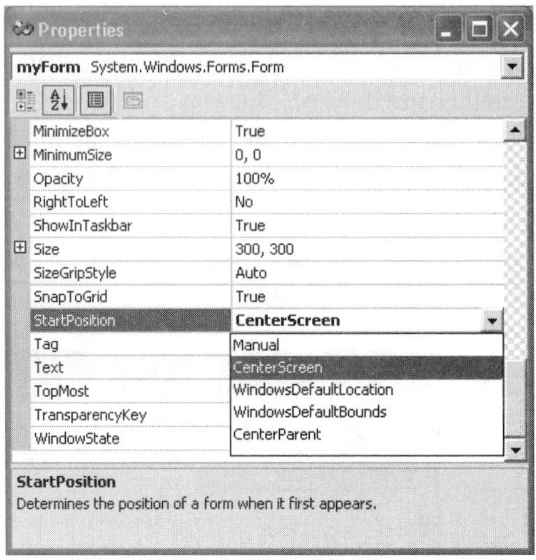

Setting the BackColor

Various color properties can be set to change the color of elements of a form. For example, the BackColor property sets the background color used in a form. By default, it is set to a color determined by the Windows System color scheme, as shown here.

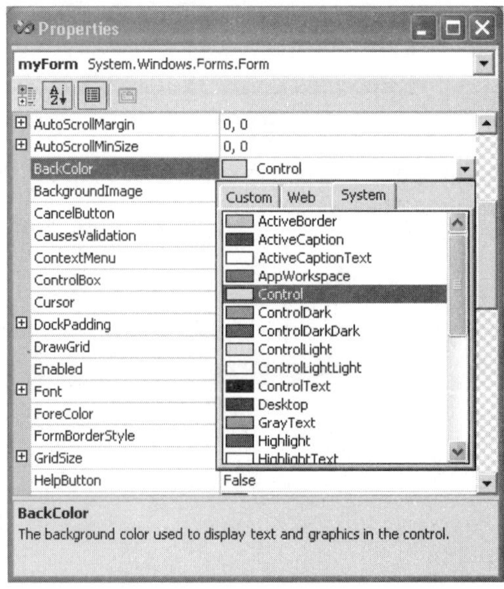

You can also set BackColor to a color of your choice using the Custom palette:

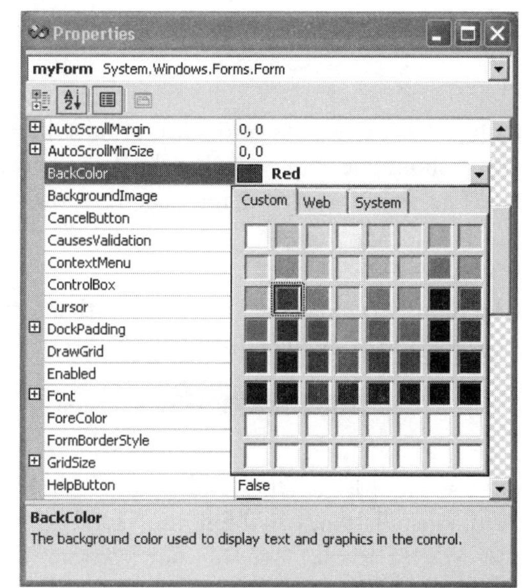

Another option is to set BackColor to a color that is designed to display well on the Web (well, actually in Internet Explorer) using the Web palette.

Setting the Text Property

The Text property controls the text that appears in a form's caption bar. When you set the Text property in the Properties window, it appears in the form's caption bar in the form designer, as shown in Figure 2.13, and when you run the form.

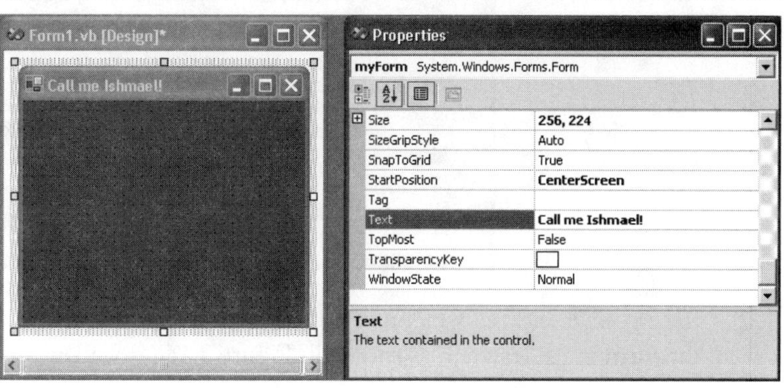

FIGURE 2.13: Setting a form's Text property

NOTE In earlier versions of VB, this was the Form.Caption property. It has been renamed the Text property to maintain consistency with the way most .NET object properties are named.

A common confusion for newcomers to VB is to mistake an object's Text property with its Name property. You should be very clear that the Text property of an object is different from the object's name. The Text property merely sets the text that is displayed.

Setting a Form's Icon

You can use the Icon property to associate an icon with a form by clicking the button with three dots on the right side of the Icon listing in the Properties window.

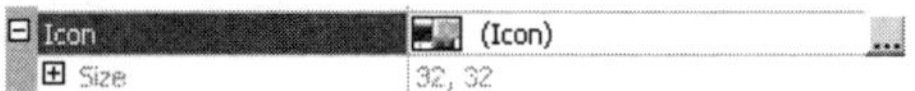

When the button is clicked, the Open dialog opens, as shown in Figure 2.14. Assuming a default Visual Studio installation, you'll find the Visual Studio .NET icon library in your `Program Files\Microsoft Visual Studio .Net\Common7\Graphics\icons` folder.

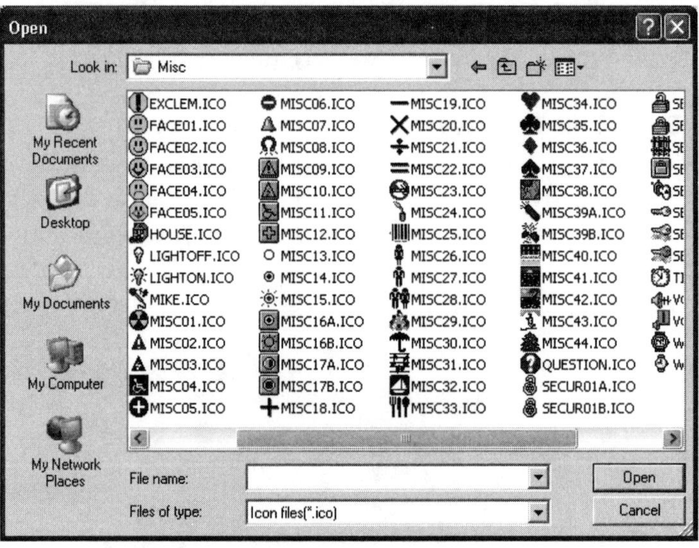

FIGURE 2.14: The Open File dialog is used to select an icon.

Once you've selected an icon, it is displayed in the Properties window and in the title bar of the form in its designer, as shown in Figure 2.15, as well as on the running form.

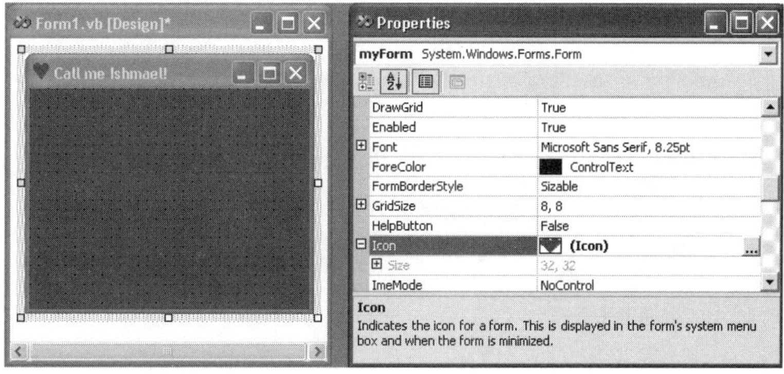

FIGURE 2.15: When an icon is selected, it is displayed in the title bar of the form.

NOTE The icon selection will not be saved with the form until you save the form's resources file. You should be prompted to do this if you close the form's designer or run the project.

Setting Form Opacity

The Form Opacity property controls how opaque or transparent a form is. In other words, can you see through the form? When the Opacity property is set to 100% in the Properties window, the form is opaque (this is the standard style we are used to). Anything less than 100% produces a window that is somewhat transparent when it runs, as shown below.

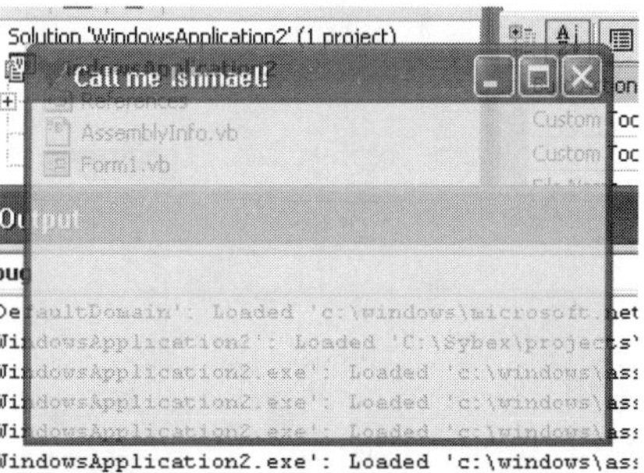

As you might expect, an Opacity setting of 0% produces an “Invisible Man” window—it is 100% transparent, and you can’t see it at all.

This effect cannot be seen at design time, so you must run your project in order to view it.

NOTE This way cool property is new with .NET. I think it’s great, but I can’t think of any way it could actually be used as part of an application’s user interface. If you come up with a good use for it, please send me an e-mail message!

Categorizing Properties

Properties can be viewed in categories or alphabetically within the Properties window. This makes it somewhat easier to find a property for which you are looking. To display the form properties grouped in categories, click the button farthest to the left in the toolbar at the top of the Properties window. The properties will be arranged in categories, such as Behavior and Data, as shown below.

To return to an alphabetized display, click the second button in the toolbar at the top of the Properties window.

Running a Project

To see how a VB .NET project actually looks and behaves, you will need to run the project. By running the project in the Visual Studio design-time environment, termed *debug mode*, you will have a great many tools that help you debug your program, and you do not need to go to the trouble of deploying a program every time you want to test it.

In VB .NET, every time you run a project, its modules are compiled and built. Only if this can be done successfully will your project run. If there are syntax or other errors, a message will be displayed so that you can correct the errors.

As I mentioned previously, before running a project, you need to select a Startup object. This specifies the first code in the application to be executed. (In a default, one-form Windows Application project, the form will be the Startup object by default.) To select a Startup object, open the Project Property pages by selecting the project in the Solution Explorer and choosing Properties from its context menu. On the General page, choose your Startup object from the drop-down list, as shown in Figure 2.16.

FIGURE 2.16: If your project has more than one module, you should select a Startup object.

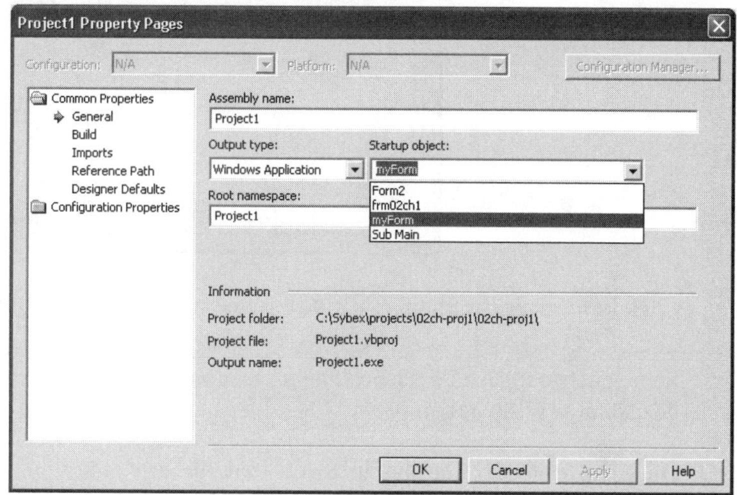

NOTE Windows Application projects must start with a form or with a `Main` procedure that has been created in a code module.

Once you have selected a Startup object, you can run your project in debug mode in a number of ways:

- Click the right arrow in the center of the primary Visual Studio toolbar.

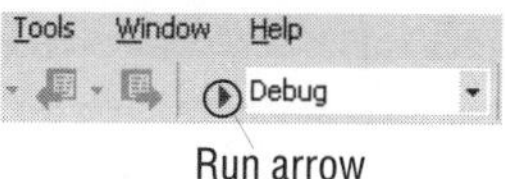

- Press the F5 key.
- Choose Debug ➢ Start from the Visual Studio menu.

If you selected Prompt to Save Changes to Open Documents in the Options dialog for the Visual Studio environment, as I advised earlier in this chapter, you will be prompted to save any unsaved changes before your project runs.

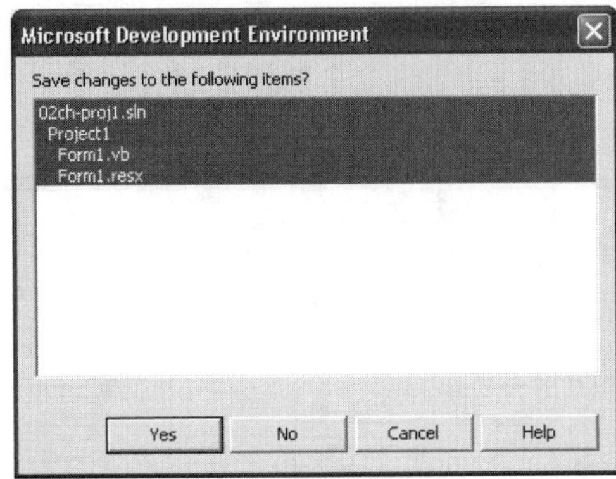

Click Yes to save the changes (or No to discard them), and your project will run.

NOTE Some changes, such as associating an icon with a form, must be saved, or they will not be displayed when a form is run.

Once the project is running, its forms look like any other running program window, as in the example shown here.

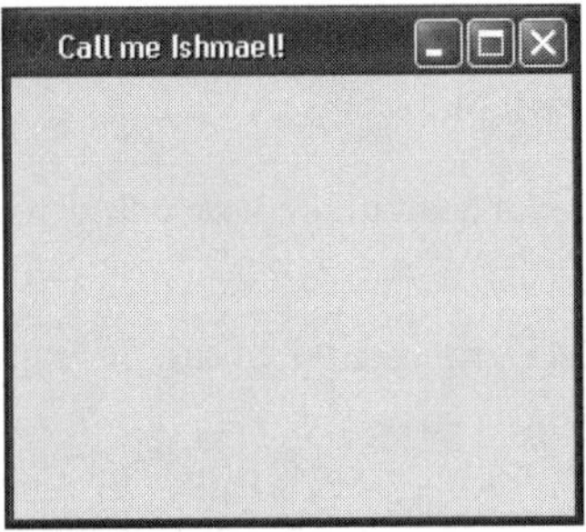

You cannot tell, based on appearance alone, that this window is running in the Visual Studio .NET environment rather than on its own.

As your project compiles and builds, and then as it runs, status messages are displayed in the Visual Studio .NET Output window, as shown in Figure 2.17. These can be very helpful for finding and fixing program problems (see Chapter 13 for more information).

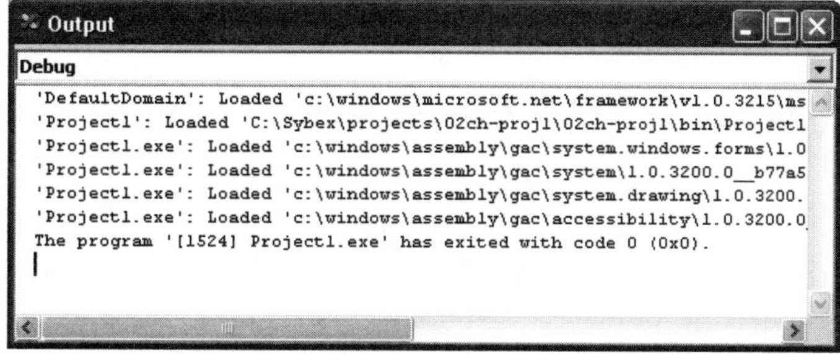

FIGURE 2.17: The Output window displays debug, build, and compilation status messages for your project.

NOTE The final message shown in Figure 2.17, stating that the program has "exited with code 0," means that the program was closed with no error conditions caused along the way.

Adding Controls

Controls are components that add functionality to forms, since forms by themselves don't do very much. In other words, a control is prepackaged functionality that can be added to a form with a few mouse clicks in the Visual Studio design-time environment.

Each control that is available to use has a graphical representation in the Visual Studio Toolbox:

If your Toolbox isn't displayed, you can open it by selecting View ➢ Toolbox from the Visual Studio menu.

NOTE The controls in the Windows Forms category generally present some sort of visual interface to the user.

To add a control, such as a button, to a form, first make sure that the Toolbox is displayed and the form is open in its designer. (If the form's designer is not open, you can open it by double-clicking the form in the Solution Explorer.) Next, either double-click the Button control in the Toolbox (it will be added to the upper-left corner of the form and you can position it later) or drag and drop the Button control into position on the form, as illustrated in Figure 2.18.

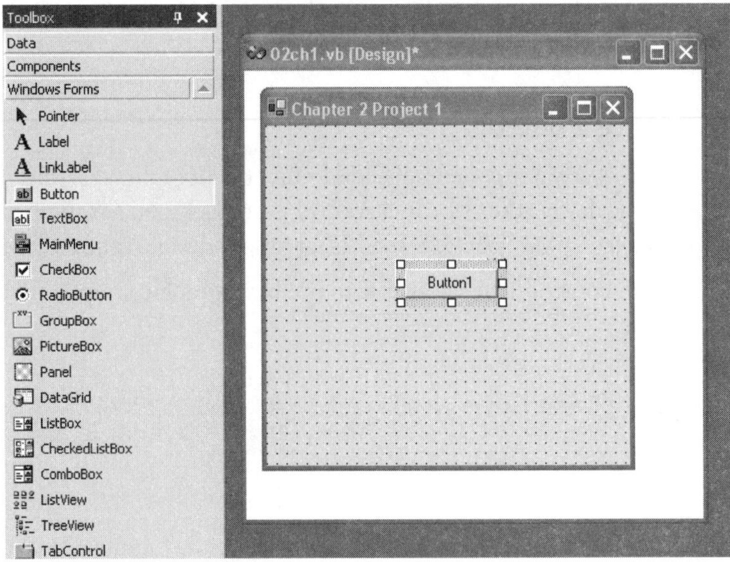

FIGURE 2.18: A control, such as a button, can be added to a form, either by double-clicking the control or by dragging and dropping the control onto the form.

Once a control has been added to a form, you can change the control's properties using the Properties window. Make sure that the control has been selected in the drop-down Objects list at the top of the Properties window. Figure 2.19 shows the Text property of a button being set in the Properties window.

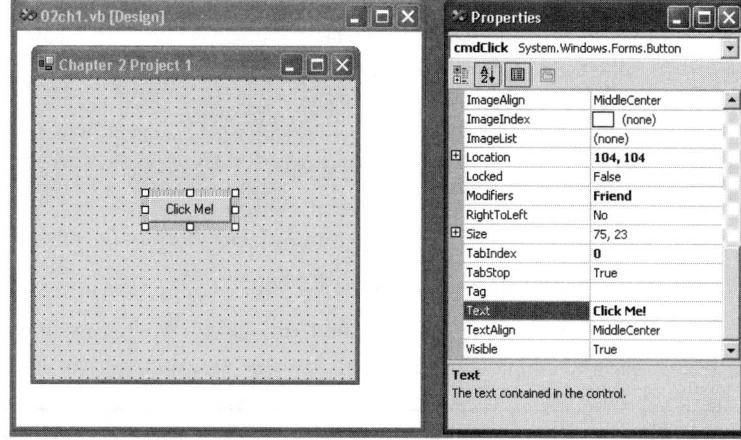

FIGURE 2.19:
The Properties window is used to change control properties.

Introducing Event Handlers

Forms, buttons, and many other VB .NET objects have *events* associated with them. Events are part of the fundamental paradigm of modern programming. As opposed to the old days, when programs were linear in direction (meaning that they went from the start of code to the finish of code), event-driven programs respond to things that happen (when the thing happens, it is said that the event is *fired* or *triggered*).

When you place an object, such as a form with buttons, programmatically onto the screen, you really don't know what the user is going to do. Event-driven code responds to the action that the user chooses to make, or to actions initiated by a program or the system. The process of creating a program largely becomes adding code to respond to various events.

VB .NET makes it very easy to associate code with events, meaning that the code is executed when the event is fired. Procedures that do this are called *event handlers*. One very common event handler is the Click event, fired when a button is clicked. You almost always want to handle this event, referred to as the `ButtonName.click` event, if a button is present; users will be disappointed if they click a button and nothing happens.

Event handling is discussed in detail in Chapter 5, "Events and the Life Cycle of Forms." Here, we will take a quick look at how to add code to a button Click event, to give you an idea of how it all works.

Using the Code Editor

Before you can add code for a specific event, you need to know how to associate code with a form. The Code Editor is used to add code to a form (or other module).

You can open the Code Editor in several ways:

- Select the form in the Solution Explorer, right-click, and choose View Code from the context menu.
- With the form module selected in Solution Explorer, choose View ➢ Code.
- With a form selected, press the F7 key.

Whatever technique you use, the Code Editor opens, as shown in Figure 2.20. You are now ready to add code to the form, its objects, and the associated events.

FIGURE 2.20:

The Code Editor is used to add code to a form.

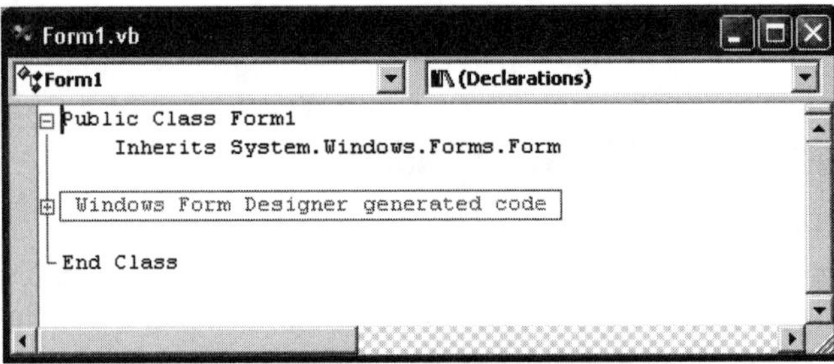

In Figure 2.20, notice two drop-down list boxes at the top of the form:

- The drop-down list on the left is the *Objects* list. You select the object you want to work with using this list.
- The drop-down list on the right is the *Procedures* list. You use this list to choose an event or other procedure.

When the Code Editor opens form code for the first time, you'll notice a plus sign (+) next to the words "Windows Form Designer generated code." (You can see this in Figure 2.20.) The + icon is used to expand hidden code in the Code Editor. Hidden code is the automatically generated code required for the basic functionality of Windows forms. You can view it by clicking the + icon.

Unlike previous versions of VB, Windows forms are true objects like other objects. The hidden code shows the objects that the Windows form inherits from, the methods used to create and destroy the object, and much more. This code is initially hidden to keep things simple for users who don't want or need to know about it. You can learn more about object-oriented programming in Chapter 15, "Object-Oriented Programming in VB .NET," but for now, you really don't need to bother with the hidden code.

Adding Code to an Event

To add code to an event, in the Code Editor, select the object with the event in the Objects list. Next, choose the event from the Procedures list, as shown in Figure 2.21.

FIGURE 2.21: Code can be added to any of the events that appear in the Procedures list for an object.

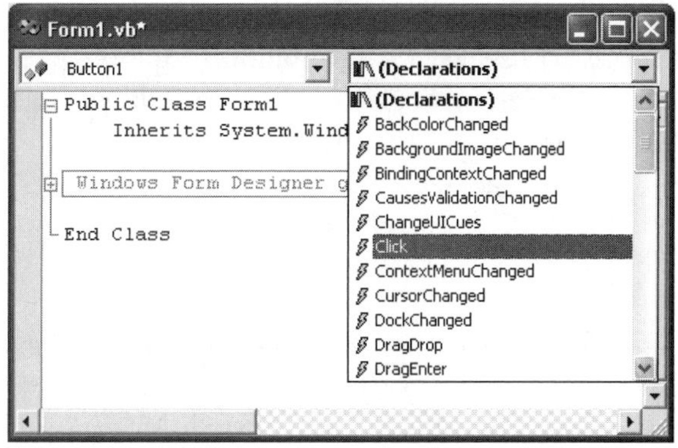

NOTE Events are indicated in the Procedures list with an icon that looks like a lightning bolt.

After you have selected the event from the Procedures list, VB .NET creates the scaffolding for the event, consisting of a procedure declaration and an `End Sub` statement to close the event procedure. Here is an example:

```
Private Sub Button1_Click(ByVal sender As Object, ByVal e _
   As System.EventArgs) Handles Button1.Click
   ...
End Sub
```

Code is added between the beginning and end of the event procedure in the area indicated by the three dots, which shows up in the Code Editor as empty white space.

NOTE A space followed by an underscore (_) is the line continuation character in VB .NET. In other words, everything before the three dots is one logical line of code, and will appear on one line in the Code Editor.

Let's have a look at an event procedure example. Start with a project named **`Project1`** containing a form named **`frm02ch1`**. Add a Button control to the form named **`cmdClick`**. If you would like, you can use the Properties window to set the `Button.Text` property to "`Click Me!`"

TIP It's a good idea to name objects starting with a prefix that says what the object is, such as `frm` for forms and `cmd` for buttons. This practice will help make your code intelligible (help with the "who is doing what to whoms") and also make sure that like objects are grouped next to each other in the Objects list.

With `frm02ch1` selected in the Solution Explorer, open the Code Editor. In the Objects drop-down list, select `cmdClick`. In the Procedures list, select Click. The scaffolding for the event procedure will be created:

```
Private Sub cmdClick_Click(ByVal sender As Object, ByVal e _
   As System.EventArgs) Handles cmdClick.Click

End Sub
```

As a first step, let's change the caption of the running window to "Lions and Tigers & Bears!" when the button is clicked. To do this, use the `Me` keyword to refer to the form and the Text property of the form. Add the following line of code:

```
Me.Text = "Lions and Tigers & Bears!"
```

Next, display a message to the user using the `MessageBox.Show` method:

```
MessageBox.Show("Oh my!")
```

By default, `MessageBox.Show` displays an OK button. It is also *modal*, meaning the user can't do anything else in the application, and the message won't go away, until the OK button is clicked. (Message boxes are discussed in detail in Chapter 3, "Building a User Interface.") So, we can add a line of code to change the caption of the form to "Chapter 2 Project 1" when the OK button is clicked:

```
Project1.frm02ch1.ActiveForm.Text = "Chapter 2 Project 1"
```

Note that this statement doesn't use the `Me` keyword. Instead, it directly uses the project and form name, combined with the dot operator, to change the value of the property.

Now you're ready to run the project and test the code. (The complete procedure is shown in Listing 2.1.) When you run the project, verify that clicking the Button control changes the caption and that a message box is displayed, as shown in Figure 2.22. When you click OK in the message box, the caption should change again.

Listing 2.1 Adding Code to a Button.click Event

```
Private Sub cmdClick_Click(ByVal sender As Object, ByVal e _
   As System.EventArgs) Handles cmdClick.Click
   Me.Text = "Lions and Tigers & Bears!"
   MessageBox.Show("Oh my!")
   Project1.frm02ch1.ActiveForm.Text = "Chapter 2 Project 1"
End Sub
```

FIGURE 2.22:
Code placed in the event procedure is executed when the user triggers, or "fires," the event by clicking the button.

TIP You don't need to stick with the events offered in the Procedures list. It is possible to "roll your own" event, but this means creating the code that fires the event as well as the code that responds to the event. For more information, see Chapter 5.

Summary

In this chapter, you learned a great deal about working with VB .NET in Visual Studio. You learned about solutions, projects, forms, controls, properties, and events. You learned how to add code to an event in the Code Editor, and created your first VB .NET program. This is a great deal of material, but there is much more to be learned! With the basic organizational concepts of VB .NET under your belt, you are ready to move on. In Chapter 3, you'll learn how to work with message boxes and a number of form controls, as you discover more about the VB .NET programming language.

CHAPTER 3

Building a User Interface

- Displaying message boxes
- Adding form controls
- Using `If` statements
- Wiring a form to determine user choice

In Chapter 2, "Introducing Projects, Forms, and Buttons," you learned how to use the Visual Studio .NET integrated development environment. You also learned how to display a text message in a simple dialog using `MessageBox.Show`.

This chapter builds on what you learned in the previous chapter. You'll learn more about message boxes, as well as how to put controls on a form and add code that lets the program interact with the user. You'll also start to learn the syntax of the VB .NET language.

The goal of this chapter is to build an application. By the end of the chapter, you will know how to put together an application that displays most VB .NET message box variations, and how to add the code that evaluates user selection of a message box variation and the response to the dialog that is generated. I think you'll be surprised by how simple and fun it is to do this!

Displaying Message Boxes

You can use message boxes to give the user a choice, depending on which button the user clicks. In the previous chapter, you used `MessageBox.Show` in a simple way to display a message to the user. You probably will not be surprised to learn that you can use `MessageBox.Show` to create "instant" dialogs that include buttons and icons. (You've undoubtedly seen dialogs of this sort when using applications.)

In Chapter 2, `MessageBox.Show` was used in a statement that does not return a value. However, `MessageBox.Show` can also be used to return a value, which usually represents the user's choice of buttons displayed by the message box.

Here is an example of a message box being used to display text:

```
MessageBox.Show("This displays a message!")
```

And here is an example that shows the use of a message box that is intended to return a value:

```
Dim answer As DialogResult
answer = MessageBox.Show("I return a value!")
```

Later in the chapter, in the "Getting a Return Value" section, I'll show you how to add the buttons to the message box that are used to send a response value back to the `DialogResult` variable.

`MessageBox.Show` has six possible parts, also called *arguments*. The first four arguments—*`Text`*, *`Caption`*, *`Buttons`*, and *`Icon`*–are the most commonly used. The text that is supplied as the *`Text`* argument appears within the MessageBox, the *`Caption`* appears in the caption bar, the *`Buttons`* argument determines which buttons will be displayed, and the *`Icon`* argument determines the icon. Only the first of these, *`Text`*, is required, and it is quite common to display a message box with text and no other individualized characteristics.

As you'll soon see, this is a lot less complicated in practice than it sounds.

Visual Basic Comments

Let's get the business of comments over with right away, because it's a good idea to put plenty of comments in your code. You'll see comments in the code throughout this book.

In VB .NET, the usual way to put a comment in code is to start the comment with single quotation mark ('), or "quote" for short. (REM followed by a space also works, although this is an older syntax going back to the roots of Basic, and it is better practice to use a single quote.) Comments can start a line, in which case, the single quote or REM should be followed by a space, although this space is not required.

Here are some examples of comments:

```
' I am a comment!
REM I am a comment, too!
Kludge = 10 'This is yet another comment!
```

A very nice feature of the VB .NET Code Editor allows you to comment and uncomment selected blocks. You can access this facility by selecting Edit ➢ Advanced and then choosing Comment Selection or Uncomment Selection.

Understanding *MessageBox.Show* Syntax

`MessageBox.Show` has the following format:

```
DialogResult = MessageBox.Show (Text, Caption, Buttons, Icon,
   DefaultButton, Options)
```

Here's the meaning of the arguments, which must be entered in the order shown above:

- *`Text`* contains the text that will be displayed in the message box. The contents of a variable in the *`Text`* position must evaluate to a *string*, meaning that it must be alphanumeric. One way to do this is with *string literals*. To create a string literal, enclose an alphanumeric sequence in quotation marks, as in, `"I am a string!"`
- *`Caption`*, which is optional, contains the text that will go in the message box caption bar. Like the *`Text`* argument, the *`Caption`* argument must be of string type.
- *`Buttons`*, which is optional, tells VB .NET which buttons will be displayed.
- *`Icon`*, which is optional, tells VB .NET which icon will be displayed.
- *`DefaultButton`*, which is optional, tells VB .NET which button is activated by default (when the user presses the Enter key).
- *`Options`*, which is optional, allows you to select some special options for the message box. These include things like making the text right-aligned, specifying a right-to-left reading order, or displaying a message box from a Windows service application.

To use `MessageBox.Show` to display a message box without returning a value, just use it in a statement without an equal sign:

```
MessageBox.Show (Text, Caption, Buttons, Icon)
```

The following sections describe how to use the `MessageBox.Show` arguments.

The MsgBox Function

For reasons of backward compatibility with VB6 (and earlier versions of VB), Microsoft has retained the `MsgBox` statement and `MsgBox()` function. Here is an example of a `MsgBox` statement:

```
MsgBox ("Hello, World!")
```

This code displays a message box containing the text "Hello, World!"

`MsgBox` works in much the same way as `MessageBox.Show`, and in most situations, there is no strong reason to prefer one mode to another. But `MessageBox.Show` does do away with some of the peculiarities of the `MsgBox` syntax, such as combining icon and button information in one argument.

Many old-time VB programmers are in the habit of dashing out quick `MsgBox` statements, and old habits die hard, even though `MessageBox.Show` is more in keeping with VB .NET's object orientation. In places in this book, where there is no reason not to, you may find that I revert to the `MsgBox` syntax.

Adding Buttons and Icons to Message Boxes

The *`Buttons`* argument, which controls the buttons that are displayed, is set using one of the enumeration constants, or members, that are part of the `MessageBoxButtons` set of values. When you start typing `MessageBox.Show` in the Code Editor, you can choose a `MessageBoxButtons` enumeration value from the drop-down list, as shown in Figure 3.1.

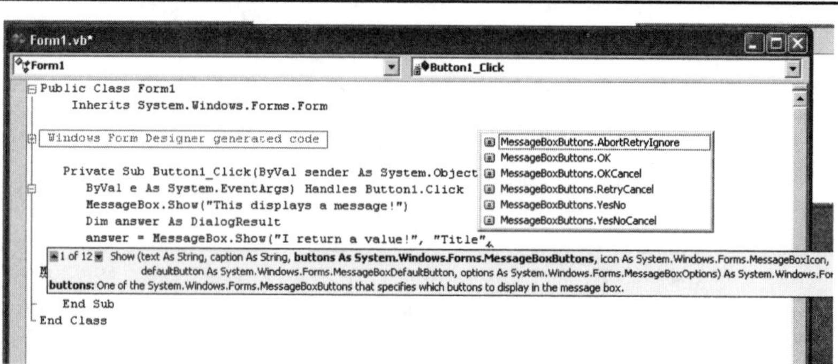

FIGURE 3.1: The syntax of the `MessageBox.Show` statement and a drop-down list of possible Button enumeration values appear when you start to type a `MessageBox.Show` statement in the Code Editor.

NOTE An *enumeration value* is one that must be chosen from a specific set of possible values.

The *Icon* argument, which sets the icon that is displayed, is specified using one of the members that are part of the MessageBoxIcon set of values.

So where do you find the values to use for buttons and icons? Look no further! Table 3.1 shows the MessageBoxButtons members, and Table 3.2 shows the MessageBoxIcon set of values. Don't worry; you often won't need to refer back to these tables, because the Code Editor's auto-completion feature provides a drop-down list of possible values as you're typing a MessageBox.Show statement. (In addition, you can view these values using the Object Browser, as explained in Chapter 14, "Using the Object Browser.")

TABLE 3.1: MessageBoxButtons Values

Members	Description
MessageBoxButtons.AbortRetryIgnore	Displays Abort, Retry, and Ignore buttons
MessageBoxButtons.OK	Displays an OK button only
MessageBoxButtons.OKCancel	Displays OK and Cancel buttons
MessageBoxButtons.RetryCancel	Displays Retry and Cancel buttons
MessageBoxButtons.YesNo	Displays Yes and No buttons
MessageBoxButtons.YesNoCancel	Displays Yes, No, and Cancel buttons

TABLE 3.2: MessageBoxIcon Values

Members	Description
MessageBoxIcon.Asterisk	Displays an information icon
MessageBoxIcon.Error	Displays an error icon
MessageBoxIcon.Exclamation	Displays an exclamation icon
MessageBoxIcon.Hand	Displays an error icon
MessageBoxIcon.Information	Displays an information icon
MessageBoxIcon.None	Does not display an icon
MessageBoxIcon.Question	Displays a question icon
MessageBoxIcon.Stop	Displays an error icon
MessageBoxIcon.Warning	Displays an exclamation icon

You also need to know what the possible return values are for `MessageBox.Show`. (I'll show you how to use return values in the "Evaluating the Response" section later in this chapter.) These values are the members of `System.Windows.Forms.DialogResult`, or `DialogResult` for short, shown in Table 3.3.

TABLE 3.3: `DialogResult` Values

Members	Description
`DialogResult.Abort`	Abort button was clicked.
`DialogResult.Cancel`	Cancel button was clicked.
`DialogResult.Ignore`	Ignore button was clicked.
`DialogResult.No`	No button was clicked.
`DialogResult.None`	None of the buttons were clicked.
`DialogResult.OK`	OK button was clicked.
`DialogResult.Retry`	Retry button was clicked.
`DialogResult.Yes`	Yes button was clicked.

Reviewing *MessageBox.Show* Examples

Let's look at some actual examples that invoke the `MessageBox.Show` method, so that you can get a better feeling for how it is used in practice.

Displaying Text and a Caption

To display text and a caption only, use code like this:

```
MessageBox.Show("This is the text!", "This is the caption!")
```

The message box displays text, a caption, and an OK button, as shown here.

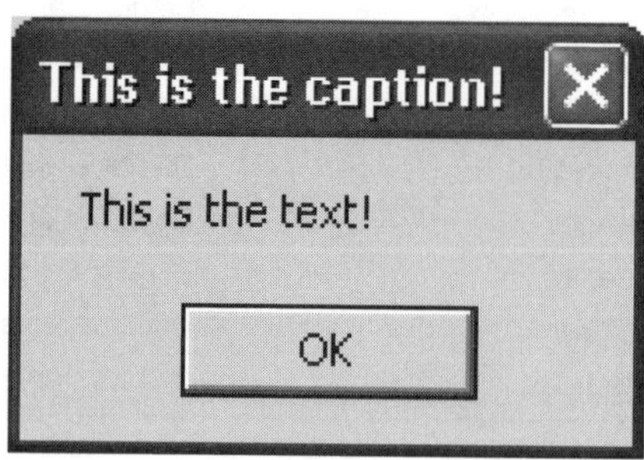

Declaring Variables Using *Dim*, *Option Explicit*, and Other Important Matters

The `Dim` statement (short for "Dimension") is used to declare variables; that is, it tells the VB .NET compiler that something is a variable and what type it is. (A *variable* is simply a name that is used to store a value.) In VB .NET, if you declare a variable using the `Dim` statement without a type, it defaults to the Object type.

It's good programming practice to always explicitly declare variables. It may seem like more work, but it will save you trouble in the long run. To force explicit variable declarations, you can turn on Option Explicit in your project's Property Pages, as explained in Chapter 2. Placing the statement `Option Explicit On` in each module before any code is the functional equivalent of turning it on in a project's Property Pages. Either way, once explicit variable declaration is required, if there are any undeclared variables in your program, it will stop with a compile-time error and not run.

A related compiler option is Option Strict. Like Option Explicit, Option Strict can be turned on for an entire project using the project's Property Pages or on a module-by-module basis by placing the statement `Option Strict` before any code. Option Strict does not relate to parenting style; rather, it compels any declared variable to be given a type at the time of declaration using the As keyword. So, using Option Strict, `Dim myVal As String` is a valid declaration, but `Dim myVal` is not.

Option Strict also makes VB a "strongly typed" language. This means that VB will not implicitly convert variables from one type to another. For example, if S is a string, and `I` is an integer, `S = I` will work if Option Strict is off, but will not work if Option Strict is on. If Option Strict is on, you need to explicitly convert `I` to a strong using the `ToString()` method: `S = I.ToString()`. For further discussion of strong typing and its implications regarding when objects are "bound," see Chapter 15, "Object-Oriented Programming in VB .NET."

Here are some examples of using the `Dim` statement, with comments:

```
Dim myText As String 'Alphanumeric string value
Dim myNum As Integer 'Number that is an integer
Dim answer As DialogResult 'Member of the DialogResult enumeration
Dim myObj 'Provided Option Strict is not turned on, this will declare a
variable
   ' of object type; if Option Strict is on this will produce a syntax error
```

Displaying OK and Cancel Buttons

You can be a little more socially couth and put a Cancel button as well as an OK button in your message box by using code along these lines:

```
MessageBox.Show("Press OK to continue, Cancel to escape!", _
   "Are you tired of this application yet?", _
   MessageBoxButtons.OKCancel)
```

Displaying an Icon and Buttons

To add an icon to the display as well as a button, simply add an argument in the *Icon* position:

```
MessageBox.Show("Press OK to continue, Cancel to escape!", _
   "Are you tired of this application yet?", _
   MessageBoxButtons.OKCancel, _
   MessageBoxIcon.Information)
```

The result is a message box with an information icon, along with OK and Cancel buttons.

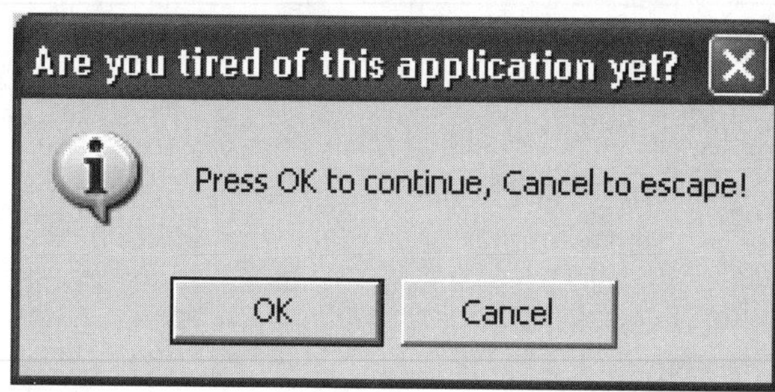

Getting a Return Value

You can easily get a return value to determine which button the user clicked by declaring a variable of type `DialogResult` and assigning the value of the `MessageBox.Show` method to it, as in this example:

```
Dim answer As DialogResult
answer = MessageBox.Show("Press OK to continue, Cancel to escape!", _
   "Are you tired of this application yet?", _
   MessageBoxButtons.OKCancel, _
   MessageBoxIcon.Information)
```

I'll show you how to do something with this return value later in this chapter, in the "Evaluating the Response" section.

Displaying Yes, No, and Cancel Buttons

You can easily display Yes, No, and Cancel buttons (and an icon, if you would like) by using the `MessageBoxButtons.YesNoCancel` value for the *Buttons* argument. Here's the code that creates the box, and returns a value:

```
Dim answer As DialogResult
answer = MessageBox.Show("Press Yes for lunch, No for dinner," & _
   "and Cancel if you are not hungry!", "What meal is it?", _
   MessageBoxButtons.YesNoCancel, MessageBoxIcon.Question)
```

This code uses the concatenation operator (&), which appends two strings of text. The resulting message box includes a question icon and Yes, No, and Cancel buttons.

Setting the Initially Selected Button

The fifth `MessageBox.Show` argument lets you specify the default button, which is the button that is initially selected in a message box. You have three choices, working from left to right: `MessageBoxDefaultButton.Button1` selects the first button, `MessageBoxDefaultButton.Button2` selects the second button, and, as you would suppose, `MessageBoxDefaultButton.Button3` selects the third button. If you don't use the argument, the first button is selected by default.

To move the initial selection to the second button, you could use the following code:

```
Dim answer As DialogResult
answer = MessageBox.Show("Press Yes for lunch, No for dinner," & _
   "and Cancel if you are not hungry!", "What meal is it?", _
   MessageBoxButtons.YesNoCancel, MessageBoxIcon.Question, _
   MessageBoxDefaultButton.Button2)
```

The resulting message box will include Yes, No, and Cancel buttons, with No (the second button) selected by default.

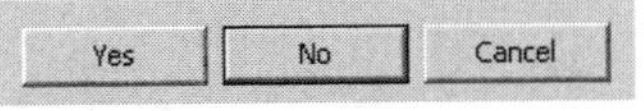

Fooling with the Appearance

There are a bunch of other things you can do with message boxes if you really want to get fancy. First, you can add the constant `MessageBoxOptions.RightAlign` to the sixth `MessageBox.Show` argument, as in this example:

```
Dim answer As DialogResult
Dim msg As String = "I AM ON THE RIGHT!"
answer = MessageBox.Show(msg, "Fooling with Appearance...", _
   MessageBoxButtons.OK, MessageBoxIcon.Information, _
   MessageBoxDefaultButton.Button1, _
   MessageBoxOptions.RightAlign)
```

This aligns the text in the message box on the right.

To play with this right-aligned appearance further, it's fun to break up lines. You can break the text in a `MessageBox.Show` *`Text`* parameter by inserting a carriage return. You can do this by using the constants that are the members of the VB .NET `ControlChars` enumeration. In this enumeration, `ControlChars.Cr` is a carriage return, and `ControlChars.CrLf` is a carriage return line feed. Here is an example that uses `ControlChars.Cr`:

```
Dim answer As DialogResult
Dim msg As String
msg = "I" & ControlChars.CrLf & "AM" & ControlChars.CrLf & _
   "ON" & ControlChars.CrLf & "THE" & ControlChars.CrLf & "RIGHT!"
answer = MessageBox.Show(msg, "Fooling with Appearance...", _
   MessageBoxButtons.OK, MessageBoxIcon.Information, _
   MessageBoxDefaultButton.Button1, _
   MessageBoxOptions.RightAlign)
```

The resulting message box displays text broken up on the right side of the box.

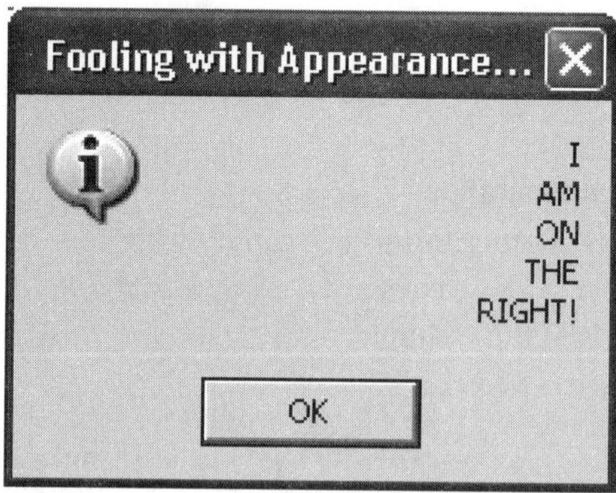

NOTE You can also insert carriage returns by using the ASCII code for a carriage return (13) and the `Chr` function. Written this way, the function `Chr(13)` inserted in the message box text causes line breaks. VB provides several built-in constants that serve the same function as `Chr(13)`, and it's a better practice to use them, because the resulting code is more transparent. The VB6 constants have been retained for backward compatibility: `vbCr` is a carriage return, or `Chr(13)`, and `vbCrLf` is a carriage return plus line feed, `Chr(13) + Chr(10)`. However, you should use the constants that are the members of the VB .NET `ControlChars` enumeration instead, as shown in the example here.

Adding a Service Notification

A really nifty MessageBox option allows you to add a notification in the System event log, provided, of course, that your application is running on a system that provides this facility. (For more information about working with event logs, see Chapter 10, "Using Timers, EventLogs, and ServiceControllers.")

To add this functionality to a message box, simply add the value `MessageBoxOptions.ServiceNotification` to the sixth argument of `MessageBox.Show`. If there is already a value for this argument, add the two values together. For example, the following code adds a service notification to the message box with right-aligned text.

```
answer = MessageBox.Show(msg, "Fooling with Appearance...", _
   MessageBoxButtons.OK, MessageBoxIcon.Information, _
   MessageBoxDefaultButton.Button1, _
   MessageBoxOptions.RightAlign + _
   MessageBoxOptions.ServiceNotification)
```

If you run this, and open the Event Viewer (found in the Administrative Tools Control Panel applet provided by Windows 2000 or Windows XP), you'll find a recent Application Popup entry in the System log. Expand the entry in the Event Viewer to find the text of the message box, as shown in Figure 3.2.

Putting Together a Form for the Examples

I've put together a form with buttons to access the message box examples presented here. The form is shown in Figure 3.3. You can find the complete source code for all the message box examples, along with event handlers to invoke them when the appropriate button is clicked, in Listing 3.1.

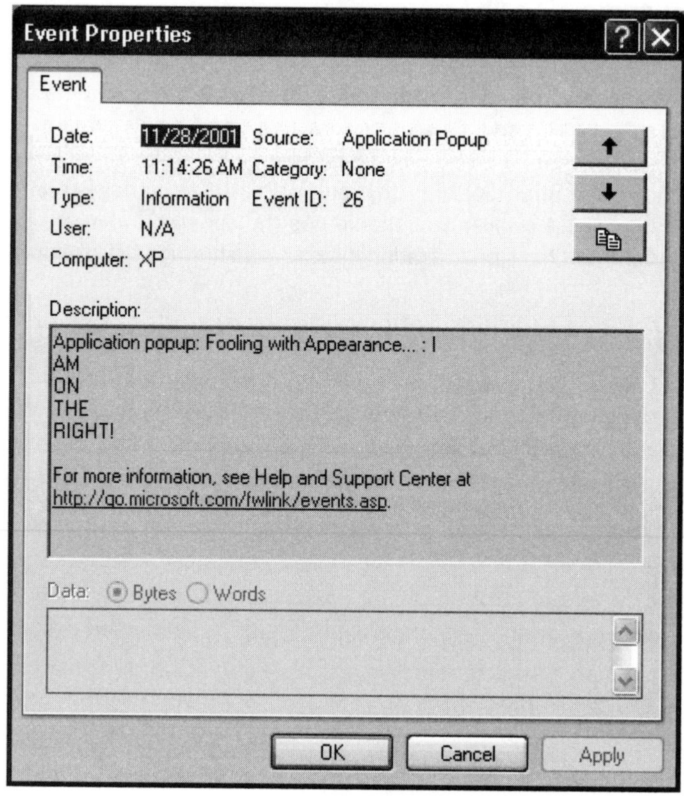

FIGURE 3.2: By adding `MessageBox-Options.Service-Notification` to the options argument of `MessageBox.Show`, you can place an entry in the System log when the message box is displayed.

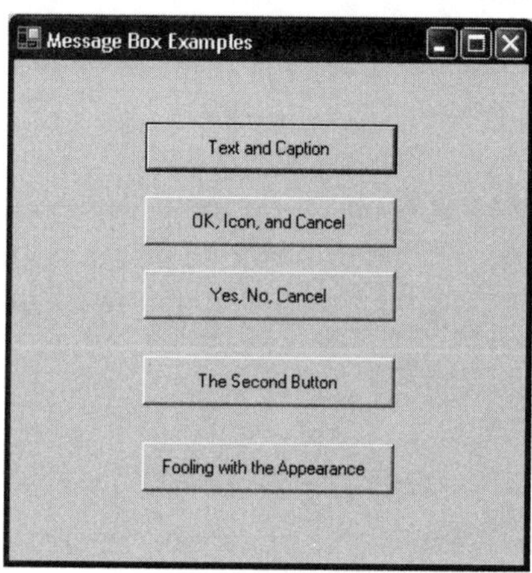

FIGURE 3.3: The buttons on the Message Box Examples form are used to display the `MessageBox.Show` examples.

Listing 3.1 Sample *MessageBox.Show* Code

```
Private Sub btnTextandCaption_Click(ByVal sender As Object, _
   ByVal e As System.EventArgs) Handles btnTextandCaption.Click
   MessageBox.Show("This is the text!", "This is the caption!")
End Sub

Private Sub btnOKIconCancel_Click(ByVal sender As Object, _
   ByVal e As System.EventArgs) Handles btnOKIconCancel.Click
   MessageBox.Show("Press OK to continue, Cancel to escape!", _
      "Are you tired of this application yet?", _
      MessageBoxButtons.OKCancel)
   Dim answer As DialogResult
   answer = MessageBox.Show("Press OK to continue, Cancel to escape!", _
     "Are you tired of this application yet?", _
     MessageBoxButtons.OKCancel, _
     MessageBoxIcon.Information)
End Sub

Private Sub btnYesNoCancel_Click(ByVal sender As Object, _
   ByVal e As System.EventArgs) Handles btnYesNoCancel.Click
   Dim answer As DialogResult
   answer = MessageBox.Show("Press Yes for lunch, No for dinner," & _
      "and Cancel if you are not hungry!", "What meal is it?", _
      MessageBoxButtons.YesNoCancel, MessageBoxIcon.Question)
End Sub

Private Sub btnSecond_Click(ByVal sender As Object, _
   ByVal e As System.EventArgs) Handles btnSecond.Click
   Dim answer As DialogResult
   answer = MessageBox.Show("Press Yes for lunch, No for dinner," & _
      "and Cancel if you are not hungry!", "What meal is it?", _
      MessageBoxButtons.YesNoCancel, MessageBoxIcon.Question, _
      MessageBoxDefaultButton.Button2)
End Sub

Private Sub btnAppear_Click(ByVal sender As Object, _
   ByVal e As System.EventArgs) Handles btnAppear.Click
   Dim answer As DialogResult
   'Dim msg As String = "I AM ON THE RIGHT!"
   Dim msg As String
   msg = "I" & ControlChars.CrLf & "AM" & ControlChars.CrLf & _
      "ON" & ControlChars.CrLf & "THE" & ControlChars.CrLf & "RIGHT!"
   answer = MessageBox.Show(msg, "Fooling with Appearance...", _
      MessageBoxButtons.OK, MessageBoxIcon.Information, _
      MessageBoxDefaultButton.Button1, _
      MessageBoxOptions.RightAlign + _
      MessageBoxOptions.ServiceNotification)
End Sub
```

Adding Form Controls

In the remainder of this chapter, I'll show you how to build an application that displays most of the possible permutations of `MessageBox.Show` icons and buttons. In addition, the application will evaluate the user response to the `MessageBox.Show` buttons.

To build the interface for this application, we're going to need to use a variety of VB .NET controls, and this provides a good excuse for getting to know what these controls do and how they work. Specifically, we will look at GroupBoxes, Panels, Splitters, Labels, TextBoxes, and RadioButtons, and how to set the tab order for moving among these controls.

Using GroupBoxes, Panels, and Splitters

For starters, we're going to use two GroupBoxes, two Panels, and a Splitter to divide form real estate by logical purpose. GroupBoxes (called Frames in previous versions of VB) and Panels are used to hold, or contain, groups of other controls; they don't do too much in and of themselves. They are similar, except that a GroupBox lets you put a line of text at the top, and a Panel does not. A Splitter lets the user resize the areas it adjoins.

The application that you'll build will have the following visual interface groups:

- A GroupBox at the top for the user to enter the prompt and title
- A Panel on the left side of the center area for the button selection
- Another Panel on the right for the icon selection, separated from the left Panel by a Splitter
- A GroupBox on the bottom used to contain the button whose Click procedure activates the application and displays the selected message box

Before you can add GroupBoxes, Panels, and the other controls, you will need to build a Windows Form project. You must start a VB .NET project and open a form in its designer, as explained in Chapter 2.

WARNING When you first run your project, if you have changed the name of your form, you will quite likely get a Build error, which somewhat inscrutably tells you that `Sub Main` was not found in your project. To fix this problem, open the project's Property Pages, as explained in Chapter 2, and set the Startup object to the form as it has been renamed.

Adding GroupBoxes

To add a GroupBox to your form, with the project and form open, select the GroupBox control in the Toolbox, as shown on the following page.

Double-click, or drag and drop, to place the GroupBox control on the form.

NOTE If the Toolbox is not displayed, choose View ➢ Toolbox from the main VB .NET menu to display it.

The next step is to set this GroupBox so that it docks to the top of the form. To do this, in the Properties window, make sure that the GroupBox is selected in the Objects list. Next, locate the Dock property. Use the drop-down area map to set the GroupBox to dock to the top of the form, as shown in Figure 3.4.

FIGURE 3.4: Use the Properties window to change the Dock property so that the GroupBox docks to the top of the form.

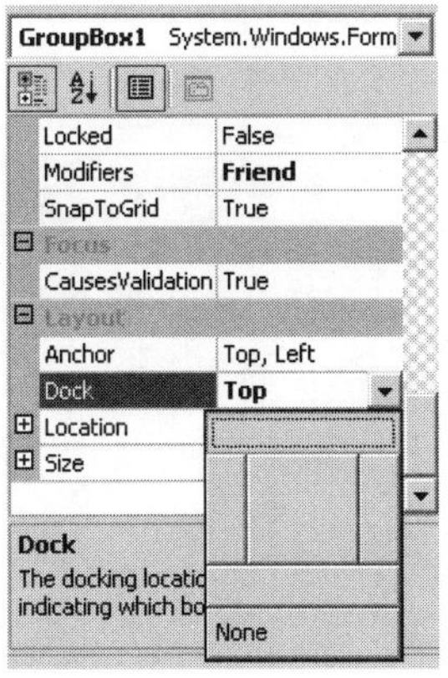

Next, change the Text property in the Properties window to the text you would like displayed. For this example, make the Text property **`Enter your text and caption:`**, as shown in Figure 3.5. That's it for the top GroupBox.

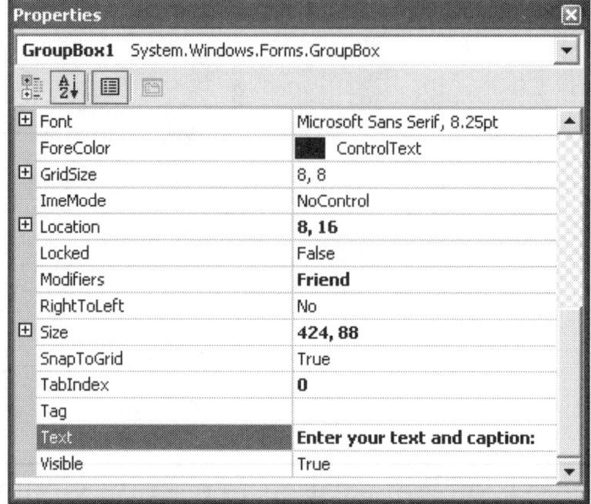

FIGURE 3.5: Use the Properties window to change the GroupBox Text property.

To add the bottom GroupBox, follow the steps for the top GroupBox, but make sure that the Text property is empty. Use the Dock property of the bottom GroupBox to align it to the bottom of the form.

You can add a button to the bottom GroupBox by dragging the Button control from the Toolbox onto the GroupBox. (Make sure that you drop it on the bottom GroupBox, *not* on the form.) Change the Button name to **`btnShow`**, and change its text to **`SHOW`**.

When the form with the two GroupBoxes is run, the GroupBoxes are docked to the top and bottom of the window, no matter how you resize it. You can see what the GroupBoxes look like in Figure 3.6.

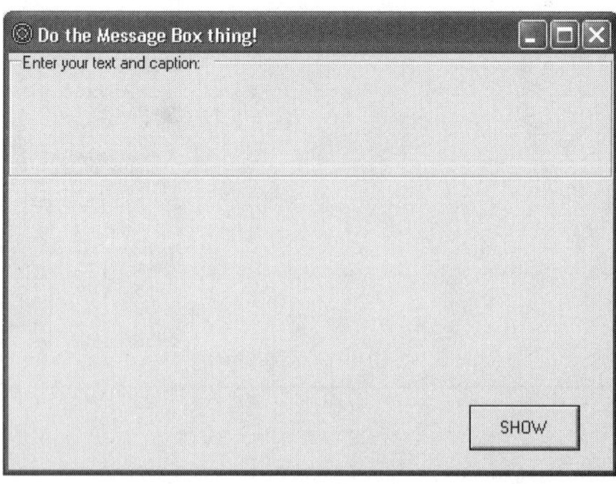

FIGURE 3.6: When you run the form, the GroupBoxes remained aligned to the top and bottom, no matter how you size the window.

Inserting Panels and Splitters

The idea behind using Panels with a Splitter control is that the user can use the Splitter to resize the width or height of Panels to best access the controls that have been placed on the Panels. For example, Windows Explorer uses a Splitter to separate the tree view and folder content panes, and you can move it to set the width of each pane.

Placing a Splitter on a form can be frustrating, so follow the steps outlined in this section to learn how to do it.

First, add a Panel control to the form by selecting it in the Toolbox and dragging it onto the form (or by double-clicking it).

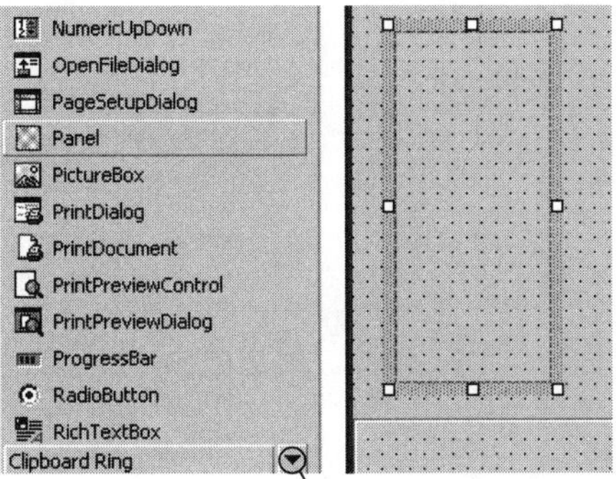

NOTE You may need to click the Toolbox expansion arrow (shown above) to get it to display tools that are toward the end of the alphabet, such as the Panel control.

Next, set the Dock property of the Panel to Left. To do this, in the Properties window, make sure that the Panel is selected in the Objects list. Find the Dock property in the list of properties on the left. Click the drop-down arrow corresponding to the Dock property (to its right). Use the position map to select the left side, as shown here.

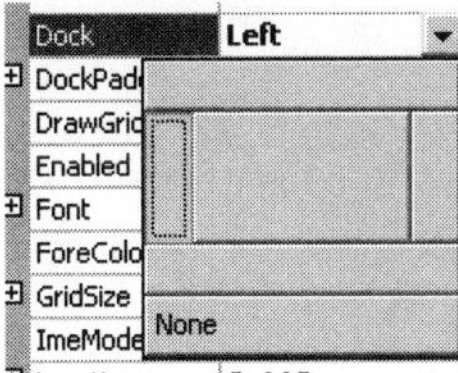

Place the Splitter control on the form. (Make sure that you site the Splitter on the form, *not* on the Panel!) It will automatically dock, as shown in Figure 3.7. Set the BackColor property of the Splitter to something vivid, such as Red, so that you will be able to clearly see it when you run the form.

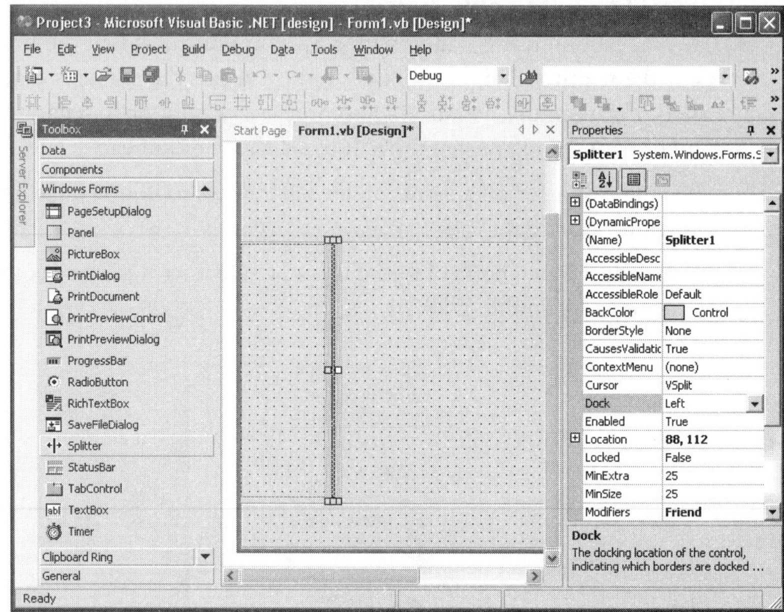

FIGURE 3.7:

Place the Splitter on the form.

Next, place another Panel on the form. This Panel will act as the right pane of the application. Use the Properties window to set the Dock property of this Panel to Fill. Figure 3.8 shows the Panel placement and Dock property setting.

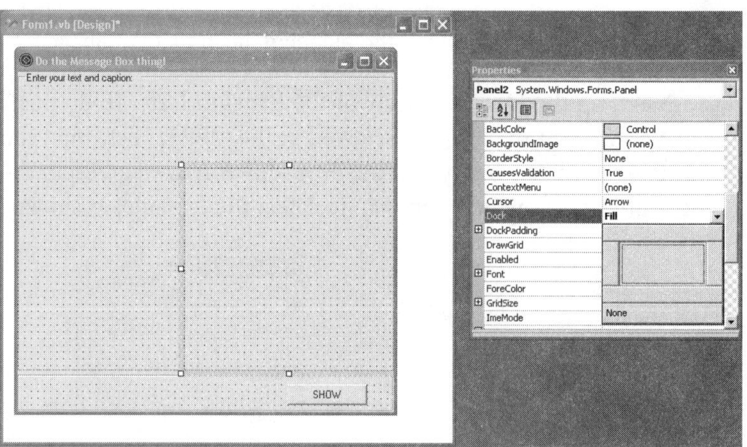

FIGURE 3.8:

Put another Panel on the form, and set its Dock property to Fill.

When you run the project as it now stands, you'll see that the two Panels create panes that fill the width of the form, no matter how you resize the form. You can use the Splitter to reallocate the relative size of the panes on the fly.

Adding Labels and TextBoxes

Label controls are used to display text on forms (usually, this text "labels" things, hence the name of the control). TextBox controls are most often used to accept text input from an application's user (in some circumstances, they are also used to display information). Together, Labels and TextBoxes are probably used in every application that interacts with users. So, let's get started adding these important controls to our program.

First, add a Label that will designate where the user inputs the text for the prompt. To do this, select the Label control in the Toolbox and drag it onto the top GroupBox. In the Properties window, make sure that the Label is selected in the Objects list. Change the Text property of the Label to **`Text:`**. Figure 3.9 shows the Label placement and Text property.

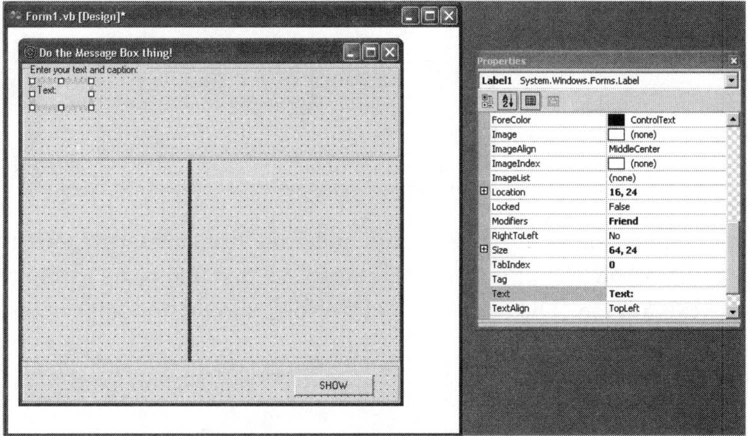

FIGURE 3.9: Add a Label to the top Panel and use the Properties window to set its Text property to Text:.

NOTE The new value of the Text property will not be displayed in the control on the form until the focus leaves the Text property in the Properties window. This happens, for example, when you click to select another property in the Properties window.

Repeat this process to add a Label that will be used to designate the place for the user to input text for the title. The Text property for this control should contain **`Caption:`**. It's a good idea to rename any control that you will need to refer to in code with a name that reflects the type of the control and its function in the application. But, in many cases, Label controls are never used in code; they are essentially "decorative" in nature. In these cases, there is no real need to change the default control name, which is Label*n*, as in Label1, Label2, and so on.

Next, add a TextBox control to the right of the Caption Label. Drag the TextBox from the Toolbox onto the form. Use the Properties window to change the Name property of the control to **txtText**. Delete all the text in the Text property. Figure 3.10 shows the TextBox on the form in design mode.

FIGURE 3.10:

Add a TextBox control, making sure to set it so that it contains no text.

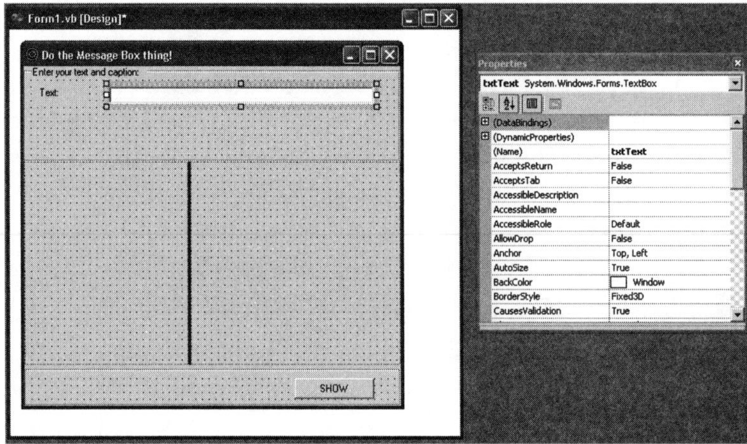

Add another TextBox control under the first one for the title text. Again, make sure to delete the default text for this control, so that it appears without text on the form. Name it **txtCaption**. The upper pane of the form should now appear as shown here.

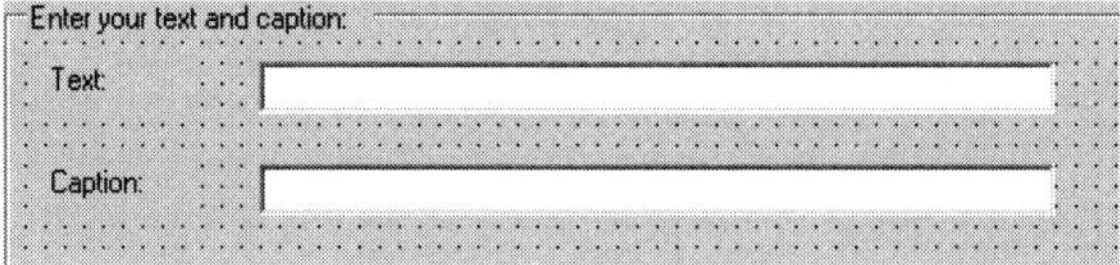

While we're adding Labels, you can make the application a little nicer by identifying the Panels. Add a Label with the Text property **Buttons** to the left Panel, and another Label with the Text property **Icon** to the right Panel.

TIP You can use the Align and Make Same Size options on the Format menu to standardize the appearance of labels and buttons on a form. Alternatively, you can use the control's position coordinates, which can be found in the Location and Size properties in the Properties window, to align controls. For example, to make sure that two controls are aligned vertically, simply set the Location property X coordinate of each control to the same number.

Adding RadioButtons

RadioButton controls are typically used when you want to let a user make one—and only one—choice from a number of options. (This is the control "formerly known" as an Option button.) When you add more than one RadioButton to a container such as a Panel or GroupBox, these RadioButtons form a kind of group in which only one can be "checked," or selected, at a time.

Let's create a group of RadioButtons to accept the user's choice of buttons. In the Toolbox, select the RadioButton control.

RadioButton

Drag the control onto the left Panel. Figure 3.11 shows its position.

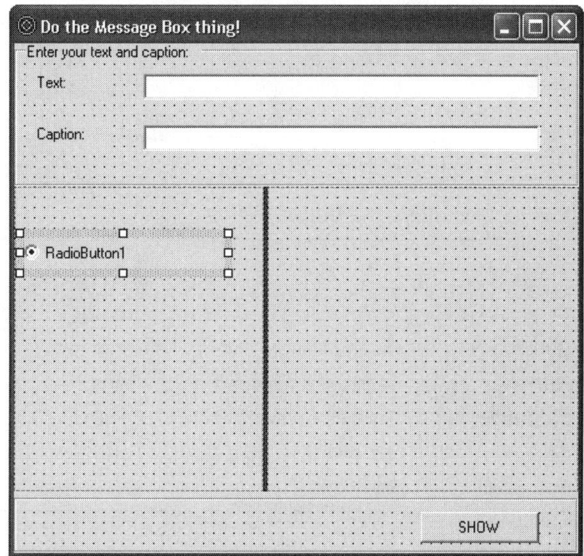

FIGURE 3.11: Place the RadioButton on the left Panel.

Using the Properties window, set the Name property of the RadioButton to **`rdoOKOnly`**, its Text property to **`Ok Only`**, and its Checked property to **`True`**, as shown in Figure 3.12. The Checked property sets the RadioButton to be selected when the form runs.

Next, repeat the steps using the Name and Text property values shown in Table 3.4, adding five more RadioButtons to the left Panel. Set the Checked property for each of the other buttons to **`False`**.

FIGURE 3.12:

Set the Checked property of the first RadioButton to True.

TABLE 3.4: Values for the Buttons Pane

Name	Text	Checked
rdoOKOnly	Ok Only	True
rdoOKCancel	Ok and Cancel	False
rdoAbRetry	Abort, Retry, Ignore	False
rdoYesNoCancel	Yes, No, Cancel	False
rdoYesNo	Yes and No	False
rdoRetryCancel	Retry and Cancel	False

When you're finished, your group of RadioButtons should appear as shown here.

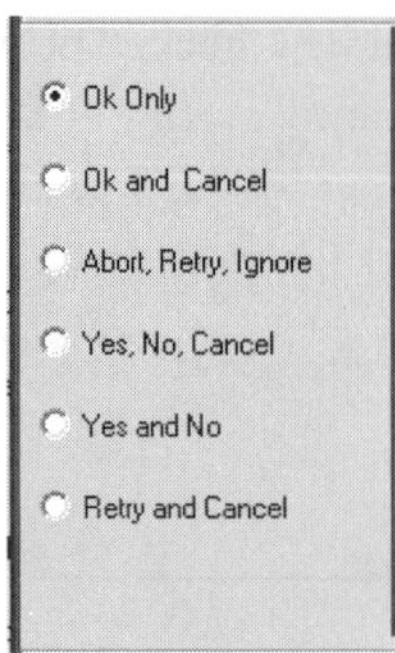

TIP You can create RadioButtons of uniform size by copying and pasting a RadioButton that has already been positioned on a form. This achieves the same results as dragging the RadioButton control from the Toolbox and can save some time.

Next, using the Name and Text values from Table 3.5, create the RadioButton group for the right (icons) pane. Be sure to set the Checked property for the first one, `rdoError`, to **`True`**, and the Checked properties for all the other RadioButtons to **`False`**.

TABLE 3.5: Values for the Icons Pane

Name	Text	Checked
rdoError	Error	True
rdoQuestion	Question	False
rdoExclamation	Exclamation	False
rdoInformation	Information	False
rdoNoIcon	No Icon	False

When you're finished, your application's form should be complete, as shown in Figure 3.13.

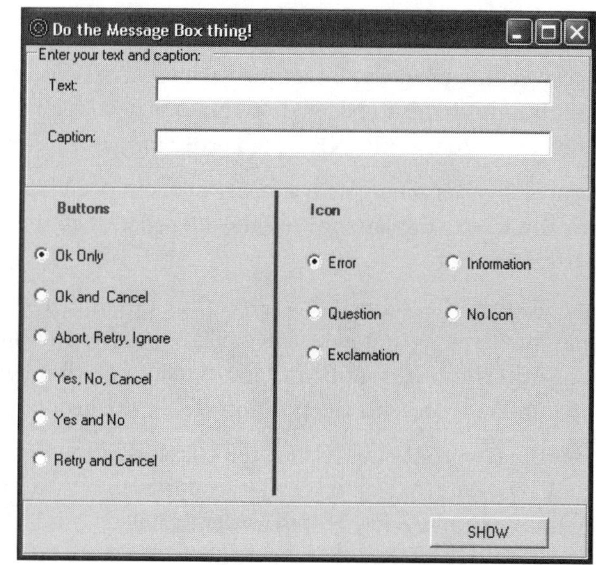

FIGURE 3.13: In all its glory! If you run the form, you can get a sense of what it looks like as a whole and make sure that the user interface is working (for example, that you can select only one RadioButton in each group).

Setting the Tab Order

It's important that all applications have an easy way to navigate that does not require the mouse. Generally, this is done using keyboard shortcuts that open menus (see Chapter 11, "Creating Menus") and with the Tab and arrow keys. When you create an application, you set the tab order, so that users who prefer to use the Tab key are taken through the controls on a form in the proper order.

VB .NET provides an easy and nifty way to set the tab order. But before we get to it, you should understand that the properties of a control are used to set where that control appears in the tab order, and if it can be reached using the Tab key at all.

If you set a control's TabStop process to False (you can use the Properties window to do this), the control is not included in the tab order. Another way of putting this is that for a control to be part of the tab order, its TabStop property must be set to True.

The TabIndex property (which can also be set in the Properties window) sets the navigation order for controls using the Tab key. So, the control with the lowest TabIndex (0) is where the tab order starts. The control with the next lowest TabIndex, provided its TabStop property is set to True, will be next.

NOTE Not all controls are included in the tab order. For example, Label controls cannot be navigated to (another way of putting this is that they cannot receive the focus) and do not have a TabIndex property.

You can set the tab order by setting each control's TabIndex property in the Properties window, but this tends to be a tedious process in which it's hard to see what you're doing. It's much easier to use VB .NET's tab order mode.

To start tab order mode, with a form open, choose View ➢ Tab Order from the VB .NET menus. You'll see a display showing the tab order of all the controls on a form, like that shown in Figure 3.14.

Controls that are grouped in a GroupBox or Panel are shown with two tab order mode position numbers, separated by a decimal point, for example, 1.2. The first number is the tab order position of the GroupBox or Panel itself, which the user accesses with the Tab key. The second number represents the position within the group, which is accessed using arrow keys.

To set the tab order, simply click the controls in the form in the order you would like. As you click each control, you'll see that its position in the tab order changes. To close tab order mode, simply choose View ➢ Tab Order again.

Once you've set the tab order, you should run the form to make sure that it works as you intended.

FIGURE 3.14:

It's easy to set the tab order using VB .NET's nifty tab order mode.

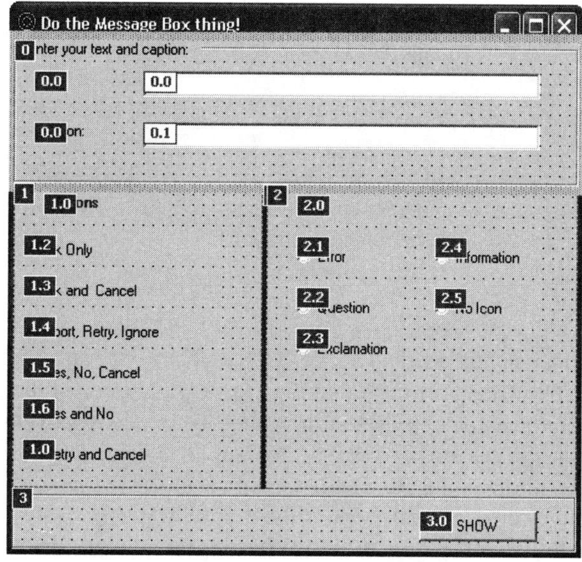

Using *If* Statements

The message box application is now ready to be "wired," meaning that the user interface is complete and in place. All that is missing is the code that ties the various pieces of the user interface together and lets the application do its thing (which in this example, in case you've lost track, is to display variations of `MessageBox.Show`).

To help achieve this wiring, we will use `If` statements. `If` statements are one type of conditional statement used in a program to allow the program to make decisions based on conditions. In other words, the program will do one thing if something (the condition) is true, and do another thing if the condition is not true.

NOTE Another conditional statement is the `Select Case` statement, which selects the code to be executed depending on a condition. `Select Case` and `If` statements are logically equivalent, but depending on the situation, one or the other can be a lot more straightforward and less convoluted to use. For more information about the `Select Case` statement, see Chapter 7, "Working with Windows Forms Controls."

To write good `If` statements, you need to understand the scaffolding and syntax of the `If` statement in a particular language, and also what it means for something to be true. (For example, the condition `0=10` will always evaluate to false.)

The structure of the VB .NET `If` statement that we will use to wire our message box form is as follows:

```
If condition1 Then
   first block of code
ElseIf condition2 Then
   second block of code
...
Else
   final block of code
End If
```

TIP

It's the best programming practice to build the complete structure of the `If` statement with the conditions and space for the blocks of code that the conditions will trigger before actually writing the code that is triggered. `If` statements can get complicated, particularly when they are nested one within another. If you try to write everything all at once, you can easily get the syntax of the statement bollixed up and cause something you didn't intend when the program launches.

VB first evaluates *`condition1`*. If it is true, the first block of code is executed, and the `If` statement is complete. If *`condition1`* is false, *`condition2`* is evaluated. If *`condition2`* is true, the code in its block is processed, and the execution of the `If` statement is complete. Otherwise, the next conditional block is evaluated, and so on until, if no conditions have evaluated to true, the final block of code following the `Else` statement is executed.

TIP

In many cases, you'll think that a condition will always be true and that execution will never "fall through" to the `Else` clause. It's still a good idea to include an `Else` clause and block of code, just to catch errors you might not have considered.

With the `If` statement out of the way, let's go ahead and get to the exciting part: wiring the form!

Wiring the Form

There are three parts to wiring the form in this example:

- Evaluating which buttons and icon were selected
- Displaying the results
- Evaluating the response to the resulting message box

You've already seen a number of different examples of displaying message boxes earlier in this chapter. The only difference is that this application will display different results depending on the choices of the user, by storing the value of those choices in a variable.

All the code for the application will be placed in the Click event of the button used to display the results, btnShow.

First, open the Code Editor by selecting the button and then choosing View Code from its context menu.

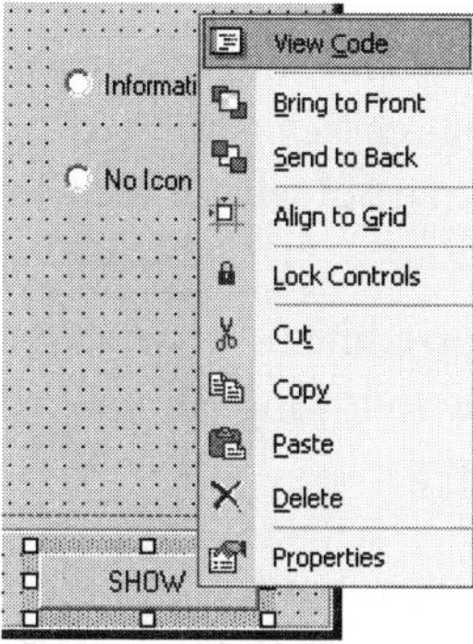

Next, create the scaffolding for the button's Click event procedure. Make sure btnShow is selected in the Objects list and choose Click from the Procedures list, as shown in Figure 3.15. The event procedure will be created for you:

```
Private Sub btnShow_Click(ByVal sender As Object, _
   ByVal e As System.EventArgs) Handles btnShow.Click

End Sub
```

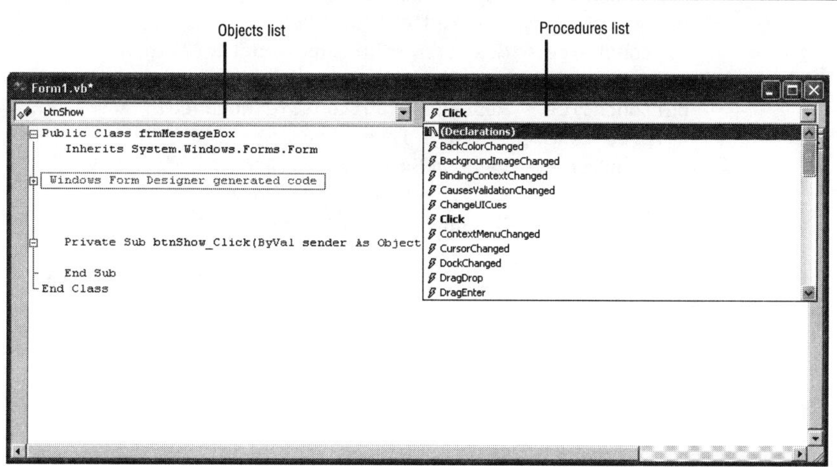

FIGURE 3.15: Select btnShow from the Objects list and the Click event from the Procedures list to create the scaffolding for the button's Click event handler.

Within the event procedure, declare three variables: one to hold the user's choice of buttons, the second to store the choice of icon, and the third for the user's selection from the message box:

```
Dim buttonchoice As MessageBoxButtons
Dim iconchoice As MessageBoxIcon
Dim answer As DialogResult
```

Determining Button Choice

In most applications, user interfaces are intended to interface with the user. This means that the user gets to do things like entering text and making choices. As a programmer, you need to be able to know what that choice was. Hence, you must determine which radio button was selected by the user as part of wiring your form. This is accomplished through an `If` statement.

After the declarations, skip a line to separate the different functional code blocks in the procedure, and then add the following comment:

```
'Determine Button Choice
```

TIP It's good practice to include a comment at the beginning of each block of code saying what the code does. If the blocks of code within the `If` conditions were complicated (in this example, each is only one line), a comment should be included to explain what each one does.

Next, add an `If` statement to determine which radio button has been selected, using the `RadioButton.Checked` property:

```
If rdoOKOnly.Checked = True Then
   buttonchoice = MessageBoxButtons.OK
ElseIf rdoOKCancel.Checked = True Then
   buttonchoice = MessageBoxButtons.OKCancel
ElseIf rdoAbRetry.Checked = True Then
   buttonchoice = MessageBoxButtons.AbortRetryIgnore
ElseIf rdoYesNoCancel.Checked = True Then
   buttonchoice = MessageBoxButtons.YesNoCancel
ElseIf rdoYesNo.Checked = True Then
   buttonchoice = MessageBoxButtons.YesNo
ElseIf rdoRetryCancel.Checked = True Then
   buttonchoice = MessageBoxButtons.RetryCancel
Else
   MessageBox.Show("Unexpected error in button selection!")
End If
```

TIP The `If` statement should never "fall through" to the `Else` block, because we know all the choices available to the user, and one must be selected. However, sometimes you cannot be so sure, so as a matter of good programming form, an `Else` block has been included just in case.

Determining Icon Choice

You will also need to know which icon was selected by the user. Skip a line and add the descriptive comment, followed by the `If` statement that determines the user's icon choice:

```
'Determine Icon Choice
If rdoError.Checked = True Then
   iconchoice = MessageBoxIcon.Error
ElseIf rdoQuestion.Checked = True Then
   iconchoice = MessageBoxIcon.Question
ElseIf rdoExclamation.Checked = True Then
   iconchoice = MessageBoxIcon.Exclamation
ElseIf rdoInformation.Checked = True Then
   iconchoice = MessageBoxIcon.Information
ElseIf rdoNoIcon.Checked = True Then
   iconchoice = MessageBoxIcon.None
Else
   MessageBox.Show ("Unexpected error in icon selection!")
End If
```

The final option, "No Icon," sets the value of the `iconchoice` variable to `MessageBoxIcon.None`. When this choice is selected, an icon isn't displayed in the message box.

Displaying the Message Box

In the real world, once you know the input and choices made by the user, your program needs to do something (hopefully, taking the user input into account). In our case, we want to display a message box based on the choices made by the user as a proxy for the more complicated things a real-world program would do with the user input.

Once again, skip a line to separate the different functional code blocks in the procedure. Add a comment stating what the block does:

```
'Display the Message Box
```

Next, add code to display the message box, using the Text property of the two TextBoxes for the text and the caption, and the variable values processed in code for the buttons and icons:

```
answer = MessageBox.Show(txtText.Text, txtCaption.Text, _
   buttonchoice, iconchoice)
```

You can run the project at this point. Test the application by trying all possible combinations of buttons and icons. Figure 3.16 shows an example of testing the Yes and No choice.

FIGURE 3.16: You should test the message box application by trying all the possibilities.

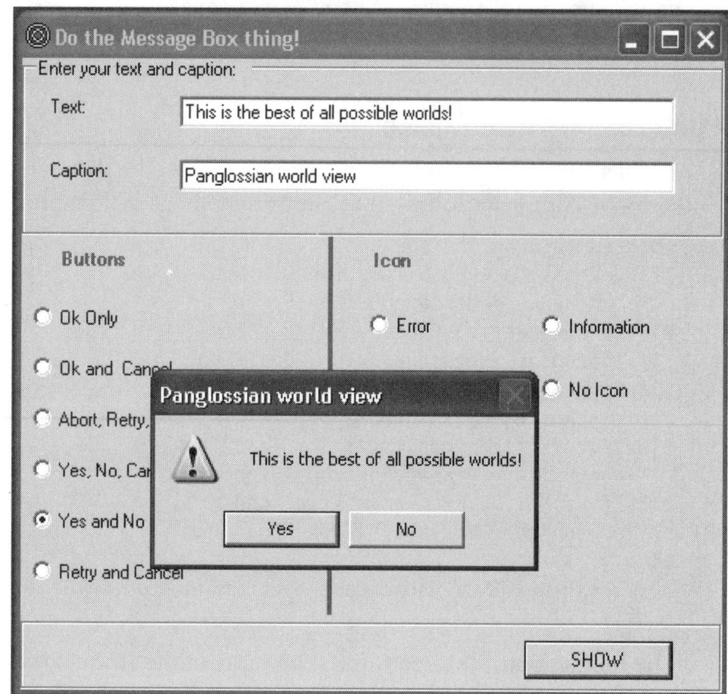

Evaluating the Response

The final step in the application is to create the code that evaluates the user choice of buttons. Back in the Code Editor once again, skip a line and add a descriptive comment:

```
'Evaluate the answer
```

You can then add an `If` statement to check which button the user selected:

```
Dim evaluate As String
If answer = DialogResult.OK Then
   evaluate = "You clicked OK!"
```

```
ElseIf answer = DialogResult.Cancel Then
   evaluate = "You clicked Cancel!"
ElseIf answer = DialogResult.Abort Then
   evaluate = "You clicked Abort!"
ElseIf answer = DialogResult.Retry Then
   evaluate = "You clicked Retry!"
ElseIf answer = DialogResult.Ignore Then
   evaluate = "You clicked Ignore!"
ElseIf answer = DialogResult.Yes Then
   evaluate = "You clicked Yes!"
ElseIf answer = DialogResult.No Then
   evaluate = "You clicked No!"
Else
   evaluate = "Nothing was clicked!"
End If
```

Finally, you should do something with the information you collected (displaying it isn't a bad start):

```
'Do something with the evaluation
MessageBox.Show(evaluate, "Message Box Evaluation", _
   MessageBoxButtons.OK, MessageBoxIcon.Information)
```

Once again, you should run the project and test all possible permutations. For example, suppose that you use the application to create a message box with Abort, Retry, and Ignore buttons. (Notice that it's easy to create alarming messages, but you should try to refrain from putting them in your applications!)

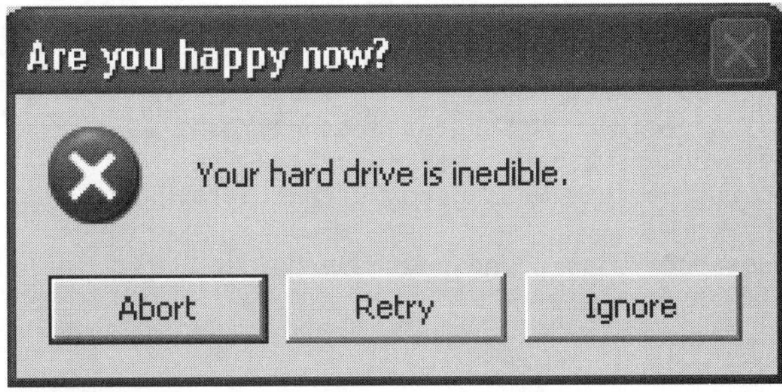

After the correct message box is built, you should make sure that the application correctly evaluates what you did when you click Retry.

The completed code for the entire Click event is shown in Listing 3.2.

Listing 3.2 Displaying Message Boxes and Evaluating the Response

```
Private Sub btnShow_Click(ByVal sender As Object, _
   ByVal e As System.EventArgs) Handles btnShow.Click
   Dim buttonchoice As MessageBoxButtons
   Dim iconchoice As MessageBoxIcon
   Dim answer As DialogResult

   'Determine Button Choice
   If rdoOKOnly.Checked = True Then
      buttonchoice = MessageBoxButtons.OK
   ElseIf rdoOKCancel.Checked = True Then
      buttonchoice = MessageBoxButtons.OKCancel
   ElseIf rdoAbRetry.Checked = True Then
      buttonchoice = MessageBoxButtons.AbortRetryIgnore
   ElseIf rdoYesNoCancel.Checked = True Then
      buttonchoice = MessageBoxButtons.YesNoCancel
   ElseIf rdoYesNo.Checked = True Then
      buttonchoice = MessageBoxButtons.YesNo
   ElseIf rdoRetryCancel.Checked = True Then
      buttonchoice = MessageBoxButtons.RetryCancel
   Else
      MessageBox.Show("Unexpected error in button selection!")
   End If

   'Determine Icon Choice
   If rdoError.Checked = True Then
      iconchoice = MessageBoxIcon.Error
   ElseIf rdoQuestion.Checked = True Then
      iconchoice = MessageBoxIcon.Question
   ElseIf rdoExclamation.Checked = True Then
      iconchoice = MessageBoxIcon.Exclamation
   ElseIf rdoInformation.Checked = True Then
      iconchoice = MessageBoxIcon.Information
```

```
        ElseIf rdoNoIcon.Checked = True Then
           iconchoice = MessageBoxIcon.None
        Else
           MessageBox.Show ("Unexpected error in icon selection!")
        End If

        'Display the Message Box
        answer = MessageBox.Show(txtText.Text, txtCaption.Text, _
           buttonchoice, iconchoice)

        'Evaluate the answer
        Dim evaluate As String
        If answer = DialogResult.OK Then
           evaluate = "You clicked OK!"
        ElseIf answer = DialogResult.Cancel Then
           evaluate = "You clicked Cancel!"
        ElseIf answer = DialogResult.Abort Then
           evaluate = "You clicked Abort!"
        ElseIf answer = DialogResult.Retry Then
           evaluate = "You clicked Retry!"
        ElseIf answer = DialogResult.Ignore Then
           evaluate = "You clicked Ignore!"
        ElseIf answer = DialogResult.Yes Then
           evaluate = "You clicked Yes!"
        ElseIf answer = DialogResult.No Then
           evaluate = "You clicked No!"
        Else
           evaluate = "Nothing was clicked!"
        End If

        'Do something with the evaluation
        MessageBox.Show(evaluate, "Message Box Evaluation", _
           MessageBoxButtons.OK, MessageBoxIcon.Information)
     End Sub
```

Summary

You should be really proud! In this chapter, you learned how to create a fairly complex application that has some syntactical complexity, as well as a decent user interface. You learned many of the most important aspects of creating user interfaces that are logical and clean in VB .NET. You used VB .NET to put together and wire a complicated form. This a great deal of material, and you are well on your way to becoming a real VB .NET maestro.

In the next chapter, you'll learn more about Windows Form projects—what they are and how to work with them.

Chapter 4

Working with Windows Form Properties

- Using form properties
- Setting form style
- Setting the default button
- Setting background and foreground colors
- Setting fonts
- Assigning icons
- Setting form size and placement
- Setting dynamic properties

In Chapter 3, "Building a User Interface," you learned how to work with the VB .NET language by using conditional statements to display message boxes. This chapter backs up and takes a different approach, focusing on Windows form properties.

Windows forms are one of the most important kinds of objects that you will be working with in VB .NET. This chapter explores Windows form properties from two viewpoints. You'll learn how to work with the most important form properties at design time using the Properties window. In addition, you'll find out how to change these properties in code—or dynamically—in response to user actions. Changing form properties, such as the BackColor of a form, in code requires understanding how to create and work with objects such as the `System.Drawing.Color` color class. As you'll see, once you get the hang of it, it's easy!

Using the Form Properties

Properties are used to represent and refer to characteristics of objects, as well as set object characteristics. For example, the BackColor property of a Windows form is used to set the background color of the form.

You can also retrieve, or *return*, a property value and store it in a variable. The property value thus contained in a variable can be tapped as needed when a program is running, often using a conditional statement.

Initially, most properties are set at design time using the Properties window. However, it is equally viable to set form properties in code. If you wish the characteristics of your form to change dynamically in response to a user action or system event, using code to change the value of form properties at runtime is the only way to go.

TIP There are many more form properties than those discussed in this chapter. Space constraints mean that I can show you only some of what is available. Be sure to browse the Properties window to view the complete list of properties. Select a property to see its description at the bottom of the Properties window.

The same properties that you use to change the characteristics of forms are also used with many other objects. This means that when you understand how these properties work with forms, you'll also know how to use them with other objects.

Additionally, controls placed on a form automatically inherit many of the property settings of the form. For example, the BackColor property controls the form background color, and the ForeColor property sets the color of the text that appears on a form. These same properties are available to customize buttons and many other controls. It's also the case that buttons placed on a form will automatically assume the BackColor and ForeColor property values of the form. Making life even easier, when you change the value of these properties for a form, they are automatically also changed for the controls sitting on the form.

NOTE A control that is placed on a form is said to be "seated" on the form.

Form and Property References

In the code examples in this chapter, the `Me` keyword is used to refer to the form whose properties are being manipulated. This keeps things really simple, which is good. However, as you may have suspected, it's often necessary to refer to forms in other ways, particularly when there is more than one form in a project. Techniques for working with multiple forms will be explored in Chapter 6, "Working with Form Methods and Modules."

As long as we are getting a little ahead of ourselves, let's take a second to define a form *method*. As opposed to a form property, which represents a characteristic of the form, a form method operates on the form. In other words, the method of an object performs an action. (You can also think of a method as a function or statement.)

In the Code Editor, object properties and methods are invoked by referencing the object (for example, by using `Me`). Next, the dot operator is used, followed by the property or method. Here is an example that sets the Text property and invokes the `Close` method (a form's `Close` method, as you would suspect, closes the form):

```
 ' Set the form's Text property
Me.Text = "I am a form!"

' Invoke the form's Close method
Me.Close
```

TIP The `Me` keyword is optional. So, you could also write `Text = "I am a form!"` (without the `Me`), and it would work.

By the way, it's useful to know that the dot operator can be stacked to refer to the properties of objects on a form, as in this example:

```
Me.Button1.Text = "I am a button on a form!"
```

This code changes the Text property of the Button control named `Button1`, not the Text property of the form.

The Code Editor Pick List

Considering how many form properties there are, you'll probably be glad to know that you really don't need to remember them. When you reference an object, such as a form, in your code, followed by the dot operator, the Code Editor automatically pops up a list of the properties, methods, and objects that you can invoke:

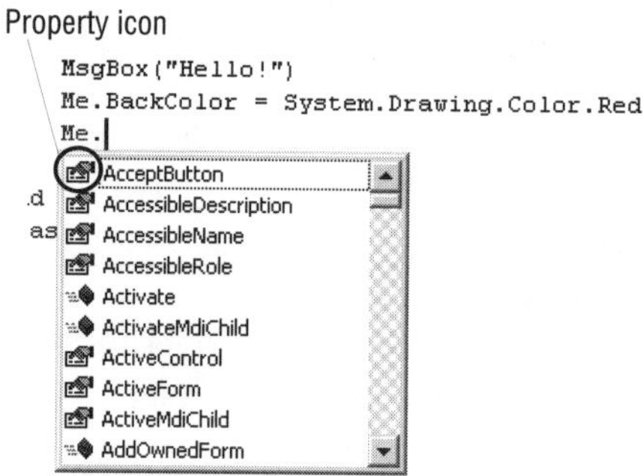

You can recognize properties in this drop-down list, as opposed to methods and objects such as controls, by the little icon showing a hand pointing to a list, which appears to the left of the property.

With the preliminaries out of the way, let's move on and start working with some form properties.

Setting the Form Style

Windows forms come in a number of different styles. These styles are set using the FormBorderStyle property. (This is the property formerly known as BorderStyle in earlier versions of VB.)

Styles change the basic appearance of the window when the form is run, and also change its behavior in significant ways. For example, depending on the FormBorderStyle setting, an icon will (or will not) be displayed in the Windows Taskbar. The FormBorderStyle setting also determines whether or not a running window is resizable. We tend to take these things for granted, but the reality is that a Windows form buys us a great deal of scaffolding in terms of behaving as users expect windows to behave. The good news for the programmer is that you don't need to do any work to get this scaffolding—just select a FormBorderStyle setting.

NOTE I considered showing pictures of windows based on each of the FormBorderStyle settings. The truth is that, by themselves, the windows don't look all that distinctive, and pictures of them don't show much. To get a sense of the different windows and how they behave, the best bet is to play with each of the FormBorderStyle settings.

To select a FormBorderStyle, open a form in its designer. In the Properties window, highlight FormBorderStyle and click the arrow in the right column to display a drop-down list of possible settings.

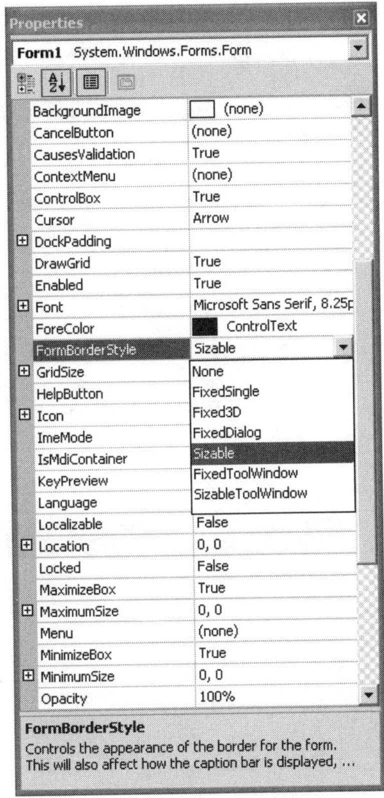

Table 4.1 describes the windows that result from the seven different FormBorderStyle choices.

TABLE 4.1: FormBorderStyle Settings

Setting	Resulting Window
None	A window without a border or any border-related elements. This is the setting to use for introductory "splash" screens.
FixedSingle	A nearly normal window with a single-line border that is only resizable using its Minimize and Maximize buttons. You cannot drag the window's borders to resize it while it is running.
Fixed3D	Like FixedSingle, except that the borders are created with a raised, 3D effect.

Continued on next page

TABLE 4.1 CONTINUED: FormBorderStyle Settings

Setting	Resulting Window
FixedDialog	Like FixedSingle, except that the borders appear recessed. This FormBorder-Style setting is commonly used for dialog boxes.
Sizable	A normal, resizable window, with Minimize and Maximize buttons if desired. This is the default and most commonly used FormBorderStyle setting.
FixedToolWindow	A non-resizable window with a Close button and small-size text in the title bar. Unlike the previous settings, this kind of window does not display an icon in the Windows Taskbar.
SizableToolWindow	Like FixedToolWindow, but sizable.

Setting the Default Button

The AcceptButton property determines which control on a form triggers, or *fires*, a Click event when the user presses the Enter key. To see this in action, place two buttons on a form, like this:

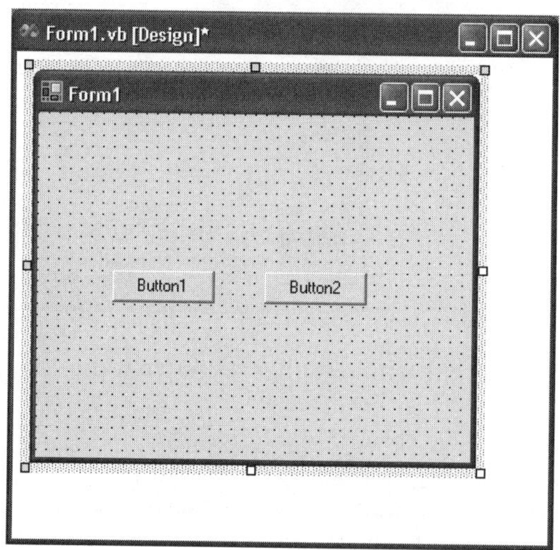

NOTE Make sure to take both Button controls off the tab order by setting their TabStop property (in the Properties window) to **False**, so that the control is not included in the tab order. Otherwise, the first button will be selected by default, and a selected control receives the "focus" and acts as the AcceptButton. See Chapter 3 for more information about setting the tab order.

Next, add code to each button's Click event, as shown in Listing 4.1, so that you can tell when a button's Click event has been triggered using `MsgBox` statements.

Listing 4.1 Testing the *AcceptButton* Property

```
Private Sub Button1_Click(ByVal sender As Object, _
   ByVal e As System.EventArgs) Handles Button1.Click
   MsgBox("I am Button1!")
End Sub

Private Sub Button2_Click(ByVal sender As Object, _
   ByVal e As System.EventArgs) Handles Button2.Click
   MsgBox("I am Button2!")
End Sub
```

NOTE As I explained in Chapter 3, to add the code to each button's Click event, start in the form designer. Using the context menu for one of the buttons, choose View Code. Next, in the Code Editor, choose the button from the Objects list. Select the Click event from the Procedures list. The procedure declaration for the event, which I have previously termed "scaffolding," will be created in the Code Editor. Add your code between the beginning and the end of the event procedure.

Next, set the AcceptButton property of the form to **`Button1`**.

If you run the form and press the Enter key, you'll find that the first button has been clicked, as shown here.

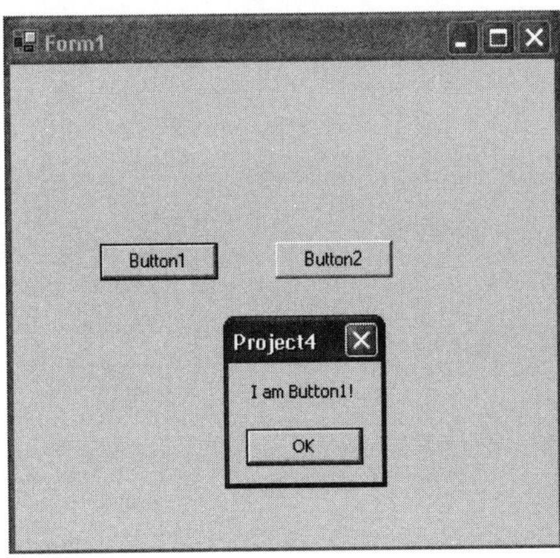

To test the AcceptButton property, with the project back in design mode, use the Properties window to change the value of the form's AcceptButton property to **`Button2`**.

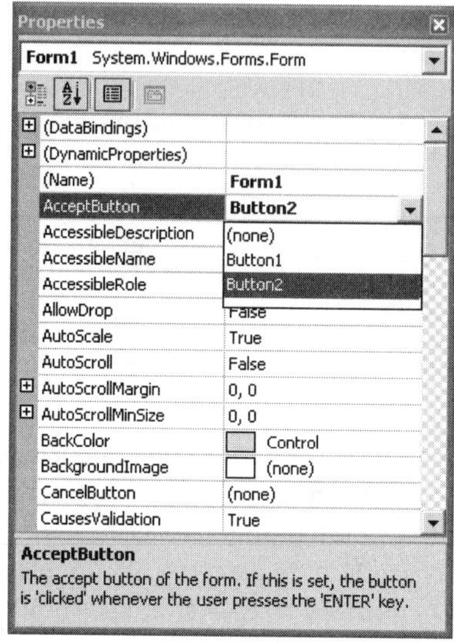

Now, run the project and press Enter again. You'll see that it's as though the second button has been clicked.

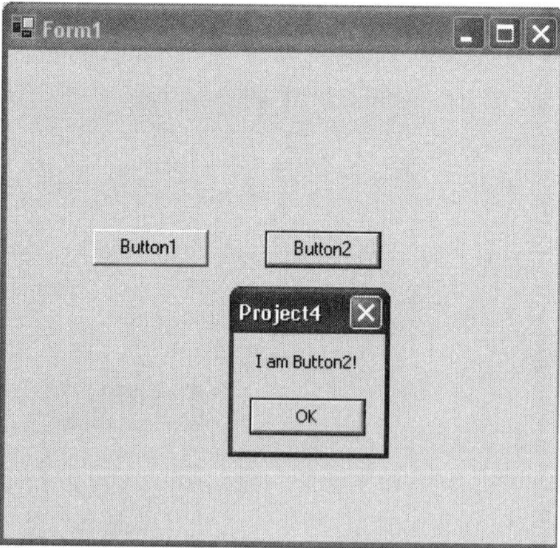

Setting Background and Foreground Colors

The BackColor property sets the background color of a form, and the ForeColor property controls the color of foreground elements. Most often, forms do not directly have any elements whose color is set using the form's ForeColor property. But this form property controls the color of text, such as that displayed by Label and Button controls placed on the form.

NOTE Controls inherit their parent's color scheme. So, if a form has its BackColor set to red and its ForeColor set to white, buttons placed on the form will have these colors as well. Furthermore, if you change these properties for the underlying form, the controls seated on the form will also change.

Using the Properties Window Palettes

It's easy to set BackColor and ForeColor property values using the three palettes built into the VB .NET Properties window: the Custom palette, the Web palette, and the System palette.

To access these palettes, in the Properties window, select the BackColor or ForeColor property. Next, click the down arrow on the right side of the Properties window to open the palettes and select a color. For example, choose the Web palette and select a color, as shown below.

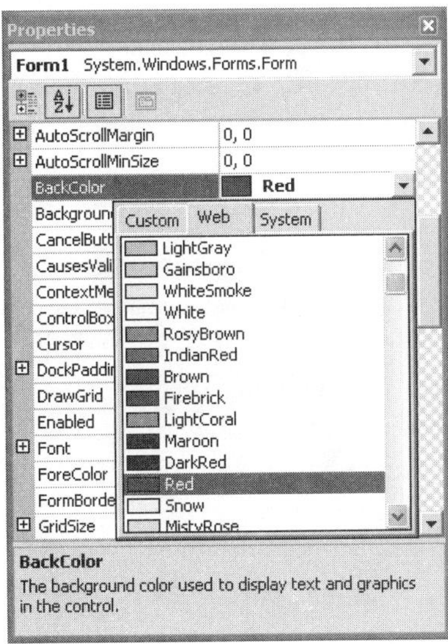

You can use these palettes to establish a color scheme for your form and its controls. For example, a reverse-color scheme in which text is white can be very effective. Setting the ForeColor property to White and the BackColor property to a solid color such as Red produces a knockout effect that is the reverse of the standard scheme, as shown below.

Using Predefined Color Values

In VB6, color values were stored as long integers (specifically, they were typed as Long). In other words, every color that you could use was reduced to a numerical value. In contrast, in VB .NET, colors are stored as two new types: `System.Drawing.Color` and `System.Drawing.SystemColors`. (Both types return a color structure that contains the color value as a 32-bit number.) You can use the members of the `System.Drawing.Color` and `System.Drawing.SystemColors` classes as predefined color values in your applications. For example, `System.Drawing.Color.Red` is a member of `System.Drawing.Color` (the VB6 equivalent was `vbRed`).

If you need them, there are a number of different ways to find the color values (or *constants*) that are the members of these classes. For one thing, the names of available colors appear beside the Web and System palettes in the Properties window, although these names appear by themselves (Red); you will need to supply the full type name (`System.Drawing.Color.Red`). As I'll show you in the "Using the RGB Function" section, coming up shortly, there is also some useful information you can gather from the Custom palette in the Properties window.

You can find a good deal of information about the VB .NET color constants in the online documentation (see Appendix A, "Using VB .NET's Help System," for more information about using online help). But the best approach is to go to the "horse's mouth" and use the Object Browser to inspect the `System.Drawing.Color` and `System.Drawing.SystemColors` classes. In the Object Browser (opened by selecting View ➢ Other Windows ➢ Object Browser), you can see a list of all the constants that are the members of these classes. Figure 4.1 shows the Object Browser's view of the VB .NET predefined color constants, and Figure 4.2 shows the system color constants. (See Chapter 14, "Using the Object Browser," for detailed instructions on how to use the Object Browser.)

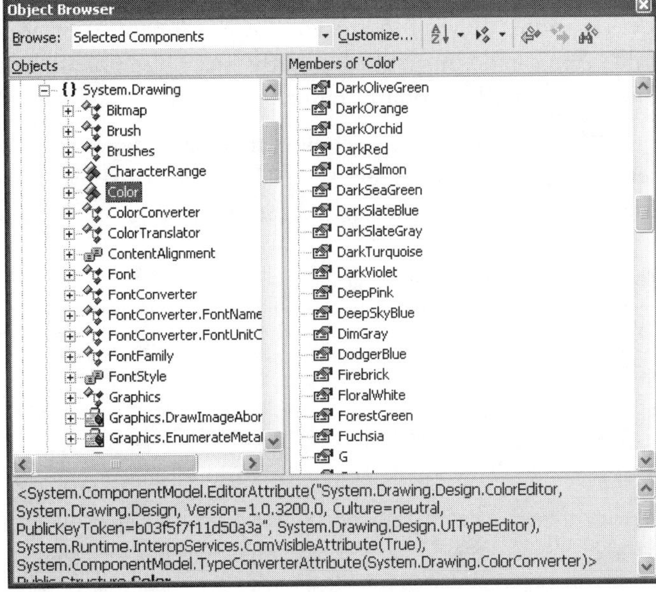

FIGURE 4.1: You can use any of VB .NET's many predefined color constants, which are the members of `System.Drawing.Color` (shown here in the Object Browser).

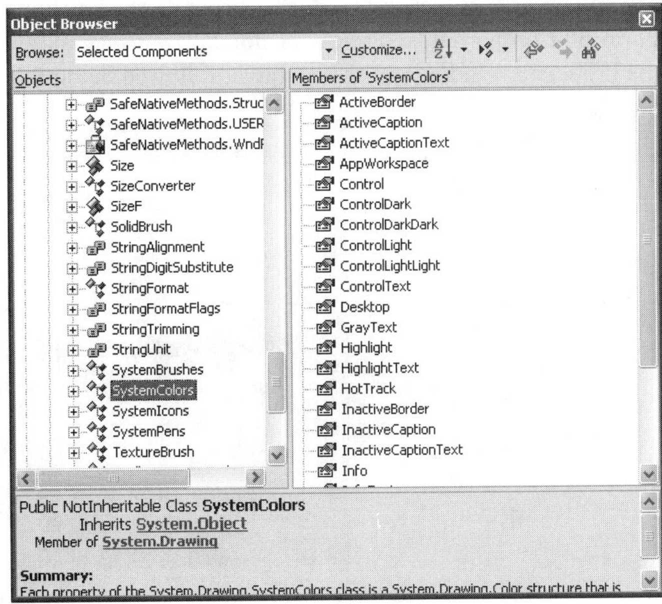

FIGURE 4.2: System color constants, which are the members of `System.Drawing.SystemColors`, can also be used.

Using the RGB Function

Let's suppose you want to mix your own colors rather than using a predefined constant value. You can do this, but it's slightly tricky. First of all, let's have a quick look at RGB, or Red Green Blue, color notation.

In RGB color notation, each primary component color (red, green, and blue) is represented by a number between 0 and 255. Table 4.2 shows some of the most common RGB values, but, of course, you can use the notation to represent almost any color.

TABLE 4.2: RGB Values and Colors

Color	Red value	Green value	Blue Value
Black	0	0	0
Blue	0	0	255
Green	0	255	0
Red	255	0	0
Yellow	255	255	0
White	255	255	255

If you use the Properties window to bring up the Custom palette for the BackColor or ForeColor properties, and select a color, you'll notice that the color you selected appears in the Properties window as a color swatch, followed by three numbers separated by commas.

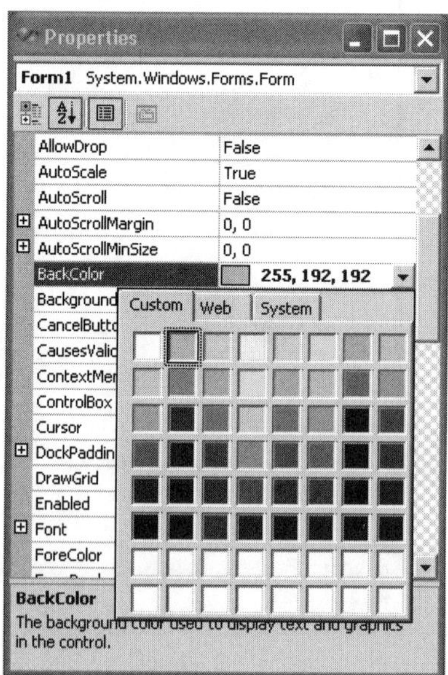

These numbers, such as 255,192,192 in the example, are the RGB values for the selected color. (Represented in this fashion, red is 255,0,0.)

To make these RGB values useful internally to VB .NET, they must be converted to a single number. Here's where the `RGB` function comes in. The following code will store the RGB value for red in a variable:

```
Dim redValue As Integer
redValue = RGB (255, 0, 0)
```

The `System.Drawing.ColorTranslator` class takes the internal RGB value generated by the `RGB` function and allows you to set a property with it. For example, let's take 255, 192, 192, which is a kind of light pink. The following value can be assigned to a BackColor or ForeColor property:

```
System.Drawing.ColorTranslator.FromWin32(RGB(255, 192, 192))
```

TIP The `ColorTranslator` class, using its `FromOle` method, can also be used to convert VB6 hexadecimal-style RGB color values so that they can be used in VB .NET.

Using Code to Set the BackColor Property

You've seen how to use the Properties window to change the color values of a form's BackColor and ForeColor properties, and understand the basics of color notation in VB .NET. It's time to get started working in code to set these properties so that they change at runtime in response to user actions, and also to store and compare color values.

Changing the BackColor Property Using a Constant

To use a color constant to change a property value in response to a user action, within an event procedure, assign the constant value. For example, add a Button control to a form and name it **`btnChangeColor`**. In the Code Editor, add a single line of code to the button's Click event procedure:

```
Private Sub btnChangeColor_Click(ByVal sender As Object, _
   ByVal e As System.EventArgs) Handles btnChangeColor.Click
   Me.BackColor = System.Drawing.Color.AliceBlue
End Sub
```

Run the project. The form will have a Change Color button.

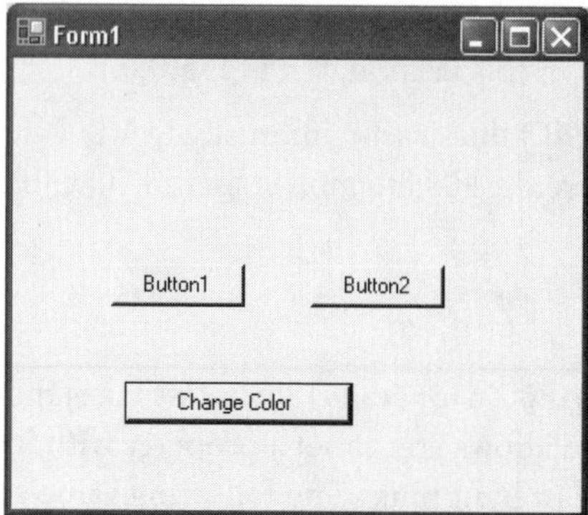

When the user clicks the Change Color button, the background color of the window will change.

Changing the BackColor Property Using an RGB Value

Assigning a color using an RGB value works pretty much the same way. You use the `RGB` function and the `ColorTranslator` class, as shown here:

```
Private Sub btnRGB_Click(ByVal sender As Object, _
   ByVal e As System.EventArgs) Handles btnRGB.Click
   Me.BackColor = ColorTranslator.FromWin32(RGB(255, 192, 192))
End Sub
```

This code assigns the RGB value 255, 192, 192 to a form's BackColor property when the user clicks the button.

Storing a Color Value

To store a color value, you need to create a variable of the correct type, as in this example:

```
Dim formcolor As System.Drawing.Color
```

Next, assign the value you want to save to the variable you created. For example, the following code assigns the current color of a form to the variable `formcolor`:

```
formcolor = Me.BackColor
```

Comparing the Color

Let's say that you've created a mechanism for the user to change the background color of a form to the color value `AliceBlue`, as explained earlier in this section. Now, you want to check to see if the user actually did change the background color. To do this, you need to compare the current form color with the value `AliceBlue`.

Start by adding a Button control for doing the comparison. Within the Click event procedure for the button, create a variable to store the form's background color and store the color in it:

```
Dim formcolor As System.Drawing.Color
formcolor = Me.BackColor
```

TIP Strictly speaking, you don't need to store the color information (you could use `Me.BackColor` for the comparison). But storing the color does help to make the code clearer.

Next, use a conditional statement and the `System.Drawing.Color op_Equality` method to compare the current form background color with `AliceBlue` and display an appropriate message:

```
If System.Drawing.Color.op_Equality(formcolor, _
   System.Drawing.Color.AliceBlue) Then
   MsgBox("You changed the color to Alice Blue!")
Else
   MsgBox("I want to be Blue, Alice Blue!")
End If
```

NOTE As you may have noticed, I use `MsgBox` statements in the examples in this chapter, rather than the newer `MessageBox.Show`. Using quick `MsgBox` statements is a habit of old-time VB programmers. See Chapter 3 for more information about `MessageBox.Show` and `MsgBox`.

Run the form. Don't change the background color and click the Compare button. You'll see this message:

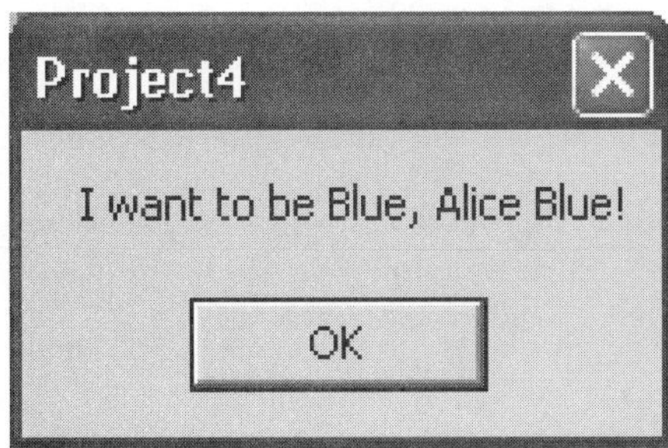

Now, go back and click the Change Color button. The form is beautiful in blue, Alice Blue! Click the Compare button, and you will get a message saying that you've changed the color.

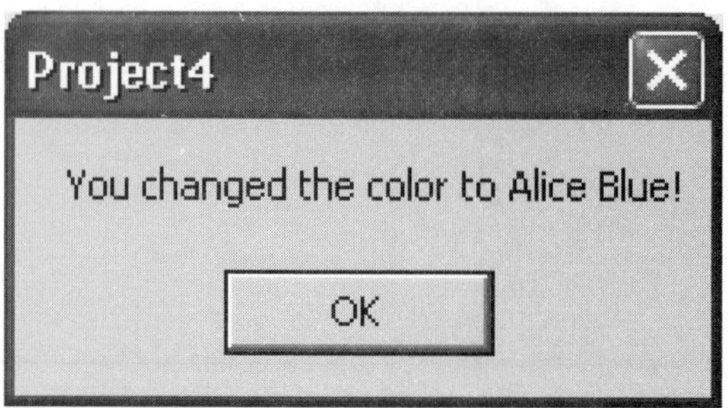

The complete code for this example is shown in Listing 4.2.

Listing 4.2 Changing, Storing, and Comparing Color Values in Code

```
Private Sub btnChangeColor_Click(ByVal sender As Object, _
   ByVal e As System.EventArgs) Handles btnChangeColor.Click
   Me.BackColor = System.Drawing.Color.AliceBlue
End Sub

Private Sub btnRGB_Click(ByVal sender As Object, _
   ByVal e As System.EventArgs) Handles btnRGB.Click
   Me.BackColor = ColorTranslator.FromWin32(RGB(255, 192, 192))
End Sub

Private Sub btnCompare_Click(ByVal sender As Object, _
   ByVal e As System.EventArgs) Handles btnCompare.Click
   Dim formcolor As System.Drawing.Color
   formcolor = Me.BackColor
   If System.Drawing.Color.op_Equality(formcolor, _
      System.Drawing.Color.AliceBlue) Then
      MsgBox("You changed the color to Alice Blue!")
   Else
      MsgBox("I want to be Blue, Alice Blue!")
   End If
End Sub
```

Setting the Font

The Font property is used to change the font display characteristics of type that appears on a form and on its controls.

When you first open the Properties window, you'll notice that a small + icon appears to the left of the Font property, which is itself an object. Click this icon to expand it so that you can see all the properties of the Font object. Each of these properties of the Font object—such as Size, Bold, and so on—can be set individually.

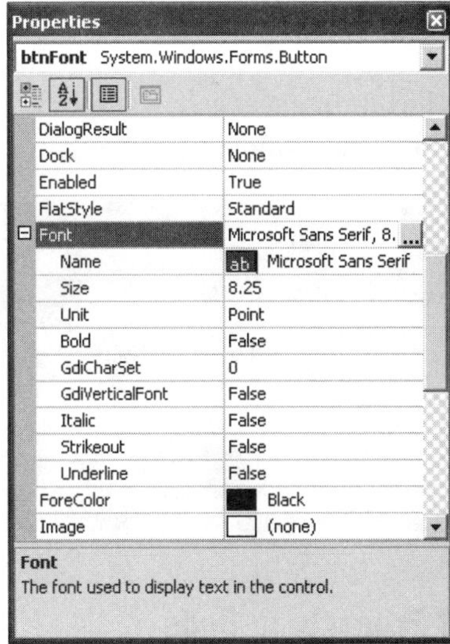

If you click the ellipses to the right of the current font value in the Properties window, the Font dialog will open, as shown in Figure 4.3.

FIGURE 4.3:

You can use the Font dialog to set Font object properties.

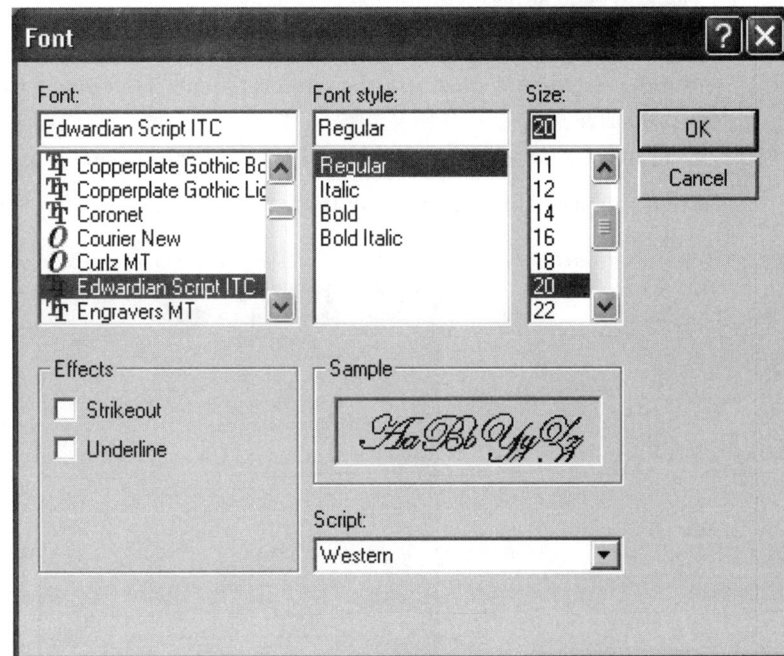

The Font dialog is an easy way to set your choice of Font property values. Once you've made your selections and clicked OK, the new font choices appear on your form. In the example shown here, the button's text is now displayed using the Font properties you selected through the Properties window.

Changing the Font Property in Code

As I'm sure you suspect, you can also change font characteristics in code. To do this, you need to create a new Font object using the `New` keyword, which you then assign as the value of the Font property:

```
New System.Drawing.Font("WingDings", 20)
```

This example creates a new Font object with the WingDings font face, in a size of 20 points.

A simple assignment statement then makes the new Font object the value of the button's Font property:

```
Me.btnFont.Font = New System.Drawing.Font("WingDings", 20)
```

When you place the code in the button's Click event procedure and run the form, it will look like this:

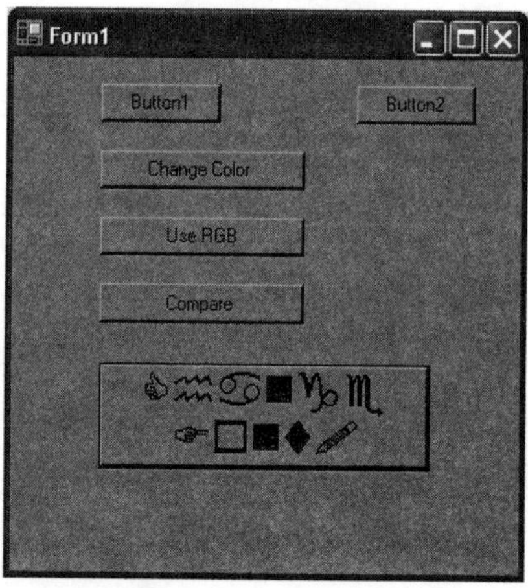

Clicking the WingDings button changes the font in which text is displayed.

NOTE This example changes the value of the Font property of a button. If, instead, you changed the value of the Font property of the form, the Font properties of all the controls on the form, including the button, would also change.

Listing 4.3 shows the complete code for this example.

Listing 4.3 Changing the Font Property in Code

```
Private Sub btnFont_Click(ByVal sender As Object, _
   ByVal e As System.EventArgs) Handles btnFont.Click
   Me.btnFont.Font = New System.Drawing.Font("WingDings", 20)
End Sub
```

Assigning Icons

Icons are used to represent windows when they are minimized and also appear in a window's caption bar.

To assign an icon to a form, with the form open, select Icon in the Properties window. Next, click the ellipses on the right side of the Properties window. The Open dialog will appear, as shown in Figure 4.4.

FIGURE 4.4: Use the Icon property in the Properties window to choose an icon to assign a form.

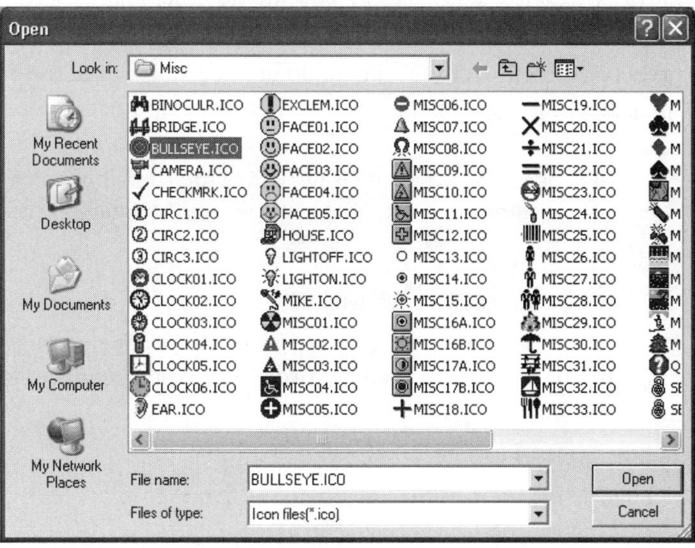

TIP

You can add a background image for a form in the same way, using the BackgroundImage property in the Properties window.

Once you've selected an icon, it will appear in the form's caption bar.

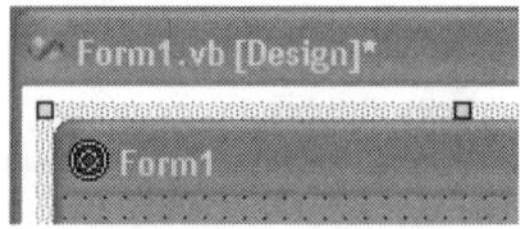

The icon will also appear on the Windows Taskbar.

NOTE

Depending on your choice of FormBorderStyle, an icon may not appear in the Windows Taskbar. For example, if FormBorderStyle is set to None, FixedToolWindow, or SizableToolWindow, no Taskbar icon will be displayed. Also, if the ShowInTaskbar property is not set to True, the window's icon will not be displayed in the Windows Taskbar.

Setting the Form's Size and Position

It's easy to change the size of a form using the Properties window. If you scroll to the Size property, you'll notice a pair of coordinates, separated by a comma. These are the width and height of the form, in pixels. You can expand the Size property by clicking the + icon, which takes you directly to the Width and Height properties of the Size object. Alternatively, you can just modify the comma-delimited pair of coordinates.

NOTE

VB .NET measures things in pixels, just as monitors do, which is a big improvement over earlier measurement units. (Can you say "twip" ten times quickly?)

Changing the Form Size in Code

You can also easily assign a new size to a form in code, to be executed while the form is running. To do this, use the `New` keyword to create a Size object with specific characteristics, as in this example:

```
New System.Drawing.Size(500, 600)
```

Then assign the new Size object to the form's Size property.

As an example of how this works, place two buttons on a form: one to make the form bigger and the other to make the form smaller. In the Click event of the `btnBigger` button, place code to make the form size large:

```
Private Sub btnBigger_Click(ByVal sender As Object, _
   ByVal e As System.EventArgs) Handles btnBigger.Click
   Me.Size = New System.Drawing.Size(500, 600)
End Sub
```

In the Click event of the other button, create a Size object and assign it to the form's Size property to make the form small:

```
Private Sub btnSmaller_Click(ByVal sender As Object, _
   ByVal e As System.EventArgs) Handles btnSmaller.Click
   Me.Size = New System.Drawing.Size(100, 150)
End Sub
```

Run the form. When you click the Bigger button, the form gets large.

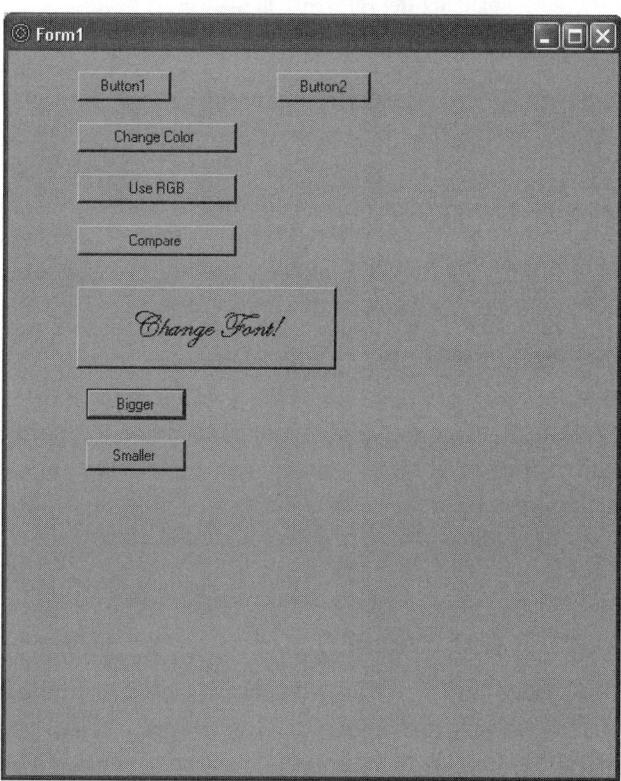

Clicking the Smaller button makes the form small.

TIP Set the AutoScroll property of the form to True for better access to controls on the form, even when it is small. This very cool form property is new with .NET.

Listing 4.4 shows the complete code for this example.

Listing 4.4 Changing the Form Size in Code

```
Private Sub btnBigger_Click(ByVal sender As Object, _
   ByVal e As System.EventArgs) Handles btnBigger.Click
   Me.Size = New System.Drawing.Size(500, 600)
End Sub

Private Sub btnSmaller_Click(ByVal sender As Object, _
   ByVal e As System.EventArgs) Handles btnSmaller.Click
   Me.Size = New System.Drawing.Size(100, 150)
End Sub
```

Setting the Form Position

The StartPosition property determines the position of the form when it is first loaded. Normally, once the form is running, the user can reposition it. Setting the form to start centered in the middle of the screen helps to make your applications appear professional. To do this, use the Properties window to set the form's StartPosition property to CenterScreen. Figure 4.5 shows an example of a form centered on the screen.

Specifying the Text Property

The Text property of a form changes the text that appears in the form's caption bar. This works in the same way that changing the Text property of a Button control changes the button's text, and changing the Text property of a Label control changes the text that a label displays.

You can change the value of a form's Text property in the Properties window, as you've seen in previous examples, or change the text property in code.

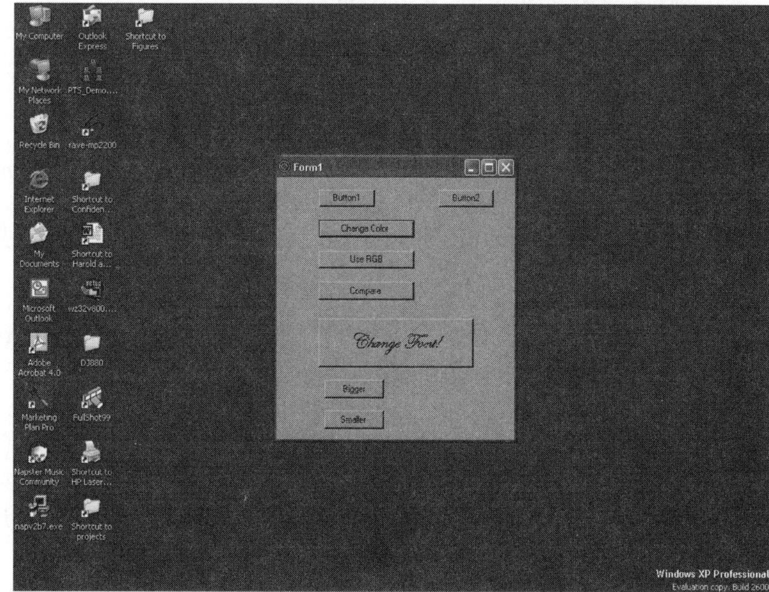

FIGURE 4.5: Setting the StartPosition property to CenterScreen gives your application a crisp appearance when it loads.

Changing the Text Property in Code

You'll often want to change the value of the Text property in code to show that something has happened. Listing 4.5 shows changing the value of the form's Text property when the user clicks a button.

Listing 4.5 Changing the Text Property in Code

```
Private Sub btnFormText_Click(ByVal sender As Object, _
   ByVal e As System.EventArgs) Handles btnFormText.Click
   Me.Text = Chr(169) & " Harold Davis"
End Sub
```

The expression `Chr(169)` evaluates to the character with the ASCII code of 169, the copyright sign. The concatenation operator, &, appends two strings together. Here are the results of clicking the Change Form Text button:

© Harold Davis

NOTE The plus operator, +, also will serve to concatenate two strings, and you may see this used in code. However, using the concatenation operator for its intended purpose is better practice because it is less confusing.

Controlling Form Appearance and Behavior

There are many other properties that have an important impact on the way forms look and behave. The best way to find out about these properties is to explore them in the Properties window, play with them, and learn by experimentation what they do.

The following are a few of these properties:

ControlBox Clicking the icon of a running window opens a *control* menu. This menu, sometimes also called the *system* menu, gives users the ability to close and resize the running window. If the ControlBox property is set to True, the user of a form can access the control menu.

MaximizeBox The Maximize button appears at the right end of a form's caption bar. Clicking the button maximizes a running form. If the MaximizeBox property is set to True, the running form has a Maximize button.

MinimizeBox The Minimize button appears at the right end of a form's caption bar, to the left of the Maximize button. Clicking the button minimizes a running form. If the MinimizeBox property is set to True, the running form has a Minimize button.

TopMost Only one running form can be in use, or *active*, at a time. Normally, the active form appears on top of all other forms. If you use the Properties window to set the TopMost property to True, the form will appear on top of all others, even when it is inactive.

Figure 4.6 shows a form with a control box, control menu, and Minimize and Maximize buttons.

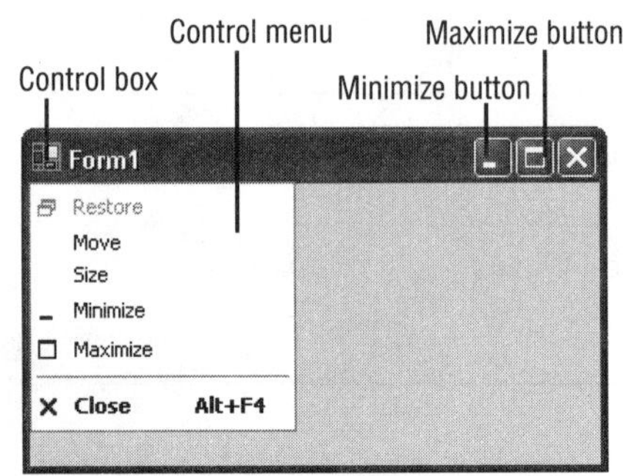

FIGURE 4.6: A window with a control box, control menu, Maximize button, and Minimize button

Setting Dynamic Properties

Words, like eels, are slippery things, so we need to be careful with many of them. One such tricky word is *dynamic*. Dynamic means, as we have correctly used it in this chapter, something that changes in response to a user action.

In the context of VB .NET properties, dynamic has an additional meaning. Dynamic properties in VB .NET can be set using an external XML file. This is done to make it easier to customize and change distributed applications. All you need to do is change an XML file, and the properties within an application will change. Changing a whole bunch of these XML files can be done via an automated program.

Let's have a quick look at this in action. To start with, find the Dynamic Properties listing in the Properties window. (If your Properties window is set to list properties alphabetically, this will be at the top of the window, not filed under the letter *D*.) Click the + icon to expand the Dynamic Properties listing. An Advanced identifier will appear below Dynamic Properties on the left, with three ellipses on the right.

Click the ellipses. The Dynamic Properties dialog will open, as shown in Figure 4.7. Check the boxes next to the properties that you want to control with the external XML file. (Figure 4.7 shows the Text property selected.)

FIGURE 4.7:

The Dynamic Properties dialog lets you designate form properties that can be set dynamically from an external XML file.

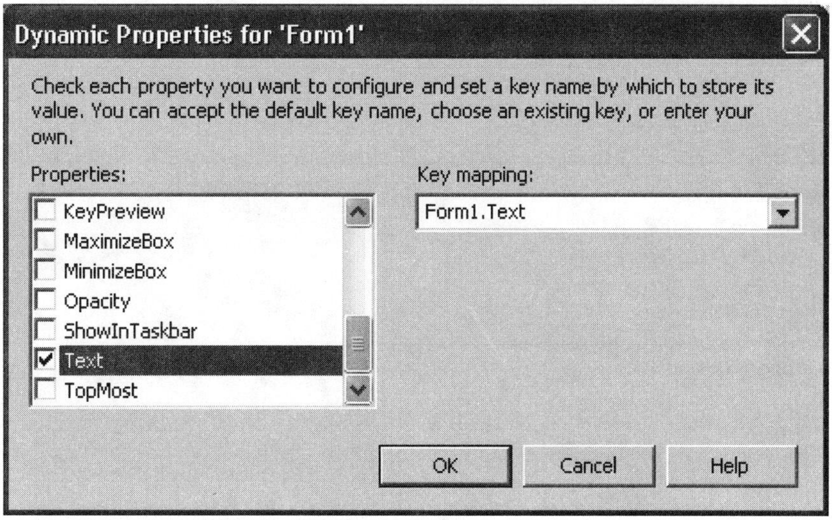

TIP

By default, each property will be accessed using a *key* consisting of the object followed by the property, for example, `Form1.Text`. Using the Key Mapping box shown in Figure 4.7, you can change this to anything you would like, as well as assign one key to multiple properties.

With a property selected, click OK. The external XML file, named `app.config`, will be created in your project directory. Note that you will not see the keys and values for dynamic properties in this file until you save your project.

The property in the Properties window will have a small file icon next to it if it is being saved in the `app.config` file.

Listing 4.6 shows an `app.config` file with one key and value, for the `Form1.Text` property. If you change the value of the `Form1.Text` key (for example, by changing it to "Goodbye!") and save the project, the next time you run it, the new value of the Text property will appear in the title bar.

Listing 4.6 An *app.config* Dynamic Property XML File with One Key/Value Pair

```
<?xml version="1.0" encoding="Windows-1252"?>
<configuration>
  <appSettings>
    <!--  User application and configured property settings go here.-->
    <!--   Example: <add key="settingName" value="settingValue"/> -->
    <add key="Form1.Text" value="Goodbye! " />
  </appSettings>
</configuration>
```

Figure 4.8 shows the form we have worked on in this chapter, after running the code in Listing 4.6.

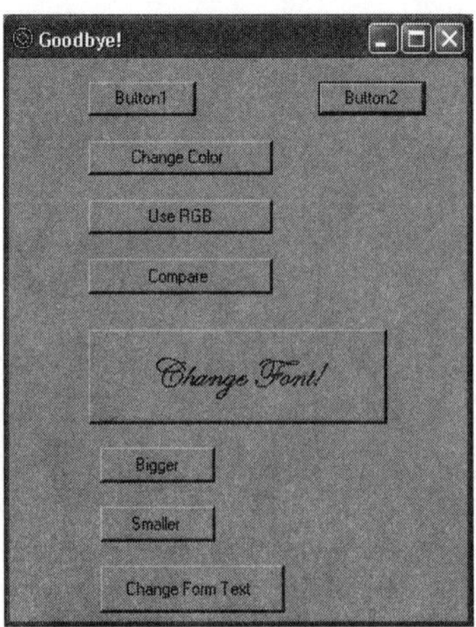

FIGURE 4.8: Changes made to the `app.config` XML file appear when you run a project and overrule any setting made in the Properties window.

Summary

In this chapter, you learned a great deal about how to change the look and feel, as well as the behavior, of forms. Along the way, you should have picked up a feeling for the concept of form properties, what they are, and how to work with them in VB .NET. It's easy enough to set properties using the Properties window, but often that won't do. For example, you might prefer to change properties in response to a user action. In this chapter, you learned how to change properties in code. Often, this requires creating objects that can be used as the new value for the property, so along the way, you began to get the feeling for the process of creating and using VB .NET objects.

The next chapter continues our exploration of objects, with an emphasis on understanding events and how to work with them, particularly in the context of forms.

CHAPTER 5

Events and the Life Cycle of Forms

- Understanding event-driven programming
- Handling events
- Monitoring events using the Debug object
- Initializing forms
- Unloading forms
- Understanding event syntax
- Avoiding event loops
- Assigning multiple events to a single handler

In the previous chapters, you learned how to work with form properties. You also used one event: the Click event, fired when a button is clicked. This chapter takes a closer look at events in general—what are they and how are they used?

Although events are an integral part of the way many objects work, the emphasis in this chapter continues to be forms. By the end of the chapter, not only will you understand events, you will also understand the birth, life, and death—or entire life cycle—of the form.

Understanding Event-Driven Programming

Event-driven coding is the primary mechanism for dealing with the essential nonlinearity of a windowing environment. Before the onset of windowing environments, most programs started in one place and ended in another. Even if users could make choices, those choices were severely limited.

In a windowing environment such as VB .NET, the programmer has basically no idea what the user is going to do once that first window opens up on the screen. Sure, you can limit the user choice in a number of ways, but usually there are a great many things the user can do along the lines of moving and resizing the window. Furthermore, you have no real way to know what event the user will trigger next. Some user actions might seem trivial, but without event-driven programming, you would need a response for each and every one in a giant conditional loop.

Event procedures give you the opportunity to place code in response to actions that are important to your particular application and let the default behavior of the form otherwise apply. An object's event procedures are placeholders for code. There is no requirement that you put code in an event procedure, but if you do, the code is processed when the event is triggered. (In the terminology of events, an event that is triggered is also said to have been *fired* or *raised*.) Events can be fired in a number of ways, including the following:

- By an action taken by a user, such as clicking an object
- By a call to the event procedure in code
- By triggering a declared event procedure using the `RaiseEvent` statement
- By the operating system

There are a number of important reasons for understanding events. Events constitute the life cycle of an object such as a form or a button. For example, a sequence of events takes place when a form is loaded, and another sequence is fired when the form is closed (or unloaded). Without understanding the events associated with a form, you cannot really understand how the form behaves, and you will not be able to get it to behave the way you want it to. You need to know which user or system action triggers which object event in order to work with the object.

Give someone a fish, they say, and you've assuaged their hunger once; teach the person to fish, and you've fed them for life. The emphasis in this chapter is showing you how you can empirically tell what is going on with events, using the form as the primary object example, so you will be able to figure out the event-firing sequence for new events you meet.

NOTE The great trinity of the VB .NET object is properties, or attributes (explained in Chapter 4, "Working with Windows Form Properties"); events (covered in this chapter); and methods, which cause an object to do something (explained in Chapter 6, "Working with Form Methods and Modules.")

Handling Events

The best way to find out which events are associated with an object in VB .NET is to inspect the object. (Sure, documentation also can provide good information, but why not go to the primary source?)

To see the events associated with a form, open the Code Editor. From the Objects list on the top left, choose (Base Class Events). The Procedures drop-down list on the top right will then display all form events, as shown in Figure 5.1.

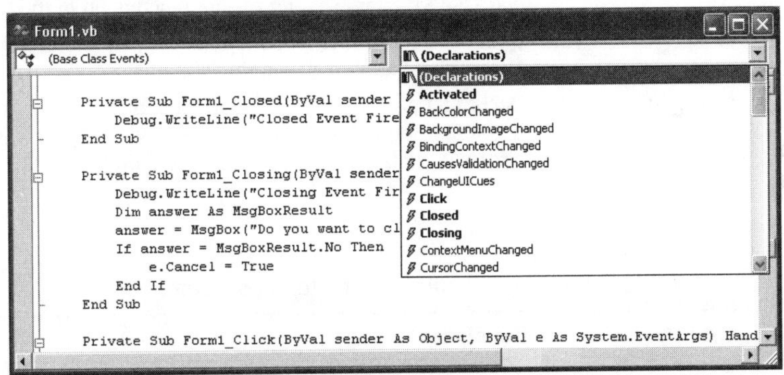

FIGURE 5.1: When you choose a Form object's (Base Class Events) from the Code Editor's Object list, all of the form's events appear in the Procedures list.

As you can see in Figure 5.1, events are denoted using a lightning bolt icon. When you click the event in the Procedures list, the event procedure framework code is automatically created within the form code. Event procedures that have been created are listed in the Procedures list in bold; event procedures that have not yet been created are in normal (not bold) type.

Once an event procedure has been created, you can add code that is activated in response to the event. This code is said to *handle* the event. It goes between the beginning and end of the procedure that has been created. For example, when you choose the form Click event, the following empty event procedure is created:

```
Private Sub Form1_Click(ByVal sender As Object, _
   ByVal e As System.EventArgs) Handles MyBase.Click

End Sub
```

Your code that handles the event goes between the procedure declaration (the line starting with `Private`) and the end of the procedure (`End Sub`, which is short for End Subroutine).

Form events fall into three general categories, as shown in Tables 5.1 through 5.3. These categories are form birth, user interaction with a running form, and form death. The birth and death sequences in these tables are shown in the order in which they occur. Not all events are shown in these tables; in particular, there are many other user-interaction events. Code Listings 5.1 through 5.5, discussed in the next section, "Monitoring Events," show you how to view these events.

TABLE 5.1: Form Constructor and Birth Events

Event	Description
New	Used to create an instance of a form. You can use this constructor to initialize data that will be used by the form. The New constructor is fired in the "hidden" form code (see Listing 5.1 and further discussion in the next section).
Load	Used for initialization code and for reading the initial values of form properties (see "Initializing Forms" later in this chapter).
Activated	Occurs as part of the birth sequence, and, later, in response to user or program actions, when the form becomes the active window. This event can occur only when a form is visible and after it has been loaded.

TABLE 5.2: Form (and Control) User-Interaction Events

Event	Description
Click	Fired when the user clicks in the form (or a control).
Enter	Fired when the form (or a control) gets the focus, meaning that it becomes the object that receives keyboard and mouse input.
Leave	Fired when the form (or a control) loses the focus.
MouseMove	Fired when the user moves the mouse over the form (or control).
Paint	Occurs when a window has been resized or uncovered, hence causing the form to require "painting."
Resize	Fired when the height or width of the form is changed.

TABLE 5.3: Form Death Events

Event	Description
Closing	The first event in the form death sequence, which allows the programmer to give the user the chance to cancel closing the form (see "Unloading Forms" later in this chapter).
Deactivate	The form becomes inactive.
Closed	The form is unloaded.
Dispose	The form is still in memory but is no longer considered a valid object. The memory for the form is not reclaimed until the garbage collector runs. However, Dispose is where you would put any cleanup code that is required, as it is your last chance to clean up. Dispose is fired in the "hidden" form code (see Listing 5.5).

Monitoring Events

The secret to monitoring events is to use the Debug object with the Output window. You can use the methods of the Debug object in your code to send a message, which is displayed in the Output window, when an event has been fired. (You'll find more information about the Debug object in Chapter 13, "Errors, Exceptions, and Debugging.")

Monitoring the New Method

The first event that we would like to monitor is actually not an event at all, strictly speaking, but rather the `New` method. The `New` method is fired when a Form object is created as an instance of the `System.Windows.Forms.Form` class. By default, the `New` method fires for the first form in a project named `Form1` (see Listing 5.1).

The `New` constructor is fired in the "hidden" form code. This hidden form code will not be visible in the Code Editor when you open it. To view the hidden form code, click the + icon to the left of the grayed text "Windows Form Designer generated code." The Code Editor window will expand to show the hidden, auto-generated form code.

NOTE "Hidden" form code reminds me of the man behind the curtains in the movie *The Wizard of Oz*. You can find out more about what the hidden form code really does, and about object constructors in general, in Chapter 15, "Object-Oriented Programming in VB .NET."

In Listing 5.1, you'll see that the base class constructor is called with this statement:

```
MyBase.New()
```

Then a procedure required by the Windows Form Designer is invoked:

```
InitializeComponent()
```

After this, there is a comment telling you to add any initialization code. It's here that you can add the line that displays a message in the Output window when the `New` method is executed by invoking the `WriteLine` method of the Debug object:

```
Debug.WriteLine("New Fired")
```

TIP This is the place to put initialization code that is not related to the appearance of the form. For example, this would be a good place to put code that uses database calls to set the values of variables that will be used by the form and its code.

Listing 5.1 The Beginning of the "Hidden" Form Code Showing the New Method

```
Public Class Form1
    Inherits System.Windows.Forms.Form

#Region " Windows Form Designer generated code "

    Public Sub New()
        MyBase.New()

        'This call is required by the Windows Form Designer.
        InitializeComponent()

        'Add any initialization after the InitializeComponent() call

        Debug.WriteLine("New Event Fired")

    End Sub
...
```

Monitoring the Form Load Sequence

Unlike the `New` method, the form `Load` and `Activated` methods do not use the hidden form code. To add monitoring statements to these events, in the Code Editor, select Base Class Events in the Objects list, and then select each event from the Procedures list. Once each event procedure has been created, add the code that invokes the `WriteLine` method of the Debug object, as shown in Listing 5.2. Now, when you run your project, the Output window will automatically be opened in debug mode, showing the form load events being fired, as shown in Figure 5.2.

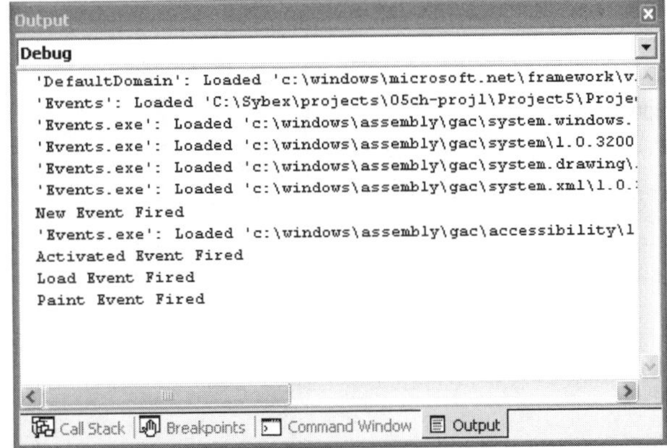

FIGURE 5.2: The Output window showing the form load sequence

Listing 5.2 **Monitoring Form Load Events**

```
Private Sub Form1_Load(ByVal sender As Object, _
   ByVal e As System.EventArgs) Handles MyBase.Load
   Debug.WriteLine("Load Event Fired")
End Sub

Private Sub Form1_Activated(ByVal sender As Object, _
   ByVal e As System.EventArgs) Handles MyBase.Activated
   Debug.WriteLine("Activated Event Fired")
End Sub
```

Monitoring User-Interaction Events

Next, let's add some code to monitor user-interaction events, as shown in Listing 5.3. You should know that it is often useful to display more information in the Output window than simply that an event has been fired. For example, it might be helpful to know what the width of the form is when a form Resize event is fired. To do this, find the width of the form, convert the number to a string using the `ToString()` method, and concatenate it with the text saying the event has been fired, for display in the Output window:

```
Debug.WriteLine("Resize Event Fired " & Me.Size.Width.ToString())
```

With the monitoring code placed in the user-interaction events, when you run the form and move your mouse around, you'll see the events being fired (and the width of the form in pixels each time a Resize event is fired), as shown in Figure 5.3.

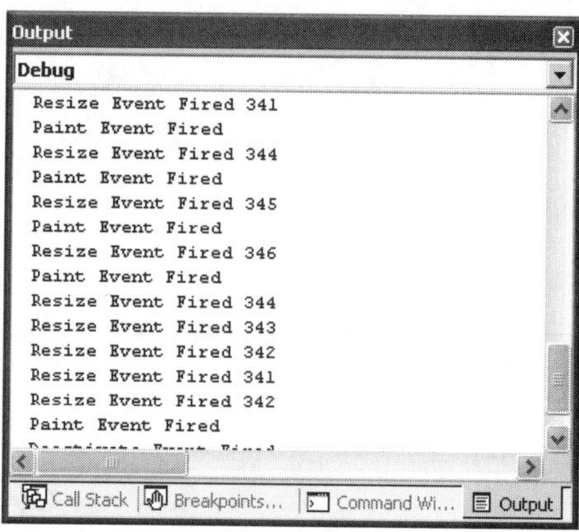

FIGURE 5.3: The Output window showing the user moving her mouse around the form.

Listing 5.3 Monitoring User-Interaction Events

```
Private Sub Form1_Click(ByVal sender As Object, _
   ByVal e As System.EventArgs) Handles MyBase.Click
   Debug.WriteLine("Click Event Fired")
End Sub

Private Sub Form1_Enter(ByVal sender As Object, _
   ByVal e As System.EventArgs) Handles MyBase.Enter
   Debug.WriteLine("Enter Event Fired")
End Sub

Private Sub Form1_Leave(ByVal sender As Object, _
   ByVal e As System.EventArgs) Handles MyBase.Leave
   Debug.WriteLine("Leave Event Fired")
End Sub

Private Sub Form1_MouseMove(ByVal sender As Object, _
   ByVal e As System.Windows.Forms.MouseEventArgs) Handles MyBase.MouseMove
   Debug.WriteLine("MouseMove Event Fired")
End Sub

Private Sub Form1_Paint(ByVal sender As Object, _
   ByVal e As System.Windows.Forms.PaintEventArgs) Handles MyBase.Paint
   Debug.WriteLine("Paint Event Fired")
End Sub

Private Sub Form1_Resize(ByVal sender As Object, _
   ByVal e As System.EventArgs) Handles MyBase.Resize
   Debug.WriteLine("Resize Event Fired " & Me.Size.Width.ToString())
End Sub
```

Monitoring Form Closing Events

Does *closing* sound more tentative to you than *closed*? In the brave new world of events, it is indeed. The Closing event gives the programmer a chance to allow the user to change her mind (see the "Unloading Forms" section later in this chapter), while the Closed event is the real thing—the form is gone. As this implies, Closed comes after Closing in the sequence, with Deactivate in between. You can add calls to the `Debug.WriteLine` method to observe this, as shown in Listing 5.4.

Listing 5.4 **Monitoring Form Closing Events**

```
Private Sub Form1_Closing(ByVal sender As Object, _
   ByVal e As System.ComponentModel.CancelEventArgs) _
   Handles MyBase.Closing
   Debug.WriteLine("Closing Event Fired")
End Sub

Private Sub Form1_Deactivate(ByVal sender As Object, _
   ByVal e As System.EventArgs) Handles MyBase.Deactivate
   Debug.WriteLine("Deactivate Event Fired")
End Sub

Private Sub Form1_Closed(ByVal sender As Object, _
   ByVal e As System.EventArgs) Handles MyBase.Closed
   Debug.WriteLine("Closed Event Fired")
End Sub
```

One more form death event remains: `Dispose`. Like `New`, `Dispose` is a method occurring in the form's hidden code. It is used to clean up after the form (and any controls that have been placed on the form). As shown in Listing 5.5, you can add a `Debug` command to the `Dispose` procedure.

With the form death events monitored, when you run the form and then close it, you'll see a display in the Output window similar to that shown in Figure 5.4.

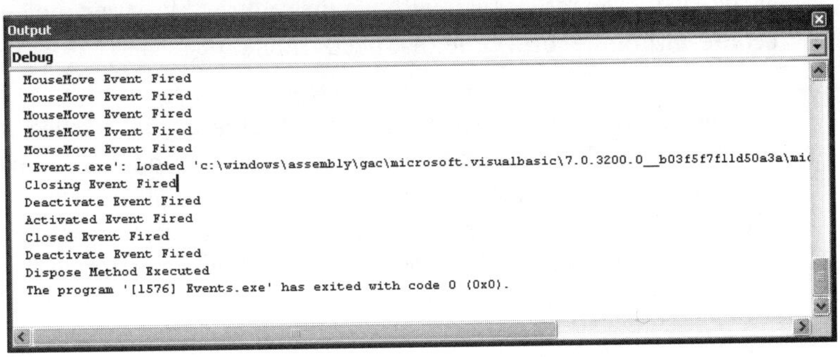

FIGURE 5.4: The Output window showing a form being closed

```
Output
Debug
MouseMove Event Fired
MouseMove Event Fired
MouseMove Event Fired
MouseMove Event Fired
MouseMove Event Fired
'Events.exe': Loaded 'c:\windows\assembly\gac\microsoft.visualbasic\7.0.3200.0__b03f5f7f11d50a3a\mi
Closing Event Fired
Deactivate Event Fired
Activated Event Fired
Closed Event Fired
Deactivate Event Fired
Dispose Method Executed
The program '[1576] Events.exe' has exited with code 0 (0x0).
```

Listing 5.5 The *Dispose* Method in the Hidden Form Code

```
'Form overrides dispose to clean up the component list.
Protected Overloads Overrides Sub Dispose(ByVal disposing As Boolean)
   Debug.WriteLine("Dispose Method Executed")
   If disposing Then
      If Not (components Is Nothing) Then
         components.Dispose()
      End If
   End If
   MyBase.Dispose(disposing)
End Sub
```

Initializing Forms in the Load Event

Events are totally a blast to work with once you understand them. To illustrate this point, and to show you how simple it is to work with events, let's create a program that stores the size and position of a form when it first loads (you can set this using the Properties window and/or by how you position and size the form at design time). Let's say the user moves and resizes the form. The program will provide a mechanism for restoring the running form to its original size and position.

Actually, this involves three different programmatic steps:

- Declaring the variables that will keep track of the original size and position
- Adding code to the form's Load event to "remember" the original size and position
- Adding a mechanism that will let the user restore the original size and position

However, before we get to coding, let's add a Button control to the form. Using the Properties window, name it **btnRemember**, and give it the Text value **Remember Position**.

The variables that will hold the original size and position information need to be declared at the form level rather than within a procedure. That way, they will be available to any procedure within the form code that needs them.

NOTE Where a variable is available to code is called the variable's *scope*. A variable declared using the `Dim` statement within a procedure is available to only that procedure. A variable declared outside any methods, but inside the form class, is available within any procedure in the form class. There are good reasons for scoping variables as *narrowly*—meaning, restricted tightly in their scope—as possible. For more information about scoping, particularly in the context of VB .NET classes, see Chapter 15.

To declare variables at form level, put the declaration statements immediately below the Windows Form Designer generated code and outside any procedures. Here are the declarations for a variable of type `System.Drawing.Size`, `formsize`, used to keep track of the form's size, and a variable of type `System.Drawing.Point`, `formlocation`, used to track the form's initial location:

```
' Variables declared at form level
Dim formsize As System.Drawing.Size
Dim formlocation As System.Drawing.Point
```

Next, add code to the form Load event that stores the initial size and location:

```
formsize = Me.Size
formlocation = Me.Location
```

Finally, use the Procedures list to create a Click event handler for `btnRemember`. Add code to the event procedure that restores the original form location and size when it is fired:

```
Private Sub btnRemember_Click(ByVal sender As Object, _
   ByVal e As System.EventArgs) Handles btnRemember.Click
   Me.Size = formsize
   Me.Location = formlocation
End Sub
```

The complete code for the program is shown in Listing 5.6.

Listing 5.6 Using Form Load Event Initialization Code to Recall Form Size and Position

```
' Variables declared at form level
Dim formsize As System.Drawing.Size
Dim formlocation As System.Drawing.Point

Private Sub Form1_Load(ByVal sender As Object, _
   ByVal e As System.EventArgs) Handles MyBase.Load
   Debug.WriteLine("Load Event Fired")
   formsize = Me.Size
   formlocation = Me.Location
End Sub

...

Private Sub btnRemember_Click(ByVal sender As Object, _
   ByVal e As System.EventArgs) Handles btnRemember.Click
   Me.Size = formsize
   Me.Location = formlocation
End Sub
```

With everything ready, it's time to take this program for a spin! Run the form, and move and resize it to your heart's content. For example, make it smaller:

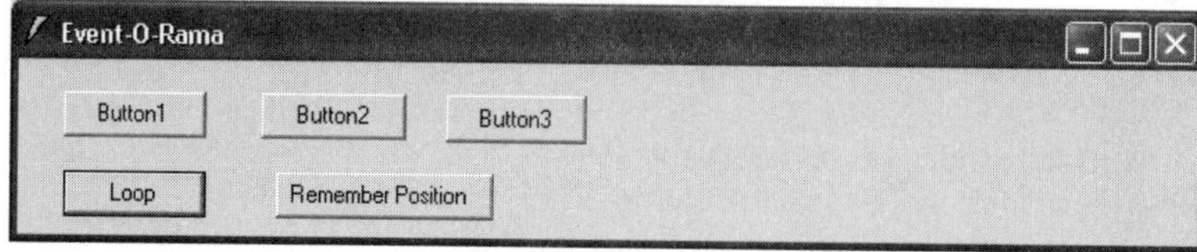

When you are ready to stop playing, click the Remember Position button. The form will be restored to its original position and size.

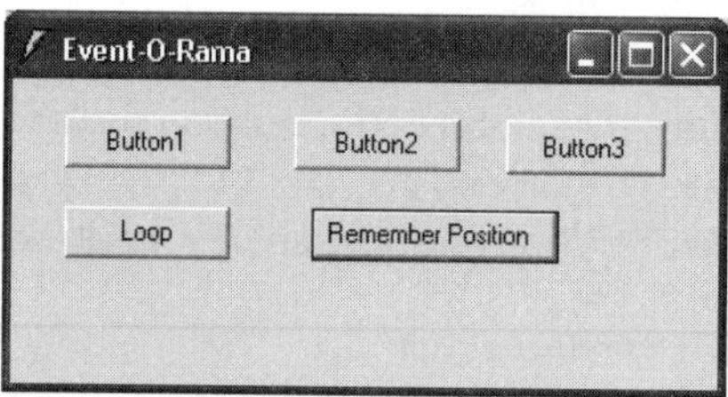

Unloading Forms

Earlier in this chapter, I mentioned that the form Closing event was not final, and that it could be used to give the user an opportunity not to close the form. (It can also be used for other purposes such as executing your own program's conditional cleanup code.)

To see how this works, create an event handler procedure for the form Closing event. Next, create a variable to return the result of a message box and display a message box asking the user if she really wants to close the window:

```
Dim answer As MsgBoxResult
answer = MsgBox("Do you want to close this window?", _
   MsgBoxStyle.YesNo, "Demonstration of the Closing event")
```

If the user clicks No, set the Cancel property of the variable `e`, which was passed to the event procedure, to True:

```
If answer = MsgBoxResult.No Then
   ' Do not close the form
   e.Cancel = True
End If
```

`e` is a variable of type `System.ComponentModel.CancelEventArgs`. By setting it to True, the unloading process is canceled.

The complete procedure code is shown in Listing 5.7.

Listing 5.7 Checking to See If the User Really Wants to Close a Form

```
Private Sub Form1_Closing(ByVal sender As Object, _
   ByVal e As System.ComponentModel.CancelEventArgs) Handles MyBase.Closing
   Dim answer As MsgBoxResult
   answer = MsgBox("Do you want to close this window?", _
      MsgBoxStyle.YesNo, "Demonstration of the Closing event")
   If answer = MsgBoxResult.No Then
      ' Do not close the form
      e.Cancel = True
   End If
End Sub
```

If you run the form and then close it, you will see this message box:

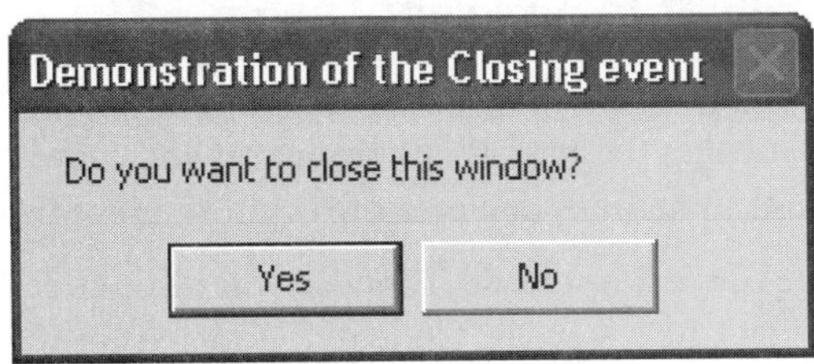

If you click No, the form stays loaded. Otherwise, the normal form death sequence of events is fired, and the form is unloaded.

Understanding Event Syntax

An event is a procedure with a name, such as `Form1_Click`, followed by parameters (also called arguments) within parentheses, followed by a `Handles` clause, which says which event or events the procedures takes care of (or handles).

You should know that it is easy to call an event procedure in code. You must be sure to pass the event procedure the number and type of arguments it expects. For example, to call a form Click event in code, you can declare a variable of type `System.EventArgs`:

```
Dim g As System.EventArgs
```

This statement will then fire the Click event:

```
Form1_Click (Me, g)
```

From within another event procedure, you don't even need to declare a new variable; you can just pass on the parameters sent to the first Click procedure. Here is an example:

```
Private Sub Form1_Resize(ByVal sender As Object, _
   ByVal e As System.EventArgs) Handles MyBase.Resize
   Form1_Click (sender, e)
End Sub
```

Now, every time the form is resized, its Click event is also fired.

There are a great many things you can do with event procedures. Writing your own events is explained in Chapter 15 and in Chapter 16, "Creating Windows Controls."

Don't Get Caught in an Event Loop

Be careful that you don't get caught in an infinite event loop! If one event invokes another, and the second invokes the first, then you are off and running. This happens more easily than it sounds, because sometimes one event fires another event in ways you don't expect.

As an example of what not to do, suppose you place code in a button's Enter event that invokes the button's Leave event. Code in the Leave event invokes the Enter event (see Listing 5.8). Put `Debug.WriteLine` statements in each event procedure as well.

NOTE Enter is the event formerly known as GotFocus in previous versions of VB. Leave is the event formerly known as LostFocus.

Listing 5.8 An Infinite Event Loop

```
Private Sub btnLoop_Enter(ByVal sender As Object, _
   ByVal e As System.EventArgs) Handles btnLoop.Enter
   Debug.WriteLine("btnLoop Enter Event Fired")
   btnLoop_Leave(sender, e)
End Sub

Private Sub btnLoop_Leave(ByVal sender As Object, _
   ByVal e As System.EventArgs) Handles btnLoop.Leave
   Debug.WriteLine("btnLoop Leave Event Fired")
   btnLoop_Enter(sender, e)
End Sub
```

Run the form. Tab to the button (the button may be the AcceptButton for the form, in which case you don't even need to manually give it the focus). You are now in an infinite loop, as shown in the Output window.

```
btnLoop Leave Event Fired
btnLoop Enter Event Fired
btnLoop Leave Event Fired
btnLoop Enter Event Fired
btnLoop Leave Event Fired
btnLoop Enter Event Fired
btnLoop Leave Event Fired
btnLoop Enter Event Fired
btnLoop Leave Event Fired
btnLoop Enter Event Fired
btnLoop Leave Event Fired
btnLoop Enter Event Fired
btnLoop Leave Event Fired
btnLoop Enter Event Fired
btnLoop Leave Event Fired
```

Assigning Multiple Events to One Event Handler

A really great thing about VB .NET event handler procedures is that a single procedure can easily handle many events. If you have a procedure that handles an event and you want it to handle a second event, just add the name of the second event to the `Handles` clause of the event procedure. For example, suppose you have a Click event handler for `Button1`, and you want it to also handle `Button2`'s Click event. It's the easiest thing in the world to add `Button2`'s Click event to the `Button1` handler:

```
Private Sub Button1_Click(ByVal sender As Object, ByVal e As _
   System.EventArgs) Handles Button1.Click, Button2.Click
```

Now, every time `Button1` or `Button2` is clicked, this one event procedure is invoked.

This gets really useful when you are working with groups of related controls, such as CheckBox and RadioButton controls, as explained in Chapter 7, "Working with Windows Forms Controls."

It is also the case that you might want to know *which* control fired the Click procedure. To determine which of three buttons the user clicked, you can use the `sender` argument of the event-handling procedure, as shown in Listing 5.9.

Listing 5.9 Handling Multiple Click Events with One Event Procedure

```
Private Sub Button1_Click(ByVal sender As Object, _
   ByVal e As System.EventArgs) Handles Button1.Click, _
   Button2.Click, Button3.Click
   MsgBox(sender.Text & " was clicked!")
End Sub
```

When you run the form, the code shown in Listing 5.9 displays a message telling you which button was clicked (and therefore activated the single event procedure).

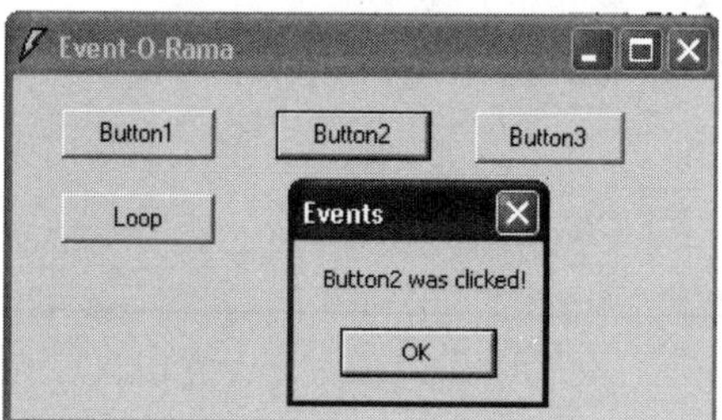

Summary

This chapter covered a lot of ground. In it, I showed you many of the events that make up the life cycle of a form, how to observe these events in action, and how to work with them. Understanding events, and how they interact with program code, is crucial to creating event-driven VB .NET programs.

In the next chapter, we will move on to explore methods, which together with properties and events define how you work with objects such as forms. We will also have a look at code modules and applications that have multiple form and/or code modules.

CHAPTER 6

Working with Form Methods and Modules

- Using form methods
- Using code modules
- Working with forms
- Working with the Graphics object
- Creating MDI applications

The previous chapters explained how to work with properties and how to program with events. This chapter is primarily concerned with the third important aspect of an object: its methods. Methods *do* something. Usually, something is done to the object whose method it is, but this isn't always the case.

As with the earlier chapters, the focus is primarily on methods in the context of the Form object. Once you understand how form methods work, you'll find that working with the methods of other objects follows basically the same principles.

In this chapter, you'll also learn how to add a code module to your project and how to use the Graphics object (and related objects such as Brush, Font, and Pen). The methods of the Graphics object allow you to use GDI+—short for Graphics Device Interface +—to place lines, shapes, and text on the background of a form or control. Finally, you'll learn how to create an MDI (Multiple Document Interface) application in VB .NET.

It is a truism that first impressions count, and you don't get a second chance to make first impressions. The appearance and behavior of the forms in your application make up a great deal of the first impressions that users will get of your programs. Using the techniques explained in this chapter, you can make sure that the users' first impression is a positive one.

Using Form Methods

Form methods are used to do something to a form. They are invoked by using a reference to an instance of the form, followed by the dot operator. For example, a form's `Show` method causes an instance of the form to be loaded into memory, complete with controls, properties, and event code. The form is also displayed on the screen as part of the `Show` method invocation.

Understanding Method Syntax

Form methods are invoked either by using the `Me` keyword or by using a variable that references an instance of the form class. Here is an example of using `Me`:

```
Me.Close()
```

And here is an example of invoking a method that references an instance of the form class:

```
Dim Form2 As New Form2
...
Form2.Close()
```

`Me` seems clear enough, and it is, in fact, the easiest way to reference properties and methods of the current form (the form in which code is currently executing).

TIP If you leave off the Me, it is implied. For example, Close() works just as well as Me.Close().

But what's this Form2 As New Form2 about? Suppose you want to add a second form to an application. The Form2 you are given by VB .NET as an automatically generated module is a *class*, or blueprint, for an object. To do anything to a second form, you need an instance of the object (that is, an object based on the blueprint). You also need to be able to refer to the object using a variable (so you can do things like invoking object methods).

The New keyword in the Dim Form2 As New Form2 statement creates an object based on the Form2 blueprint (of the Form2 class). The Dim Form2 As part of the statement stores a reference to the new Form object in a variable named Form2. This means that there are both a class and a variable named Form2. Arguably, this is somewhat confusing, and you could actually use any variable name you like, as in this example:

```
Dim Frodo As New Form2
...
Frodo.Hide()
```

This example hides an instance of Form2 referenced by the variable Frodo (provided, of course, that Frodo is a currently displayed form). So, while it may seem odd to have a variable named Form2 that holds an instance of the Form2 class, think of it as a kind of shorthand that is often used in VB .NET.

Whatever variable name you use for your Form2, creating a variable to hold an instance of the Form2 class is what you need to do to manipulate one form from another one (or manipulate a form from a code module). If you are finding yourself a little puzzled by this discussion, the examples in this chapter should help to make it clearer.

NOTE VB6 provided both the class and a variable containing an instance of the class when you added a form, such as Form1, to a project, ready to go. VB .NET just requires a bit more work in this area in the interest of being more object-oriented.

In many cases, invoking a method does the same thing as changing a property value. For example, this code makes a form invisible on the screen without unloading it:

```
Me.Hide()
```

You can achieve the same result by using a form's Visible property:

```
Me.Visible = False
```

As you've already seen, in many cases, you will want to use methods (and set properties) of controls or other objects that "belong to" a form. This is done using the dot operator, both between the form and the object and between the object and the method to be invoked. For example, if you have placed a button named `Button1` on a form, the following code makes the button invisible on the form, or "hides" it.

```
Me.Button1.Hide()
```

Notice the parentheses used with the `Hide` method. Methods can be thought of as functions, which normally require parentheses, even if they don't have any arguments within the parentheses. But you don't need to worry about this very much. The VB .NET Code Editor will automatically supply the parentheses if you leave them off a method call that doesn't take arguments (of course, you must supply any required arguments).

Introducing Important Form Methods

Table 6.1 shows some of the most frequently used form methods and describes what they do.

TABLE 6.1: Commonly Used Form Methods

Method	Purpose
`Activate`	Moves the focus to the form and makes it active. (Called the `SetFocus` method in previous versions of VB.)
`Close`	Unloads the form.
`BringToFront`	Moves the form on top of all other forms. (Set using the `ZOrder` method in previous versions of VB.) See also `SendToBack`.
`Hide`	Makes a form invisible, or hides it, without unloading the form.
`Refresh`	Updates the appearance of a form by repainting the form.
`SendToBack`	Moves the form beneath all other forms. (Set using the ZOrder method in previous versions of VB.) See also `BringToFront`.
`SetBounds`	Used to position a form.
`Show`	Loads and displays a modeless form (a normal window). See the "Showing a Modal Form" section later in this chapter for an explanation of modal and modeless forms.
`ShowDialog`	Loads and displays a modal form, such as a dialog box.

Using Code Modules

So far, all of the examples in this book have involved forms. Forms are objects that include code and are displayed on the screen. In other words, forms have a visual display at runtime, as well as a visual representation at design time. The design-time aspect of the Form object—or module—allows you to use the Properties window, Toolbox, and other graphical aspects of the .NET development environment to visually modify the form (of course, these visual changes are then reflected in the underlying code that constitutes the form).

In contrast, a *code module*—often referred to as a *module*—just consists of code. A code module does not have an automatic representation on the screen.

A procedure named `Sub Main` in a code module can be used to start a project. (The starting point of a project is referred to as the project's *entry point*.) So, if you have a project that does not need a screen presence, or a project with a number of forms, it's likely that you will want to start it from `Sub Main()` in a code module. In addition, if you write procedures that are used by a number of different forms in your project, it's a good idea to keep them separate from your Windows form modules. One way to do this is to create classes, placed in class modules, as explained in Chapter 15, "Object-Oriented Programming in Visual Basic .NET." But it is also simple enough to just place procedure code in ordinary code modules and invoke the procedure from form events. (You can put as many procedures as you would like in a code module.)

Once a procedure has been created in a module, it can be invoked using the module name, followed by the dot operator, followed by the procedure name (if you leave the module name off, the current module is implied). Here's an example:

```
myModule.myProcedure()
```

Adding Code Modules

To add a code module, choose Project ➢ Add Module from the VB .NET menu. The Add New Item dialog will appear, as shown in Figure 6.1. Make sure that Module is selected in the right pane of the Add New Item dialog, and give the module a name. Click Open, and a code module will be added to your project.

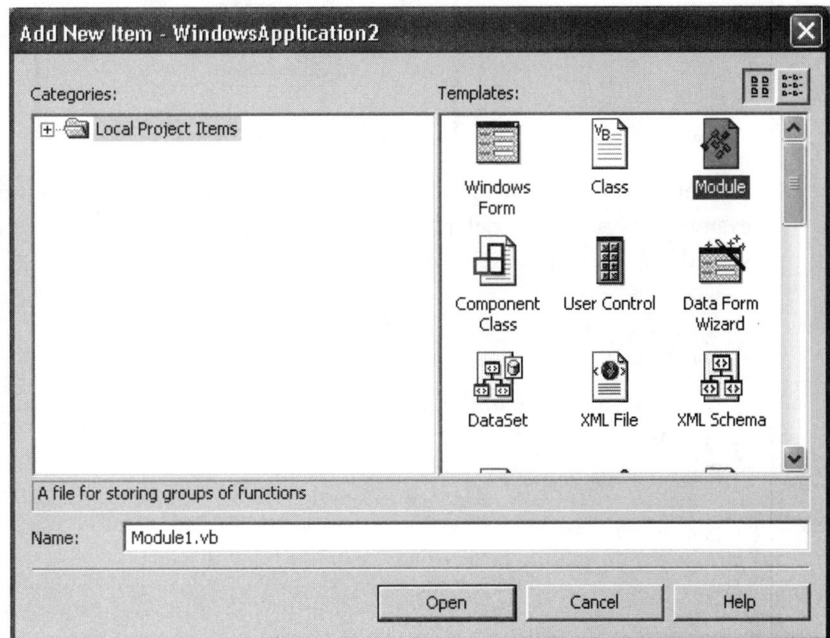

FIGURE 6.1: To add a code module, select Module in the Add New Item dialog.

TIP You can get to the Add New Item dialog in a number of ways. Almost any of the Add items on the Project menu brings up the Add New Item dialog. Just be careful that the module type you want is selected. Alternatively, in the Solution Explorer, select a Project and right-click. Next, choose Add ➢ Add New Item from the context menu. The Add New Item dialog will open.

Renaming a Module

Once you've added the code module, there are a number of ways to rename it. You can use the context menu in the Solution Explorer, as shown here.

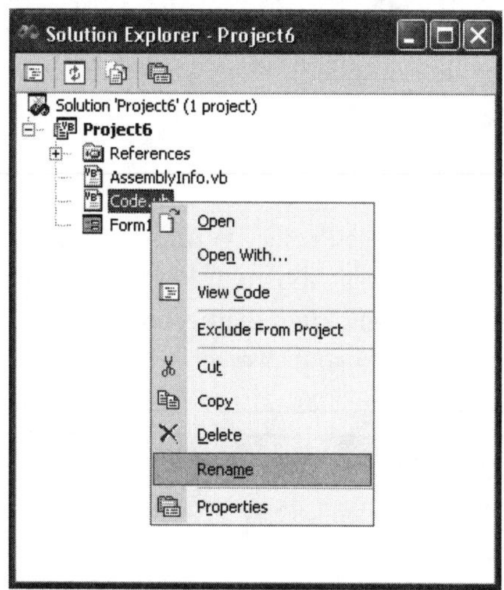

Alternatively, you can simply change the name of the module in the Code Editor. For example, if you left the default name of the code module when it was created, it will look something like this in the Code Editor:

```
Module Module1

End Module
```

To change the name of the module, just change `Module1`. For example, here's how to rename the module to `Code`:

```
Module Code

End Module
```

Creating *Sub Main*

The next step, if you want to use the code module as the starting point for your program (the application's entry point), is to create a procedure named `Sub Main` in the module.

NOTE Sub is short for Subroutine. It's a kind of procedure that performs an action, but does not return a value to the calling code.

To create a `Sub Main` procedure, in the Code Editor, within the code module, type **`Sub Main`**. The Code Editor will automatically add parentheses and an `End Sub` statement, so your `Sub Main` code will look like this:

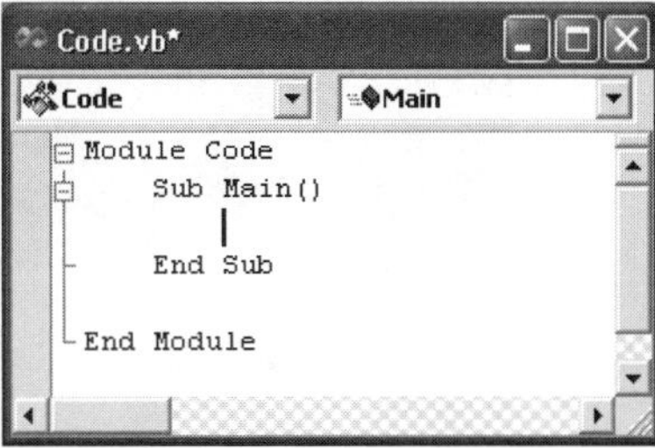

Setting the Startup Object

To set the application entry point to the newly created `Sub Main`, in the Solution Explorer, use the context menu for the project to open the project's Property Pages, as shown in Figure 6.2. Use the Startup object drop-down list to designate `Sub Main` as the Startup object.

FIGURE 6.2: Use the Project Property Pages to designate `Sub Main` as the Startup object.

With the Startup object designated, let's test it by adding `MessageBox.Show` to the `Sub Main` procedure, as shown in Listing 6.1.

Listing 6.1 Displaying a Message Box from *Sub Main*

```
Module Code
   Sub Main()
      MessageBox.Show("I am starting from Sub Main!", "Main!", _
         MessageBoxButtons.OK)
   End Sub
End Module
```

When you run the project, the message box will be displayed. Note that when you click OK in the message box, program execution terminates.

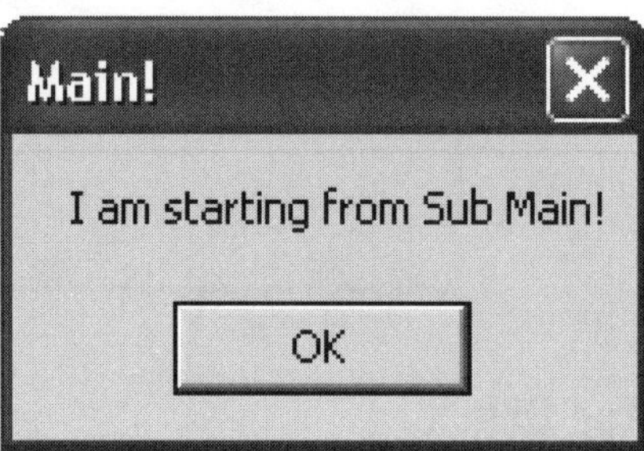

Working with Forms

If you added the code module to a default project, it also has a Windows form module, named *`Form1`* by default. (Don't worry if `Form1` isn't there because you deleted it; you can always add forms to your project using the Add New Item dialog.) You'll often want to load and display forms, even though your project has started from `Sub Main`.

Opening and Closing Forms

To display a normal form from `Sub Main`, declare a variable that holds an instance of the form class and use the `Run` method of the Application object to load and display it:

```
Dim Form1 As New Form1()
Application.Run(Form1)
```

To make it clear that this form display is optional and under the control of the programmer, you can let the user decide to load the form or not by using a conditional statement:

```
Dim answer As DialogResult
   answer = MessageBox.Show("Do you want to see Form1?", "Main!", _
      MessageBoxButtons.YesNo)
   If answer = DialogResult.Yes Then
      Dim Form1 As New Form1()
      Application.Run(Form1)
   End If
```

This displays a message box with Yes and No buttons.

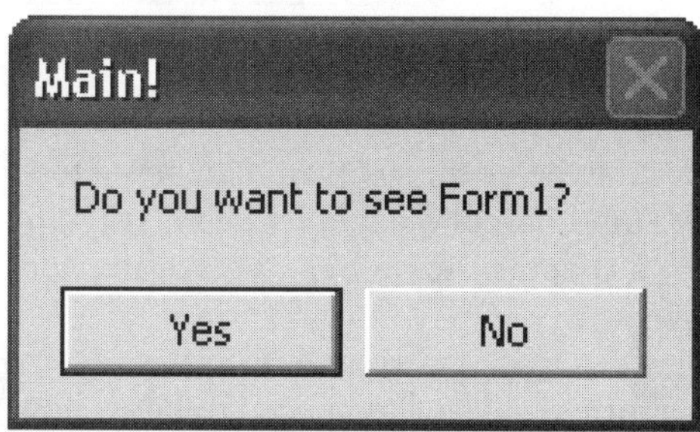

The complete code is shown in Listing 6.2.

Listing 6.2 Showing a Form from *Sub Main*

```
Module Code
    Sub Main()
      MessageBox.Show("I am starting from Sub Main!", "Main!", _
         MessageBoxButtons.OK)
      Dim answer As DialogResult
      answer = MessageBox.Show("Do you want to see Form1?", "Main!", _
         MessageBoxButtons.YesNo)
      If answer = DialogResult.Yes Then
         Dim Form1 As New Form1()
         Application.Run(Form1)
      End If
    End Sub
End Module
```

The form that loads displays a telltale triangle in the lower-right corner, meaning that it is primarily intended for use as a dialog box.

NOTE If you try to display Form1 on the screen using just its Show method, it will not stay on the screen long enough to be seen, and the program will terminate. There is another option: You can display Form1 modally, using its ShowDialog method (see "Showing a Modal Form" later in this chapter). To do this, replace the Application.Run statement with Form1.ShowDialog().

Once you have a form displayed, you need to know how to use code to close the form. If you add a Close button to the form, you can invoke the form's Close method to shut down the form, as shown in Listing 6.3.

Listing 6.3 Closing a Form

```
Private Sub Button1_Click(ByVal sender As Object, _
   ByVal e As System.EventArgs) Handles Button1.Click
   Me.Close()
End Sub
```

The form now includes a Close button.

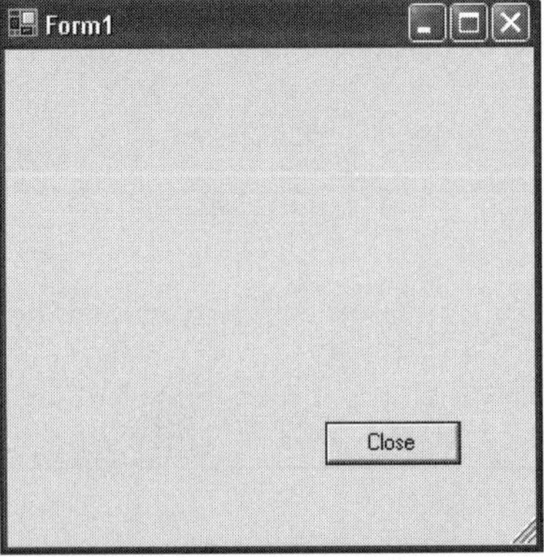

Things get interesting when you add more than one form to a project (use the Add New Item dialog to add as many Windows form modules to your project as you would like). Here's an example of a project with two form modules:

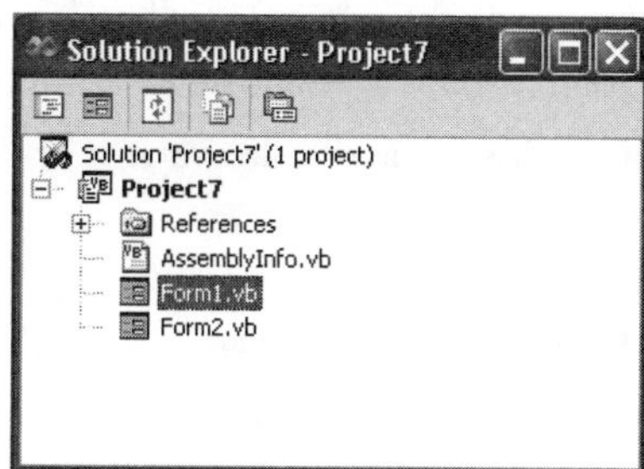

The first thing you might want to do is open a second form (`Form2`) from the first form (`Form1`). It's easy to imagine many real-world situations in which you need to do this. For example, you might want a user's choice to open a new dialog that covers some specifics in detail.

To open `Form2` from `Form1`, within `Form1`, declare a variable to hold an instance of `Form2`:

```
Dim Form2 As New Form2()
```

Next, invoke `Form2`'s `Show` method:

```
Private Sub btnShow_Click(ByVal sender As Object, _
   ByVal e As System.EventArgs) Handles btnShow.Click
   Form2.Show()
End Sub
```

To close `Form2` from `Form1`, just invoke `Form2`'s `Close` method:

```
Form2.Close()
```

The user can now open and close `Form2` from `Form1`, as shown in Figure 6.3.

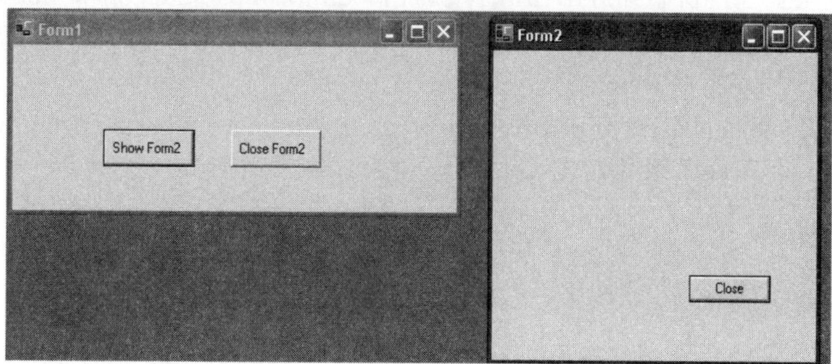

FIGURE 6.3: You can open and close one form from another form.

It's also sometimes useful to hide Form2, which you can do by using the Hide method:

```
Form2.Hide()
```

This keeps Form2 loaded without it being visible. You might do this if you wanted to perform operations on the form or its objects and later make use of these without needing to reload them (which would probably reset values to their initial state).

The code for opening, closing, and hiding one form from another form is shown in Listing 6.4.

Listing 6.4 Opening, Closing, and Hiding *Form2* from *Form1*

```
Dim Form2 As New Form2()
...

Private Sub btnShow_Click(ByVal sender As Object, _
   ByVal e As System.EventArgs) Handles btnShow.Click
   Form2.Show()
End Sub

Private Sub btnClose_Click(ByVal sender As Object, _
   ByVal e As System.EventArgs) Handles btnClose.Click
   Form2.Close()
End Sub

Private Sub btnHide_Click(ByVal sender As Object, _
   ByVal e As System.EventArgs) Handles btnHide.Click
   Form2.Hide()
End Sub
```

Manipulating Another Form

While Form2 is hidden, you might want to change some things about it, and then show it again. For example, you could use text input by the user on Form1 to change the Text property of Form2 and to display the hidden form using its Show method:

```
Form2.Text = txtNewText.Text
Form2.Show()
```

When Form2 is displayed again, the text entered by the user appears in its caption bar, as illustrated in Figure 6.4.

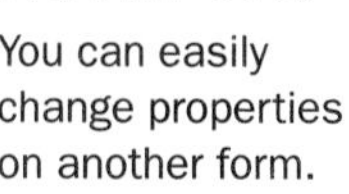

FIGURE 6.4:

You can easily change properties on another form.

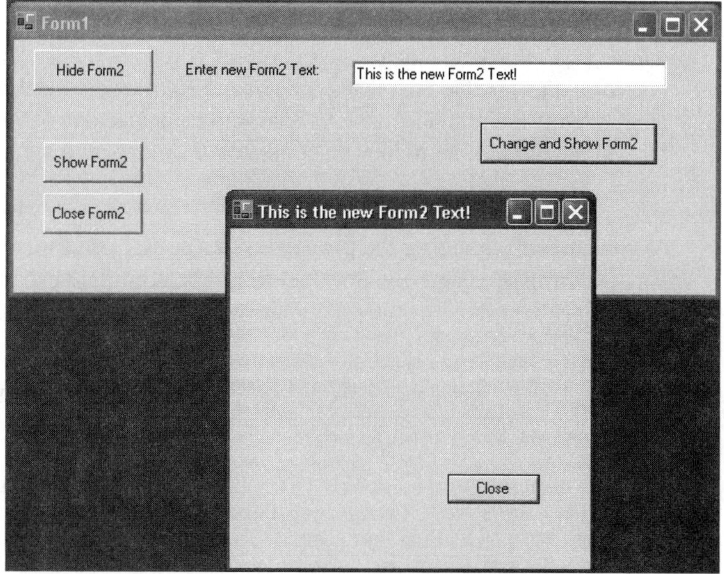

You can also use the same technique to change the property values of controls that are on the other form. For example, you could change the Text property of the Close button on `Form2` to something a little wilder:

```
Form2.Button1.Text = "Come on and close me!"
```

When you run the form, the button appears with its new text.

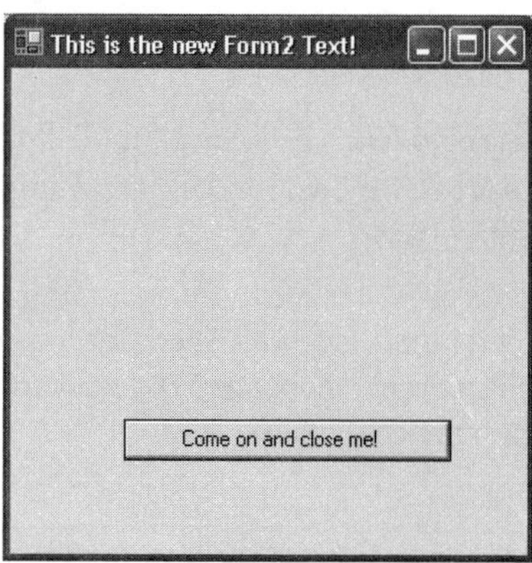

NOTE As a truly object-oriented language, VB .NET requires that you instantiate an object, such as a form, in a variable to manipulate the object. If you are manipulating a second form from a first form, the variable containing the second Form object must be declared (and instantiated) within the first form. Those familiar with older versions of VB will want to keep in mind that, within the first form, they must declare a variable and store an instance of the other form in it.

As you can see, changing the properties of a control on the other form just requires referencing the property using the dot operator. The complete event procedure for changing form properties and form control properties of another form is shown in Listing 6.5.

Listing 6.5 Changing *Form2* and *Form2* Control Properties from *Form1*

```
Dim Form2 As New Form2()
...
Private Sub btnChangeandShow_Click(ByVal sender As Object, _
   ByVal e As System.EventArgs) Handles btnChangeandShow.Click
   Form2.Text = txtNewText.Text
   Form2.Button1.Text = "Come on and close me!"
   Form2.Show()
End Sub
```

Showing a Modal Form

A *modal* form waits for the user to close the form before proceeding with the program. From a modal form, the user cannot work on another form belonging to the application. In contrast, if a form is *modeless* (the opposite of modal), the user can click another form belonging to the application to make it active.

As you can see in Listing 6.6, to show `Form2` modally from `Form1`, just use `Form2`'s `ShowDialog` method. Once `Form2` has been shown modally, as in Figure 6.5, the user must close it before she can use `Form1`, or any other form.

WARNING If you try to invoke a method, such as Show, for a form that has been unloaded, or disposed of, you will get an error message. The workaround is to hide forms that you may need to use later in an application.

Listing 6.6 Showing *Form2* Modally from *Form1*

```
Dim Form2 As New Form2()
...
Private Sub btnShowModal_Click(ByVal sender As Object, _
```

```
    ByVal e As System.EventArgs) Handles btnShowModal.Click
    Form2.ShowDialog()
End Sub
```

FIGURE 6.5:

If you use the ShowDialog method to load Form2 modally, the user must close Form2 before using Form1.

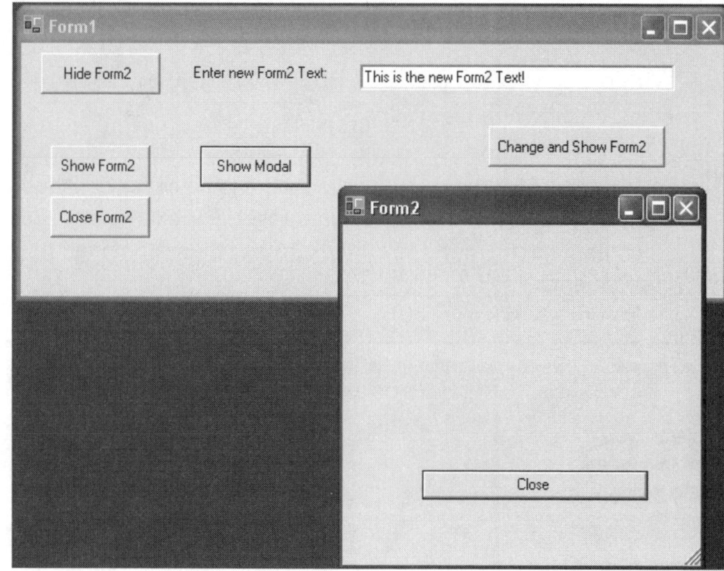

Positioning Forms

It's easy to use the Size and Location properties of `Form2` to move and resize it from `Form1`. To see this in action, add TextBox controls to `Form1` to hold the new location and size, as follows:

Name	Contents
`txtLocX`	Location X
`txtLocY`	Location Y
`txtWidth`	Width
`txtHeight`	Height

Also add a Button control, named `btnChange`, to make the changes when the user clicks. Within `btnChange`'s Click event, create a new Size object and assign it to `Form2`'s Size property:

```
Form2.Size = New System.Drawing.Size(CInt(txtWidth.Text), _
    CInt(txtHeight.Text))
```

When the Size object is created, as arguments it takes the new Width and Height values entered by the user. These values are converted from strings (since they are entered as text values) to integers using the `CInt` function.

Next, create a Point object. As you probably have anticipated, the new Point object is created using the values entered by the user in the `txtLocX` and `txtLocY` boxes. These string values are converted to integers using the `CInt` function, and the newly created Point object is assigned to `Form2`'s Location property:

```
Form2.Location = New System.Drawing.Point(CInt(txtLocX.Text), _
     CInt(txtLocY.Text))
```

With the code complete (see Listing 6.7), the user can move `Form2` around to her heart's content, as shown in Figure 6.6.

WARNING This is not production code because there is no checking that the user has entered something that can be converted to an integer. For example, if the user enters a text string (such as a name) in the Width box, rather than a number, running the program will produce an error.

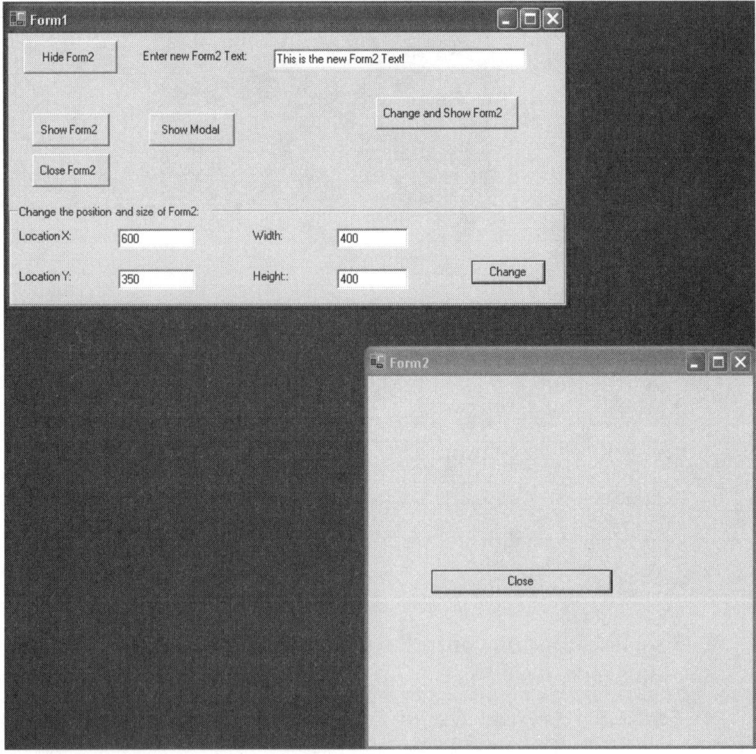

FIGURE 6.6: Using Size and Location objects, you can easily manipulate `Form2`'s dimensions and position.

Listing 6.7 Sizing and Positioning *Form2* from *Form1* in Response to User Input

```
Dim Form2 As New Form2()
...
Private Sub btnChange_Click(ByVal sender As Object, _
   ByVal e As System.EventArgs) Handles btnChange.Click
   Form2.Size = New System.Drawing.Size(CInt(txtWidth.Text), _
      CInt(txtHeight.Text))
   Form2.Location = New System.Drawing.Point(CInt(txtLocX.Text), _
      CInt(txtLocY.Text))
End Sub
```

Using Form Inheritance Features

It's easy to use VB .NET's inheritance features so that a new form can inherit the characteristics of the first form—lock, stock, properties, methods, events, and code.

Changing Form Inheritance in Code

Normally, if you look at the first line of code in a form, you will see something like this:

```
Public Class Form3
    Inherits System.Windows.Forms.Form
```

If you want `Form3` to inherit from `Form1`, the only thing you need to do is change this line, as follows:

```
Public Class Form3 Inherits Form1
```

NOTE If you would like your form to inherit from a form in another project, you must reference it by namespace, for example, `Project7.Form1`. You can set the namespace for a project in the project's Property Pages. By default, the namespace is the name of the project.

To view your inherited form, show it the normal way:

```
Private Sub btnShowForm3_Click(ByVal sender As Object, _
   ByVal e As System.EventArgs) Handles btnShowForm3.Click
   Dim Form3 As New Form3()
   Form3.Show()
End Sub
```

As shown in Figure 6.7, you'll see that `Form3` has inherited everything from `Form1`.

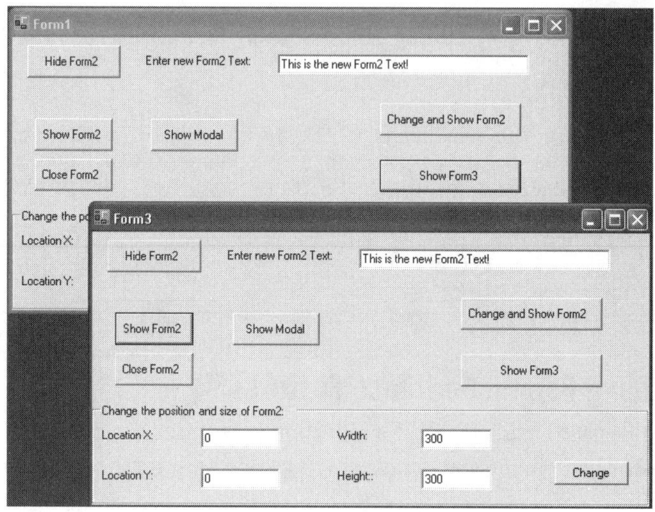

FIGURE 6.7: It's easy to use form inheritance to give a new form all the characteristics of an existing form.

Using Visual Inheritance

You can also create a new form that inherits its characteristics from another form by using a VB .NET feature called *visual inheritance*. To do this, open the Add New Item dialog and select Inherited Form, as shown in Figure 6.8.

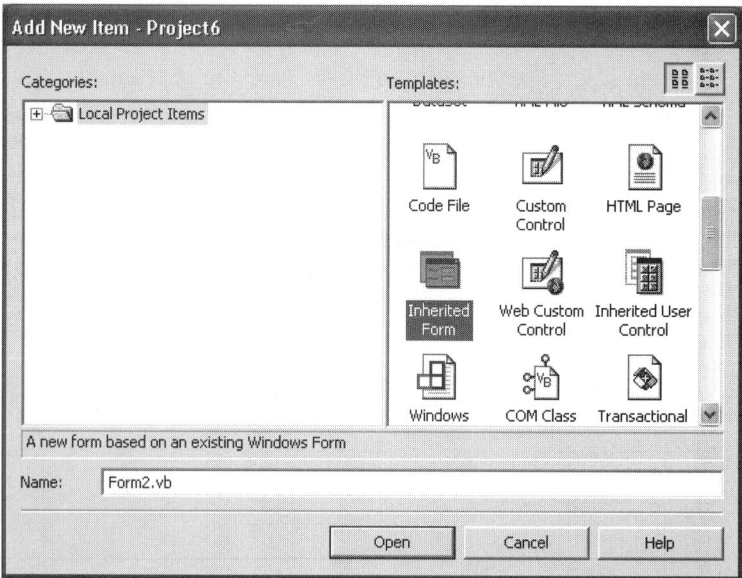

FIGURE 6.8: You can select Inherited Form in the Add New Item dialog.

TIP If you select Add Inherited Form from the Project menu, the Add New Item dialog opens with the Inherited Form module type selected.

Click Open. The Inheritance Picker dialog opens, as shown in Figure 6.9. You can use the Inheritance Picker to select the form that will be inherited from. Use the Browse button to inherit from a form in a project other than the current one.

FIGURE 6.9: Select the form to inherit from using the Inheritance Picker dialog.

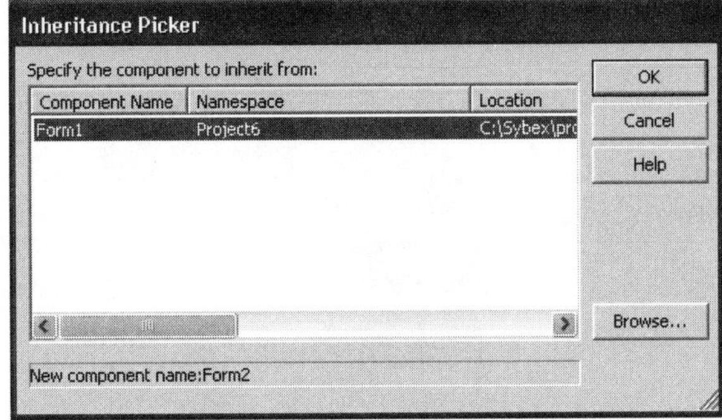

When you click OK in the Inheritance Picker, the inherited form will be added to your project. Note that the form that has been added uses an `Inherits` clause in its declaration to create the inheritance relationship, so the visual inheritance process leads to the same place as adding an `Inherits` clause in code (as described in the previous section).

Working with the Graphics Object

The Graphics object is used to draw text and graphics on a form. In theory, the methods of the Graphics object are used with related objects—such as Brushes, Fonts, and Pens—to draw on a graphics *context* (which you can think of as a canvas).

The good news is that Graphics object, methods, and related objects provide you with immensely powerful ways to create graphics on a form (and other objects). The not-so-good news is that these powerful tools are a little tricky to use and almost overwhelming in their variety. When you just want to do something simple like drawing a line, this can be a bit of a drawback.

NOTE No longer will you find form methods—such as VB6's `Line` and `Circle` methods—that let you easily put simple shapes on a form.

One thing you will need to think about before getting started with the Graphics object is the persistence of what you draw. If you use the Graphics object to draw something on a form's graphics context, it will disappear as the form is repainted; for example, it will be gone when the user resizes the form. As I'll show you, you can make your graphics persist by placing the code that renders your drawing in the form Paint event.

Before we get too far into the Graphics object, it would be a good time to beautify the form we have already created to manipulate other forms. In VB .NET, it's easy to let the IDE align and space controls, and make selected controls the same size. As shown in Figure 6.10, you'll find the tools needed to achieve great form layouts on the Format menu.

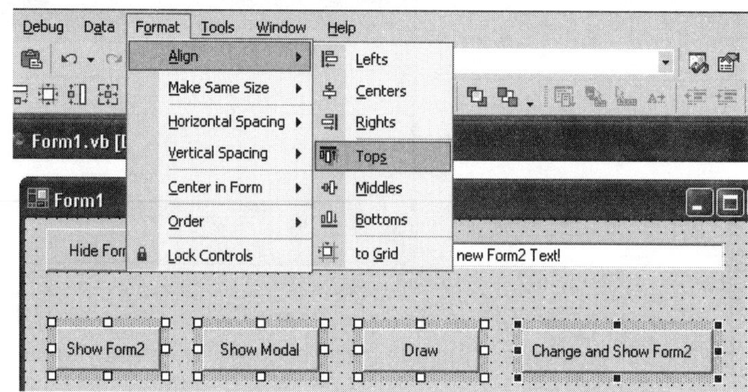

FIGURE 6.10: You can easily align and space controls on a form using the Format menu (the buttons are shown being top-aligned).

Drawing Text on a Form

Let's start by drawing some fancy text on the background of a form. Within a button Click event, create a Graphics object variable named `g`:

```
Dim g As Graphics
```

Next, create a Brush object called `theBrush`. For this example, I chose to create something called a HatchBrush, and I filled it with blue and red plaid. I assigned this to `theBrush`. (I don't necessarily recommend the aesthetics of this choice, and there are many, many brush options to choose from.)

```
Dim theBrush As New Drawing2D.HatchBrush _
   (Drawing.Drawing2D.HatchStyle.Plaid, _
    Color.RoyalBlue, Color.DarkRed)
```

Next, create a Font object variable and give it initial values:

```
Dim theFont As New Font("Arial", 60)
```

Use the form's `CreateGraphics` method to associate the Graphics object with the form:

```
g = Me.CreateGraphics
```

Finally, use the `DrawString` method of the Graphics object to draw a text string on the form, using the Font and Brush objects previously created:

```
g.DrawString(".NET is cool!", theFont, theBrush, 40, 190)
```

As shown in Figure 6.11, when the user invokes the event procedure, the text is drawn on the form (although you can't quite see the garish plaid colors in all their glory in black and white).

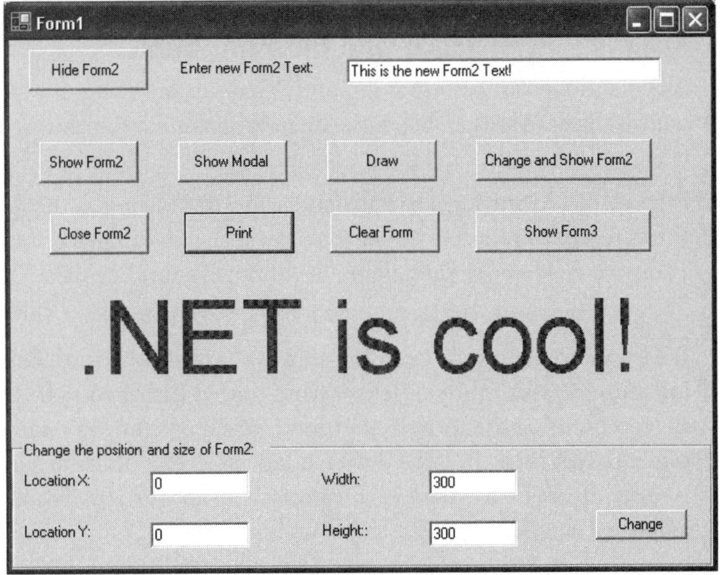

FIGURE 6.11: The Graphics object's `DrawString` method is used to render text on the background of a form.

The complete event procedure is shown in Listing 6.8.

Listing 6.8 Printing Text on a Form

```
Private Sub btnPrint_Click(ByVal sender As Object, _
   ByVal e As System.EventArgs) Handles btnPrint.Click
   Dim g As Graphics
   Dim theBrush As New Drawing2D.HatchBrush _
      (Drawing.Drawing2D.HatchStyle.Plaid, _
      Color.RoyalBlue, Color.DarkRed)
   Dim theFont As New Font("Arial", 60)
   g = Me.CreateGraphics
   g.DrawString(".NET is cool!", theFont, theBrush, 40, 190)
End Sub
```

By the way, you may also wish to have a way to clear your form, or to give users the opportunity to do so (particularly if you've used red and blue plaid letters!).

To clear a form, you need to repaint it, which you can do by invoking the form's `Refresh` method. The following button Click event will clear the background of a form:

```
Private Sub btnClear_Click(ByVal sender As Object, _
   ByVal e As System.EventArgs) Handles btnClear.Click
   Me.Refresh()
End Sub
```

Achieving Persistence with the Paint Event

As I mentioned at the beginning of this section, anything drawn on a form background is normally subject to erasure when the form is repainted. Repainting happens a lot; for example, it occurs when the user minimizes or resizes a form. Fortunately, there is a way around this.

If you want your form background art to last as long as the form does (using proper lingo, this is to say you want to *persist* the drawing), you can place your drawing code in the form's Paint event. Here are the arguments of the event procedure:

```
ByVal sender As Object, ByVal e As System.Windows.Forms.PaintEventArgs
```

Listing 6.9 shows the code for drawing text in the form's Paint event. Note that the code in Listing 6.9 is slightly different from that in Listing 6.8. In Listing 6.8, the device, or canvas representing the form background, was created by invoking the form's `CreateGraphics` method. In Listing 6.9, the device is passed as one of the arguments of the Paint event procedure. To create the device, or canvas, `e.Graphics` is assigned to the Graphics object that will be drawn on.

Listing 6.9 Drawing the Text in the Form's Paint Event

```
Private Sub Form1_Paint(ByVal sender As Object, _
   ByVal e As System.Windows.Forms.PaintEventArgs) Handles MyBase.Paint
   Dim theBrush As New Drawing2D.HatchBrush _
      (Drawing.Drawing2D.HatchStyle.Plaid, _
       Color.RoyalBlue, Color.DarkRed)
   Dim theFont As New Font("Arial", 60)
   Dim g As Graphics
   g = e.Graphics
   g.DrawString(".NET is cool!", theFont, theBrush, 40, 190)
End Sub
```

Drawing Circles and Lines

It's fairly easy to draw simple shapes such as circles and lines on a form background. The general steps will seem familiar from drawing text on the form:

- Declare a variable as a Graphics object.

- Give it a device context using the form `CreateGraphics` method (or using the arguments passed to the Paint event).
- Create pens (and/or brushes).
- Use the methods of the Graphics object, with the pens and brushes you have created, to do your drawing.
- As a final step, you should reclaim the memory occupied by the pen(s) you have created.

Taking these steps in order, declare the variable:

```
Dim g As Graphics
```

Then give it the device context of the form background:

```
g = Me.CreateGraphics
```

To draw a red ellipse 10 pixels wide using the dimensions specified:

```
Dim thePen As New Drawing.Pen(System.Drawing.Color.Red, 10)
g.DrawEllipse(thePen, 200, 190, 100, 100)
```

To draw a blue horizontal line (5 pixels wide, 600 pixels horizontally, and located 235 pixels below 0,0):

```
thePen.Dispose()
thePen = New Drawing.Pen(System.Drawing.Color.Blue, 5)
g.DrawLine(thePen, 0, 235, 600, 235)
```

To reclaim the memory occupied by the Pen object, using the object's `Dispose` method:

```
thePen.Dispose()
```

When the user invokes the code in an event procedure, as shown in Listing 6.10, a circle and a line will be drawn on the form background, as shown in Figure 6.12.

Listing 6.10 Drawing a Circle and a Line on a Form

```
Private Sub btnDraw_Click(ByVal sender As Object, _
   ByVal e As System.EventArgs) Handles btnDraw.Click
   Dim g As Graphics
   g = Me.CreateGraphics
   Dim thePen As New Drawing.Pen(System.Drawing.Color.Red, 10)
   g.DrawEllipse(thePen, 200, 190, 100, 100)
   thePen.Dispose()
   thePen = New Drawing.Pen(System.Drawing.Color.Blue, 5)
   g.DrawLine(thePen, 0, 235, 600, 235)
   thePen.Dispose()
End Sub
```

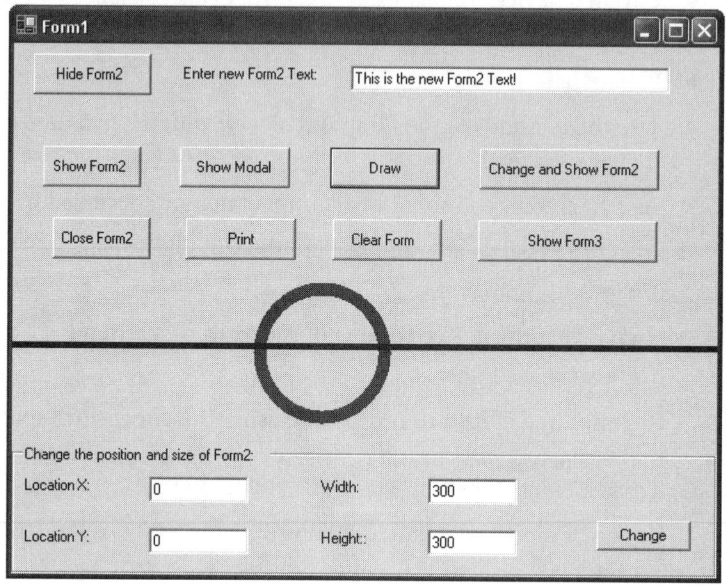

FIGURE 6.12: You can easily use GDI+ and the Graphics object to render shapes such as circles and lines.

Why Be Square?

One of the great things about .NET is that it is easy to make visual objects, such as Windows forms, any shape that you would like. For example, an elliptical window might make users think your application is really cool!

Let's do this with the form we've been working with in this chapter. To start, at the top of the form module, import the `System.Drawing.Drawing2D` namespace to make referring to the Drawing2D library members easier:

```
Imports System.Drawing.Drawing2D
Public Class Form1
    Inherits System.Windows.Forms.Form
```

Next, immediately below the form declaration, create a subroutine, `ApplyInitialRegion`. Within `ApplyInitialRegion`, define a GraphicsPath object using its `AddEllipse` method, and assign it to the Region property of the Form object.

```
Private Sub ApplyInitialRegion()
   Dim myGraphicsPath As GraphicsPath
   myGraphicsPath = New GraphicsPath()
   myGraphicsPath.AddEllipse(New Rectangle(0, 0, 700, 300))
   Me.Region = New Region(myGraphicsPath)
End Sub
```

All that remains is to create a way to call the form, which you can do in a button Click event, as shown in Listing 6.11.

WARNING Depending on the shape you choose for your form, it may not have the normal mechanisms for closure, as in the example here. Make sure that you provide a way to close the form, such as Button control for this purpose (see Listing 6.11).

Listing 6.11 Creating an Elliptical Form

```
Imports System.Drawing.Drawing2D
Public Class Form1
    Inherits System.Windows.Forms.Form
Private Sub ApplyInitialRegion()
    Dim myGraphicsPath As GraphicsPath
    myGraphicsPath = New GraphicsPath()
    myGraphicsPath.AddEllipse(New Rectangle(0, 0, 700, 300))
    Me.Region = New Region(myGraphicsPath)
End Sub
...
Private Sub btnShape_Click(ByVal sender As System.Object, _
   ByVal e As System.EventArgs) Handles btnShape.Click
   ApplyInitialRegion()
End Sub

'Provide a way to shut down the form
Private Sub btnExit_Click(ByVal sender As System.Object, _
   ByVal e As System.EventArgs) Handles btnExit.Click
   Application.Exit()
End Sub
```

When you run the form and click the Why Be Square? button, you'll find that it has a pretty nifty oval shape.

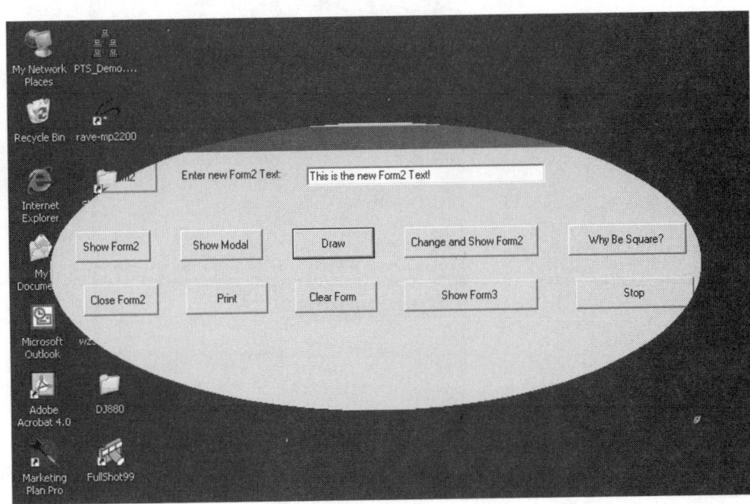

TIP You can load a form with whatever shape you'd like by placing the call to the procedure that shapes the form in the form's `New` subroutine (found within the Windows Form Designer generated code).

Creating MDI Applications

In MDI (Multiple Document Interface) applications, there is one MDI, or parent, form. There are usually many MDI child forms. There can be more than one type of MDI child form, but all children, whatever their type, must fit into the client space of the parent MDI window.

NOTE The *client space* of a form is the form background area, exclusive of title bar, toolbars, menus, and border.

Application styles go, well, in and out of style. MDI applications used to be very hot indeed. These days, they are perhaps less highly regarded. In fact, so far, all the forms I've shown you are SDI (Single Document Interface) forms rather than part of an MDI application. But you should know about MDI applications, which are simple and easy to rig in VB .NET.

Start with a new project with two forms. Leave the form names `Form1` and `Form2`. `Form1` will be our MDI parent, and `Form2` will be used as the basis for the application's MDI children.

To make `Form1` the MDI parent, in the Properties window, set its IsMDIContainer property to True. (*Container* is an alternative term for parent.)

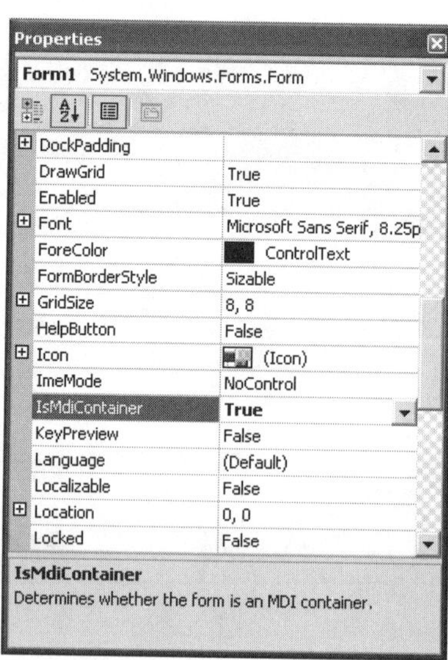

TIP You'll find information about creating MDI menus, an important part of MDI look and feel, in Chapter 11, "Creating Menus."

Setting the IsMDIContainer property takes care of the MDI parent. Now, let's get to work on the MDI children.

First, add a button to the parent form, `Form1`, that will be used to open child form instances. Name it **`btnShowChild`**.

TIP If you place the button on a Panel control in `Form1`, the Panel is not treated as part of `Form1`'s client area.

Next, in the `btnShowChild` Click event, declare a variable to hold an instance of `Form2` in the usual fashion:

```
Dim Form2 As New Form2()
```

Here's the crucial step: Assign the value of `Form2`'s MDIParent property to `Form1` (in this case, using the `Me` keyword, which means `Form1`):

```
Form2.MdiParent = Me
```

Finally, show the child form:

```
Form2.Show()
```

To make this a little more elegant, let's add a counter variable so we know how many children have been created. Declare the counter variable at the form level:

```
Public Class Form1
    Inherits System.Windows.Forms.Form
    Dim i As Integer
```

Next, initialize the variable so that the first child is number one:

```
'This call is required by the Windows Form Designer.
InitializeComponent()
i = 1
'Add any initialization after the InitializeComponent() call
```

Finally, back in the Click event procedure, change the Text property of the child form (`Form2`) to reflect which number it is, and increment the child counter:

```
Form2.Text = Form2.Text & " #" & CStr(i)
i = i + 1
```

Listing 6.12 shows the complete code for this example.

Listing 6.12 Creating MDI Children with an Incremental Counter

```
Public Class Form1
    Inherits System.Windows.Forms.Form
    Dim i As Integer

#Region " Windows Form Designer generated code "

    Public Sub New()
        MyBase.New()

        'This call is required by the Windows Form Designer.
        InitializeComponent()
        i = 1
        'Add any initialization after the InitializeComponent() call

    End Sub
...
Private Sub btnShowChild_Click(ByVal sender As Object, _
   ByVal e As System.EventArgs) Handles btnShowChild.Click
   Dim Form2 As New Form2()
   Form2.MdiParent = Me
   Form2.Show()
   Form2.Text = Form2.Text & " #" & CStr(i)
   i = i + 1
End Sub
```

When you run the project, you can click the Show a Child! button to create as many child forms as you would like.

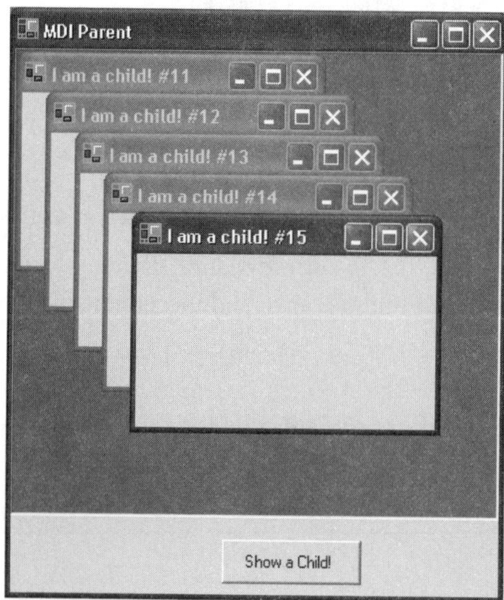

Organizing Code with *#Region*

The code that is automatically generated to create a visual form is initially hidden from view in the Code Editor using a #Region command. By expanding the region—clicking the + icon next to the Region description—the hidden code is expanded.

You can use the same facility yourself to help organize your code. Start the code you want to be hidden and expandable with a #Region command:

```
#Region "My Expandable Code"
```

After the code you want to be expandable, put the following command:

```
#End Region
```

The next time you open the module, you'll see "My Expandable Code" with an expansion icon, treated just the way the "hidden" form code is treated.

Summary

This chapter showed you how to work with forms. You learned how to open forms, close forms, manipulate forms, and draw on them. Understanding this material is necessary for any project. In addition, you learned a great deal about working with methods, an important part of the VB .NET object interface. In passing, I showed you a great deal about working with VB .NET objects.

The next chapter picks up where this one left off. In the real world, forms achieve most of their functionality using controls. In Chapter 7, "Working with Windows Forms Controls," you'll learn how to create forms that are professional in appearance and functionality using the most important form controls.

Chapter 7

Working with Windows Forms Controls

- Working with the ToolBox
- Adding PictureBox controls
- Adding CheckBox controls
- Working with control collections and arrays
- Working with ComboBoxes, ListBoxes, and CheckedListBoxes
- Working with the ErrorProvider

In the previous three chapters, you've had a good look at how you work with forms. You learned about form properties, events, and methods. However, things get really interesting when you start adding controls to your forms. Fortunately, the things you have learned about form properties, events, and methods apply—for the most part—to controls as well. In this chapter, you will learn how to build rich applications by working with some of the most important Windows forms controls.

Using the Toolbox is the easiest way to add controls to a form. Notice that I said "easiest" and not "only," because you can also add a control to a form using code. In this chapter, you'll learn both approaches to adding controls.

Working with the Toolbox

As you've already seen, the Toolbox allows you to add controls to a form visually. It's important to understand in detail all that you can do with the Toolbox because it will make your life as a .NET developer much easier.

By default, the Toolbox comes "out of the box" with a number of different tabs used for organizing controls and components. You can navigate between these tabs by clicking their title bar.

NOTE The essential difference between a *control* and a *component* is that a control is able to have a visual appearance when seated on a form, and a component is not. In other words, a control is a component (the more general term) that is able to present a visual interface.

By default, the Toolbox has Data, Components, Windows Forms, Clipboard Ring, and General tabs. The General tab appears by default whenever the Toolbox opens, but is empty except for the Pointer. The Data tab contains components for working with databases (discussed in Chapter 17, "Working with Data and ADO.NET"). The Clipboard Ring tab (referring to an Office 2000–style Clipboard Ring) is used to store recently cut or copied Clipboard items for easy access.

The Components tab, shown on the following page, gives you access to controls that do not have a visual representation at runtime.

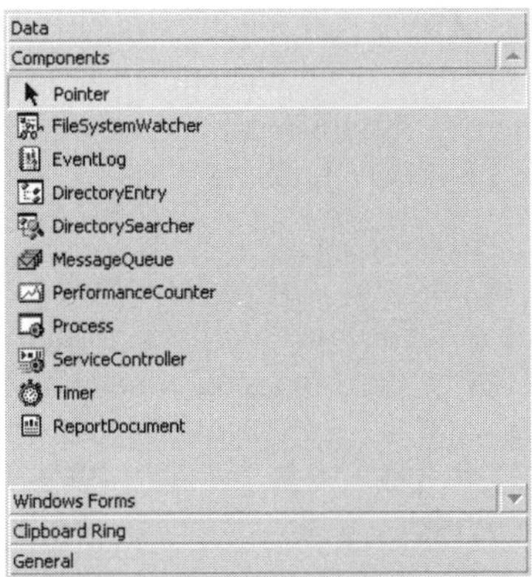

The components on the Components tab are used for nonvisual programming jobs, such as adding information to event logs, message queuing, and firing timed events. When you add one of these components to a form, they appear on the tray below the form, rather than on the form itself. You'll find more information about working with some of these components in Chapter 10, "Using Timers, EventLogs, and ServiceControllers."

The Windows Forms tab of the Toolbox, shown below, gives you access to the standard .NET controls that you can use with forms.

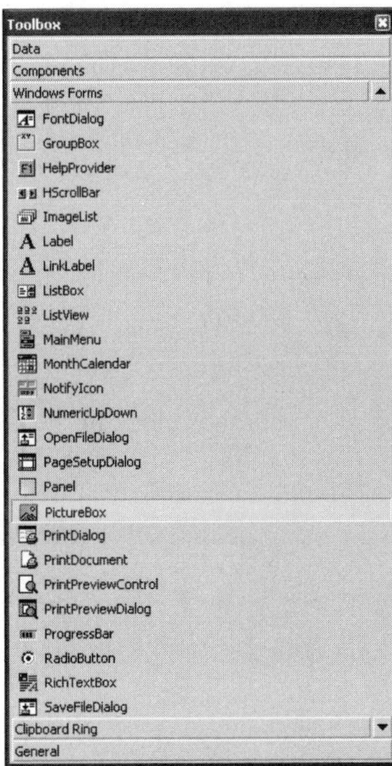

In addition to these tabs, there are a number of other tabs that appear when they are needed because they are appropriate to your current working mode. You can view all the tabs by selecting Show All Tabs from the Toolbox's context menu. Items that are inappropriate for the current working mode are disabled (shown in gray).

NOTE Generally, you will see only the Toolbox tabs that are applicable to your current working situation. For example, if you have no form modules open in their designers, and are working in the Code Editor, the Windows Forms controls tab will not be displayed.

Toolbox tabs are very customizable. You can add news tabs, rename tabs, add items to tabs, delete items from tabs, and reorganize items on a tab. It's up to you to make your Toolbox work best for you.

Adding Frequently Used Code to the Toolbox

One of the coolest features of the Toolbox is that you can drag code that you frequently use to a Toolbox tab. Once code is placed on the tab, you can drag and drop it into any program you are writing. This is a great way to retrieve frequently used code blocks.

For example, suppose you have a standardized comment block that you use to start all your modules (you might be part of a development team where the form of the initial comment block is specified for you). You could create a comment block template that looks something like this:

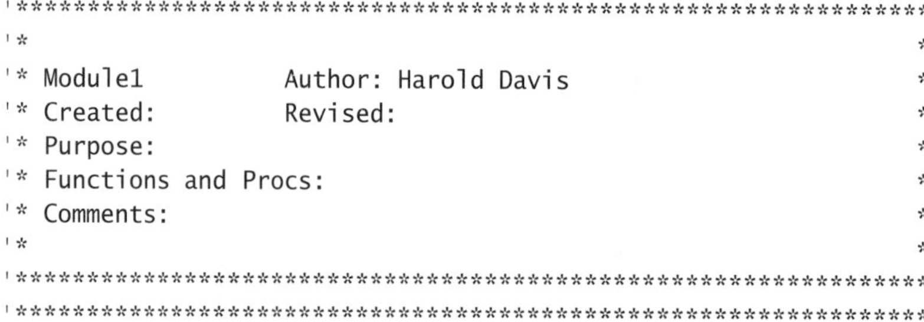

```
'*******************************************************************
'*                                                                 *
'* Module1          Author: Harold Davis                           *
'* Created:         Revised:                                       *
'* Purpose:                                                        *
'* Functions and Procs:                                            *
'* Comments:                                                       *
'*                                                                 *
'*******************************************************************
'*******************************************************************
```

Next, you could select the comment block in the Code Editor and drag it to a Toolbox tab, as shown here.

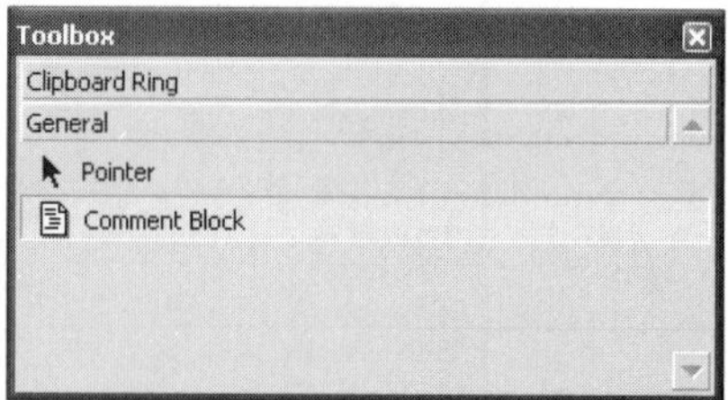

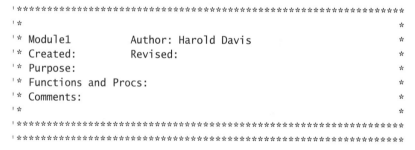

To reuse the comment block code, simple drag it from the Toolbox to where you want it in the Code Editor.

TIP By default, code dragged to the Toolbox will be designated with the first characters of the code. You can change it to something more user friendly by selecting Rename Item from the item's context menu in the Toolbox.

Customizing the Toolbox

Using the Toolbox's context menus, you can completely customize the appearance of Toolbox tabs and their items. Actions you can take include the following:

- Adding and removing custom tabs
- Adding and removing items on a tab
- Renaming tabs and items on the tab
- Showing all tabs or concealing those that you are not using
- Displaying items on the tab as icons or in labeled lists
- Sorting items on a tab alphabetically
- Moving items on a tab to another position

For example, it's easy to organize things within the Toolbox by adding your own special tabs. To add a tab to the Toolbox, select Add Tab from the Toolbox's context menu. It will appear in the Toolbox with the name you specified, as in the example (My Tab) shown here:

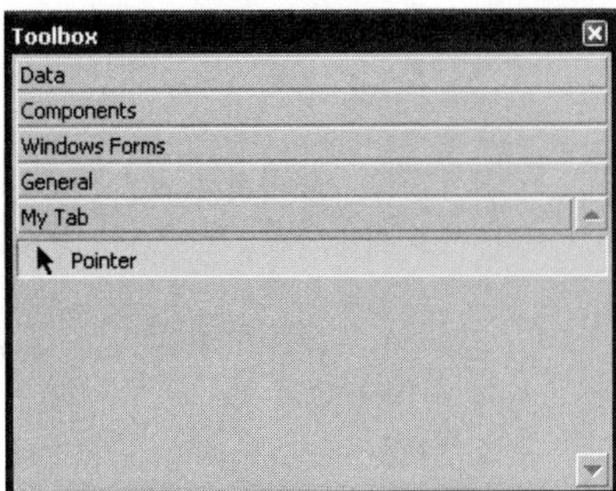

You can also easily add existing components and controls on your system to the Toolbox by selecting Customize Toolbox from the Toolbox's context menu. As you can see in Figures 7.1 and 7.2, there are separate tabs in the Customize Toolbox dialog for COM components (also known as ActiveX components) and .NET Framework components. Components that are checked in the Customize Toolbox dialog (you'll see checked and unchecked components in Figure 7.1) appear in the Toolbox and are ready for use.

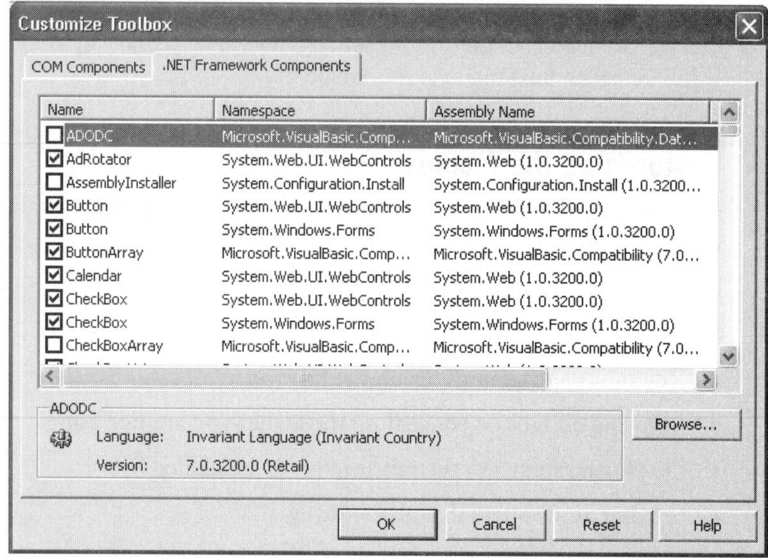

FIGURE 7.1: Within the Customize Toolbox dialog, the .NET Frameworks Components tab shows the native .NET controls you can add to your Toolbox.

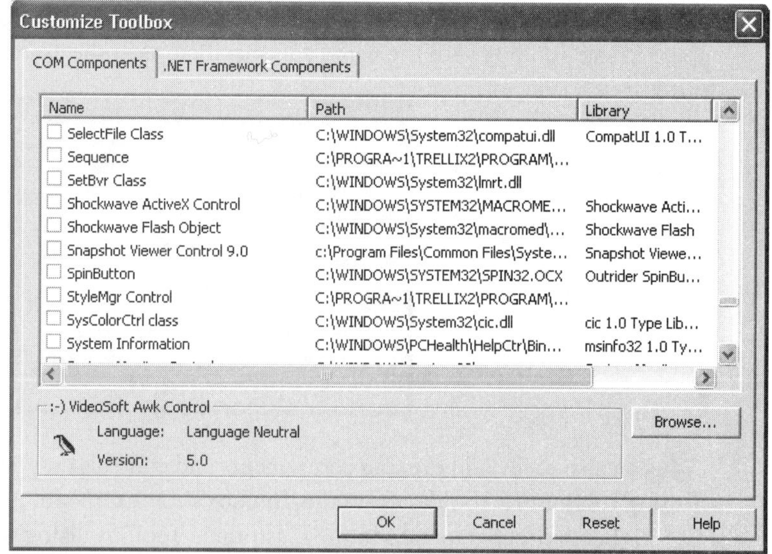

FIGURE 7.2: You can use the COM Components tab to add ActiveX controls to your Toolbox.

TIP As you can see in the Customize Toolbox dialog, the Windows Forms .NET controls are part of the `System.Windows.Forms` namespace. An interesting group of controls, which are not enabled by default, belong to the `Microsoft.Visual Basic.Compatability.VB6` namespace. As the namespace implies, these controls are intended to help with backward compatibility; in other words, they're helpful for converting from VB6 to VB .NET projects. For more information, see Appendix B, "Migrating Applications from VB6 to VB .NET."

It's easy to perform these and other customizations using the Toolbox's context menus. I recommend you play with the Toolbox until you find the configuration that works best for you.

.NET Framework and COM Components

The .NET Framework is designed to allow you to use either .NET components or COM (ActiveX) components. For that matter, you can create either kind of component using .NET. Possibly, it might be useful to create COM components in .NET for use with legacy development environments. However, you need to go through the extra step of creating a Client Callable Wrapper (CCW) to make your .NET class look like a COM object, and this is a nontrivial task. Generally, .NET is intended for working with .NET components, although COM has not been entirely eliminated (to help development projects that must use this legacy mechanism for interoperability).

The fact that you can use existing ActiveX controls is a good thing if you have substantial legacy code in (possibly custom) COM components. However, there are some disadvantages to using COM components within a .NET application, including the following:

- Increased overhead
- Decreased performance (because of the performance hit that you take by going through the COM interoperability layer)
- Much more complicated deployment (you have the worst of both worlds: the nasty issues that surround deploying COM objects and also the need to have the .NET runtime installed)
- Possible loss of "managed code" benefits for applications that include COM components, such as type checking, identity checking, and fully automated memory management
- The things that drove us crazy about COM components in the first place, such as the way they worked (or didn't) with the Windows Registry

For these reasons, your policy should probably be "in with the new and out with the old." Unless you have very good reasons to the contrary, I recommend that you use only .NET components in your .NET applications. This book makes the assumption that you are following this advice, and there will be no further discussion of COM.

Adding PictureBox Controls

One of the most commonly employed controls, the PictureBox, is used to display pictures. The PictureBox control can be used to display bitmap graphic files in BMP, GIF, ICO, JPG, and PNG formats, as well as Windows metafiles (WMF files).

Loading a Picture

A PictureBox's Image property is used to control the graphics file that is displayed by the PictureBox. To load a picture, select the Image property in the Properties window. Click the button marked with ellipses on the right side of the Properties window. The Open dialog will appear, as shown in Figure 7.3.

FIGURE 7.3: The PictureBox's Image property lets you load an image from the filesystem at design time.

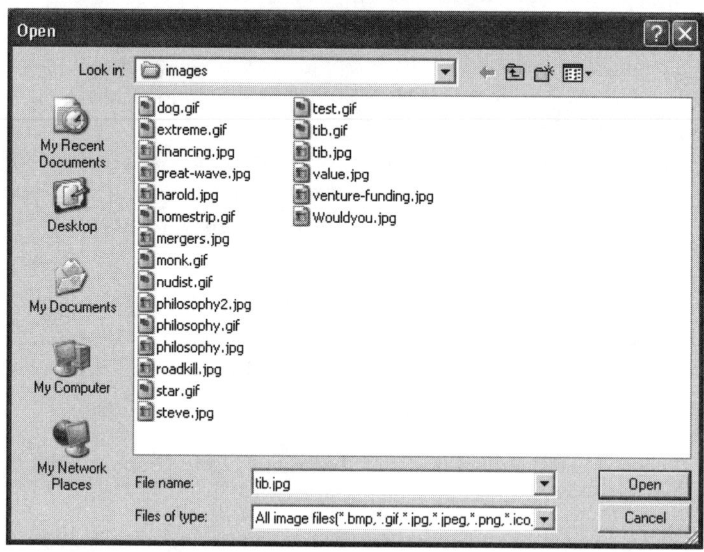

Once you have selected a graphics file, it will appear in the PictureBox control at both design time and runtime.

Sizing and Positioning Pictures

After you've added a PictureBox to a form, make sure to size and position it as you would like. Pay particular attention to its Dock, Anchor, and SizeMode properties.

Setting the Dock Property

The size of the displayed image depends on how you set the PictureBox control's properties. For example, if the PictureBox's Dock property is set to Full, the picture will occupy the entire client area of the form at design time and runtime, as shown next.

Setting the Anchor Property

Anchor is a nifty property that does a lot of work for you. By default, controls anchor in the top-left area of the form. You can use the Anchor property to set a PictureBox (or any other control) to anchor elsewhere (for example, the bottom right). You can set the Anchor property using the graphical interface in the Properties window.

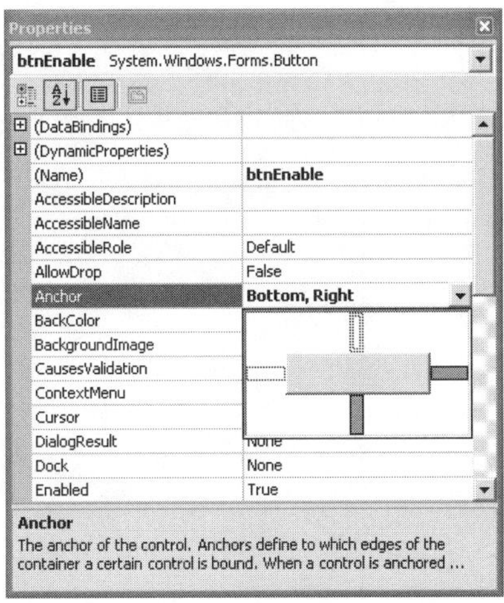

Setting the SizeMode Property

The PictureBox's general positioning properties can be used to position the contents of the PictureBox in relationship to the form. You can also use the PictureBox's SizeMode property to manipulate the graphics file in relationship to the PictureBox. For example, suppose the PictureBox is bigger than the graphic and you want to stretch the graphic to fill the PictureBox. Setting the SizeMode property of the PictureBox to StretchImage will achieve this.

You can set the SizeMode property in the Properties window or in code. To set it in code, add this statement (for a PictureBox control named `PictureBox1`) to an event handler or at initialization:

```
PictureBox1.SizeMode = PictureBoxSizeMode.StretchImage
```

It's a good thing that you don't need to remember the possible SizeMode values. The Code Editor's auto-completion feature will supply the possible values in a drop-down list:

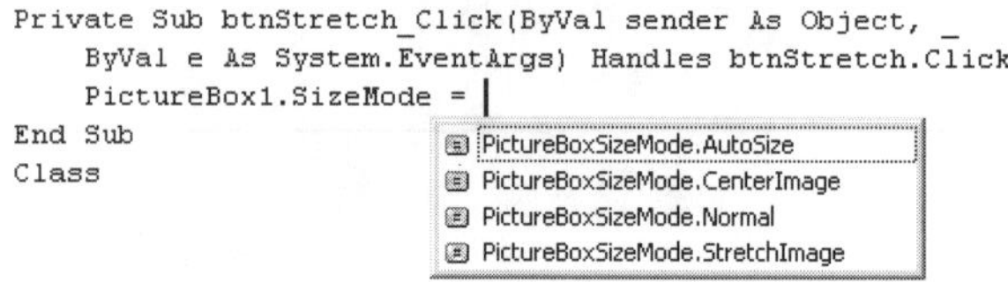

Changing PictureBox Properties in Code

You will often want to load, size, and unload a graphic in response to user actions at runtime. You can do this by changing the PictureBox properties in code. To see how this works, add a PictureBox control to a form. For the time being, leave its Image property empty. Add buttons to the form for loading the picture, stretching the picture, and removing the picture, as shown here.

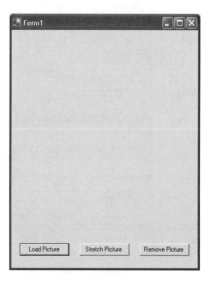

To load a picture, add code to the Load Picture button's Click event, using the `FromFile` method of the Image class to assign a graphics file to the PictureBox's Image property:

```
Private Sub btnLoad_Click(ByVal sender As Object, _
   ByVal e As System.EventArgs) Handles btnLoad.Click
   Dim Path As String = "C:\WINDOWS\Soap Bubbles.bmp"
   PictureBox1.Image = Image.FromFile(Path)
End Sub
```

WARNING Depending on your system, the file `Soap Bubbles.bmp` may not be located in the Windows directory (or may not even be present on your system). If necessary, change the path string to correctly point to an image file that is present on your system.

When you run this code, provided the file supplied to the `FromFile` method is a valid graphics file in the specified location, the picture will be loaded into the PictureBox control and displayed in its actual size:

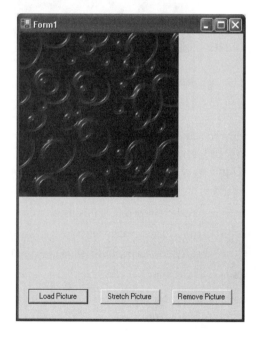

To stretch the picture to fill the PictureBox control, change the PictureBox's SizeMode property in the Stretch button's Click event:

```
Private Sub btnStretch_Click(ByVal sender As Object, _
   ByVal e As System.EventArgs) Handles btnStretch.Click
   PictureBox1.SizeMode = PictureBoxSizeMode.StretchImage
End Sub
```

When you run the project, load the picture, and then click the Stretch button, the graphic is resized to fill the PictureBox:

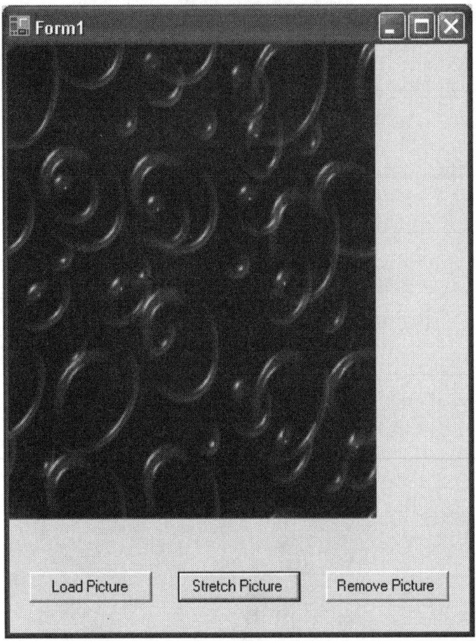

You also may want to remove a graphics file from a PictureBox at runtime. Bearing in mind that everything in .NET is an object, you cannot do this simply by setting the PictureBox's Image property to an empty string:

```
PictureBox1.Image = ""
```

Attempting to run this code will produce a compiler error along the lines of:

```
Value of type 'String' cannot be converted to 'System.Drawing.Image'
```

You must use "object speak," by setting the PictureBox's Image property to `Nothing`:

```
PictureBox1.Image = Nothing
```

Listing 7.1 shows the complete event procedure code for loading, stretching, and deleting a graphic from a PictureBox at runtime.

Listing 7.1 Loading, Stretching, and Deleting an Image at Runtime

```
Private Sub btnLoad_Click(ByVal sender As Object, _
   ByVal e As System.EventArgs) Handles btnLoad.Click
   Dim Path As String = "C:\WINDOWS\Soap Bubbles.bmp"
   PictureBox1.Image = Image.FromFile(Path)
End Sub
```

```
Private Sub btnStretch_Click(ByVal sender As Object, _
   ByVal e As System.EventArgs) Handles btnStretch.Click
   PictureBox1.SizeMode = PictureBoxSizeMode.StretchImage
End Sub

Private Sub btnDelete_Click(ByVal sender As Object, _
   ByVal e As System.EventArgs) Handles btnDelete.Click
   PictureBox1.Image = Nothing
End Sub
```

Adding CheckBox Controls

Check boxes are an important part of many, if not most, user interfaces. As opposed to radio buttons, which are intended for situations in which the user can make one choice from a number of possibilities, check boxes are used when the user can say yes or no to one or more questions, with each check box independent of the others. For example, "Do you want your pizza delivered?" and "Do you want anchovies on your pizza?" would be asked using check boxes, because it is (thankfully for those who do not love anchovies) not an either/or choice. On the other hand, "Do you want to pay with cash, check, or a credit card?" would be asked with radio buttons, because you must choose one, and only one, of the options.

Determining the CheckBox State

The VB .NET CheckBox control can be used in a two-state or three-state mode, depending on whether its ThreeState property is True or False. When ThreeState is False, the control's Checked property is used to determine the state of the CheckBox. The Checked value can be either True (the CheckBox is checked or indeterminate) or False (the CheckBox is not Checked).

When ThreeState is True, the control's CheckState property is used to determine the control's state. The CheckState value can be Checked (the CheckBox is checked), Unchecked (the CheckBox is unchecked), or Indeterminate (the CheckBox is displayed with a dimmed appearance to indicate that the option is not available). Note that when ThreeState is True, the Checked property is True for both `CheckState.Checked` and `CheckState.Indeterminate`.

You should also know about a couple of other control properties. If AutoCheck is set to True, then the CheckBox automatically changes state: It becomes checked if it is not checked, and unchecked if it is checked when you click on the check box itself or on its associated text. The Enabled property enables (or disables) the control. A disabled control cannot be accessed by the user and is shown with a dimmed appearance.

To see how this works, let's put two CheckBoxes on a form: one named chkBonus ("Do you want the bonus feature?") and the other named chkLottery ("Check here to win the lottery."). The first one, chkBonus, is a two-state CheckBox. The other one, chkLottery, starts with its ThreeState property set to True.

Start by creating a variable to hold the state value of the CheckBoxes:

```
Dim status As String
```

Determining the status of chkBonus, and assigning it to the display variable, is easy:

```
If chkBonus.Checked = True Then
   status = "chkBonus is checked. " & ControlChars.Cr
Else
   status = "chkBonus is unchecked. " & ControlChars.Cr
End If
```

We want to be a little more careful with chkLottery because it's currently a three-state CheckBox, but it might turn into a two-state one. To assign the state of a chkLottery check box in its three-state mode to the display variable, we can use a statement like this:

```
status = "chkLottery's CheckState is " & _
   chkLottery.CheckState.ToString & "."
```

Wrapping this in conditional code so that we can determine the state of the check box no matter whether it is two-state or three-state, it becomes:

```
If chkLottery.ThreeState = True Then
   status = status & "chkLottery's CheckState is " & _
      chkLottery.CheckState.ToString & "."
Else
   If chkLottery.Checked = True Then
      status = status & "chkLottery is checked."
   Else
      status = status & "chkLottery is unchecked."
   End If
End If
```

Add a statement to display the results:

```
MessageBox.Show(status)
```

Also, set the CheckState property of chkLottery to Indeterminate in the Properties window. When you run the project and click the button, you'll see a message showing the status of both check boxes.

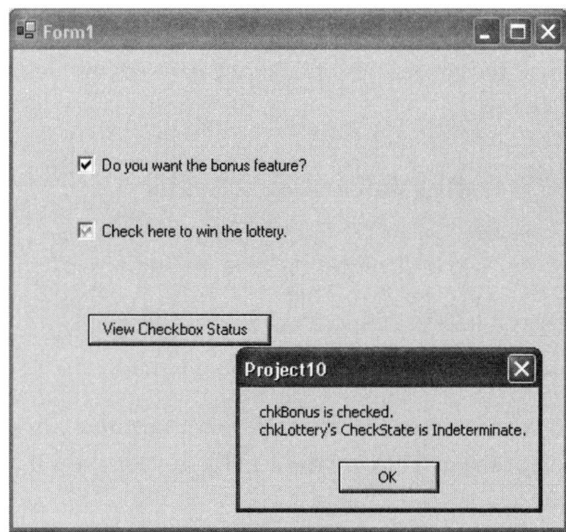

TIP You don't need to set the CheckBox to ThreeState to use the CheckState property.

Note that chkBonus can be changed by the user, with results reflected in the status message, but chkLottery cannot be changed by the user.

Listing 7.2 shows the complete code for determining the status of the two check boxes.

Listing 7.2 Determining CheckBox State

```
Private Sub btnStatus_Click(ByVal sender As Object, _
   ByVal e As System.EventArgs) Handles btnStatus.Click
   Dim status As String
   If chkBonus.Checked = True Then
      status = "chkBonus is checked. " & ControlChars.Cr
   Else
      status = "chkBonus is unchecked. " & ControlChars.Cr
   End If
   If chkLottery.ThreeState = True Then
      status = status & "chkLottery's CheckState is " & _
         chkLottery.CheckState.ToString & "."
   Else
      If chkLottery.Checked = True Then
         status = status & "chkLottery is checked."
      Else
         status = status & "chkLottery is unchecked."
      End If
   End If
   MessageBox.Show(status)
End Sub
```

Enabling a CheckBox at Runtime

It's easy to change the properties of `chkLottery` to dynamically enable it at runtime, as shown in Listing 7.3.

Listing 7.3 Enabling the Checkbox at Runtime

```
Private Sub btnEnable_Click(ByVal sender As Object, _
    ByVal e As System.EventArgs) Handles btnEnable.Click
    chkLottery.AutoCheck = True
    chkLottery.CheckState = CheckState.Checked
End Sub
```

If you add the code shown in Listing 7.3 to a button's Click event, run the project, and enable the `chkLottery` by clicking the Enable button, you'll now be able to check and uncheck both boxes.

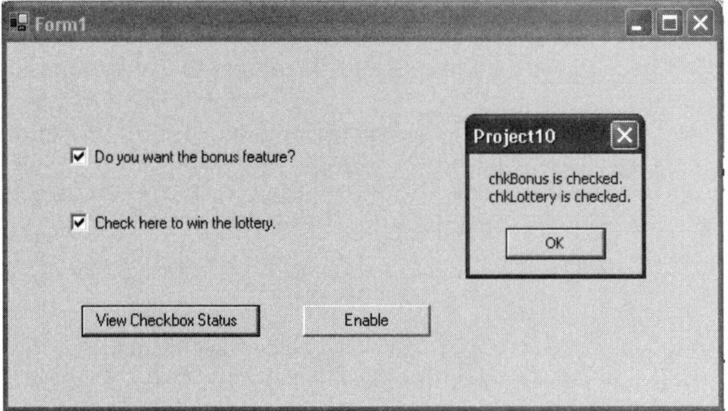

Setting CheckBox Appearance

As noted earlier in the chapter, in the "Sizing and Positioning Pictures" section, the Anchor property of a control lets you set where the control anchors on a form. To see how this works, set the Enable button's Anchor property to Bottom, Right. Now, if you increase the width of the form, it will migrate with the form, creating a much more reasonable interface than if it were anchored to the top left (the default).

Figure 7.4 shows the Enable button anchored to the form's bottom-right side. It also illustrates another way of configuring a CheckBox control: as a button that is either raised or not raised. To have your check boxes appear as buttons, set their Appearance property to Button.

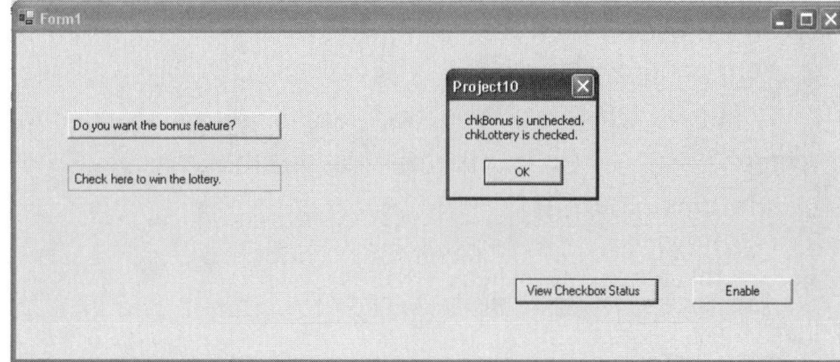

FIGURE 7.4: CheckBoxes can be shown as two-state buttons by setting their Appearance property to Button.

Working with Groups of Controls

As you saw in Chapter 3, "Building a User Interface," if you add a number of controls to a GroupBox or a Panel, they become a group. The controls behave as a group, meaning that only one RadioButton can be checked. If you move the containing control, the grouped controls move together as a block.

In the examples in Chapter 3, the state of the radio buttons was determined using a series of `If` statements. There's nothing wrong with this, but it doesn't scale. If you have a large group of controls of the same type, particularly if they are RadioButtons in which only one of the group can be checked, you'll want to be able to programmatically determine which control is checked, without needing to individually poll each control for its Checked property value. This becomes particularly essential if you plan to dynamically add controls at runtime. You need a way to check the property values of all controls, without even knowing which controls will be present. One way to do this is to cycle through the controls collection. Arrays offer another way to access items.

Collections are data structures that hold objects and give you ways to access, add, and remove objects in the collection. An *array* is an object used to store objects of the same type and access them using an index.

Accessing Controls through Collections

Each Windows Form class comes with a prebuilt controls collection that gives you a way to programmatically access the controls on a form. However, controls that have been placed on a container control used to group them are accessed through the controls collection of that container, rather than the controls collection of the form.

To see this in action, place a GroupBox on a form. Add a bunch (it doesn't matter how many) of RadioButton controls to the GroupBox. Add a Button control to the form (its Click event procedure will be used to display the selected RadioButton).

Within the Click procedure, declare an object variable that will be used to find the selected control:

```
Dim c As Object
```

Next, cycle through the GroupBox's controls collection using a `For Each...Next` statement:

```
For Each c In Me.GroupBox1.Controls

Next
```

This statement will look at all the controls that are seated on `GroupBox1`. Next, check to see whether the control is a RadioButton:

```
If TypeOf (c) Is RadioButton Then

End If
```

If it is a RadioButton, bingo, we're in luck. The next step is to use the `CType` function to cast the generic control (c) to a RadioButton:

```
Dim rb As RadioButton = CType(c, RadioButton)
```

WARNING The `CType` function converts one type to another type (*casts*). If you write a procedure like the one shown here without casting the general control (`c`) to a RadioButton object (`rb`), the object must be bound at runtime (*late bound*), rather than when the project is compiled (*early bound*). Late binding has several disadvantages compared to early binding (it is slower and more bug prone). Furthermore, it is illegal if you are compiling your programs with Option Strict on, as you should, and will cause a compilation error when you try to run the program.

Finally, we need to determine the state of the RadioButton (see if it is selected) by testing its Checked property:

```
If rb.checked = True Then

End If
```

If it is checked, then we should do something with the information. In this example, we'll use the `CStr` conversion function to display the name of the checked control. (In a real-life application, the program would take some action depending on which RadioButton was checked.) In addition, there's no point to looking at more controls, since only one RadioButton can be checked, so exit the `For Each...Next` loop.

```
MsgBox(CStr(rb.name) & " is selected")
Exit For
```

The complete code for the Click event procedure is shown in Listing 7.4.

Listing 7.4 Cycling through a Control Collection to Determine the Selected RadioButton

```
Option Strict On
...
Private Sub Button1_Click(ByVal sender As Object, _
    ByVal e As System.EventArgs) Handles Button1.Click
    Dim c As Object
    For Each c In Me.GroupBox1.Controls
        If TypeOf (c) Is RadioButton Then
        Dim rb As RadioButton = CType(c, RadioButton)
           If rb.checked = True Then
               MsgBox(CStr(rb.name) & " is selected")
               Exit For
           End If
        End If
    Next
End Sub
```

If you run the program, you'll see that the code can determine programmatically which RadioButton has been selected.

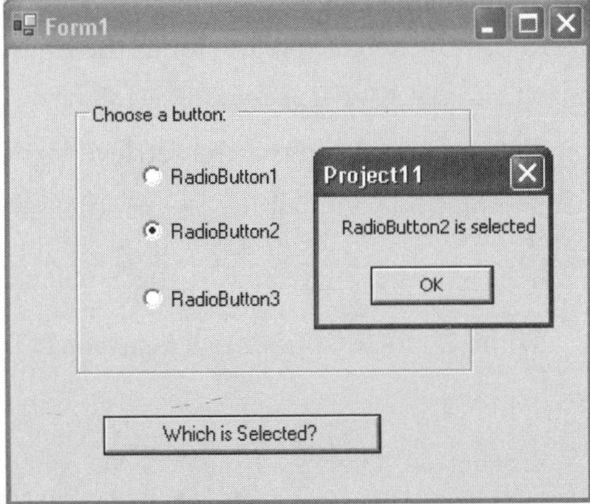

CType and Casting

As you saw in Listing 7.4, the CType function explicitly converts an expression to the specified type. Here's an example:

```
Dim rb As RadioButton = CType(sender, RadioButton)
```

This converts the object stored in `sender` to type RadioButton and assigns it to the variable `rb`.

Continued on next page

The process of converting one type to another is often called *casting*. In strictly typed languages, which VB .NET is when you run it with Option Strict on, all casts must be made explicitly. This is where CType comes in.

It's interesting to know that CType is a little unlike most VB .NET functions, in that it's compiled inline using a kind of preprocessing, rather than compiled with the rest of a program.

Wiring Multiple Controls to the Same Handler

Another approach that works to determine which control is checked (the problem solved in Listing 7.4) is to wire multiple controls to the same handler. This process is in keeping with the spirit of VB .NET, with the only possible drawback being that you need to know the names of the controls you are checking at the time you write the event handler.

To use the same handler for multiple controls, declare a string to hold the name of the control. Next, in the CheckChanged event of the first RadioButton and the CheckChanged events of the subsequent RadioButton controls to the `Handles` clause. This one event handler now handles the CheckChanged event for the three controls, as explained in Chapter 5, "Events and the Life Cycle of Forms."

Next, use `Ctype` to cast the `sender` parameter of the event procedure to a RadioButton type:

```
Dim rb As RadioButton = CType(sender, RadioButton)
```

The RadioButton control's name can now be retrieved from `rb.name`.

The code for wiring multiple controls to one handler and retrieving the checked control is shown in Listing 7.5.

Listing 7.5 Wiring Multiple Controls to a Handler and Determining the Checked Control

```
Dim rbName As String

Private Sub RadioButton1_CheckedChanged(ByVal sender As Object, _
   ByVal e As System.EventArgs) Handles RadioButton1.CheckedChanged, _
   RadioButton2.CheckedChanged, RadioButton3.CheckedChanged
   Dim rb As RadioButton = CType(sender, RadioButton)
   rbName = rb.Name
End Sub

Private Sub Button1_Click(ByVal sender As Object, _
   ByVal e As System.EventArgs) Handles Button1.Click
   MessageBox.Show(rbName)
End Sub
```

Using *For...Next* Statements

Closely related to the `For Each...Next` statement used in Listing 7.4 is the `For...Next` statement, which is designed to repeat a group of statements a specified number of times.

A `For...Next` loop uses a variable called a *counter* that increases or decreases in value during each repetition of the loop. In its simplest form, the `For` loop counter increases by one each time the loop is passed through.

The `For...Next` statement has the following syntax. The square brackets indicate optional parts, and the parts in boldface are VB keywords.

```
For counter = start To end [Step Increment]
   statements
[Exit For]
   statements
Next [counter]
```

When it first encounters the `For` loop, VB sets `counter` equal to `start`. It then tests whether the counter is greater than `end`. If so, the loop is exited. If not, the statements are executed. If an `Exit For` statement is encountered, the loop is exited. If not, when the `Next` keyword is reached, which signifies the end of one cycle through the loop, `counter` is incremented by one, unless some other increment has been specified following the `Step` keyword. (Note that the increment could be negative, in which case it should logically be called a "decrement.")

Execution is passed back to the beginning of the loop, and the incremented counter is compared with `end`. If `counter` is still less than `end`, the statements are executed once more, and so on.

Here's a very simple example of a `For...Next` statement (the ending value of `j` is 55):

```
Dim i,j As Integer
j = 0
For i = 1 To 10
   j = j + 1
Next i
```

Using Arrays in VB .NET

Arrays are very much like the collection object, except that you can easily access the items in the area using the index.

The elements within an array are referred to using parentheses, as in this example:

```
myArray(1) = 10
myArray(2) = 20
myArray(3) = 30
```

This code assigns the value 10 to the array element with an index of 1, the value of 20 to the element with an index of 2, and the value of 30 to the element with an index of 3. You can see that this functions like a single-column lookup table, although you can have multidimensional arrays with many index columns, and the elements can be any type of object. (They are not limited to being integers.)

Arrays go very nicely with `For...Next` loops, which can be used to cycle through them. Here's a simple example that defines a ten-element integer array:

```
Dim i,j As Integer
Dim myArray(10) As Integer
j = 0
For i = 1 To 10
   j = j + 1
   myArray(i) = j
Next i
```

To check your understanding of this, you might want to verify that if you displayed the value of `myArray(10)`, it would be 55.

See the "Adding and Removing Items from a ListBox" section later in this chapter for an example of using an array in an application.

Working with ComboBoxes, ListBoxes, and CheckedListBoxes

ComboBoxes, ListBoxes, and—new to VB .NET—CheckedListBoxes are user interface controls for dealing with lists of items. These are extremely important to almost every program interface.

If you place one of each kind of control on a form, you'll see that they look a little different. However, for the most part, they all function in the same way.

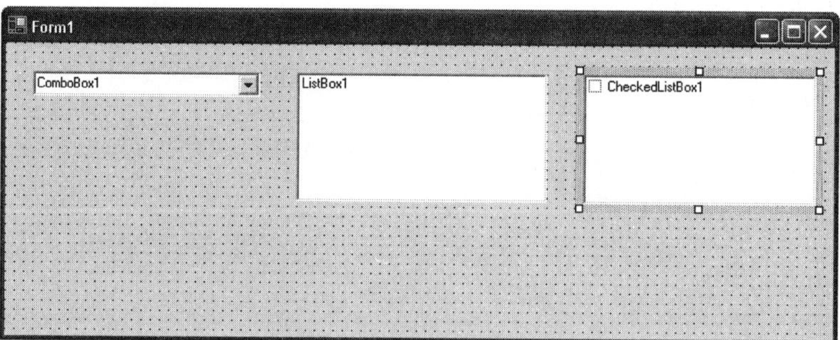

The ComboBox looks the most different, although if you change the value of the `ComboBox.DropDownStyle` property, it will look pretty much like the others.

A CheckedListBox is almost exactly like a ListBox whose SelectionMode property has been set to enable multiple selections. The difference then becomes one of interface. Items in the CheckedListBox are selected by checking them. Selected items in the ListBox are, well, selected and appear marked by a dark bar. A ComboBox is like a ListBox with a text box for user entry. This means that the items in a ListBox are strictly limited, whereas users can enter their own items into a ComboBox, provided the DropDownStyle of the ComboBox is not set to `ComboBoxStyle.DropDownList`.

To return a single selected item from one of these controls, use the SelectedItem property:

```
ComboBox1.SelectedItem
```

To sort the contents alphabetically, use the control's Sorted property:

```
CheckedListBox1.Sorted = True
```

Note that you can set the Sorted property at design time in the Properties window as well as in code.

Adding and Removing Items from a ListBox

Despite their differences in appearance, the ListBox, ComboBox, and CheckedListBox controls are programmed in an almost identical fashion. So, while the example in this section shows a ListBox in action, the same code will work with all three controls. However, there is one wrinkle with CheckedListBoxes, which I'll tell you about in the "Determining the Status of a CheckedListBox" section later in this chapter.

Let's set up an application as a lab for looking at how to add and remove items from a ListBox in code. You should know that you can assign items to the items collections of these controls at design time using the Properties window. In this example, we will use `Select…Case` statements, so let's look at them first.

Using *Select…Case* Statements

`Select…Case` statements are used to simplify conditional logic. It is axiomatic that every time a `Select…Case` statement is used, you could use multiple `If` statements instead. (The converse is also true.) In fact, if you ever have trouble with understanding a `Select…Case` statement, it may help to think of it this way.

Here is the general syntax of the `Select…Case` statement (the keywords are in bold):

```
Select Case expression
   Case value1
      statements
   Case value2
      statements
   ...
   Case valueN
      statements
```

```
    [Case Else]
        statements
End Select
```

The expression can be just about anything. It is often a function, as in the simple example described in the next section.

When the value of the Case clause equals the expression, the statements are executed. When there are no matches, the optional Case Else statements are executed.

Select...Case statements are an improvement over multiple If statements because they are clearer to understand. Clear code tends to be less buggy and is easier to maintain.

Adding Items

As a first task, let's get our interface to add a text item to the bottom of the items in the ListBox. (Since there currently are no items in the ListBox's items collection, the newly added item will be on top by default.)

Before we get to programming the ListBox addition, let's write a function that returns a string indicating what action to take based on the RadioButton selected by the user. The point of this is to do it once, so we can refer to it from both the Remove and Add buttons without needing to rewrite code.

The function's *signature*, which means its type and the arguments it takes, is as follows:

```
Function DoWhat() As String
```

To live up to the contract that this implies, the function will need to return a string value. This is done using the Return keyword. Here's the function, wrapped in a #Region directive, so it can be hidden from view to keep things simple when we are working on the rest of the code (see Chapter 6, "Working with Form Methods and Modules," for more on #Region):

```
#Region "What action are we taking today?"
   Function DoWhat() As String
      'Find out what action we are taking
      Dim whichAct As String
      If rdoItem.Checked = True Then
         whichAct = "item"
      ElseIf rdoByIndex.Checked = True Then
         whichAct = "byindex"
      ElseIf rdoArray.Checked = True Then
         whichAct = "array"
      ElseIf rdoDeleteSelection.Checked = True Then
         whichAct = "delete"
      End If
   Return whichAct
   End Function
#End Region
```

Now, let's write the `Select...Case` statement that calls the `DoWhat()` function to determine what we are adding to the ListBox:

```
Private Sub btnAdd_Click(ByVal sender As Object, _
   ByVal e As System.EventArgs) Handles btnAdd.Click
   Select Case DoWhat()
      Case "item"

      Case "byindex"

      Case "array"

      Case "delete"

   End Select
End Sub
```

All that remains is to add text entered by the user in a TextBox to the ListBox, which takes one line:

```
...
Case "item"
ListBox1.Items.Add(txtItem.Text)
```

To see this in action, run the project and enter something in the Item Text box. When you click Add, the item will be added to the ListBox's items collection, as shown in Figure 7.5.

FIGURE 7.5:

You can use the Add method to add a string or an object.

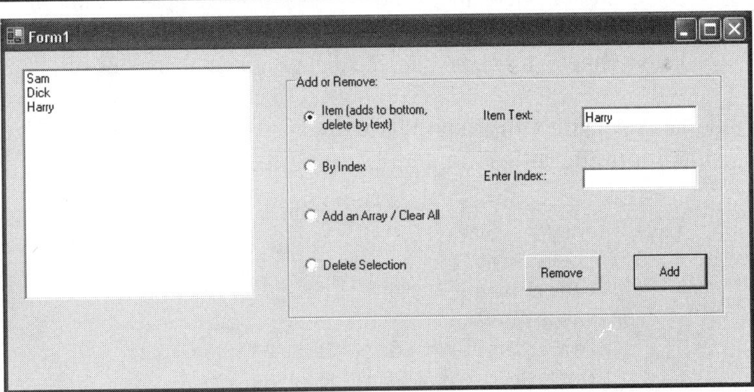

Suppose you don't want to add the new item at the bottom of the items collection. To pick the location in the items collection for a new item, it must be added by using an index. Here's the code, added to the `Select...Case` statement:

```
...
Case "byindex"
   ListBox1.Items.Insert(CInt(txtIndex.Text), txtItem.Text)
```

First, the `Insert` method of the items collection is used, as opposed to the `Add` method used previously. An integer value is required to position the new item, hence the `CInt()` type-conversion function. You should also know that the items collection is zero-based, meaning that the first item in the collection has an index of 0. If there are *n* items in the collection, this also implies that the last item has an index of *n* – 1.

To test the `Insert` method in action, run the project and enter text and an index. The new item will be added to the ListBox, as shown in Figure 7.6.

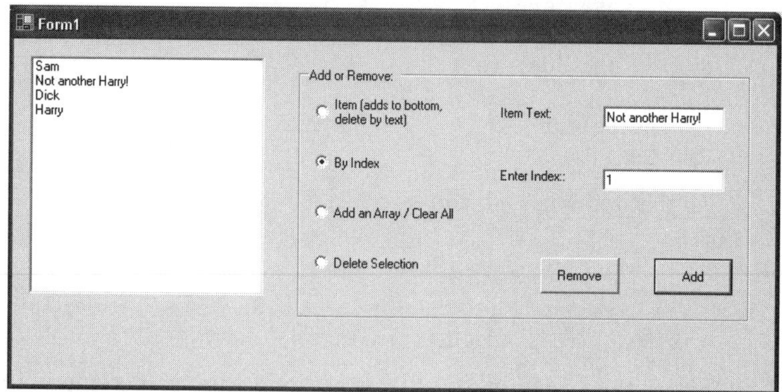

FIGURE 7.6: If you use the `Insert` method, the text will be inserted in the position supplied.

WARNING If you enter an index that is out of range, for example, greater than the current highest index value plus one, you will generate a runtime error. See "Working with the ErrorProvider" later in this chapter for some simple input-validation techniques.

Let's say you want to populate the ListBox in a big hurry. It's easy to put an entire array of items into the collection. Here's the code:

```
...
Case "array"
   Dim itemString(25) As String
   Dim i As Integer
   For i = 0 To 24
      itemString(i) = CStr("Item #") & i
      ListBox1.Items.Add(itemString(i))
   Next i
```

Note that this array is zero-based (the first element of each is zero), like the items collection.

TIP You don't really need to use an array to do this. You could use the `For...Next` loop to just assign item values to the ListBox with the intermediate step of assigning the values to the array.

Go ahead and run the form. You can see that it is easy to add an entire array of items to the ListBox, as shown here.

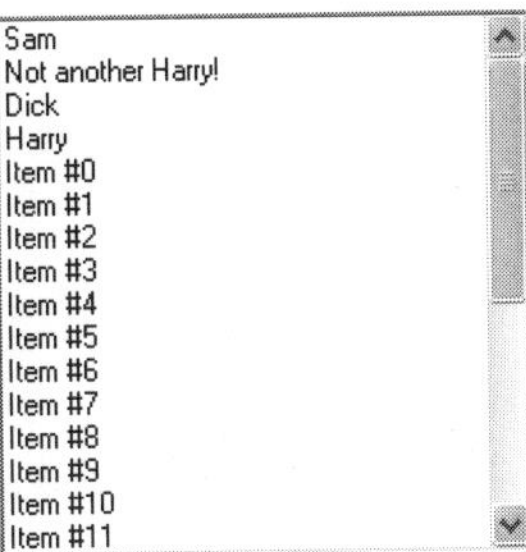

Removing Items

It's time to move to the other side of the equation: removing items from the ListBox's items collection. Once again, we'll use the `Select…Case` framework, but within the Remove button's Click event procedure.

Here's the code for removing a selected item:

```
...
Case "delete"
   ListBox1.Items.Remove(ListBox1.SelectedItem)
```

Run the project and select an item, as shown in Figure 7.7. (In the figure, Item #1 is selected.)

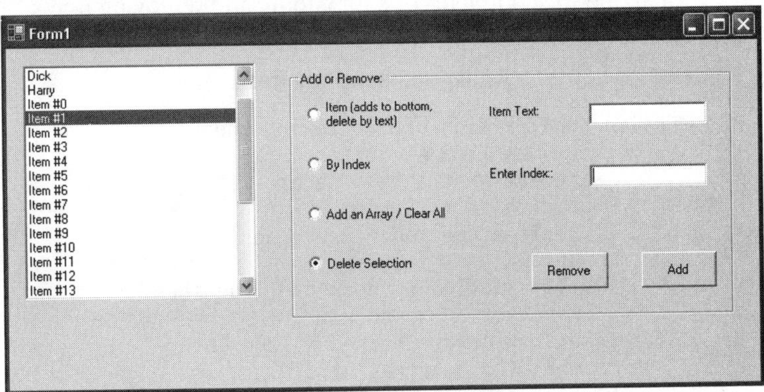

FIGURE 7.7: The selected item can be removed by using the `SelectedItem` property.

When you click Remove, Item #1 is no longer in the ListBox.

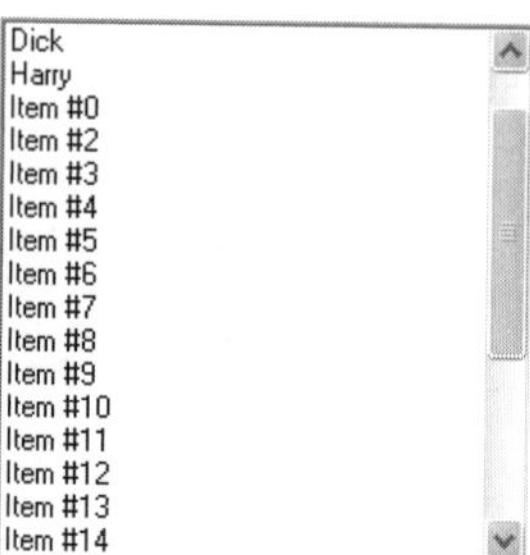

We might also want to remove an item if we know its text. Here's how:

```
...
Case "item"
   ListBox1.Items.Remove(txtItem.Text)
```

Next, you could delete an item if you know its index:

```
...
Case "byindex"
   ListBox1.Items.RemoveAt(CInt(txtIndex.Text))
```

Finally, just as it was nice to add an array in one fell swoop, you might decide to get rid of everything in the ListBox using the `Clear` method of its items collection:

```
...
Case "array"
   ListBox1.Items.Clear()
```

You'll find the complete code for adding and removing items from the ListBox in Listing 7.6.

Listing 7.6 Adding and Removing Items

```
#Region "What action are we taking today?"
   Function DoWhat() As String
      'Find out what action we are taking
      Dim whichAct As String
      If rdoItem.Checked = True Then
         whichAct = "item"
      ElseIf rdoByIndex.Checked = True Then
         whichAct = "byindex"
      ElseIf rdoArray.Checked = True Then
         whichAct = "array"
      ElseIf rdoDeleteSelection.Checked = True Then
         whichAct = "delete"
      End If
   Return whichAct
```

```
   End Function
#End Region

Private Sub btnAdd_Click(ByVal sender As Object, _
   ByVal e As System.EventArgs) Handles btnAdd.Click
   Select Case DoWhat()
      Case "item"
         ListBox1.Items.Add(txtItem.Text)
      Case "byindex"
         ListBox1.Items.Insert(CInt(txtIndex.Text), txtItem.Text)
      Case "array"
         Dim itemString(25) As String
            Dim i As Integer
            For i = 0 To 24
               itemString(i) = CStr("Item #") & i
               ListBox1.Items.Add(itemString(i))
            Next i
      Case "delete"
         MsgBox("Cannot delete if you are adding!")
   End Select
End Sub

Private Sub btnRemove_Click(ByVal sender As System.Object, _ [TE]
   ByVal e As System.EventArgs) Handles btnRemove.Click
   Select Case DoWhat()
      Case "item"
         ListBox1.Items.Remove(txtItem.Text)
      Case "byindex"
         ListBox1.Items.RemoveAt(CInt(txtIndex.Text))
      Case "array"
         ListBox1.Items.Clear()
      Case "delete"
         ListBox1.Items.Remove(ListBox1.SelectedItem)
   End Select
End Sub
```

Retrieving the Text of an Item

One more thing that it might be nice to add to the form developed in Listing 7.6 is the ability to retrieve the text of an item based on its index. Here's how:

```
Private Sub btnShow_Click(ByVal sender As System.Object, _
   ByVal e As System.EventArgs) Handles btnShow.Click
   MsgBox(ListBox1.Items(CInt(txtShowIndex.Text)).ToString)
End Sub
```

If you run the project, enter an index value, and click the Show button, the item text will be displayed.

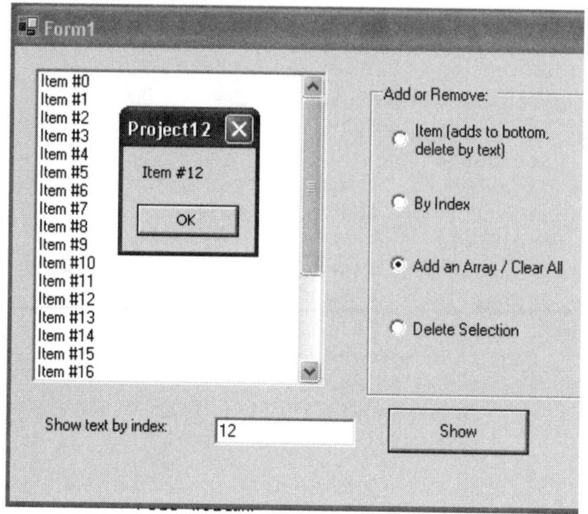

Determining the Status of a CheckedListBox

I mentioned earlier that CheckedListBoxes were not very different from ListBoxes, with the addition of check boxes. Because of this addition, you will need to know how to determine if a particular item in a CheckedListBox is checked (or not). You'll find the code to do this in Listing 7.7.

Listing 7.7 Is a CheckedListBox Item Checked?

```
Private Sub Button1_Click(ByVal sender As System.Object, _
   ByVal e As System.EventArgs) Handles Button1.Click
   If CheckedListBox1.GetItemChecked(CInt(TextBox1.Text())) = True Then
      MsgBox("Item # " & TextBox1.Text & " checked.")
   Else
      MsgBox("Item # " & TextBox1.Text & " NOT checked.")
   End If
End Sub
```

Suppose that you run this code in an event procedure in a form with a populated CheckedListBox and a TextBox for entering the index number of the item you want to inspect. You'll see that it does indeed programmatically determine if an item has been checked.

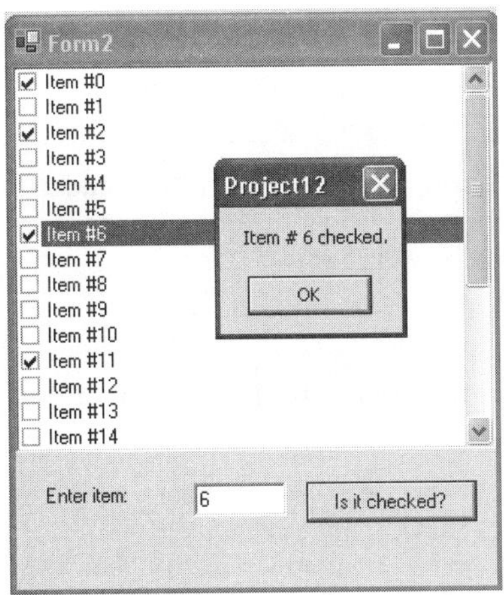

NOTE To take this one step further, you might want to ask the question, "How many items in the CheckedListBox are checked?", since you can check multiple boxes in the list.

Working with the ErrorProvider

One problem with the code in the ListBox example is that the user input has not been validated. The user might try to add an item without supplying text for the item. This would produce an item with blank text; somewhat silly, perhaps, but not tragic.

But the index values for the items collection present a somewhat worse problem. A user could try to enter non-numeric text in the index field. Or, the user could enter an index value that was out of range for the collection. Either case would produce a runtime error and, quite possibly, crash the application.

This is a situation the ErrorProvider control lives to deal with!

You'll find the ErrorProvider on the Windows Forms tab of the Toolbox. When you add it to a form, it appears seated in an area below the form that is normally reserved for components with no visual interface, as shown here.

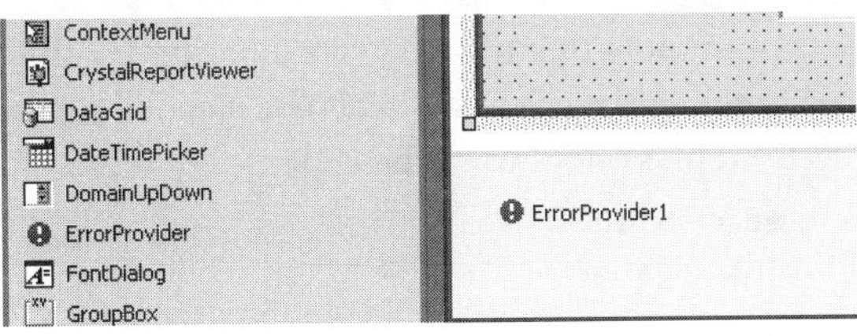

Checking for Numeric Entries

To start with, let's use the ErrorProvider to make sure that only numeric values can be added in the index TextBox. First, create a framework for the `txtIndex Validating` event procedure:

```
Private Sub txtIndex_Validating(ByVal sender As Object, _
   ByVal e As System.ComponentModel.CancelEventArgs) _
   Handles txtIndex.Validating

End Sub
```

Next, invoke the `SetError` method of the ErrorProvider if the contents of the TextBox are not numeric:

```
If Not IsNumeric(txtIndex.Text) Then
   ErrorProvider1.SetError(txtIndex, _
      "You must enter a numeric value for the index!")
End If
```

Note that you must supply a message to the user about the validation problem.

Finally, you must clear the ErrorProvider if there are no validation problems:

```
If Not IsNumeric(txtIndex.Text) Then
   ErrorProvider1.SetError(txtIndex, _
      "You must enter a numeric value for the index!")
Else
   'Clear the error
   ErrorProvider1.SetError(txtIndex, "")
End If
```

Run the project and try entering something non-numeric in the input box. Now, try to tab away from the box (or use any other control). The ErrorProvider will put a blinking warning next to the input box and display the message you designated.

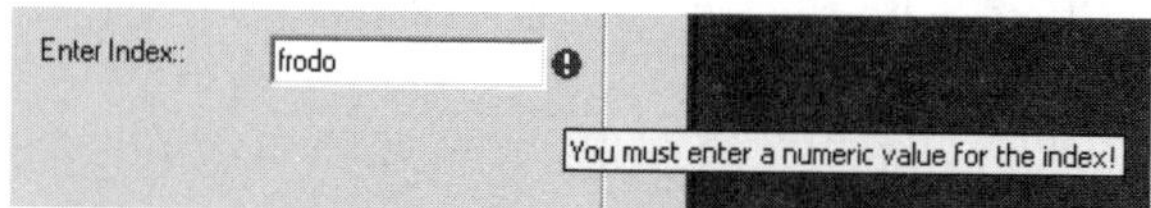

Validating the Range

It's a little more work to validate the index range against the ListBox's collection size, but it's a job worth doing. Assuming that the entry is numeric, we want to be sure that it is greater than zero and within the range of the `ListBox.Items.Count` property (the number of elements in the items collection) plus one. Here's the code:

```
If Not IsNumeric(txtIndex.Text) Then
   ErrorProvider1.SetError(txtIndex, _
      "You must enter a numeric value for the index!")
ElseIf (CInt(txtIndex.Text) >= ListBox1.Items.Count + 1 _
```

```
      Or CInt(txtIndex.Text) < 0) Then
      ErrorProvider1.SetError(txtIndex, _
         "You have entered an index that is out of range!")
   Else
      'Clear the error
      ErrorProvider1.SetError(txtIndex, "")
   End If
```

If you run this code and enter a value that is out of range, you'll see that the ErrorProvider does its job well.

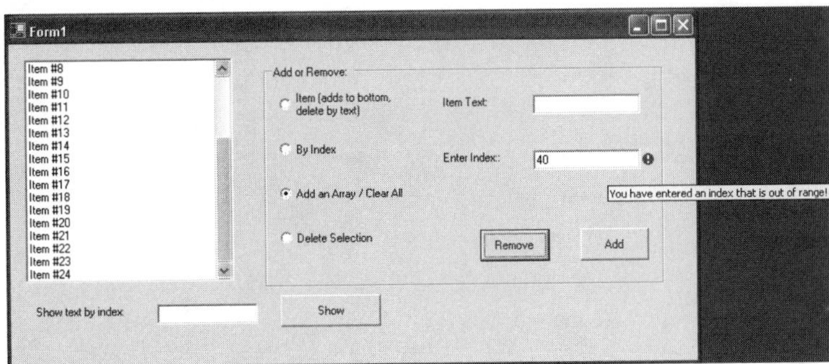

The complete code for the validating event procedure is shown in Listing 7.8.

Listing 7.8 **Validating Input as Numeric and within the Range of the ListBox**

```
Private Sub txtIndex_Validating(ByVal sender As Object, _
   ByVal e As System.ComponentModel.CancelEventArgs) _
   Handles txtIndex.Validating
   If Not IsNumeric(txtIndex.Text) Then
      ErrorProvider1.SetError(txtIndex, _
         "You must enter a numeric value for the index!")
   ElseIf (CInt(txtIndex.Text) >= ListBox1.Items.Count + 1 _
      Or CInt(txtIndex.Text) < 0) Then
      ErrorProvider1.SetError(txtIndex, _
         "You have entered an index that is out of range!")
   Else
      'Clear the error
      ErrorProvider1.SetError(txtIndex, "")
   End If
End Sub
```

Summary

The devil, they say, is in the details, and as you read this chapter, you may have felt as if you were stumbling through many details! Be of good cheer—you have come a long way. The material in this chapter provides a lot of the information you need to put together any application that uses controls, as well as nuts and bolts around concepts such as collections, arrays, loops, and `Select...Case` statements. In addition, you'll be able to use controls such as the ListBox and the really nifty ErrorProvider in a great many contexts.

In the next chapter, we move onto some of the other controls that give Windows applications their distinctive look and feel, including StatusBars, Toolbars, ToolTips, and TabControls.

Chapter 8

Adding StatusBars, ToolBars, ToolTips, and Tabbed Dialogs

- Working with StatusBar controls
- Working with ToolBar controls
- Adding ToolTip controls
- Adding tabbed pages

The controls discussed in this chapter are an integral part of most Windows form user interfaces. All of these controls, with the exception of the ToolTip, are implemented around collection classes. As you learned in the previous chapter, collections are integral to VB .NET. The StatusBar has a collection of Panels, the ToolBar has a Buttons collection, and the TabControl has a TabPages collection. You'll find it easy to use these controls and their collections, which have been implemented in a simple and consistent way.

Working with StatusBars

StatusBar controls are used to display all kinds of application status information. They are usually positioned along the bottom of a form. For example, Microsoft Internet Explorer uses a status bar to display the URL of a page when the mouse passes over a hyperlink, and Microsoft Word displays an animation on its status bar to indicate that a document is being saved.

StatusBars contain a collection of Panels, and each Panel can display different information.

TIP You can have a really simple StatusBar without Panels that just displays a text message. To do this, in the Properties window, set the StatusBar's ShowPanel property to False, and use the StatusBar's Text property to enter the text you want to display.

Adding a Panel to a StatusBar

To add a Panel to a StatusBar's Panel collection using the Properties window, first make sure that the StatusBar's ShowPanel property is set to True. Then, in the Properties window, select the Panels property. By clicking the button with the ellipses in the right column of the Properties window, you will open the StatusBarPanel Collection Editor, shown in Figure 8.1.

You can use the StatusBarPanel Collection Editor for the following tasks:

- Adding and removing Panels
- Ordering the Panels in a StatusBar Panel collection
- Giving each Panel a name and text
- Setting the visual display style for the Panel

TIP You can customize the appearance of a Panel by setting its Style property to OwnerDraw and then adding the code you want to the DrawItem event of the StatusBar.

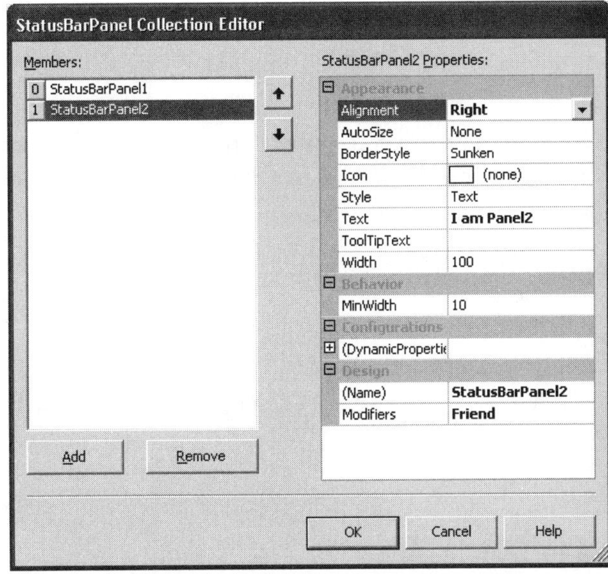

FIGURE 8.1: You can use the StatusBarPanel Collection Editor to add panels to the StatusBar Panel collection.

Toggling a StatusBar

Many applications allow users to decide whether they want to see the status bar. In other words, sometimes a user may find the information provided by the status bar useful; other times, she may find it a waste of screen "real estate."

It's easy to dynamically toggle whether or not a StatusBar is displayed by setting its Visible property. For example, if you have a StatusBar named `StatusBar1`, you can turn off its display as follows:

```
StatusBar1.Visible = False
```

To make it reappear, set Visible to True:

```
StatusBar1.Visible = True
```

Dynamically Adding StatusBar Panels

You might want to add another Panel to display information when a user activates new application features. It's easy to dynamically add and remove Panels in code using the StatusBar Panels collection. To show how this is done, let's add a Panel to the Panels collection for

StatusBar1. This example assumes that the Panels collection already has three members (Panels). Note that the Panels collection is zero-based, meaning that the first item in the collection has an index of 0, the second has an index of 1, and so on.

First, use the Toolbox to add a Button control named btnAddPanel to the form. Next, in the Code Editor, in the Click event procedure, use the Add method of the Panels collection to add a new Panel. It's nice to use StatusBar Panels to display the time, so let's use that as the text for the new panel:

```
StatusBar1.Panels.Add(Now.ToShortTimeString)
```

Using the index value of the new Panel, which is 3, set some of its display properties:

```
StatusBar1.Panels(3).AutoSize = StatusBarPanelAutoSize.Spring
StatusBar1.Panels(3).BorderStyle = StatusBarPanelBorderStyle.Sunken
```

Run the program and click the Add Panel button. You'll see the new panel displaying the current time.

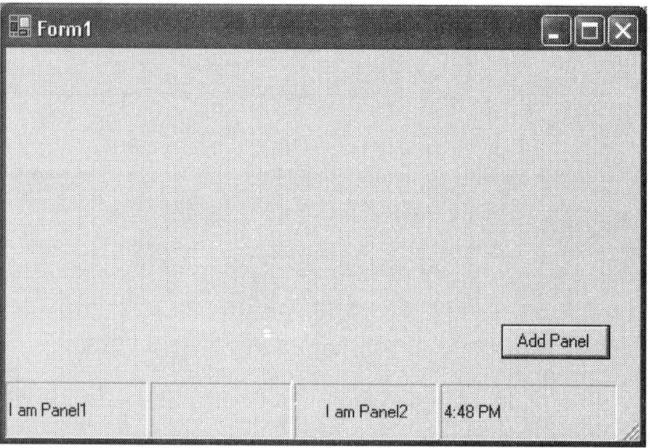

The code for the Click event procedure is shown in Listing 8.1.

Listing 8.1 Dynamically Adding a StatusBar Panel That Displays the Current Time

```
Private Sub btnAddPanel_Click(ByVal sender As System.Object, _
   ByVal e As System.EventArgs) Handles btnAddPanel.Click
   StatusBar1.Panels.Add(Now.ToShortTimeString)
   StatusBar1.Panels(3).AutoSize = StatusBarPanelAutoSize.Spring
   StatusBar1.Panels(3).BorderStyle = StatusBarPanelBorderStyle.Sunken
End Sub
```

TIP The example in Listing 8.1 displays the time only at the instant that the user clicks to add a Panel. To keep the time current, you need to update it using a Timer control, as explained in Chapter 10, "Using Timers, EventLogs, and ServiceControllers."

If you just want to add a Panel "after" all the current Panels and set its properties, you don't need to know or use the index of the Panels collection. The following code is in some ways preferable to that shown in Listing 8.1. It adds a new Panel with an index one greater than the current Panels collection index and sets its properties:

```
Dim sbp As StatusBarPanel
sbp = StatusBar1.Panels.Add(Now.ToShortTimeString)
sbp.AutoSize = StatusBarPanelAutoSize.Contents
sbp.BorderStyle = StatusBarPanelBorderStyle.Sunken
```

If your StatusBar is an integral part of your application, you might want to be able to respond when the user clicks the control. In particular, you might want to be able to respond differently depending on which Panel was clicked. You can determine which Panel was clicked using the arguments passed to the StatusBar's PanelClick event handler. Using the `Select...Case` syntax (explained in Chapter 7, "Working with Windows Forms Controls"), you can check the index of the StatusBar Panel collection, and act accordingly, as shown in Listing 8.2.

Listing 8.2 Determining Which Panel Was Clicked

```
Private Sub StatusBar1_PanelClick(ByVal sender As System.Object, _
   ByVal e As System.Windows.Forms.StatusBarPanelClickEventArgs) _
   Handles StatusBar1.PanelClick
   Select Case StatusBar1.Panels.IndexOf(e.StatusBarPanel)
      Case 0
         MsgBox("You clicked StatusBarPanel1!")
      Case 1
         MsgBox("You clicked StatusBarPanel2!")
      Case 2
         MsgBox("You clicked StatusBarPanel3!")
      Case 3
         MsgBox("You clicked myPanel!")
   End Select
End Sub
```

If you run this code and click a Panel, you'll get a message indicating which Panel was clicked.

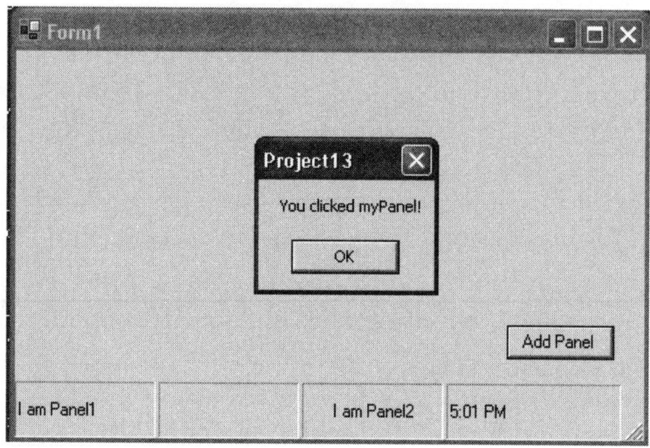

Working with ToolBars

You'll be pleased to know that the ToolBarButtons collection of the ToolBar control works in the same way as the StatusBarPanels collection of the StatusBar, with one interesting wrinkle. The point of the ToolBar control is to display graphical buttons. The graphic images are associated with the ToolBarButtons collection by using a related control, the ImageList. The ImageList itself has a collection, Images, so the first step in creating a ToolBar is to populate the Images collection of the ImageList control. You should think of the ImageList as a library of imagery that can be used by other controls.

Adding an ImageList

To see this in action, use the Toolbox to add an ImageList to your form. It will appear in the tray beneath the form, rather than on your form. (The ImageList control never appears visually within the form.)

Next, in the Properties window, with the ImageList selected, choose the Images property, and then click the button in the right column to open the Image Collection Editor. Click Add, and the Open dialog will let you select an image file from the filesystem, as shown in Figure 8.2.

TIP In this example, I've used icons that show the elements. These are supplied with Visual Studio .NET, and in a default installation, they can be found in the Elements folder of the `Microsoft Visual Studio .NET\Common7\Graphics\icons` directory.

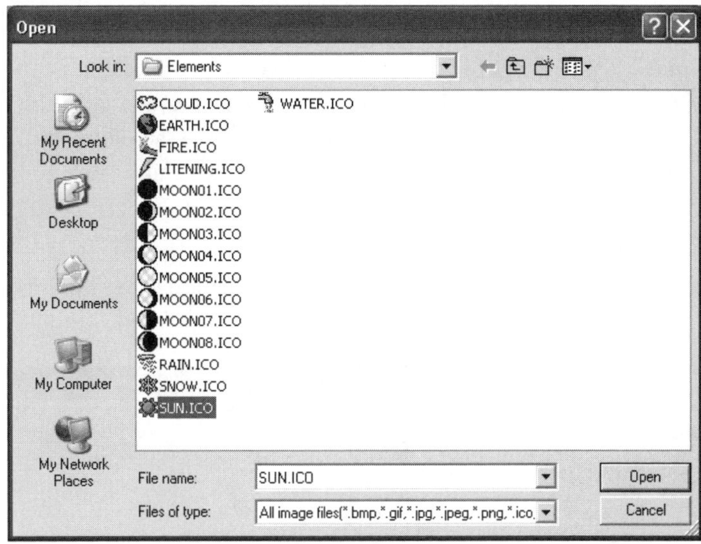

FIGURE 8.2: Image files from the filesystem are added to the ImageList.

When you are finished adding image files to the ImageList, they will appear in the Image Collection Editor, which can be used to reorder the images, as shown in Figure 8.3.

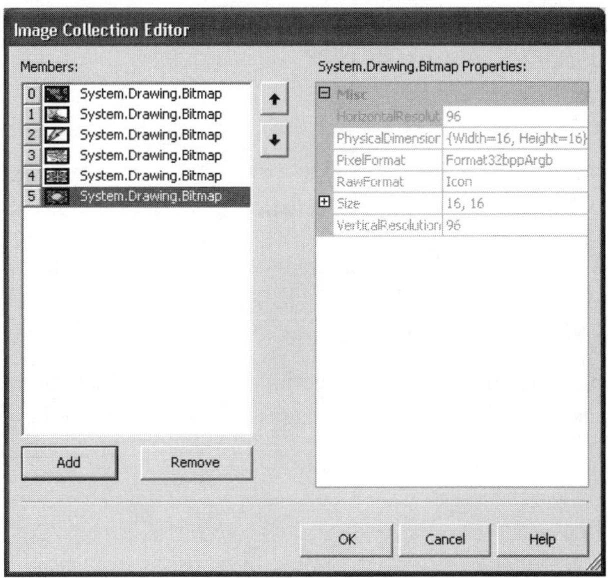

FIGURE 8.3: The Images that have been added to the ImageList image collection appear in the Image Collection Editor.

Click OK. You will be returned to the ImageList in the Properties window. You should note the ImageSize property of the ImageList, which reflects the maximum dimensions in pixels of the images in the Images collection. (In the case of the element icons, they will all be the same size.) Then, when you set the ToolBar properties, as described in the next section, you can set its ButtonSize property to the same dimensions as the ImageSize property of the ImageList, to avoid extra blank spaces around your ToolBar buttons.

Adding Buttons to the ToolBar

Next, select the ToolBar in the Properties window. Set the ImageList property of the ToolBar to the ImageList control that you have just populated.

With the ImageList associated with the ToolBar, select the Buttons property of the ToolBar in the Properties window. Click the button with the ellipses in the right column of the Properties window to invoke the ToolBarButton Collection Editor, as shown in Figure 8.4.

In the ToolBarButton Collection Editor, use the ImageIndex property to associate a button with an image stored in the ImageList. When you are finished adding buttons, click OK to view your completed ToolBar.

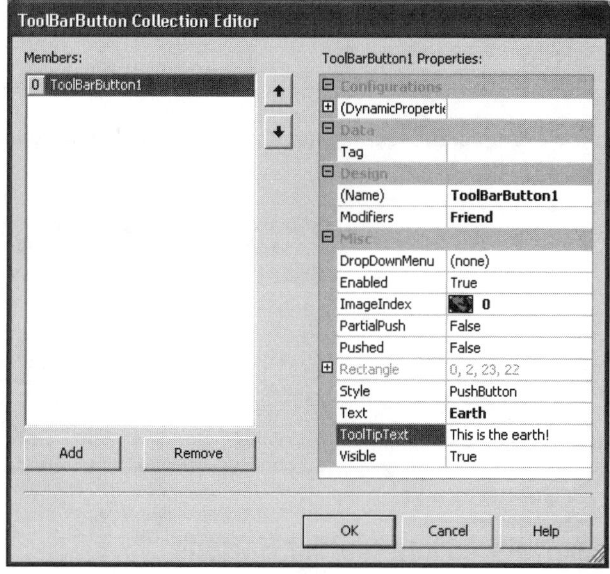

FIGURE 8.4: With the ImageList associated with the ToolBar, the ToolBarButton Collection Editor is used to add buttons to the ToolBar.

Determining Which ToolBar Button Was Clicked

Generally, you will need to know which ToolBar button the user clicked. As shown in Listing 8.3, this can be done with a `Select...Case` statement in the ToolBar button Click event handler. The `Select...Case` statement checks the index value of the passed Buttons collection argument.

Listing 8.3 Determining which ToolBar Button Was Clicked

```
Private Sub ToolBar1_ButtonClick(ByVal sender As System.Object, _
   ByVal e As System.Windows.Forms.ToolBarButtonClickEventArgs) _
   Handles ToolBar1.ButtonClick
   Select Case ToolBar1.Buttons.IndexOf(e.Button)
      Case 0
         StatusBar1.Panels(0).Text = "EARTH"
      Case 1
         StatusBar1.Panels(0).Text = "FIRE"
      Case 2
         StatusBar1.Panels(0).Text = "LIGHTNING"
      Case 3
         StatusBar1.Panels(0).Text = "CLOUDS"
      Case 4
         StatusBar1.Panels(0).Text = "SNOW"
```

```
        Case 5
            StatusBar1.Panels(0).Text = "SUN"
    End Select
End Sub
```

In the example, the text of the first StatusBar Panel is changed depending on which ToolBar button was clicked.

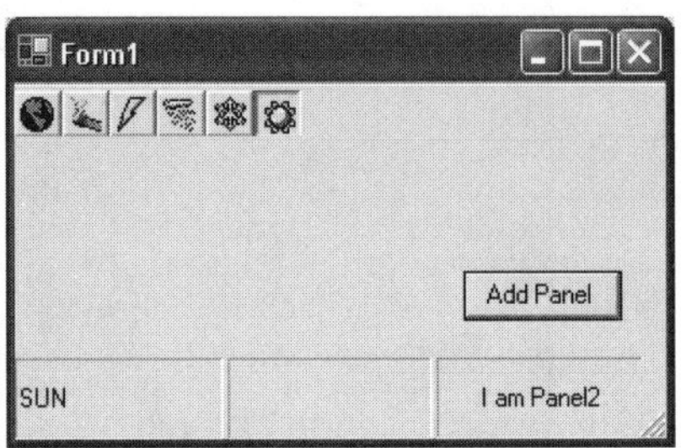

Dynamically Adding ToolBar Buttons

You might also want to add or remove a button from the ToolBar in response to a user action. To get a feeling for how this is done, add a button named `btnAddButton` to your form. The Click event handler of this control will be used to add a ToolBar button.

The first step is to instantiate a string variable and assign it the path of the graphic file that the ToolBar button will use:

```
Dim fileName As String = "C:\Program Files\Microsoft Visual " & _
    "Studio .NET\Common7\Graphics\icons\Elements\MOON02.ICO"
```

Next, instantiate a `System.Drawing.Image` object, and then use its `FromFile` method to load the graphic file:

```
Dim myImage As System.Drawing.Image = _
    Image.FromFile(fileName)
```

Use the `ImageList.Images` collection's `Add` method to add the new graphic to the ImageList:

```
ImageList1.Images.Add(myImage)
```

Instantiate a new ToolBarButton, and use the ToolBar Buttons collection's `Add` method to add it to the ToolBar:

```
Dim myToolBarButton As New ToolBarButton()
ToolBar1.Buttons.Add(myToolBarButton)
```

Finally, use the new ToolBarButton's ImageIndex property to assign to it the image loaded in the ImageList:

```
myToolBarButton.ImageIndex = 6
```

The complete code for the event handler is shown in Listing 8.4.

Listing 8.4 Dynamically Adding a ToolBar Button

```
Private Sub btnAddButton_Click(ByVal sender As System.Object, _
   ByVal e As System.EventArgs) Handles btnAddButton.Click
   Dim fileName As String = "C:\Program Files\Microsoft Visual " & _
      "Studio .NET\Common7\Graphics\icons\Elements\MOON02.ICO"
   Dim myImage As System.Drawing.Image = _
      Image.FromFile(fileName)
   ImageList1.Images.Add(myImage)
   Dim myToolBarButton As New ToolBarButton()
   ToolBar1.Buttons.Add(myToolBarButton)
   myToolBarButton.ImageIndex = 6
End Sub
```

If you run this code and click the Add Button, you'll see the new ToolBar button in place.

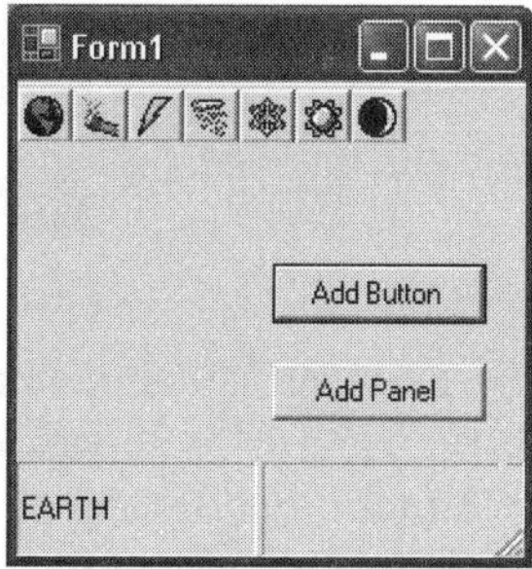

Adding ToolTips

ToolTip text appears next to a control when the cursor hovers over the control. Generally, it is used to help the user understand the purpose or functionality of the associated control.

Like the ImageList, when you add a ToolTip control to a form, the ToolTip sits on the tray beneath the form, rather than on the form itself.

Assuming you have added a ToolTip to your form, to set the ToolTip text for a control, select the control in the Properties window, for example, a Button. You'll see a property labeled ToolTip on `ToolTip1`, where `ToolTip1` is the name of the ToolTip you added to the form.

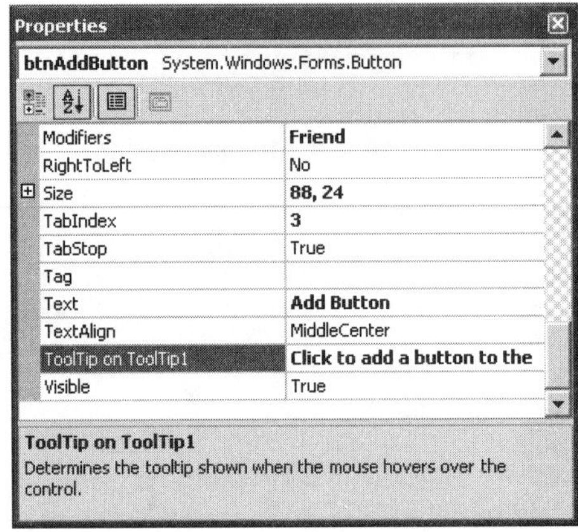

Simply enter the ToolTip text for the Button control in the Properties window, and it will appear next to the control at runtime when your cursor hovers over the control.

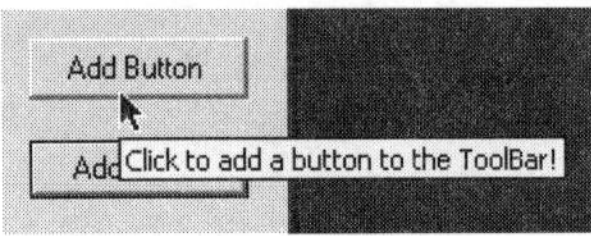

TIP One ToolTip control can be used for all the controls on a form. Emphatically, you do not need to add multiple ToolTip controls to service multiple controls. However, if you wish some ToolTips to have different properties from others—for example, the delay before displaying the text, which can be set in the Properties window—then you will need to use multiple ToolTip controls.

Dynamically Changing ToolTip Text

It's easy to use the `SetToolTip` method of the ToolTip control to set new ToolTip text dynamically in code. The `SetToolTip` method takes two arguments: the control whose ToolTip text is to be changed and the new text. Listing 8.5 shows the code for resetting the ToolTip text for `btnAddButton` when the user clicks the first ToolBar button.

Listing 8.5 Programmatically Changing a Control's ToolTip Text (from the ToolBar ButtonClick Event)

```
Private Sub ToolBar1_ButtonClick(ByVal sender As System.Object, _
   ByVal e As System.Windows.Forms.ToolBarButtonClickEventArgs) _
```

```
    Handles ToolBar1.ButtonClick
    Select Case ToolBar1.Buttons.IndexOf(e.Button)
       Case 0
         ToolTip1.SetToolTip(btnAddButton, _
            "This is the new ToolTip text...")
       ...
    End Select
 End Sub
```

After the code is run, the new ToolTip text appears.

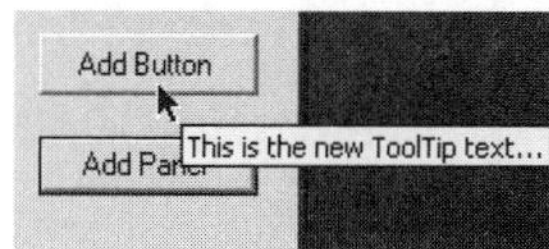

Adding Tabbed Pages

The TabControl control is used to add tabbed pages to a Windows Forms interface. It works in much the same way as the StatusBar and ToolBar controls. You can use the TabPage Collection Editor, accessed through the Properties window, to add, edit, and remove TabPages within a TabControl's TabPages collection, as shown in Figure 8.5.

FIGURE 8.5: You can use the TabPage Collection Editor to add members to the TabPages collection of a TabControl.

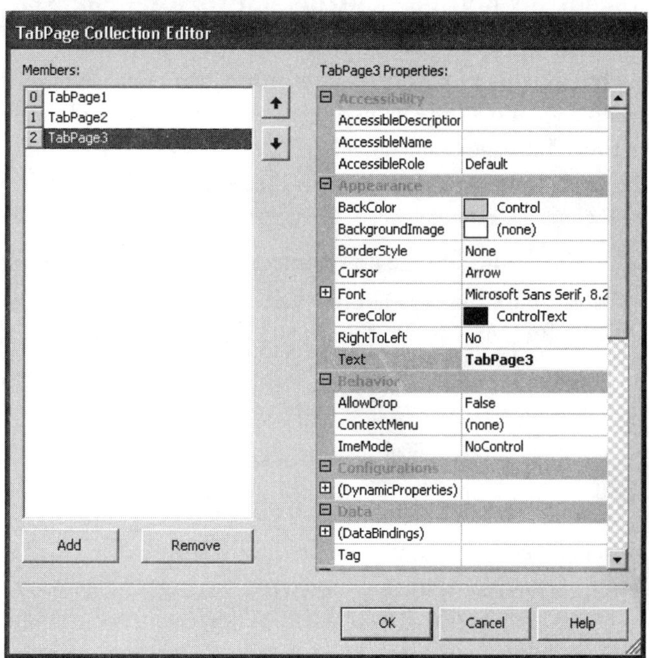

TIP You can also add and remove TabPages directly using the TabControl's context menu. Note that this is a little tricky to do, because you need to right-click in the area where the tabs are, but not on an existing tab.

TabPages added in the TabPage Collection Editor are wired and fully functional. You don't need to add any code to allow the user to use the mouse to navigate between the tabs. (VB6 users will note this as a really cool improvement!)

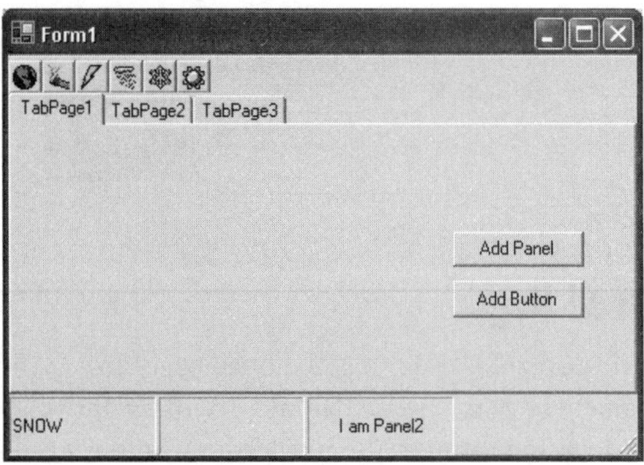

Dynamically Moving Controls between TabPages

Each TabPage has a collection of the controls contained by that TabPage. You can use these collections to dynamically move controls from one TabPage to another. For example, the following code moves the named controls, which I placed on the first TabPage (`TabPages(0)`) to the third TabPage (`TabPages(2)`):

```
TabControl1.TabPages(2).Controls.Add(btnAddPanel)
TabControl1.TabPages(2).Controls.Add(btnAddButton)
```

You can also instantiate new controls, and then add them to a TabPage, as in this example:

```
Dim myButton As New Button()
Dim myText As New TextBox()
TabControl1.TabPages(2).Controls.Add(myButton)
TabControl1.TabPages(2).Controls.Add(myText)
```

TIP In the real world, you will want to assign some property values, such as Text and Location, to the new controls.

Place the code to move and add the controls in the Click event handler of a Button control named `btnMoveControls`, as shown in Listing 8.6. The Move Controls button is positioned on the first tab page (`TabPages(0)`). When the user clicks the button, the controls are moved, new ones are created on the third tab page (`TabPages(2)`), and a message box tells the user to check the tab page to which the controls were relocated.

Listing 8.6 Switching Controls from One Tab to Another and Adding New Control Instances to a Tab

```
Private Sub btnMoveControls_Click(ByVal sender As System.Object, _
   ByVal e As System.EventArgs) Handles btnMoveControls.Click
   ' Move buttons from TabPages(0) to TabPages(2)
   TabControl1.TabPages(2).Controls.Add(btnAddPanel)
   TabControl1.TabPages(2).Controls.Add(btnAddButton)
   Dim myButton As New Button()
   Dim myText As New TextBox()
   TabControl1.TabPages(2).Controls.Add(myButton)
   TabControl1.TabPages(2).Controls.Add(myText)
   MessageBox.Show("Now open TabPage3 to see the controls!", "Tabs!")
End Sub
```

When you run the project and click the TabPage, the controls are moved (and created).

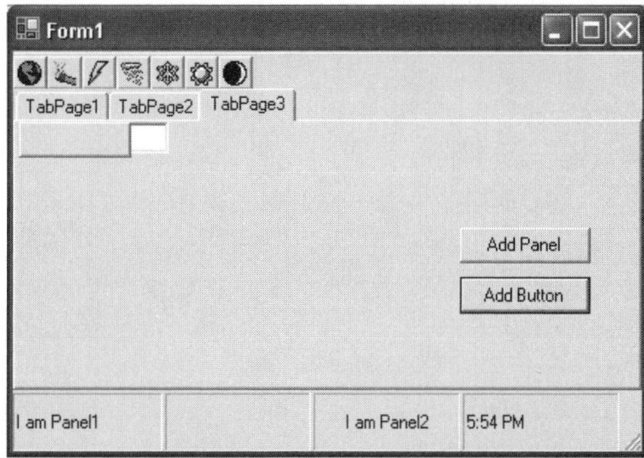

Summary

This chapter has shown you how to use some of the most important Windows Forms interface controls. As you've seen, working with these controls mostly involves knowing how to navigate VB .NET's collections, which, fortunately, have been implemented in a clear and consistent way. Using the material presented in this chapter, you should have no problems using StatusBars, ToolBar, ToolTips, and TabPages in your own applications. Let's move onto another important part of most applications' user interfaces—using the common dialog controls.

Chapter 9

Working with Common Dialogs

- Using the common dialog controls
- Working with the ColorDialog control
- Working with the FontDialog control
- Using the SaveFileDialog and OpenFileDialog controls
- Working with FileStream, StreamWriter, and StreamReader objects

Common dialog controls provide a "wrapper" for dialogs that perform commonly needed tasks, which means that they provide easy access to the functionality of standard dialog boxes. For example, the SaveFileDialog control displays the standard Save As dialog for naming and locating a file to be saved. It's the same dialog box you see in Microsoft Word and other applications.

By using the VB .NET common dialog controls to display these dialog boxes, the appearance of your applications becomes standardized. Users see dialog boxes that they recognize and already know how to use. However, although the common dialog controls show dialog boxes allowing the user to make choices, they don't actually do the work. For example, the SaveFileDialog control doesn't save the contents of a file after the user chooses to save a file. In this chapter, I will not only show you how to use the common dialog controls to get user input, but also how to do some very useful things with that input.

This chapter explains how to work with the ColorDialog, FontDialog, SaveFileDialog, and OpenFileDialog controls. Some other common dialog controls related to printing are covered in Chapter 12, "Printing from an Application."

Using Common Dialog Controls

To use a common dialog control, drag it from the Toolbox to your form, where it will appear in the tray along the bottom of the form. Figure 9.1 shows the result of adding ColorDialog, FontDialog, SaveFileDialog, and OpenFileDialog controls to a form.

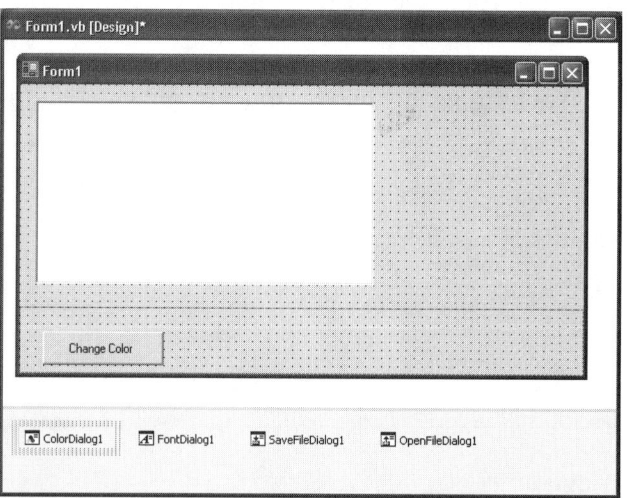

FIGURE 9.1: When you add common dialogs to a Windows form, they appear in the bottom tray.

Once you have added the common dialog to the tray, you can use that dialog multiple times within your application. In other words, you need to add only one ColorDialog control to your application, no matter how many times you plan to show the Color dialog, and even if the characteristics for each dialog will change a bit.

You can set many of a dialog's initial characteristics using the Properties window. For example, if the AllowFullOpen property of the ColorDialog is set to True, the user is allowed to define custom colors (and not allowed to do so if it is set to False).

You can also set these properties in code prior to displaying the dialog, as in this example:

```
ColorDialog1.AllowFullOpen = True
```

The advantage to setting dialog properties in code is that it makes one common dialog control conceptually more reusable, because you don't need to think about what may or may not have been set in the Properties window—you can just look at the code. In the examples in this chapter, the Properties window will not be used to set common dialog properties.

NOTE It's worth noting that, under the hood, VB .NET is different from VB6 in the respect that all form and control property values, even if set in the Properties window, are written to form module code (although you may need to expand the generated code region to see it).

Once you've configured the dialog to your liking, the common dialog's `ShowDialog` method is used to actually display the dialog:

```
FontDialog1.ShowDialog()
```

This chapter explores how to use four common dialog controls:

- ColorDialog, which allows the user to select a color
- FontDialog, which allows the user to select a font and its related characteristics
- OpenFileDialog, which allows the user to pick a file to open from the filesystem
- SaveFileDialog, which allows the user to select a filename and location in the filesystem for saving a file

The RichTextBox Control

The examples in this chapter use a control that we haven't used in the previous chapters: the RichTextBox control. The RichTextBox control displays multiple lines of text that can be formatted with fonts, size, and color.

When the content of the RichTextBox is saved, the formatting information can be retained in RTF (Rich Text File) format. In other words, the RichTextBox control quickly and easily provides the nucleus of a text-processing program with roughly the capabilities of WordPad—well beyond the simple, text only, capabilities of a program like Notepad.

You can easily use the RichTextBox control to provide text-processing capabilities within your .NET applications. You'll see some uses of RichTextBoxes in the examples in this chapter.

Working with the ColorDialog Control

The ColorDialog control is used to invoke the Color dialog, which obtains a color selection from the user.

To see how this works, add a RichTextBox control and a button named `btnChangeColor` to your form.

Open the Change Color button's Click event handler in the Code Editor. Set the initial characteristics of the ColorDialog:

```
ColorDialog1.AllowFullOpen = True
ColorDialog1.AnyColor = True
```

As mentioned earlier, when the AllowFullOpen property of the ColorDialog control is set to True, the user can use the Color dialog to define custom colors. If the AnyColor property is set to True, the dialog displays all available colors; if not, only solid colors are selectable.

Next, show the dialog:

```
ColorDialog1.ShowDialog()
```

If you run the code and click the Change Color button, you'll see the Color dialog.

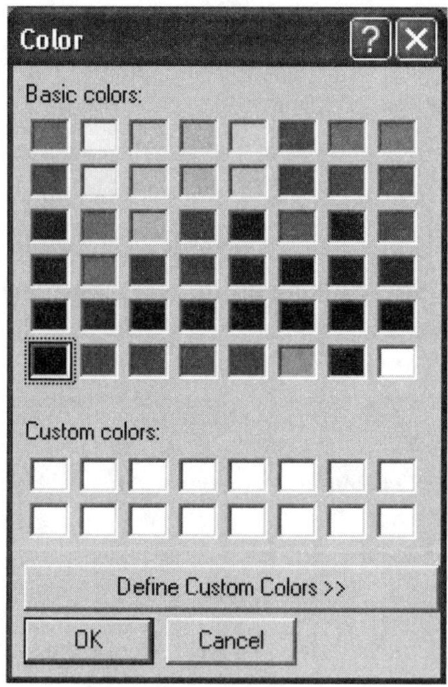

The next step is to capture the user's choice of color (or what good is a dialog that lets the user select a color?). First, declare a variable of type `System.Drawing.Color` to hold the color value selected:

```
Dim theColor As System.Drawing.Color
```

Next, after showing the ColorDialog, assign the Color property of the ColorDialog to the variable:

```
theColor = ColorDialog1.Color
```

Now that we have the user's choice of color captured in the variable, let's do something with it! We can change the color of the text on the button to the color selected:

```
btnChangeColor.ForeColor = theColor
```

We can also use the SelectionColor property of the RichTextBox to change the color of any selected text in the RichTextBox:

```
RichTextBox1.SelectionColor = theColor
```

If you try this out, you'll see that it works. The color change doesn't show up very well in black and white, but you can get the idea from Figure 9.2. You'll find the complete Click event code for showing the Color dialog, capturing the user's choice, and applying it to the button text and RichTextBox selection in Listing 9.1.

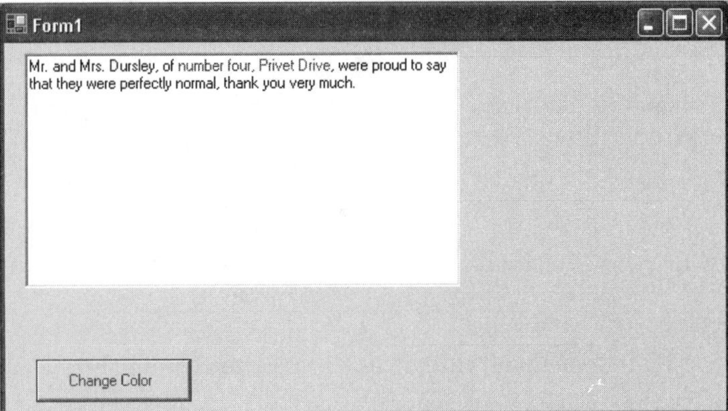

FIGURE 9.2: The color of the selected text in the RichTextBox and the Button's text has been changed according to the user's selection.

Listing 9.1 Using the ColorDialog to Change the Color of Button Text and Selected Text in a RichTextBox

```
Private Sub btnChangeColor_Click(ByVal sender As System.Object, _
   ByVal e As System.EventArgs) Handles btnChangeColor.Click
   Dim theColor As System.Drawing.Color
   ColorDialog1.AllowFullOpen = True
   ColorDialog1.AnyColor = True
```

```
    ColorDialog1.ShowDialog()
    theColor = ColorDialog1.Color
    'Change the color of the Button to the dialog selection
    btnChangeColor.ForeColor = theColor
    'Change the color of selected text in the RichTextBox
    RichTextBox1.SelectionColor = theColor
End Sub
```

Working with the FontDialog Control

The FontDialog control works in much the same way as the ColorDialog control. To see it in action, add a Button control named `btnChangeFont` to the form. Within the button's Click event handler, add the following code:

```
FontDialog1.ShowDialog()
```

This displays the standard Font dialog.

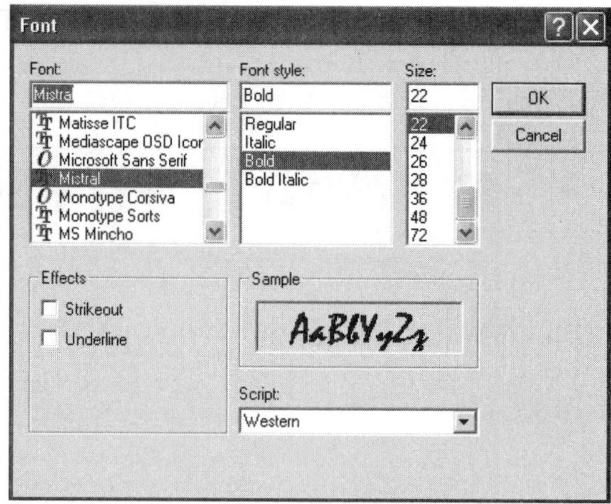

To do something with the user's font choice in the FontDialog, first declare a variable of type `System.Drawing.Font`:

```
Dim theFont As System.Drawing.Font
```

Next, assign the value of `FontDialog1.Font` to the variable, after the dialog has been shown:

```
theFont = FontDialog1.Font
```

Having captured the user's font choice in the variable, we can now change the font of the button's text and any selected text in the RichTextBox accordingly:

```
btnChangeFont.Font = theFont
RichTextBox1.SelectionFont = theFont
```

The complete code for the Click event procedure is shown in Listing 9.2.

Listing 9.2 Using the FontDialog to Allow the User to Select the Font and Attribute

```
Private Sub btnChangeFont_Click(ByVal sender As System.Object, _
   ByVal e As System.EventArgs) Handles btnChangeFont.Click
   Dim theFont As System.Drawing.Font
   FontDialog1.ShowDialog()
   theFont = FontDialog1.Font
   'Change the font of the Button to the dialog selection
   btnChangeFont.Font = theFont
   'Change the font of selected text in the RichTextBox
   RichTextBox1.SelectionFont = theFont
End Sub
```

If you run the program, select some text in the RichTextBox, and click the Change Font button, you'll see that the font has changed.

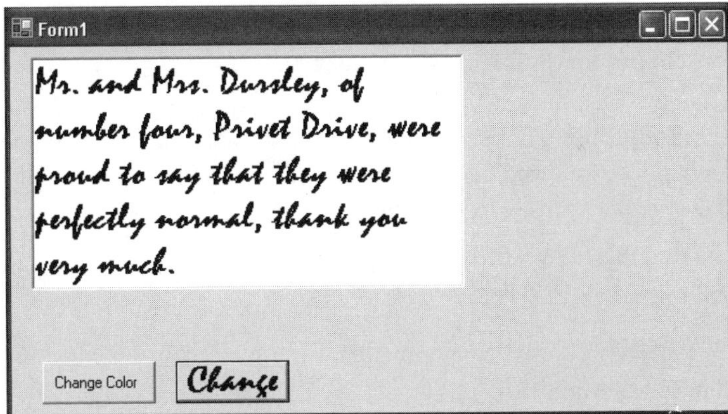

Using the SaveFileDialog and OpenFileDialog Controls

The SaveFileDialog control allows the user to pick a filename and location for saving a file via the standard Save As dialog. The OpenFileDialog control lets the user select a file for opening using the Open dialog. Once again, designating the file is all these dialogs do; they don't do any of the actual work of saving or loading. But not to worry—I'll show you how to save and load files, as well as how to use the file dialogs.

As a first exercise, we'll save the contents of the RichTextBox and then retrieve its contents, formatting and all. Note that the functionality for saving the rich text contents is implemented before the functionality for opening it. It's generally easier to do things in this order rather than scrounging around for an RTF file (and, even when you find one, you can't be absolutely sure what it should look like).

To implement the code for saving and opening rich text from the RichTextBox, add two buttons to the form, named `btnSaveRTF` and `btnOpenRTF`.

Saving the Contents of a RichTextBox

It's really very easy to use the SaveFileDialog to implement saving the contents of the RichTextBox. First, set some of the initial characteristics of the Save As dialog.

```
SaveFileDialog1.InitialDirectory = Application.ExecutablePath
```

This sets the initial directory to the application's executable path (in the case of a VB .NET application running in the development environment, this is the `/bin` directory that stores the application's EXE file). Next, set the initial filename to `Dursley.rtf`.

```
SaveFileDialog1.DefaultExt = "rtf"
SaveFileDialog1.FileName = "Dursley"
```

Finally, set a filter to determine the choices that are available to the user in the Save As Type drop-down list.

```
SaveFileDialog1.Filter = "Rich Text Files" _
   & " (*.rtf)|*.rtf|All Files (*.*) | *.*"
```

The Filter property is a text string separated by the "pipe" character (`|`). Each item consists of a description, followed by a pipe, followed by the file suffix, usually using wildcard characters. Another pipe is used to start the next item.

In the example above, the following is one item:

```
Rich Text Files (*.rtf)|*.rtf
```

It is the description followed by the specification, namely `*.rtf`.

And here's another item:

```
All Files (*.*) | *.*
```

This has the specification, `*.*`, displaying files of all types.

WARNING Be careful not to include extra spaces between the end of one item and the beginning of the next. Otherwise, the filter may not work properly.

Next, show the dialog:

```
SaveFileDialog1.ShowDialog()
```

The contents of the RichTextBox are saved using the RichTextBox's `SaveFile` method, with the filename selected by the user as its argument:

```
RichTextBox1.SaveFile(SaveFileDialog1.FileName)
```

To see how this works, run the program and enter some heavily formatted text in the RichTextBox, as in the example shown here.

Next, click the Save RTF button. The Save As dialog will open, suggesting a filename, type, and location: `Dursley.rtf` in the `/bin` directory.

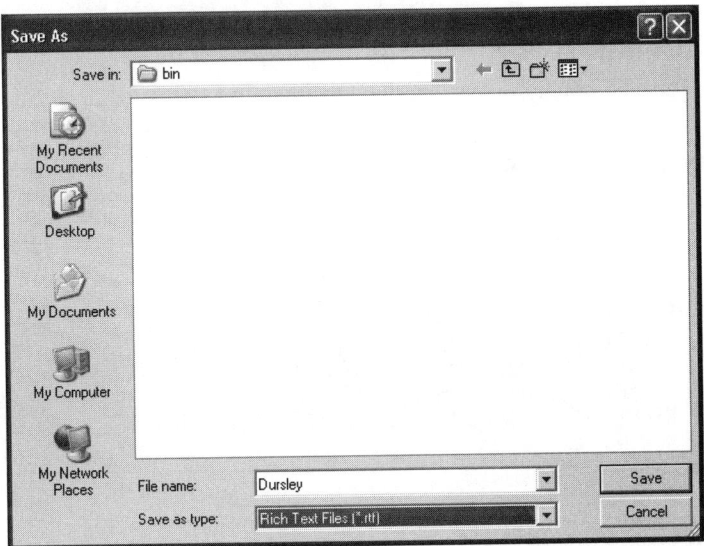

WARNING Unless you set the OverwritePrompt property of the SaveFileDialog to True (either in code or the Properties window), the user can pick an existing file, possibly resulting in overwriting its contents. Setting the OverwritePrompt property to True causes a message with a warning to appear, allowing the user to proceed if she still wants to.

Accept the filename, type, and location suggestions. Click Save. A file with the rich text contents will be created at the indicated location. To verify this, you can locate the file and open it in Microsoft Word.

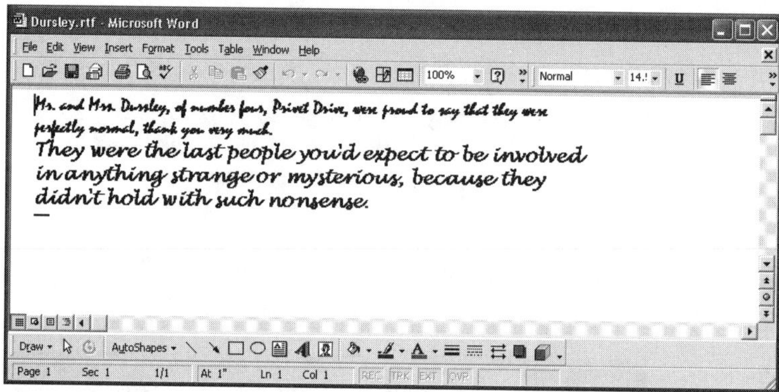

The complete Click event handler is shown in Listing 9.3.

Listing 9.3 **Saving the Contents of a RichTextBox**

```
Private Sub btnSaveRTF_Click(ByVal sender As System.Object, _
    ByVal e As System.EventArgs) Handles btnSaveRTF.Click
    SaveFileDialog1.InitialDirectory = Application.ExecutablePath
    SaveFileDialog1.DefaultExt = "rtf"
    SaveFileDialog1.FileName = "Dursley"
    SaveFileDialog1.Filter = "Rich Text Files" _
       & " (*.rtf)|*.rtf|All Files (*.*) | *.*"
    SaveFileDialog1.ShowDialog()
    RichTextBox1.SaveFile(SaveFileDialog1.FileName)
End Sub
```

Retrieving Rich Text into a RichTextBox

The next step is to create the event handler that will load rich text into the RichTextBox in the application. To do this, we will display an Open dialog using the OpenFileDialog control.

Initializing the OpenFileDialog works in the same way as initializing the SaveFileDialog (see Listing 9.3). With the OpenFileDialog's properties set, we then need to show the dialog and use the `LoadFile` method of the RichTextBox to load the contents of the file selected by the user into the control:

```
OpenFileDialog1.ShowDialog()
RichTextBox1.LoadFile(OpenFileDialog1.FileName)
```

Listing 9.4 shows the code for retrieving the rich text and loading it into the text box.

Listing 9.4 Retrieving Rich Text and Loading It into a RichTextBox

```
Private Sub btnOpenRTF_Click(ByVal sender As System.Object, _
   ByVal e As System.EventArgs) Handles btnOpenRTF.Click
   OpenFileDialog1.InitialDirectory = Application.ExecutablePath
   OpenFileDialog1.DefaultExt = "rtf"
   OpenFileDialog1.FileName = "Dursley"
   OpenFileDialog1.Filter = "Rich Text Files" _
      & " (*.rtf)|*.rtf|All Files (*.*) | *.*"
   OpenFileDialog1.ShowDialog()
   RichTextBox1.LoadFile(OpenFileDialog1.FileName)
End Sub
```

If you run the code shown in Listing 9.4 and click the Open RTF button, you can choose a rich text file from the Open dialog.

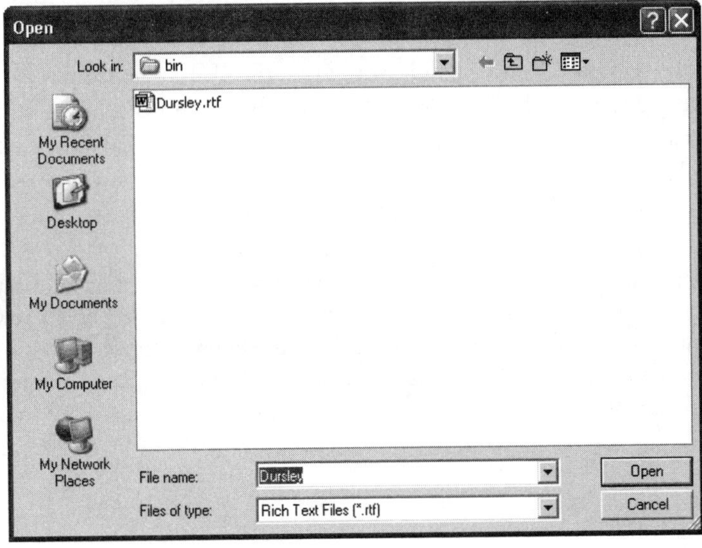

If you select the file you previously created and click Open, it will be loaded into the RichTextBox on the form.

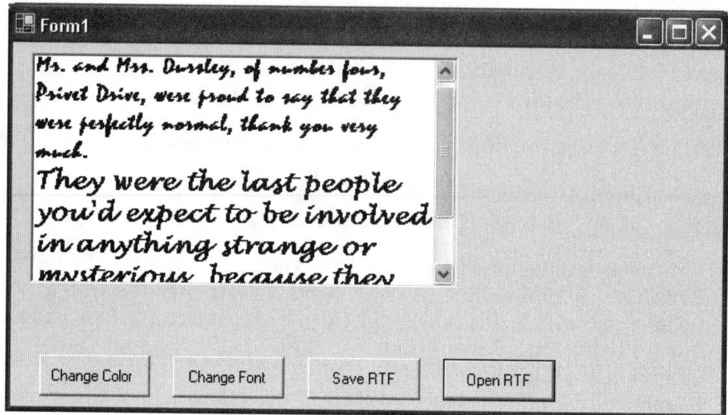

Working with Files

In some ways, the previous examples, which show you how to save and retrieve rich text using a RichTextBox are "cheating," because they let the methods of the RichTextBox do all the actual work of saving to the file and opening from the file. There's no need to cheat in this way (unless you want to).

In this section, I'll show you how to use VB .NET's FileStream and StreamWriter objects to save the value of the Text property of TextBoxes to a file, along with the control the property is associated with. Of course, once you know how to save this content, you'll also need to know how to retrieve it and load it into the controls it is associated with, and I'll also show you how to use a StreamReader object to do this.

NOTE The process explained in this section involves saving name/value pairs in a text file. This might be useful in some circumstances, but unless you have only a few control values you want to save, it's normal practice to use data-bound controls and a database for associating saved values with controls. For more information, see Chapter 17, "Working with Data and ADO.NET."

Streams, FileStreams, StreamWriters, and StreamReaders

A *stream* is an abstract concept representing streams of bytes, or streams of information. You can think of a stream as the information at a granular level that makes up a file or other object (such as a component that is instantiated over the Web).

A FileStream is a .NET object that makes this abstraction more concrete, and it is used to hold instances of streams that constitute files. StreamWriters are .NET objects used to write information to a stream, such as a FileStream. StreamReaders are used to decode the information carried by a stream, such as a FileStream.

Another way of looking at this is that FileStreams force you to work with bytes, or arrays of bytes. When dealing with text, this is cumbersome. StreamReader and StreamWriter give you the more convenient `WriteLine`, `ReadLine`, and `ReadToEnd` methods.

Using a StreamWriter to Save Control Values to a File

To get started with saving the Text values of controls, add two buttons to the form, called `btnWriteControls` and `btnReadControls`. Next, add a bunch of TextBoxes to the form. These will be used for writing and retrieving values. It really doesn't matter what they are called or what values they show initially, so you can accept the default names and values (`TextBox1`, `TextBox2`, and so on). It also doesn't matter how many or few there are, because the StreamWriter object, using the code I'll show you, will save any number of TextBox values to the stream.

TIP The example uses TextBoxes, but it will work with any control, provided you adjust the code. In addition, the example stores and retrieves the Text value of the control, but you could store and retrieve any property, once again, making the appropriate adjustments to the code.

With the controls in place on the form, open the Code Editor. This Click event procedure uses many of the objects found in the `System.IO` namespace, such as the StreamWriter. So, at the very top of the Code Editor, above the form declaration, add a statement to import `System.IO`:

```
Imports System.IO
```

NOTE You could keep entering the fully qualified name for the object, `System.Io.StreamWriter`, and, in this case, wouldn't need the `Imports` statement. However, it is less cumbersome and makes your code clearer to simply be able to refer to `StreamWriter`.

With that out of the way, in btnWriteControl's Click event handler, use the SaveFileDialog control to obtain a name and location for the file being saved:

```
Dim theFile As String
SaveFileDialog1.InitialDirectory = Application.ExecutablePath
SaveFileDialog1.DefaultExt = "hld"
SaveFileDialog1.FileName = "myFile"
SaveFileDialog1.Filter = "HLD Files" _
   & " (*.hld)|*.hld|All Files (*.*)| *.*"
SaveFileDialog1.OverwritePrompt = True
SaveFileDialog1.ShowDialog()
theFile = SaveFileDialog1.FileName
```

Note that the user is encouraged to select an HLD file, which is a made-up type (using my initials).

Next, create a FileStream object named fs.

```
Dim fs As FileStream = New FileStream(theFile, FileMode.OpenOrCreate)
```

This gives the FileStream object the name (and path) obtained from the SaveFileDialog. It also uses the FileMode enumeration value OpenOrCreate, telling it to open the file if it exists, or create it if it does not.

Now, create a StreamWriter object named w to actually write the text to the file:

```
Dim w As StreamWriter = New StreamWriter(fs)
```

Finally, cycle through the form's control collection. (The control collection code is explained in Chapter 7, "Working with Windows Forms Controls.") When a TextBox control is reached, use the StreamWriter w to write the name of the control, followed by an equal sign, followed by the value of its Text property:

```
Dim c As Object
For Each c In Me.Controls
   If TypeOf (c) Is TextBox Then
      Dim tbox As TextBox = CType(c, TextBox)
      w.WriteLine(tbox.name & "=" & tbox.text)
   End If
Next
```

Note that the WriteLine method adds a line break after each line is written; the w.Write() method does not add line breaks.

Finally, close the StreamWriter, which saves the file and its contents:

```
w.Close()
fs.Close()
```

WARNING This code involves a loose type conversion and will fail with an error message if Option Strict is turned on. For details on cycling through a collection, see Chapter 6, "Working with Form Methods and Modules."

To try this out to see if it works, run the program and enter some text in the TextBoxes on the form.

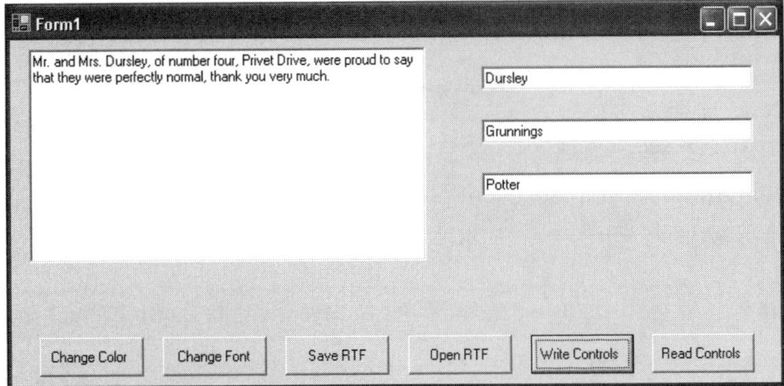

Next, click the Write Controls button. The Save As dialog opens.

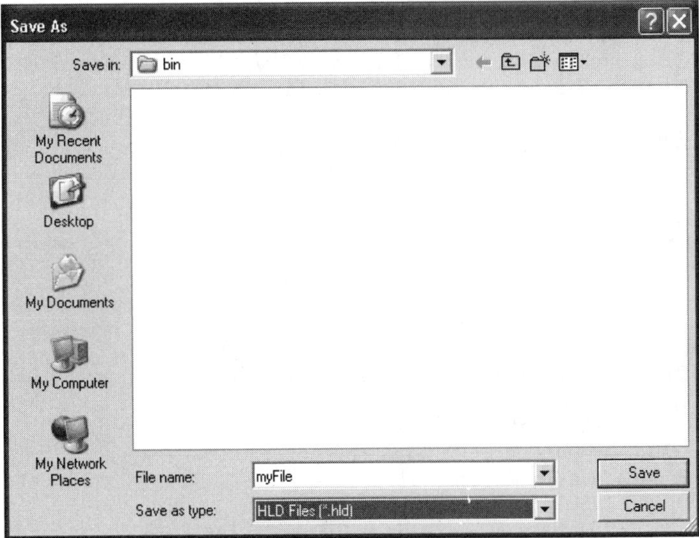

Pick a name for the file (the default suggestion, `myFile.hld`, is fine). Click Save. To make sure that the StreamWriter did what it was supposed to do, you can locate the file and open it in Notepad.

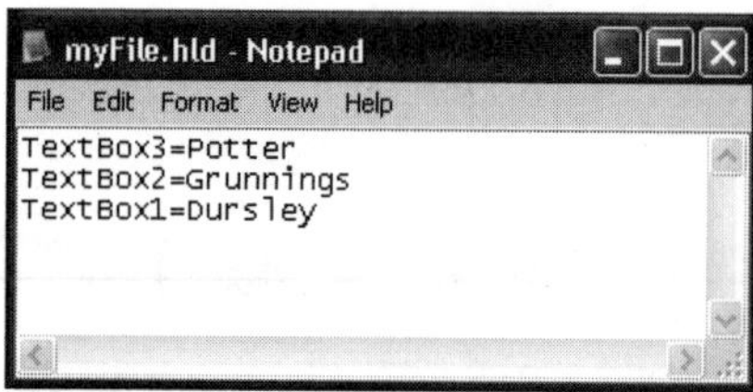

As you can see, it has been saved in the format we designated.

You'll find the complete event procedure code for using the StreamWriter to write multiple control values to a file in Listing 9.5.

Listing 9.5 Using a StreamWriter to Save Multiple Control Values to a File

```
Option Strict On
Imports System.IO
...
Private Sub btnWriteControls_Click(ByVal sender As System.Object, _
   ByVal e As System.EventArgs) Handles btnWriteControls.Click
   'Get a file name
   Dim theFile As String
   SaveFileDialog1.InitialDirectory = Application.ExecutablePath
   SaveFileDialog1.DefaultExt = "hld" 'custom format
   SaveFileDialog1.FileName = "myFile"
   SaveFileDialog1.Filter = "HLD Files" _
      & " (*.hld)|*.hld|All Files (*.*)| *.*"
   SaveFileDialog1.OverwritePrompt = True
   SaveFileDialog1.ShowDialog()
   theFile = SaveFileDialog1.FileName

   'Grab an IO stream
   Dim fs As FileStream = New _
      FileStream(theFile, FileMode.OpenOrCreate)
   Dim w As StreamWriter = New StreamWriter(fs)

   'Write the controls
   Dim c As Object
   For Each c In Me.Controls
      If TypeOf (c) Is TextBox Then
         Dim tbox As TextBox = CType(c, TextBox)
         w.WriteLine(tbox.name & "=" & tbox.text)
      End If
   Next
```

```
    'Close the StreamWriter
    w.Close()
    fs.close()
End Sub
```

Using a StreamReader to Restore Control Values

Obviously, it is all well and good to save the values of the TextBox text, but you also need to know how to retrieve and restore the values. As I'll show you, it's easy to use the `ReadLine` method of a StreamReader object to read a file line, but you need to do a little work to get the Text value parsed out of the line.

To start with, once more, make sure you have an `Imports System.IO` statement as the first line of your form module code.

Next, within the `btnReadControl`'s Click event procedure, use the OpenFileDialog control to get the name of the file to be opened:

```
Dim theFile As String
OpenFileDialog1.InitialDirectory = Application.ExecutablePath
OpenFileDialog1.DefaultExt = "hld" 'custom format
OpenFileDialog1.FileName = "myFile"
OpenFileDialog1.Filter = "HLD Files" _
   & " (*.hld)|*.hld|All Files (*.*) | *.*"
OpenFileDialog1.ShowDialog()
theFile = OpenFileDialog1.FileName
```

Next, instantiate a FileStream, using the name of the file selected in the OpenFileDialog, in Open mode:

```
Dim fs As FileStream = New FileStream(theFile, FileMode.Open)
```

Create a StreamReader, `r`, to read the contents of the FileStream:

```
Dim r As StreamReader = New StreamReader(fs)
```

Cycle through the controls on the form. When a TextBox is reached, use the `ReadLine` method of the StreamReader to read the line into an array, `tmpArray`. The `Split` function is used to separate each file line into two elements in the array, with an equal sign as the delimiter. If the first element of the array (`tmpArray(0)`) matches the name of the TextBox, then the value for the Text property of the control is supplied by the second array element (`tmpArray(1)`):

```
Dim c As Object
Dim tmpArray() As String
For Each c In Me.Controls
   If TypeOf (c) Is TextBox Then
      Dim tbox As TextBox = CType(c, TextBox)
      tmpArray = Split(r.ReadLine(), "=")
```

```
        If tbox.name = tmpArray(0) Then
            tbox.text = tmpArray(1)
        End If
    End If
Next
```

Finally, the StreamReader is closed:

```
r.Close()
fs.Close()
```

WARNING There are many things that could go wrong with this code. It assumes that the file being opened is in the right format, and that the order and number of controls on the form have not changed since the file was saved. In other words, there is no error checking whatsoever.

To test this procedure, run the form. Click the Read Controls button to make sure that the values you previously saved in `myFile.hld` are read into the appropriate TextBoxes.

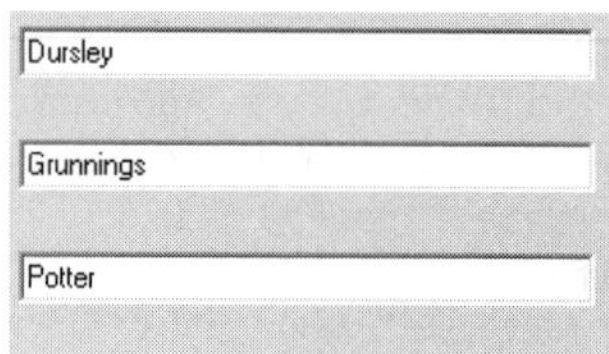

The code for using a StreamReader to restore the text values to the controls is shown in Listing 9.6.

Listing 9.6 Using a StreamReader to Restore the Text Values to the Controls

```
Option Strict On
Imports System.IO
...
Private Sub btnReadControls_Click(ByVal sender As System.Object, _
    ByVal e As System.EventArgs) Handles btnReadControls.Click
    'Get the file
    Dim theFile As String
    OpenFileDialog1.InitialDirectory = Application.ExecutablePath
    OpenFileDialog1.DefaultExt = "hld" 'custom format
    OpenFileDialog1.FileName = "myFile"
    OpenFileDialog1.Filter = "HLD Files" _
        &" (*.hld)|*.hld|All Files (*.*) | *.*"
    OpenFileDialog1.ShowDialog()
    theFile = OpenFileDialog1.FileName

    'Grab an IO stream
    Dim fs As FileStream = New FileStream(theFile, FileMode.Open)
    Dim r As StreamReader = New StreamReader(fs)
```

```
    'Read the controls and write property values
    Dim c As Object
    Dim tmpArray() As String
    For Each c In Me.Controls
       If TypeOf (c) Is TextBox Then
           Dim tbox As TextBox = CType(c, TextBox)
           tmpArray = Split(r.ReadLine(), "=")
           If tbox.name = tmpArray(0) Then
              tbox.text = tmpArray(1)
           End If
       End If
     Next
     'Close the StreamReader
     r.Close()
  End Sub
```

Summary

In this chapter, you've seen that the common dialog controls are easy to use and produce the standardized dialog boxes that users have come to expect. I also showed you how to respond to user selection of color and font, and to save the contents of a RichTextBox control to a file. Next, you were introduced to the concept of a stream and to the FileStream, StreamWriter, and StreamReader objects. You learned how to use these objects to save control values to a file and retrieve them. This is great stuff!

In Chapter 10, you'll learn how to work with notification components, such as the Timer, EventLog, and ServiceController. These are components that set off an alarm or perform actions related to services and events.

CHAPTER 10

Using Timers, EventLogs, and ServiceControllers

- Working with the Timer component
- Creating animations with the Timer
- Using the Server Explorer
- Writing to an event log
- Creating a timed audit trail in an event log
- Working with the ServiceController component
- Starting and stopping services

This chapter explains how to use three important .NET controls, or components, that appear on the Components tab of the Toolbox: the Timer, EventLog, and ServiceController.

The Timer component is used to fire an event after an elapsed interval of time. You'll find this surprisingly useful and ubiquitous component used in a great variety of applications.

The EventLog allows you to write events to System, Security, and Application logs. Keeping track of program events by logging them can help you to debug problems when they arise and lets you create an application audit trail.

The ServiceController gives you access to applications that run as services on a system, and lets you stop and start them.

These components share the characteristic that they do not present a visual interface in a form-based application. Nevertheless, they can be added to a form when it is in its designer, and they appear in design-time mode on the tray beneath the form (rather than on the form itself).

Working with the Timer Component

The Timer component, like the other components discussed in this chapter, is found on the Components tab of the Toolbox.

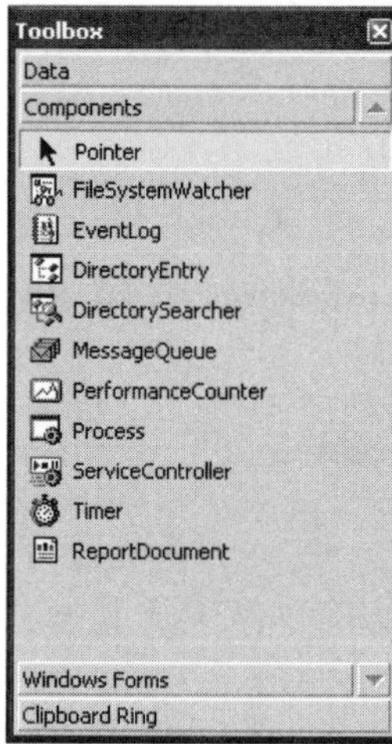

NOTE Most of the components on the Components tab of the Toolbox are server-based applications that the .NET developer can access in a client application that instantiates the server component. Some of these components, such as the MessageQueue, are primarily intended as part of the architecture of a distributed application. However, the Timer, EventLog, and ServiceController components are potentially helpful to any application, whether it has a distributed architecture or is operating strictly locally.

The Timer component is easy to use because it has so few properties and events. There are two properties that matter:

- Enabled, which turns the Timer off and on
- Interval, which sets the interval that elapses between fired events, in milliseconds

You can set these properties programmatically, or you can set them at design time in the Properties window.

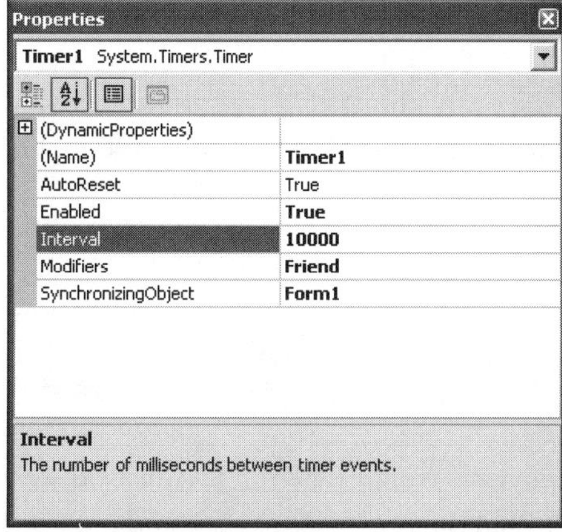

The Timer has one event procedure, Elapsed. When the Timer is enabled, code placed in the Elapsed event procedure is executed repeatedly every time the interval elapses.

Keeping the Time Current

Back in Chapter 8, "Adding StatusBars, ToolBars, ToolTips, and Tabbed Dialogs," I showed you how to display the current time on a StatusBar Panel, and noted that you need to use a Timer control to keep the time display current. This section describes how to do that.

Drag the Timer control from the Toolbox to your form to add it to the form's tray. In the Properties window, set the Enabled property of the Timer to False and its Interval property to 100.

Next, add a StatusBar to the form. In the Properties window, set the StatusBar's ShowPanels property to True, and use the StatusBarPanel Collection Editor to add three empty panels. (See Chapter 8 for detailed instructions on how to work with StatusBar controls.)

Add a Button control to your form. Name the Button `btnTimer` and give it the Text value **`Enable`**. Double-click the Button control to open the Code Editor and create a framework for the button's Click event procedure. Within the Click event procedure, add code that toggles the Timer's Enabled setting and the button's Text property:

```
Private Sub btnTimer_Click(ByVal sender As System.Object, _
   ByVal e As System.EventArgs) Handles btnTimer.Click
   If btnTimer.Text = "Enable" Then
      Timer1.Enabled = True
      btnTimer.Text = "Disable"
   Else
      Timer1.Enabled = False
      btnTimer.Text = "Enable"
   End If
End Sub
```

TIP By toggling the Button control's Text property value, you can use one Button control to turn the Timer on and off, rather than two (one to turn it on and the other to turn it off).

Next, add code to the Timer's Elapsed event procedure that writes the current time to the StatusBar Panel:

```
Private Sub Timer1_Elapsed(ByVal sender As Object, _
   ByVal e As System.Timers.ElapsedEventArgs) Handles Timer1.Elapsed
   StatusBar1.Panels(2).Text = Now.ToLongTimeString
End Sub
```

When you run the project and click the Enable button, you'll see that the button text has changed to Disable, and the time is displayed on the status bar, updated every 100 milliseconds (once every tenth of a second), almost faster than you can see.

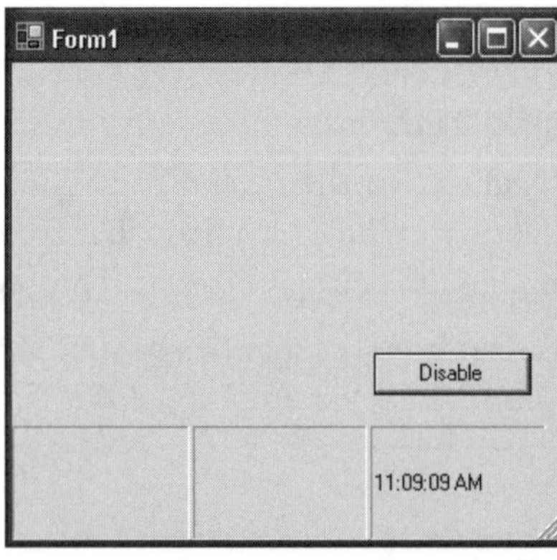

Counting the Number of Times the Timer Has Fired

To learn a bit more about the Timer control, let's get it to display a counter showing the number of times it has fired. We can use the same button to enable and disable this counter, and display the results in the form's caption bar.

For starters, we'll set up an integer variable `i`, declared using the `Static` keyword in the Timer Elapsed event:

```
Static i As Integer
```

By using `Static` instead of `Dim`, the variable's value persists throughout the scope of the application, not just within a procedure. In other words, a variable declared with `Dim` would be reset every time the Elapsed procedure was terminated, so it would never count up. In contrast, a variable declared using `Static` maintains its incremental value between calls to the Elapsed procedure.

TIP Another way to achieve the goal of having a variable act as a persistent counter is to declare it using `Dim` at the module level rather than within a procedure. That way, the variable's value will persist as long as the module is loaded.

With our `Static` variable declared, within the Elapsed event, add a line of code to display the number of times the Timer has fired, and then increment the counter:

```
Me.Text = "The Timer has been fired " & CStr(i) & " times."
i = i + 1
```

The complete code for keeping the time current on a StatusBar Panel and displaying the number of times a Timer has fired is shown in Listing 10.1.

Listing 10.1 **Displaying the Current Time and Counting the Number of Times the Timer Has Fired**

```
Private Sub btnTimer_Click(ByVal sender As System.Object, _
   ByVal e As System.EventArgs) Handles btnTimer.Click
   If btnTimer.Text = "Enable" Then
      Timer1.Enabled = True
      btnTimer.Text = "Disable"
   Else
      Timer1.Enabled = False
      btnTimer.Text = "Enable"
   End If
End Sub

Private Sub Timer1_Elapsed(ByVal sender As Object, _
   ByVal e As System.Timers.ElapsedEventArgs) Handles Timer1.Elapsed
   Static i As Integer
   StatusBar1.Panels(2).Text = Now.ToLongTimeString
```

```
    Me.Text = "The Timer has been fired " & CStr(i) & " times."
    i = i + 1
End Sub
```

When you run the program and click Enable, the number of times the Timer has been fired will be displayed in the form's caption bar.

Using the Timer for Simple Animations

Another handy use of a Timer is to power animations. By placing code in the Timer's Elapsed event, you can give objects the appearance of motion.

In this section, I'll show you how to use a Timer to animate a Label control that has been loaded with a graphic portraying a (very small) rocket ship. The rocket will travel up and down, and all around the form.

> **TIP** You can create much more interesting animations than the one shown in this example by using (and animating) the Graphics objects associated with GDI+. See Chapter 6, "Working with Form Methods and Modules," for some examples of the use of the Graphics object. While what you "draw" with the Graphics object is considerably more flexible than the label with graphic shown in this example, the animation technique is the same.

As a first step, add a new Timer control to your form. Set its Enabled property to **`False`** and its Interval property to **`100`** milliseconds.

Add a Label control to the form. Set its Size property to **`16, 16`** (16×16 pixels), the size of the graphic that will be loaded into it.

First, add an `Imports` statement at the top of the form module code to import the `System.Drawing` namespace (making it easier to refer to the objects that belong to this namespace):

```
Imports System.Drawing
```

Declare increment variables, which will be used to determine the size of each movement by the animated rocket, at the form module level, just after the form class declaration:

```
Public Class Form1
   Inherits System.Windows.Forms.Form
   Dim xIncrement, yIncrement As Integer
```

Next, add a Button control named **`btnAnimate`** to the form, with the Text property value **`Animate`**. In the button's Click event procedure, load the rocket icon into an Image object:

```
Dim filename As String = "C:\Program Files\Microsoft Visual" _
   & " Studio .NET\Common7\Graphics\icons\arrows\POINT10.ICO"
Dim theImage As Image = Image.FromFile(filename)
```

Set up a framework, as in the previous example, to use the button to turn the animation on and off:

```
If btnAnimate.Text <> "Animate" Then
   ...
Else
   ...
End If
```

To start the animation, load the image into the Label's Image property, set the increment of motion, and activate the Timer. You'll also want to change `btnAnimate`'s text to Stop:

```
lblAnimate.Image = theImage
xIncrement = 5
yIncrement = 10
Timer2.Enabled = True
btnAnimate.Text = "Stop"
```

Next, let's write the code to stop the animation, by setting the Label's Image property to `Nothing`, disabling the Timer, and resetting the button's Text value:

```
lblAnimate.Image = Nothing
Timer2.Enabled = False
btnAnimate.Text = "Animate"
```

The main engine for movement in the Timer's Elapsed event procedure is the assignment of a new Point object to the Label's Location property:

```
lblAnimate.Location = New Point(lblAnimate.Location.X + _
      xIncrement, lblAnimate.Location.Y + yIncrement)
```

The value of the new Point is based on the current location of the Label, with the addition of the specified increment in both dimensions.

This works well enough by itself, with only one hitch. When the Label reaches the edge of the form, the increments just keep going. To the user, this will mean that the rocket goes off the form, never to reappear.

To remedy this situation, in the Elapsed event procedure, we need to add code that adjusts the increment variables when the rocket reaches the edge of the form. Note that this adjustment changes the increment from positive to negative, and if it's already negative, back to positive:

```
If lblAnimate.Location.X > Me.Size.Width - 30 Then
   xIncrement = -5
End If
If lblAnimate.Location.Y > Me.Size.Height - 50 Then
   yIncrement = -10
End If
If lblAnimate.Location.X <= 0 Then
   xIncrement = 5
End If
```

```
If lblAnimate.Location.Y <= 0 Then
   yIncrement = 10
End If
```

The complete code for animating the Label is shown in Listing 10.2.

Listing 10.2 Animating a Label

```
Imports System.Drawing
Public Class Form1
   Inherits System.Windows.Forms.Form
   Dim xIncrement, yIncrement As Integer
...
Private Sub btnAnimate_Click(ByVal sender As System.Object, _
   ByVal e As System.EventArgs) Handles btnAnimate.Click
   Dim filename As String = "C:\Program Files\Microsoft Visual" _
      & " Studio .NET\Common7\Graphics\icons\arrows\POINT10.ICO"
   Dim theImage As Image = Image.FromFile(filename)
   If btnAnimate.Text <> "Animate" Then
      'Turn off the animation
      lblAnimate.Image = Nothing
      Timer2.Enabled = False
      btnAnimate.Text = "Animate"
   Else
      'Start the animation
      lblAnimate.Image = theImage
      xIncrement = 5
      yIncrement = 10
      Timer2.Enabled = True
      btnAnimate.Text = "Stop"
   End If
End Sub

Private Sub Timer2_Elapsed(ByVal sender As System.Object, _
   ByVal e As System.Timers.ElapsedEventArgs) Handles Timer2.Elapsed
   If lblAnimate.Location.X > Me.Size.Width - 30 Then
      xIncrement = -5
   End If
   If lblAnimate.Location.Y > Me.Size.Height - 50 Then
      yIncrement = -10
   End If
   If lblAnimate.Location.X <= 0 Then
      xIncrement = 5
   End If
   If lblAnimate.Location.Y <= 0 Then
      yIncrement = 10
   End If

   lblAnimate.Location = New Point(lblAnimate.Location.X + _
      xIncrement, lblAnimate.Location.Y + yIncrement)
End Sub
```

With the code in place, you can run the project and click the Animate button to watch the rocket.

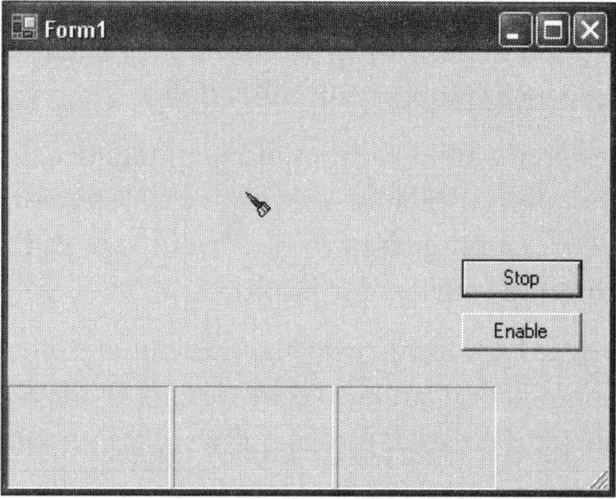

Multiple Variable Declarations in a Single Statement

The statement `Dim xIncrement, yIncrement As Integer` declares both variables, `xIncrement` and `yIncrement`, as type Integer, which makes sense. In VB6 and earlier versions, this statement would produce one Variant variable, `xIncrement`, and one integer, `yIncrement`. In other words, all variables in the declaration other than the last one were assumed to be the default type, which is Variant.

So, in VB6, the statement `Dim xIncrement, yIncrement As Integer` would be equivalent to `Dim xIncrement As Variant, yIncrement As Integer`; in VB .NET, it is equivalent to `Dim xIncrement As Integer, yIncrement As Integer`. This is a difference with consequences. While the VB .NET interpretation is clearly superior, if you are involved in converting legacy code, you should watch for this.

In addition to the change (for the better) in the way the `Dim` statement works, VB .NET no longer has the Variant variable type, which essentially said, "This is a variable and it can hold anything." The closest thing to using a Variant is to declare a variable as an Object type, which allows the variable to be almost anything in VB .NET, since all types inherit from the Object class.

Using the Server Explorer

So far, we've been able to use objects such as components and controls via two mechanisms in our application code. When you drag and drop an object from the Toolbox, VB .NET takes care of creating an instance of the object, and the instance can be referred to via the name given in the Properties window. Alternatively, you can create objects in code using the `New` keyword.

Many of the components on the Components tab can be added in a third way: by dragging and dropping them on the form tray from the Server Explorer. To access the Server Explorer, choose View ➢ Server Explorer from the VB .NET menu.

The Server Explorer is used to view and manipulate database connections, services, and system programs that are available on your local system or on any server to which you have network access. For example, you will find event logs and system services, as well as data connectivity, as you browse your Server Explorer.

Items in the Server Explorer are displayed in an expandable tree structure, as shown in Figure 10.1. When you drag an item that appears in the Server Explorer onto a form, an instance of the object is created, just as if it were a component in the Toolbox.

FIGURE 10.1:

You can drag a server component from the Server Explorer to use an instance of the component in your application.

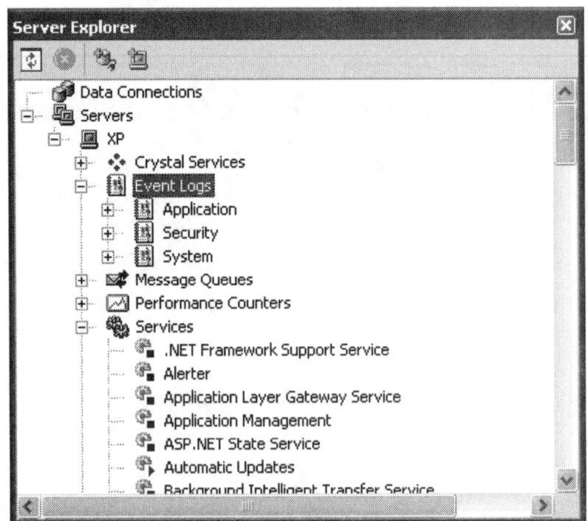

Writing to an Event Log

Event logs provide a standardized way to write and view messages from programs. One common use of the event log is to write an entry when a program encounters an error condition. This can help you debug the problem. Another scenario is to write the program status and key variable values periodically, probably using a Timer's Elapsed event to write the information.

This creates an audit trail, which will clearly tell an observer what the program was doing. If designed correctly, this kind of audit trail is an important aspect of application security. However, you should be careful how much data you write to the event log, because it has a finite size.

Writing an Event Log Entry

It's easy to write an entry in an event log by using the EventLog component. To write a message in an event log, first drag an EventLog component to your form. In the Properties window, set the Log property of the EventLog to System, meaning this EventLog component will write to the System log.

Next, add a TextBox (for the message that will be written) and a Button control (to actually write the message). Within the button's Click event procedure, add a call to a subroutine, `WriteLog`:

```
Private Sub btnOnce_Click(ByVal sender As System.Object, _
   ByVal e As System.EventArgs) Handles btnOnce.Click
   WriteLog()
End Sub
```

To create the subroutine `WriteLog`, type **`Private Sub WriteLog`** in the Code Editor. The Code Editor will automatically supply the parentheses and the `End Sub` statement to make the subroutine's framework.

Within the framework, supply a descriptive value for the Source property of the EventLog, and use the EventLog's `WriteEntry` method to create the entry in the event log:

```
Private Sub WriteLog()
   EventLog1.Source = "mySource"
   EventLog1.WriteEntry(txtEventLog.Text)
End Sub
```

NOTE The call to the `WriteEntry` method was placed in a subroutine so that we could easily call it multiple times in the next example (which creates multiple, timed event log entries).

That's all there is to it. (You may want to explore writing custom Application event log entries, rather than writing to the System log.)

Listing 10.3 shows the code for writing an entry to an event log.

Listing 10.3 Writing to the Event Log

```
Private Sub btnOnce_Click(ByVal sender As System.Object, _
   ByVal e As System.EventArgs) Handles btnOnce.Click
   WriteLog()
End Sub

Private Sub WriteLog()
   EventLog1.Source = "mySource"
   EventLog1.WriteEntry(txtEventLog.Text)
End Sub
```

To test this program, run the project and enter some text in the text box.

Click the Once button. Your message has been written to the System event log. To view the message and verify that it is there, in Windows XP, open the Control Panel, then Administrative Tools, and then Event Viewer. Within Event Viewer, highlight the System log in the left pane, as shown in Figure 10.2. Your mySource entry will appear as a recent entry in the right pane.

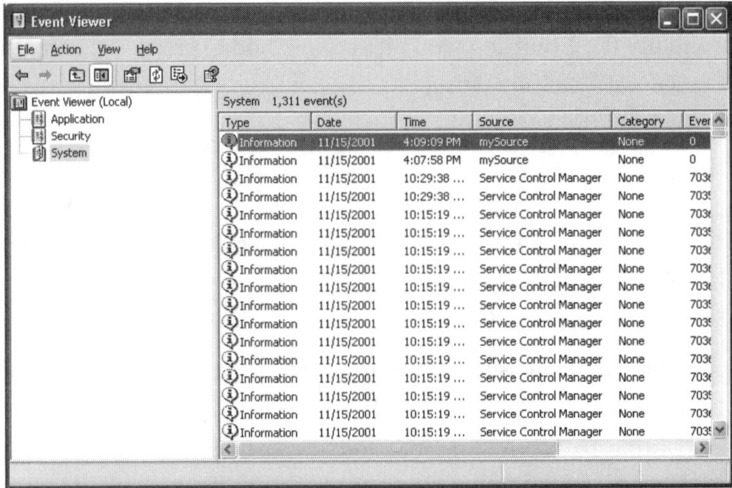

FIGURE 10.2: The message is displayed by time, date, and source in the System log.

To view the event text, double-click the event item in the Event Viewer. The Event Properties dialog will open, as shown in Figure 10.3. In the Description field, you will see the event text.

FIGURE 10.3: You can view event details, including the text description, by double-clicking in the Event Viewer.

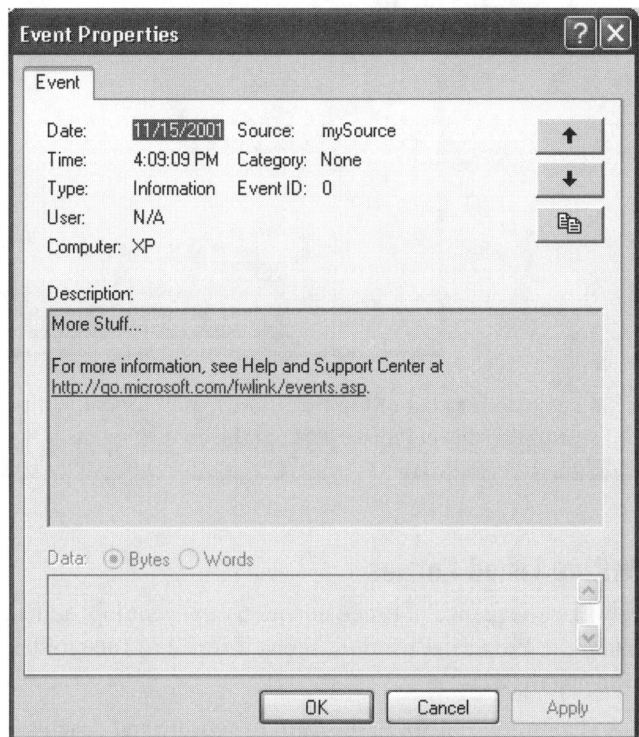

Viewing Event Logs in the Server Explorer

Rather than using Window XP's Event Viewer to view event log entries, you can see them in the Server Explorer. To do this, open the Server Explorer (choose View ➢ Server Explorer from the VB .NET menu) and expand the node for the system running the application to display the Event Logs node. Beneath this node, expand the event log of interest: Application, Security, or System. Finally, expand the application node to see the event log entries. For example, you can expand the mySource application node in the System log (created in Listing 10.3) to see the entries, as shown next.

Continued on next page

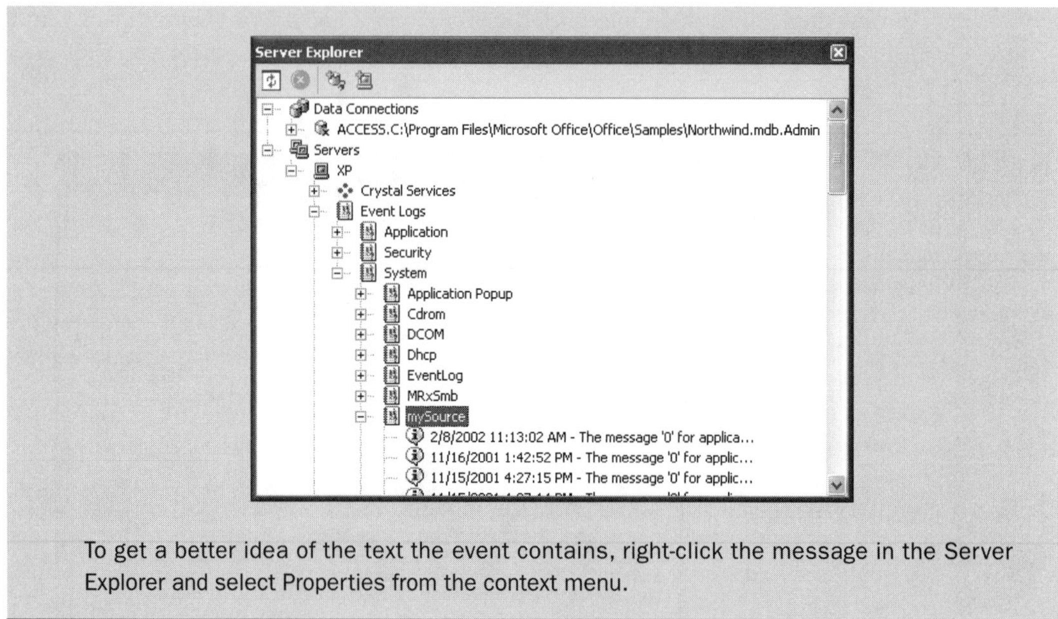

To get a better idea of the text the event contains, right-click the message in the Server Explorer and select Properties from the context menu.

Writing Timed Entries

To write a sequence of timed entries to an event log, add a new Timer control to your form. Using the Properties window, set its interval to **1000** milliseconds (1 second) and its Enabled property to **False**.

Add a Button control to the form to activate and deactivate the repeated entry writing. We'll use the same TextBox as in the previous example for entering the descriptive text to be written to the event log.

In the Timer's Elapsed event handler, add code to write the entry using the same `WriteLog` subroutine as in the previous example:

```
Private Sub Timer3_Elapsed(ByVal sender As Object, _
   ByVal e As System.Timers.ElapsedEventArgs) Handles Timer3.Elapsed
   WriteLog()
End Sub
```

Next, add code to the button's Click event handler that enables the Timer (and disables it when the user wants to stop writing to the event log):

```
Private Sub btnKeep_Click(ByVal sender As System.Object, _
   ByVal e As System.EventArgs) Handles btnKeep.Click
```

```
    If btnKeep.Text = "Keep Writing" Then
       Timer3.Enabled = True
       btnKeep.Text = "Stop"
    Else
       Timer3.Enabled = False
       btnKeep.Text = "Keep Writing"
    End If
 End Sub
```

WARNING Be careful of allowing a program—or the program's users—to have indefinite and unlimited access to writing to an event log. It's easy to use this kind of access to fill the event log, after which, no events are written. If your application attempts to write to a full log, an exception is generated.

The code for writing timed entries to an event log is shown in Listing 10.4.

Listing 10.4 Writing Timed Entries to the Event Log

```
Private Sub btnKeep_Click(ByVal sender As System.Object, _
   ByVal e As System.EventArgs) Handles btnKeep.Click
   If btnKeep.Text = "Keep Writing" Then
      Timer3.Enabled = True
      btnKeep.Text = "Stop"
   Else
      Timer3.Enabled = False
      btnKeep.Text = "Keep Writing"
   End If
End Sub

Private Sub Timer3_Elapsed(ByVal sender As Object, _
   ByVal e As System.Timers.ElapsedEventArgs) Handles Timer3.Elapsed
   WriteLog()
End Sub

Private Sub WriteLog()
   EventLog1.Source = "mySource"
   EventLog1.WriteEntry(txtEventLog.Text)
End Sub
```

Run the project, enter some text, and click Keep Writing. When you open Event Viewer (as described in the previous section), you'll see an event written to the System event log every second, as shown in Figure 10.4.

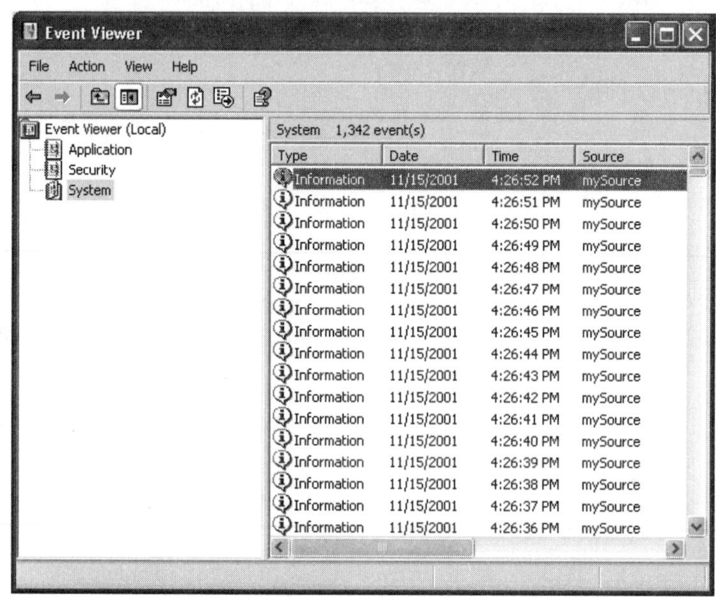

FIGURE 10.4: You can use the Timer control to add a regular time-based entry (depending on the Timer's Interval property) to an event log, such as the System log.

TIP In a real-world application, if you were creating a timed audit trail, you would probably also want to write crucial values as part of the event log entry. For example, you might record the current user ID and access levels.

Working with a ServiceController

A Windows service application generally has no visual interface, runs in the background as a kind of system utility, and is controlled by the Services applet in the Administrative section of the Windows Control Panel. The ServiceController component is used to connect to, and control the behavior of, existing services.

To see how this works, we'll create an application that displays the services on a system and lets the user start and stop them.

Displaying Services

To display the services, drag a ServiceController component from the Toolbox onto your form's tray. Next, add a ListBox control and four Button controls. The first button will be used to load the services into the ListBox, the second to start a service, the third to stop a service, and the fourth to clear the contents of the ListBox.

In the Load button's Click event handler, declare an array, `services`, of type `ServiceProcess.ServiceController`. Use the `GetServices` method of the ServiceController component to load the services into the array:

```
Dim services() As ServiceProcess.ServiceController
services = ServiceController1.GetServices
```

Next, use a `For` statement to loop through the array and add each item to the ListBox. The ServiceName property of each ServiceController contains the name of the description. The integer value of the Status property is converted into an English message to provide the current status of the service. The two properties are separated by a pair of dashes (--) as delimiters in the ListBox:

```
For i = 0 To services.Length - 1
   tmp = services(i).ServiceName
   If CInt(services(i).Status) = 1 Then
      tmp2 = "Status is stopped."
   ElseIf CInt(services(i).Status) = 4 Then
      tmp2 = "Status is started."
   End If
   lstServices.Items.Add(tmp & "--" & tmp2)
Next
```

Listing 10.5 shows the complete code for displaying services and their status.

Listing 10.5 Displaying Services and Their Status

```
Private Sub btnLoad_Click(ByVal sender As System.Object, _
   ByVal e As System.EventArgs) Handles btnLoad.Click
   Dim services() As ServiceProcess.ServiceController, i As Integer
   Dim tmp, tmp2 As String
   services = ServiceController1.GetServices
   lstServices.Items.Clear()
   For i = 0 To services.Length - 1
      tmp = services(i).ServiceName
      If CInt(services(i).Status) = 1 Then
         tmp2 = "Status is stopped."
      ElseIf CInt(services(i).Status) = 4 Then
         tmp2 = "Status is started."
      End If
      lstServices.Items.Add(tmp & "--" & tmp2)
   Next
End Sub
```

Run the project and click the Load button. You'll see a list of services and their status in the ListBox.

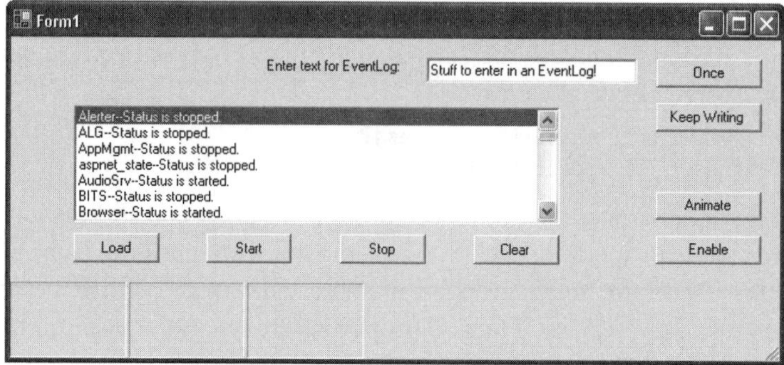

You can open the Services applet in the Administrative Tools section of Windows Control Panel to verify that the services displayed and their status correspond to those loaded by the ServiceController. Figure 10.5 shows an example of a Services window.

FIGURE 10.5: You can verify that the services displayed in your application match the Services applet.

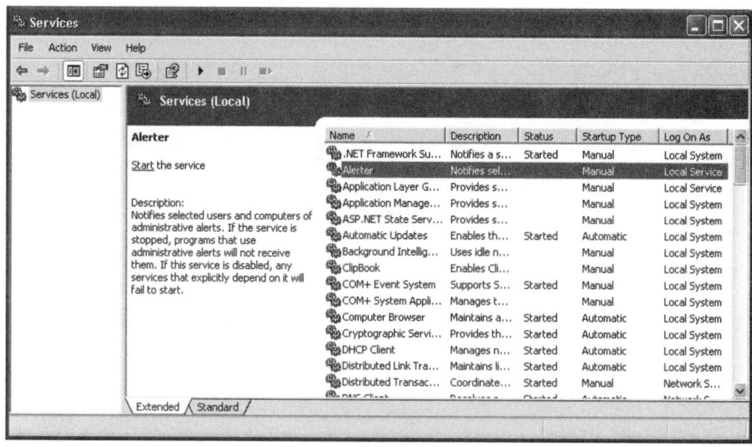

Taking this one step further, why not give users the opportunity to clear the ListBox if they want to start over without restarting the application? To do so, place the following code in the Clear button's Click event procedure:

```
Private Sub btnClear_Click(ByVal sender As System.Object, _
   ByVal e As System.EventArgs) Handles btnClear.Click
   lstServices.Items.Clear()
End Sub
```

Starting a Service

To start a service displayed in the ListBox, first create a function to parse the name of the service from the combined string representing the service's name and status (with the name and status separated by a pair of dashes). I've called the function `doTheSplit`, because it uses the `Split` string-manipulation function:

```
Function doTheSplit(ByVal inString As String) As String
   Dim tmpArray() As String
   tmpArray = Split(inString, "--")
   Return tmpArray(0)
End Function
```

The function declares an array of strings and reads the parameter passed to the function, `inString`, into the array using `--` as the delimiter for the `Split` function. It then returns the first element of the array.

All this is simply to obtain the name of the service. Back in the Click event handler for the Start button, create a new instance of a `ServiceProcess.ServiceController` object named `myController`. When `myController` is created, it takes as its argument the name of the selected item in the ListBox, passed through the `doTheSplit` function:

```
Dim myController As New ServiceProcess.ServiceController _
   (doTheSplit(lstServices.SelectedItem.ToString()))
```

Finally, invoke the `Start` method for the new ServiceController:

```
myController.Start()
```

The complete code for starting a service is shown in Listing 10.6.

Listing 10.6 Starting a Service

```
Private Sub btnStart_Click(ByVal sender As System.Object, _
   ByVal e As System.EventArgs) Handles btnStart.Click
   Dim myController As New ServiceProcess.ServiceController _
     (doTheSplit(lstServices.SelectedItem.ToString()))
   myController.Start()
End Sub

Function doTheSplit(ByVal inString As String) As String
   Dim tmpArray() As String
   tmpArray = Split(inString, "--")
   Return tmpArray(0)
End Function
```

Run the project, load the ListBox, and select a stopped service in the ListBox. The previously stopped service will start.

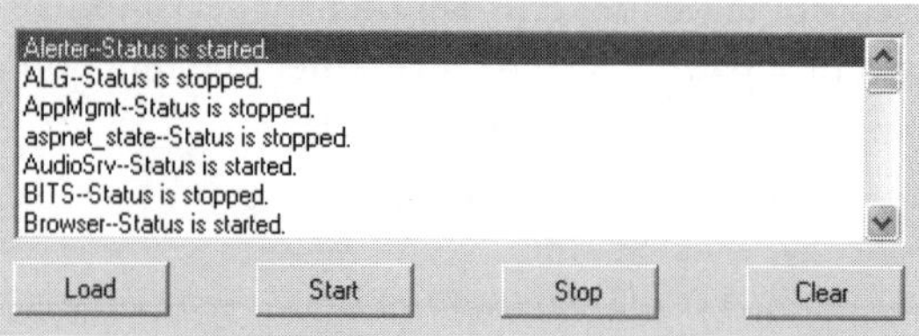

Stopping a Service

Shutting down a service works just like starting a service, except that a ServiceController property, CanStop, and a ServiceController method, `Stop`, are used instead of the ServiceController `Start` method. The CanStop property is interrogated to see if the service can be shut down. If the ServiceController's CanStop property evaluates to True, then a message is displayed and the service is shut down. Otherwise, a message is displayed stating that the service cannot be stopped:

```
If myController.CanStop Then
   MsgBox("Shutting down service " & _
      myController.ServiceName.ToString())
   myController.Stop()
Else
   MsgBox("Cannot shut service " & _
      myController.ServiceName.ToString())
End If
```

The complete code for stopping a service is shown in Listing 10.7.

Listing 10.7 Stopping a Service

```
Private Sub btnStop_Click(ByVal sender As Object, _
   ByVal e As System.EventArgs) Handles btnStop.Click
   Dim myController As New ServiceProcess.ServiceController _
      (doTheSplit(lstServices.SelectedItem.ToString()))
   If myController.CanStop Then
      MsgBox("Shutting down service " & _
         myController.ServiceName.ToString())
      myController.Stop()
   Else
      MsgBox("Cannot shut service " & _
         myController.ServiceName.ToString())
   End If
End Sub
```

```
Function doTheSplit(ByVal inString As String) As String
   Dim tmpArray() As String
   tmpArray = Split(inString, "--")
   Return tmpArray(0)
End Function
```

If you run the project, select a service in the ListBox, and click Stop, you will see a message letting you know that the service is stopping (if the service can be stopped).

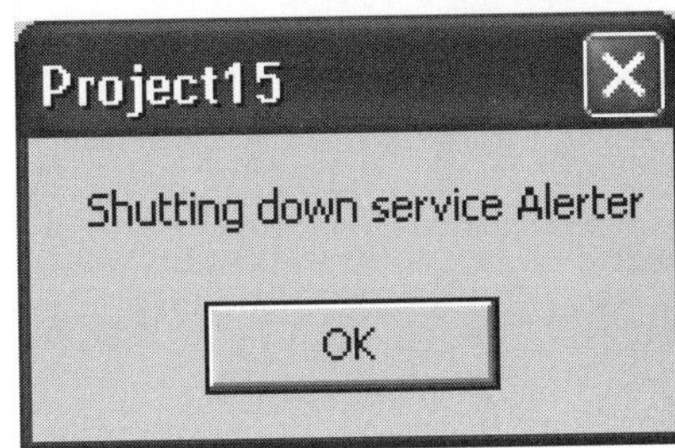

You can then reload the services back into the ListBox to verify that the service has indeed been stopped.

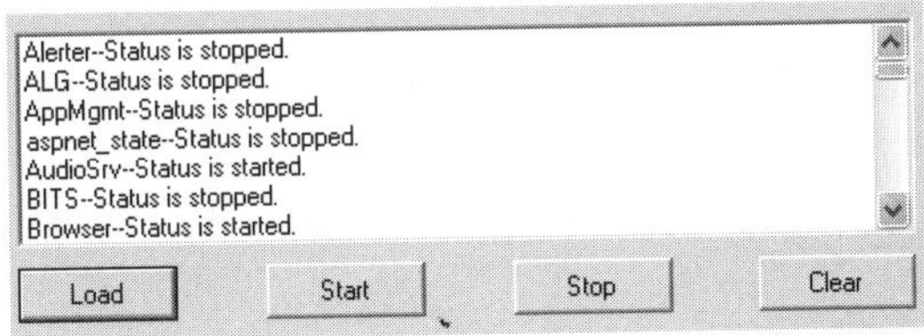

Summary

This chapter explained how to work with the Timer control, an all-around utility component that is a "most valuable player." You've also learned how to work with some of VB .NET's server components, specifically the EventLog and ServiceController components. These components give you easy access to a great deal of exciting functionality that previously took considerable work to program.

In the next chapter, you'll learn how to work with VB .NET's menu objects. Menus are necessary to almost all applications, and you'll find the .NET menu controls very easy to work with.

Chapter 11

Creating Menus

- Using the MainMenu control
- Creating an MDI Window menu
- Adding context menus
- Working with checked menu items
- Manipulating menus in code
- Reviewing auto-generated menu code
- Creating a menu structure dynamically at runtime

Menus are basic to most applications, and VB .NET provides two menu controls in the Toolbox: MainMenu and ContextMenu. The MainMenu control is used to add menu items, which are a form's top-level menu choices, such as a File menu. Each menu item itself has a menu items collection, such as the Save and Save As items on the hypothetical File menu. And each of these menu items can have their own menu items collection (if they have submenus), and so on. This may sound confusing, but in practice, it is not difficult to add menus.

The ContextMenu control is used to add pop-up menus, which are menu structures that are displayed when the user right-clicks an object, such as a button or form, associated with the ContextMenu control.

You can use these controls at design time, and in many cases create professional menus without ever needing to know anything about the underlying code. At the other extreme, you can instantiate menus in code at runtime without ever working with the menu design-time tools. In between the two poles, you can create a menu using the design-time tools associated with the menu controls, and then modify the menus dynamically, using program code, in response to changing application conditions.

This chapter takes you through all three scenarios. We'll start by looking at how to use the menu controls without any programming. Next, we'll look at some easy ways to modify menus on the fly once an application is running. Finally, I'll show you how to dynamically instantiate your own menus and menu items at runtime.

Using the MainMenu Control

When you add a MainMenu control from the Toolbox to a form, the control rests on the tray beneath the form along with the other nonvisual Toolbox controls. Figure 11.1 shows the MainMenu control added to the tray of the form used to demonstrate common dialogs in Chapter 9, "Working with Common Dialogs." (Since every common dialog that can be accessed by clicking a button should also be accessible using a menu, it makes sense to add a menu to this application.)

By adding a MainMenu control to the form, you automatically get the code that instantiates the menu and its objects. (For a look at that code, see the "Looking at the Code behind the Menus" section later in this chapter.) In addition, you get the design-time menu-creation tool "for free."

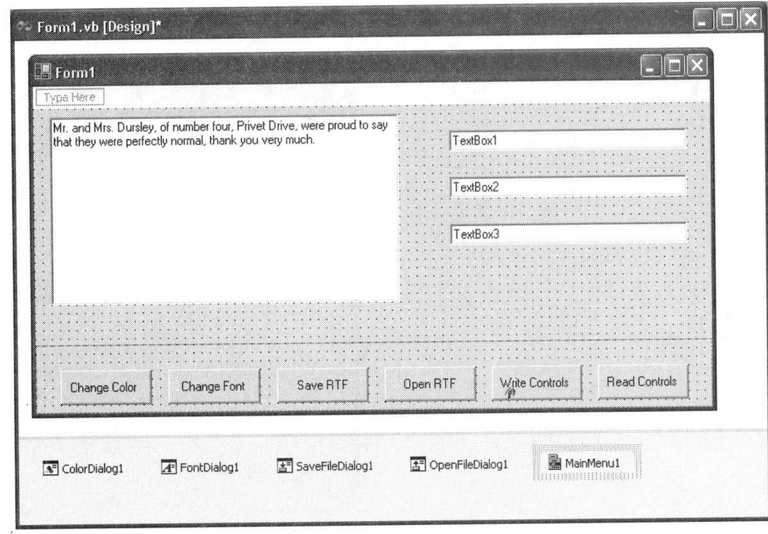

FIGURE 11.1: When you add a MainMenu control to a form, you can start typing in a menu (notice the Type Here box just below Form1 on the caption bar).

To get started with this, start entering menu text (also called a menu's *caption*). The first menu caption goes in the square marked Type Here, which you can see in the upper left of the form shown in Figure 11.1.

As you continue entering menu captions, more Type Here boxes appear.

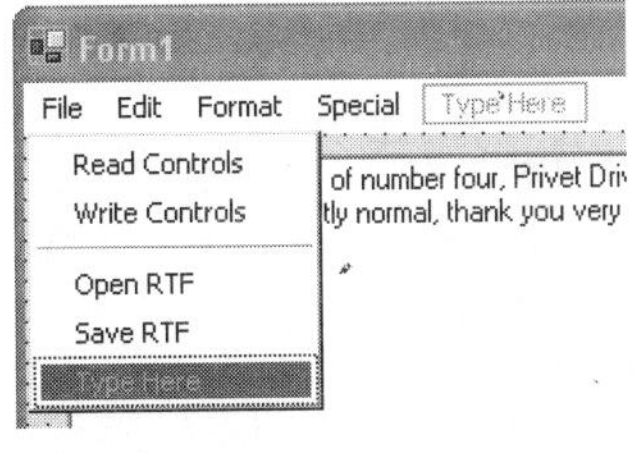

TIP To enable Alt key access to a menu item, use the & character, which will appear at runtime as an underline. For example, `&File` appears at runtime as File, and is accessed by holding down the Alt and F keys.

Generally, you can type in a menu item's text to the right of the last item in a row and at the bottom of a column of existing items.

You can also use the context menu to insert a new item between existing items, insert a separator, and to go into the edit names mode.

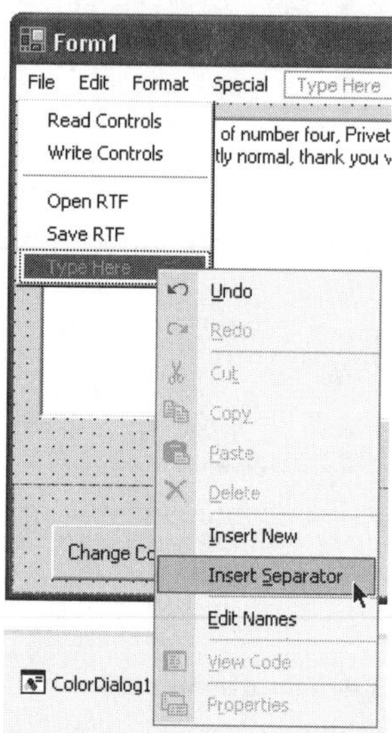

TIP You can also enter a menu separator the same way you could in VB6: just enter a hyphen (–) for the menu text.

Using MenuItems Collections

Using the MainMenu control, you can type in menu text to any depth you like. Here's an example of a Special menu with an Options menu item. Color, Fonts, and File Types are menu items "below" Options.

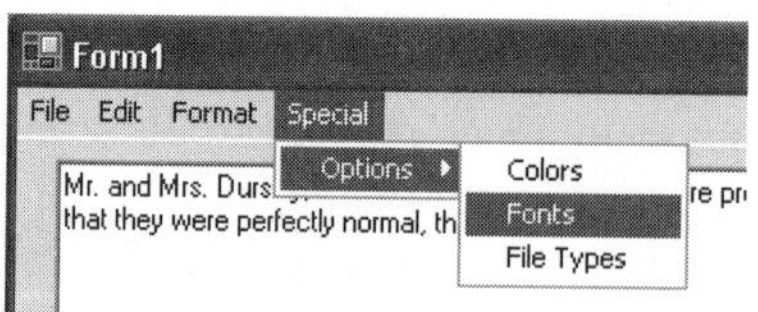

TIP As a matter of usability and user interface design, you should not create menus that contain more than three levels. In the example shown here, you could add one more level of "fly-out" menus, but that would be the limit.

This looks like a completely organic process of adding menu items. However, behind the scenes, .NET is creating menu items, known as MenuItem objects, and collections of MenuItems. In our example, File, Edit, Format, and Special are MenuItems that are part of the MenuItems collection of the MainMenu control. Options belongs to the MenuItems collection of Special. In turn, Colors, Fonts, and File Types belong to the MenuItems collection of Options.

This hierarchy may seem a wee bit complex, but as you'll see in the "Creating Menus Interactively" section later in this chapter, it does allow you to address every menu item in code by using the appropriate methods of the various MenuItems collections.

Each time you create the text for a menu item using the design-time interface, a MenuItem object is created and named. These MenuItems are named `MenuItem1`...`MenuItemN`, in the order in which they were created. You can see this in the Properties window.

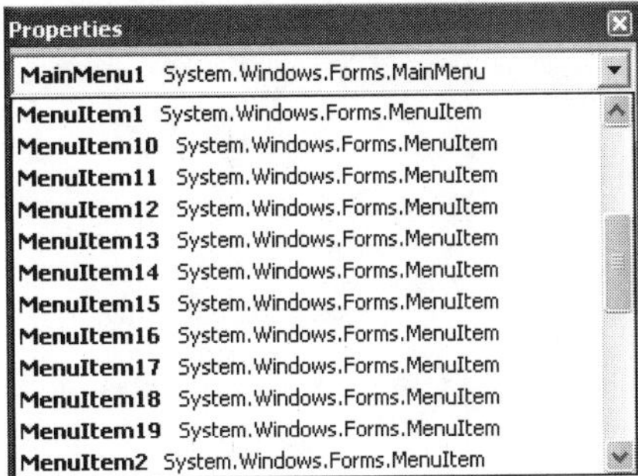

This naming convention produces a degree of opacity. There's no real way to know what, for example, `MenuItem15` is without individually inspecting its Text property using the Properties window.

Clearly, the names of at least those MenuItems that you plan to use in code should be changed to something intelligible. You can make these changes in the Properties window, or, more simply, in the MainMenu's edit names mode, which is accessed using the MainMenu's context menu.

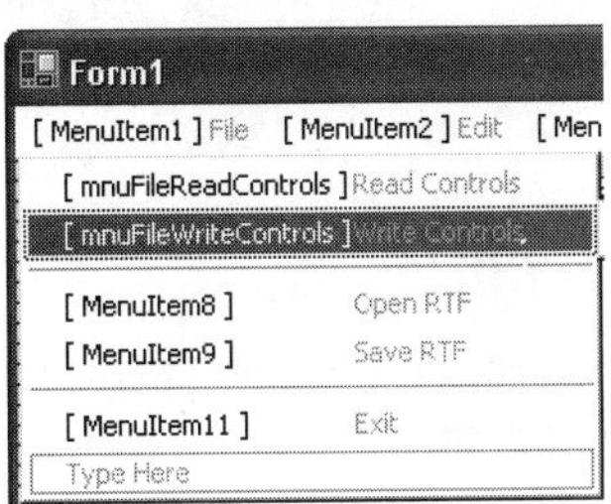

TIP It's a good idea to name MenuItems hierarchically, so you can tell where they fit in a menu structure at a glance (and so that "siblings" are near one another alphabetically in the Properties window). For example, on an Edit menu, the menu items Copy, Cut, and Paste might be named `mnuEditCopy`, `mnuEditCut`, and `mnuEditPaste`.

You can change the names of individual menu items using the Properties window. Another interesting property you'll see in the Properties window of a menu item is Shortcut, which sets the keyboard shortcut for access to that menu item.

If the ShowShortcut property is set to True, then the shortcut keys are displayed next to the menu item.

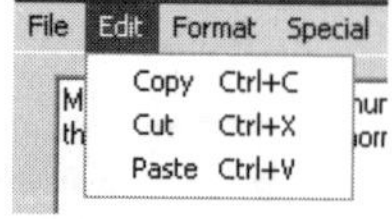

Responding to Menu Clicks

If you've named your menu items intelligibly, it becomes very easy to add their Click event handlers to existing event procedures, as shown in Listing 11.1. There's no need to rebuild functionality that already exists. The Code Editor's auto-completion feature will help you add menu item handlers to existing procedures.

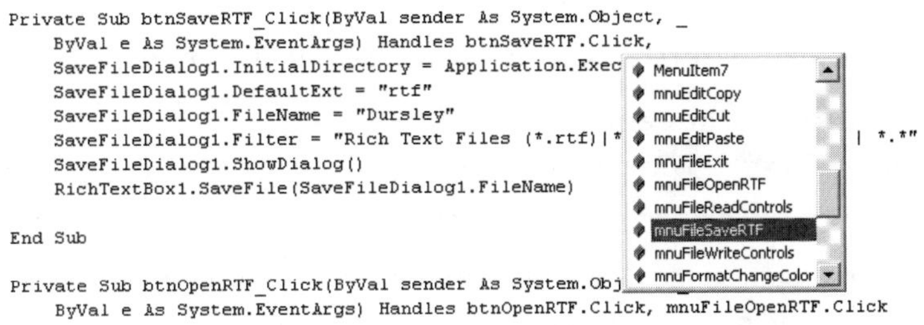

```
Private Sub btnSaveRTF_Click(ByVal sender As System.Object, _
    ByVal e As System.EventArgs) Handles btnSaveRTF.Click,
    SaveFileDialog1.InitialDirectory = Application.Exec
    SaveFileDialog1.DefaultExt = "rtf"
    SaveFileDialog1.FileName = "Dursley"
    SaveFileDialog1.Filter = "Rich Text Files (*.rtf)|*          | *.*"
    SaveFileDialog1.ShowDialog()
    RichTextBox1.SaveFile(SaveFileDialog1.FileName)

End Sub

Private Sub btnOpenRTF_Click(ByVal sender As System.Obj
    ByVal e As System.EventArgs) Handles btnOpenRTF.Click, mnuFileOpenRTF.Click
```

MenuItem7
mnuEditCopy
mnuEditCut
mnuEditPaste
mnuFileExit
mnuFileOpenRTF
mnuFileReadControls
mnuFileSaveRTF
mnuFileWriteControls
mnuFormatChangeColor

Listing 11.1 Adding a Menu Event to an Existing Event Handler

```
Private Sub btnSaveRTF_Click(ByVal sender As System.Object, _
   ByVal e As System.EventArgs) Handles btnSaveRTF.Click, _
   mnuFileSaveRTF.Click
   ...
End Sub
```

If you don't have an existing event procedure that does what your menu Click handler needs, it's easy to add new menu item Click event handlers in the usual fashion.

For a menu item named `mnuEditCopy`, the form, or *signature*, of the Click event procedure is as follows:

```
Private Sub mnuEditCopy_Click(ByVal sender As Object, _
   ByVal e As System.EventArgs) Handles mnuEditCopy.Click
```

But be of good cheer; you don't need to remember this. In the Code Editor, simply select the menu item from the drop-down Objects list. With the menu item selected in the Objects list, choose Click from the procedures drop-down list. The framework—signature and `End Sub` statement—for the Click event will be created for you.

TIP Just as with a control like a Button, you can double-click a menu in the designer, and the event handler will be created for you, which saves some steps.

Listing 11.2 shows Click event handlers created for the Copy, Cut, and Paste menu items.

Listing 11.2 Creating New Menu Item Click Event Handlers

```
Private Sub mnuEditCopy_Click(ByVal sender As Object, _
   ByVal e As System.EventArgs) Handles mnuEditCopy.Click
   RichTextBox1.Copy()
End Sub
```

```
Private Sub mnuEditCut_Click(ByVal sender As Object, _
   ByVal e As System.EventArgs) Handles mnuEditCut.Click
   RichTextBox1.Cut()
End Sub

Private Sub mnuEditPaste_Click(ByVal sender As Object, _
   ByVal e As System.EventArgs) _
   Handles mnuEditPaste.Click
   RichTextBox1.Paste()
End Sub
```

You can often respond to multiple events in a single "multicast" event procedure. Internal conditional statements determine the object that gives rise to the event (and which code should be processed). Listing 11.3 shows a single event procedure with the same functionality as the three procedures shown in Listing 11.2 (provided the menu items have the indicated text). Combining menu event handling code into a single procedure can often lead to more manageable code.

Listing 11.3 Handling Multiple Menu Items in One Procedure

```
Private Sub multiMenu(ByVal sender As Object, ByVal e As _
   System.EventArgs)Handles mnuEditCopy.Click, _
   mnuEditCut.Click, mnuEditPaste.Click
   Dim tmpSender As MenuItem = CType (sender, MenuItem)
   Select Case tmpSender.text
      Case "Copy"
         RichTextBox1.Copy()
      Case "Cut"
         RichTextBox1.Cut()
      Case "Paste"
         RichTextBox1.Paste()
   End Select
End Sub
```

Wiring an MDI Menu

In Chapter 6, "Working with Form Methods and Modules," I showed you how to create an MDI (Multiple Document Interface) application. An important part of the look and feel of an MDI application is a special MDI Window menu. This menu displays a list of all open MDI children and places a check mark next to the currently active child window.

To create an MDI Window menu, add a MainMenu control to the MDI parent form. Add a top-level menu item with the text **Window** (or **&Window**, for Alt key access).

Next, in the Properties window, select the Window menu item. Set its MdiList Property to True.

When you run the project, at the bottom of the Window menu, all open children forms are listed, with the active child form checked.

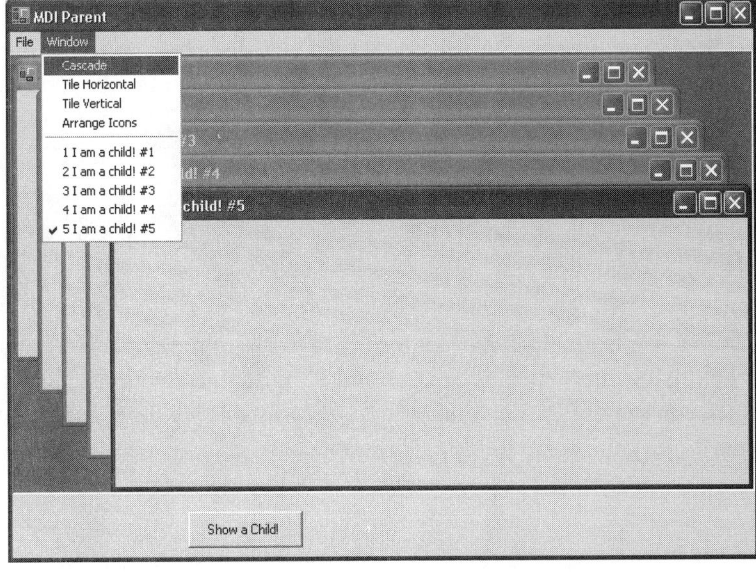

In an MDI application, it's also conventional to include the ability to arrange the child forms on the MDI Window menu. The code in Listing 11.4 shows how to use the `LayoutMdi` method and the enumeration constants that are the members of MdiLayout to arrange the child forms in an MDI application.

Listing 11.4 Coding the MDI Window Menu

```
Private Sub arrangeWin(ByVal sender As System.Object, _
   ByVal e As System.EventArgs) Handles mnuCascade.Click, _
   mnuArrangeIcons.Click, mnuTileHorizontal.Click, _
   mnuTileVertical.Click
   Select Case sender.text
      Case "&Cascade"
         Me.LayoutMdi(MdiLayout.Cascade)
      Case "&Tile Horizontal"
         Me.LayoutMdi(MdiLayout.TileHorizontal)
      Case "Tile &Vertical"
         Me.LayoutMdi(MdiLayout.TileVertical)
      Case "&Arrange Icons"
         Me.LayoutMdi(MdiLayout.ArrangeIcons)
   End Select
End Sub
```

Adding Context Menus

To add a context menu to your application, add a ContextMenu control to the form. Like the MainMenu control, the ContextMenu control will appear on the tray below the form. Next, select the ContextMenu control. You'll then be able to start entering menu item text for the context menu items, just as you can for MainMenu control menu item captions.

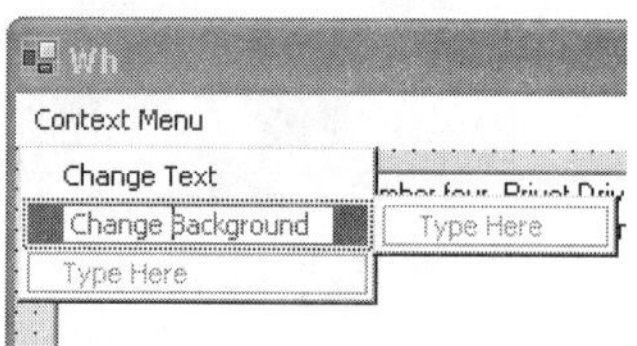

In other words, the ContextMenu control works in the same way as the MainMenu control, by organizing MenuItem objects and MenuItem collections. As with the MainMenu control, you can use the edit names mode—accessible via the ContextMenu control's context menu—to give the menu items recognizable names.

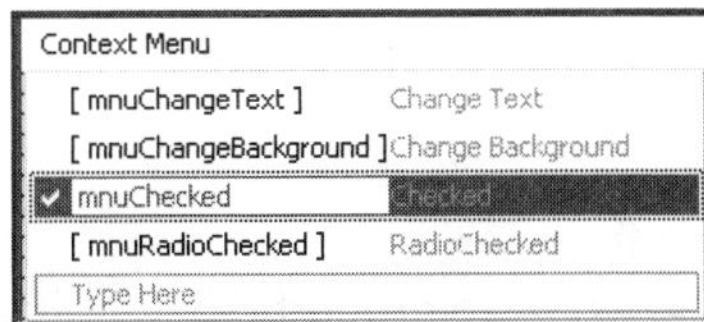

With the ContextMenu and its menu items in place, use the Properties window to connect it to a control (or form) by setting the ContextMenu property of the control to which you want to connect the context menu. Here is an example of assigning a context menu to a Change Color button:

With the ContextMenu property set, when the user right-clicks the connected object, the context menu will open.

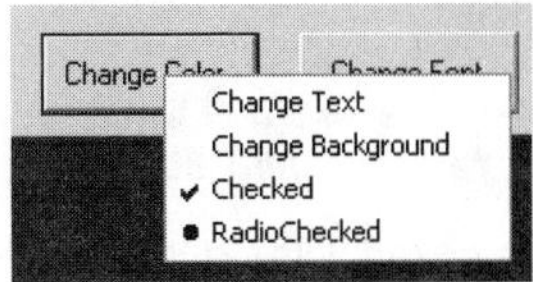

Working with Checked Menu Items

The context menu shown in the previous section shows two other MenuItem properties in action:

- Checked, which is a two-state property that, if True, displays a check mark next to the menu item
- RadioCheck, which is a three-state property that displays a round mark next to the menu item

For the RadioCheck mark to be displayed, both Checked and RadioCheck must be True.

Listing 11.5 demonstrates how to determine whether a menu item is checked and how to reverse its state (as well as the text for the menu item).

Listing 11.5 Checking and Unchecking a Menu Item

```
Private Sub mnuChecked_Click(ByVal sender As Object, _
   ByVal e As System.EventArgs) Handles mnuChecked.Click
   If mnuChecked.Checked = True Then
      mnuChecked.Checked = False
      mnuChecked.Text = "Unchecked"
   Else
      mnuChecked.Checked = True
      mnuChecked.Text = "Checked"
   End If
End Sub
```

NOTE It's often the case that you'll want to put some kind of logic in the procedure that toggles a menu item's check mark (it may be as simple as the change of menu item text shown in Listing 11.5, or it may be a lot more complex). But if all you need to do is toggle the menu item's checked state, you can do it more simply with this command: `mnuChecked.Checked = Not mnuChecked.Checked`.

Listing 11.6 shows how to reverse the state of a menu item with a RadioCheck mark (and change the text accordingly).

Listing 11.6 Working with a Menu Item's RadioChecked Property

```
Private Sub mnuRadioChecked_Click(ByVal sender As Object, _
   ByVal e As System.EventArgs) Handles mnuRadioChecked.Click
   If mnuRadioChecked.RadioCheck = False Then
      mnuRadioChecked.RadioCheck = True
      mnuRadioChecked.Checked = True
      mnuRadioChecked.Text = "RadioChecked"
   Else
```

```
        mnuRadioChecked.RadioCheck = False
        mnuRadioChecked.Checked = False
        mnuRadioChecked.Text = "UnRadioChecked"
    End If
End Sub
```

Manipulating Menus in Code

One of the easiest ways to manipulate menus in response to application state is to add a second MainMenu control to the form and toggle between the two menu structures. To see an example of this in action, add a Toggle Menus menu item to the original MainMenu structure we've created.

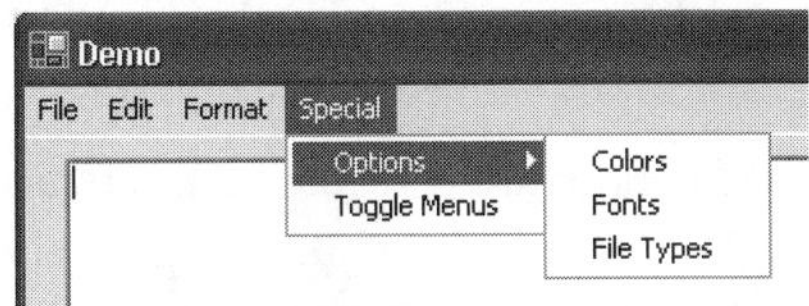

Next, add a new MainMenu control to the form. As you can see, the menu items that make up this menu structure are pretty fantastic, so let's give the menu item that toggles back to the first menu the text "Back to Reality."

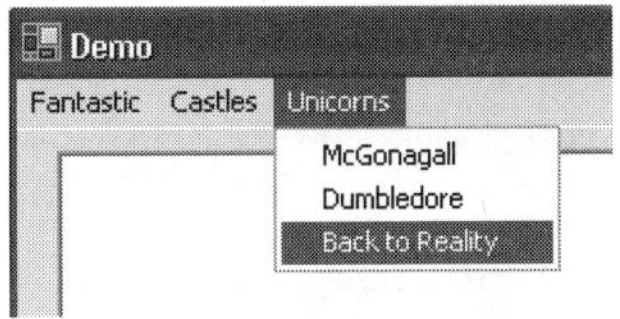

NOTE By default, the first MainMenu control added to a form will be displayed for you to add and edit menu items. To add (and edit) menu items that are part of the second MainMenu structure, make sure that the second MainMenu control is selected.

To toggle between the two MainMenu controls, assign the menu you want to be active to the form's Menu property, as shown in Listing 11.7.

Listing 11.7 Toggling between Menus

```
Private Sub mnuToggle_Click(ByVal sender As Object, _
   ByVal e As System.EventArgs) Handles mnuToggle.Click
   Me.Menu = MainMenu2
End Sub

Private Sub mnuBackToReality_Click(ByVal sender As System.Object, _
   ByVal e As System.EventArgs) Handles mnuBackToReality.Click
   Me.Menu = MainMenu1
End Sub
```

It's also easy to use a variety of coding techniques to add one or more menu items to a menu structure dynamically at runtime. For a first example, let's add the Change Background menu item from the context menu structure (created in the "Adding Context Menus" section earlier in this chapter) to the fantastic `MainMenu2`. The item will be added to the Unicorns menu.

Remembering that collections are zero-based, the Unicorns menu item can be referred to as `MainMenu2.MenuItems(2)` because it is the third top-level menu item in `MainMenu2`. We can use the `Add` method of the `MainMenu2.MenuItems(2)` MenuItems collection to add and position the Change Background menu item. To place it in the final, or fourth, position on the Unicorns menu, give it an index value of 3. The following line of code adds the Change Background item in the fourth position of `MainMenu2`'s Unicorn menu:

```
MainMenu2.MenuItems(2).MenuItems.Add((3), mnuChangeBackground)
```

Similarly, the MenuItems collection `AddRange` method can be used to add a set of MenuItems to a MenuItem. The following statement adds two more menu items to the bottom of the Unicorns menu:

```
MainMenu2.MenuItems(2).MenuItems.AddRange (New _
   System.Windows.Forms.MenuItem() {mnuChangeText, mnuRadioChecked})
```

Finally, the `CloneMenu` method appends an entire menu item structure to a menu item. For example, let's take the Options menu—consisting of the Options menu item and three subitems (shown at the beginning of this section)—and clone it to the bottom of the Unicorns menu. The Options menu item happens to be named `MenuItem17`. Here's the code for replicating the Options menu structure on the bottom of the Unicorns menu:

```
MainMenu2.MenuItems(2).MenuItems.Add(MenuItem17.CloneMenu)
```

TIP Whatever method you use to add menu items to an existing menu structure, you get the existing functionality of the added menu items—such as Click event handlers—with no extra work.

Listing 11.8 shows placing code in the mnuToggle Click event handler that uses the `Add`, `AddRange`, and `CloneMenu` methods to add these menu items.

Listing 11.8 Programmatically Adding Menu Items (Using the *Add*, *AddRange*, and *CloneMenu* Methods)

```
Private Sub mnuToggle_Click(ByVal sender As Object, _
   ByVal e As System.EventArgs) Handles mnuToggle.Click
   'Add the item
   MainMenu2.MenuItems(2).MenuItems.Add((3), mnuChangeBackground)
   'Add a set of items using AddRange
   MainMenu2.MenuItems(2).MenuItems.AddRange (New _
      System.Windows.Forms.MenuItem() {mnuChangeText, mnuRadioChecked})
   'Clone a menu structure
   MainMenu2.MenuItems(2).MenuItems.Add(MenuItem17.CloneMenu)
   Me.Menu = MainMenu2
End Sub
```

When you run this code, you'll see the Unicorns menu with the additional items.

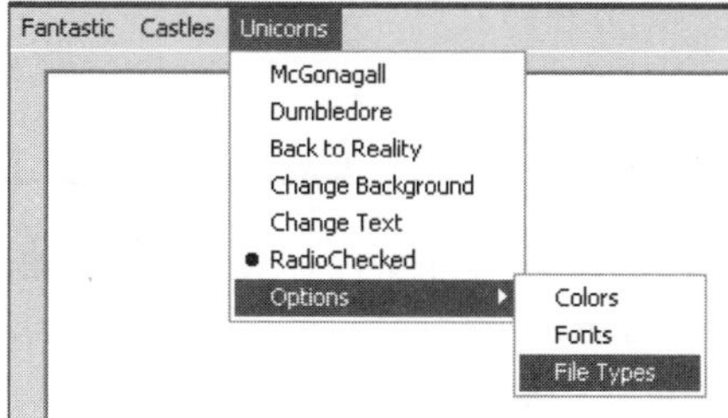

Looking at the Code Behind the Menus

By now, we've got some fairly complex menu structures going. Before the end of this chapter, I plan to show you how to instantiate your own menu structures in code without using the Toolbox and without visually adding controls to a form.

In order to understand how to do this, let's create a new form with a very simple menu structure, as shown in Figure 11.2.

This simple menu structure has two top-level menu items, named `mnuFile` and `mnuSpecial`. Beneath the `mnuFile` menu are two menu items: `mnuFileNew` and `mnuFileExit`. Beneath `mnuSpecial` is the `mnuSpecialOptions` item. So, this simple menu structure has a total of five menu items.

All of the auto-generated menu code is in the Windows Form Designer–generated code, so you'll need to click to expand this region in the Code Editor to view the code. (For an explanation of hidden regions in the Code Editor, see Chapter 6.)

First, the MainMenu and each MenuItem are declared as of type MainMenu (or MenuItem). To keep this simpler, we'll be following a MenuItem object through the auto-generated code.

FIGURE 11.2: A very simple menu structure

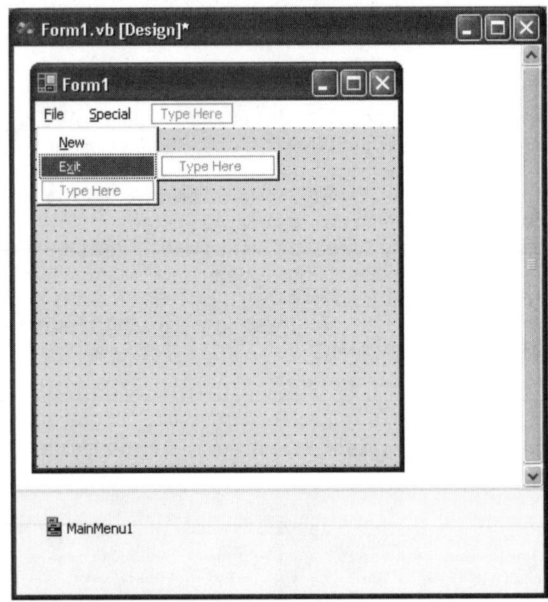

The declaration uses the `Friend` access modifier (restricted to the program) and the `WithEvents` keyword to indicate that event procedures will be associated with the object:

```
Friend WithEvents MainMenu1 As System.Windows.Forms.MainMenu
Friend WithEvents mnuFile As System.Windows.Forms.MenuItem
```

Next, each object is instantiated using the `New` keyword:

```
Me.mnuFile = New System.Windows.Forms.MenuItem()
```

The properties of each MenuItem are assigned, along with MenuItems that belong in its MenuItems collection:

```
'mnuFile
'
Me.mnuFile.Index = 0
Me.mnuFile.MenuItems.AddRange _
  (New System.Windows.Forms.MenuItem() {Me.mnuFileNew, Me.mnuFileExit})
Me.mnuFile.Text = "&File"
```

Other properties, if they were not the default (such as `Checked = True`), would appear in this section.

Finally, after all of the properties have been assigned, and the MenuItem collections has been properly set up, the MainMenu object is assigned as the value of the form Menu property.

```
Me.Menu = Me.MainMenu1
```

Put this way, the code for creating the menu structures does not seem very difficult (you'll find the code in Listing 11.9). As I'll show you in the next section, you can follow a similar track to create menus dynamically at runtime.

Listing 11.9 Auto-generated Code for the Simple Menu

```
...
Friend WithEvents MainMenu1 As System.Windows.Forms.MainMenu
Friend WithEvents mnuFile As System.Windows.Forms.MenuItem
Friend WithEvents mnuSpecial As System.Windows.Forms.MenuItem
Friend WithEvents mnuSpecialOptions As System.Windows.Forms.MenuItem
Friend WithEvents mnuFileNew As System.Windows.Forms.MenuItem
Friend WithEvents mnuFileExit As System.Windows.Forms.MenuItem
...
'NOTE: The following procedure is required by the Windows Form Designer
'It can be modified using the Windows Form Designer.
'Do not modify it using the code editor.
<System.Diagnostics.DebuggerStepThrough()>
Private Sub InitializeComponent()
Me.MainMenu1 = New System.Windows.Forms.MainMenu()
Me.mnuFile = New System.Windows.Forms.MenuItem()
Me.mnuSpecial = New System.Windows.Forms.MenuItem()
Me.mnuSpecialOptions = New System.Windows.Forms.MenuItem()
Me.mnuFileNew = New System.Windows.Forms.MenuItem()
Me.mnuFileExit = New System.Windows.Forms.MenuItem()
'
'MainMenu1
'
Me.MainMenu1.MenuItems.AddRange _
   (New System.Windows.Forms.MenuItem() {Me.mnuFile, Me.mnuSpecial})
'
'mnuFile
'
Me.mnuFile.Index = 0
Me.mnuFile.MenuItems.AddRange _
  (New System.Windows.Forms.MenuItem() {Me.mnuFileNew, Me.mnuFileExit})
Me.mnuFile.Text = "&File"
'
'mnuSpecial
'
Me.mnuSpecial.Index = 1
Me.mnuSpecial.MenuItems.AddRange _
   (New System.Windows.Forms.MenuItem() {Me.mnuSpecialOptions})
Me.mnuSpecial.Text = "&Special"
'
'mnuSpecialOptions
'
Me.mnuSpecialOptions.Index = 0
Me.mnuSpecialOptions.Text = "&Options"
'
```

```
'mnuFileNew
'
Me.mnuFileNew.Index = 0
Me.mnuFileNew.Text = "&New"
'
'mnuFileExit
'
Me.mnuFileExit.Index = 1
Me.mnuFileExit.Text = "E&xit"
...
Me.Menu = Me.MainMenu1
```

Creating Menus Interactively

Now that you understand how the auto-generated menu code works, you should be able to implement your own version. Let's work through an example. The form shown in Figure 11.3 will serve as the user interface. Clicking the button on the top left will create the MainMenu. Using this form, you can also create top-level menus and assign menu items to them.

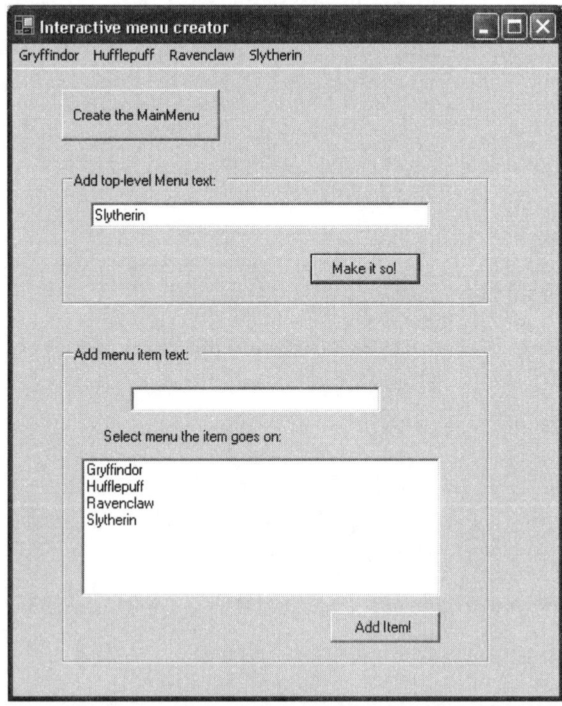

FIGURE 11.3: Once the MainMenu has been instantiated, you can use the Add method of the MenuItems collection to add top-level menus.

Creating the Main Menu

To create the MainMenu, declare a variable, `ourMenu`, of type MainMenu:

```
Private ourMenu As MainMenu
```

Next, instantiate the MainMenu and assign it to the form's Menu property:

```
ourMenu = New MainMenu()
Me.Menu = ourMenu
```

The code for creating a MainMenu is shown in Listing 11.10. To create the MainMenu, run the project and click the Create the MainMenu button.

WARNING If you attempt to add menu items before instantiating the MainMenu object, you will get a runtime error.

Listing 11.10 Creating a MainMenu

```
Public Class Form1
    Inherits System.Windows.Forms.Form
Private ourMenu As MainMenu
...
Private Sub btnMainMenu_Click(ByVal sender As System.Object, _
   ByVal e As System.EventArgs) Handles btnMainMenu.Click
   ourMenu = New MainMenu()
   Me.Menu = ourMenu
End Sub
```

Adding Top-Level Menus

Next, write the procedure for adding top-level menus. Declare a variable of type MenuItem for holding top-level menu items:

```
Private ourTop As MenuItem
```

Instantiate it with the text supplied by the user and add the text to the ListBox (so that users can pick top-level menus for the menu items they create):

```
Dim itemString As String = txtTopLevel.Text
ourTop = New MenuItem(itemString)
ourMenu.MenuItems.Add(ourTop)
lstTopLevel.Items.Add(itemString)
```

Listing 11.11 shows the code for creating top-level menus.

Listing 11.11 Creating Top-Level Menus

```
Private ourTop As MenuItem
...
Private Sub btnTopMnu_Click(ByVal sender As System.Object, _
   ByVal e As System.EventArgs) Handles btnTopMnu.Click
   Dim itemString As String = txtTopLevel.Text
   ourTop = New MenuItem(itemString)
   ourMenu.MenuItems.Add(ourTop)
   lstTopLevel.Items.Add(itemString)
End Sub
```

Adding Menu Items

Next, write the procedure for adding menu items. First, `ourItem`, a variable of type MenuItem, is declared `WithEvents`, so VB .NET knows that an event procedure may be associated with the object:

```
Private WithEvents ourItem As MenuItem
```

Next, instantiate the MenuItem with the text supplied by the user and associate it with an event handler named menuClick:

```
ourItem = New MenuItem(txtItemText.Text, New System.EventHandler _
      (AddressOf Me.menuClick))
```

Finally, add the new menu item to the top-level menu chosen in the ListBox:

```
ourMenu.MenuItems(i).MenuItems.Add(ourItem)
```

This uses the `Add` method to add `ourItem` at the bottom of the top-level menu item, using the `Count` method of the MenuItems collection of the top-level menu item selected.

The code for creating menu items is shown in Listing 11.12.

Listing 11.12 Creating Menu Items

```
Private WithEvents ourItem As MenuItem
...
Private Sub btnAddItem_Click(ByVal sender As System.Object, _
   ByVal e As System.EventArgs) Handles btnAddItem.Click
   Dim i As Integer
   i = lstTopLevel.SelectedIndex
   ourItem = New MenuItem(txtItemText.Text, New System.EventHandler _
      (AddressOf Me.menuClick))    ourMenu.MenuItems(i).MenuItems.Add(ourItem)
End Sub
```

When you run the project, start by creating the MainMenu. Next, add some top-level menu items. Finally, add menu items beneath the top-level menus, as shown in Figure 11.4.

FIGURE 11.4:
Menu items can be added to each top-level menu and positioned using the index argument of the Add method.

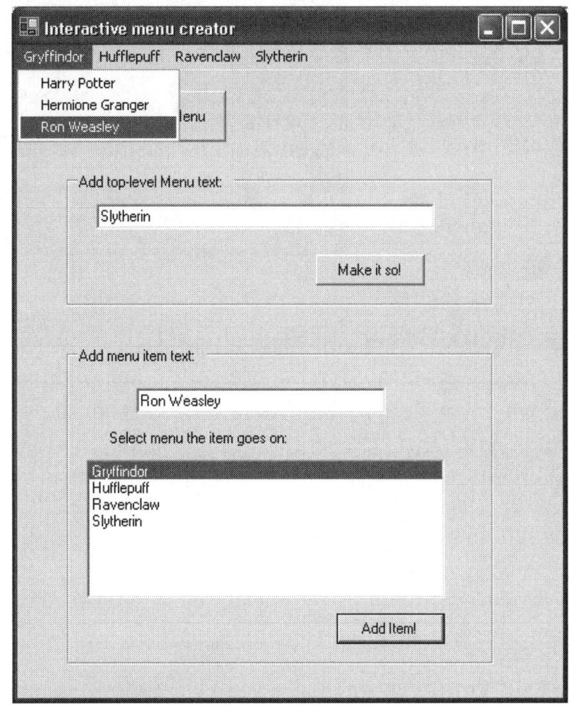

Creating an Event Handler for Menu Items

We still need to create an event handler for the `ourItem` menu items. The code for doing this, and for identifying the menu that triggered the event, is shown in Listing 11.13.

Listing 11.13 Creating an Event Handler for the Menu Items

```
Private Sub menuClick(ByVal sender As Object, ByVal e As System.EventArgs)
      MessageBox.Show ("You clicked " & sender.text & ".", _
      "Interactive Menu Creator!"
   End Sub
```

With the project running, when you click a menu item, you'll see the appropriate message.

Coded Menus versus Menu Controls

The menu objects created in the previous example differ somewhat from the menu objects created when you drag a MainMenu control from the Toolbox to your form's tray and start entering menu items. The menu objects created in usual drag-and-drop fashion do not distinguish between top-level menu items and lower-level menu items, whereas the code in this example does. Top-level menu items were declared:

```
Private ourTop As MenuItem
```

Lower-level menu items were declared as follows:

```
Private WithEvents ourItem As MenuItem
```

So, in the object hierarchy in this example, `ourItem` menu items have an event handler associated with them, and `ourTop` menu items do not. This is a not unreasonable distinction, as there is usually no reason to use a top-level menu item's event handler. However, it is also reasonable to go the other way, as does the form-generated code, and create only one kind of menu item.

The moral here is that .NET's visual development environment is not black magic. Everything that the form designer and Toolbox do for you, you can do yourself in code. Whether it makes more sense to do this or to rely on .NET's visual design facility depends on the circumstances. However, some important functionality requires object instantiation on the fly in response to a change in a program condition (or user action). It's important that the ability to do this is part of your programming toolkit. And, as you've seen in this example, it is not necessarily very hard to do.

Summary

In this chapter, you've learned how to use the MainMenu control to create application menus (more technically, structures of MenuItems). You've also learned how to create context menus using the ContextMenu control and how to programmatically control MenuItems.

Menus are very important—almost every application has one—and it is necessary to learn how to add them to your programs. This chapter showed you how to work with menus, but there was also a subtext. Think of the controls in the Toolbox as objects that cause code auto-generation in a form. You can create this code yourself, meaning that the objects involved can be instantiated dynamically at runtime.

The next chapter covers an important facility that, like menus, is found in a great many applications: printing.

CHAPTER 12

Printing from an Application

- Using printing components and controls
- Adding a PrintDocument component
- Coding the PrintPage event
- Displaying the Page Setup dialog
- Displaying the Print dialog
- Adding a print preview

A great many applications need a print facility of some sort, so enabling printing from an application is an important subject. When it comes to printing from a VB .NET project, there is good news and bad news.

First, the bad news: You are programmatically responsible, using the methods of the .NET Graphics object, for creating the content that will be printed. This works in the same way as using the Graphics object to draw on the screen, as explained in Chapter 6, "Working with Form Methods and Modules."

The good news is that VB .NET supplies a number of controls and components that encapsulate the dialogs and interface that involve printing. This means that a great deal of the interface work is done for you. For example, you can have print preview functionality for the price of adding a control to your form and making a Properties window setting. In addition, your print-related dialogs, like the other common dialogs covered in Chapter 9, "Working with Common Dialogs" will have standard features and a look and feel familiar to users.

This chapter explains the mechanics of using the controls and components that are related to printing.

Using Printing Components and Controls

VB .NET provides five components and controls for printing-relating tasks, including three common dialogs. Table 12.1 shows the components and controls in the Toolbox (on the Windows Forms tab) that are related to printing and briefly explains their functionality.

TABLE 12.1: Printing Components and Controls

Object	Purpose
PrintDocument	Used to add the logic that sends a Graphics object to the printer.
PageSetupDialog	A common dialog control used to set page properties such as orientation and margins.
PrintDialog	A common dialog control used to select the printer and set printer properties.
PrintPreviewControl	Used to display a preview of a PrintDocument. However, it is without user interface (other than the document display). Unless you want to build your own user interface, you should use the PrintPreviewDialog instead.
PrintPreviewDialog	A common dialog control used to display the previewed image. It provides standard user interface tools for displaying and printing the preview.

Printing a Page

In its simplest form, printing a page involves three steps:

1. Add a PrintDocument component to a form.

2. Add code to the PrintDocument's PrintPage event that specifies what is to be printed.
3. Call the `Print` method of the PrintDocument.

To see this in practice, let's go through the three basic steps.

Adding a PrintDocument Component

Add a PrintDocument component to an open form by double-clicking PrintDocument in the Toolbox. The PrintDocument component will appear below the form, rather than on the form itself. Step one is now complete.

Adding Code to the PrintPage Event

In the Code Editor, create the event-handling framework for the PrintDocument's PrintPage event in the usual fashion (select the PrintDocument in the Objects list in the upper left of the Code Editor, then select PrintPage from the upper-right Procedures list):

```
Private Sub PrintDocument1_PrintPage(ByVal sender As Object, _
   ByVal e As System.Drawing.Printing.PrintPageEventArgs) Handles _
   PrintDocument1.PrintPage
   ...
End Sub
```

The Graphics property of PrintPageEventArgs is used to get the Graphics object that will "paint" the page that is printed, as in this example:

```
e.Graphics.DrawString("Harold", New Font("Arial", 12, _
      FontStyle.Regular), Brushes.Black, 100, 100)
```

This will print the text string "Harold" in 12-point Arial, starting at position 100, 100. Listing 12.1 shows the PrintPage event procedure for printing this (important to the author) text string.

Listing 12.1 Using the PrintPage Event to Print Text

```
Private Sub PrintDocument1_PrintPage(ByVal sender As Object, _
   ByVal e As System.Drawing.Printing.PrintPageEventArgs) Handles _
   PrintDocument1.PrintPage
   e.Graphics.DrawString("Harold", New Font("Arial", 12, _
      FontStyle.Regular), Brushes.Black, 100, 100)
End Sub
```

Invoking the Print Method

The third, and final, step is to invoke the `Print` method of the PrintDocument object, typically in a MenuItem or Button control Click event handler. For example, in `mnuPrint`'s Click event handler, add the following:

```
Private Sub mnuPrint_Click(ByVal sender As System.Object, _
```

```
    ByVal e As System.EventArgs) Handles mnuPrint.Click
    PrintDocument1.Print()
End Sub
```

If you run this and fire the mnuPrint Click event, your default printer will print "Harold" in 12-point Arial.

So far, this is pretty easy. But note that you are responsible for using the Graphics object passed by the PrintPage event to generate anything you want to print.

In addition to text, you can easily use the passed Graphics object to print shapes. For example, using code explained in Chapter 6, you could print a red circle:

```
Private Sub PrintDocument1_PrintPage(ByVal sender As Object, _
    ByVal e As System.Drawing.Printing.PrintPageEventArgs) Handles _
    PrintDocument1.PrintPage
    Dim thePen As New Drawing.Pen(System.Drawing.Color.Red, 10)
    e.Graphics.DrawEllipse(thePen, 200, 190, 100, 100)
End Sub
```

More on Print Events

The PrintDocument control has some additional events, BeginPrint and EndPrint, that can be used for preprint and postprint processing. For example, EndPrint can be used to display a message stating that printing has completed.

The logic within a PrintPage event can get fairly complex, and, as I've already disclaimed, this chapter explains only simple cases. More advanced printing code might loop through multiple controls in a form's control collections, printing the contents of each in a standard way. In addition, a StreamReader might be used to parse each line of a file so that it could be printed. For an example that loops through an entire control collection and employs a StreamReader (in the context of saving, rather than printing, control contents), see Chapter 9, "Working with Common Dialogs."

Building a Simple Printing Demo

The printing functionality described in the previous section will generally be wrapped in a standardized user interface. To see how this works, add a TextBox control to a form. Name the TextBox txtTextToPrint and set its Multiline property to True using the Properties window. This TextBox will be used to allow the user to enter text that will be printed.

Next, add a MainMenu control and four MenuItems: PageSetup, PrintSetup, PrintPreview, and Print.

Finally, add a PrintDocument component and PageSetupDialog, PrintDialog, and PrintPreviewDialog controls to the form. Your form should look like Figure 12.1 in design mode. It is now ready to be wired.

FIGURE 12.1: The menu items in the simple printing demo application access the functionality of the printing controls and components.

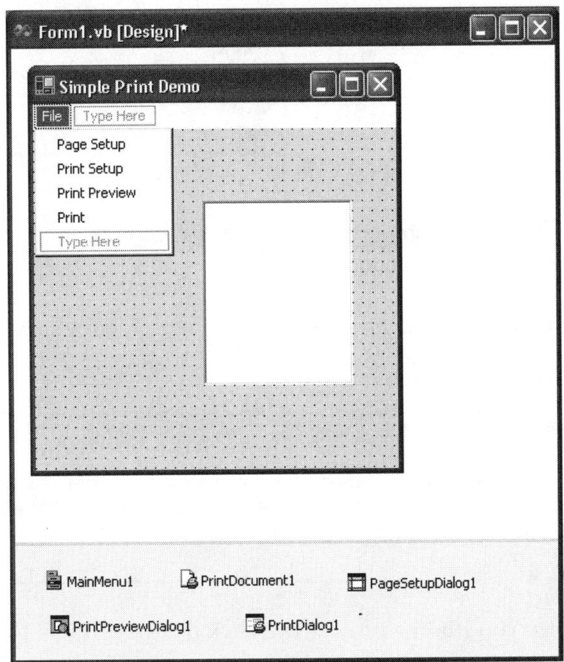

Using the PageSetupDialog Control

The PageSetupDialog control is used to select paper, orientation, and page margin options. Also, a number of properties change the runtime appearance and behavior of the Page Setup dialog. For example, if AllowPrinter is set to False, the Printer button in the lower-right corner of the Page Setup dialog box is disabled. When AllowPrinter is True, the Printer button invokes a printer selection dialog.

To activate the PageSetupDialog control, use the Properties window to set the Document property of this object to the PrintDocument.

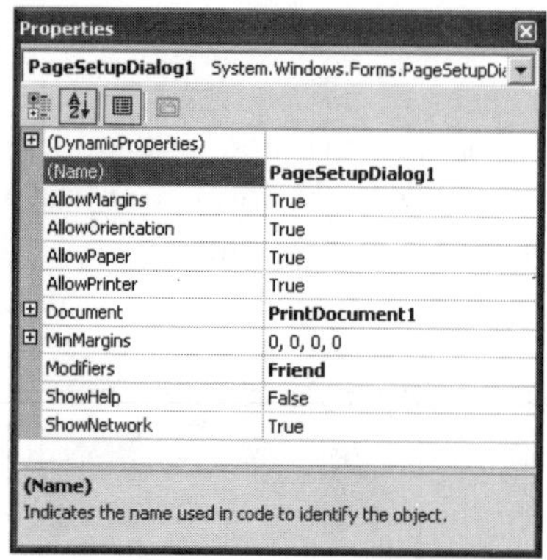

TIP

The Document property of the PageSetupDialog (and other print-related dialog controls) can also be set in code.

Next, add an invocation to the PageSetupDialog's `ShowDialog` method in the Page Setup menu Click event handler, as shown in Listing 12.2.

Listing 12.2 Displaying the Page Setup Dialog

```
Private Sub mnuPageSetup_Click(ByVal sender As System.Object, _
   ByVal e As System.EventArgs) Handles mnuPageSetup.Click
   PageSetupDialog1.ShowDialog()
End Sub
```

When you run the project and click the menu item, the Page Setup dialog is displayed.

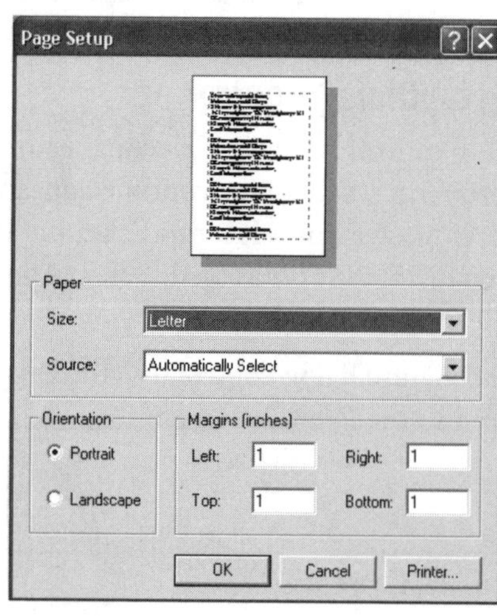

Changing the options in the Page Setup dialog changes the way the Graphics object in the associated PrintDocument PrintPage handler is printed.

TIP The easiest way to verify that changing the settings in this dialog box is having an effect is to change the paper orientation and then preview the page. Previewing the page is explained in the "Using the PrintPreviewDialog Control" section later in this chapter.

Using the PrintDialog Control

The PrintDialog control is used to select a printer and set its properties. The Document property of the PrintDialog must be associated with the related PrintDocument, either using the Properties window or in code.

In addition, at design time, you can set some properties that change the runtime behavior of the dialog. For example, if AllowPrintToFile is set to False, then the Print to File check box is not displayed.

Once the Document property has been set, the dialog can be displayed via its `ShowDialog` method, as shown in Listing 12.3.

Listing 12.3 Displaying the Print Dialog

```
Private Sub mnuPrintSetup_Click(ByVal sender As System.Object, _
   ByVal e As System.EventArgs) Handles mnuPrintSetup.Click
   PrintDialog1.ShowDialog()
End Sub
```

When the user invokes this method, a standard Print dialog is displayed.

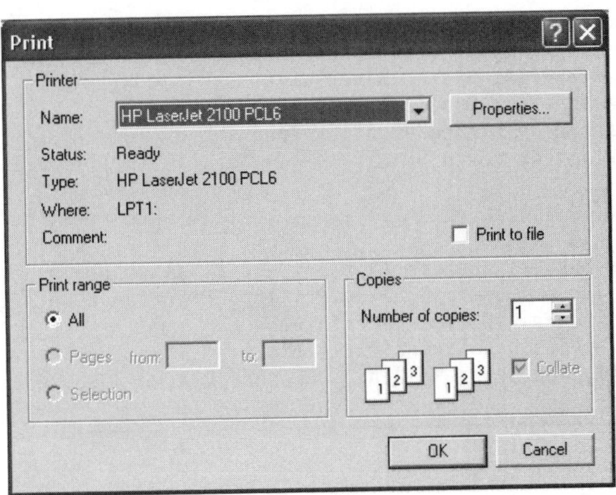

Printing

To print the contents of the multiple-line TextBox, first use the DrawString method of the Graphics object passed to the PrintDocument's PrintPage event:

```
Private Sub PrintDocument1_PrintPage(ByVal sender As Object, _
   ByVal e As System.Drawing.Printing.PrintPageEventArgs) _
   Handles PrintDocument1.PrintPage
   e.Graphics.DrawString(txtTextToPrint.Text, New Font("Arial", _
      40, FontStyle.Regular), Brushes.Black, 200, 200)
End Sub
```

NOTE This code prints the contents of the TextBox, rather than a predetermined text string as shown in the PrintPage event example in the "Printing a Page" section earlier in this chapter.

Next, invoke the PrintDocument's Print method:

```
PrintDocument1.Print()
```

When you choose to print something from an application such as Microsoft Word, usually you'll see a Print dialog offering you printer options. In other words, normally the Print command does not print immediately, but only after the user clicks OK in the Print dialog. It's a good idea to set up your own applications in a similar fashion. To do this, declare a variable of type DialogResult. Show a PrintDialog by assigning its return value to the variable. Invoke the PrintDocument's Print method only if the return value equals DialogResult.OK.

The code for displaying a Print dialog, as well as actually printing the contents of the multiple-line TextBox if the user clicks OK, is shown in Listing 12.4.

Listing 12.4 Printing the Contents of a TextBox, with User Choice, from the Print Dialog

```
Private Sub mnuPrint_Click(ByVal sender As System.Object, _
   ByVal e As System.EventArgs)Handles mnuPrint.Click
   Dim answer As System.Windows.Forms.DialogResult
   answer = PrintDialog1.ShowDialog()
   If answer = DialogResult.OK Then
      PrintDocument1.Print()
   End If
End Sub

Private Sub PrintDocument1_PrintPage(ByVal sender As Object, _
   ByVal e As System.Drawing.Printing.PrintPageEventArgs) _
   Handles PrintDocument1.PrintPage
   e.Graphics.DrawString(txtTextToPrint.Text, New Font("Arial", _
      40, FontStyle.Regular), Brushes.Black, 200, 200)
End Sub
```

Using the PrintPreviewDialog Control

For the PrintPreviewDialog control to work, it, too, must be wired so that its Document property is assigned to the related PrintDocument component. You can do this in the Properties window or in code.

WARNING For the PrintPreviewDialog to display anything, the related PrintDocument's PrintPage event must contain Graphics object code that would result in a page being printed. Otherwise, the PrintPreview control will display a blank page.

With the Document property set, the `ShowDialog` method is used to display the Print Preview dialog, as shown in Listing 12.5.

Listing 12.5 Displaying a Print Preview Dialog

```
Private Sub mnuPrintPreview_Click(ByVal sender As System.Object, _
   ByVal e As System.EventArgs) Handles mnuPrintPreview.Click
   PrintPreviewDialog1.ShowDialog()
End Sub
```

This works with the PrintDocument code shown in Listing 12.4. The user enters lines of text in the text box, like this:

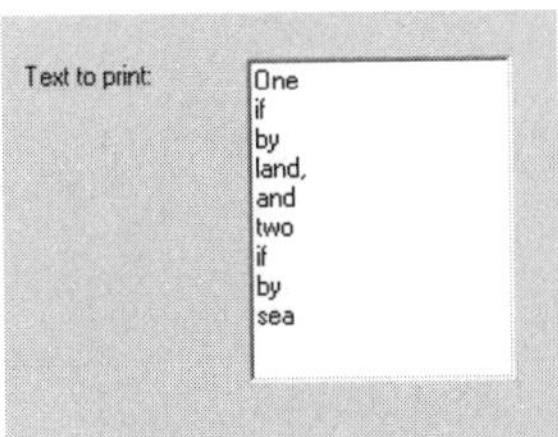

When the user chooses Print Preview, the text will be displayed in the Print Preview dialog.

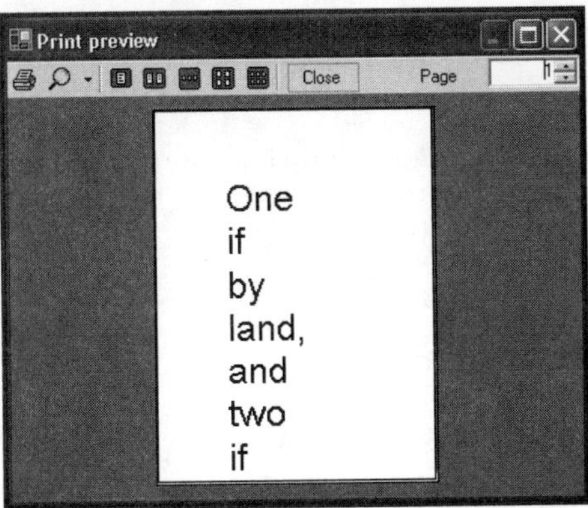

Note that clicking the printer icon on the left side of the Print Preview dialog will cause the document to be printed.

Summary

This chapter explained the mechanics of adding simple printing functionality to your VB .NET programs. It's easy to add a great-looking user interface to this printing functionality. As you learned in the chapter, adding simple printing functionality is easy. However, complex printing functionality is complicated, because you are responsible for programmatically creating the content that will be printed. Truly sophisticated printing routines need to add facilities to determine if the content will fit on the page, arrange page breaks and margins, and much more.

The next chapter explains how to write code that works with exceptions. You'll also learn more about how to use the sophisticated debugging tools that ship as part of the VB .NET development environment.

CHAPTER 13

Errors, Exceptions, and Debugging

- Understanding errors and exceptions
- Recognizing VB6 error handling
- Understanding VB .NET structured exception handling
- Throwing exceptions
- Following testing guidelines
- Using debug tools

Of course, programmers would like to be able to write programs without any defects—or "bugs," as they are often called. In the real world, as projects become complicated, this is close to impossible. In addition, good programs can go bad because of unforeseen conditions. (A common example is an expected resource being unavailable.) The implication is that, in the real world, you must plan for program errors. In fact, you can get exceptions even if you do everything right, due to circumstances beyond your control, such as a disk being full, a computer running out of memory, or a network being down.

This chapter looks at a number of important topics related to program defects in applications created in VB .NET. First, what are the different kinds of program errors and their consequences? Next, how should programs be written to gracefully deal with error conditions? VB .NET's structured exception-handling capability is a big improvement on the facilities for working with errors in previous versions of VB, but the older methods still work. I'll briefly explain the legacy error-handling techniques, and then explain how to effectively use structured exceptions as an integral part of your programs. Next, we'll have a look at how to test programs for errors. Finally, I'll take you on a tour of the debugging tools available to VB .NET programmers.

Understanding Errors and Exceptions

It's helpful to distinguish between three different kinds of problems, or errors: syntax errors, runtime errors, and logical errors. Syntax errors are easily dealt with, and runtime errors should not pose too great a problem to properly structured code. On the other hand, logical errors can be very difficult to detect and fix. Along with the types of errors, you also need to understand what the terms *exception* and *exception handling* mean.

What Causes Syntax Errors?

Syntax errors are caused by code that has been improperly constructed. Put another way, a syntax error occurs when a program statement fails to meet the requirements of the formal language definition, and therefore cannot be compiled. (Syntax errors are also called *compile-time errors*.)

Obviously, there are many different kinds of syntactical errors that a programmer can make. Common examples in VB .NET include using undeclared variables (when Option Explicit is on), mismatched type assignments, and calling a procedure with the wrong number of arguments.

The good news is that the Visual Studio development interface intercepts syntax errors for you. As shown next, syntax errors are underlined in the Code Editor almost as soon as you've made the error, with a message explaining what is wrong.

```
Public Class Form1
    Inherits System.Windows.Forms.Form

 Windows Form Designer generated code 
thisVarNotDeclared = 2004
   Public Sub Lucy(ByVal mertz As String, ByVal ricardo As String)
      ' Do something
   End Sub
   Private Sub Button1_Click(ByVal sender As System.Object, _
      ByVal e As System.EventArgs) Handles Button1.Click
      Lucy("baby")
   End Sub         Argument not specified for parameter 'ricardo' of 'Public Sub Lucy(mertz As String, ricardo As String)'.
End Class
```

If you go ahead and try to build an application that contains syntax errors, a message box will warn you that there are build errors and ask if you want to continue. If you decide to build the application with errors, it may or may not run. Whenever there are build errors, they will be displayed in the Task List window, as in this example:

In the Task List window, you can double-click each syntax error to be taken to the place in your code where you made the error.

TIP Select Show Task Help from the context menu for an error in the Task List window to see the documentation (and fix) for the problem. Usually, this documentation is informative and will help put you on the right track for fixing the problem.

When Do Runtime Errors Occur?

In contrast to syntax errors, which are caught at compile time, *runtime errors* occur when a running, previously compiled program attempts to perform an operation that is impossible to perform. When a runtime error occurs, you'll generally see a message box noting an "unhandled exception." The classic example is code that attempts to divide by zero:

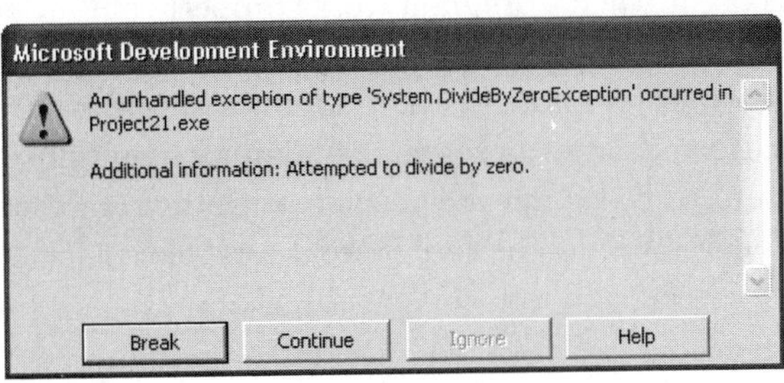

There's nothing syntactically illegal about the code that does the division; it's just that dividing by zero is impossible.

Other common examples of problems that may cause runtime errors include an attempt to use a resource that isn't present (for example, a file on a network drive) and users entering data of an unexpected sort, causing a type cast error:

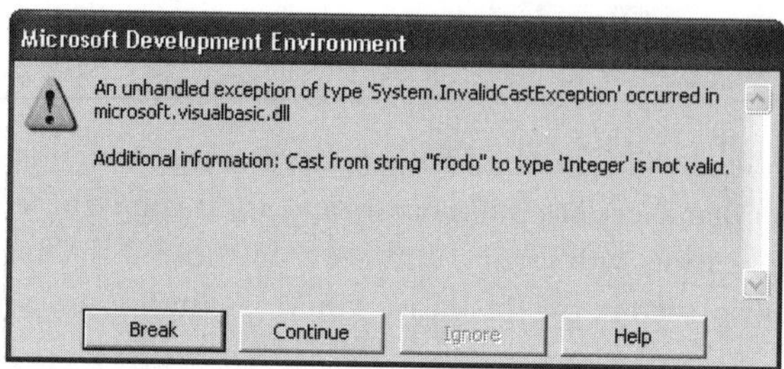

NOTE Of course, the underlying issue when a user enters the wrong kind of data is that the program has insufficiently validated the user input.

Runtime errors rarely occur on your desktop when you're testing the program. The embarrassing thing is that they frequently pop up the first time a client runs the program on her own system.

The key to dealing with runtime errors is to think through all the possible things that might go wrong. As you'll learn in this chapter, each potential runtime error can be handled. If possible, the problem can be recovered from and program execution can continue. If not, a reasonably literate message can explain the problem and whom to contact. If appropriate, information helpful to debugging the problem can be saved or logged.

TIP There is no substitute for thinking through all the likely (and unlikely) potential problems a program may encounter.

What Can You Do About Logical Errors?

Logical errors occur when a program works properly but produces wrong results. Logical errors can be much harder to debug than runtime errors, because they don't necessarily produce an obvious symptom like a program crash. (In contrast, you *will* get a program crash if you attempt to run a program containing a runtime error such as an unhandled division by zero.) The subtler the problem with the results of the program, the harder it can be to debug (or even to be sure there is a problem).

For resolving a logical problem, your three most important weapons will be clarity of thought about the program's operations, intelligent testing, and making good use of the debugging tools available to understand exactly what your program is doing. Testing and the excellent debugging tools provided by VB .NET—and how to use them to squash those pesky logical bugs—are covered in the "Testing and Debugging" section later in this chapter.

Why Is an Error a "Bug?"

It's a piece of generally believed programmer folklore that the expression "bug" comes from a literal insect that was creating havoc with the innards of an old-time computer. Supposedly, Admiral Grace Hopper, one of the creators of the language COBOL, first used the term *bug* in the 1950s to describe a moth that was causing a vacuum-tube monster to malfunction. These days, *bug* means any error that causes a program or computer to malfunction (essentially, it is synonymous with *error*).

As a matter of historical fact, the word *bug* was used prior to the invention of the computer to mean a glitch or problem with an industrial or scientific process. (Thomas Edison is on record as having used the term this way.) However, Admiral Hopper is probably the first to use the term in connection with a computer (whether or not the context really involved a moth, I will not conjecture).

What Is an Exception?

An *exception* is an unexpected condition in a program. For example, an exception may occur if you attempt to connect to the database but can't, because it's down. When you work with exceptions in VB .NET, you can think of them as synonymous with errors.

What does it mean to "handle" an exception (or error)? Users need to be insulated from the consequences of a runtime error; your program should not crash under any circumstances. If the situation can be recovered from, and the program can continue execution, it should. If execution cannot continue, a reasonably comprehensible message should explain that the program is terminating, and if appropriate, explain why. Then the program should shut down gently. In any case, information necessary for debugging the problem should be saved, either to a file or the system log, as explained in Chapter 10, "Using Timers, EventLogs, and ServiceControllers."

NOTE If at all possible, a program should try to run if it can, even with reduced functionality. (This scenario is one that Microsoft has dubbed "degrading gracefully.")

As you'll learn in the "Throwing Exceptions" section later in this chapter, you can *throw* (also called *raise*) an exception any time you like, and it need not be because of an error condition. For example, exceptions could be used as an application communication mechanism, keeping track of the current state of the application. However, just because something can be done doesn't mean it should be. This use of exceptions is not recommended. In practice, the Exception object in VB .NET and all the classes derived from it represent runtime errors. If you create your own exceptions, they also should represent either a runtime or (in some cases) a logical error.

A Blast from the Past: *On Error GoTo*

VB6 programmers will recall that errors were handled using the Err object and a series of (infamous) `On Error GoTo` statements. The `On Error GoTo` *`label`* statement turned on error handling within a procedure. When a runtime error occurred within the procedure, execution was passed to the location specified by *`label`*.

`On Error Resume Next`, another VB6 statement, cleared the runtime error and transferred execution to the statement following the one that caused the runtime error. (Essentially, using `On Error Resume Next` says "I want execution to just continue, even if there are runtime errors," and this is a dangerous way to proceed.)

The Err object and `On Error GoTo` syntax have been retained by VB .NET for backward compatibility. You should not use this approach for new VB .NET applications that you write. However, you may wish to know about this syntax so that you recognize what it is when you see it (or in case you need to convert legacy projects).

WARNING The Err object and `On Error GoTo` cannot be used in the same procedure with .NET's structured error handling.

Some commonly used properties and methods of the Err object are shown in Table 13.1.

TABLE 13.1: Commonly Used Properties and Methods of the Err Object

Property or Method	Purpose
Number	Returns or sets the error number
Description	Returns a description of the error
Clear	Clears all properties of the Err object (should be called after you have handled an error)
Raise	Generates a runtime error

Generally, when you are using the Err object, you begin a routine with an `On Error GoTo label` statement. The label consists of an identifier beginning a line, followed by a colon, as in this example:

```
Sub WhatEver
   On Error GoTo ErrHandler
   ...
   Exit Sub
ErrHandler:
   ' Handle the error
   ...
Exit Sub
```

In the code above, the `Exit Sub` statement is used to make sure that code that does not trigger the error condition does not drop down into the error-handling code.

For example, if you added a TextBox control named `txtDivisor` and a Button control named `btnCauseProblem` to a form, you could use the code in Listing 13.1 to display the number and description of an error that occurs.

Listing 13.1 Using the Err Object's Number and Description Properties

```
Private Sub btnCauseProblem_Click(ByVal sender As System.Object, _
   ByVal e As System.EventArgs) Handles btnCauseProblem.Click
   On Error GoTo ErrHandler
   Dim result As Integer
   result = 1000 \ CInt(txtDivisor.Text)
   MessageBox.Show(result.ToString)
   Exit Sub
ErrHandler:
   MessageBox.Show("Error Number: " & Err.Number.ToString & _
      ControlChars.CrLf & "Description: " & Err.Description, _
      "The Err Object", MessageBoxButtons.OK, _
      MessageBoxIcon.Information)
End Sub
```

The obvious error is division by zero, when the user enters 0 in the text box and clicks the button, but some other runtime errors are also possible. For example, suppose the user enters a text string, such as “frodo,” which cannot be converted to an integer. In this case, a message box explaining the error will appear.

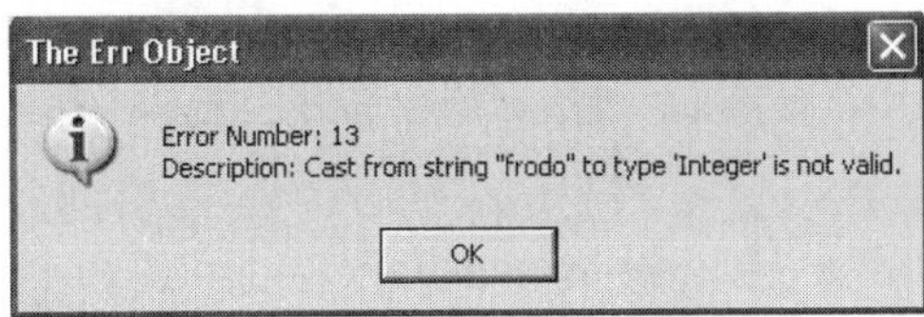

If you write this kind of error-handling code for your applications, you'll soon realize that you need to do different things, depending on what the problem is. Listing 13.2 shows various errors being handled differently, using a `Select...Case` statement. A more-or-less user-friendly message is displayed, alerting the user to the problem so that it can be corrected, and the `Err.Clear` method is used to wipe the slate clean.

Listing 13.2 A *Select...Case* Structure That Handles and Clears Multiple Errors

```
Private Sub btnCauseProblem_Click(ByVal sender As System.Object, _
   ByVal e As System.EventArgs) Handles btnCauseProblem.Click
   On Error GoTo ErrHandler
   Dim result As Integer
   result = 1000 \ CInt(txtDivisor.Text)
   MessageBox.Show(result.ToString)
   Exit Sub
ErrHandler:
   Select Case Err.Number
      Case 11
         ' Do something
         MessageBox.Show("I told you not to divide by zero!", _
            "The Err Object", MessageBoxButtons.OK, _
            MessageBoxIcon.Information)
         Err.Clear()
      Case 13
         ' Do something different
         MessageBox.Show("Next time, enter a number!", _
            "The Err Object", MessageBoxButtons.OK, _
            MessageBoxIcon.Information)
         Err.Clear()
      Case Else
         ' Handle the universe of unknown errors
   End Select
End Sub
```

For example, if the user persists in entering a text string in the text box, she is told to try a number instead.

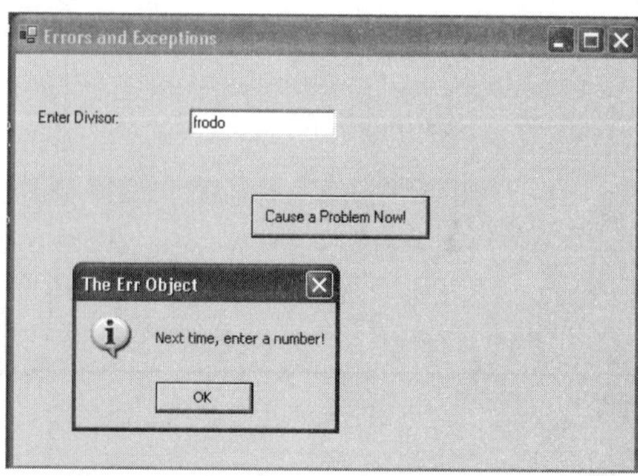

Understanding Structured Exception Handling

The kind of code shown in the previous section is not elegant, quickly becomes difficult to maintain, and tends to be very application-specific (not a good thing). Over the years, VB's kludgy error-handling mechanisms have become a major source of problems in creating industrial-strength applications in VB. Structured exception handling is recognized as the best way for a programming language to deal with common errors, and it is finally supported by VB!

Exception handling has many advantages compared to the hoary Err object, including these:

- You can nest error handlers.
- You can use `Finally` to call, close, or dispose of objects that you opened in the `Try` block.
- The Exception class contains far richer error information than was available in the past.
- You can come up with your own custom exception classes and develop rich, robust error handling in a way not possible before.
- You can transmit your own custom information using exceptions.

Let's explore VB .NET's structured exception handling to see how modern exception handling is finally incorporated into VB.

Using *Try...Catch...Finally*

When an exception does occur, you can use the `Try...Catch...Finally` statement to handle it. Let's look at its syntax and then some examples.

Understanding *Try...Catch...Finally* Syntax

The general form of the `Try...Catch...Finally` statement is as follows (the elements enclosed in brackets are optional):

```
Try
   Program statements
   ...
[Catch1 [exception [As type]] [When expression]
...
[CatchN [exception [As type]] [When expression]
...
[Finally
   Final program statements]
End Try
```

The program statements in the `Try` block are the body of the program that is being monitored for errors, and the `Catch` statements are executed in response to VB catching a particular kind of error in the `Try` block. As you would expect, code in the optional `Finally` block is executed, whether or not an error has been caught.

Within each Catch block, you can have an Exit Try statement, which exits the entire Try...End Try structure.

For example, if you have a form with a TextBox control and a Button control, you could add the following code in the button's Click event to catch different kinds of problems:

```
Private Sub Button1_Click(ByVal sender As System.Object, _
   ByVal e As System.EventArgs) Handles Button1.Click
   Dim i As Integer, d As Double
   Try
      i = CInt(TextBox1.Text)
      d = 42 \ i
   Catch excep As DivideByZeroException
      MessageBox.Show("Don't Divide By Zero!")
   Catch except As InvalidCastException
      MessageBox.Show("Enter a number!")
   End Try
End Sub
```

In the example, Catch clauses within the Try block deal with the situation if the user enters text instead of a number or enters zero (which would cause a division by zero).

It's possible to have the first Catch filter without any conditions:

```
Catch
   code
```

You could also just catch the general Exception type:

```
Catch excep as Exception
```

In these cases, the filter will catch all errors. In some situations, you can use this as a centralized error-processing mechanism along the lines of "if any error happens, go here and take care of it." Often, however, it is a better idea to use specific Catch clauses to handle certain types of exceptions. A final, generic Catch clause could deal with all nonspecific exceptions. Written like this, the Try...Catch...Finally structure should look like this (leaving off the Finally clause in the interest of simplicity):

```
Try
   Program statements
   ...
Catch excep As DivideByZeroException
   ' Handle divide by zero
Catch other specific errors
...
Catch excep As Exception
    ' Catch any exception not handled above
End Try
```

What if this was written the other way around?

```
...
Catch excep As Exception
   ' Clear all exceptions
...
Catch excep As DivideByZeroException
   ' Handle divide by zero
Catch other specific errors
```

Then none of the specific exception filters, such as the divide by zero exception, would ever be triggered.

Reviewing *Try...Catch...Finally* Examples

Let's have a look at working with exceptions and `Try...Catch...Finally` in practice.

Starting with a form with a TextBox control named `txtDivisor` and a Button control named `btnCauseProblem`, the code in Listing 13.3 uses the `ToString` method of the Exception object to display a great deal of information about a type-conversion error.

Listing 13.3 Displaying a Type Cast Error Using the *Exception.ToString* Method

```
Private Sub btnCauseProblem_Click(ByVal sender As System.Object, _
   ByVal e As System.EventArgs) Handles btnCauseProblem.Click
   Try
      Dim result As Integer
      result = 1000 \ CInt(txtDivisor.Text)
      MessageBox.Show(result.ToString)
   Catch excep As InvalidCastException
      MessageBox.Show(excep.ToString)
   End Try
End Sub
```

The message box includes details, including the procedure and line of code causing the error.

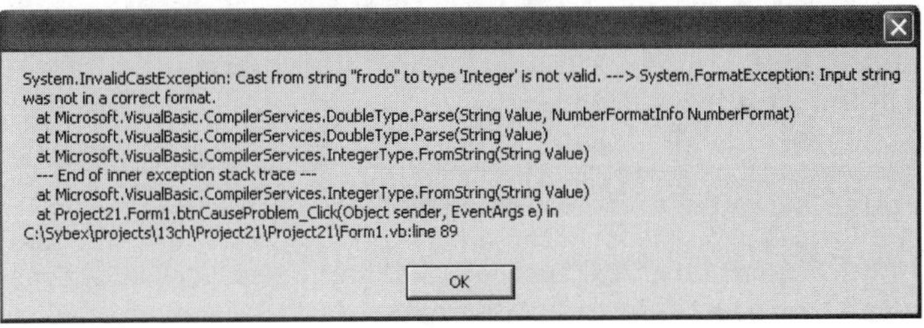

If you want to add clean-up code that executes whether or not the type-cast exception has been thrown, you can add a `Finally` block, as shown in Listing 13.4.

Listing 13.4 Adding a *Finally* Block

```
Private Sub btnCauseProblem_Click(ByVal sender As System.Object, _
   ByVal e As System.EventArgs) Handles btnCauseProblem.Click
   Try
      Dim result As Integer
      result = 1000 \ CInt(txtDivisor.Text)
      MessageBox.Show(result.ToString)
   Catch excep As InvalidCastException
      MessageBox.Show(excep.ToString)
   Finally
      MessageBox.Show("I get executed, no matter what!", _
         "Structured Exception Handling", MessageBoxButtons.OK, _
         MessageBoxIcon.Information)
   End Try
End Sub
```

With this addition, a message box appears to indicate that execution will continue.

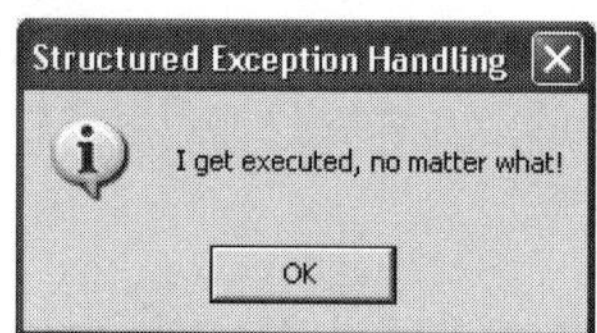

Different `Catch` blocks are used to handle different errors, and you can add messages that are clearer than the information provided by the `ToString` method. Listing 13.5 demonstrates using `Catch` blocks in this fashion.

Listing 13.5 Using *Catch* Blocks to Handle Different Errors

```
Private Sub btnCauseProblem_Click(ByVal sender As System.Object, _
   ByVal e As System.EventArgs) Handles btnCauseProblem.Click
   Try
      Dim result As Integer
      result = 1000 \ CInt(txtDivisor.Text)
      MessageBox.Show(result.ToString)
   Catch excep As DivideByZeroException
      MessageBox.Show("Enter a non-zero integer and try again!", _
         "Structured Exception Handling", MessageBoxButtons.OK, _
         MessageBoxIcon.Information)
   Catch excep As InvalidCastException
      MessageBox.Show(excep.ToString)
   Catch excep As Exception
```

```
        ' Handles everything else
        MessageBox.Show(excep.ToString)
    Finally
        MessageBox.Show("I get executed, no matter what!", _
            "Structured Exception Handling", MessageBoxButtons.OK, _
            MessageBoxIcon.Information)
    End Try
End Sub
```

Using this approach, you can help the user to clear up the specific problem. For example, the code in Listing 13.5 shows a (possibly) helpful message when a divide by zero error is attempted:

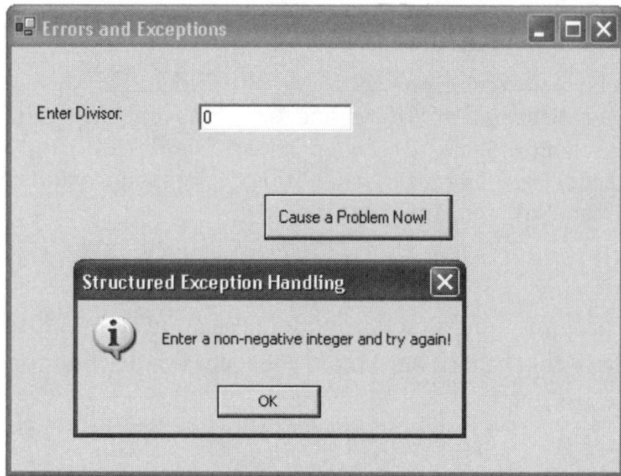

Throwing Exceptions

Throwing an exception means creating your own exception under certain conditions. (It is comparable to raising an error in VB6.) Throwing custom exceptions should not be done to facilitate normal program communication, but it may make sense as part of a scheme for dealing with logical errors, and it is what your application should do in many circumstances if it asked to do something impossible.

To throw an exception, use the `Throw` keyword with a new instantiation of the Exception class, or one of the classes derived from Exception. (The Exception object and classes are described in the next section.) A text string is used to create the new exception, which can then be used to catch it, as in this example:

```
Throw New Exception("Foo")
```

This exception could be caught within a `Catch excep As Exception` block using a conditional:

```
If excep.Message = "Foo"
```

TIP

In the real world, if you plan to make extensive use of throwing custom events, you will probably want to create your own Exception objects, based on Exception or its subclasses, which provide some additional facilities. For more information on creating custom objects in VB .NET, see Chapter 15, "Object-Oriented Programming in VB .NET."

Let's look at an example of throwing and catching an exception in practice. Suppose, in the example we've used so far in this chapter, something terrible happens if the user types the word "Gremlins" in the text box. We can then throw the exception:

```
If txtDivisor.Text = "Gremlins" Then
   Throw New ApplicationException("There are Gremlins in the text box!")
End If
```

Then catch it to handle the situation specially:

```
Catch excep As Exception
   If excep.Message = "There are Gremlins in the text box!" Then
      MessageBox.Show("Clean up those Gremlins!", _
      "Structured Exception Handling", MessageBoxButtons.OK, _
      MessageBoxIcon.Information)
   Else
...
```

As a good programming practice, your application should throw only `ApplicationException` objects, or those that inherit `ApplicationException`. It's not good practice to throw instances of `System.Exception`.

NOTE

If you're wondering why you should avoid throwing `System.Exception`, keep in mind the code that will catch the exceptions. Often, you catch specific exceptions and deal with them appropriately, and then catch `System.Exception` for the "and everything else" condition. If your application logic throws `System.Exception`, the catcher has no way to distinguish between application exceptions and everything else. On the other hand, if you get in the habit of throwing `ApplicationException`, the catcher can look for this specifically and handle it differently.

Listing 13.6 shows the complete code for the example, including throwing and catching the exception related to gremlins.

Listing 13.6 Throwing and Catching an Exception

```
Private Sub btnCauseProblem_Click(ByVal sender As System.Object, _
   ByVal e As System.EventArgs) Handles btnCauseProblem.Click
   Try
      Dim result As Integer
      result = 1000 \ CInt(txtDivisor.Text)
      If txtDivisor.Text = "Gremlins" Then
```

```
            Throw New ApplicationException("There are Gremlins in the text box!")
         End If
         MessageBox.Show(result.ToString)
      Catch excep As DivideByZeroException
         MessageBox.Show("Enter a non-negative integer and try again!", _
            "Structured Exception Handling", MessageBoxButtons.OK, _
            MessageBoxIcon.Information)
      Catch excep As InvalidCastException
         MessageBox.Show(excep.ToString)
      Catch excep As Exception
         If excep.Message = "There are Gremlins in the text box!" Then
            MessageBox.Show("Clean up those Gremlins!", _
            "Structured Exception Handling", MessageBoxButtons.OK, _
            MessageBoxIcon.Information)
         Else
            MessageBox.Show(excep.ToString)
         End If
      Finally
         MessageBox.Show("I get executed, no matter what!", _
            "Structured Exception Handling", MessageBoxButtons.OK, _
            MessageBoxIcon.Information)
      End Try
   End Sub
```

If a user enters "Gremlins" in the text box, he gets to clean them up.

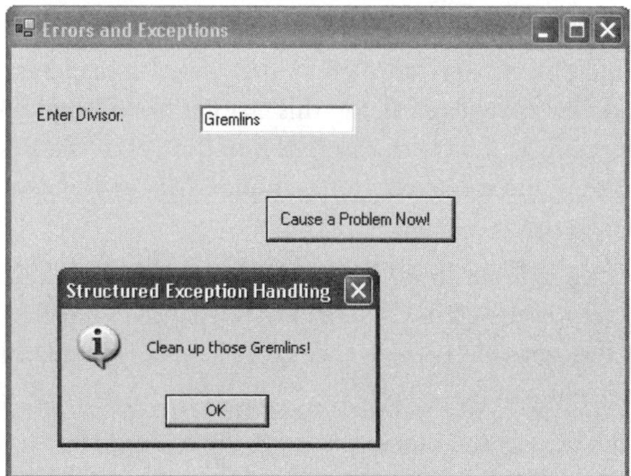

Exploring the Exception Object and Classes

The first thing you should know about the Exception object and the classes that inherit from Exception is that (for the most part) the subclasses do not vary from Exception by implementing additional members or functionality. This means that the only difference between the parent and child classes is the name of the class. (An important exception to this is `SqlException`, which is thrown when SQL Server returns a warning or error.) The implication is that if you have a compelling reason to add information to the Exception class, you certainly can; however, it still makes sense to deal with your exception as a generic exception (meaning, no matter how much information you add, you should still implement a meaningful Message property.)

Table 13.2 shows some of the commonly used properties and methods of the Exception object.

TABLE 13.2: Commonly Used Properties and Methods of the Exception Object

Property or Method	Purpose
Message	Gets a message that describes the current exception
StackTrace	A string that contains the stack trace immediately before the exception was thrown
TargetSite	The method that threw the current exception
ToString	A string that contains the name of the exception and a great deal of other information, such as the error message and the stack trace (see Listing 13.3, earlier in this chapter)

In general, the Exception class has two subclasses: `ApplicationException` and `System-Exception`. In theory, `ApplicationException` subclasses are created by your application, and `SystemException` subclasses are created by the runtime (CLR) and operating environment.

As you would expect, there are a great many subclasses of `SystemException`, some of which you've seen in the examples earlier in this chapter (for example, `InvalidCastException`). Most of these Exception classes are the members of the `System` namespace, but others are located further down the namespace tree (for example, `IOException` is a member of `System.IO` rather than `System` directly).

The best place to learn about individual exceptions and their class relationships is the Object Browser (discussed in Chapter 14, "Using the Object Browser"). For example, in Figure 13.1, you can see `DivideByZeroException` and its members (the members are displayed in the right pane).

If you look at the information displayed at the bottom of the Object Browser window shown in Figure 13.1, you'll see that `DivideByZeroException` is, itself, a member of `System` and that it inherits from `System.ArithmeticException`. If you click the `System.ArithmeticException` link at the bottom of the Object Browser window, you'll see that `ArithmeticException` is another member of `System` and that it inherits from `System.SystemException`. `SystemException` inherits from `System.Exception`, and that's the top of this inheritance chain. In other words, you don't need to catch just generic `System.Exception`, or the very specific `DivideByZeroException`; you can catch classifications of exceptions, like all `ArithmeticException`.

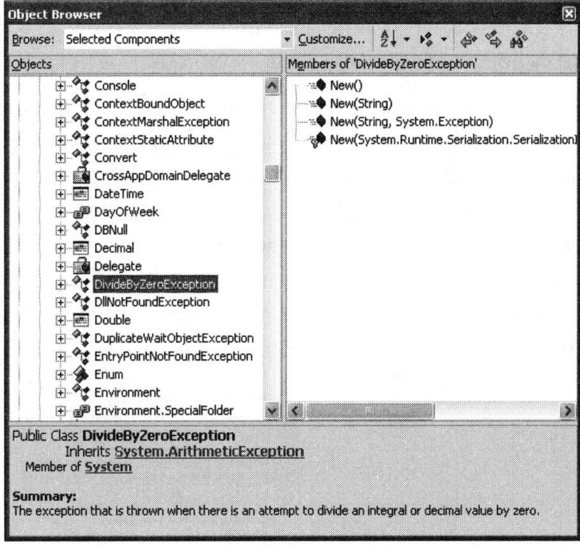

FIGURE 13.1: The class relationships of exceptions can be traced using the Object Browser.

Using the Exceptions Dialog

The Exceptions dialog, shown in Figure 13.2, is another way to look at a list of the Exceptions that come prebuilt with VB .NET, although that is not the primary purpose of the dialog. To open the Exceptions dialog, choose Debug ➢ Exceptions.

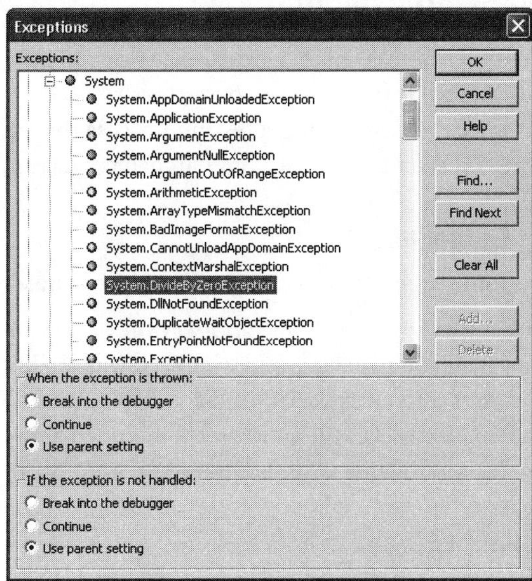

FIGURE 13.2: The Exceptions dialog is used to set what happens when an exception is thrown.

The Exceptions dialog is used to set the behavior of the development environment when an exception is thrown. The choices are to continue or to break into the debugger. This can happen when an exception is thrown, whether or not it is handled.

The individual exceptions can be set to Use Parent Setting, as they all are by default. The default setting for the parent, Common Language Runtime Exceptions, is to continue when an exception is thrown and to break into the debugger if the exception is not handled. You might want to modify this behavior for one or more exceptions; for example, you could set the Break Into the Debugger option for a handled exception to see exactly what is going on when it is thrown. When you change the setting for a particular exception, the icon to the left of the exception changes, as shown here next to `DivideByZeroException` set to Break Into the Debugger.

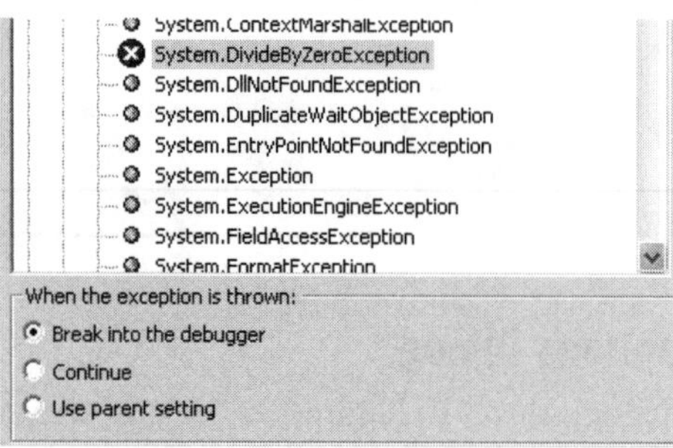

Testing and Debugging

The remainder of this chapter explains the debugging tools provided by the VB .NET environment. You will primarily use these tools to detect and fix logical errors. It's much better to detect logical errors during a testing process than after a program has been distributed. Therefore, I'll start by sharing some high-level testing guidelines.

Testing Guidelines

Here are some suggestions for testing your programs:

Work hard at breaking your application. Approach testing a program with a different mindset than you may have had when creating it. Testing is a relentless pursuit whose best practitioners often partake of Murphy's laws and their corollaries: Everything you can think of that can go wrong, will go wrong—and then some things you haven't thought of will go wrong. It's worthwhile to make strenuous attempts to "break" your application to see how it will react.

Track your testing steps. Keep careful track of the steps you take in testing, paying particular attention to the test values of variables. (In formal quality assurance situations, keeping track is done rigorously, using scripts.) At the level of the individual developer, this implies that being rigorous and disciplined pays.

Consider data boundaries. Programs usually operate on ranges of data. For example, the user might input an integer, which is saved as a variable. By definition, this integer variable varies in value; if it did not, you would use a constant rather than a variable. But integer variables in VB .NET have bounds—they can range from a low of –2,147,483,648 to a high of 2,147,483,648. When you construct your testing scenarios, it's smart to consider these bounding values. You should test at the low end, the high end, and any other values that you have reason to believe might cause problems.

Check for one-off conditions. "One-off" conditions are probably the single biggest cause of logical program errors. A one-off error occurs whenever a counter or loop is off by one. You should suspect and test for one-off errors whenever a logical error occurs and a loop or counter is present.

Test vigorously for runtime errors. Try to consider all possible runtime problems and understand your program's reactions. For example, reading and writing to files is a common cause of real-life failures. What happens if a file doesn't exist, or the appropriate permissions are not present? In .NET, this is an acute problem. If you forget to close a FileStream object, the file remains locked for the life of the application, even if the application doesn't think it's using it any more.

Although it's hard to foresee all problems in advance, the time you spend attempting to do so will save you time spent piecemeal responding to individual logical errors.

Using the Debugging Tools

The primary debugging tools provided by VB .NET include the following:

- Using the methods of the Debug object (and observing their output in the Watch window)
- Working with the Trace object
- Stepping through a program statement by statement
- Setting breakpoints to stop program execution at a particular point (or to begin stepping)
- Interactively executing program statements using the Command window

The best way to learn about these tools is by using them in actual projects. That way, you will see how they fit in with your debugging strategy. In the remaining sections of this chapter, I'll provide a high-level tour of some of the debugging tools that you'll find useful in VB .NET development environment.

Using the Methods of the Debug Object

The methods of the Debug object are used to display messages, usually including variable values, in the Watch window (described in the "Viewing Variables in the Watch Window" section later in this chapter). Table 13.3 shows the most commonly used methods of the Debug object, which are discussed in the following sections.

TABLE 13.3: Commonly Used Methods of the Debug Object

Method	Purpose
`Assert`	Used to check whether a logical condition is false when a program is running
`Write`	Writes to the Watch window
`WriteLine`	Writes a line to the Watch window
`WriteIf`	Writes to the Watch window if the condition is true
`WriteLineIf`	Writes a line to the Watch window if the condition is true

Debug.Write

`Debug.Write` and its variants are used to examine the values of variables during program execution. `Debug.WriteLine` is probably the single most useful variant, because the output is clearer when things are presented line by line, rather than in a jumble.

The trick is to insert a `Debug.Write` statement at the point where you want to know the variables' values. In this sense, using `Debug.Write` to repeatedly display the value of `myVariable` is much like displaying the value of `myVariable` in a message box, except that with the far cruder message box, you run the risk of needing to repeatedly click OK.

For example, suppose you were concerned about the values of the counter variables in a nested loop that looked like this:

```
Dim i, j, k As Integer
For i = 1 To 1000
   For j = 2500 To 1 Step -1
      For k = -10000 To 10000 Step 10
         ...
      Next
   Next
Next
```

You could add `Debug` statements to send the values of the counter variables to the Output window:

```
Dim i, j, k As Integer
For i = 1 To 1000
   For j = 2500 To 1 Step -1
      For k = -10000 To 10000 Step 10
```

```
            Debug.WriteLine("The value of i is " & i.ToString)
            Debug.WriteLine("The value of j is " & j.ToString)
            Debug.WriteLine("The value of k is " & k.ToString)
            ...
        Next
    Next
Next
```

If you ran this code and looked at the Output window, you would see the running values of the three counter variables:

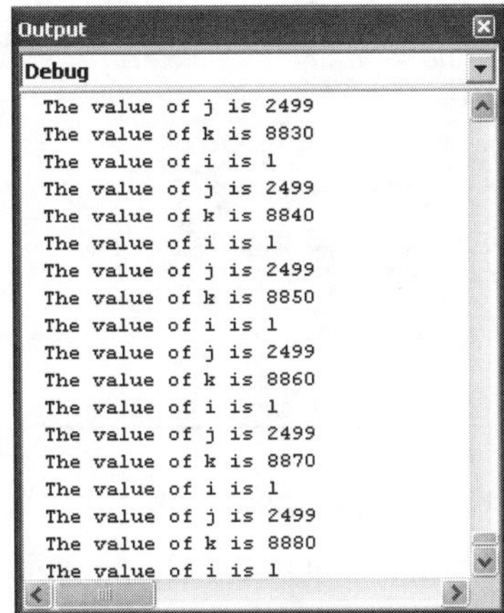

In this particular case, you probably won't learn much beyond the obvious: that the outer counter doesn't start to move until the inner loops are complete.

Debug.Assert

The `Debug.Assert` method checks a condition, also called an *assertion*. If the assertion evaluates to false, a message is displayed. You can use assertions to check that your assumptions about the values of variables are correct. One of the most common uses of `Debug.Assert` is to check the values of arguments that are passed to a method.

For example, suppose you were concerned that there might be problems in the `i`, `j`, `k` looping example (in the previous section) when the value of `k` was positive (of course, we know that `k` will be positive!). You could modify the looping code to add a `Debug.Assert` statement:

```
Dim i, j, k As Integer
For i = 1 To 1000
    For j = 2500 To 1 Step -1
        For k = -10000 To 10000 Step 10
            Debug.Assert (k < 0)
            ...
```

```
        Next
    Next
Next
```

If you run the code, an assertion failure message box containing a great deal of information (the call stack) will be supplied.

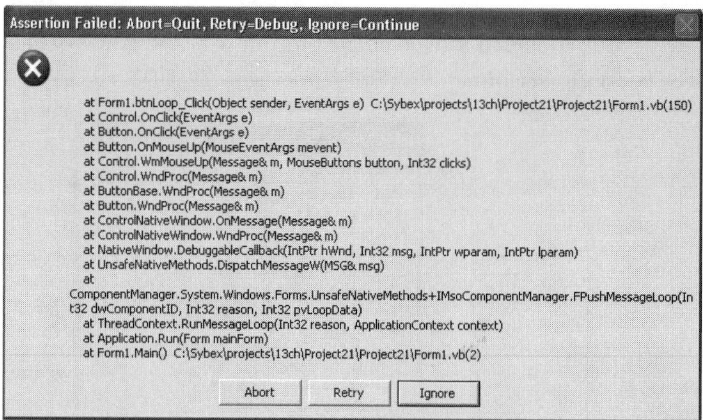

You can continue program operation, quit, or break into the debug mode.

You'll find the same information in the Output window following program termination.

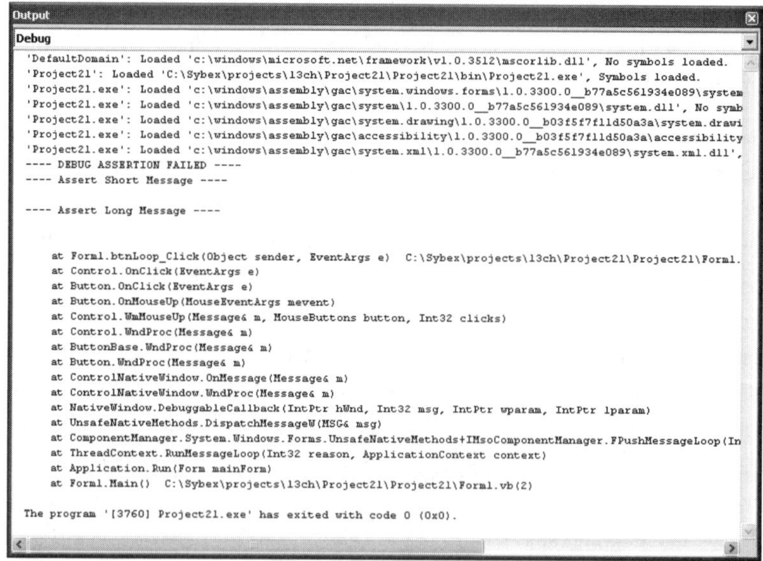

You can also add your own text to the assertion failure information. You can append one or two strings as arguments after the assertion clause, and they will appear along with the call stack information. For example, the following statement prints the text message and the value of k:

```
Debug.Assert (k < 0, "k is positive or equal to zero ", k.ToString)
```

TIP Using the Debug object's Listener collection and a StreamWriter object, you can easily write Debug (or Trace) output to a file rather than to the Watch window. For information about how to do this, see the "Introduction to Instrumentation and Tracing" topic in online help.

Working with the Trace Object

The Trace object is the same as the Debug object, except that code involving Trace classes is compiled by default into release builds (and Debug code is not). The Trace object uses the same methods as the Debug object (see Table 13.3).

An implication is that Trace methods have a negative impact on performance, whereas Debug methods do not. Debug statements are intended for use within the development environment, and tracing is used when you will need to monitor a program after it has been released.

Stepping through a Program

Stepping is the process of executing a program line by line, pausing between lines. You can learn some very interesting things by stepping through a program.

There are three variants of stepping:

- Step Into, which executes every line of code and pauses after each line
- Step Over, which executes a function call as one line (rather than going into the function)
- Step Out, which breaks out of a function call

The Step commands are available on the Debug menu. The shortcut keys are also useful to know: F11 for Step Into and F10 for Step Over.

Setting Breakpoints

Suppose you know that a function isn't giving you the desired output, but you don't know why. If only you could step through the function one line at a time, you might be able to determine where the problem is occurring. That's what breakpoints are for. They let you halt execution on a specific line, and then step through the following lines, one at a time. While you're stepping from one line to the next, you can examine the values of variables, and even step into called functions, to hunt for the problem.

To insert a breakpoint, place the cursor at the place in the Code Editor you want to break and choose Debug ➢ New Breakpoint. The New Breakpoint dialog will open, as shown in Figure 13.3. You can also set, or remove, a breakpoint using the F9 key.

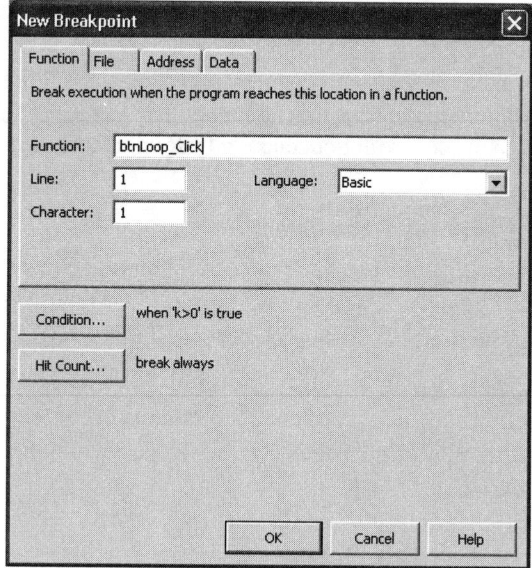

FIGURE 13.3: The New Breakpoint dialog is used to insert breakpoints in code.

To set up a condition under which the break is triggered, click the Condition button. In the Breakpoint Condition dialog, specify the condition, as shown in this example:

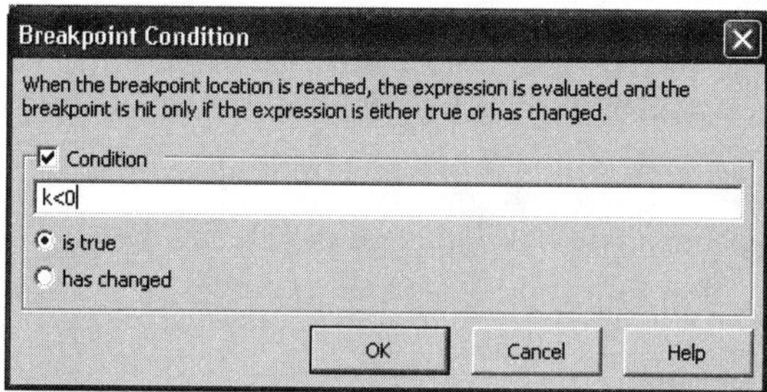

Once you've set a breakpoint, it appears highlighted in the Code Editor.

```
Private Sub btnLoop_Click(ByVal sender As System.Object, _
    ByVal e As System.EventArgs) Handles btnLoop.Click
    Dim i, j, k As Integer
    For i = 1 To 1000
        For j = 2500 To 1 Step -1
            For k = -10000 To 10000 Step 10
                'Debug.Assert(k < 0, "k is positive or equal to zero ", k.ToString)
            Next
        Next
    Next
```

The Breakpoints window, shown in Figure 13.4, allows you to view and modify all breakpoints. (To open the Breakpoints window, choose Debug ➢ Windows ➢ Breakpoints.)

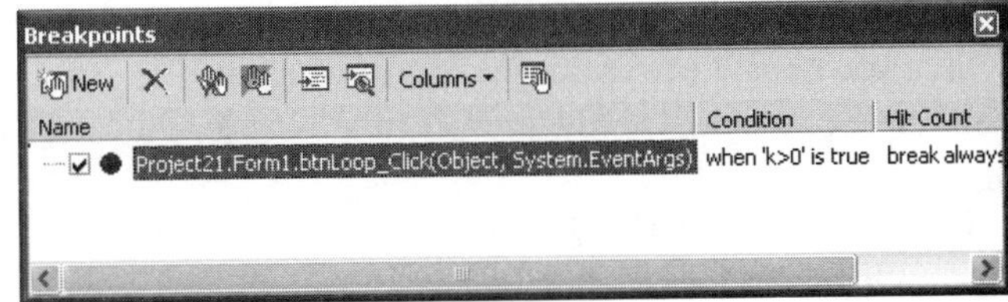

FIGURE 13.4: The Breakpoints window displays all project breakpoints and allows their properties to be modified.

Viewing Variables in the Watch Window

The Watch window, shown in Figure 13.5, displays the values of variables when a program is running in debug mode. To open a Watch window with a program running in debug mode, select Debug ➢ Windows ➢ Watch.

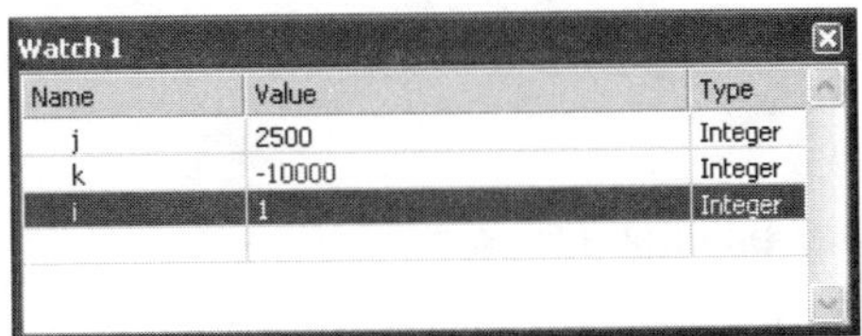

FIGURE 13.5: The Watch window can display the values of variables as you step through a program.

When a program is in break mode, you can open the QuickWatch window, shown in Figure 13.6. To open the QuickWatch window, choose Debug ➢ QuickWatch.

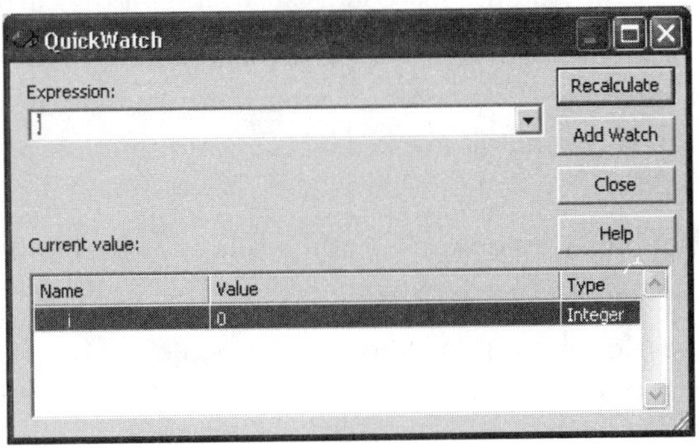

FIGURE 13.6: The QuickWatch window can be used to provide the current value of a variable at a breakpoint and to add variables to the regular Watch window.

TIP Expressions viewed in the QuickWatch window can be added to a regular Watch window by clicking the Add Watch button.

Executing Statements Using the Command Window

The Command window in Immediate mode, shown in Figure 13.7, allows you to execute programming statements against a program in break mode (meaning that the variables used start with their values at the time of the break). This provides a valuable facility for quickly determining the impact of various program commands at different stages of your program. (To open the Command window in Immediate mode, choose Debug ➢ Windows ➢ Immediate.)

NOTE Along with Immediate mode, the Command window also operates in Command mode, which is used to enter command-line Visual Studio commands against the Visual Studio .NET environment.

FIGURE 13.7:

The Command window in Immediate mode is used to run code against a project in break mode.

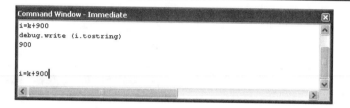

Using Other Debugging Tools

VB .NET provides many more debugging features and tools. The tools listed below can be opened from the VB .NET Debug menu, provided the debugger is running; in other words, a program must be running in debug mode.

- The Autos window allows you to display and modify the values of variables in the current statement (and the statements surrounding the current statement).
- The Call Stack window displays the functions or procedures that are currently on the stack. In other words, if `theMethod` is currently running because it was called from another object's method, which was invoked by `Sub Main`, all these procedures will appear in the Call Stack window.
- The Locals window displays the value of variables local to the current context (usually the function or procedure being executed).
- The Modules window shows the modules—DLLs and EXEs—used by the program running in debug mode.

Summary

Architecting effective error handling, instituting good testing processes, and sanely debugging are all demanding disciplines that take one part art and one part science. This chapter has provided an overview of the facilities that are available for each of these important activities in VB .NET. The debugging and exception-handling facilities in .NET are extraordinarily rich. The trick is to not get overwhelmed and to stick with the features that you understand and find useful.

In the next chapter, I'll show you how to use the Object Browser to learn about .NET classes and program more effectively in .NET.

Chapter 14

Using the Object Browser

- Opening the Object Browser
- Setting the Object Browser scope
- Using the Object Browser interface
- Exploring namespaces and classes

The Object Browser lets you determine the members of .NET objects, or classes, and the relationships of objects to each other. You can easily use the Object Browser to learn about the objects available for use in your programs.

The Object Browser also teaches about the structure of the .NET framework. You can use it to discern the hierarchy of classes and members of classes, as well as the properties, events, and methods of each object. Thus, the Object Browser is a tool of discovery, rather than a tool you use to actually do anything. But it's probably the single most important discovery tool included in the VB .NET development environment.

This chapter describes the basics of using the Object Browser: opening it, setting its scope, and navigating its interface. You'll also learn how to explore VB .NET namespaces and classes in the Object Browser.

Opening the Object Browser

To open the Object Browser, use one of the following methods:

- Choose View ➢ Other Windows ➢ Object Browser from the VB .NET menus.
- Press the keyboard shortcut, Ctrl+Alt+J.
- In the Code Editor, place the cursor on a .NET object, right-click, and choose Go To Definition from the context menu. (See the following discussion.)

The opening Object Browser window is shown in Figure 14.1.

FIGURE 14.1:

The Object Browser window

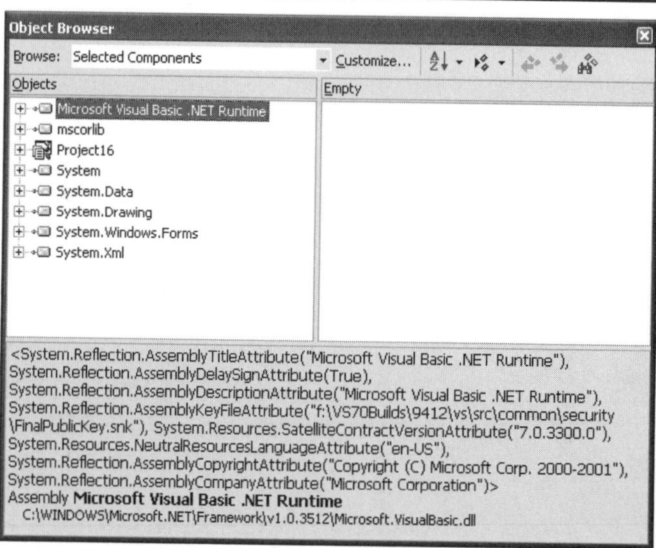

Opening the Object Browser Using Go To Definition

When you open the Object Browser from the Code Editor (by choosing Go To Definition from a .NET object's context menu), the Object Browser will open with the highlighted object defined. Note that this does not work if the cursor is hovering over a variable or keyword. In the case of a keyword, Go To Definition does nothing. In the case of a variable, Go To Definition takes you to the variable declaration.

For example, suppose you have a component in your project named `ColorDialog1`. With the cursor over a statement using `ColorDialog1`, right-click and select Go To Definition.

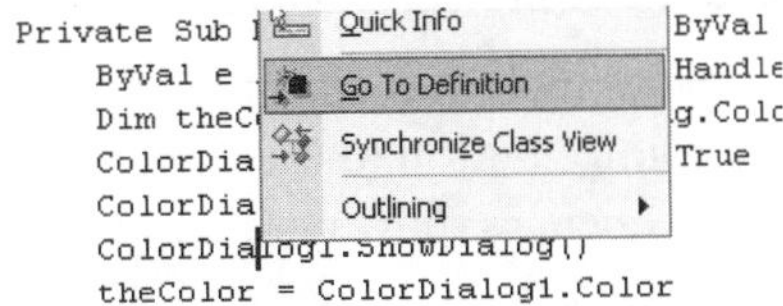

You will be taken to the declaration for `ColorDialog1` at the beginning of the module. Likely, this declaration was generated for you when you added a ColorDialog control to your form. It's probably along these lines:

```
Friend WithEvents ColorDialog1 As System.Windows.Forms.ColorDialog
```

If you move the cursor to `ColorDialog` at the end of this declaration statement, and then select Go To Definition again, the Object Browser will open to the definition of the ColorDialog class, as shown in Figure 14.2.

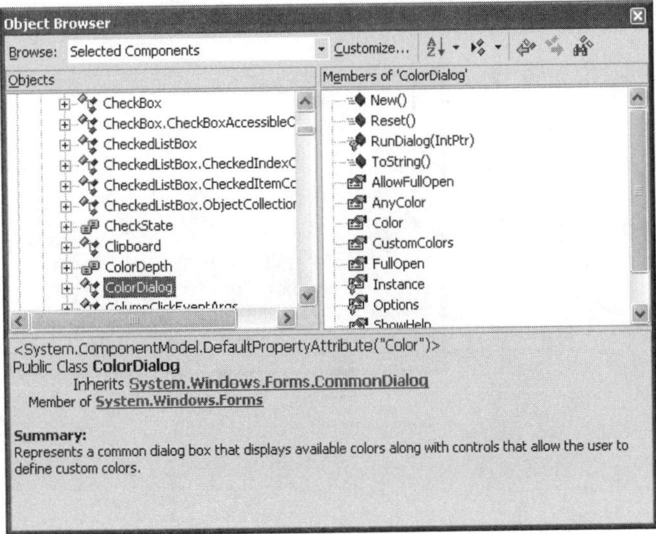

FIGURE 14.2: The class definition of an object is shown in the Object Browser.

Setting Browser Scope

When the Object Browser opens, you have a choice regarding the scope of the browser (or which objects it will see). The two scope options are available in the Browse drop-down list in the upper-left corner of the Object Browser. Selected Components is the default initial selection. You can customize the objects included in this scope.

The other scope option is Active Project, which includes the active project and its references (for example, `System`, and, in the case of a form-based application, `System.Windows.Forms`). The Active Project setting does not allow any customization of the objects that can be browsed. (But you could go back to the project and add or remove a reference in the Solution Explorer.)

To customize the objects included within the Selected Components scope of the Object Browser, click the Customize button to the right of the Browse drop-down list. The Selected Components dialog will open, as shown in Figure 14.3.

FIGURE 14.3:

You can use the Selected Components dialog to determine which components to browse.

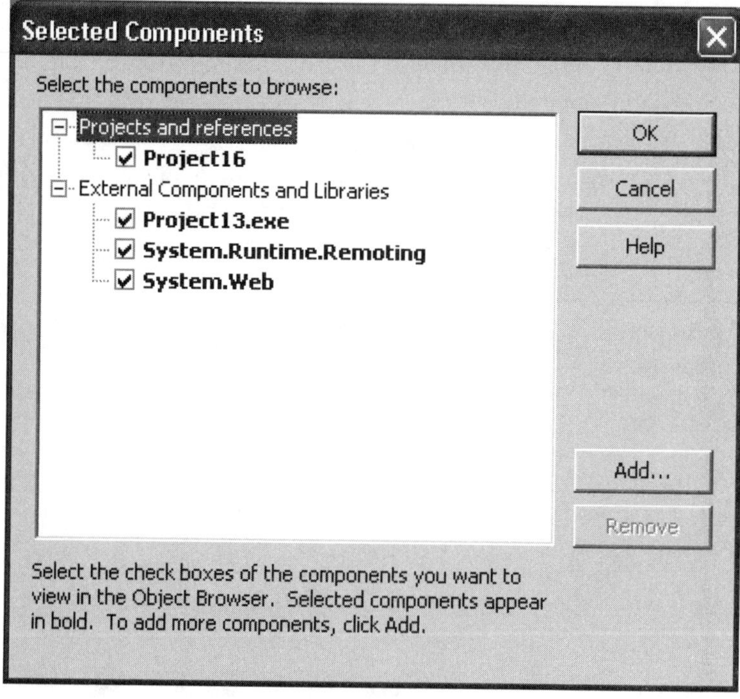

Click the Add button in the Selected Components dialog to open the Component Selector dialog, shown in Figure 14.4. You can use the Component Selector to choose .NET and COM components to add. To add projects, executables, and other types of files (such as OLB or TLB type libraries or DLLs), click the Browse button. Components added to the Selected Components box at the bottom of the Component Selector dialog will appear in the Selected Components dialog. Check the components that you want to be available to browse in the Object Browser.

FIGURE 14.4: You can use the Component Selector dialog to add components to the Selected Components dialog.

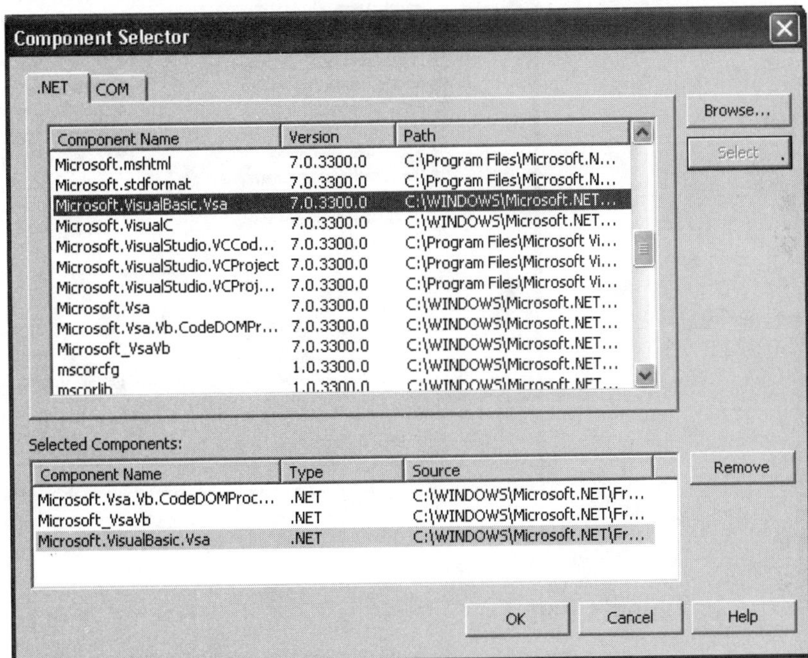

Using the Object Browser Interface

The Object Browser interface consists of a toolbar and three windows, or panes: the Objects pane, the Members pane, and the Description pane. Figure 14.5 shows the full Object Browser interface, with information for the MessageBox class.

FIGURE 14.5: The Members pane shows the members of an object selected in the Objects pane, and the Description pane provides information about the selected object.

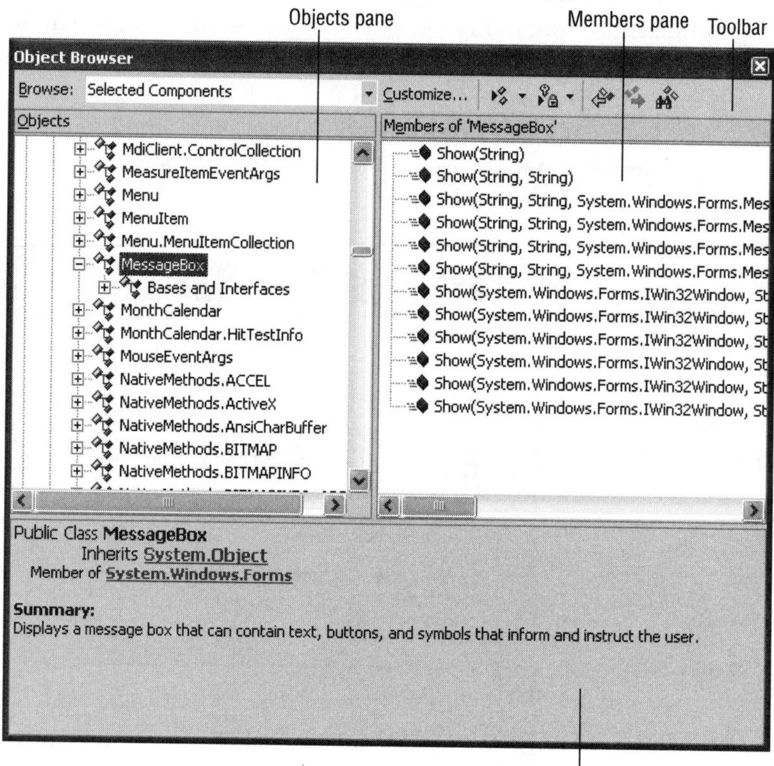

The Objects Pane

The Objects pane provides a hierarchical view of the objects (or classes) contained in the namespaces that are within the scope of the Object Browser. Here is an example of the Objects pane with some of the Color objects (part of the `System.Drawing` namespace):

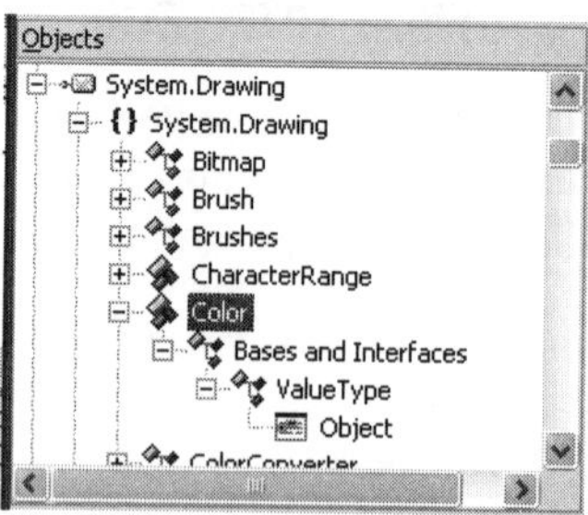

Clicking the + or – icons in the Objects pane expands or contracts the tree view of objects. (Color is a member of `System.Drawing`, so expanding `System.Drawing` shows the Color class.)

If you fully expand an object in the Objects pane, a great deal about the object—such as the classes that it is based on—will be displayed in the Objects pane.

The Members Pane

The Members pane shows the members of an object selected in the Objects pane. *Members* mean properties, methods, events, variables, constants, and enumeration values. Here is the Members pane with some of the members of the Color object:

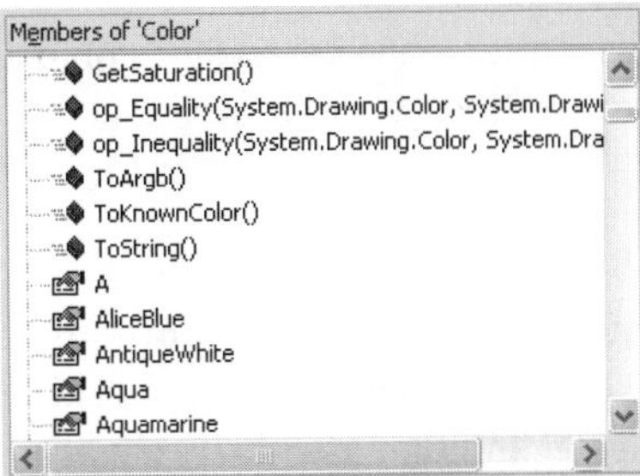

An icon indicates each different kind of member. These icons are shown in Table 14.1. In addition, one other icon, a key (also shown in Table 14.1), means that the member is protected, or only accessible from within its own (or a derived class). (For more on this topic, see Chapter 15, "Object-Oriented Programming in VB .NET.")

TABLE 14.1: Member Pane Icons

Icon	Member Type
	Property or procedure
	Method
	Event
	Variable
	Constant
	Enumeration Value
	Protected

The Description Pane

The Description pane provides a great deal of information about the object currently selected in the Objects pane. This information isn't the same for all objects, but it usually includes the following:

- A description of the object
- The name of the object and its parent object
- The object syntax
- Links to related objects and members

TIP The links in the Description pane take you to objects that are related to the selected object. They are immensely valuable for quickly gathering information about an object.

The Toolbar

The Object Browser toolbar is used to customize the Object Browser scope (as explained in the "Setting Browser Scope" section earlier in this chapter), arrange the contents of the Object Browser, navigate, and find identifiers (such as object names, but called *symbols* here).

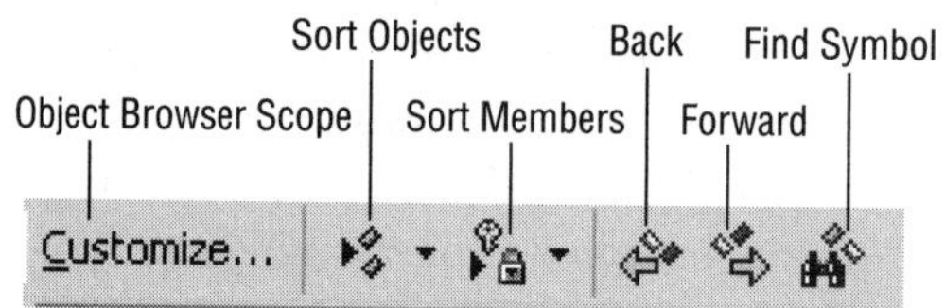

It's likely that the most useful toolbar button is Find Symbol (the button with the binoculars icon). When you click the Find Symbol button, the Find Symbol dialog opens, as shown in Figure 14.6.

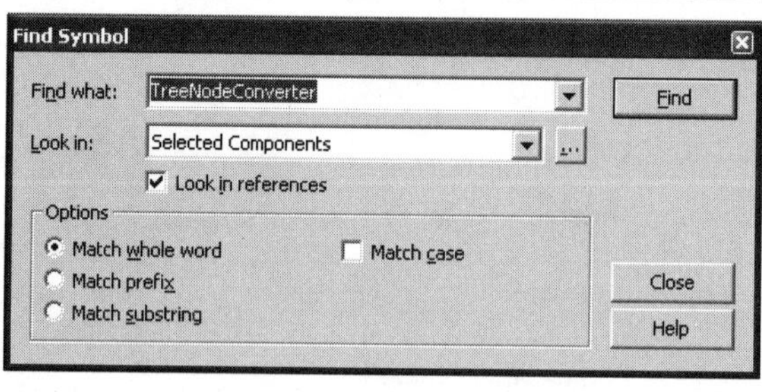

FIGURE 14.6: The Find Symbol dialog lets you search for objects using the object's name.

The Find Symbol dialog allows you to search for objects including namespaces, classes, and structures—and the members of these objects—using the object's name.

TIP Obviously, Object Browser tools, such as the Find Symbol dialog, are the easiest way to locate specific objects within the Object Browser. But pure recreational browsing can teach you a great deal about the way .NET is structured, how to work with it, and even the best way to construct your own object hierarchies.

Exploring Namespaces

When you first open the Object Browser, provided you have not selected an object to define, the objects you see in the Objects pane will all be *assemblies*, as shown here.

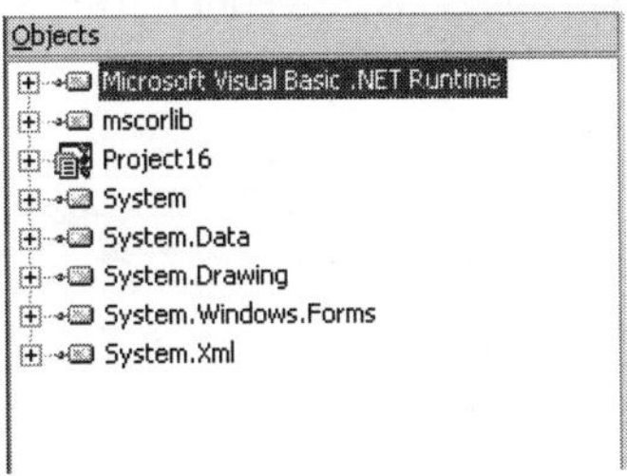

As explained in Chapter 1, "Understanding Visual Basic .NET," assemblies are deployable units of code that correspond to stand-alone executable files or DLLs. Each compiled VB .NET program has at least one related assembly.

If you drill down one step below the assembly level, you'll find that the members of a given assembly are namespaces. Another way of putting this is that namespaces organize the objects defined in an assembly. For example, `Microsoft.VisualBasic` is a namespace that is part of the `Microsoft Visual Basic .NET Runtime` assembly. What can get a little confusing is that a namespace and an assembly can have the same name. For example, here is an Objects pane listing of namespaces that are members of the `System.Windows.Forms` assembly:

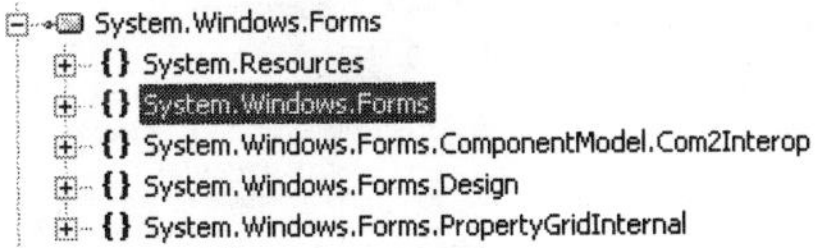

Notice that one of the namespaces is also named `System.Windows.Forms`.

Each project you build is organized in the same fashion, with an assembly that corresponds to the overall executable and one or more namespaces that are the members of the assembly.

Exploring Classes

If you continue drilling down through namespaces in the Objects pane, you'll find the members of each namespace. These include classes, interfaces, enumeration constants, and methods.

Viewing Classes in the Object Browser

A class is a blueprint for an object. You can learn a lot about objects by studying their blueprints in the Object Browser. For example, the Button class is a member of the `System.Windows.Forms` namespace. If you select the Button object in the Objects pane and expand it as shown below, you will learn that Button is descended from Object (like all classes) by way of Component, Control, and ButtonBase.

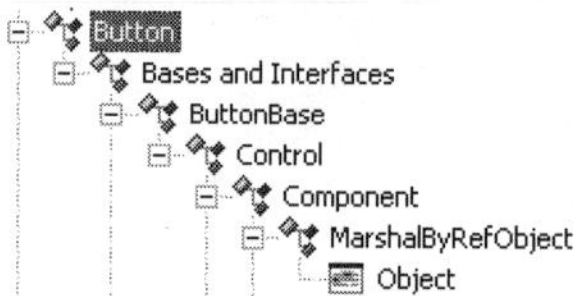

If you look at ButtonBase, you will discover that it implements the basic functionality common to Button controls. Exploring the members of ButtonBase will show you what this functionality is and a great deal about how it has been implemented.

Using the Class View Window

You can also explore the class relationships in your projects using the Class View window. Choose View ➢ Class View to open this window.

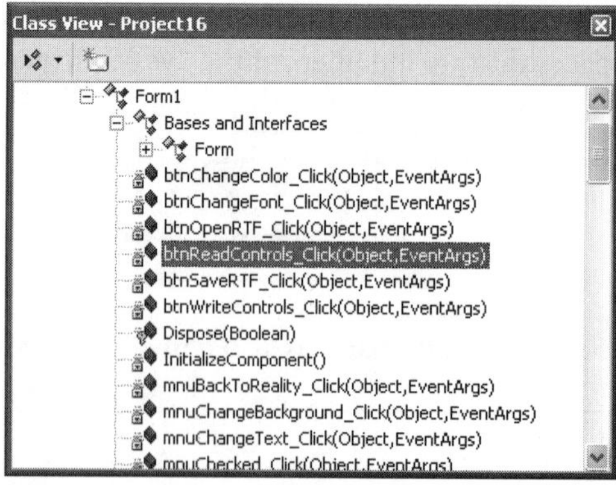

Select a class in the Class View window, right-click, and choose Browse Definition from the context menu. This takes you to the object, and its related information, in the Object Browser.

Summary

The Object Browser is the best tool for learning about the guts of VB .NET and your programs. While relatively intuitive to use, this discovery engine is powerful, informative, and neglected in documentation. For example, what exactly do all those funny little icons mean? You certainly won't find out from the program documentation or Help files.

Browsing objects, namespaces, and classes, and understanding how they relate, brings us to the topic of the next chapter: object-oriented programming in VB .NET.

Chapter 15

Object-Oriented Programming in VB .NET

- Understanding object-oriented programming
- Creating a class
- Building a class library
- Using class modules
- Working with class properties, methods, and events
- Creating a collection class

The previous chapter showed you how to browse the objects, and the classes that are the blueprints for objects, that make up VB. The next step is to effectively use object-oriented programming techniques.

This chapter briefly explains object-oriented programming (OOP for short) concepts. I'll then go on to show you how to use OOP in VB .NET by creating and using classes in your programs. While advanced OOP issues are beyond the scope of this book, by the time you finish this chapter, you should understand how OOP works in VB .NET.

Understanding Object-Oriented Programming

In real-world applications, some aspects of OOP should probably be used wherever possible. These include fostering code reuse and practicing object encapsulation (which means to expose only the members of an object that are specifically designed for accessing that object, as explained a bit later in this chapter). However, a "full-tilt boogie" OOP approach may be overkill for small projects, and it might not always be appropriate even for large projects.

Large projects that involve many objects that may behave in a great variety of ways are probably best tackled in a fully OOP fashion. For example, systems that simulate markets, the weather, or even complex development environments are good candidates for OOP.

In VB6 and earlier versions of VB, you could certainly encapsulate objects, and there were various good strategies for fostering code reuse. (For that matter, you could create and use classes.) However, in certain significant respects, VB was not a truly object-oriented development environment. For example, you were handed a form, which was an object, but the form was a black box—you could neither view nor alter the code that created the form, nor inherit the form and customize its behavior.

VB .NET is a completely object-oriented development environment, in the way that earlier versions of VB were not. Every object that you use in a program is instantiated (created) in your code. VB .NET now includes real object-oriented features, including full inheritance, function overloading, and true polymorphism. (These and other OOP-related terms are described in the following sections.)

It's also the case that VB .NET allows you to create elegant OOP programs with the same features that were formerly available only in languages such as C++ or Java.

Finally, classes—and objects created around classes, such as controls—built in VB .NET can be used in C# .NET, and vice versa. This means that teams of mixed-language developers can use an OOP design to work in the language of their choice, and can even inherit from objects written in another language.

The Case for OOP (and VB .NET)

I've been around programming long enough to see projects written using every conceivable methodology fail, and some written using no methodology or process succeed. Let's just put it this way: I'm not a card-carrying, or Kool-Aid–drinking, member of anything. But writing code in VB .NET is writing OOP code. Therefore, it's important to understand the case for OOP and why VB .NET has been redesigned from the ground up to be an elegant and powerful OOP language.

The .NET Framework intentionally makes you put everything in classes. In .NET, everyone is doing OOP, whether they like it or not. But will developers think about how to organize those classes? Are they doing good OOP or bad OOP? As a .NET programmer, it's important that you understand OOP, so you can do good OOP.

If you look at the genesis for OOP, you'll find that it arose because software projects grew in complexity. Developers were spending more and more time communicating with each other because they needed to have such intimate knowledge of what everyone else was doing. People realized that eventually developers would need to spend all their time in meetings, and no time programming. OOP provided a solution, by allowing the problem to be broken down into chunks, so that developers needed to understand only the internals of their code and the interface to other code.

Proponents believe that the advantages of OOP and its "divide-and-conquer" approach are significant. Used correctly, it will result in a more elegant solution, with code that's more likely to be reused, easier to maintain, and easier to understand.

Abstraction

Abstraction means that you can use code with no knowledge of the internal operation of the object you are accessing. For example, when you use the `StreamWriter.WriteLine` method, you don't need to know anything about how the StreamWriter actually does what you ask. Implementation details are hidden.

In other words, if I've created an OOP abstraction, from the outside of a given object, I need to know what it does and how to invoke a given method; I do not need to know *how* the action is achieved. In fact, I'm better off as an OOP programmer if I simply think of each object as a black box. Object members should do what they have contracted to do. If an object—let's call it `theMath`—performs arithmetic operations, and the `Sum` method of `theMath` is supposed to return the sum of two numbers, then all I need to know is that if I invoke `theMath.Sum (Number1, Number2)`, I'll get the sum back. Abstraction keeps me from worrying about what is going on inside.

Each object may have attributes, which in OOP-speak are known as *properties* and *fields*. For example, a property of the Employee object might be Salary, and an Invoice might have a property called Amount_Due.

In addition to attributes, most objects will be able to take actions, which correspond to the programming concept of methods. For example, the Employee object might be able to `LogBillableHours`, and an Accounting object might be able to `MarkAsPaid(Invoice)`.

A successful OOP abstraction of a programming problem breaks up a problem into objects that interact with each other using their properties and methods, and send each other messages.

TIP I've found it works well to start by writing the name of each object and a one-sentence description on a separate sheet of paper (or a 3-by-5 card). Then I sketch in the object's interface (properties and methods), concentrating on the responsibilities of each object without worrying about implementation details. Later on, I can turn this specification into real code and work out the implementation details that are hidden within the object (see the discussion of encapsulation, coming up shortly).

Classes

Classes are probably the single most important OOP concept. A class is a blueprint, factory, or template—depending on your choice of metaphor—from which objects are made. Every object you create from a class is an *instance* of the class, and the object is said to be *instantiated* when it is created from the class "blueprint" in code.

As an example, think of a Car as a class. A Car has certain attributes—including a year, make, model, color, and more—and is abstract in the sense that it could represent many different cars. In contrast, MyCar (which is a 2001, Mercedes, 430E, Gold) is a specific thing. It is not an abstract concept that could take many forms.

MyCar is said to be an instance of the Car class. In other words, the class is the concept. An actual instance of the concept, such as my specific car, is an object.

The variables, properties, methods, and events within a class are the *members* of the class. The *exposed* members—that is, members available externally to an object of the class—are the *interface* of the class. A *shared* member, indicated using the `Shared` keyword, can be accessed without creating an instance of the class. On the other hand, some interface members do not have any implementation. These are intended to be implemented only in derived classes (see the "Inheritance" section) and are called *abstract members*.

Containment

Containment, or *aggregation*, means that one object contains another object. For example, an Invoice object would likely contain LineItem objects. *Delegation* means handing off a task to a contained object. For example, a method of the Invoice object might invoke a method of a contained LineItem object to perform an inventory adjustment.

Containment is an alternative strategy to inheritance for reusing code. Generally, inheritance should be used if, and only if, an "is a" relationship applies. As an example, a Dog "is an" Animal, so Dog should inherit from Animal. On the other hand, a Customer "has an" address, so containment should be used, and a Customer class should contain an Address class.

Encapsulation

Encapsulation means that you've grouped related attributes and methods to make a cohesive entity. Put somewhat more formally, an object should be a stand-alone unit of code that has as few dependencies on other code as possible. For example, you might build a data access component called dbCustomer. This component exists only to store and retrieve customers from the database. You should be able to use this class in a desktop (Windows Forms) application, web application, or web service. There should be nothing in this class that makes it dependent on a particular user interface implementation.

Ideally, the class should not be dependent on other business rule or data access classes, either. dbCustomer should not be dependent on dbEmployee, for example. In "OO-speak," this is said to be "loosely coupled." Also, since dbCustomer is designed to encapsulate the database operations, it should contain all the code needed to create, read, update, and delete a customer. If so, dbCustomer is said to be "highly cohesive." Loosely coupled and highly cohesive are the hallmarks of good classes. Consider the classes in the Base Class Library. For example, the String class encapsulates all aspects of storing and manipulating an array of characters. It's a stand-alone class. When designing your own classes, keep in mind the goal of making them as independent as possible.

Inheritance

Inheritance means being able to create a new class based on an existing class. The existing class is called the *base*, or *parent*, class, and the new class is called the *child*, or *derived*, class. The child class starts out with all the members of the parent class. You can then *override* some of the methods of the parent class to implement different functionality.

Inheritance enables you to implement classes in a hierarchical fashion. For example, the class used to create Employee objects is probably a good parent for the class used to create Programmer objects. The test is whether a child object has an "is a" relationship with the parent object. If a programmer is an employee, then the example used a few sentences ago shows a good inheritance relationship. On the other hand, if a programmer is a contractor, then it does not.

Part of the power of inheritance comes from the fact that derived classes inherit functionality based on their "ancestors." For example, suppose you have a Mammal class with a BodyTemp property. The Dog class inherits from Mammal, and the Cocker Spaniel class inherits from Dog. A cocker spaniel named Fred is an instance of the Cocker Spaniel class; Fred automatically has a BodyTemp property.

Here's another example that is a little more realistic. Suppose you want to have a TextBox control that will only allow the user to enter dates. You can use inheritance to create a DateBox that inherits all the characteristics of a TextBox with one line of code, and then fairly easily add the logic to check that the input is a date.

Polymorphism

Polymorphism means that objects know what appropriate actions to take, provided they are sent a message they can understand. In other words, different objects that have inherited from the same base class will likely take different actions when sent the same message, because they implement the method difference.

In VB .NET, polymorphism is implemented via inheritance (or through interfaces, as in VB6).

As an example, a `LogBillableHours` method that is a member of an Employee object would probably be implemented differently with various child classes of Employee, such as President, Consultant, and Dishwasher. (The President might tell his assistant, the Consultant might submit a weekly time sheet, and the Dishwasher might punch a time clock.)

Polymorphism is important because it is a mechanism for anticipating future changes. When you add a new object into a system that inherits code from an existing parent, you need to write code only for the methods you need to change (override or, possibly, add). This is a lot easier than needing to change multiple long `Select...Case` statements.

An issue related to polymorphism (but not restricted to OOP) is *overloading*. A function, or method, is overloaded, indicated by the `Overloads` keyword, when two functions have the same name but different signatures. (The *signature* of a function is the number and type of its arguments.) Overloading is used to create methods that differ in signature from the method inherited from a base class.

Creating a Class

Creating a class in VB .NET couldn't be simpler. You start by opening a module of any sort within the Code Editor. As an example, we'll use a form module, as we have done for many of the examples so far in this book.

Creating the Class Framework

With a form module in the Code Editor, take a look at the form code:

```
Public Class Form1
    Inherits System.Windows.Forms.Form
...
End Class
```

You can see that this is just a class, like any other.

Move the cursor past the `End Class` statement for the form. Create the framework for your class, named `ShowMe`, by typing the following:

```
Public Class ShowMe
```

VB .NET completes the framework by adding an `End Class` statement, so you now have an empty class structure:

```
Public Class ShowMe

End Class
```

Adding a Method

The next thing to do is to add a method, or procedure, that does something, so that we can demonstrate using the class. Let's create a simple one named, logically enough, `displayMessage`, which takes a string argument and uses it to display a MessageBox:

```
Public Sub displayMessage(ByVal txt As String)
   MessageBox.Show(txt, "I am a class!", _
   MessageBoxButtons.OK, MessageBoxIcon.Information)
End Sub
```

Listing 15.1 shows the code for the `ShowMe` class and its method.

Listing 15.1 A Class That Displays a MessageBox

```
Public Class ShowMe
   Public Sub displayMessage(ByVal txt As String)
      MessageBox.Show(txt, "I am a class!", _
      MessageBoxButtons.OK, MessageBoxIcon.Information)
   End Sub
End Class
```

NOTE The `Public` keyword determines the scope of class members. For more information, see the "Working with Class Properties, Methods, and Events" section later in this chapter.

Invoking a Class

Now, let's invoke the class. Add a button to your form, and in the button's Click event procedure, create an object, named `x`, that is an instance of the `ShowMe` class:

```
Dim x As New ShowMe()
```

Next, invoke the `x` object's `displayMessage` method with a text argument:

```
x.displayMessage("Hello!")
```

The complete method invocation code is shown in Listing 15.2.

Listing 15.2 Invoking a Method of the Class from a Click Event Procedure

```
Private Sub btnDoIt_Click(ByVal sender As Object, _
   ByVal e As System.EventArgs) Handles btnDoIt.Click
   Dim x As New ShowMe()
   x.displayMessage("Hello!")
End Sub
```

If you run the project, and click the button, a message will be displayed.

Using a Shared Member

If a member of a class is marked using the `Shared` keyword, you don't need to instantiate an object based on the class to use the class member. One way of thinking of this is that shared members belong to the class as a whole, rather than to a single instance of the class. (Of course, you can still use a shared member in an instantiated object based on the class if you want to.)

Creating a shared member is a useful thing to do with utility methods that will be used by a great many different objects. An example in VB .NET is `MessageBox.Show`—you do not need to create an instance of the `MessageBox` class to use the `Show` method.

To use our `displayMessage` method as a shared member, add the `Shared` keyword:

```
Public Shared Sub displayMessage(ByVal txt As String)
```

It can then be invoked without instantiating an object by using the class name, the dot operator, and the method:

```
ShowMe.displayMessage ("This works without instantiating an object!")
```

NOTE Once you declare a method as shared, you can invoke it only from the class type. You can no longer call it for an actual instance of an object based on the class.

Listing 15.3 shows the code from Listings 15.1 and 15.2 revised so that `ShowMe` is a shared member, invoked without object instantiation.

Listing 15.3 Invoking a Shared Member

```
Private Sub btnDoIt_Click(ByVal sender As Object, _
   ByVal e As System.EventArgs) Handles btnDoIt.Click
   ShowMe.displayMessage ("This works without instantiating" & _
     " an object!")
End Sub
...
Public Class ShowMe
   Public Shared Sub displayMessage(ByVal txt As String)
      MessageBox.Show(txt, "I am a class!", _
      MessageBoxButtons.OK, MessageBoxIcon.Information)
   End Sub
End Class
```

If you run the revised code, you'll see this message box:

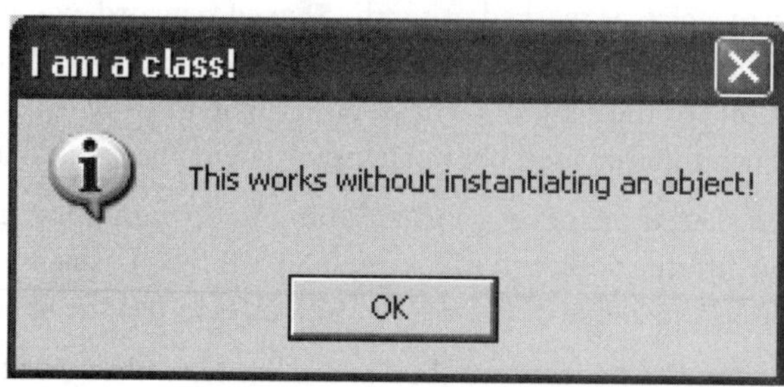

Building a Class Library

For a class to be usable externally, the project that it is in must be compiled into a library (DLL) rather than an executable file (EXE). You may find it useful to build a library of code that you can include in multiple applications.

To create a class library, open the Property Pages for your project and set the Output type to Class Library (rather than Windows Application), as shown in Figure 15.1.

FIGURE 15.1: To access a class externally, it should be compiled into a library.

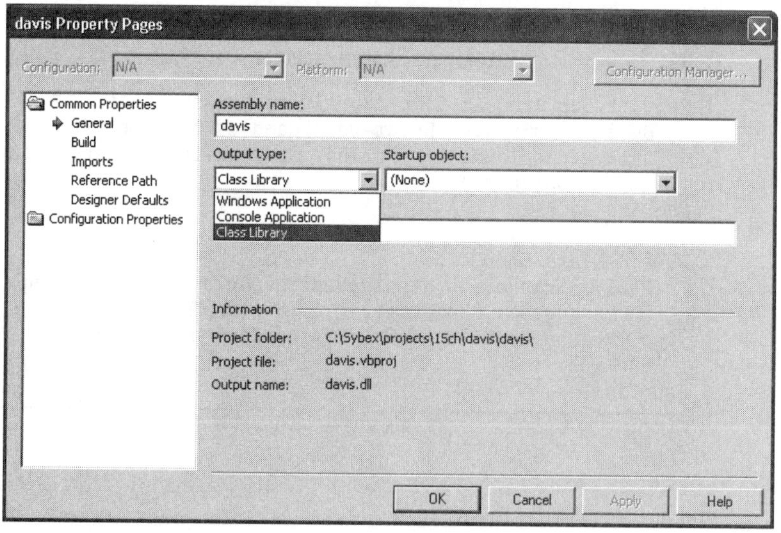

Next, build the library. Note that you should *build* it, rather than *run* the project (which starts by creating a build). A library cannot be run; it is said to have "no entry point," because it is intended to be run by from other programs, not as a stand-alone executable.

In fact, normally, you would not include a form module in a class library. Class modules are intended to be compiled into a class library (see the "Using Class Modules" section later in this chapter for more information about class modules).

Invoking a Class Using Its Namespace

At the head of the class, so to speak, are namespaces. Every class—and every module—must be part of a namespace. If you want to access a class that is external to your project, you'll need to invoke it using its namespace.

Each project that becomes a program is represented by an assembly. By default, both the assembly, and the *root*, or starting, namespace have the same name as the project. For example, if I name a project `davis`, as shown in Figure 15.2, both the assembly and root namespace are named `davis`.

FIGURE 15.2:
The project name will become the name of the root namespace.

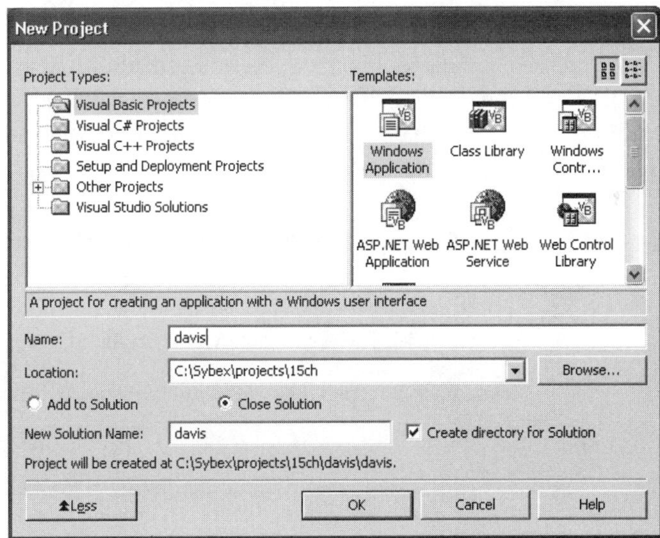

Namespaces help to organize class libraries and avoid ambiguity between class names. There needs to be a way to uniquely identify classes (you can have two different classes with the same name but residing in different namespaces).

You can change the name of the project and related assembly and root namespace by using the project's Property Pages, as shown in Figure 15.3.

FIGURE 15.3: The root namespace can be changed using the project's Property Pages.

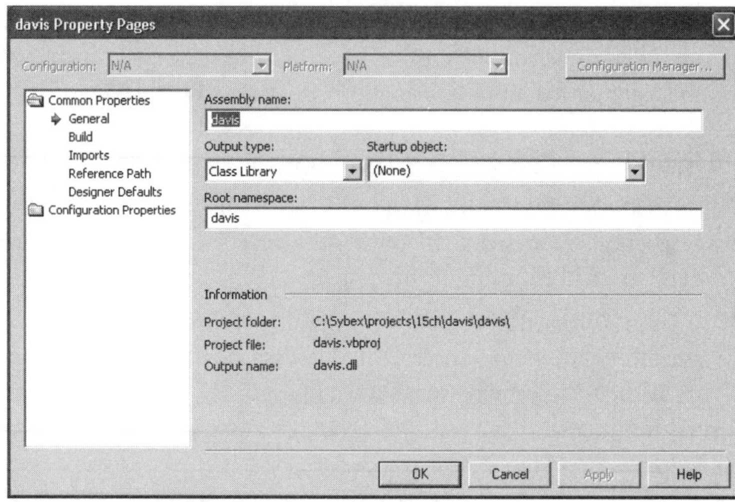

Within the project's root namespace, you can add whatever namespaces—and namespace hierarchies—you would like using the `Namespace` and `End Namespace` keywords. For example, within the `davis` root namespace, let's put our `ShowMe` class in a namespace named `harold`. This is shown in Listing 15.4.

Listing 15.4 Creating a New Namespace That Contains the *ShowMe* Class

```
Namespace harold
   Public Class ShowMe
      Public Sub displayMessage(ByVal txt As String)
         MessageBox.Show(txt, "I am a class!", _
         MessageBoxButtons.OK, MessageBoxIcon.Information)
      End Sub
   End Class
End Namespace
```

Let's rebuild the `davis` project containing the `harold` namespace, which contains the `ShowMe` class, and close the project.

WARNING You need to comment out the instantiation based on the ShowMe object in the Do It button's Click event project before you can rebuild the project. This is because it is now `harold.ShowMe`, rather than just ShowMe.

The next step is to open a new project that will instantiate an object using the `ShowMe` class as a blueprint.

Referencing and Instantiating the Class

To use a class in your class library, you need to add a reference to it. For our example, the next step is to add a reference to the `davis` project. First, open a new Windows Application solution and project (one that has a form). Then open the Add Reference dialog by selecting Project ➢ Add Reference or by right-clicking References in the Solution Explorer. With the Add Reference dialog open, select the Projects tab, as shown in Figure 15.4.

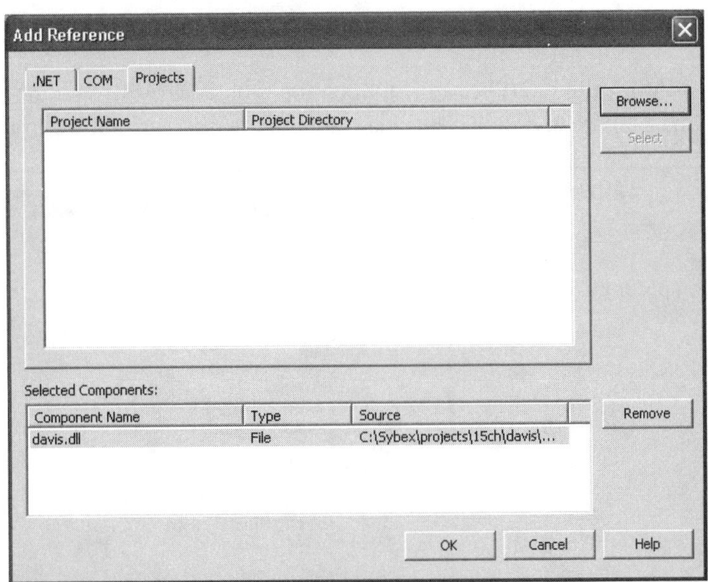

FIGURE 15.4: The Projects tab of the Add Reference dialog is used to add a reference to a project.

Click the Browse button, and then select `davis.dll`. It will be added to the Selected Components list at the bottom of the Add Reference dialog.

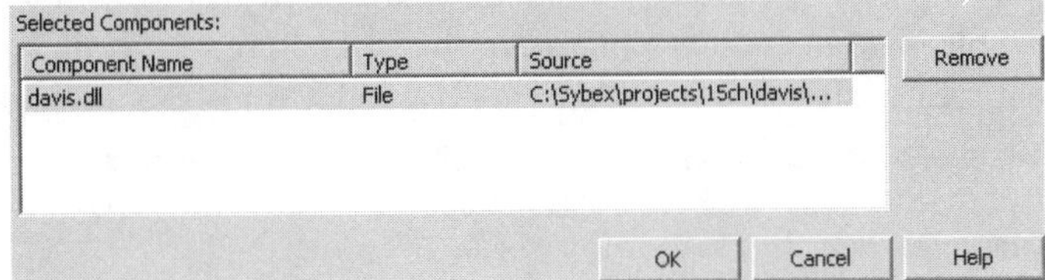

Click OK. The reference to the `davis` project will now appear under References in the Solution Explorer.

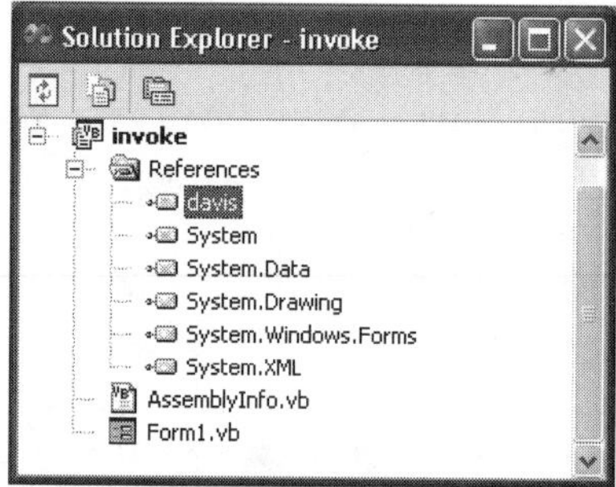

With the reference added, open the Object Browser. There, you'll see the `davis.harold` namespace and the `ShowMe` class and its members, as shown in Figure 15.5.

FIGURE 15.5: The classes and members of the new library now appear in the Object Browser.

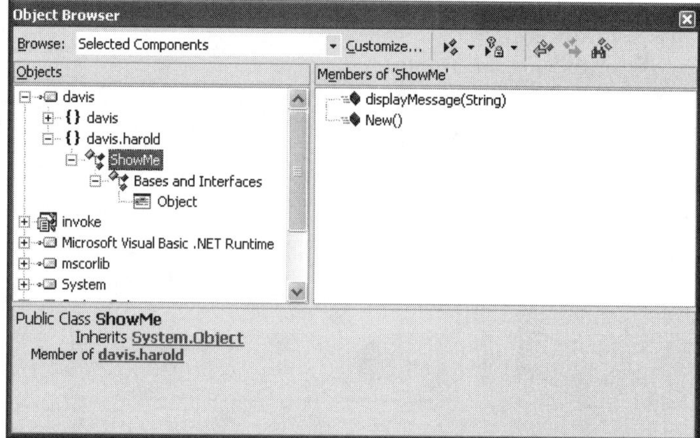

You can go about creating an object of the `ShowMe` class in the new project in the normal fashion, although you do need to remember where the class fits in its namespace hierarchy. For example, if you've added a button to the form, here's the code in its Click event procedure that creates an object based on the class and invokes the method:

```
Private Sub btnCallClass_Click(ByVal sender As System.Object, _
   ByVal e As System.EventArgs) Handles btnCallClass.Click
   Dim x As New davis.harold.ShowMe()
   x.displayMessage("I'm in another project!")
End Sub
```

If you run this code, the external class will be invoked to instantiate an object based on it, the `displayMessage` method will be called, and the appropriate MessageBox will appear on the screen.

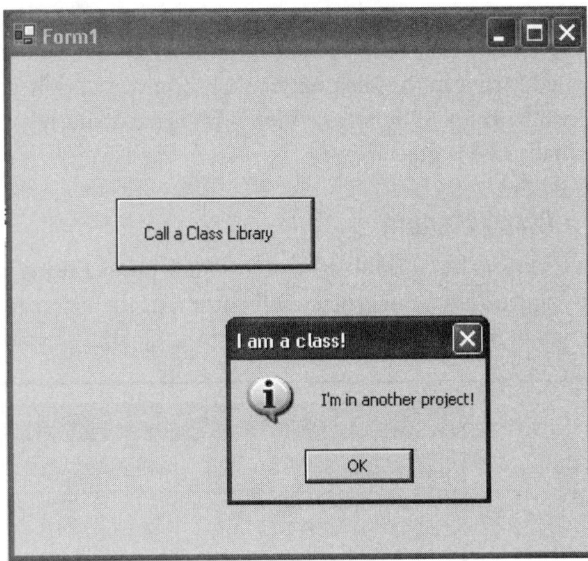

Using the *Imports* Keyword

Suppose you get tired of using the namespace hierarchy every time you want to instantiate an object. It could, of course, be a great deal worse than `davis.harold`. I could add some middle names to get to `davis.harold.leon.fair-weather.virgil.william`. Well, maybe not, but you get the idea that needing to repeatedly use the namespace hierarchy can be annoying.

The solution is to use an `Imports` statement at the top of your module. In examples in earlier chapters, you've seen `Imports` used to make coding with .NET classes simpler. You can also use it with the class libraries that you create. Using an `Imports` statement, the code snippet in the previous section is rewritten as follows:

```
Imports davis.harold
...
Private Sub btnCallClass_Click(ByVal sender As System.Object, _
   ByVal e As System.EventArgs) Handles btnCallClass.Click
   Dim x As New ShowMe()
   x.displayMessage("I'm in another project!")
End Sub
```

If you had a number of references to classes within the `davis.harold` namespace, this would make your life simpler (and the code easier to read).

Using Class Modules

As I mentioned earlier in this chapter, classes should generally go in a class module (rather than one already occupied by form code). This is particularly true if you plan to access the classes externally to a project.

Creating a Class Module

One way to create a class module is to start a new project using the Class Library template, as shown in Figure 15.6. The project will automatically be created with a class module. Also, the project will be set to build into a class library, or DLL, by default.

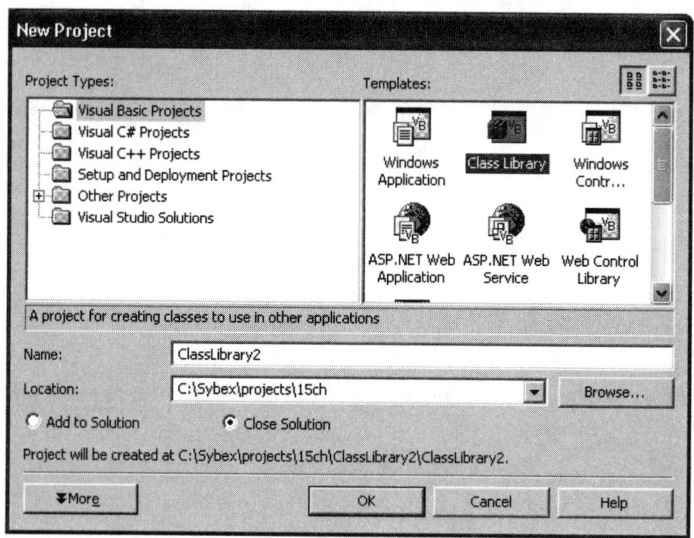

FIGURE 15.6: You can start a new project using the Class Library template that will include a class module.

It's also easy to add a new class module to any project with the Add New Item dialog. Just make sure Class is selected in the Templates pane, as shown in Figure 15.7.

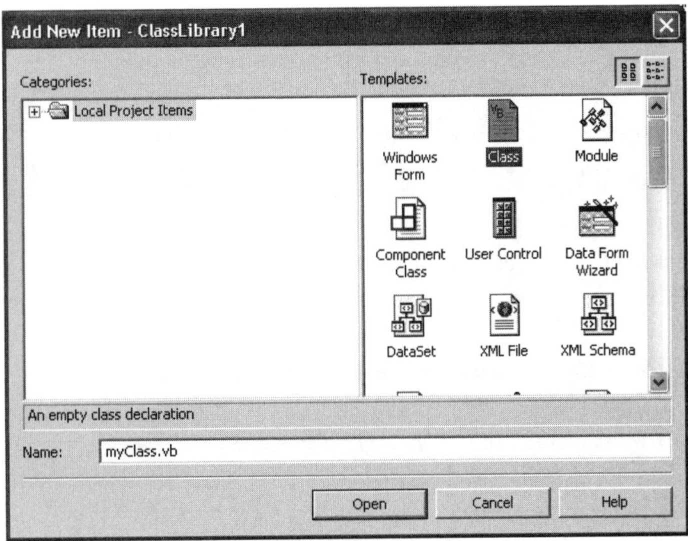

FIGURE 15.7: You can add a class module to any project using the Add New Item dialog.

Adding Classes to the Module

Once you have a class module, you should open it in the Code Editor. You'll see that one class framework has already been created in the module:

```
Public Class Class1

End Class
```

You can change the name of the class to anything you like.

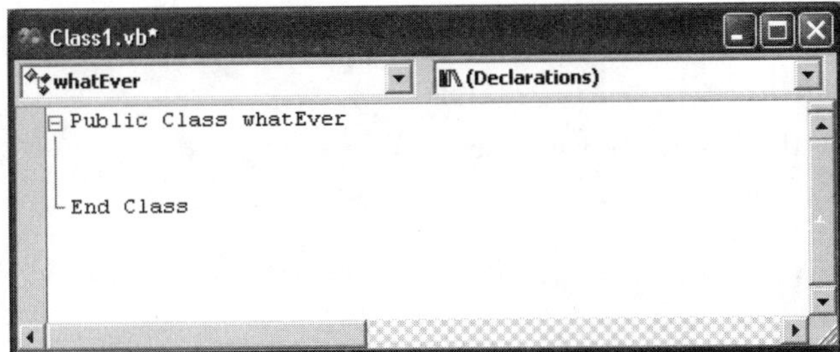

Then add class members, as explained earlier in the chapter. You can also add other classes to the module, with or without hierarchies of namespaces.

TIP The easiest way to test classes is to create a normal Windows Application project that includes code to test the classes in a class module.

Working with Class Properties, Methods, and Events

Before you implement class members, you need to understand their access scope. There are five possible access scopes for members of a class, shown in Table 15.1. The default access scope for a member is `Public`, except for variables, which default to `Private`.

TABLE 15.1: Access Keywords for Class and Member Scope

Keyword	Meaning
`Public`	`Public` allows access without restrictions.
`Private`	`Private` access is the most restricted; access is restricted to within its class (including any nested classes).
`Protected`	Members specified using the `Protected` keyword have, logically enough, protected access. They can be accessed from within the class or from a derived class.
`Friend`	`Friend` access means that access is restricted to the assembly that contains the class or member.
`Protected Friend`	`Protected Friend` members can be accessed only from within the class or a derived class, or access is restricted to the assembly that contains the member. In other words, access to a `Protected Friend` member is the union of `Protected` and `Friend` access to that member. (`Protected Friend` does not apply to a class.)

Implementing Class Properties

You might think that you could define a class property using a variable declared with `Public` access, as in this example:

```
Public Class cPerson
   Public Age As Integer

End Class
```

Sure enough, any program that can instantiate a cPerson object can access the Age variable. But wait! This violates a number of the principles of OOP, particularly encapsulation. We don't want a user to be able to enter any value for age; it must be within a range, and this validation—as an implementation detail—should be hidden.

The proper way to implement properties within classes is by using Property procedures. Validation (or any other implementation) is done within the class using private variables. Listing 15.5 shows the framework for a Property procedure.

Listing 15.5 The Framework for a Property Procedure

```
Public Class cPerson
   Property Age() As Integer
      Get

      End Get
      Set(ByVal Value As Integer)

      End Set
   End Property
End Class
```

Listing 15.6 shows a possible implementation of an Age property with a bit of validation code.

Listing 15.6 Implementing the Age Property

```
Public Class cPerson
   Private iAge As Decimal
   Property Age() As Decimal
      Get
         Age = iAge
      End Get
      Set(ByVal Value As Decimal)
         ' Do some validation
         If Value <= 0 Or Value > 140 Then
            MessageBox.Show("Too old or too young!")
         Else
            iAge = Value
         End If
      End Set
   End Property
End Class
```

You'll note that in Listing 15.6, I've changed the property type from Integer to Decimal (I'll show you why soon, when we get to Listing 15.8). Listing 15.7 adds a new property, Name, to the class. The Property Name procedure contains no validation code, but in theory, you could use pattern-matching techniques to make sure that the name entered met certain criteria.

Listing 15.7 The cPerson Class with Two Properties

```
Public Class cPerson
   Private iAge As Decimal
   Private iName As String
   Property Age() As Decimal
      Get
         Age = iAge
      End Get
      Set(ByVal Value As Decimal)
         ' Do some validation
         If Value <= 0 Or Value > 140 Then
            MessageBox.Show("Too old or too young!")
         Else
            iAge = Value
         End If
      End Set
   End Property
   Property Name() As String
      Get
         Name = iName
      End Get
      Set(ByVal Value As String)
         iName = Value
      End Set
   End Property
End Class
```

Listing 15.8 shows code that could be used to create an object based on the class. (It's a very young cPerson object; hence, the need for a Decimal rather than Integer value.) Note that the `MessageBox.Show` statement at the end of the event procedure in Listing 15.8 tests the Property procedure by making sure that the new values are in effect.

Listing 15.8 Creating a cPerson Object and Using the Properties

```
Private Sub btnDoIt_Click(ByVal sender As Object, _
   ByVal e As System.EventArgs) Handles btnDoIt.Click
   Dim Nicholas As New cPerson()
   Nicholas.Age = 0.1
   Nicholas.Name = "Nicholas Davis"
   MessageBox.Show(Nicholas.Name & " is " & Nicholas.Age.ToString & _
      " years old.", "I am a cPerson Object", _
      MessageBoxButtons.OK, MessageBoxIcon.Information)
End Sub
```

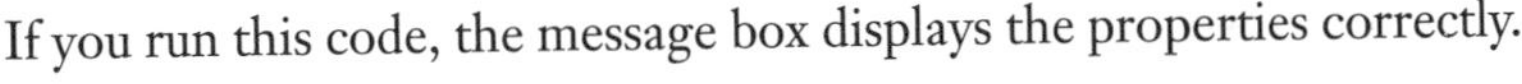
If you run this code, the message box displays the properties correctly.

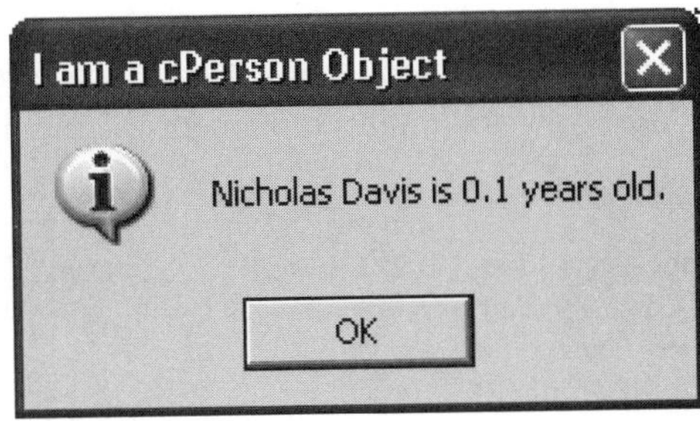

What if you substitute an invalid value for the Age property, like this?

```
Nicholas.Age = 180
```

You will get the class-generated error message, as shown here.

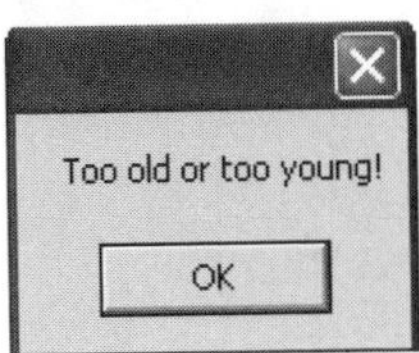

Implementing Class Methods

Methods, as you've already seen, are implemented using procedures or functions. For example, the MessageBox display shown in Listing 15.8 could be moved over to the cPerson class. Here's how it would be implemented using the `Me` keyword within the class:

```
Public Class cPerson
...
   Public Sub Show()
      MessageBox.Show(Me.Name & " is " & Me.Age.ToString & _
         " years old.", "I am a cPerson Object", _
         MessageBoxButtons.OK, MessageBoxIcon.Information)
   End Sub
End Class
```

You could then invoke it:

```
Dim Nicholas As New cPerson()
Nicholas.Age = 0.1
Nicholas.Name = "Nicholas Davis"
Nicholas.Show()
```

The message box displayed would be the same as the one generated by Listing 15.8.

You use a function instead of a procedure when the method needs to return a value. For example, suppose you want a method in the class that checks a passed argument to see if an entity is a baby. Here's how you might implement the method:

```
Public Class cPerson
...
   Public Function IsBaby(ByVal howOld As Decimal) As Boolean
      If howOld < 3 Then
         Return True
      Else
         Return False
      End If
   End Function
End Class
```

Invoking the method is matter of calling the method with an appropriate argument and evaluating it.

You could use the return value from the method to decide whether to do something, for example, to display a MessageBox:

```
If Nicholas.IsBaby(0.875) Then
   MessageBox.Show("Nicholas is a baby!", "Baby Method", _
   MessageBoxButtons.OK, MessageBoxIcon.Information)
End If
```

If `IsBaby` returns True, you see the message box.

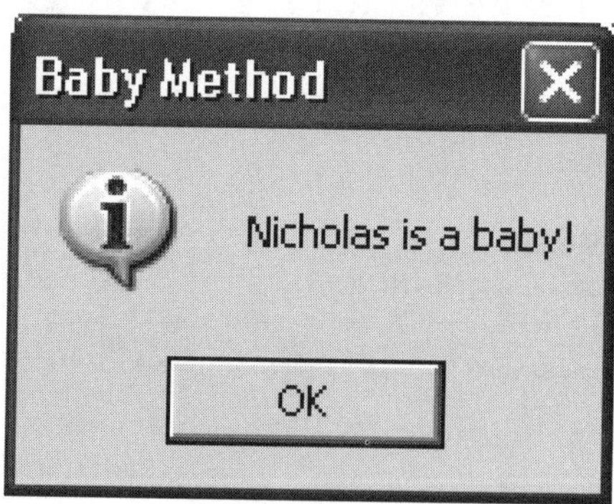

This is a good place to mention one of the great things about using class members in VB .NET: As soon as you add them to the class, they show up in the Code Editor as an object's members. Here, you see `IsBaby` as an auto-completion option.

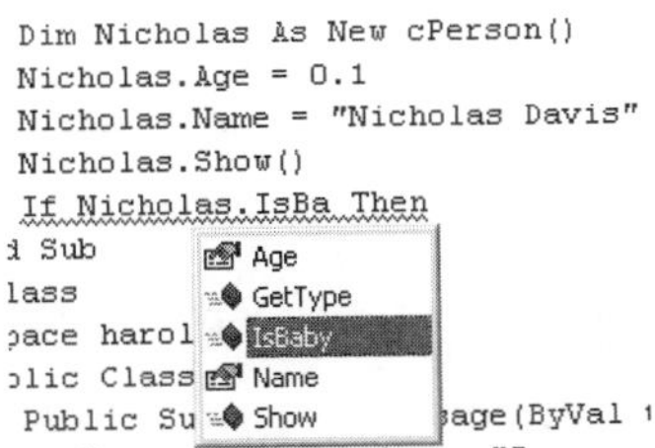
Dim Nicholas As New cPerson()
Nicholas.Age = 0.1
Nicholas.Name = "Nicholas Davis"
Nicholas.Show()
If Nicholas.IsBa Then
Age
GetType
IsBaby
Name
Show

Adding Events to a Class

As you'll recall, an event is a procedure that is a special kind of placeholder for code that is triggered, or *fired*, when something occurs. Chapter 5, "Events and the Life Cycle of Forms," explained a great deal about how events work in VB .NET.

It's easy to add events to a class, and I'll show you how it's done in this section, using our cPerson class as an example. When an object is instantiated based on the class with an event, event-handling procedure code can be executed when the event is fired—just like, for example, a form or button event.

Declaring Events

Events are declared in the class module using the `Event` keyword. For example, we might want an event to be fired when the Name property for an instantiated object is changed. We could declare it this way:

```
Public Event Name_Changed(ByVal event_number As Integer)
```

NOTE It is up to you to decide what information you want your event to provide when it is fired. This information is passed as the arguments of the event procedure. In the example presented here, the information is an event number.

You are completely responsible for firing the event, which is done using the `RaiseEvent` keyword. I've placed a `RaiseEvent` statement that fires the Name_Changed event in the Property Set procedure:

```
RaiseEvent Name_Changed(42)
```

NOTE Strictly speaking, this event is fired when the Name property is set. It doesn't actually need to change.

Listing 15.9 shows the code for the cPerson class, including the code used to add the Name_Changed event.

Listing 15.9 The cPerson Class Module Including the Name_Changed Event

```
Option Strict On
Public Class cPerson
   Public Event Name_Changed(ByVal event_number As Integer)
   Private iAge As Decimal
   Private iName As String
   Property Age() As Decimal
      Get
         Age = iAge
      End Get
      Set(ByVal Value As Decimal)
         ' Do some validation
         If Value <= 0 Or Value > 140 Then
            MessageBox.Show("Too old or too young!")
         Else
            iAge = Value
         End If
      End Set
   End Property
   Property Name() As String
      Get
         Name = iName
      End Get
      Set(ByVal Value As String)
         RaiseEvent Name_Changed(42)
         iName = Value
      End Set
   End Property
   Public Sub Show()
      MessageBox.Show(Me.Name & " is " & Me.Age.ToString & _
        " years old.", "I am a cPerson Object", _
        MessageBoxButtons.OK, MessageBoxIcon.Information)
   End Sub
   Public Function IsBaby(ByVal howOld As Decimal) As Boolean
      If howOld < 3 Then
         Return True
      Else
         Return False
      End If
   End Function
End Class
```

Instantiating an Object with an Event

Next, we need to make a few modifications to the form code that instantiates the cPerson object. First, let's include a few text boxes on the form, so that the user can add new names and ages to the object (it's easier to test for the Name_Changed event that way).

Next, the object to be instantiated, which I've named Nicholas, must be declared using the `WithEvents` keyword at the beginning of the module:

```
Public WithEvents Nicholas As cPerson
```

Since Nicholas has already been declared as type cPerson, we no longer want to use this statement:

```
Dim Nicholas As New cPerson()
```

Instead, we simply instantiate a new cPerson object, which is pointed to by the previously declared Nicholas object:

```
Nicholas = New cPerson()
```

One-Step or Two-Step Instantiation

Let's do the instantiation two-step rumba! Seriously, folks, it's helpful to remember that the statement `Dim Nicholas As New cPerson()` combines two steps—declaring the variable and instantiating it—in a single shorthand statement. It is precisely equivalent to the following two statements, which are each one of the two steps:

```
Dim Nicholas As cPerson()
Nicholas = New cPerson()
```

Creating the Event Procedure

The next step is to go find the Name_Changed event for the Nicholas object, which works in the same way as finding the Click event for a Button control. With the form open in the Code Editor, select the Nicholas object in the Objects list. The Name_Changed event will appear in the Procedures list.

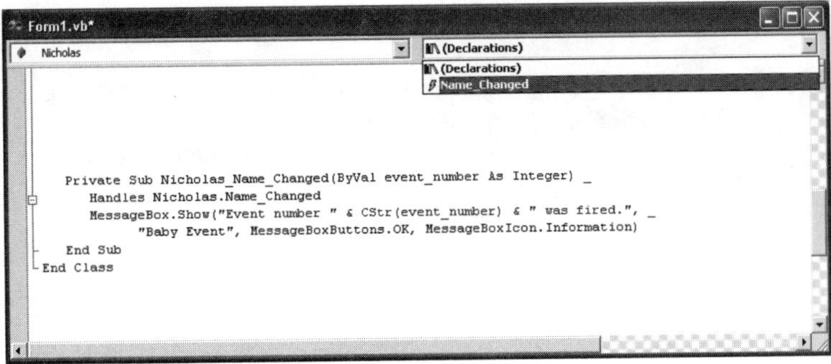

As with a button Click event, when you click the Name_Changed event in the Procedures list, the framework for the event procedure will be created for you:

```
Private Sub Nicholas_Name_Changed(ByVal event_number As Integer) _
   Handles Nicholas.Name_Changed

End Sub
```

Let's add a `MessageBox.Show` statement to this event handler, so we can see when it is fired:

```
Private Sub Nicholas_Name_Changed(ByVal event_number As Integer) _
   Handles Nicholas.Name_Changed
   MessageBox.Show("Event number " & CStr(event_number) & _
   " was fired.", "Baby Event", MessageBoxButtons.OK, _
   MessageBoxIcon.Information)
End Sub
```

Listing 15.10 shows the form module code that instantiates a Nicholas object (based on the cPerson class) and then displays a message box when the Name_Changed event is fired.

Listing 15.10 Invoking the Class and Firing the Event

```
Option Strict On
Public Class Form1
   Inherits System.Windows.Forms.Form
   Public WithEvents Nicholas As cPerson
...
   Private Sub btnDoIt_Click(ByVal sender As Object, _
      ByVal e As System.EventArgs) Handles btnDoIt.Click
      Nicholas = New cPerson()
      Nicholas.Age = CDec(txtAge.Text)
      Nicholas.Name = txtName.Text
      Nicholas.Show()
      If Nicholas.IsBaby(CDec(txtAge.Text)) Then
         MessageBox.Show("Nicholas is a baby!", "Baby Method", _
         MessageBoxButtons.OK, MessageBoxIcon.Information)
      End If
   End Sub

   Private Sub Nicholas_Name_Changed(ByVal event_number As Integer) _
      Handles Nicholas.Name_Changed
      MessageBox.Show("Event number " & CStr(event_number) & _
      " was fired.", "Baby Event", MessageBoxButtons.OK, _
      MessageBoxIcon.Information)
   End Sub
End Class
```

If you run the project, each time you enter a name in the Name text box and click the Do It! button, you'll see that the Name_Changed event has been fired.

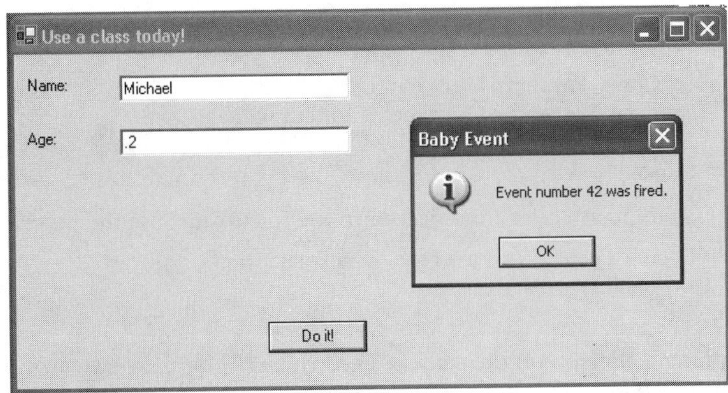

TIP The cPerson class event uses the `New` constructor and the `Finalize` destructor method, which are built into all classes to instantiate and finalize objects. However, it is often the case that you may wish to override these methods and add initialization (and clean-up) code before the base-class methods are called.

Creating a Collection Class

As you learned in Chapter 8, "Adding StatusBars, ToolBars, ToolTips, and Tabbed Dialogs," a *collection* is a way to contain and access objects of all kinds. Using the VB .NET collection object allows you to easily and powerfully organize the objects built using your custom classes.

To demonstrate the use of collections with classes, let's organize a structure around our cPerson object that uses a collection to behave like a stack.

NOTE A *stack* is a data structure with the property that each new item added to it ("pushed" on it) becomes the next item accessed ("popped") off it. In other words, a stack is not a random-access structure. Only the top item in the stack is available to the program at any given time.

Implementing a Collection Class

To implement a collection class, the first step is to create the class in our class module. If the collection class inherits from `System.Collection.CollectionBase`, it will automatically have available all of the methods and properties that you may be familiar with from dealing with ListBoxes, such as `Clear` and `Add` methods, and an Items property (itself a collection).

Let's name our collection class `PersonCollection`. So the framework declaration for the class that allows it to inherit from `System.Collection.CollectionBase` looks like this:

```
Public Class PersonCollection
   Inherits System.Collections.CollectionBase

End Class
```

It's easy to push a cPerson object onto the stack—just use the inherited `List.Add` method:

```
Public Sub Push(ByVal aPerson As cPerson)
   List.Add(aPerson)
End Sub
```

Popping a cPerson off the stack is a bit trickier. There are two aspects to this: We need to return the cPerson object that is being popped, and we also need to remove it from the stack.

First, declare a function that will handle the "popping" and also return the object:

```
Public Function Pop() As cPerson

End Function
```

Next, make sure that the collection has at least one member using the inherited `Count` property (otherwise, trying to remove a member will produce a runtime error):

```
Public Function Pop() As cPerson
   If Count >= 1 Then

   End If
End Function
```

Next, create a temporary variable, `iPerson`, of type cPerson. The conversion function `CType` will be used, with the collection's `List.Item` property, to store the most recently added cPerson object in `iPerson`:

```
Dim iPerson As cPerson
iPerson = CType(List.Item(Count - 1), cPerson)
```

NOTE The CType function converts an expression to the specified type (often called *type casting*). See Chapter 7, "Working with Windows Form Controls," for more information about using CType.

Finally, use the inherited `List.RemoveAt` method to delete the current object, and then return the temporary `iPerson` object (it is the object that has been popped from the stack).

The complete code for implementing a stack as a collection class is shown in Listing 15.11.

Listing 15.11 Implementing a Stack As a Collection Class

```
Option Strict On
...
Public Class PersonCollection
   Inherits System.Collections.CollectionBase

   Public Sub Push(ByVal aPerson As cPerson)
      List.Add(aPerson)
   End Sub

   Public Function Pop() As cPerson
      If Count >= 1 Then
         Dim iPerson As cPerson
         iPerson = CType(List.Item(Count - 1), cPerson)
         List.RemoveAt(Count - 1)
         Return iPerson
      End If
   End Function
End Class
```

Using the Collection Class

To actually push and pop from the stack, we must do a little work. We'll use the same form module that we've been using to work with cPerson objects all along, adding a button for pushing and a button for popping. The Name and Age property of each `cPerson` object will be entered in the existing Name and Age text boxes.

WARNING The project includes no validation code to make sure that user input is of appropriate type, or even that the user has entered anything at all.

In the form module code, a new `PersonCollection` object needs to be declared and created:

```
Dim myPersonCollection As New PersonCollection()
```

It's easy to push the stack by creating a new cPerson object and using it to invoke the `Push` method we just wrote:

```
Dim X As New cPerson()
X.Age = CDec(txtAge.Text)
X.Name = txtName.Text
myPersonCollection.Push(X)
```

Popping the stack is equally simple, but we do need to check that there is something on the stack before we pop:

```
If myPersonCollection.Count >= 1 Then
   Dim X As New cPerson()
   X = myPersonCollection.Pop
   ...
   ' Do something with the popped object
Else
   ' Nothing to pop
End If
```

The complete code that uses the collection stack is shown in Listing 15.12.

Listing 15.12 Pushing and Popping the Stack

```
Option Strict On
Public Class Form1
   Inherits System.Windows.Forms.Form
   Dim myPersonCollection As New PersonCollection()
...
   Private Sub btnPush_Click(ByVal sender As Object, _
      ByVal e As System.EventArgs) Handles btnPush.Click
      Dim X As New cPerson()
      X.Age = CDec(txtAge.Text)
      X.Name = txtName.Text
      myPersonCollection.Push(X)
   End Sub

   Private Sub btnPop_Click(ByVal sender As System.Object, _
      ByVal e As System.EventArgs) Handles btnPop.Click
      If myPersonCollection.Count >= 1 Then
         Dim X As New cPerson()
         X = myPersonCollection.Pop
         MessageBox.Show(X.Name & ", aged " & X.Age & _
            " years, was popped off the stack!", _
            "Stack event", MessageBoxButtons.OK, _
            MessageBoxIcon.Information)
      Else
         MessageBox.Show("Nobody left on the stack!", _
         "Stack error", MessageBoxButtons.OK, _
         MessageBoxIcon.Information)
      End If
   End Sub
End Class
```

If you run the project, you can click the Push button to "push" as many cPerson objects on the stack as you would like.

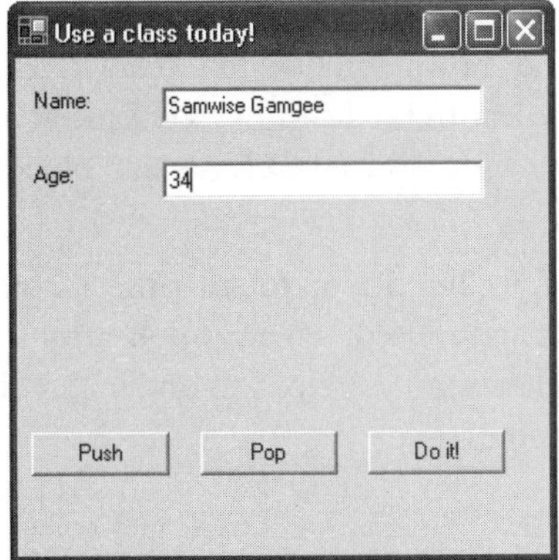

Popping the stack removes the most recent addition to the stack and returns it to the calling function. You'll see this message:

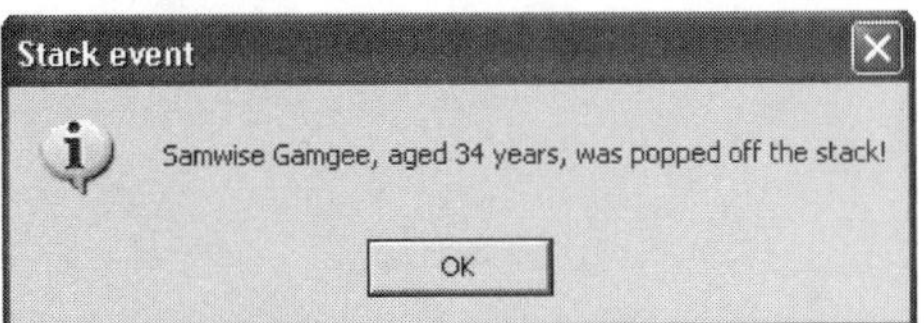

If there is nobody left on the stack, this is trapped so that a runtime error is not generated by attempting to remove an item that doesn't exist. In this case, the message box lets the user know what happened.

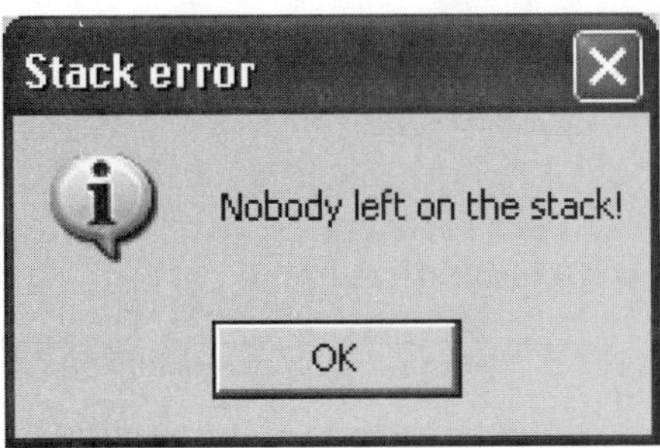

Summary

Classes, and the objects created from them, are integral to VB .NET and programs created in VB .NET. This chapter has explained the basic concepts and theory of object-oriented programming (OOP), and shown you how to work with classes in VB .NET. This is an important topic that is near and dear to the heart of .NET programming. There is a lot more that could be said about working with VB .NET classes and objects, but this chapter should give you a running start.

In the next chapter, we'll move on to creating custom VB .NET controls, which can be added to the Toolbox and reused in many applications. As you'll see, the internals of a control are made up of classes, so you need to understand how to work with classes before you can create your own controls.

Chapter 16

Creating Windows Controls

- Creating an inherited control
- Adding Toolbox bitmaps
- Testing custom controls
- Creating a composite control
- Implementing properties for custom controls

Controls are represented visually in the Toolbox and are instantiated in auto-generated code when they are moved onto a form (or the tray beneath the form). As you've seen in previous chapters, VB .NET provides many prebuilt controls. However, you may want to create your own "custom" controls to contain reusable code for use (often visual) in the development environment.

You can create your own controls—which may or may not have a runtime appearance—in three ways:

- By extending the functionality of an existing control using inheritance
- By combining the functionality of two or more existing controls
- By basing your control on the Control class and building it from scratch

This chapter explains the basics of the first two techniques for creating custom controls.

The controls discussed in this chapter are intended for use with Windows forms. It is also possible to create custom web controls. See Chapter 19, "Building ASP.NET Web Applications," for details.

NOTE Windows controls cannot be created using the Professional Edition of VB .NET (you cannot create a Windows Control Library project). You must have at least the Enterprise Developer Edition to create Windows controls.

Creating an Inherited Control

The easiest way to create a custom control is to base the new control on a single, inherited control that in some way modifies or extends the functionality of the base control. Extending the functionality of controls in this fashion is a form of code reuse that is particularly appropriate to team development. If a piece of extended functionality must be used over and over again by team members, encapsulating it in a control makes sure that it has been tested and is consistent. In addition, some team members may be more comfortable with instantiating an object by dragging it from the Toolbox, rather than by creating it in code.

As a simple example, I'll show you how to extend the functionality of a TextBox control by limiting the user to numeric input. If the user tries to enter anything other than a number in the NumTextBox, a warning message is displayed, and focus is returned to the control. The `OnLeave` method of the base TextBox control is used to check the contents of the NumTextBox. The base TextBox's `Focus` method (in VB6, this was the `SetFocus` method) is used to return focus to the control.

WARNING The examples in this chapter are simplistic and intended to give you a feeling for how to create your own custom controls. They are not intended as complete production controls.

Creating a New Windows Control Project

To create a new Windows control project, open the New Project dialog and choose Windows Control Library from the Templates pane. Name your project **NumTextBoxLib**, as shown in Figure 16.1. Then click OK.

FIGURE 16.1:
In the Add New Project dialog, select the Windows Control Library template and name your project.

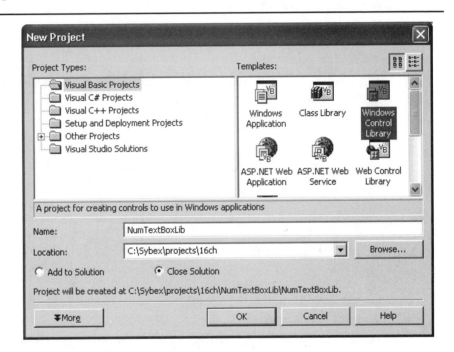

When the new project is created, it will contain a UserControl module. You can see this in the Solution Explorer.

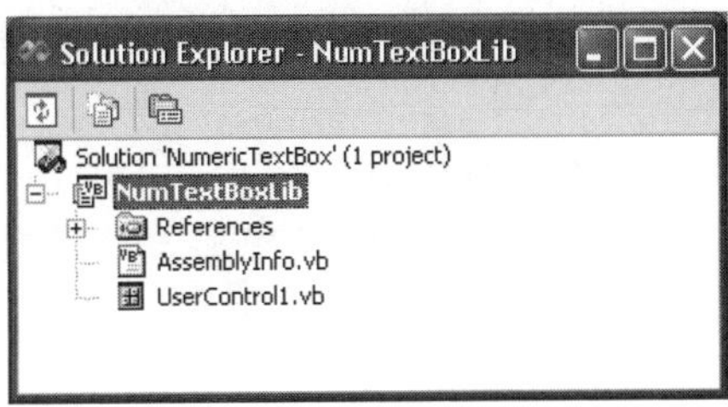

Right-click the UserControl module and change its name to **NumTextBox.vb**.

NOTE As an alternative to creating separate user control and test projects, which is what I show you here, you can add a UserControl module to an existing project. In some ways, this is easier, because the new user control appears in the Toolbox immediately. However, certain features, such as the custom Toolbox bitmap, do not work this way, and I think it is easier in the long run to start with two projects.

Inheriting from a Single Control

After you've created a Windows Control Library project, you can edit its code to create the new control. Right-click the NumTextBox module and select View Code to open the module in the Code Editor.

Change the name of the class to **NumTextBox**. In the `Inherits` clause, delete `UserControl`. The Code Editor's auto-completion feature will show you the classes that are members of `System.Windows.Forms` from which your control can inherit.

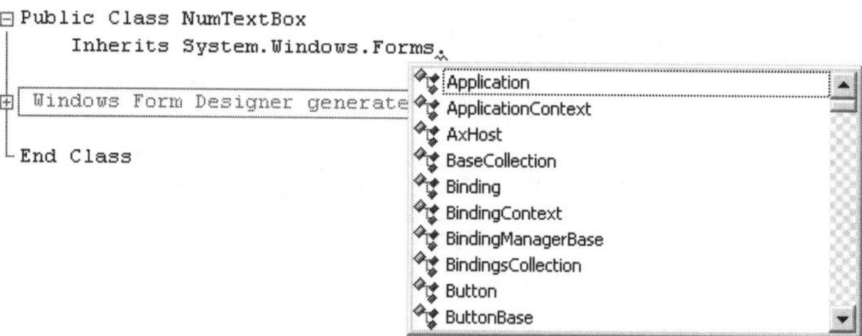

Choose TextBox, so that the opening lines of the module look like this:

```
Public Class NumTextBox
    Inherits System.Windows.Forms.TextBox
```

Adding a Toolbox Bitmap

A control is represented in the Toolbox by a bitmap. It is this bitmap that the user drags onto a form (or other container) to auto-generate the code that instantiates the object based on the control.

By default, if you do not specify a Toolbox bitmap, your control will be represented by a round, wheel-like image. It's much better to pick an image, which should be a 16×16-pixel bitmap.

You specify the Toolbox image by using a metadata tag called an *attribute*. Using attribute tags, you can set the Toolbox image to a specific image file or to an icon supplied for any existing type of control.

In this case, it makes sense to use the TextBox control's icon, since the NumTextBox is essentially a TextBox. Listing 16.1 shows the class declaration with the attribute tag that uses the TextBox's Toolbox image. (See the "Creating a Composite Control" section later in this chapter for an example that shows how to load a Toolbox image from a file.)

Listing 16.1 The Class Declaration with a Toolbox Image Attribute

```
<ToolboxBitmap(GetType(TextBox))> Public Class NumTextBox
   Inherits System.Windows.Forms.TextBox
```

Adding Code

The next step is to add the code that gives functionality to objects based on the NumTextBox class. In a real-world application, this might involve quite a bit of functionality. In this example, it is simply a matter of testing the contents of the control using the `IsNumeric` function, and if the entry is not a number, setting the focus back within the control.

This new code will override the `OnLeave` method. To create the skeleton for the event, in the Code Editor, select (Overrides) from the Objects list, and then select OnLeave from the Procedures list. The skeleton will be created:

```
Protected Overrides Sub OnLeave(ByVal e As System.EventArgs)
End Sub
```

Next, add the code to implement event functionality, as shown in Listing 16.2.

Listing 16.2 The NumTextBox Leave Event

```
Protected Overrides Sub OnLeave(ByVal e As System.EventArgs)
   If Not IsNumeric(Me.Text) Then
      MessageBox.Show("You must enter a numeric value!", _
         "Please try again....", MessageBoxButtons.OK, _
         MessageBoxIcon.Exclamation)
      Me.Focus()
   End If
   MyBase.OnLeave(e)
End Sub
```

Since this is all that we are adding to the control, it's time to build the project (choose Build ➢ Build Solution).

Adding a Test Project to the Solution

Like the class libraries you worked with in Chapter 15, "Object-Oriented Programming in VB .NET," Windows Control Library projects cannot be run (or tested) on their own. A Windows Application project must be used to test adding the new control to the Toolbox and making sure that it works correctly.

You can add a test project, named **`TestNumTextBox`**, to the current solution from the New Project dialog. Make sure that Windows Application is selected in the Templates pane and that Add to Solution (rather than Close Solution) is selected, as shown in Figure 16.2.

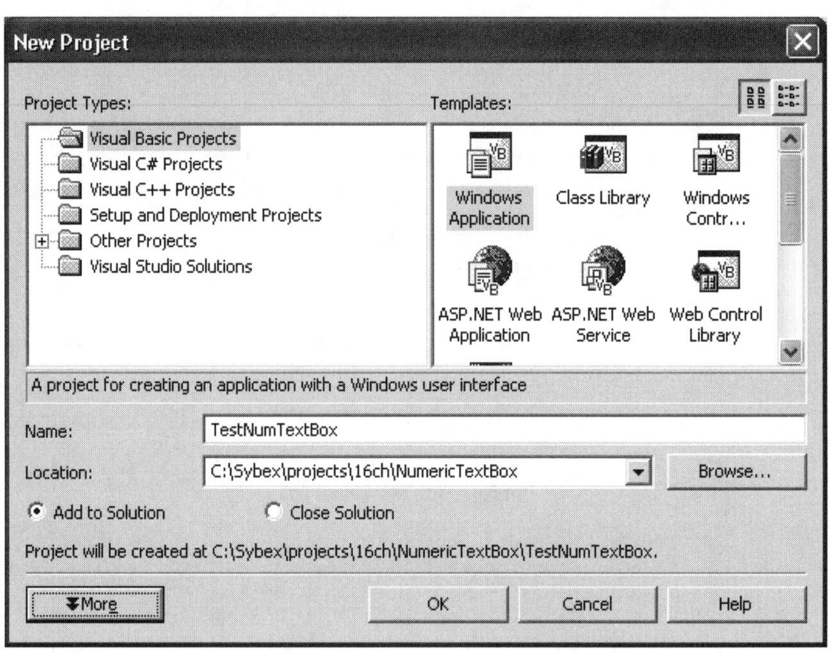

FIGURE 16.2: You can add a Windows Application project to the current solution to test the new control.

TIP You can also use the File ➢ Add Project ➢ New Project menu command to add a new project to the solution.

The new project, and its form module, will appear in the Solution Explorer.

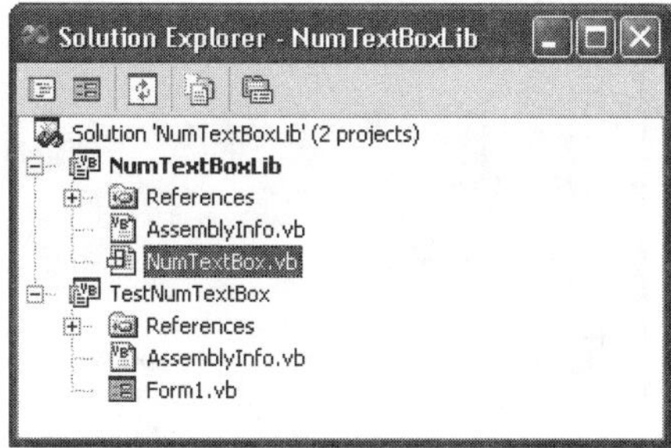

Use the Property Pages for the solution to set the Startup project to the test project (TestNumTextBox), as shown in Figure 16.3.

FIGURE 16.3:

Make sure to set the solution's Startup project to the test project.

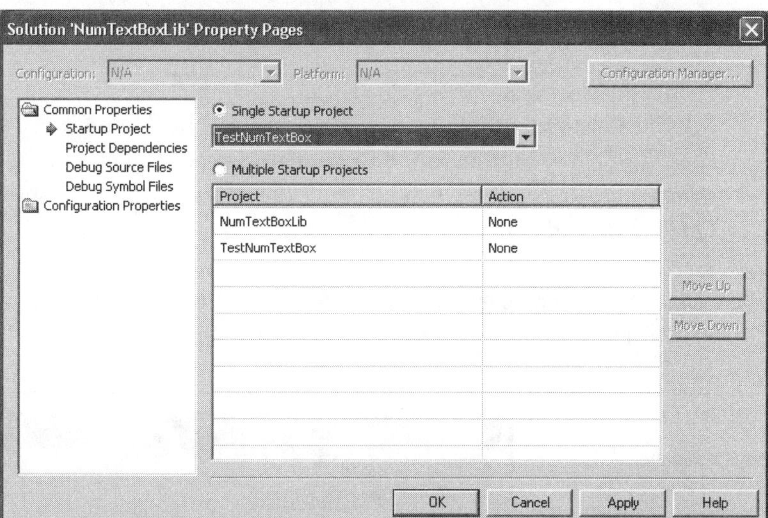

Adding the Control to the Toolbox

In the test project, open the form in its designer. Make sure the Toolbox is displayed. In the Windows Forms tab of the Toolbox, right-click and select Customize Toolbox. The Customize Toolbox dialog will open, as shown in Figure 16.4.

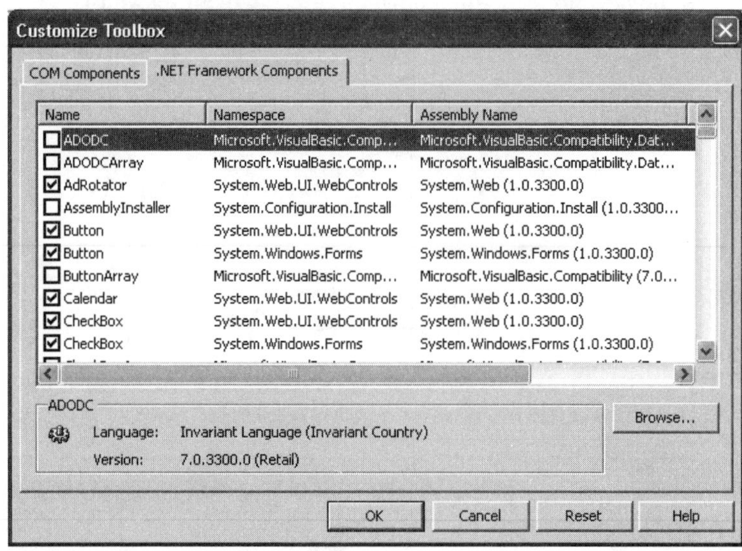

FIGURE 16.4: The Customize Toolbox dialog shows the installed controls.

In the Customize Toolbox dialog, select the .NET Framework Components tab. Next, click the Browse button. In the Open dialog, select the library file (with a `.dll` extension) that you created earlier when you built the control project, as shown in Figure 16.5. Click Open to open the file.

NOTE The built, or compiled, file based on the control project will be located in the bin folder associated with that project.

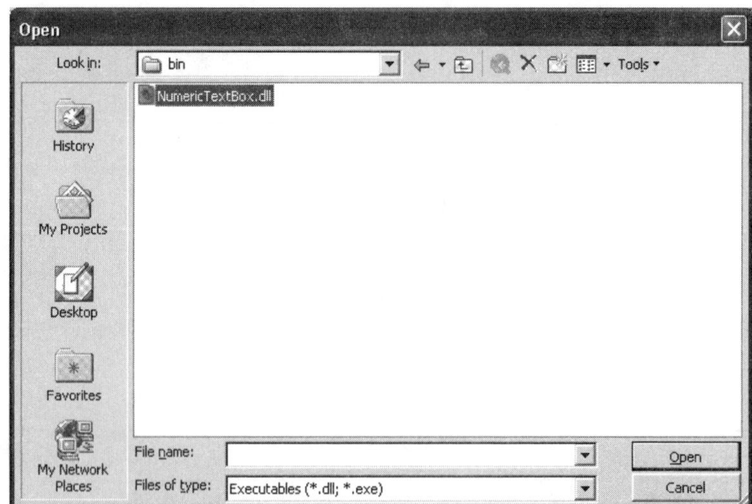

FIGURE 16.5: Use the Open dialog to select the new control.

The NumTextBox control will now be shown selected (with a check mark) in the .NET Frameworks Components tab of the Customize Toolbox dialog.

☑ MonthCalendar	System.Windows.Forms	System.Windows.Forms (1.0.3300.0)
☑ NotifyIcon	System.Windows.Forms	System.Windows.Forms (1.0.3300.0)
☑ NumericUpDown	System.Windows.Forms	System.Windows.Forms (1.0.3300.0)
☑ NumTextBox	NumericTextBox	NumericTextBox (1.0.717.19822)
☑ OleDbCommand	System.Data.OleDb	System.Data (1.0.3300.0)
☐ OleDbCommandBuilder	System.Data.OleDb	System.Data (1.0.3300.0)
☑ OleDbConnection	System.Data.OleDb	System.Data (1.0.3300.0)
☑ OleDbDataAdapter	System.Data.OleDb	System.Data (1.0.3300.0)
☑ OpenFileDialog	System.Windows.Forms	System.Windows.Forms (1.0.3300.0)

Click OK. You'll see that the control has been added to the Toolbox.

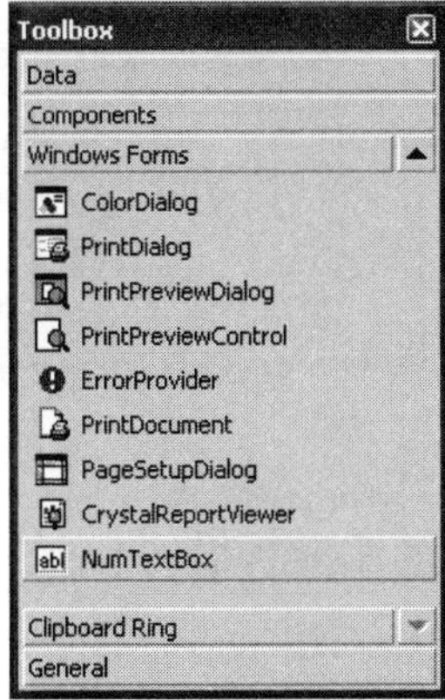

Testing the Control

You can drag and drop your custom control from the Toolbox onto a form, just like any other control, such as a TextBox. Do that now to put a NumTextBox control on the form.

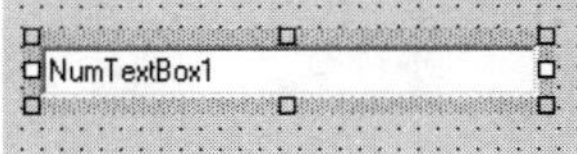

Once the control is seated on the form, it doesn't take much to test the control's new characteristics. You'll need to add at least one other control to the form, such as a Do It! button.

Run the project. Enter a number in the NumTextBox. Click the Do It! button. There is no problem.

Now, go back to the NumTextBox and enter some non-numeric text. Click the Do It! button again. This time, a warning message box will be displayed, and focus will be set back to the NumTextBox.

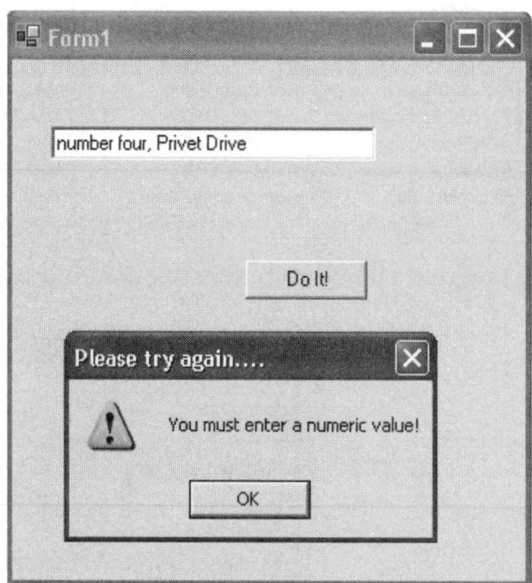

Creating a Composite Control

In the previous section, you saw that VB .NET makes it easy to create a control by modifying a single existing control. You can also create a custom control by combining the functionality of two or more existing controls.

As an example of creating a composite control, we will animate a bitmap (sometimes called a *sprite*) using a Label control as its background. This animation control, named Animate, will use a Timer control in addition to the Label. The logic behind the code for animating a sprite is explained in Chapter 10, "Using Timers, EventLogs, and ServiceControllers."

Adding Multiple Controls

Unlike the previous example, the Animate control will use elements from more than one control, so the best starting place is the UserControl class, which provides a container for multiple controls.

Start by creating a Windows Control Library project (as in the previous example). Name the project **`AnimateLib`**, and modify the class declaration for the control module so that it is named `Animate` and inherits from `System.Windows.Forms.UserControl`:

```
Public Class Animate
   Inherits System.Windows.Forms.UserControl
```

Next, open the control module in its designer (either by double-clicking the module or by selecting View Designer from its context menu in the Solution Explorer). What you see looks very much like a form in its designer, except that this is the UserControl, or container for multiple controls.

Add a Label control and a Timer to the UserControl, as shown in Figure 16.6. Just as with forms, the Timer control sits on a tray beneath the UserControl, rather than on the UserControl itself.

FIGURE 16.6:

Add the controls that will be used to create the composite control to the control's designer as if it were a form.

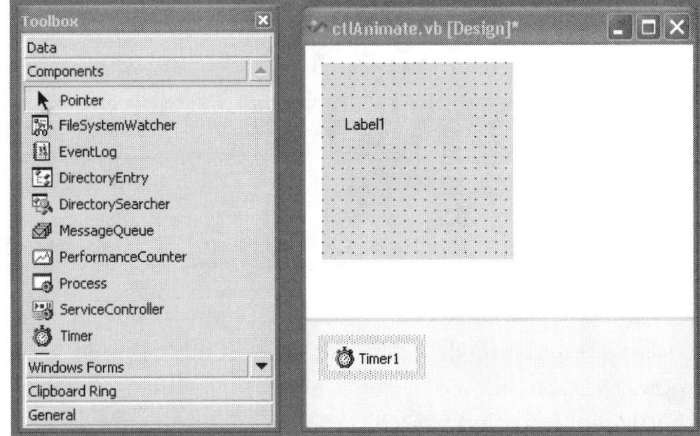

Implementing Control Functionality

Now that we have the two controls that we want to use on the UserControl, we can implement the functionality of the composite control.

First, with the UserControl still open in its designer, use the Properties window to set the Enabled property of the Timer to False. Still using the Properties window, change the name of the Label to `lblAnimate`, delete the text in its Text property, and use its Image property to select a bitmap file to animate (the sprite). Figure 16.7 shows selecting a file (`FACE02.ICO`) to animate.

TIP FACE02.ICO is part of the icon library that ships with VB .NET. You should find it in the `Program Files\Microsoft Visual Studio .NET\Common7\Graphics\icons\Misc` folder.

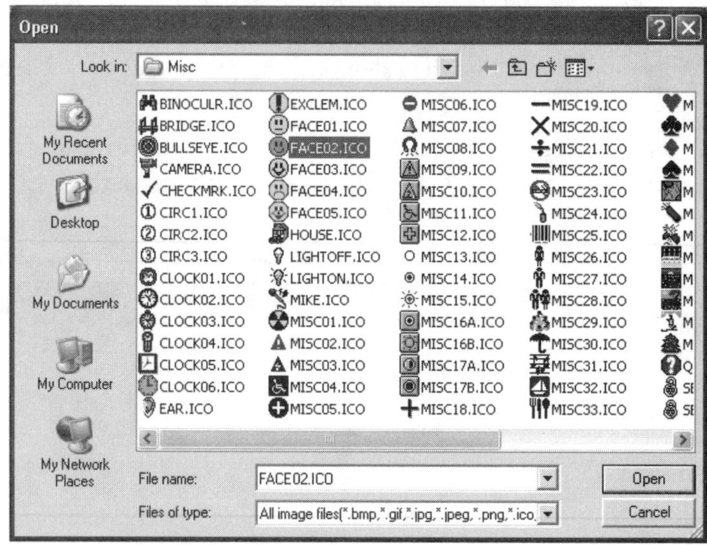

FIGURE 16.7: The Image property of the constituent Label control can be used to load an image.

Next, switch to the Code Editor to view the Animate control module's code. We've already declared the class module, but let's add a ToolboxBitmap attribute to the class statement that shows the same bitmap in the Toolbox as the one that will be animated (in the interests of shortening the path, I have copied it to my `C:` directory):

```
<ToolboxBitmap("C:\FACE02.ICO")> Public Class Animate
   Inherits System.Windows.Forms.UserControl
```

To actually implement the animation, use the Timer's Elapsed event and the logic explained in Chapter 10, as shown in Listing 16.3.

Listing 16.3 Implementing the Animation

```
Imports System.Drawing
<ToolboxBitmap("C:\FACE02.ico")> Public Class Animate
   Inherits System.Windows.Forms.UserControl
   Private xIncrement As Integer = 5
   Private yIncrement As Integer = 10
   ...

   Private Sub Timer1_Elapsed(ByVal sender As Object, _
      ByVal e As System.Timers.ElapsedEventArgs) Handles Timer1.Elapsed
      If lblAnimate.Location.X > Me.Size.Width - 30 Then
         xIncrement = -5
      End If
      If lblAnimate.Location.Y > Me.Size.Height - 50 Then
         yIncrement = -10
```

```
        End If
        If lblAnimate.Location.X <= 0 Then
           xIncrement = 5
        End If
        If lblAnimate.Location.Y <= 0 Then
           yIncrement = 10
        End If
        lblAnimate.Location = New Point(lblAnimate.Location.X _
           + xIncrement, lblAnimate.Location.Y + yIncrement)
     End Sub
     ...
  End Class
```

The Control and UserControl Classes

It's somewhat confusing, but there are two base classes related to control development:

- The UserControl class, which you've already met as the basis for composite controls
- The Control class, which you would use if you were building a control from scratch

Note that "building a control from scratch" means implementing special functionality not inherently related to any existing control. A control built from scratch must draw its own interface and implement its own logic.

Both Control and UserControl are part of the `System.Windows.Forms` namespace. In fact, most classes within the `System.Windows.Forms` namespace derive from the Control class, another way of saying that the Control class is the base class for controls, which are components, or class libraries, with a visual representation.

Another important class that you might want to inherit from is Component, which you would use if you wanted to build something like the Timer (it shows up in the Toolbox but has no user interface).

Implementing Properties

If you want to define properties for your custom control, these properties are implemented using Property procedures, as explained in Chapter 15's discussion of class modules. Each property consists of an internal variable, a `Get` procedure that gets the value, and a `Set` procedure that sets the value.

At a minimum, our Animate control should have two properties: one to turn the animation on and off, named Go, and one to set the animation interval, named Speed. Listing 16.4 shows the implementation of the Go and Speed properties.

Listing 16.4 Implementing the Go and Speed Properties

```
Imports System.Drawing
<ToolboxBitmap("C:\FACE02.ico")> Public Class Animate
   Inherits System.Windows.Forms.UserControl
   ...
   Private iSpeed As Integer = 1000
   Private iGo As Boolean = False
   ...
   Property Go() As Boolean
      Get
         Return iGo
      End Get
      Set(ByVal Value As Boolean)
         iGo = Value
         Timer1.enabled = iGo
      End Set
   End Property
   Property Speed() As Integer
      Get
         Return iSpeed
      End Get
      Set(ByVal Value As Integer)
         iSpeed = Value
         Timer1.enabled = iSpeed
      End Set
   End Property
End Class
```

Testing the Control

Now that the composite control is created, it's time to test it. First, you need to build the control project so that it is compiled into a library file. Next, add a test Windows Application project to the solution, making sure that the test project is set to be the Startup project for the solution. (See the "Adding a Test Project to the Solution" section earlier in the chapter for details.)

With the form module of the test project open, use the .NET Frameworks Components tab of the Customize Toolbox dialog to add the Animate control to the Toolbox, as shown in Figure 16.8.

FIGURE 16.8:

When the control has been added, it appears checked in the Customize Toolbox dialog.

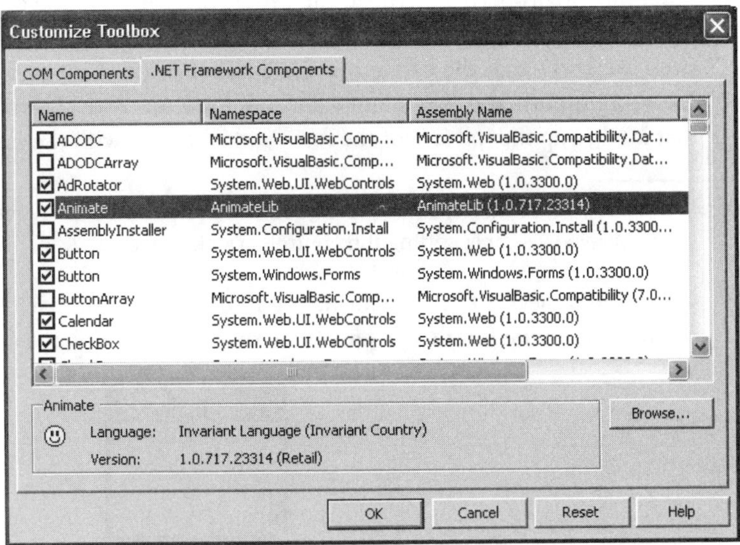

Once the Animate control has been added to the Toolbox, you can double-click it (or drag and drop it) to seat it on a form. Next, open the Properties window to make sure that the Go and Speed properties appear, as shown in Figure 16.9.

FIGURE 16.9:

Custom properties for the control appear in the Properties window.

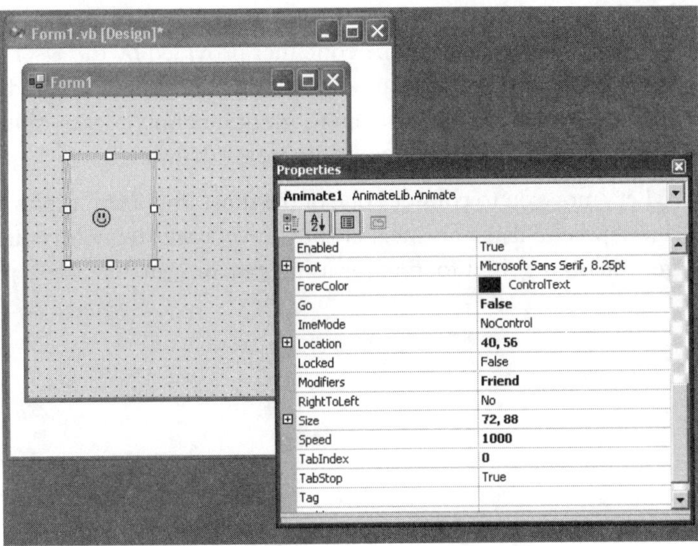

Set the Go property to True in the Properties window (you could also turn this property on and off using a Button control). The bitmap will start moving around on its background (well, we know that the background is a Label constituent of this composite control, but users might not). You also might want to set the Animate control's Dock property to Fill, so that it takes up the full size of the form and is resized with the form.

NOTE In VB6, you would have needed to code the form's Resize event to get the functionality you obtain by simply setting the control's Dock property.

Run the project. Resize the form. You'll see that the Animate control keeps on moving—rolling around the form like a basketball on a court—until you shut the project down.

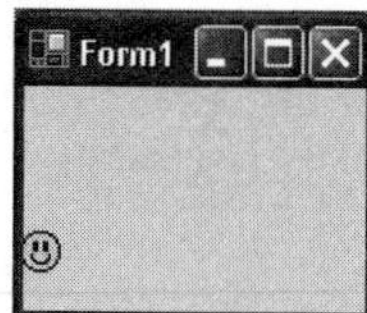

Summary

This chapter has shown you how to build two rather basic custom controls. One was built by inheriting directly from another control class (the TextBox). The other was created from composite controls using the container provided by the UserControl class. The point of these examples was to explain the underlying mechanisms and give you the taste for control creation, which is very useful and a lot of fun. You'll learn more about a related kind of control creation, used in web applications, in Chapter 19.

Let's move on to consider one of the most important topics in the universe of software development: data. The next chapter covers working with data and ADO.NET, and it will get you on the right footing for using data in your VB .NET programs.

CHAPTER 17

Working with Data and ADO.NET

- Reviewing database basics
- Using .NET Data components
- Creating datasets
- Binding controls to data
- Updating a database

In the long run, you cannot do anything very sophisticated or useful without the ability to save and retrieve data between program sessions. Although there are a variety of ways you could go about doing this, it makes the most sense to use the software designed for this purpose—databases. In effect, the great majority of real-world programs are designed to query databases to populate the programs' objects. Programs that perform jobs such as managing payrolls or reservations must also be able to save their work and pick up where they left off.

In many cases, the program will also use user input to update data stored in the database. In this capacity, VB has become known as an extraordinarily versatile and powerful "front end" for database applications. This appellation, often used in a derogatory fashion, is a touch misleading, because there are actually at least three layers involved. In addition to the user interface (front end) and database, there is a connectivity layer.

This chapter provides an overview of how the connectivity layer is used in VB .NET and how data carried in the connectivity layer is *bound* to controls in a VB .NET application. The chapter's primary focus will be the tools available to help you create the database connectivity layer in .NET. At first glance, these tools may seem to be somewhat confusing because there are so many powerful objects and interfaces available. The aim of this chapter is to keep it simple and help you find your way through this maze.

Reviewing Database Basics

It's true that you can create database applications in VB .NET without needing to program and without possessing a deep understanding of databases. (Obviously, willingness to program and having a sophisticated understanding of databases does help!)

You do need to know that databases are organized in tables. Each table contains rows and columns, called *fields*, of information. A row across a table is called a *record*.

Each table usually contains a *primary key*, which is used to uniquely identify records. In other words, within a table, the value of a primary key cannot be duplicated across records. For example, a primary key might be a social security number, an e-mail address, or another unique identifier.

In addition to primary keys, *foreign keys*, which do not need to be unique, are used to establish relationships between the data in tables. For example, suppose you have a Customers table in which `cust_ID` is the primary key. You could also have an Orders table in which the same `cust_ID` showed up a number of times as a foreign key (because one customer made multiple orders).

Data organized in this fashion in independent tables is called *relational*. The software used to contain it is, logically, a relational database. SQL (Structured Query Language) is the common language used to manipulate and retrieve information stored in relational databases. High-powered databases are organized as servers and referred to as *database management systems* (DBMS). You'll also see the term *relational database management system* (RDBMS). In effect, the access layer of a VB .NET program is a client of the database server (in the same sense that an Internet browser is the client of a web server).

Good architecture of databases often funnels access through special programs internal to the database. These programs are written in an internal, database-specific language intended for this purpose, and they are called *stored procedures*. From the viewpoint of a VB .NET program, what you want to do to a database is either execute SQL statements against it or run a stored procedure in the database intended for access purposes (in large part, the stored procedure itself executes SQL).

NOTE In production applications, running stored procedures is generally far more scalable and secure than executing ad hoc SQL statements against a DBMS. Stored procedures are beyond the scope of this chapter, but you can find more information in publications devoted to databases and DBMS.

Using the Data Components

Each new version of VB has shipped with a new model for the data connectivity layer, and VB .NET is no exception. The changes from one version to the next have been evolutionary or revolutionary, depending on whom you ask, and constitute a veritable soup of acronyms (DAO, ADO, ADO+, and now ADO.NET). The latest incarnation is, of course, ADO.NET. (It's no longer clear that it matters very much what the letters *ADO* are short for—or if, indeed, they are short for anything.)

Since space in this chapter is limited, I'll forgo historical discussion and concentrate on how ADO.NET provides data access in VB .NET.

NOTE Older data-access layers used COM to communicate. You can still use these access methods by including a COM *wrapper* in your programs.

Working with Managed Providers

The .NET Data components are supplied as a separate set of four Data components for each data source. Each set of objects, targeted at a particular data source, is known as a *managed provider*.

Currently, the only managed providers that ship with VB .NET are a set for Microsoft's SQL Server DBMS and a set that work with any OLE database (OLE DB) source—in other words, a managed provider for all the rest. Undoubtedly, Data components that provide a specific connectivity layer for IBM, Oracle, Sybase, and so on will become available.

TIP An ODBC managed provider is currently available for download. To download it, or for further information, go to `http://msdn.microsoft.com` and search for ODBC .NET Data Provider.

The two sets of Data components (one set for SQL Server and one set for OLE DB) are functionally identical. The purpose of each of the components is shown in Table 17.1.

TABLE 17.1: ADO.NET Data Components Available in the Toolbox

Component	Purpose
OleDbDataAdapter SqlDataAdapter	Contains and controls Command objects (see Table 17.2).
OleDbConnection SqlConnection	Provides a connection to a database server (or source).
OleDbCommand SqlCommand	Executes SQL statements (or stored procedures). The `ExecuteReader` method of this object is used to create a DataReader object (see the following section).
DataSet	Contains an in-memory cache of data (sometimes called a *data store*) made up of one or more tables. This fundamental ADO.NET object is filled using one or more managed provider data adapters.
DataView	Contains filtered and sorted data based on a DataSet. Controls can be bound to a DataView.

The Data components belong to the `System.Data` namespace. SQL Server components are part of `System.Data.SQLClient`, and OLE DB components belong to `System.Data.OleDB`.

The examples in this chapter use the OLE DB provider with the sample Northwind database tables that ship with Microsoft Access. (After all, not everyone has SQL Server available, but most people who have ever installed Microsoft Office Professional have some version of the Northwind database.)

NOTE The specific location and name of the `Northwind.mdb` sample database depend on your system and the software that you have installed on it. For example, if you have Office XP installed in the default location, you can find a copy of the database at `C:\Program Files\Microsoft Office\Office10\1033\FPNWind.mdb`. Those with older versions of Office may find it at `C:\Program Files\Microsoft Office\Office\Samples\Northwind.mdb`.

Displaying Data with a DataReader

The OleDbDataReader and OleSqlDataReader allow you to return read-only result sets from a database. If you need to quickly cycle through all the values in a field, but have no need to update or change the values, using the DataReader is probably the easiest route. DataReader objects are created in code using the `ExecuteReader` method of either the OleDbCommand or SqlCommand objects.

Before we get down to more specifics about how to use the ADO.NET Data components, let's run through a simple code example. The task is to display the company names in the CompanyName field of the Suppliers table of the sample Northwind database. We'll use a DataReader object to display this data.

As a preliminary, start a new Windows Application project. Add a Button control named `btnGetData` and a TextBox control named `txtData` to the Windows form. Set `txtData`'s Multiline property to True. The button's Click procedure will be used to retrieve the data. The TextBox will be used to display the results gathered by the DataReader.

The first step in the code module is to import the `System.Data.OleDb` namespace:

```
Imports System.Data.OleDb
```

NOTE When you are working with a SQL Server data source and the SQL DataReader (instead of the OLE DB DataReader), you will need to import the `System.Data.SqlClient` namespace.

Next, within `btnGetData`'s Click event procedure, create the query string and define a new OleDbConnection object:

```
Dim mySelectQuery As String = "SELECT CompanyName FROM Suppliers"
Dim myConnection As New & _
    OleDbConnection("Provider=Microsoft.Jet.OLEDB.4.0;" & _
    "Data Source=C:\Program Files\Microsoft " & _
    "Office\Office10\1033\FPNWind.mdb")
```

Using the query string and the OleDbConnection, create a new OleDbCommand:

```
Dim myCommand As New OleDbCommand(mySelectQuery, myConnection)
```

Open the connection:

```
myConnection.Open()
```

Declare an OleDbDataReader, and then use the `ExecuteReader` method of the OleDbCommand to populate it:

```
Dim myReader As OleDbDataReader
myReader = myCommand.ExecuteReader()
```

Use the `Read` method of the OleDbDataReader to retrieve the data, and use its `GetString` method to display the data:

```
While myReader.Read()
   txtData.Text = txtData.Text & myReader.GetString(0) _
      & ControlChars.CrLf
End While
```

Finally, close the OleDbDataReader and the OleDbConnection:

```
myReader.Close()
myConnection.Close()
```

Listing 17.1 shows the complete procedure that uses the ADO.NET components to create an OleDbDataReader, and then uses the OleDbDataReader to display the specified data.

Listing 17.1 Displaying Data with an OleDbDataReader Component

```
Imports System.Data.OleDb
...
Private Sub btnGetData_Click(ByVal sender As System.Object, _
   ByVal e As System.EventArgs) Handles btnGetData.Click
   Dim mySelectQuery As String = "SELECT CompanyName FROM Suppliers"
   Dim myConnection As New & _
      OleDbConnection("Provider=Microsoft.Jet.OLEDB.4.0;" & _
      "Data Source=C:\Program Files\Microsoft " & _
      "Office\Office10\1033\FPNWind.mdb")
   Dim myCommand As New OleDbCommand(mySelectQuery, myConnection)
   myConnection.Open()
   Dim myReader As OleDbDataReader
   myReader = myCommand.ExecuteReader()
   ' Always call Read before accessing data.
   While myReader.Read()
      txtData.Text = txtData.Text & myReader.GetString(0) _
      & ControlChars.CrLf
   End While
   ' Always call Close when done reading.
   myReader.Close()
   ' Close the connection when done with it.
   myConnection.Close()
End Sub
```

If you run the project and click the button, the company name information will be displayed in the text box.

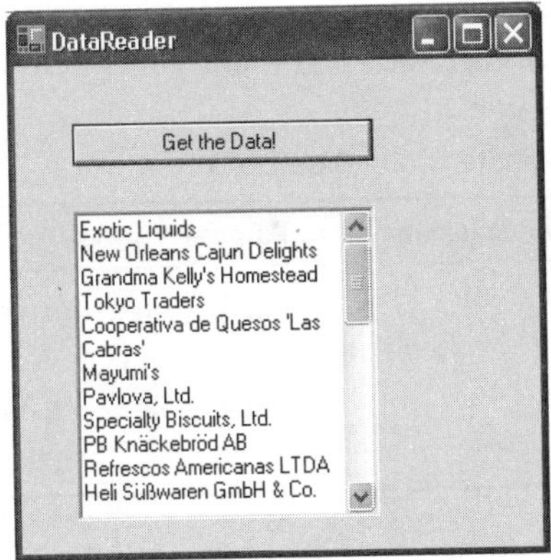

Adding Data Components

The Data components are found on the Data tab of the Toolbox.

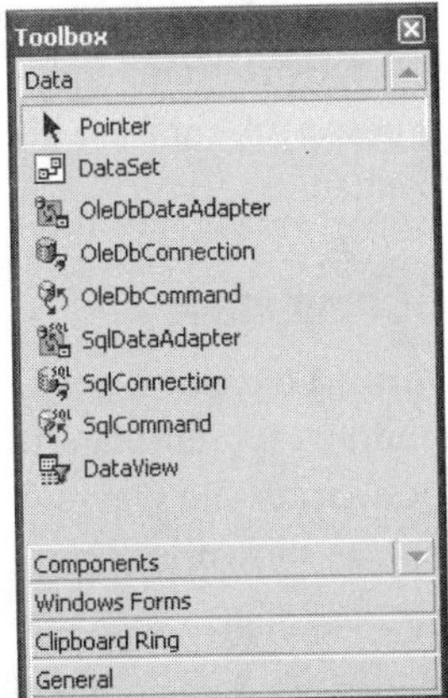

To use a Data component, drag it from the Toolbox to a form. Like the other nonvisual components, Data components sit on the tray beneath the form. (Of course, you can also instantiate these components in code, instead of using the Toolbox.)

Setting Data Adapter Properties

ADO.NET DataAdapter components (OleDbDataAdapter and SqlDataAdapter) each support four properties, which are Command objects of type OleDbCommand or SqlCommand, respectively, as shown in Table 17.2.

TABLE 17.2: DataAdapter Command Objects

OleDbDataAdapter / SqlDataAdapter	Purpose
SelectCommand	Retrieves data from a database
InsertCommand	Inserts data into a database
UpdateCommand	Updates data in a database
DeleteCommand	Deletes data in a database

Creating a Dataset with Data Components

A *dataset* is one or more tables of data. The data connectivity layer "pulls" data from a database and uses it to create a dataset. Items in the tables in the dataset are manipulated to perform the actions required by the program, and, in some cases, saved back to the database. Although datasets are very powerful, they are disconnected tables of data. If you need to be continuously connected to a database, you will need to use the legacy ADO COM objects.

Adding a DataAdapter Component

The first step toward creating a dataset is to add a DataAdapter component. With a form open in its designer, add an OleDbDataAdapter to the form by double-clicking the OleDbDataAdapter component on the Data tab of the Toolbox. The Data Adapter Configuration Wizard will open, as shown in Figure 17.1.

Click Next to start the Wizard. The next panel, shown in Figure 17.2, allows you to choose a data connection from the existing data connections or to create a new connection.

FIGURE 17.1:

When you add a DataAdapter component to your form, the Data Adapter Configuration Wizard will open.

FIGURE 17.2:

You can choose a data connection from the list of current data connections or create a new connection.

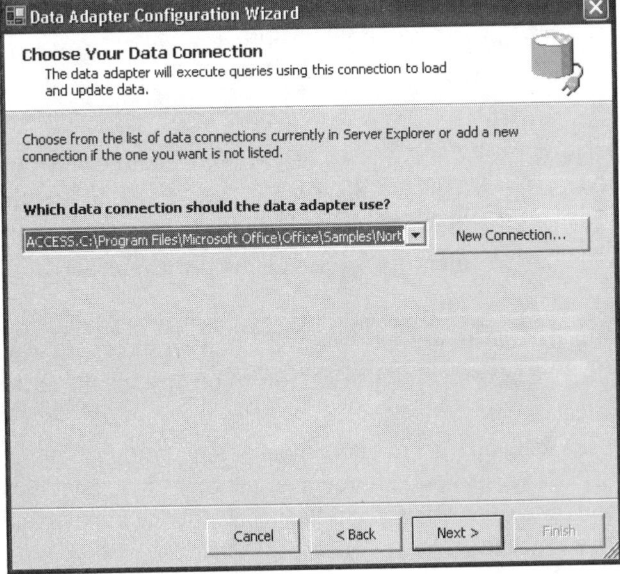

Creating a New Data Connection

To create a new connection, follow these steps:

1. Click the New Connection button in the Data Adapter Configuration Wizard. The Data Link Properties dialog will open, as shown in Figure 17.3.

FIGURE 17.3:

The Data Link Properties dialog allows you to create a new data connection.

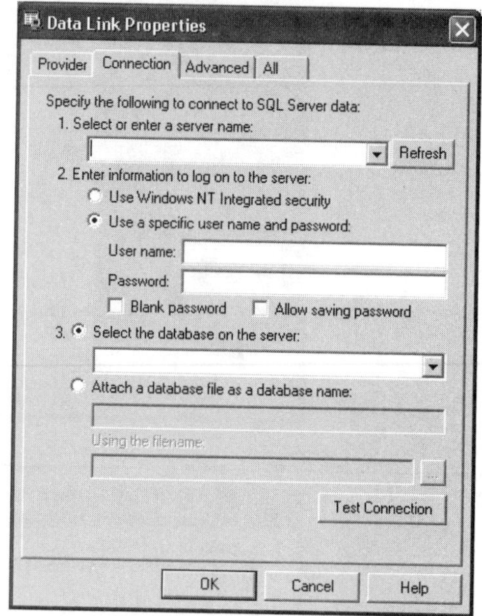

2. The first step in using the Data Link Properties dialog is to select the OLE DB provider you want to use to connect to the data. Click the Provider tab and select your provider. Figure 17.4 shows the Provider tab with the Microsoft Jet 4.0 OLE DB Provider selected (the Jet providers are commonly used with Access databases).
3. Click Next. The Connection tab will open, as shown in Figure 17.5. Use this tab to select the database you are connected to, either by typing in a database name or by browsing for it. The next two steps show how to browse for the database file.

NOTE Depending on the provider you selected, the Connection tab is also used when a username and password are required for accessing a database server, to specify file types and connection strings, and to supply other information that may be required to successfully connect.

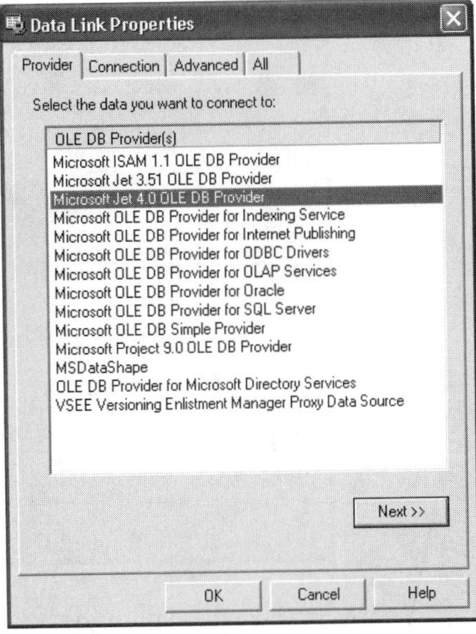

FIGURE 17.4: The Provider tab is used to select an OLE DB Provider.

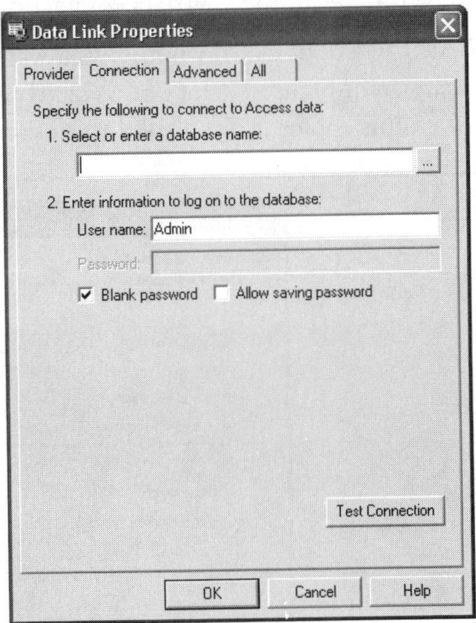

FIGURE 17.5: You can use the Connection tab to select the database you are accessing.

4. Click the button to the right of the database name box (it is marked with an ellipsis). The Select Access Database dialog will open, as shown in Figure 17.6. Use this dialog to choose an Access database file.

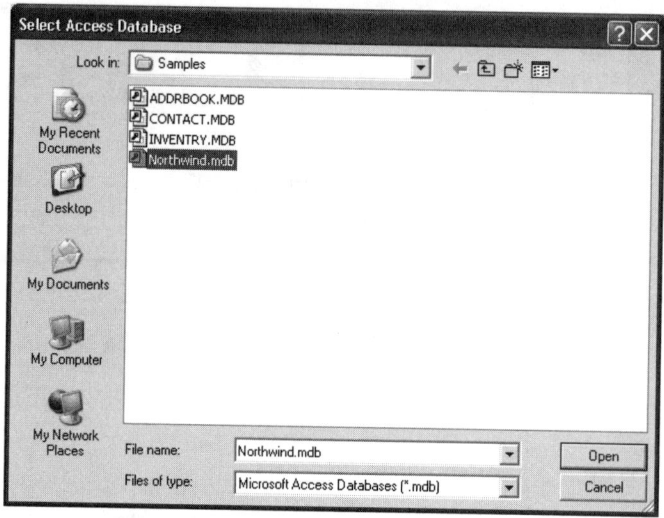

FIGURE 17.6: The Select Access Database dialog is used to select a database file.

5. Select the `Northwind.mdb` database file and click Open. The path to the file will have been placed in the database name box. Click OK. You will be returned to the Data Adapter Configuration Wizard, with the new data connection active.
6. Click Next. You will be asked whether you want to use SQL statements or stored procedures, as shown in Figure 17.7. (The Wizard cannot create stored procedures for Access databases, so this choice is disabled in this example.)

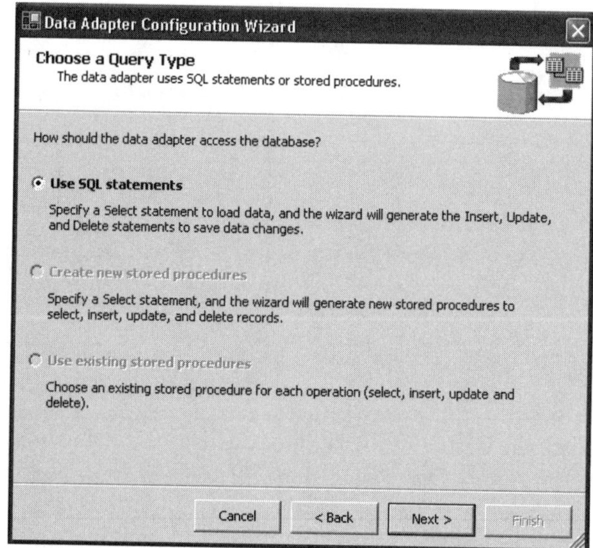

FIGURE 17.7: The Choose a Query Type panel lets you choose between SQL and stored procedure DBMS access.

Building a Query

The next Data Adapter Configuration Wizard panel, shown in Figure 17.8, asks you to enter a SQL statement that will be used to create the dataset. Many people find it easier to use a visual tool to create their SQL statement rather than entering one by hand.

FIGURE 17.8:

A SQL statement is used to determine which data will be used to create the dataset.

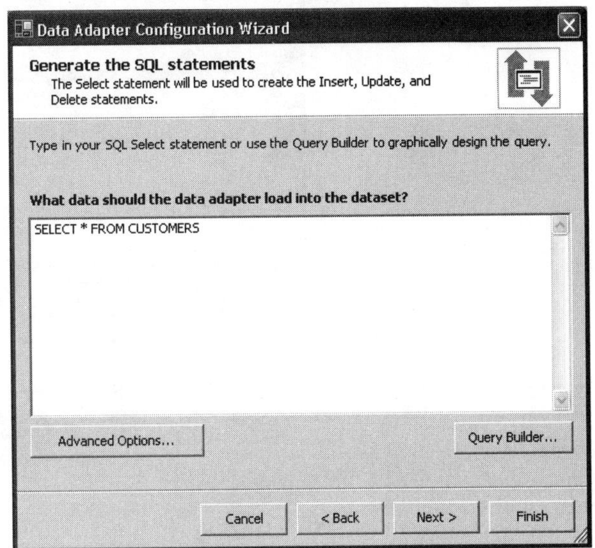

To visually generate a query, follow these steps:

1. Click the Query Builder button in the Data Adapter Configuration Wizard.
2. The Add Table dialog appears, as shown in Figure 17.9. The Query Builder lets you add a table or view. Select a table and click Add.
3. Once you have added a table, select the fields you would like to include, as shown in Figure 17.10. (The primary key for the table is shown in bold in the Query Builder.)
4. You can add multiple tables to your query by right-clicking in the upper pane and selecting Add Table from the context menu. In the new tables that you added, select the fields you would like to include, as shown in Figure 17.11.
5. When you are satisfied with your query, click OK. The SQL statement will appear in the Data Adapter Configuration Wizard, as shown in Figure 17.12.

NOTE Figure 17.12 shows a relatively complex Select query. For the example that follows, I'll use the simple query `SELECT * FROM PRODUCTS`.

…GURE 17.9:

You can add tables and views using the Query Builder.

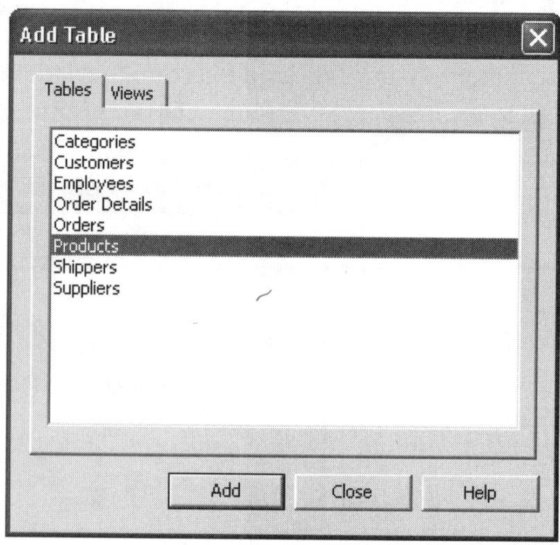

FIGURE 17.10:

You can include fields by selecting them in the Query Builder.

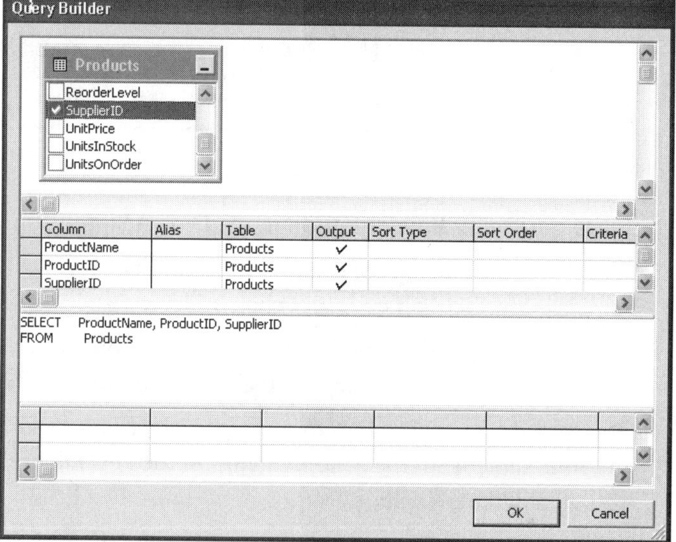

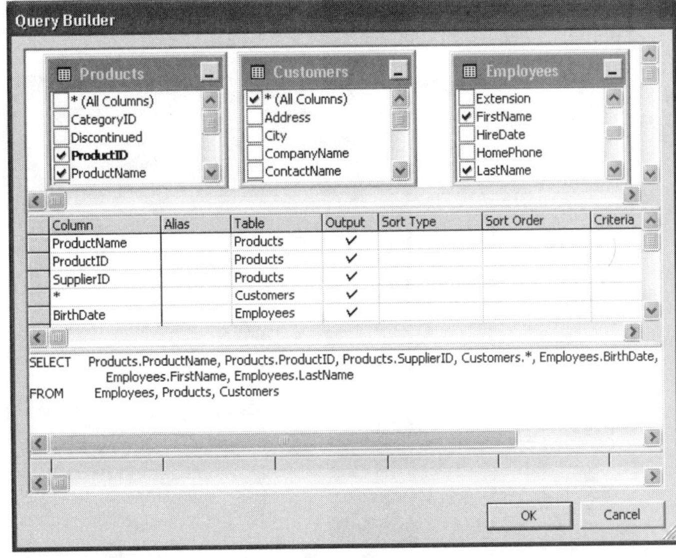

FIGURE 17.11: Queries built in the Query Builder can include multiple tables.

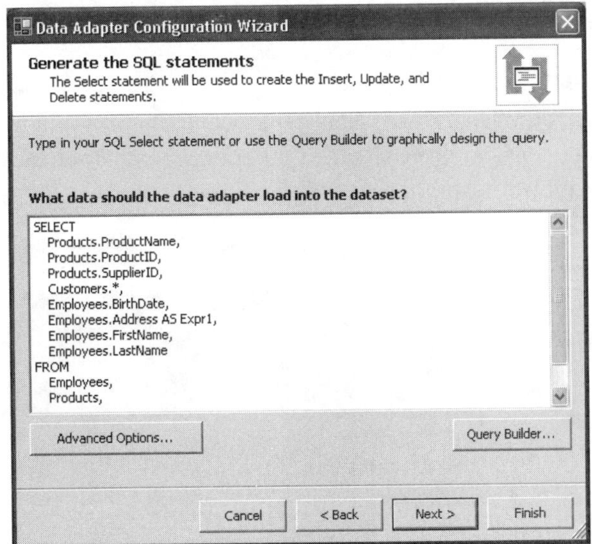

FIGURE 17.12: SQL generated by the Query Builder appears in the Data Adapter Configuration Wizard.

6. Click Next. The final panel of the Wizard will list the tasks that the Wizard has performed, as shown in Figure 17.13.

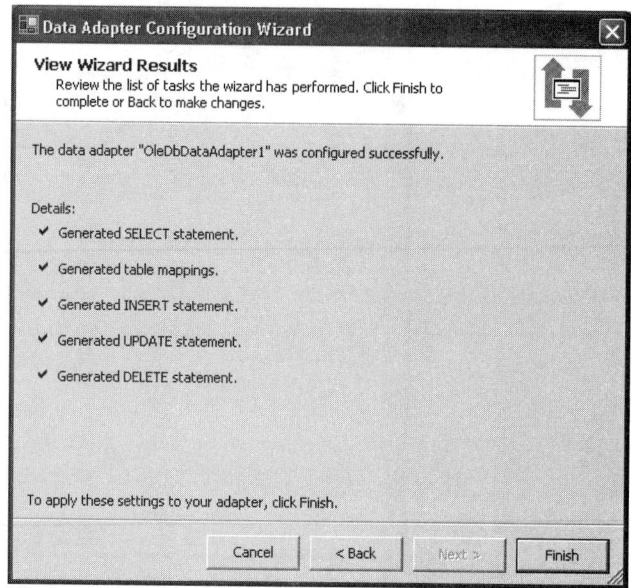

FIGURE 17.13: The final Wizard panel shows the tasks accomplished by the Wizard.

7. Click Finish. The Wizard will complete its work.

Working with the Data Adapter

After you've added the DataAdapter component, you'll notice that an OleDbConnection component has been added to the tray beneath your form and synchronized with the OleDbDataAdapter's connection string.

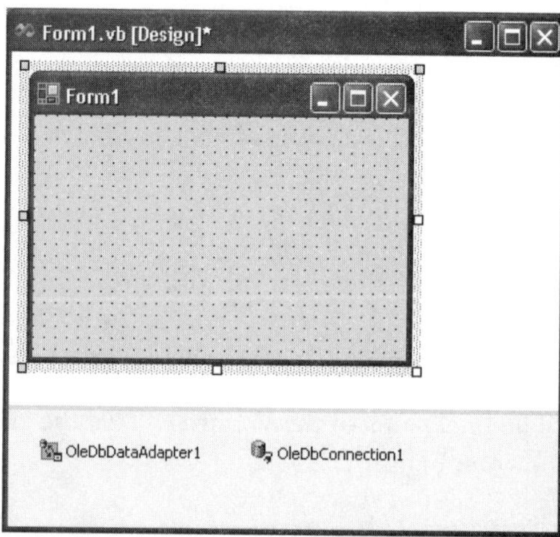

TIP If you need to reconfigure the DataAdapter, you can restart the Wizard by right-clicking the OleDbDataAdapter and selecting Configure Data Adapter from its context menu.

Note that the properties of the OleDbDataAdapter are accessible in the normal fashion in the Properties window. For example, if you've forgotten what your SQL query was (or wish to modify it), you can look at the CommandText property of the OleDbDataAdapter's SelectCommand.

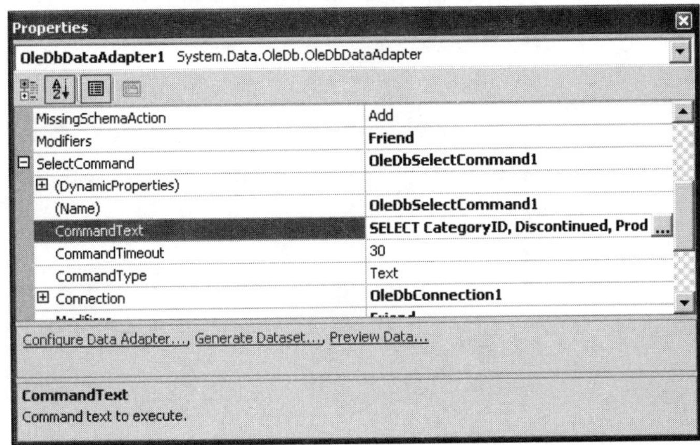

TIP Clicking the button in the right column of the Properties window of the CommandText property opens the Query Builder interface.

Previewing the Dataset

Your next step will likely be to preview the dataset. To preview the dataset, choose Data ➢ Preview Data from the VB .NET menus (or use the OleDbDataAdapter's context menu). The Data Adapter Preview dialog, shown in Figure 17.14, will open.

In the Data Adapter Preview dialog, make sure that OleDbDataAdapter1 is selected in the Data Adapters drop-down list. Next, click Fill Dataset. The Results panel will preview the dataset.

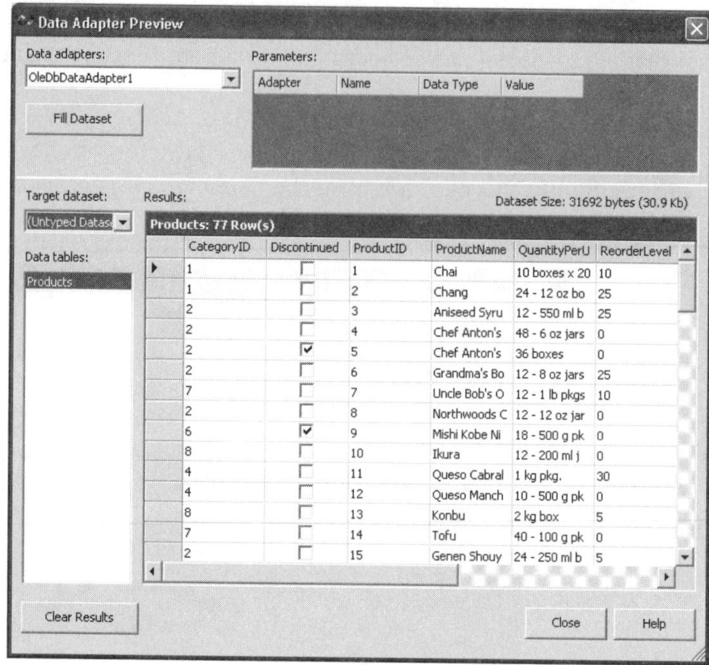

FIGURE 17.14: The Data Adapter Preview dialog allows you to preview the dataset.

Generating the Dataset

Finally, generate the dataset by selecting Data ➢ Generate Dataset (or use the OleDbDataAdapter's context menu). The Generate Dataset dialog, shown in Figure 17.15, will open. Select New, and give the dataset a name (for example, `DataSet1`). Make sure that the tables you want are selected. Also, make sure that the Add This Dataset to the Designer check box is checked. Click OK. The DataSet component will be added to the tray beneath your form.

You can also generate a dataset by adding a DataSet component from the Toolbox to your form.

WARNING Each time you generate a dataset and add a DataSet component to your form, an autogenerated source file is added to your project. For example, for `DataSet1`, the code file is named `DataSet1.vb`. This code file does not appear in the Solution Explorer. If you delete a dataset (for example, `DataSet1.xsd`) from the Solution Explorer, without first removing the DataSet component from the designer, the code file is not automatically deleted. References to it remain in the project file (`.vbproj`), which will keep the project from building. You will need to manually edit the `.vbproj` file to remove these references. (If you remove the DataSet component from the designer before you delete the `.xsd` file from the Solution Explorer, you will not have this problem.)

FIGURE 17.15:

The Generate Dataset dialog adds a DataSet component to your form.

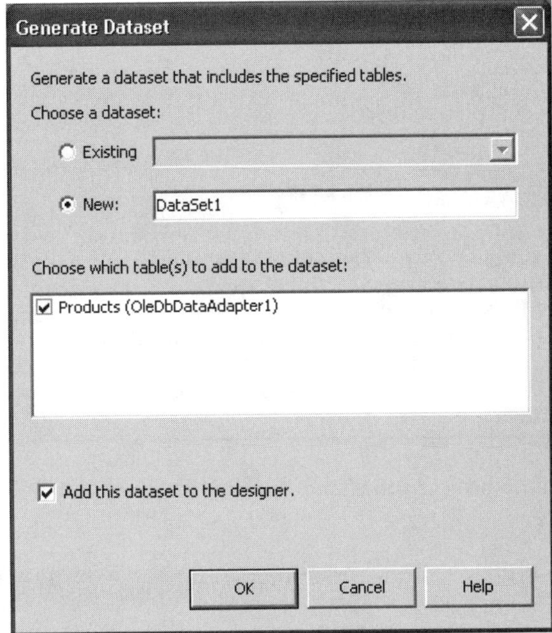

Binding Controls to Data

Now that we have our Data components in place, it's time to do something with them. As a simple example, I'll show you how to feed the ProductName and ProductID fields from the Northwind Products table into two ListBoxes. For this example, the query `SELECT * FROM PRODUCTS` was used to create the dataset.

Add two ListBoxes to the form. Also add a Button control, named `btnFill`, with the text `Fill`. With `btnFill`'s Click event, the first step is to fill the DataSet using the OleDbDataAdapter's `Fill` method:

```
OleDbDataAdapter1.Fill(DataSet1, "Products")
```

Next, set the DataSource property for each ListBox to the Products table, as in this example:

```
ListBox1.DataSource = DataSet1.Tables("Products")
```

Finally, set the DisplayMember property of the ListBox to the field you want displayed:

```
ListBox1.DisplayMember = "ProductName"
ListBox2.DisplayMember = "ProductID"
```

NOTE You may need to change the properties of the OleDbConnection object to get this to work on your particular system.

The complete Click event code for filling the two ListBoxes is shown in Listing 17.2.

Listing 17.2 Filling ListBoxes

```
Private Sub btnFill_Click(ByVal sender As System.Object, _
   ByVal e As System.EventArgs) Handles btnFill.Click
   OleDbDataAdapter1.Fill(DataSet1, "Products")
   ListBox1.DataSource = DataSet1.Tables("Products")
   ListBox1.DisplayMember = "ProductName"
   ListBox2.DataSource = DataSet1.Tables("Products")
   ListBox2.DisplayMember = "ProductID"
End Sub
```

Run the project and click Fill. The two ListBoxes will display data from the appropriate fields.

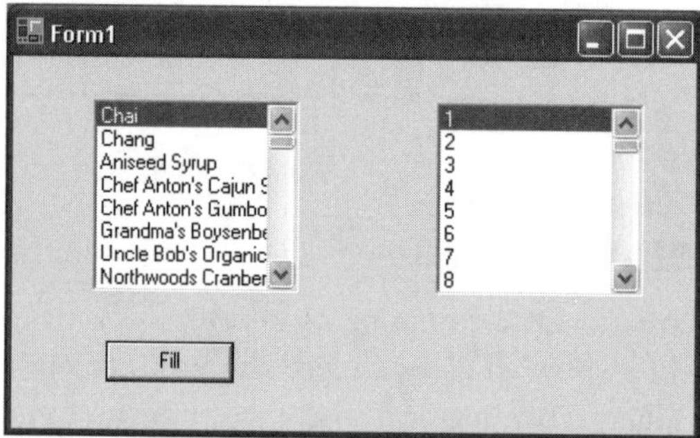

Creating a Dataset in Code

Obviously, there is a great deal to the Visual Studio .NET interface for working with data objects. This interface complexity being what it is, you will probably be pleasantly surprised to learn that you can easily build and use datasets and related data objects in code, without using the interface Microsoft provides.

As an example, let's load the CompanyName data from the Northwind Customers table into a third ListBox (named `lstFillCode`). Within the event procedure that will fill the ListBox, declare variables to hold the DataSet and OleDbDataAdapter objects:

```
Dim theData As DataSet
Dim theAdapter As OleDb.OleDbDataAdapter
```

Next, declare variables for the connection string and the SQL command:

```
Dim connectString, sqlStr As String
```

Set the connection string and SQL command (note that the location of the `Northwind.mdb` file may differ on your system):

```
connectString = "Provider=Microsoft.Jet.OLEDB.4.0;Data" & _
   "Source=C:\Program Files\Microsoft " & _
   "Office\Office\Samples\Northwind.mdb;"
sqlStr = "SELECT * FROM Customers"
```

TIP You can use the ConnectionString property of an auto-generated OleDbConnection object to get a pretty good idea of the connection string you need to use.

Next, instantiate the DataSet and set up the DataAdapter, using the connection string and SQL command:

```
theData = New DataSet()
theAdapter = New OleDb.OleDbDataAdapter(sqlStr, connectString)
```

Fill the DataSet using the DataAdapter:

```
theAdapter.Fill(theData, "Customers")
```

Load the ListBox:

```
lstFillCode.DataSource = theData.Tables("Customers")
lstFillCode.DisplayMember = "CompanyName"
```

You'll find the complete code for creating the DataSet and filling the ListBox in Listing 17.3.

Listing 17.3 Creating a DataSet in Code

```
Private Sub btnFillCode_Click(ByVal sender As System.Object, _
   ByVal e As System.EventArgs) Handles btnFillCode.Click
   Dim theData As DataSet
   Dim theAdapter As OleDb.OleDbDataAdapter
   Dim connectString, sqlStr As String
   connectString = "Provider=Microsoft.Jet.OLEDB.4.0;Data " & _
      "Source=C:\Program Files\Microsoft " & _
      "Office\Office\Samples\Northwind.mdb;"
   sqlStr = "SELECT * FROM Customers"
   theData = New DataSet()
   theAdapter = New OleDb.OleDbDataAdapter(sqlStr, connectString)
   theAdapter.Fill(theData, "Customers")
   lstFillCode.DataSource = theData.Tables("Customers")
   lstFillCode.DisplayMember = "CompanyName"
End Sub
```

If you run the project and click the Fill Code button, the customer names will appear in the ListBox.

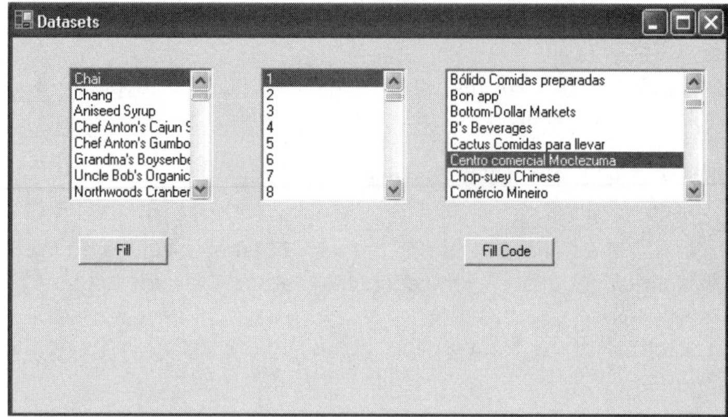

Binding to a DataGrid and Updating a Database

DataGrids are wonderful controls for displaying tabular data and for allowing the user to interact with that data. In this section, I'll show you how to bind a DataGrid to a DataSet, fill the DataSet (and thereby fill the grid), and update the database with changes that the user has made within the grid.

First, add a DataGrid control to the form. Then add two buttons: one to load the form and one to update the database.

Next, bind the DataGrid to the existing DataSet, which—as you'll recall—contains the Northwind Products table. To do this, with the DataGrid selected, open the Properties window. Set the DataSource property of the DataGrid to `DataSet1`. Next, set the DataMember property to `Products` (the drop-down arrow will show you all the tables within the DataSet).

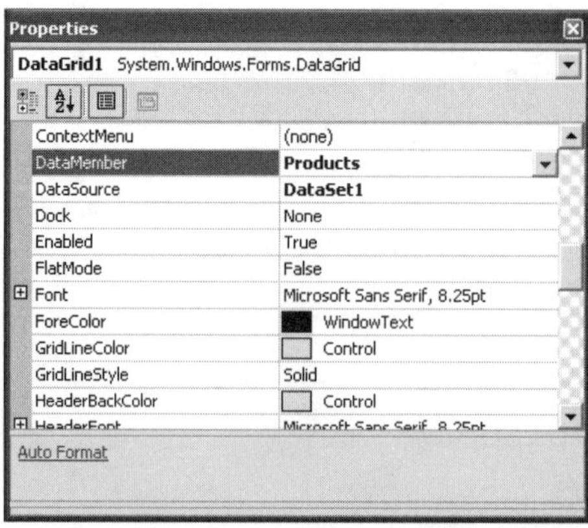

WARNING Make sure the DataSource property is set to `DataSet1` and not `DataSet1.Products`.

The DataGrid has now been bound to the DataSet, but the DataSet still needs to be filled. Within the Load button's Click procedure, add a line of code using the OleDbDataAdapter's `Fill` method to fill the DataSet:

```
Private Sub btnLoad_Click(ByVal sender As System.Object, _
   ByVal e As System.EventArgs) Handles btnLoad.Click
   OleDbDataAdapter1.Fill(DataSet1)
End Sub
```

Run the project and click the Load button. The grid will be populated with data from the Products table.

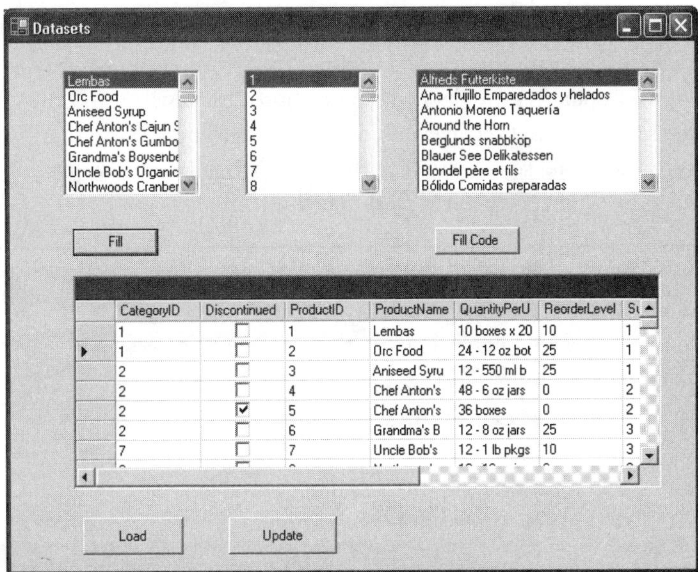

TIP Instead of making users explicitly fill a dataset by clicking a Load button, you can fill the dataset in the Form's `New` procedure when the form is created.

Next, add code to the Update button's Click event to write any changes made by the user back to the database. This is done using the `Update` method of the OleDbDataAdapter:

```
Private Sub btnUpdate_Click(ByVal sender As System.Object, _
   ByVal e As System.EventArgs) Handles btnUpdate.Click
   OleDbDataAdapter1.Update(DataSet1)
   MessageBox.Show("Database has been updated!", "Data", _
      MessageBoxButtons.OK, MessageBoxIcon.Information)
End Sub
```

Run the project again, load the data into the grid, and make some changes (for example, to the Product Name data). When you click Update, a message will be displayed to let you know the database has been updated.

You'll also note that changes made in the grid are instantly reflected in the ListBox in the upper left of the form. Figure 17.16 shows the addition of the Waybread product. This happens without updating the database, since both the ListBox and the grid are taking their data from the same DataSet. However, you may wish to make sure that the changes are actually written to the database by verifying that the changes persist when you shut down the application and start it up again (you'll find that they do!).

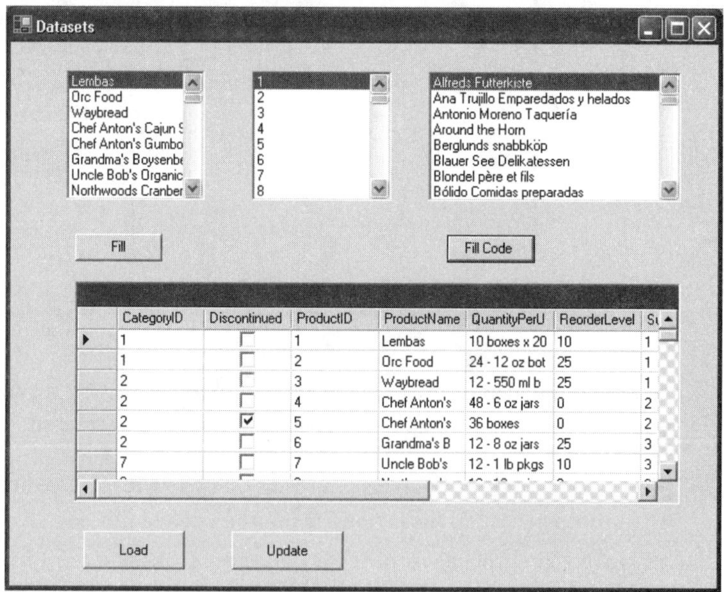

FIGURE 17.16: Changes made in the grid are instantly made to the DataSet and written to the database when the Update button is clicked.

Using the Data Form Wizard

You may be interested to know that Visual Studio .NET comes with a Data Form Wizard that can do a great deal of the work in binding controls to data. To start the Wizard, open the Add New Item dialog, and select the Data Form Wizard, as shown in Figure 17.17.

FIGURE 17.17: The Data Form Wizard can be selected from the Add New Item dialog.

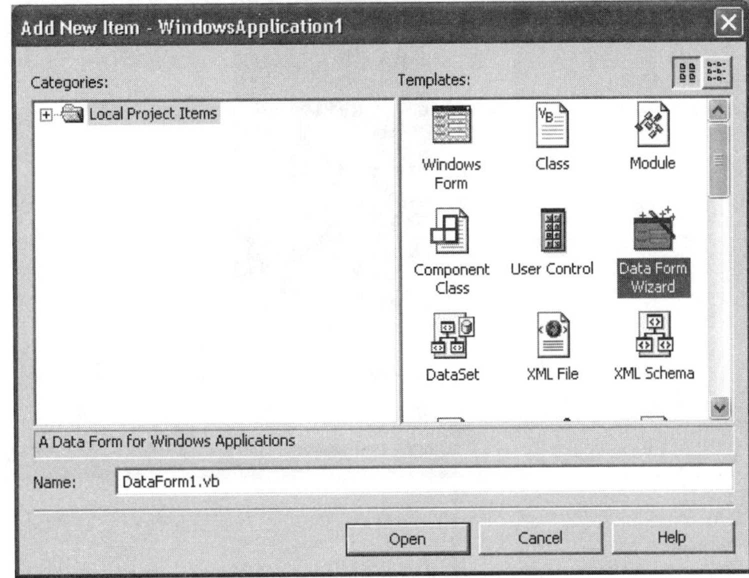

A Wizard interface gathers information from you about the dataset you want to use and the bound controls you want to create. Its opening screen is shown in Figure 17.18.

At the end of the process, a regular form is created. This form may contain a great deal of data functionality, such as the ability to load and update data, add and delete records, and cycle through data. You can specify the fields you want included in the form. See Figure 17.19 for an example of a form created by the Data Form Wizard. You may find it very handy to have this Wizard do a great deal of the "heavy lifting" in creating a data-centric user interface, and then to modify the forms as required.

FIGURE 17.18: The Data Form Wizard will create forms that contain data-bound controls.

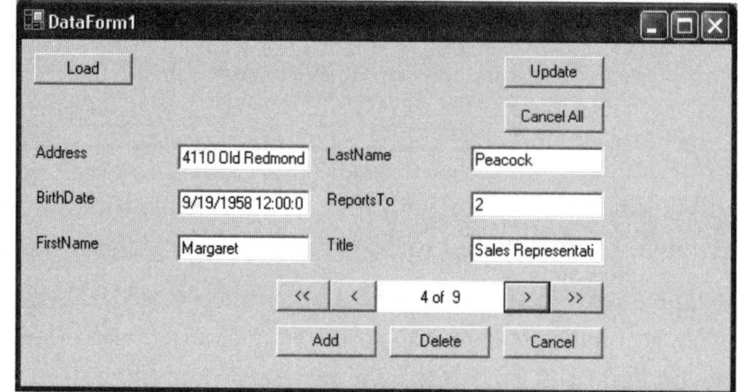

FIGURE 17.19: A great deal of functionality will be auto-generated for you.

Summary

Data is everywhere, and most modern software applications live, eat, and breathe data. The ADO.NET data components in VB .NET make it easy to add data awareness to your user interfaces. This chapter has provided you with an introduction to using these rich tools, so that you can start experimenting on your own. (I cheerfully acknowledge that this chapter has only scratched the surface.)

The next chapter looks at another important aspect of working with data in VB .NET: working with XML. As you'll see, XML provides much of the underpinnings of .NET (and its relationship to data), so this is an important topic.

Chapter 18

Working with XML

- Understanding XML
- Viewing XML schemas
- Reading XML data into a dataset
- Creating an XML schema and data file
- Serializing XML with XMLSerializer
- Writing an XML file with XMLTextWriter
- Reading an XML file with XMLTextReader

Of all the tools, technologies, and languages that have emerged in the past few years, none has had a greater impact on the interoperability of applications and data than XML (eXtensible Markup Language). XML is deceptively simple. It's easy to understand, and you can easily construct XML documents and schemas. This simplicity belies a great deal of power and sidesteps the complexity of using XML.

A great deal of XML and XML-related capabilities are built into the .NET Framework. There are literally hundreds of classes you can use to generate and manipulate XML in VB .NET. Complete information about all these classes (and objects) is clearly beyond the scope of this book (for one thing, it can hardly be expected to fit in a single chapter). Here, I'll provide an overview of XML and show you some of the most important ways of working with XML in VB .NET.

Understanding XML

As you probably know, HTML and XML are both mark-up languages, meaning that they consist of tags that describe content. That's about where the similarity ends. HTML tags are fixed in nature (at least in each version of HTML) and used to describe the elements that make up an HTML page. HTML elements are usually visual. In contrast, XML tags are custom in nature and are used to describe data. In other words, an HTML tag, such as `<h1></h1>`, is used to describe the appearance of the contents within the tag. (The `<h1>` tag means that the tag content is a level 1 heading.) On the other hand, an XML tag such as `<phone_num></phone_num>` identifies the contents as a phone number. XML tags can be used for anything that you might logically use when structuring data.

One hand may make a sound clapping, but there is little use for data description (such as XML) without the ability to communicate. The response to this within specific business communities has been to create XML structures specific to that community. These structures, called *schemas* (in the same spirit that the tabular structure of relational databases are also called schemas), are used to standardize XML communications. As long as you mark your data as elements following the industry-specific schema, all participants will know what you are talking about.

Another possibility is to create and distribute the schema for your own XML data files. These custom schemas are themselves written in XML and saved as XSD files. (DTD, or Document Type Definition, and XDR, a proprietary Microsoft schema specification, are older schema definition formats, replaced in .NET by XSD.)

NOTE XSD is a standard specified by the World Wide Web Consortium (W3C), `www.w3c.org`. In keeping with the goals of the W3C, XSD is vendor-neutral and not controlled by any one company.

XML is tightly integrated with .NET as its underlying mode of interoperability. In addition, the .NET Framework contains a great many classes (literally, hundreds of classes) to help you work with XML. You can use the Object Browser (discussed in Chapter 14, "Using the Object Browser") or the Help system (discussed in Appendix A, "Using VB .NET's Help System") to start learning about these classes. To help you start exploring, Table 18.1 shows some of the most important namespaces that contain classes related to XML development.

TABLE 18.1: VB .NET Namespaces Related to XML

Namespace	Description
`System.XML`	Provides primary support for a variety of XML functions.
`System.XML.Serialization`	Contains the classes used to serialize and deserialize XML.
`System.XML.Serialization.Schema`	Provides classes related to serializing schemas and to SOAP (Simple Object Access Protocol). SOAP is an open-standard mechanism for wrapping XML and other content so that it can be transmitted over HTTP. SOAP is used as a mechanism for invoking methods on a remote server using XML documents.
`System.Xml.XPath`	Provides an XPath parser and evaluation engine. XPath (XML Path Language) enables you to easily write queries that retrieve particular subsets of XML data.
`System.Xml.Xsl`	Provides the tools needed to work with XSLT (XML Stylesheet Language Transformations). Essentially, XSLT lets you create templates that can be used to manipulate XML documents. One use of XSLT is to transform XML into HTML so that it can be rendered in a web browser.

Viewing XML Schemas

In Chapter 17, "Working with Data and ADO.NET," I showed you how to add datasets to your projects to communicate with data sources. Unlike previous versions of Microsoft development products, which used COM for communication between distributed applications, .NET uses an underlying transport mechanism based on XML. This implies that you should be able to view the XML schema created from each DataSet object, which is, in fact, the case.

The XML schemas are saved as XML Schema Definition files (ending in an `.XSD` suffix). XSD files do not contain the XML data, but rather the structure of the XML file, including elements, attributes, and data type of the attributes.

With a DataSet object selected in the Solution Explorer, right-click and choose View in Browser from the context menu. The XML schema used by the DataSet will be displayed in the internal .NET browser, as shown in Figure 18.1.

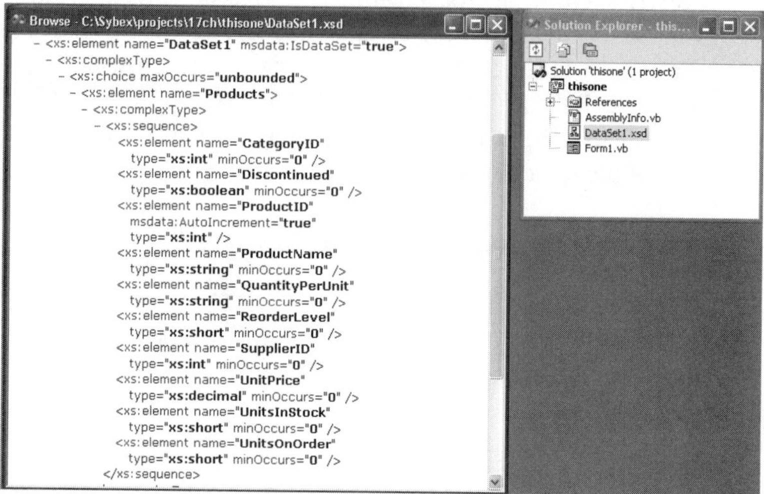

FIGURE 18.1: If you select View in Browser in the Solution Explorer, a DataSet's underlying XML schema will be displayed.

Another way to view the schema is to open a DataSet object from the Solution Explorer (select Open from the DataSet's context menu or double-click the object). The DataSet structure will be displayed in standard tabular format (rows and columns), as shown here.

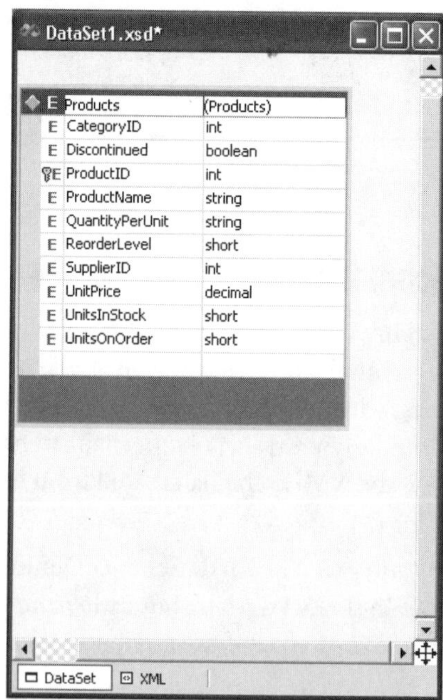

To view the same schema in XML form, click the XML icon at the bottom of DataSet window (shown previously). The DataSet's schema will be shown as an XML XSD file.

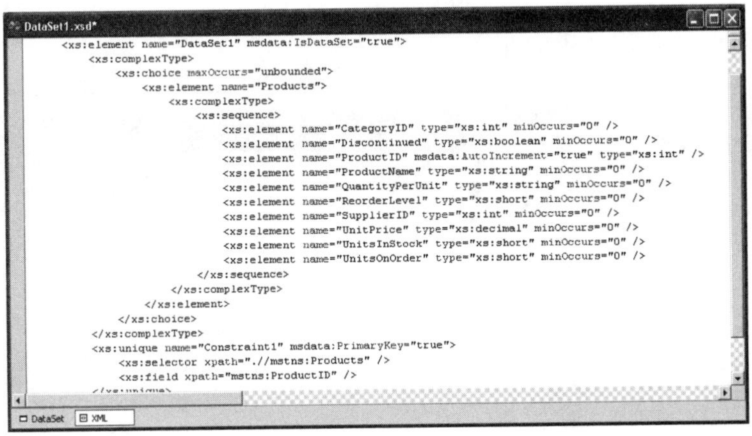

```
DataSet1.xsd*
<xs:element name="DataSet1" msdata:IsDataSet="true">
    <xs:complexType>
        <xs:choice maxOccurs="unbounded">
            <xs:element name="Products">
                <xs:complexType>
                    <xs:sequence>
                        <xs:element name="CategoryID" type="xs:int" minOccurs="0" />
                        <xs:element name="Discontinued" type="xs:boolean" minOccurs="0" />
                        <xs:element name="ProductID" msdata:AutoIncrement="true" type="xs:int" />
                        <xs:element name="ProductName" type="xs:string" minOccurs="0" />
                        <xs:element name="QuantityPerUnit" type="xs:string" minOccurs="0" />
                        <xs:element name="ReorderLevel" type="xs:short" minOccurs="0" />
                        <xs:element name="SupplierID" type="xs:int" minOccurs="0" />
                        <xs:element name="UnitPrice" type="xs:decimal" minOccurs="0" />
                        <xs:element name="UnitsInStock" type="xs:short" minOccurs="0" />
                        <xs:element name="UnitsOnOrder" type="xs:short" minOccurs="0" />
                    </xs:sequence>
                </xs:complexType>
            </xs:element>
        </xs:choice>
    </xs:complexType>
    <xs:unique name="Constraint1" msdata:PrimaryKey="true">
        <xs:selector xpath=".//mstns:Products" />
        <xs:field xpath="mstns:ProductID" />
DataSet  XML
```

TIP The XSD file generated by the DataSet contains the XML definition of the schema in standard format. This is a plain text file that is part of your project. It can be opened and inspected using an application such as Notepad.

Since a DataSet object supports XML schema files that define the data stored in the dataset, you may wonder if the reverse relationship is also true. In other words, can the structure of a dataset be created from an XML schema, and can XML data be read into a DataSet object? The answer to these questions is a resounding "Yes," as I'll show you in the next section.

Reading XML Data into a Dataset

If you want to structure a dataset from an XML schema, you first need to be able to create the XML schema. VB .NET makes it easy to create XML schemas and raw XML files. In fact, you can populate a DataSet object from a straight XML file, without referencing a schema, and the DataSet will do its best to "figure out" the structure of the XML. The advantage to loading a schema before loading XML data is that you can be sure that the data will conform to the schema. It is important to have well-formed XML data when communicating between applications.

In this section, I'll show you how to create an XML schema and how to create a straight XML file within .NET (which can be used to automatically generate an XML schema file). Next, I'll show you how to load a dataset with the XML schema and data, and populate a grid based on the dataset.

Creating an XML Schema

To create an XML schema within Visual Studio .NET, choose Add New Item from the Project menu. When the Add New Item dialog opens, select XML Schema, as shown in Figure 18.2, and click Open.

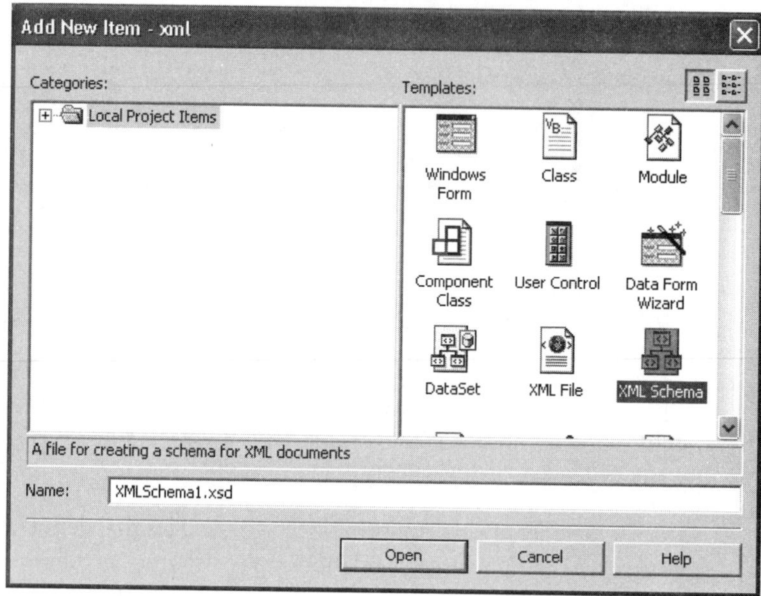

FIGURE 18.2: You can create an XML schema by adding an XML Schema module to your project.

The XML schema designer will open, as shown in Figure 18.3. The designer is empty when it first opens.

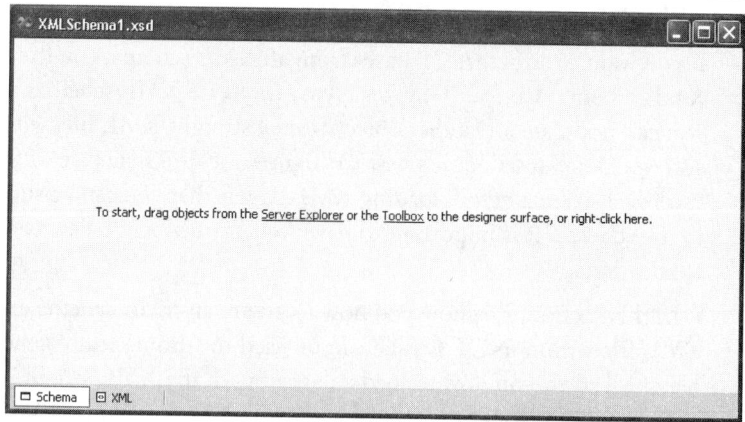

FIGURE 18.3: The XML designer is empty when it opens. To add elements and attributes to your schema, right-click the designer and choose Add.

With the schema designer open, you can add elements and attributes to your schema in several ways:

- Right-click the surface of the designer and choose Add from the context menu.
- Use the Server Explorer to drill down into a database and its tables. Then just drag and drop a table onto the schema designer, and the schema will be generated automatically.
- Open the Toolbox, which will display XML schema elements, types, attributes, and relationships. Then just drag and drop items from the Toolbox onto the schema designer.

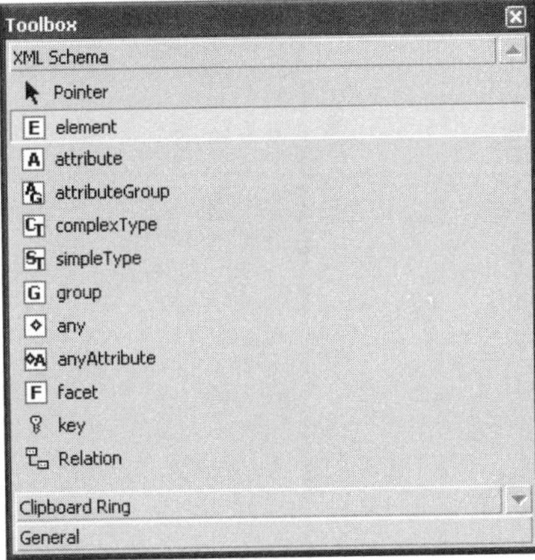

The resulting schema appears in tabular form in the designer and as an XSD file in the Solution Explorer, as shown in Figure 18.4.

FIGURE 18.4:

The schema appears in tabular form in the designer and is saved as an XSD file that is shown in the Solution Explorer.

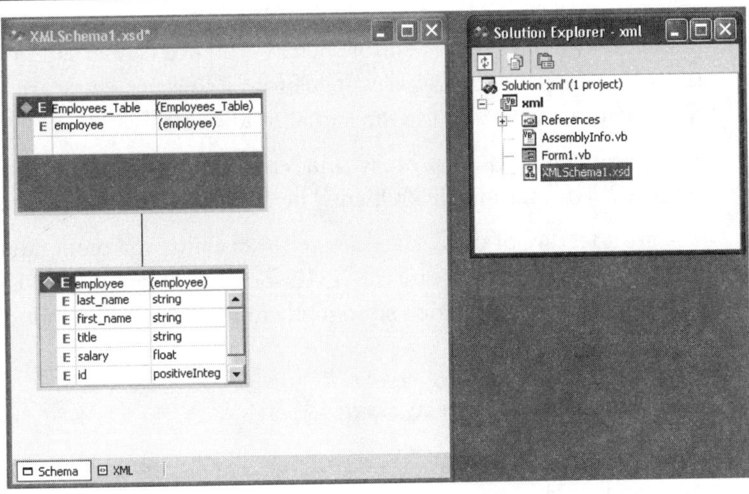

TIP To add a subelement, first add an element to your schema. Select the element. Next, right-click in the margin to the left of the element (shown under the diamond in Figure 18.4). Choose Add ➢ New Element from the context menu. You can now enter the elements and types of the subelement, which will be shown linked to its parent element with a connecting line.

Note that if you click the XML tab of the XML schema designer, the schema will appear in XML form in the color-coded XML editor, as shown in Figure 18.5.

FIGURE 18.5: You can directly edit the XML schema.

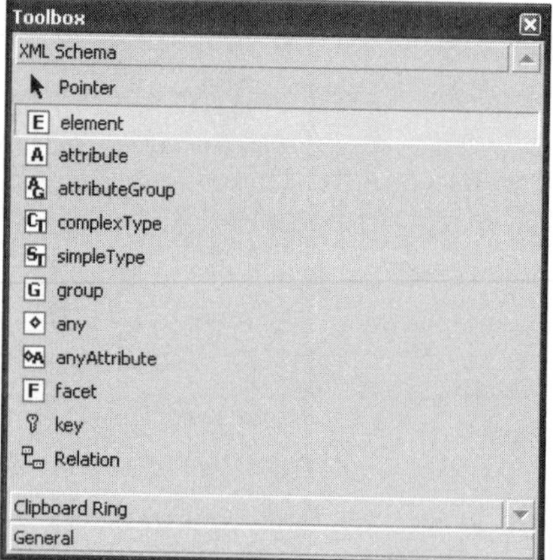

Creating an XML Data File

You can create an XML file containing data in a number of different ways, including by generating it by hand in a text editor such as Notepad (or perhaps importing it from an application that supplies data to your application). However, there are a number of features that make it advantageous to use the Visual Studio .NET XML designer.

To create an XML data file within Visual Studio .NET, select Project ➢ Add New Item ➢ XML File and click Open. The new XML file will appear in the Solution Explorer.

A great feature of the XML designer is its ability to accept tabular data. In order to use this feature, you must first create the XML for a table using the XML tab of the XML designer. For example, the XML for a simplified employee table might look like this:

```
<employee>
   <last_name></last_name>
   <first_name></first_name>
   <title></title>
   <salary></salary>
   <id></id>
</employee>
```

With this in place, if you switch to the Data tab of the XML designer, shown in Figure 18.6, you can start entering your data using the table provided. This approach is a great deal faster than constructing each XML data element.

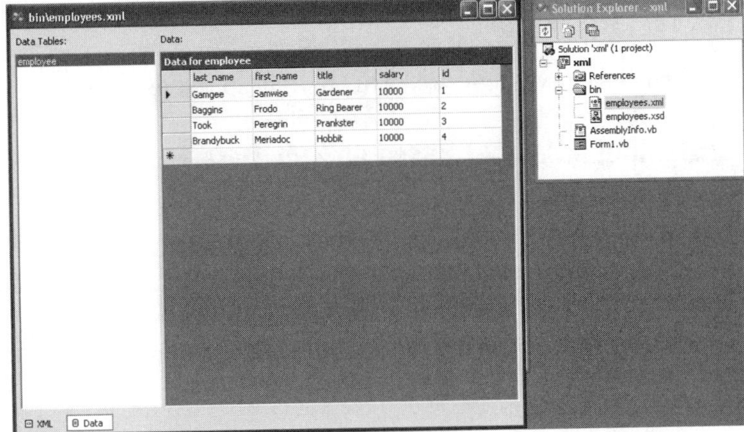

FIGURE 18.6: You can enter XML data using a table once the element has been constructed.

Once you have entered your data in tabular fashion, you can view it as straight XML by clicking the XML tab, as shown in Figure 18.7.

FIGURE 18.7: You can view data entered in the table as "straight" XML.

bin\employees.xml

```
<?xml version="1.0" encoding="utf-8" ?>
<Employees_Table xmlns="http://tempuri.org/employees.xsd">
    <employee>
        <last_name>Gamgee</last_name>
        <first_name>Samwise</first_name>
        <title>Gardener</title>
        <salary>10000</salary>
        <id>1</id>
    </employee>
    <employee>
        <last_name>Baggins</last_name>
        <first_name>Frodo</first_name>
        <title>Ring Bearer</title>
        <salary>10000</salary>
        <id>2</id>
    </employee>
    <employee>
        <last_name>Took</last_name>
        <first_name>Peregrin</first_name>
        <title>Prankster</title>
        <salary>10000</salary>
        <id>3</id>
    </employee>
    <employee>
        <last_name>Brandybuck</last_name>
        <first_name>Meriadoc</first_name>
        <title>Hobbit</title>
        <salary>10000</salary>
        <id>4</id>
    </employee>
</Employees_Table>
```

XML | Data

As I mentioned earlier in this chapter, you don't need to create an XML schema. If you don't set up a schema, the DataSet will do the best it can to create a schema on the fly from an XML data file. The reasons to create an XML schema are to ensure consistency and to make the schema available to remote applications that may communicate with your application.

It's a neat feature that you can auto-generate an XML schema based on your XML data file. To do this, right-click in the XML designer and choose Create Schema from the context menu. The newly generated XSD file will appear in the Solution Explorer.

Creating a Dataset Based on XML Data

It's easy to read XML data into a dataset, which can then be used to perform many functions with the data. For example, you could display the data contained in the dataset in a grid.

To see one way this could work, add DataGrid and Button controls to a form.

TIP If you want to populate the grid when the form loads, rather than when the button is clicked, place the code in the `Form1_Load` event.

In the button's Click event procedure, declare and instantiate a new DataSet object:

```
Dim dsEmployees As New DataSet()
```

Use the DataSet's `ReadXmlSchema` method to read the file that contains the schema:

```
dsEmployees.ReadXmlSchema("employees.xsd")
```

Next, read the actual XML data into the DataSet:

```
dsEmployees.ReadXml("employees.xml")
```

WARNING If you read the XML schema and data from files, be sure to include the path when you specify the file location. If no path is specified (as in the example), the files must be in the project `bin` directory, along with the executable.

Finally, populate the grid based on the DataSet and table that it contains:

```
DataGrid1.SetDataBinding(dsEmployees, "employee")
```

The complete Click event procedure that loads the XML data into the dataset and binds the grid to the dataset is shown in Listing 18.1.

Listing 18.1 **Reading an XML Schema and XML Data into a Dataset and Displaying It in a Grid**

```
Private Sub btnLoad_Click(ByVal sender As System.Object, _
   ByVal e As System.EventArgs) Handles btnLoad.Click
   Dim dsEmployees As New DataSet()
   dsEmployees.ReadXmlSchema("employees.xsd")
```

```
    dsEmployees.ReadXml("employees.xml")
    DataGrid1.SetDataBinding(dsEmployees, "employee")
End Sub
```

Run the project and click the Load button. The populated grid appears, as in the example shown here.

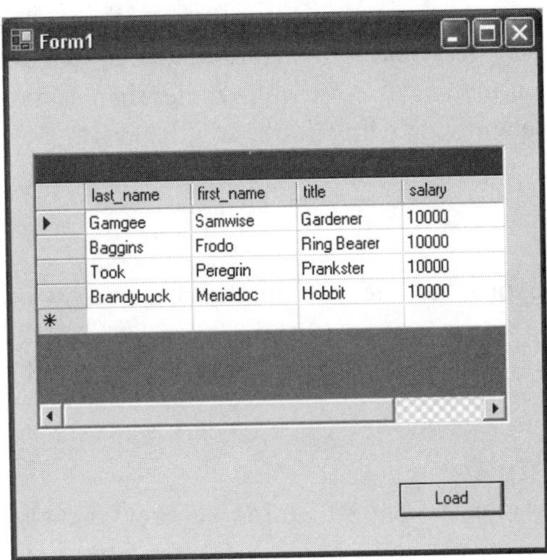

Writing and Reading XML Content

There are several ways to write and read XML content. Here, we will look at the use of the XMLSerializer object and the XMLTextWriter and XMLTextReader classes.

Using XMLSerializer

Under the hood, VB .NET and XML work hand and glove together. This can be seen in a quite simple example: using an XMLSerializer object to serialize an instance of a class to a StreamReader (which can save it as file). The XMLSerializer can also be used in a reverse fashion to convert (or "deserialize") an I/O stream, pulled from a file with a StreamWriter object, back to an instance of a class, making the members of the object programmatically available. (For more information about working with StreamReaders and StreamWriters, see Chapter 9, "Working with Common Dialogs.")

To see this in action, add two buttons to a form, one to serialize and the other to deserialize, as shown here.

Next, create a simple class module (see Listing 18.2). The class needs to implement a default constructor (`Public Sub New()`). In addition, for the sake of simplicity, the class that is shown implements properties as Public variables rather than using Property procedures. (For more information about working with classes, see Chapter 15, "Object-Oriented Programming in VB .NET.")

Serializing XML

At the top of the form module with the Serialize and Deserialize buttons, add an `Imports` statement to import the `System.IO` and `System.XML.Serialization` namespaces:

```
Imports System.Xml.Serialization, System.IO
```

Next, in the Serialize button's Click event, instantiate an XMLSerializer object based on the employee class:

```
Dim theSerializer As New XmlSerializer(GetType(employee))
```

Create an Employee object, supplying property values:

```
Dim SGamgee As New employee("Samwise", "Gamgee", "Gardener")
```

Instantiate a StreamWriter, naming the file (including the path) that you want to serialize the data to as an argument:

```
Dim sw As New StreamWriter("data.xml")
```

Finally, call the `Serialize` method of the XMLSerializer, supplying the StreamWriter and the Employee object as arguments:

```
theSerializer.Serialize(sw, SGamgee)
```

The complete procedure, along with the class code, is shown in Listing 18.2.

Listing 18.2 A Class and the Code to Serialize to XML an Object Based on the Class

```
Public Class employee
   Public first_name As String
   Public last_name As String
   Public title As String

   Public Sub New()
   End Sub

   Public Sub New(ByVal first_name As String, _
```

```
        ByVal last_name As String, _
        ByVal title As String)
        Me.first_name = first_name
        Me.last_name = last_name
        Me.title = title
    End Sub
End Class

Imports System.Xml.Serialization, System.IO
...
Private Sub btnSerial_Click(ByVal sender As System.Object, _
    ByVal e As System.EventArgs) Handles btnSerial.Click
    Dim theSerializer As New XmlSerializer(GetType(employee))
    Dim SGamgee As New employee("Samwise", "Gamgee", "Gardener")
    Dim sw As New StreamWriter("data.xml")
    theSerializer.Serialize(sw, SGamgee)
End Sub
```

If you run this code and click the Serialize Class button, you'll find that a file named `data.xml` has been created. The file looks like this:

```
<?xml version="1.0" encoding="utf-8"?>
<employee xmlns:xsd="http://www.w3.org/2001/XMLSchema"
xmlns:xsi="http://www.w3.org/2001/XMLSchema-instance">
  <first_name>Samwise</first_name>
  <last_name>Gamgee</last_name>
  <title>Gardener</title>
</employee>
```

Notice that the XML element has been named, like the class, `<employee>`. Elements have been named for each class member, for example `<title>`.

Deserializing XML

The same steps as just described are used, but backwards, to reverse the serialization process. In this way, you can deserialize XML data based on a class instance that you serialized. This is not a common requirement, but it might be useful if you are maintaining application state information, for example.

In the Click event for the Deserialize button, instantiate an XMLSerializer and a StreamReader:

```
Dim theSerializer As New XmlSerializer(GetType(employee))
Dim sw As New StreamReader("data.xml")
```

Declare an object variable based on the employee class and assign the deserialized StreamReader to it:

```
Dim theWorker As employee
theWorker = theSerializer.Deserialize(sw)
```

You can now access the properties of the object based on the employee class, which have been populated from the XML file:

```
MessageBox.Show(theWorker.first_name & " " & theWorker.last_name & _
   " is a " & theWorker.title & ".", "Deserialize!", _
   MessageBoxButtons.OK, MessageBoxIcon.Information)
```

The complete deserialization code is shown in Listing 18.3.

Listing 18.3 Deserializing and Displaying the XML

```
Imports System.Xml.Serialization, System.IO
...
Private Sub btnDeSerialize_Click(ByVal sender As System.Object, _
   ByVal e As System.EventArgs) Handles btnDeSerialize.Click
   Dim theSerializer As New XmlSerializer(GetType(employee))
   Dim sw As New StreamReader("data.xml")
   Dim theWorker As employee
   theWorker = theSerializer.Deserialize(sw)
   MessageBox.Show(theWorker.first_name & " " & theWorker.last_name & _
      " is a " & theWorker.title & ".", "Deserialize!", _
      MessageBoxButtons.OK, MessageBoxIcon.Information)
End Sub
```

If you save this code, and then click the Deserialization button, a message that uses the serialized XML data will be displayed (provided the XML file is appropriately located).

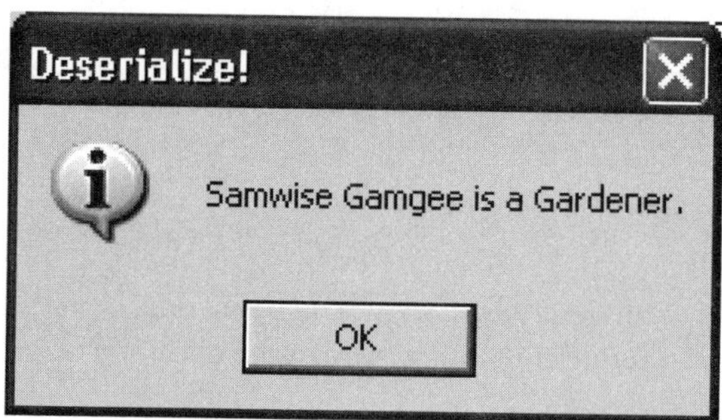

Writing XML with XMLTextWriter

You don't need to serialize XML content to write (and read) XML documents. The XMLTextWriter class allows you to write whatever XML you care to generate. (The XMLTextReader, which lets you read the contents of an XML document, is discussed in the next section.)

Using the XMLTextWriter, an XML document is written from top to bottom. In other words, you get a single forward pass at creating the XML document.

To see this in action, I've set up a simple interface, shown in Figure 18.8, which lets the user decide the name for XML nodes and the values that those nodes enclose.

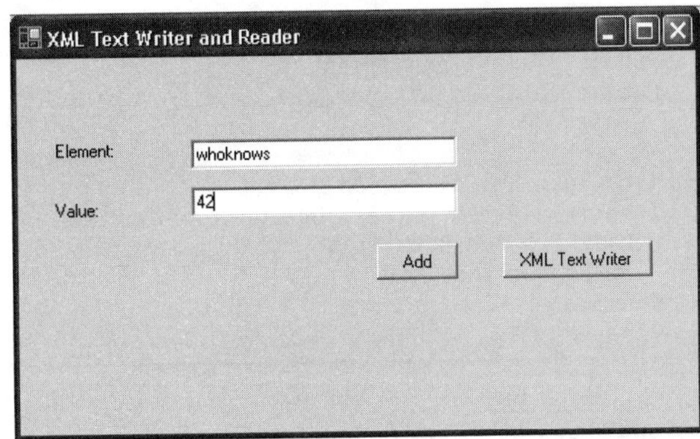

FIGURE 18.8: Users can enter as many element-value pairs as they want. When all the pairs have been entered, the XML document is created.

The text entered by the user in the Element text box will become the XML tag, and the text entered in the Value text box will become its value:

```
<element>
   value
</element>
```

In the interests of simplicity, all the element-value pairs entered by the user will fall under one root XML node, `<UserChoice>`. So the structure of the XML document will look like this, with each element-value combination chosen by the user:

```
<UserChoice>
   <element>
      value
   </element>
   <element>
      value
   </element>
   ...
</UserChoice>
```

Creating the Class and Collection Class

If the user can enter multiple element-value pairs before the XML document is generated, the application must have some way to store the information. Perhaps the easiest way to do this is to use a collection class (see Chapter 15 for more information about collections). Listing 18.4 shows the bare-bones class that will be used for each element-value pair and the collection class that will be used to store the user's XML choices until the XML document is ready to be generated.

Listing 18.4 An Element-Value XML Class and a Collection Class Used to Store Element-Value Pairs

```
Public Class XML
   Public element As String
   Public value As String
End Class

Public Class XmlCollection
   Inherits System.Collections.CollectionBase
   Public Sub Add(ByVal aXML As XML)
      List.Add(aXML)
   End Sub
End Class
```

Using the Class and Collection

After you've set up the class and collection, create an interface with text boxes for the user input of elements and values, like that shown in Figure 18.8. The Add button will be used to add an element-value pair to the collection, and the XML Text Writer button will be used to generate the relevant XML document.

At the top of the form module, import the `System.XML` namespace (it contains the XMLTextReader and XMLTextWriter classes):

```
Imports System.Xml
```

Next, declare and instantiate a Collection object based on the collection class defined in Listing 18.4:

```
Dim theXML As New XmlCollection()
```

In the Click event procedure of the Add button, instantiate an element-value object, assign the values of the text boxes to it, and add it to the collection:

```
Dim aXML As New XML()
aXML.element = txtElement.Text
aXML.value = txtValue.Text
theXML.Add(aXML)
```

That takes care of adding element-value pairs to the collection. Now let's write an XML document based on the contents of the collection!

In the Click event procedure for the Write button, declare and instantiate a XMLTextWriter, specifying a file (including the path) and the encoding to use:

```
Dim myXmlTextWriter As New XmlTextWriter("doc.xml", Nothing)
```

Setting the encoding to `Nothing` causes it to be written out as UTF-8. If no path is provided, by default, the file will be written to the executable, or `bin`, directory of the project.

WARNING The XMLTextWriter will overwrite the specified file if it already exists.

Next, declare an element-value XML object based on the class defined in Listing 18.4.

Getting to the good stuff, using the methods and properties of the XMLTextWriter object, tell the XMLTextWriter to format the XML with three spaces for indentation, place a comment at the start of the document, and create a root XML element called `<UserChoice>`:

```
With myXmlTextWriter
   .Formatting = Formatting.Indented
   .Indentation = 3
   .IndentChar = " "
   .WriteStartDocument()
   .WriteComment("This is a sample XML document generated" & _
      " using an XMLTextWriter object.")
   .WriteStartElement("UserChoice")
```

Here, we start with the `With` keyword, which allows us to refer to the object without repeatedly typing its name.

Next, use the `For Each...Next` syntax to cycle through the collection to write each item in the collection:

```
For Each aXML In theXML
   .WriteElementString(aXML.element, aXML.value)
Next
```

Finally, close the root element, document, and `With` block (with `End With`):

```
   .WriteEndElement()
   .Close()
End With
```

The complete code for adding XML element-value pairs to the collection and writing an XML document based on the collection items that have been added is shown in Listing 18.5.

Listing 18.5 **Creating a Collection of Element-Value Pairs and Writing Them to an XML Document**

```
Imports System.Xml
Public Class Form1
   Inherits System.Windows.Forms.Form
   Dim theXML As New XmlCollection()
   ...
   Private Sub btnAdd_Click(ByVal sender As System.Object, _
      ByVal e As System.EventArgs) Handles btnAdd.Click
      Dim aXML As New XML()
      aXML.element = txtElement.Text
      aXML.value = txtValue.Text
      theXML.Add(aXML)
   End Sub
```

```
    Private Sub btnWrite_Click(ByVal sender As System.Object, _
       ByVal e As System.EventArgs) Handles btnWrite.Click
       Dim myXmlTextWriter As New XmlTextWriter("doc.xml", Nothing)
       Dim aXML As XML
       With myXmlTextWriter
          .Formatting = Formatting.Indented
          .Indentation = 3
          .IndentChar = " "
          .WriteStartDocument()
          .WriteComment("This is a sample XML document generated" & _
             " using an XMLTextWriter object.")
          .WriteStartElement("UserChoice")
          For Each aXML In theXML
             .WriteElementString(aXML.element, aXML.value)
          Next
          .WriteEndElement()
          .Close()
       End With
    End Sub
...
End Class
```

Run the project and enter some element-value pairs, clicking Add each time. Next, click the XML Text Writer button. You'll find that an XML document containing the elements and values you added has been created. It will look something like this:

```
<?xml version="1.0">
<!-This is a sample XML document generated using an XMLTextWriter object.->
<UserChoice>
   <hope>experience</hope>
   <triumph>3</triumph>
   <whoknows>42</whoknows>
</UserChoice>
```

The *With* Keyword

The `With` keyword is used as a shorthand way to refer to an object without needing to continually retype the object's name. `With` blocks start using the `With` keyword and an object, and end using `End With`. Here's a simple example:

```
With TextBox1
   .Text = "Hello, With!"
End With
```

This code allows you to assign a string to the Text property without needing to retype the name of the TextBox.

Reading XML with XMLTextReader

The counterpart to the XMLTextWriter class is the XMLTextReader class. Realize that this is by no means the only class available in .NET to read (or parse) XML files; XMLNodeReader and XMLValidatingReader are also powerful classes.

Much of the time, you will know a great deal about the formatting of the XML file you want to read. That's certainly the case with the example that I'll show you, in which we know that the root element is named `<UserChoice>` and is followed by elements and values:

```
<UserChoice>
   <element>
      value
   </element>
   <element>
      value
   </element>
   ...
</UserChoice>
```

If you are interested in only the elements and values, it's an easy thing to instantiate a new XMLTextReader object and start it past the root element:

```
Dim myXMLTextReader As New XmlTextReader("doc.xml")
myXMLTextReader.ReadStartElement("UserChoice")
```

You could then set up a loop reading the rest of the document and exiting only when the `</UserChoice>` tag is reached:

```
Do While myXMLTextReader.Read()
   If myXMLTextReader.Name = "UserChoice" Then Exit Do
   ...
Loop
```

Within the loop, you can use the `ReadOuterXml` method to read tags and values into a multiline text box (the `CrLf` character makes sure that each element appears on its own line):

```
Do While myXMLTextReader.Read()
   If myXMLTextReader.Name = "UserChoice" Then Exit Do
   TextBox1.Text = TextBox1.Text & _
      Microsoft.VisualBasic.ControlChars.CrLf & _
      myXMLTextReader.ReadOuterXml
Loop
```

Finally, the XMLTextReader should be closed:

```
myXMLTextReader.Close()
```

The code, placed in an XMLTextReader button's Click event, is shown in Listing 18.6.

Listing 18.6 Reading an XML File

```
Private Sub btnReader_Click(ByVal sender As System.Object, _
   ByVal e As System.EventArgs) Handles btnReader.Click
   Dim myXMLTextReader As New XmlTextReader("doc.xml")
   myXMLTextReader.ReadStartElement("UserChoice")
   Do While myXMLTextReader.Read()
      If myXMLTextReader.Name = "UserChoice" Then Exit Do
      TextBox1.Text = TextBox1.Text & _
         Microsoft.VisualBasic.ControlChars.CrLf & _
         myXMLTextReader.ReadOuterXml
   Loop
   myXMLTextReader.Close()
End Sub
```

If you run the project and click the XML Text Reader button, the elements and values in the doc.xml file contained between the beginning <UserChoice> tag and the ending </UserChoice> tag will be shown in the text box.

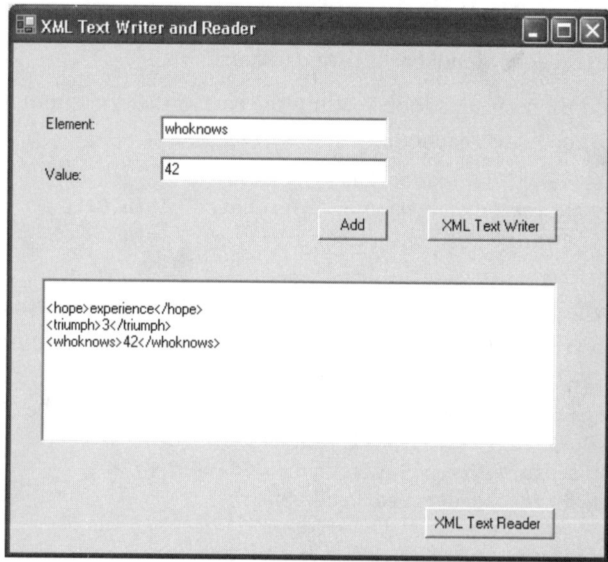

Summary

This chapter has provided a sampler of the extent to which VB .NET is integrated with XML, uses XML as an underlying means of communication, and gives the developer powerful tools for working with XML. But we have only scratched the surface of working with XML.NET, and much has been omitted. (For one thing, the samples in this chapter have left out any error-handling code.) XML and working with XML in VB .NET are big topics, and there are entire books devoted to them.

The next chapter shows how to use the skills you have learned in this book to easily and quickly create powerful web applications.

CHAPTER 19

Building ASP.NET Web Applications

- Creating web form applications
- Using web form events
- Adding web controls
- Creating and consuming a web service

From the viewpoint of VB programmers, ASP.NET is truly revolutionary. As opposed to the older ASP technology, which processed uncompiled scripts in a linear, top-to-bottom fashion, Visual Studio .NET provides a development environment in which you can create web applications in a visual, event-driven fashion. The manner in which you build an ASP.NET web application is completely analogous to the way in which you create a Windows application using VB .NET. The resulting web application is compiled into a single, unified library file.

It's really easy to create web applications using VB .NET. In this chapter, I'll show you how it's done, starting with a clichéd "Hello, World!" application. Next, we'll cover the controls you can use with web applications. There are a number of different kinds of web controls, and the nomenclature can be confusing. I'll sort this out for you. Finally, I'll show you how to create and use web services.

Creating Web Forms Applications

Perhaps you recall questions from standardized tests that are phrased as comparative analogies. These run along the lines of "A is to B as C is to D," and you are given A, B, and C. If you know what D is, you can get into the college of your choice.

In the current context, the comparative analogy is: Windows forms are to Windows applications as web forms are to X. As you probably suspect, X is an ASP.NET Web Application project. In other words, ASP.NET web applications are built around web forms in the same way that Windows applications are built around Windows forms.

A web form represents a web page in the browser (in the same way that a Windows form represents an application window on the Desktop). Just like Windows forms, web forms have properties, methods, and events that can be used to modify the appearance and behavior of the page in the browser. By default, an ASP.NET Web Application project has one web form, which becomes a web page in the Internet Explorer browser when the project is run.

NOTE Web forms and Windows forms are mutually exclusive within a project. You must pick one or the other, so it makes sense to be careful about the choice. If your project uses web forms, it will have a great deal of web functionality prebuilt. However, you will not be able to use much of the functionality that is part of Windows, such as dialog boxes, message boxes, and more.

Requirements for Running an ASP.NET Application

In order to run web forms (ASP.NET) applications, you'll need to have Internet Information Server (IIS) version 5 (or later) and the FrontPage Server Extensions. In order to install

Visual Studio .NET, you should be running Windows 2000 Server or Professional, or Windows XP Professional. (See Chapter 1, "Understanding Visual Basic .NET," for more information about software requirements for Visual Studio .NET.)

The Windows 2000 and Windows XP software ship with current versions of IIS, and your installation of Visual Studio .NET should have automatically configured it correctly to work with ASP.NET applications. You should have no problems running web forms applications from the Visual Studio .NET development environment. (The default web server is designated using the URL `http://localhost/`.)

NOTE If your web forms application is not running locally, and is deployed on an external server running IIS, the server needs to have the .NET Framework and the FrontPage Server Extensions installed.

Starting a New Web Application

To start a new web application, open the New Project dialog. With Visual Basic Projects selected in the left pane as the Project Type, choose ASP.NET Web Application from the right pane as the project template, as shown in Figure 19.1.

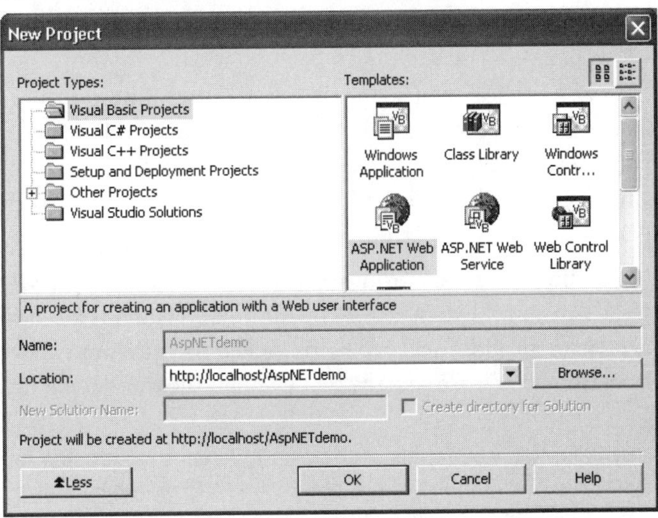

FIGURE 19.1: To create a web application, choose ASP.NET Web Application in the New Project dialog.

In the New Project dialog, name the project using the Location box. As you'll notice in Figure 19.1, the Name box is disabled. The part of the location entry following the server name, typically `http://localhost/`, becomes the project name. In Figure 19.1, the location is shown as `http://localhost/AspNETdemo`, and the project name becomes `AspNETdemo`.

When you click OK, a new Web Application project will be created. Depending on how you have set your development environment preferences, it will look more or less like Figure 19.2.

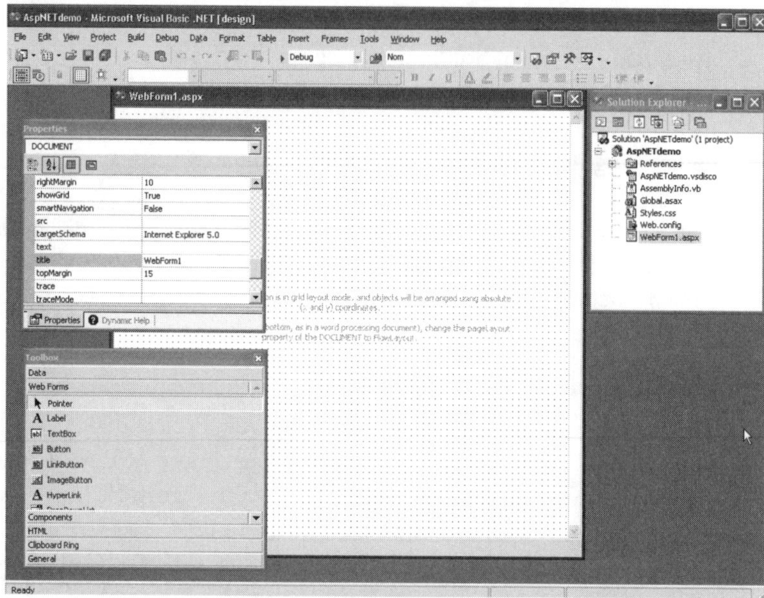

FIGURE 19.2: The new Web Application project features a web form.

What has happened so far? First, a Visual Studio project containing a web form has been created. By default, this web form is named `WebForm1` and is saved with an `.aspx` suffix (`WebForm1.aspx`). The web form provides a precise layout grid that can be used to host controls (as you'll see in the "Adding Controls to a Web Form" section later in this chapter). In this mode, the web form can be treated pretty much like a normal Windows form.

In addition, the web form can be edited in straight HTML. You can place VB code related to the form in the connected code module, which is a file with the same name as the web form, with an additional `.vb` suffix tacked on (`WebForm1.aspx.vb`). The connected code file, for reasons you'll see shortly, is also called the *code-behind* file.

TIP By default, a web form's code-behind file does not appear in the Solution Explorer. To display the code-behind file in the Solution Explorer, click the Show All Files button in the Solution Explorer's Toolbar and expand the `.aspx` file node.

Visual Studio has also created a directory named for the project (AspNETdemo) and solution file in the default Visual Studio Projects directory. A duplicate project directory and source files for the project's modules have been created for IIS under `\inetpub\wwwroot\` (if serving from your local machine, for the AspNETdemo project, it's probably `C:\inetpub\wwwroot\AspNETdemo`).

You can also see the new web application in the Internet Information Services administrative application, shown in Figure 19.3. To open the Internet Information Services administrative application, open the web server's Control Panel, select Administrative Tools, and then select Internet Information Services. (If you are running locally, "the web server" means your local system.)

FIGURE 19.3: Newly created web applications can be administered using the Internet Information Services administrative application.

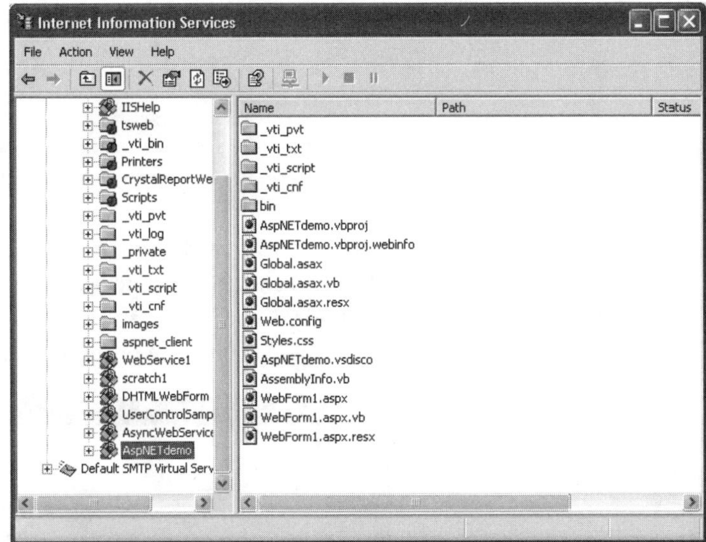

Creating a Hello, World! Application

To demonstrate how web forms work, we'll create the classic Hello, World! program as a web application. First, start a new ASP.NET Web Application project, as described in the previous section.

The next step in creating a Hello, World! application is to place a Label control on the web form. This is done in the same way that you would add a control to a Windows form—by dragging the Label from the Toolbox onto the web form. Note that the controls in the Toolbox are not the same as those that are available for Windows applications. You'll also observe that there are two different Label controls available: one on the Web Forms tab of the Toolbox and the other on the HTML tab. For now, use the Web Forms version. (The difference between Web Forms and HTML controls will be discussed later in this chapter, in the "Adding Controls to Web Forms" section.)

With the Label placed on the web form, use the Properties window in the normal fashion to enter the value **Hello, World!** for the Label's Text property.

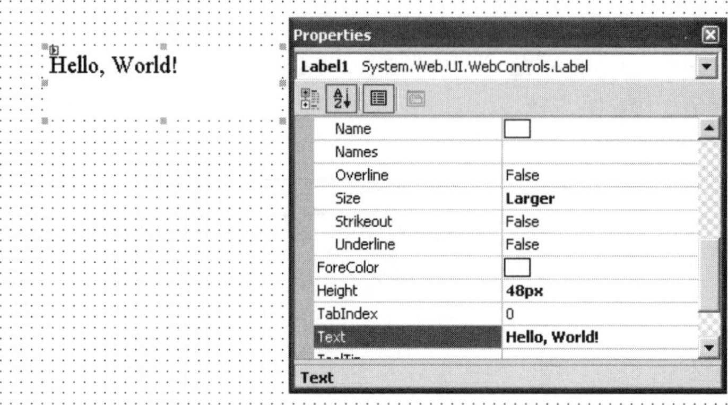

To make things just a bit more interesting, change the `Font.Size` property of the Label to **`Larger`**. (The possible values for the `Font.Size` property are expressed in relative web terms rather than in absolute point size.) In addition, use the Objects list in the Properties window to select the DOCUMENT object and set its title property to **Show how it works!**.

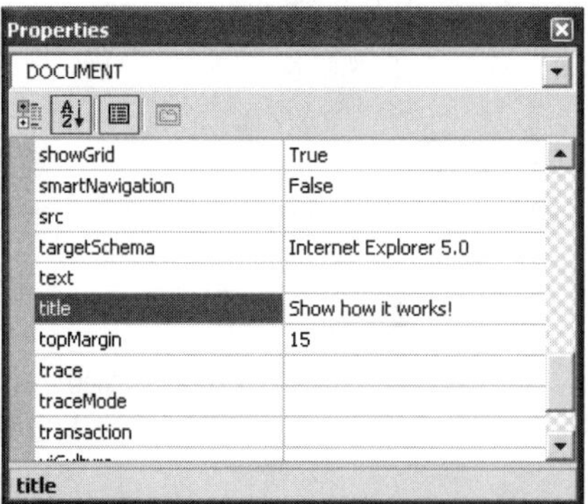

This sets the title of the web page based on the `.aspx` file as it will appear in the title bar of the browser window.

Now, run the project. The web form will be opened as a web page in the browser, as shown in Figure 19.4.

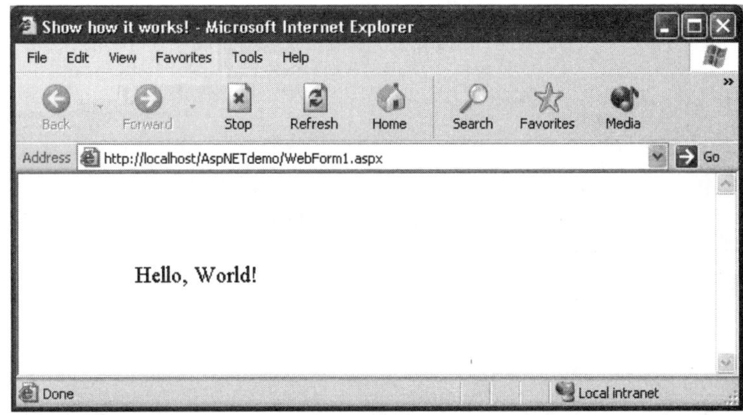

FIGURE 19.4: When you run a web form, it opens as a page in the browser.

There are a couple of things to note about the web page shown in Figure 19.4. Obviously, the "Hello, World!" text appears as it was positioned and sized on the web form. You'll also notice that the title shown for the page is the title set in the Properties window. Finally, the file "opened" in the browser is, indeed, `WebForm1.aspx`. I have put "opened" in quotation marks, because, in fact, the HTML file that is served when `WebForm1.aspx` is requested is generated by the compiled analog of `WebForm1.aspx` and its code-behind at runtime, which functions like an executable.

Viewing the Browser's HTML Source

You can see the HTML source for the page that is open in the browser by selecting View ➢ Source from Internet Explorer's menu. The HTML code generated by `WebForm1.aspx` is shown in Listing 19.1.

Listing 19.1 The HTML Returned When *WebForm1.aspx* Is Requested

```
<!DOCTYPE HTML PUBLIC "-//W3C//DTD HTML 4.0 Transitional//EN">
<HTML>
   <HEAD>
      <title>Show how it works!</title>
      <meta content="Microsoft Visual Studio.NET 7.0" name="GENERATOR">
      <meta content="Visual Basic 7.0" name="CODE_LANGUAGE">
      <meta content="JavaScript" name="vs_defaultClientScript">
      <meta content="http://schemas.microsoft.com/intellisense/ie5"
                    name="vs_targetSchema">
   </HEAD>
   <body MS_POSITIONING="GridLayout">
      <form name="Form1" method="post" action="WebForm1.aspx"
         id="Form1">
         <input type="hidden" name="__VIEWSTATE"
```

```
                value="dDwtMTU3ODAzNTQ4MDs7Pg==" />
            <span id="Label1" style="font-size:Larger;height:48px;
                width:174px;Z-INDEX: 101; LEFT: 94px; POSITION: absolute;
                         TOP: 69px">Hello, World!</span>
          </form>
      </body>
   </HTML>
```

There are a few intriguing things about this code. First, an HTML form has been inserted in the <body> section of the page:

```
<form name="Form1" method="post" action="WebForm1.aspx"
         id="Form1">
...
</form>
```

Note that if this form contained a Submit button, it would post the form contents to WebForm1.aspx (using an HTTP POST rather than an HTTP GET). Since this page is called WebForm1.aspx, this means that the form posts back to itself (rather than to some other web page). This arrangement is referred to as a *postback*.

NOTE Postbacks are important because your form will probably need to be populated with some initial values, but this initialization should take place only the first time the form is loaded. You can use the IsPostBack property to check if a postback is being processed. If not, the form initialization code should run; if it is a postback, you don't want to reinitialize the form.

Within the form, a hidden HTML element has been placed:

```
<input type="hidden" name="__VIEWSTATE"
           value="dDwtMTU3ODAzNTQ4MDs7Pg==" />
```

This hidden element is used to track the state of the page using an identifier generated following postback submissions.

Finally, the Hello, World! Label has been wrapped in a <span> tag:

```
<span id="Label1" style="font-size:Larger;height:48px;
   width:174px;Z-INDEX: 101; LEFT: 94px; POSITION: absolute;
            TOP: 69px">Hello, World!</span>
```

The <span> tag serves to hold the size, position, and style attributes for the Label in one package.

Viewing the HTML in the Designer

Let's go back to the Visual Studio interface and have another look at the HTML side of the WebForm1.aspx designer. Click the HTML tab of the designer. Here, you'll see much of the same HTML code that is displayed as the browser's source when the project is run, as shown in Figure 19.5.

FIGURE 19.5: The HTML displayed in the web form's designer is, for the most part, the same as the source displayed by the browser.

```
WebForm1.aspx *
Form1                                   onclick
<%@ Page Language="vb" AutoEventWireup="false" Codebehind="WebForm1.aspx.vb" Inheri
<!DOCTYPE HTML PUBLIC "-//W3C//DTD HTML 4.0 Transitional//EN">
<HTML>
    <HEAD>
        <title>Show how it works!</title>
        <meta content="Microsoft Visual Studio.NET 7.0" name="GENERATOR">
        <meta content="Visual Basic 7.0" name="CODE_LANGUAGE">
        <meta content="JavaScript" name="vs_defaultClientScript">
        <meta content="http://schemas.microsoft.com/intellisense/ie5" name="vs_targ

</HEAD>
    <body MS_POSITIONING="GridLayout">
        <form id="Form1" method="post" runat="server">
            <asp:Label id="Label1" style="Z-INDEX: 101; LEFT: 94px; POSITION: absol
        </form>
    </body>
</HTML>
Design  HTML
```

One difference between the source HTML and the HTML that appears in the designer is that the designer includes a tag at the top of the page that "wires" the HTML in `WebForm1.aspx` to its code-behind, `WebForm1.aspx.vb`:

```
<%@ Page Language="vb" AutoEventWireup="false"
   Codebehind="WebForm1.aspx.vb" Inherits="AspNETdemo.WebForm1"%>
```

Adding Client-Side Scripting

You may also be interested to know that the HTML tab of the designer provides a framework—via the Objects and Procedures lists—for adding client-side scripting, using JavaScript. For example, try selecting Window from the objects shown under Client Objects & Events drop-down list in the upper-left side of the designer. Next, choose Onclick from the drop-down list of events in the Procedures list.

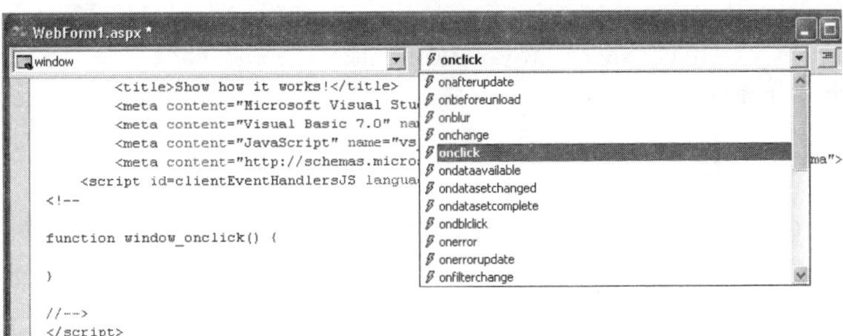

The following JavaScript framework is now auto-generated and added to the page:

```
...
<script id=clientEventHandlersJS language=javascript>
<!-
function window_onclick() {

}
//->
</script>
</HEAD>
   <body MS_POSITIONING="GridLayout" language=javascript onclick="return
window_onclick()">
...
```

To test this, add a JavaScript `alert` statement within the function scaffolding:

```
function window_onclick() {
   alert("You have visited the client-side!")
}
```

Run the page and click it within the browser. The alert box will be displayed.

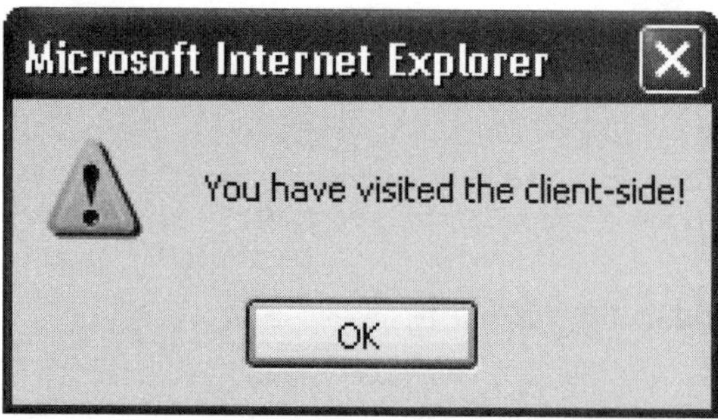

As you can see, the development environment can help you add client-side scripts as required. This example should also make clear that you can mix and match by creating your own client-side HTML (and JavaScript), or by using the code generated by an environment such as Dreamweaver, and pasting it into the HTML tab of the web forms designer. Just make sure that you don't alter the `<%@ Page ...%>` tag at the top of the page or the server control tags.

Using Events

Let's turn up the juice a little and create a web page that does more than displaying the text "Hello, World!" (well, maybe only a wee bit more). To up the excitement level, let's change our "Hello, World!" web page so that it also has TextBox and Button controls. When the page is running in the browser, the user can enter text in the text box and click the button to change the text in the "Hello, World!" label to the text entered.

First, use the Toolbox to add TextBox and Button controls to the form, as shown here.

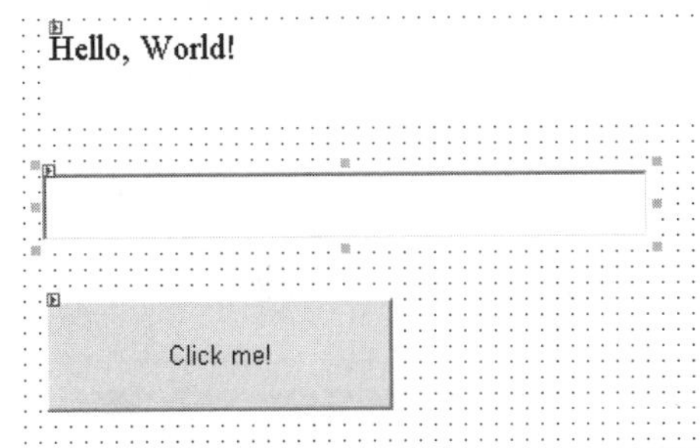

Use the Properties window to name the button **`btnClickMe`** and give it the text value **`Click Me!`**. Also using the Properties window, name the TextBox **`txtShow`** and make sure it has no text value to display.

Next, open the Code Editor for the code-behind file, `WebForm1.aspx.vb`. Just as with Windows forms, there are a number of ways to open the Code Editor with the code-behind module loaded and generate the scaffolding for an event procedure:

- Add a Button control to a form and then double-click the Button control. The Code Editor will open, and the scaffolding for the Click event will be auto-generated.
- Right-click within the designer and select View Code from the context menu.
- Double-click the code-behind module in the Solution Explorer (this assumes that the Show All Files option has been selected).

TIP You can also use the F7 key to toggle from the designer to the Code Editor, and Shift+F7 to toggle back from the Code Editor to the designer.

You'll see that the Code Editor looks almost exactly as it does when you are editing the code behind a Windows form. Once the Code Editor has been opened, you can create the event procedure scaffolding in the normal fashion: Select an object, such as a Button control, in the Objects list, and then select an event procedure, such as Click, from the Procedures list.

For this example, create a Click event handler framework for `btnClickMe`. Listing 19.2 shows the single line of code needed to change the Label's text when the user clicks. It's interesting to note that an event that has been raised on the client-side (in the browser) is processed on the server, using server-side code. This occurs because the browser is posting a form to the server. The server processes the form fields, parses out all the data, creates instances of the objects, and populates their properties with the data from the form fields. Then one of those objects determines that it is the cause of the POST, and it fires the appropriate event (a Click event in this case).

Listing 19.2 Changing the Text of a Label in a Web Form Click Event

```
Private Sub btnClickMe_Click(ByVal sender As System.Object, _
   ByVal e As System.EventArgs) Handles btnClickMe.Click
   Label1.Text = txtShow.Text
End Sub
```

Figure 19.6 shows the event code in the Code Editor.

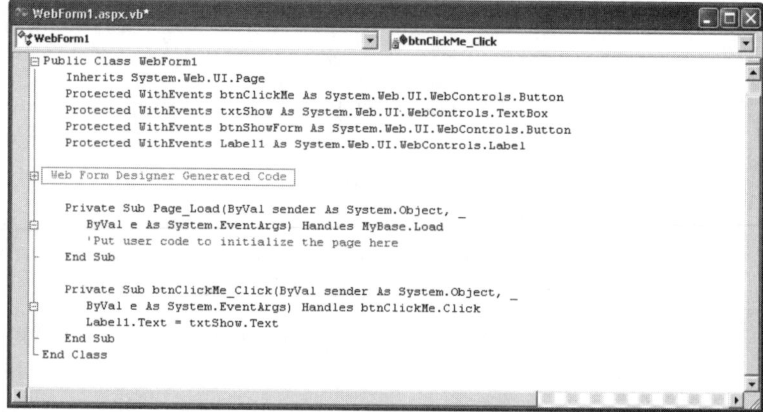

FIGURE 19.6: The Code Editor, with the code-behind for a Web form loaded, looks the same as it does when the code that generates a Windows form is being edited.

Run the project, and you'll see the controls in the browser.

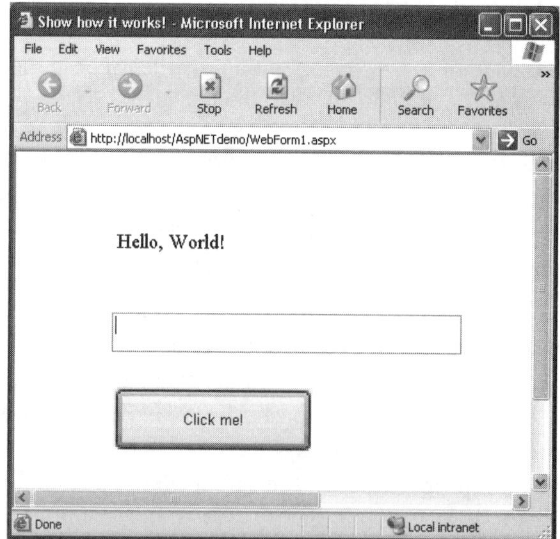

If you enter some text in the text box and click the Click Me! button, the text you entered will be displayed in the Label control.

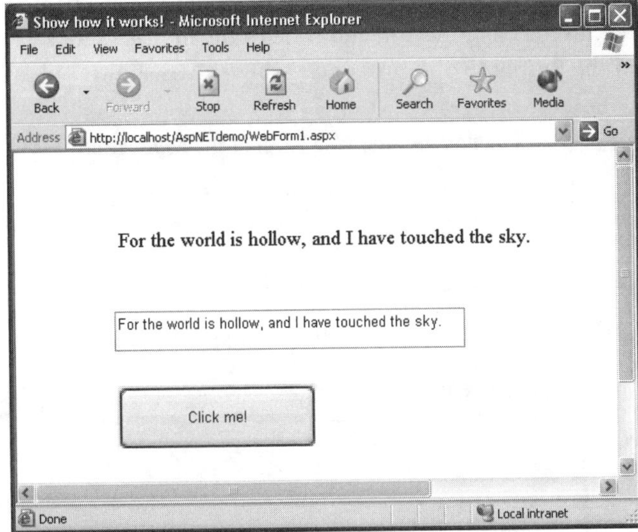

To expand on this example, let's put a Button control on our form that opens a second web form (part of the same application) when the button is clicked. First, use the Add New Item dialog to add a new web form, named `WebForm2.aspx`, to the application, as shown in Figure 19.7.

FIGURE 19.7:

The Add New Item dialog is used to add a new web form to the application.

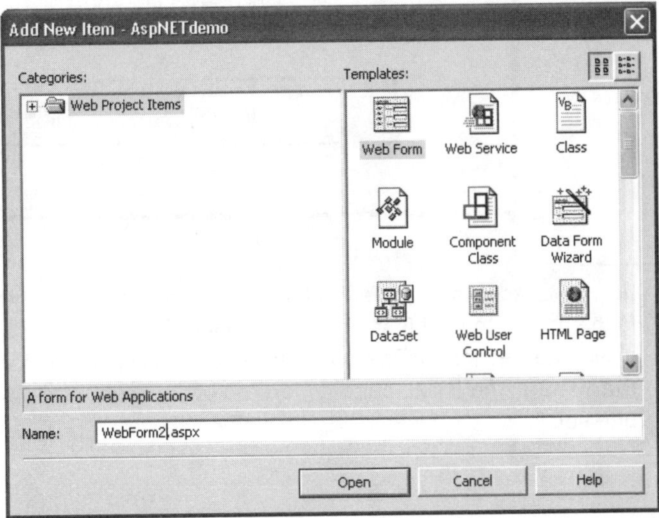

Open `WebForm2.aspx` in its designer and add a Label or two so that it is distinctive when it is running.

Returning to `WebForm1`, add a Button control to the form named **`btnShowForm`** with the text **`Show Form2`**. In the Code Editor, add code to the button's Click event that uses the `Redirect` method of the Response object to open `WebForm2`, as shown in Listing 19.3.

Listing 19.3 Opening Another Web Form in the Application

```
Private Sub btnShowForm_Click(ByVal sender As System.Object, _
   ByVal e As System.EventArgs) Handles btnShowForm.Click
   Response.Redirect("WebForm2.aspx")
End Sub
```

Run the project. `WebForm1.aspx` will open in the browser.

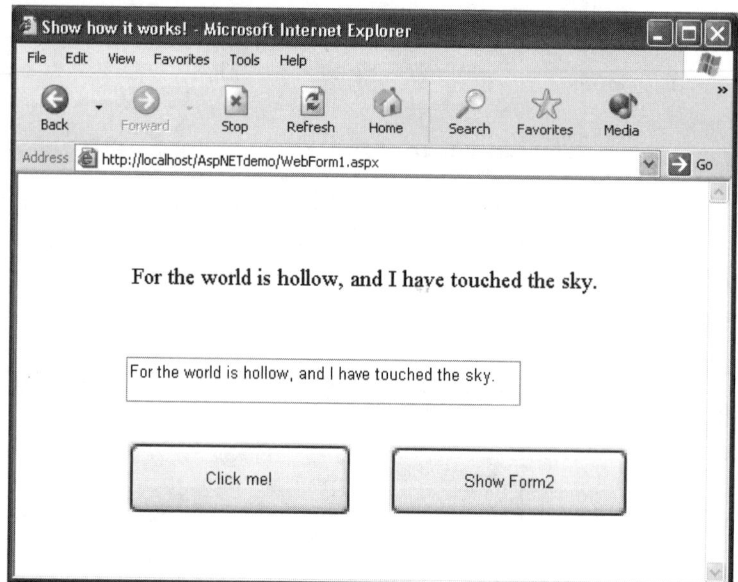

TIP `WebForm1.aspx` is the default Start page in the project, but you can choose any web form in the project to load first. To set a web form to be the first to open when a project runs, select the web form in the Solution Explorer. Right-click the web form and choose Set As Start Page. The HTML page generated by the web form will be the first to load in the browser.

Click the Show Form2 button. The page generated by `WebForm2.aspx` will appear in the browser.

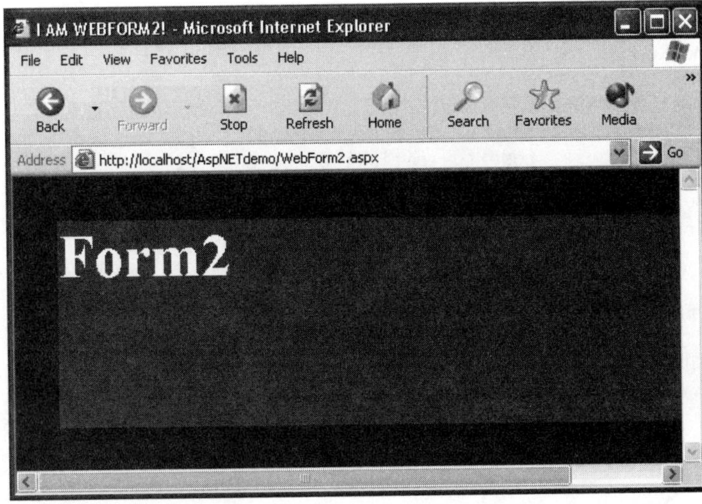

Now that we've done a couple of pretty easy things with the events that ASP.NET controls placed on `WebForm1` and looked at the event-handling procedures in the code-behind module, let's take a peek at the entire code-behind code. Listing 19.4 shows the code-behind module, `WebForm1.aspx.vb`, with the region that would normally be hidden expanded. (Although the hidden auto-generated code doesn't really do anything relevant in this example, you might be interested in seeing it.)

Listing 19.4 The Entire *WebForm1.aspx.vb* Code-Behind Module

```
Public Class WebForm1
   Inherits System.Web.UI.Page
   Protected WithEvents btnClickMe As System.Web.UI.WebControls.Button
   Protected WithEvents txtShow As System.Web.UI.WebControls.TextBox
   Protected WithEvents btnShowForm As System.Web.UI.WebControls.Button
   Protected WithEvents Label1 As System.Web.UI.WebControls.Label

#Region " Web Form Designer Generated Code "

   'This call is required by the Web Form Designer.
   <System.Diagnostics.DebuggerStepThrough()> Private Sub _
      InitializeComponent()

   End Sub

   Private Sub Page_Init(ByVal sender As System.Object, _
      ByVal e As System.EventArgs) Handles MyBase.Init
```

```
        'CODEGEN: This method call is required by the Web Form Designer
        'Do not modify it using the code editor.
        InitializeComponent()
    End Sub

#End Region

    Private Sub Page_Load(ByVal sender As System.Object, _
        ByVal e As System.EventArgs) Handles MyBase.Load
        'Put user code to initialize the page here
    End Sub

    Private Sub btnClickMe_Click(ByVal sender As System.Object, _
        ByVal e As System.EventArgs) Handles btnClickMe.Click
        Label1.Text = txtShow.Text
    End Sub

    Private Sub btnShowForm_Click(ByVal sender As System.Object, _
        ByVal e As System.EventArgs) Handles btnShowForm.Click
        Response.Redirect("WebForm2.aspx")
    End Sub
End Class
```

Notice that the class is derived from `System.Web.UI.Page`, and that the controls placed on the web form, declared `WithEvents` at the top of the module, are members of `System.Web.UI.WebControls`.

Also notice that a Page_Load event procedure has been automatically generated. You can use this procedure for page-initialization code.

As you can see, the structure of the code-behind module for a web form resembles that of a Windows form code module. So, working with the code-behind module is a great deal like working with a Windows form code module.

The ASP.NET Process and Best Practices

It's not a bad time to sit back and ask, "What exactly is going on here?" When anything beyond static HTML is required, the typical web scenario uses custom tags embedded in HTML pages. (There are many examples of this approach, such as earlier versions of ASP, ColdFusion, and JSP.) A page containing mixed HTML and these custom tags answers an HTTP request. The custom tags are processed and expanded on the server, often using database elements. This processing generally occurs in a top-down linear fashion. When it is complete, a new set of "straight" HTML—probably including client-side programs written in a scripting language such as JavaScript—is sent back to the browser. This means that if you look at the source code in a browser, you will not see the server-side scripting tags or language, although you will probably see form POSTs and GETs to other server-side pages.

Continued on next page

The ASP.NET approach is radically different from this traditional approach. True, all the real action still happens on the server-side. As you've seen earlier in this chapter, the source code that can be viewed in the browser is all traditional HTML (and client-side scripting). In other words, in the end, it's still plain HTML that gets sent to the browser.

ASP.NET's source can be seen in some other ways:

- A compiled program is created, which is essentially an executable that creates HTML.
- Within the compiled program, flow control is organized around an event model, and not limited to top-down page processing.
- A radical separation of the HTML (and other client-side) content from the server-side programming has been effected, with the HTML placed in the ASPX file and the server-side code in the related code-behind module.

The last point is extremely important to creating applications that are maintainable. In the past, the client-side interface has been mixed up with the server-side programming logic in a way that makes maintenance a nightmare. (It doesn't help matters that HTML interface designers and those responsible for coding program logic are usually different kinds of people.)

Now that non-spaghetti code web applications can be created using ASP.NET, it's important that good design principles that would be followed in a Windows application are also followed in a web application. For example, data-access routines—at least those that will be used more than once—should be placed in class modules, rather in the code-behind modules attached to web forms.

In any complicated web application, it's likely that you'll be repeating the same elements many times on different pages. It's a good idea to use templates so that design divergences don't creep into your applications. One easy way to do this is to create web user controls (discussed later in this chapter) that encapsulate the desired functionality and appearance, and can be reused.

Adding Controls to Web Forms

There are a plethora of controls that can be used with ASP.NET web forms (the examples so far in this chapter have used only a few intrinsic ASP.NET controls). It's easy to get confused about all these controls, so let's sort them all out:

- Good, old-fashioned HTML form `<INPUT>` elements can be used, but they impact only the client-side and cannot communicate with ASP.NET (they become server controls if you add a `runat=server` attribute).

- HTML server controls, found on the HTML tab of the Toolbox when a web form is open in its designer, are HTML <INPUT> form elements "rejiggered" to work as server-side components by adding a `runat=server` attribute.
- Web forms controls are the intrinsic ASP.NET server-side controls. These controls can be found on the Web Forms tab of the Toolbox.
- Data-related .NET controls, such as the DataSet, can be found on the Data tab of the Toolbox. These controls are discussed in detail in Chapter 17, "Working with Data and ADO.NET."
- .NET classes that are registered on your system can be used on web forms. These cannot provide a Windows-derived visual interface. Many available components can be found on the Components tab of the Toolbox.
- Web user controls are reusable portions of ASPX pages (and, optionally, the related code-behind).
- Custom web controls are the web forms' analog to custom Windows controls (discussed in Chapter 16, "Creating Windows Controls") and can be added to the Toolbox.

Using HTML Server Controls

If you add a control such as a Button from the HTML tab of the Toolbox to a web form, it will look pretty much like a regular Button control. As you can see in Figure 19.8, the properties of the control can be edited using the Properties window, although the names of some properties are not what we are used to (for example, Value rather than Text, because a standard HTML <INPUT> tag has a Value attribute).

FIGURE 19.8: The properties of an HTML Button can be edited using the Properties window.

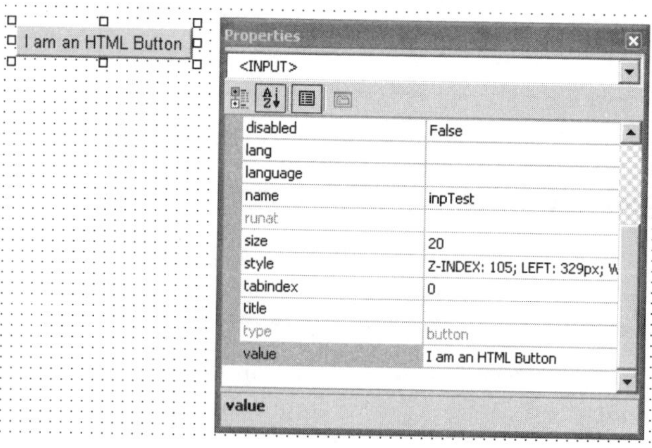

If you look on the HTML tab of the web form designer, you'll see that HTML has been added for the control. It will look something like this (note that the positioning attributes will depend on where you place the control on your form):

```
<INPUT style="Z-INDEX: 105; LEFT: 329px; WIDTH: 138px; POSITION:
   absolute; TOP: 239px; HEIGHT: 24px" type="button" value="I am an
   HTML Button" id="HTMLServerButton">
```

To use this <INPUT> element as a server-side control, you need to take one additional step. With the control selected on the form, right-click the control to open its context menu. Select Run As Server Control. (A check mark will appear next to Run As Server Control to show that this option is enabled.)

If you go back to the HTML tab, the HTML attributes for the control have been modified by adding a `runat` attribute: `runat="server"`. The tag now looks something like this:

```
<INPUT style="Z-INDEX: 105; LEFT: 329px; WIDTH: 138px; POSITION: absolute; TOP:
239px; HEIGHT: 24px" type="button" value="I am an HTML Button"
id="HTMLServerButton" runat="server">
```

You can now use the control pretty much as you would a web forms control, adding code to its event procedures in the code-behind module. In particular, if you open the code-behind module, you'll observe that a new declaration has been added at the top of the module for the control:

```
Protected WithEvents HTMLServerButton As _
   System.Web.UI.HtmlControls.HtmlInputButton
```

The HTML server controls that are available correspond to the HTML form <INPUT> elements. They are included in ASP.NET to make it easier to convert legacy applications from ASP to ASP.NET. Everything that can be done with HTML server controls can also be done—and generally done better—with web forms controls.

Using Web Forms Controls

Web forms controls, available on the Web Forms tab of the Toolbox, are the controls intrinsic to ASP.NET. Table 19.1 shows the ASP Server controls, organized into controls with a visual interface, validation controls, and miscellaneous controls.

TABLE 19.1: Web Forms Controls

Control	Description
Controls with a Visual Interface	
Label	Displays text
TextBox	Displays user-editable text
Button	Displays a button that the user can click

Continued on next page

TABLE 19.1 CONTINUED: Web Forms Controls

Control	Description
LinkButton	Displays a hyperlink; behaves like a button
ImageButton	Displays a button with an image rather than text
Hyperlink	Creates a hyperlink for navigation
DropDownList	Displays a list in a drop-down box
ListBox	Displays a scrollable list of items
DataGrid	Displays a table of information
DataList	Displays a list of items using templates
Repeater	Displays a rendered list of items
CheckBox	Displays a check box, which can be checked on or off
CheckBoxList	Displays a group of check box items
RadioButton	Displays an option button
RadioButtonList	Displays a group of option buttons
Image	Displays an image
Panel	Creates a container for other controls on a web form
Calendar	Displays an interactive calendar
AdRotator	Displays a sequence of images, either in random or predetermined order
Table	Displays a table
Web Forms Validation Controls	
RequiredFieldValidator	Makes sure that the user does not leave a field blank
CompareValidator	Compares the user's entry in a field with a value such as a variable or constant
RangeValidator	Makes sure that the user's entry is between a specified range of values
RegularExpressionValidator	Validates the user's entry against a regular expression
CustomValidator	Makes sure that the user's entry complies with validation logic you have coded
ValidationSummary	Displays a summary of all validation errors
Miscellaneous Controls	
Xml	Reads XML and displays it on a web form page, optionally applying an XSLT transformation before rendering the XML
Literal	Used to place text on a web form page, which can be programmatically manipulated on the server-side (for static text that is not programmatically changed, you can use HTML rather than this control)
CrystalReportViewer	Allows you to create, manipulate, and view reports

It's easy to use the validation controls shown in Table 19.1, and beats the blue blazes out of using reams of client-side JavaScript code for validation purposes. To see how these controls work, add a RequiredFieldValidator control to the `WebForm1` example developed earlier in this chapter. Using the Properties window, set the ErrorMessage property of the Required-FieldValidator to something like **`You must enter some text!`**. Use the drop-down list to set the ControlToValidate property to **`txtShow`**, the TextBox on the form.

Next, run the form. If you try to click a button without having entered text in the text box, the error text you entered will be displayed, and the code in the button's Click event will not be executed.

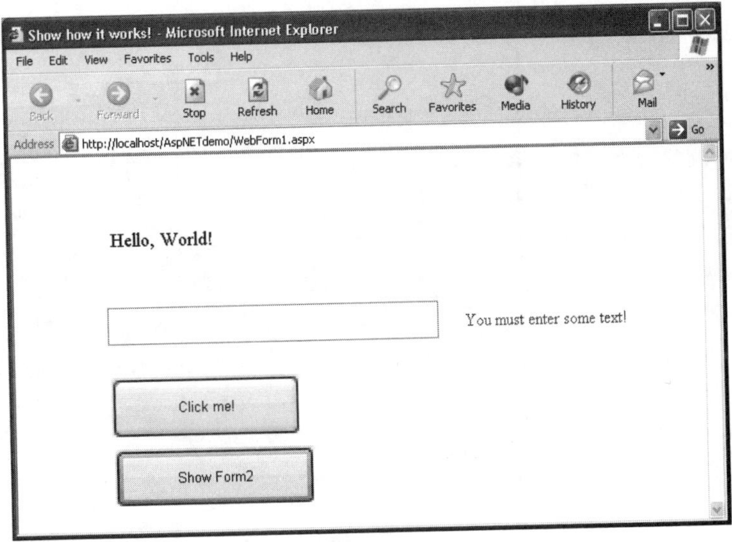

TIP You can tell a control not to interact with the validation control by setting its CausesValidation property to False. This is useful when you have multiple buttons on a form and only one of them is related to the user input that requires validation.

In the next section, you'll see how to use the Hyperlink and Literal types of web forms controls.

Using Web User Controls

The best way to think of web user controls is as a kind of supercharged server-side include that lets you reuse controls and related code. Essentially, a web user control is a portion of a web form (including controls and code-behind) that can be reused in ASPX pages.

Although these controls are quite easy to create, they are limited in some important respects. For example, they do not present a customized appearance when they are added to a web form at design time (they are not bound until the project is run). They are somewhat cumbersome to use across multiple projects (you cannot just add one to the Toolbox).

As a simple example, suppose you would like to start each of your pages with the current date and a hyperlink to (where else?) `www.sybex.com`. You don't need to manually add the controls (and related code) to implement this on each page in your project.

To set this up, first use the Add New Item dialog to add a Web User Control template to the project containing `WebForm1`. Keep the default name, `WebUserControl1.ascx`, as shown in Figure 19.9.

FIGURE 19.9: The Add New Item dialog is used to add a Web User Control template to a project.

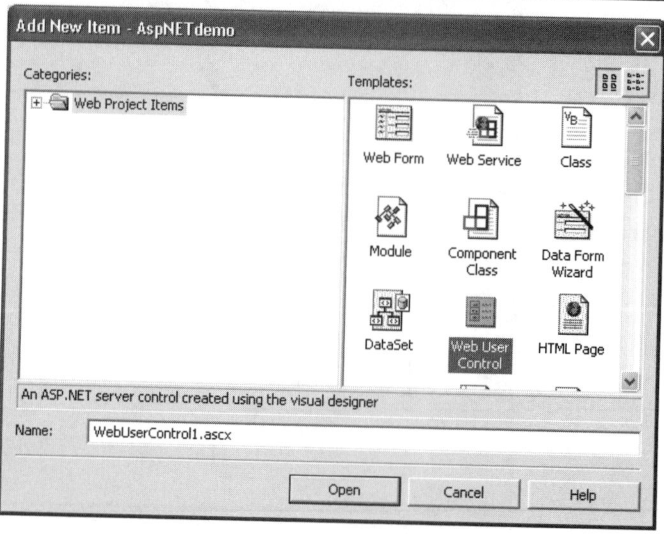

Once the user control has been added to the project, it will appear in the Solution Explorer. If you expand its node in the Solution Explorer, you will see its code-behind file, named `WebUserControl1.ascx.vb`.

Double-click the user control in the Solution Explorer to open it in its designer, which works pretty much the way a web form designer does. Use the Toolbox (Web Forms tab) to add a Literal control and a HyperLink control to the designer. Your web control should look like this:

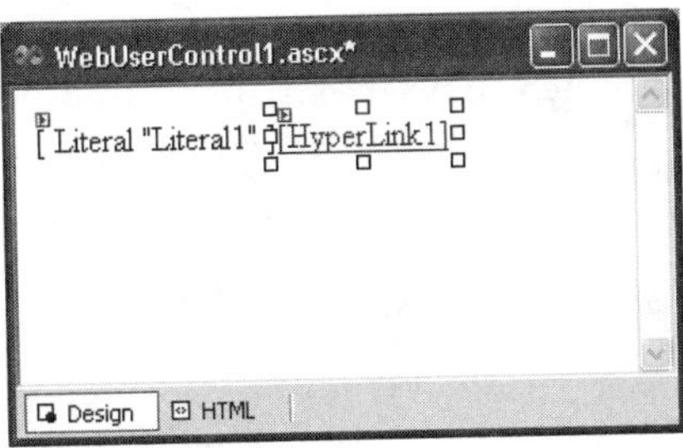

Use the Properties window to appropriately change the Text and NavigateURL properties of the HyperLink control.

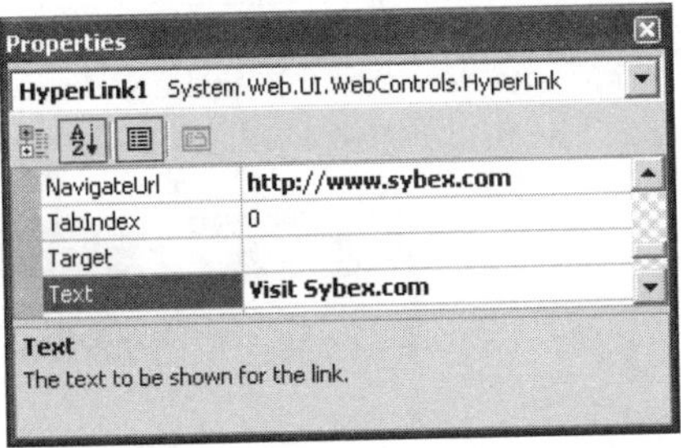

Next, open the user control's code-behind file, `WebUserControl1.ascx.vb`, in the Code Editor (either by double-clicking the code-behind file in the Solution Explorer or by selecting View Code from the right-mouse context menu in the user control's designer). In the Page_Load event, which is used to initialize the page, set the value of the Literal control's Text property to the current date:

```
Literal1.Text = DateTime.Now.ToLongDateString & "   "
```

NOTE The spaces are added at the end of the Literal control so that it doesn't appear to run right into the HyperLink control.

Listing 19.5 shows the code-behind module with the code that sets the value of the Literal (the region of generated code is not shown in the listing).

Listing 19.5 Setting the Literal with the Current Date

```
Public MustInherit Class WebUserControl1 _
   Inherits System.Web.UI.UserControl
   Protected WithEvents HyperLink1 As _
       System.Web.UI.WebControls.HyperLink
   Protected WithEvents Literal1 As System.Web.UI.WebControls.Literal

#Region " Web Form Designer Generated Code "

   Private Sub Page_Load(ByVal sender As System.Object, _
      ByVal e As System.EventArgs) Handles MyBase.Load
      'Put user code to initialize the page here
      Literal1.Text = DateTime.Now.ToLongDateString & "   "
   End Sub
End Class
```

Next, open `WebForm1` in its designer. Drag the web user control module from the Solution Explorer to `WebForm1`. The user control will look like a gray bar at the top of `WebForm1`.

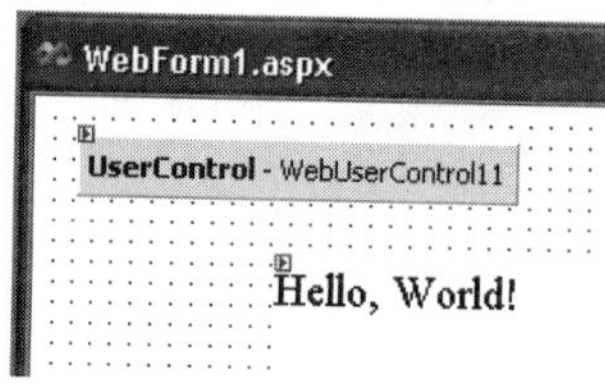

NOTE The appearance of a web user control on a web form is always the same: a gray block with `UserControl -`, followed by the name of the control.

Run the project. The current date and the appropriate hyperlink appear at the top of the page in the browser.

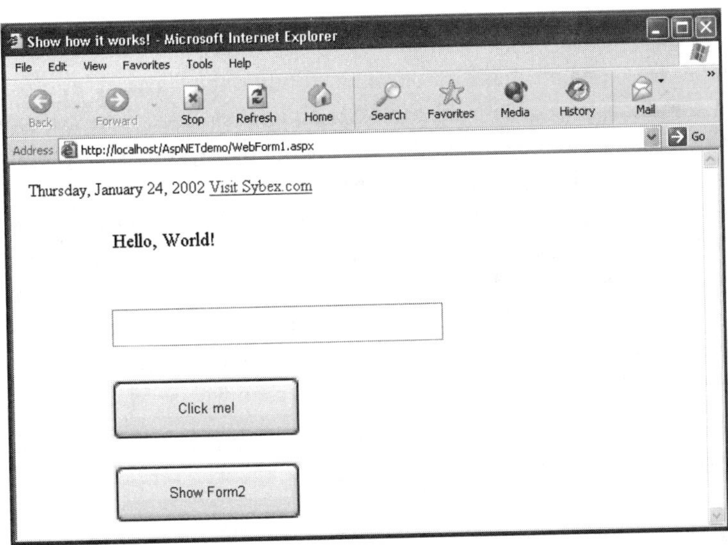

It's worth noting the way the web user control and the web form are "wired together" under the hood. When you drag the user control to the web form, a directive that registers the user control is placed at the top of HTML pane of the web form. It will look something like this:

```
<%@ Register TagPrefix="uc1" TagName="WebUserControl1"
    Src="WebUserControl1.ascx" %>
```

Significantly, the `Src` attribute tells the web form where the web user control is located, so this is something you may need to manually edit depending on the situation. The `TagPrefix` and `TagName` attributes are used in the tag that actually inserts the user control (which is placed in the body of the HTML in the form), along these lines:

```
<uc1:WebUserControl1 id="WebUserControl11" runat="server"></uc1:WebUserControl1>
```

Creating Custom Web Controls

In addition to creating web user controls, you can create "real" controls that can be used with web forms and appear on the Toolbox. As with custom .NET controls that are used with Windows forms (discussed in Chapter 19), you can create web controls in several ways.

You can extend the functionality of an existing control using inheritance by subclassing `System.Web.UI.WebControl` (for controls with a user interface) or `System.Web.UI.Control` (for controls without a user interface). You can also subclass a derivative of one of these classes (such as a `System.Web.UI.WebControl.TextBox`). Finally, you can combine the functionality of two or more existing controls, creating a composite control.

Working with Web Services

Web services are a mechanism for making components available across the Internet using open-standards such as HTTP and XML. The idea is to create components that can communicate with each other, regardless of the operating system or programming language. In essence, this can be a large-scale, client-server model, in which the web service is the "server" and the program that uses, or "consumes," the service is the client, although it can also be much more distributed in nature. Standard Internet transport models and communication protocols have replaced proprietary communication systems (such as DCOM—not that you should use a web service everywhere you used DCOM in the past). Web services carry a significant performance overhead and require IIS. (There is also .NET Remoting, which is more directly equivalent to DCOM than web services are.)

It's easy to get started with web services using .NET. In this section, I'll show you how to create a simple web service and then consume the web service.

Creating a Web Service

In theory, a sample web service could do anything you can do in a class module, from the trivial to the very useful. Our web service will determine if the number input is a prime (not evenly divisible by another number except one or itself).

First, use the New Project dialog to create an ASP.NET Web Service project named **IsPrime**, as shown in Figure 19.10.

FIGURE 19.10: Web services are based on ASP.NET Web Service projects.

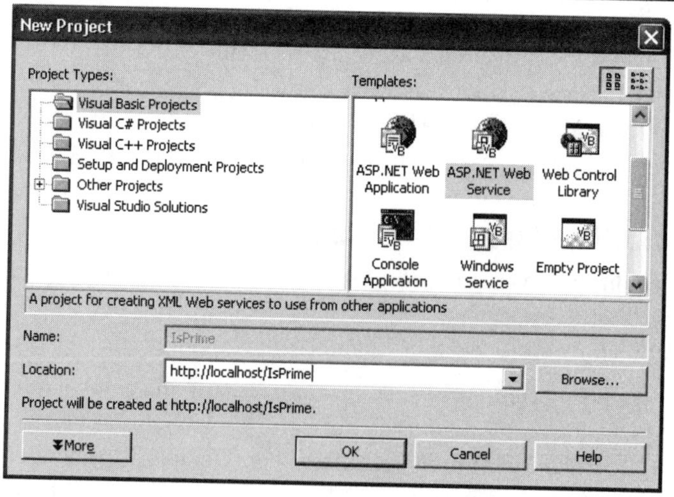

When the new project has been created, if you open the Solution Explorer, you'll see a number of modules created specifically for the web service. One of these, the ASMX file named `Service1.asmx`, has been specially created to house web service code.

Open the ASMX module in the Code Editor. Essentially, you'll find a class module that inherits from `System.Web.Services.WebService`. The sample code to create a Hello, World! web service is also included (commented out). You can delete the Hello World! sample. Then add the function that determines if the input is a prime following a `<WebMethod()>` tag, as shown in Listing 19.6 (with the generated code region hidden).

Listing 19.6 A Web Service Determining If a Number Is a Prime

```
Option Strict On
Imports System.Web.Services

<WebService(Namespace := "http://tempuri.org/")> _
Public Class Service1
    Inherits System.Web.Services.WebService

#Region " Web Services Designer Generated Code "

   <WebMethod()> Public Function IsPrime(ByVal NumToCheck As Long) _
      As Boolean
      Dim i As Long
      For i = 2 To CLng(Math.Sqrt(NumToCheck))
         If NumToCheck Mod i = 0 Then
            Return False
         End If
      Next
      Return True
   End Function
End Class
```

Note that this web service returns a Boolean value (true or false), depending on whether the number input is a prime.

Run the project. You'll see a web service informational message, along with a link for the IsPrime web service.

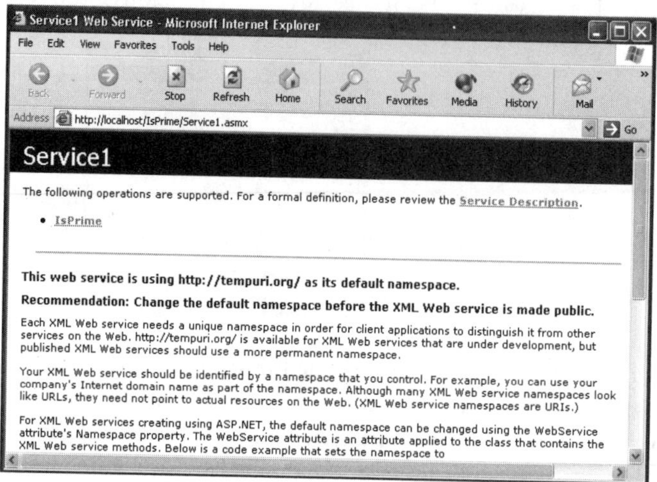

NOTE The web service, by itself, has no user interface (it is just a class). The .NET framework generates the test page on the fly.

You can test the web service by clicking the `IsPrime` link in the browser screen. When you click the link, a test page will open.

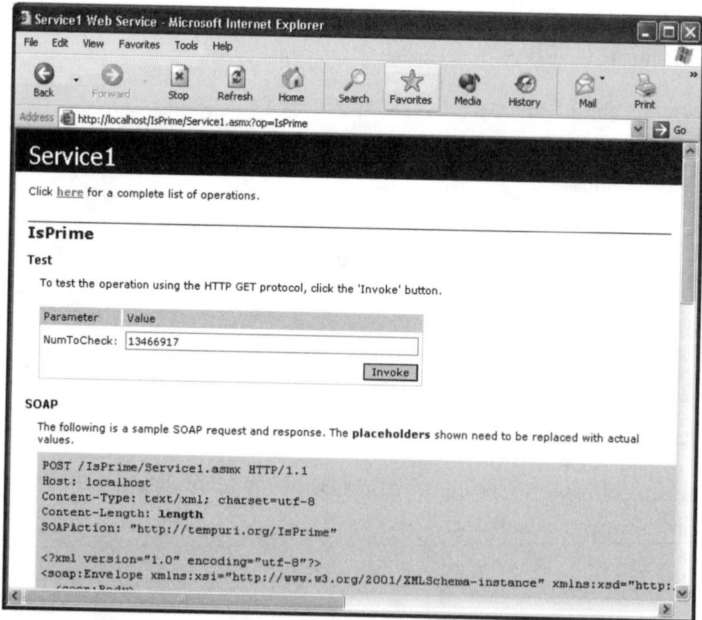

Enter a number in the box (13466917, a somewhat large prime, is shown), and click Invoke. You'll see an XML page, showing the Boolean value returned by the web service.

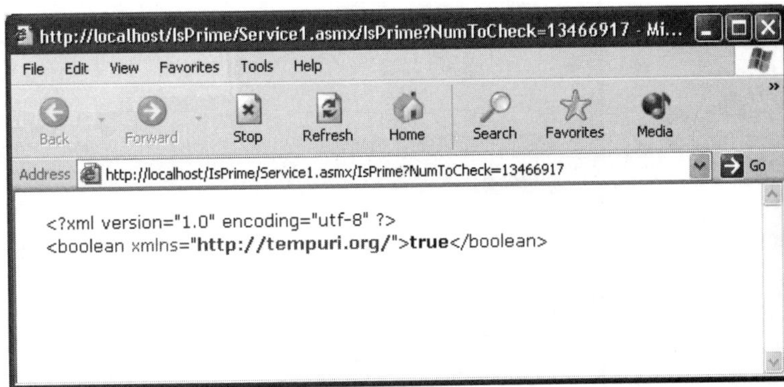

Consuming the Web Service

A web service would not be of much use if it could only be consumed with an inelegant interface like that shown in the previous section. The next step is to consume, or use, the web service from a normal application.

NOTE The example shows consuming the web service from a Windows application, but web applications can also consume web services.

To see how this works, open a new Windows Application project. Create a simple interface for checking a number on the application's form by adding TextBox and Button controls. (Note that there is no need for the IsPrime web service to be running.)

Next, choose Project ➢ Add Web Reference. The Add Web Reference dialog will open, as shown in Figure 19.11.

You can enter the address for the web service in the Address box at the top of the dialog. You could also use the UDDI directory links in the left-hand pane to search for published web services.

For our example, enter the URL for the web service we created, `http://localhost/IsPrime/Service1.asmx`, in the Address box at the top of the Add Web Reference dialog and press Enter. The Service description will appear in both panes of the dialog, as shown in Figure 19.12.

FIGURE 19.11: The Add Web Reference dialog is used to locate web services.

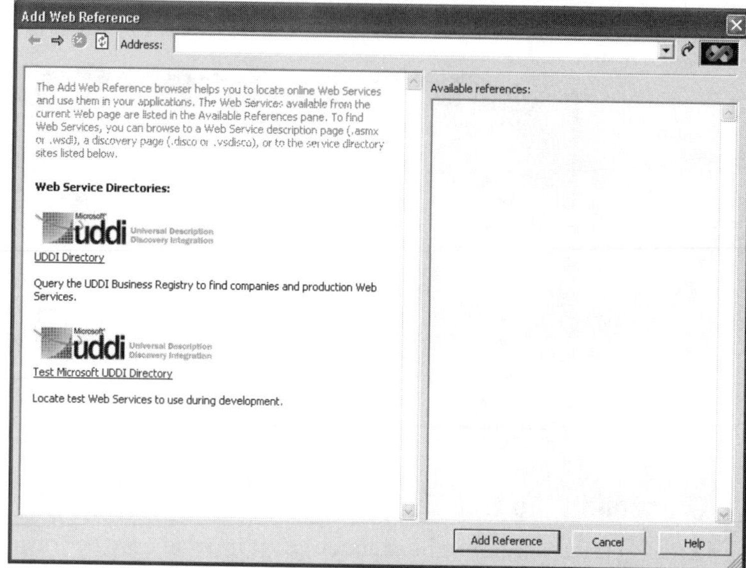

FIGURE 19.12: The description of the web service is displayed.

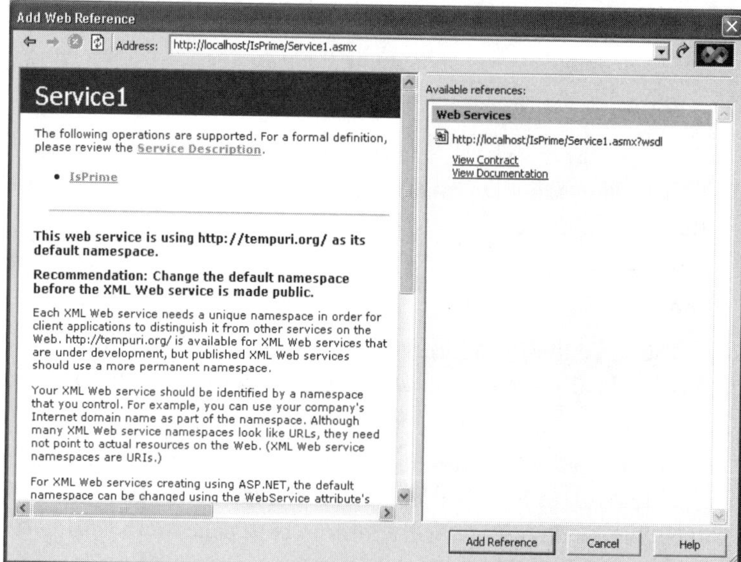

Click the Add Reference button to add the reference to the web service to the project.

Next, open the Solution Explorer. You'll see a Web References section. This reference is organized with a host, in our case named `localhost`, indicated by a globe-like icon.

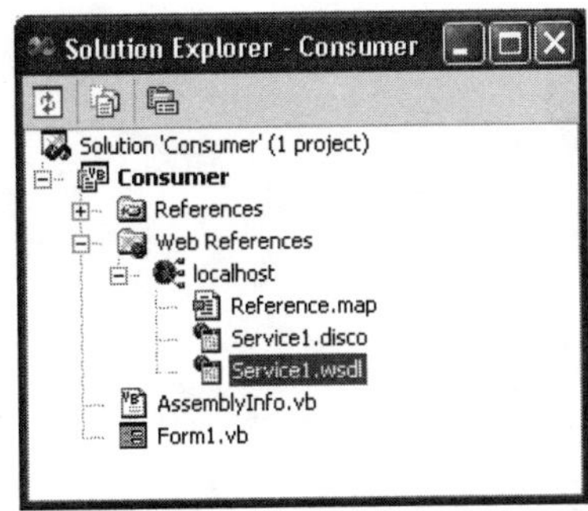

Returning to the project and form, open the Code Editor so that code can be added to the button's Click event. Instantiate a service object, using the host and service name found in the Web References section of the Solution Explorer:

```
Dim theService As New localhost.Service1()
```

Using the service object, the IsPrime service can now be queried:

```
If theService.IsPrime(qNum) Then
   ' Is a prime
Else
   ' Not a prime
End If
```

The complete Click event code for querying the web service is shown in Listing 19.7.

Listing 19.7 Consuming a Web Service from a Windows Application Form Module

```
Private Sub btnConsumeService_Click(ByVal sender As System.Object, _
   ByVal e As System.EventArgs) Handles btnConsumeService.Click
   Dim qNum As Long
   Dim theService As New localhost.Service1()
   qNum = CLng(txtNum.Text)
   If theService.IsPrime(qNum) Then
      MessageBox.Show(CStr(qNum) & " is a prime!", _
         "Consume that service today.", _
         MessageBoxButtons.OK, MessageBoxIcon.Information)
   Else
      MessageBox.Show(CStr(qNum) & " is NOT a prime!", _
         "Consume that service today.", _
         MessageBoxButtons.OK, MessageBoxIcon.Information)
   End If
End Sub
```

If you run the project, you can enter a number and then click Check to invoke the web service and determine if the number is a prime.

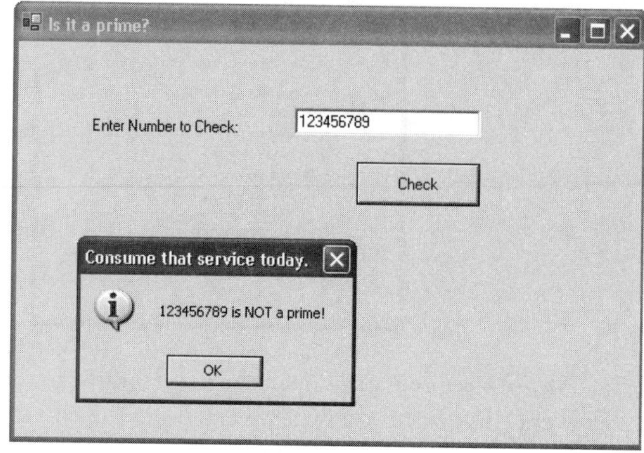

TIP You'll find a great many public web services that you can play with in your applications at `www.xmethods.com`.

Summary

ASP.NET and VB are great tools for developing web applications. You can create web applications holistically in this environment in a way never before possible. While .NET is designed to cover the gamut of application development, it's likely that developers will be extremely enthusiastic about the quantum improvement in web development afforded by these tools. In addition, web services, which are very easy to create using VB .NET, will play a big role in application interoperability and distributed applications generally. This chapter has given you the information you need to get started with these important applications.

Chapter 20

Deploying Applications

- Introducing no-touch deployment
- Choosing setup and deployment project types
- Adding a Setup project to a Windows application
- Running the Setup Wizard
- Creating a Web Setup project

As they say, you don't get a second chance to make a first impression. If your program cannot reliably be deployed (installed), the impression left by a flawed installation will not be a good one. And your application probably will not be used for the job it was intended.

Fortunately, VB. NET has installation capabilities that range from the sublimely simple—so-called "no-touch" deployment—to being gloriously filled with options and capabilities. Whatever your deployment needs, VB .NET can take care of them for you. This chapter covers the deployment options.

Introducing No-Touch Deployment

No-touch deployment means that all that is required to deploy a project is to open your executable file from a system that has the CLR installed. The application can be run in Microsoft Internet Explorer or from Windows without any further work, even across a network. This is very, very cool!

For example, to launch an application in Internet Explorer, you can simply type the full path and executable filename in the Address bar and press Enter (as though it were a URL). Alternatively, choose File ➢ Open. In the Open dialog, click Browse to find the file.

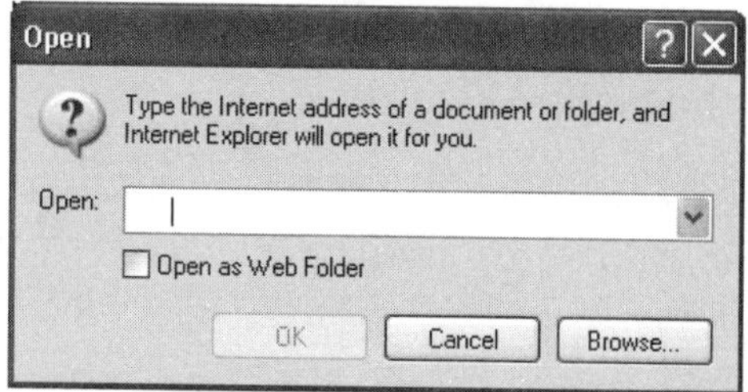

Use the Internet Explorer browse window to locate the .NET executable file locally or on the network, as shown in Figure 20.1. (Make sure to set the Files of Type drop-down list to All Files, so that .exe files are displayed.)

TIP Figure 20.1 shows a file being opened using a file path. Another way no-touch deployment can be used is to open an executable file using a URL over HTTP (for example, `http://localhost/theapp.exe`). The idea is that you could have a corporate intranet portal in which people could link to the applications they need. A default Start page in Internet Explorer could open the portal page, which could include links to the URLs for the various applications users might want to launch.

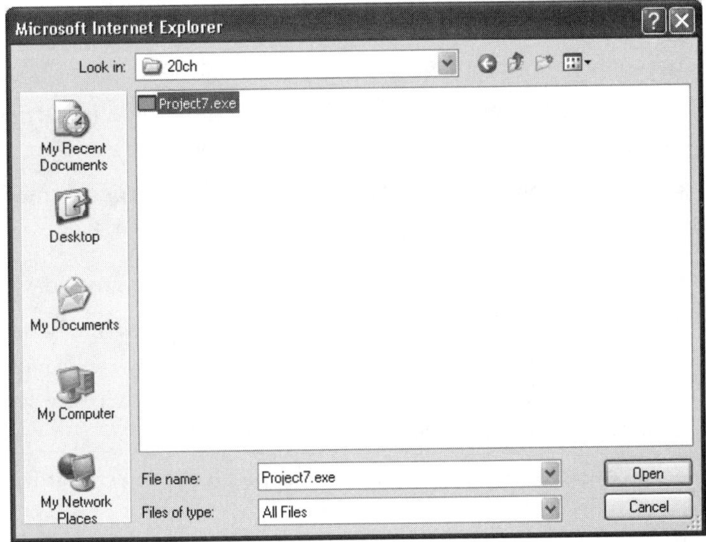

FIGURE 20.1: In no-touch deployment, executable applications can be opened using a file path or URL.

With the executable file selected, click Open, and the application will launch in Internet Explorer, as shown in Figure 20.2. When the application launches, the previously loaded page remains loaded in Internet Explorer, as you can see in the background in Figure 20.2.

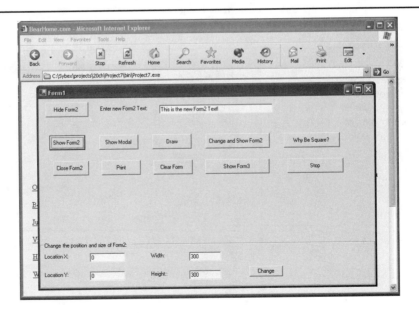

FIGURE 20.2: .NET applications can be launched in Internet Explorer by opening the application's `.exe` file.

As you would expect, you can also use no-touch deployment to launch .NET executables from the Windows Desktop in a number of ways, including from Windows Explorer, from the command prompt, or by using the Run dialog.

Convenient as no-touch deployment in this fashion is, particularly for small-scale distributions, it's essentially a manual process, and there are some limitations, such as the following:

- The application is not added to the Windows Program menu.
- An icon is not added to the Desktop.
- Directories for program data files have not been created.
- The distributed executable is uncompressed, which may be a drawback for remote copying or for placing on distribution media (although .NET executables are much smaller than VB6 executables or ActiveX controls, and there are several reasonable strategies for ameliorating this issue).

You can easily create a setup and deployment project that will take care of these needs and many more!

Choosing a Setup and Deployment Project Type

As you may have noticed when you started a new VB .NET project, one category of project type is Setup and Deployment Projects. Figure 20.3 shows this category selected in the Project Types pane of the New Project dialog.

FIGURE 20.3:
In the New Project dialog, you can select from a number of different types of setup and deployment projects.

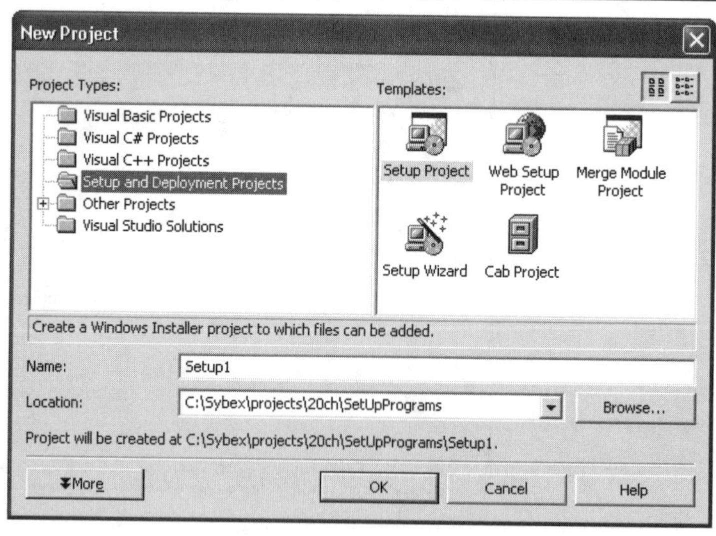

As you can see in the Templates pane of the New Project dialog, there are four different types of setup and deployment projects: Setup, Web Setup, Merge Module, and CAB. The following sections explain—in alphabetical order, and not necessarily in the order of importance—what each kind of setup and deployment project does.

Another icon you see in the Templates pane is for the Setup Wizard. This Wizard is used to guide the developer through the selection of one of the four kinds of setup and deployment projects, and through selecting options for the resulting project. For more information about the Setup Wizard, see the "Using the Setup Wizard to Create a Web Setup Project" section later in this chapter.

NOTE In addition to creating a setup and deployment project as its own solution, you can add a setup and deployment project to an existing project (such as a Windows application) within the existing solution by selecting File ➢ Add Project ➢ New Project, and then selecting the setup and deployment project type from the New Project dialog.

Cab Projects

Cab projects are used to create cabinet (`.cab`) files, which are compressed archives containing any number of files. Cabinet files are often used to package applications, such as a control, so that a single file can be placed on a web server. The cabinet file can then be downloaded by a web browser.

When the browser is Internet Explorer, a web page using the control will include a reference to the location of the cabinet file. If the control is already installed on the user's computer, the page executes normally. If it is not present, Internet Explorer downloads the cabinet file using the link supplied, decompresses it, and installs the control.

Merge Module Projects

Merge modules are similar to cabinet files in that they are compressed and can be used to package a group of files. However, they cannot be used to "self-extract" and install an application (such as the web control scenario explained in the discussion of Cab projects). Instead, the `.msm` file created by a Merge Module project is used with Microsoft Windows Installer.

The idea is to package all files and other resources required into one `.msm` library file. For example, suppose a component is used by a number of applications. If the component is packaged in an `.msm` file, that file could be used as part of the installation by each of the applications.

Setup Projects

A Setup project is used to package and install a Windows application, normally to a location within the Program Files directory structure using the Microsoft Windows Installer. This kind of project will look very familiar to VB6 developers, because it is the deployment approach conventionally used with Windows applications.

Setup projects are particularly well targeted to distribution via conventional media, such as removable disks. For more information about Setup projects, see the "Adding a Setup Project to a Windows Application" section, coming up shortly.

Web Setup Projects

A Web Setup project creates a Microsoft Windows Installer program intended to install an ASP.NET Web Application project under the virtual directory of Internet Information Server (IIS).

The major difference between a Web Setup project and a Setup project is that a Web Setup project targets the virtual directory of the web server on which the setup program is run as the place to install files (by default, `Inetpub\wwwroot\`). A Setup project creates a setup program that targets the Program Files directory by default.

There is, of course, an important distinction between Windows and web applications: Web applications are by definition client-server in nature. The client is a web browser. Installation in a web browser should normally mean simply pointing the browser at a URL.

Web Setup projects create a setup program that installs the server-side of the equation. A lot of things that you would need to set manually in IIS—restarting the web server, setting the security model, enabling or disabling site logging, allowing or disallowing directory browsing—can be done automatically for you by a Web Setup project. This type of project also will create the "web application" that IIS and ASP.NET need for your site to function.

You may be interested to know that VB .NET comes with a mechanism for automatic uploading of .NET web projects to various web service providers. Web Setup projects and automatic uploading are discussed in more detail in the "Using the Setup Wizard to Create a Web Setup Project" section later in this chapter.

Adding a Setup Project to a Windows Application

As I've already mentioned, Setup projects are used to package and install Windows applications. Let's take a closer look at creating, configuring, and building a Setup project.

Creating a Setup Project

To add a Setup project to an existing solution, select File ➢ Add Project ➢ New Project. Choose Setup and Deployment Projects as the project type, and select Setup Project as the project template. The Setup project will be added to the Solution Explorer.

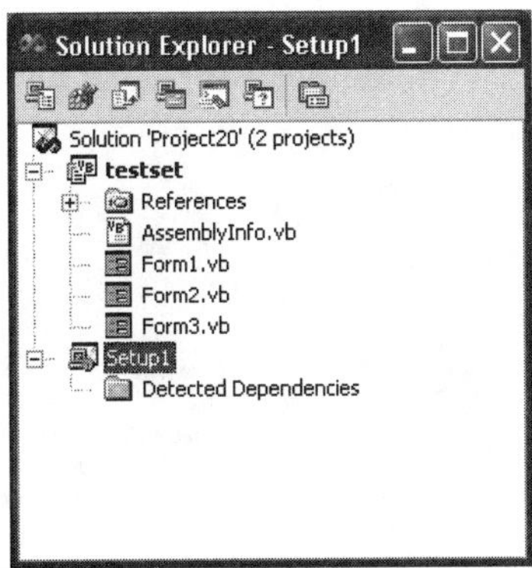

At this point, the Setup project is basically empty. The next step is to select the root node of the Setup project in the Solution Explorer, right-click, and choose Add from the context menu. A submenu will open, offering four choices: Project Output, File, Merge Module, and Assembly.

TIP The File option can be used to add any file from the filesystem to a Setup project. For example, you might want to include HTML files with the Setup project for a web application.

Select Project Output, which is used to add the output (such as EXE or DLL files) of the other project to the solution where the Setup project was added. The Add Project Output Group dialog will open, as shown in Figure 20.4.

FIGURE 20.4: The Add Project Output Group is used to add the output of the Setup project to the solution.

Make sure that Primary Output is selected and click OK. VB .NET adds the primary output from the other project to the solution. It also adds a dependency, which is the .NET Framework (`dotnetfxredist_x86_enu.msm`).

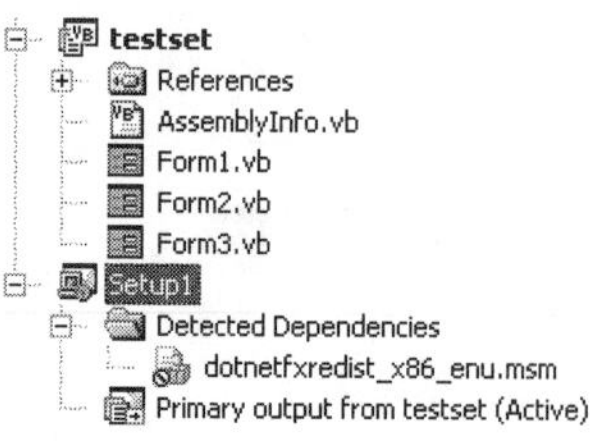

Including the .NET Framework

The .NET Framework is required to run a .NET application. A .NET application is written to the .NET Framework in the same sense that a Java application is written to a Java Virtual Machine (JVM), rather than written to an operating system.

Many systems will already have the .NET Framework installed. So, by default, the .NET Framework is excluded from the setup program that will be created. This makes for smaller setup programs, which is a good thing.

If you are not sure whether your target systems will have the .NET Framework already installed, you should plan to install it, if necessary, by including it in your setup program. To include it, select `dotnetfxredist_x86_enu.msm`, right-click, and clear the Exclude check mark.

Configuring the Setup Project

If you think that you can get to the significant properties of the Setup project by selecting the root node of the Setup project, right-clicking, and selecting Properties, surprise—you're wrong! Yes, the Property Pages dialog for the Setup project does open, as shown in Figure 20.5, but here you can set only some general properties, like the kind of compression used and the packaging format for files.

You get the real "bang for your buck" when you right-click the root node of the Setup project and select View (rather than Properties). There are six options on the View submenu, each of which can be used to configure important aspects of the setup program that will be created from the Setup project:

- File System
- Registry

- File Types
- User Interface
- Custom Actions
- Launch Conditions

Each of these choices opens a window, called an editor that allows you to set properties and configure actions that will shape the setup program. (With the root node of the Setup project selected, you can also launch these editors by clicking the icons on the Solution Explorer toolbar.)

There are far too many Setup project properties to possibly discuss them all here (it would take a whole book). This section just shows you how to change two properties and their impact on the setup program, to give you an idea of how Setup project properties work. You should explore the other Setup project properties as needed.

FIGURE 20.5: You can choose the file package type and set the kind of compression using the Setup project's Property Pages dialog.

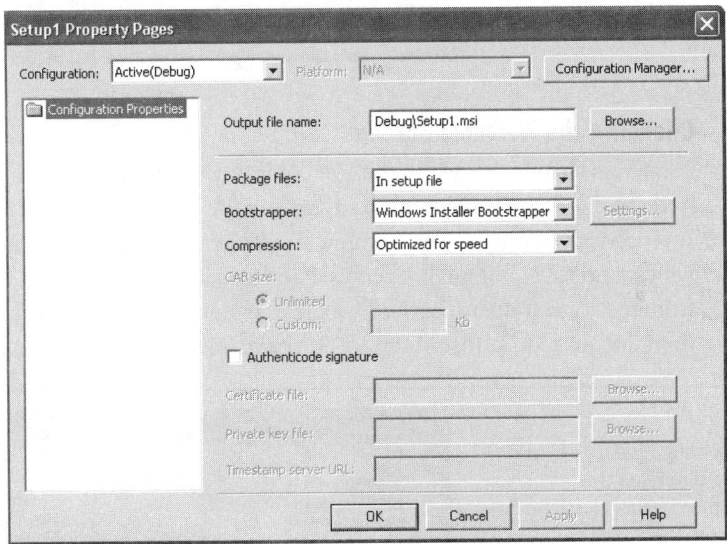

Changing the Installation Location

To start with, let's change the default location for the setup program installation to `Program Files\harold`. Select File System from the Setup project's View submenu. The File System editor for the Setup project will open. The left pane of this interface is a representation of the filesystem on a hypothetical target machine. Select Application Folder in this pane, right-click, and choose Properties from the context menu. In the Properties window, change the Default Location property to **`[ProgramFilesFolder]harold`**, as shown in Figure 20.6.

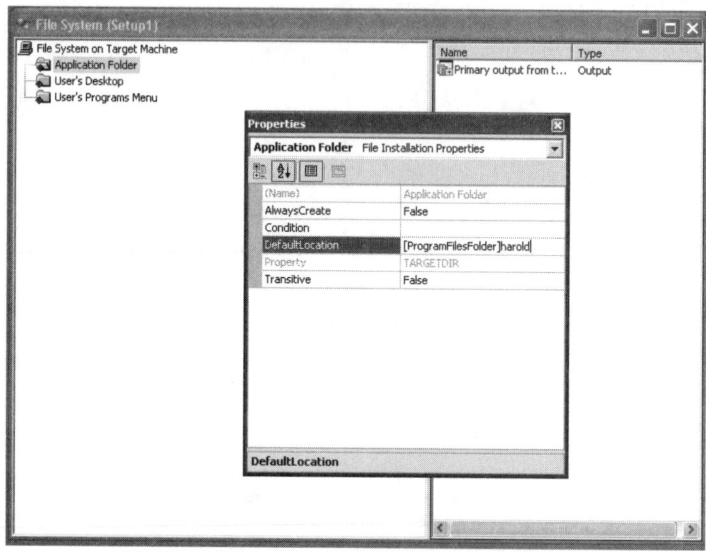

FIGURE 20.6: You change the destination that is targeted for installation by editing the properties of the objects in the Setup project's File System editor.

Changing the Welcome Screen

Next, let's change the text in the Welcome screen of the setup program. To do this, with the root node of the Setup project selected, right-click and choose View ➢ User Interface. The User Interface editor opens. This window displays each screen in the setup program in the order in which it appears. Highlight the Welcome screen icon, right-click, and select Properties Window from the context menu. In the Properties window, change the WelcomeText property to something fun, like `This installer will treat you nicely!`, as shown in Figure 20.7.

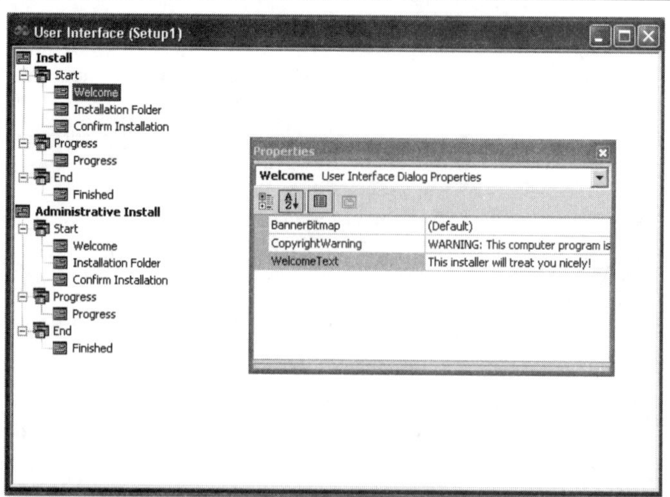

FIGURE 20.7: You can change the message displayed by the setup program by changing the WelcomeText property.

Building the Setup Program

Let's have a look at the changes we've made to the setup program. To do this, we need to build the setup program by selecting the root node for the Setup project, right-clicking, and selecting Build. (Alternatively, you can build the setup program from the VB .NET Build menu.)

When you build the setup program, you'll get the normal VB .NET build messages in the Output window, telling you whether the build has succeeded or failed. You may also get a warning—for example, telling you that the setup program does not include the .NET Framework, which may be necessary.

With the setup program built, it's time to see what it looks like. The easiest way to do this is to select the root node of the setup program in the Solution Explorer, right-click, and choose Install. Alternatively, you can run `Setup.exe` from the Windows Desktop. You'll find this executable file in either the Debug or Release directory (depending on the release configuration) made for the Setup project.

When you run the setup program, you'll see the changed text on the Welcome screen, as shown in Figure 20.8.

FIGURE 20.8: You can easily customize many aspects, such as the welcome message on the initial screen, of the setup program display.

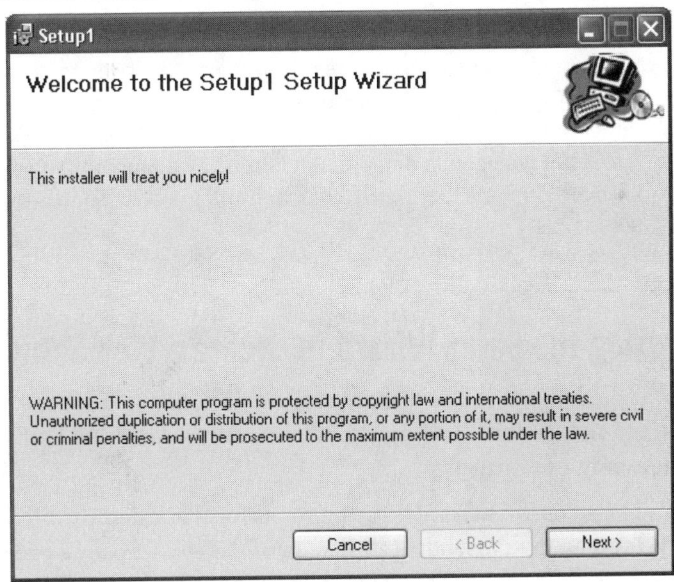

You'll also see that the location for installation has been modified, as you specified in the File System editor, as shown in Figure 20.9.

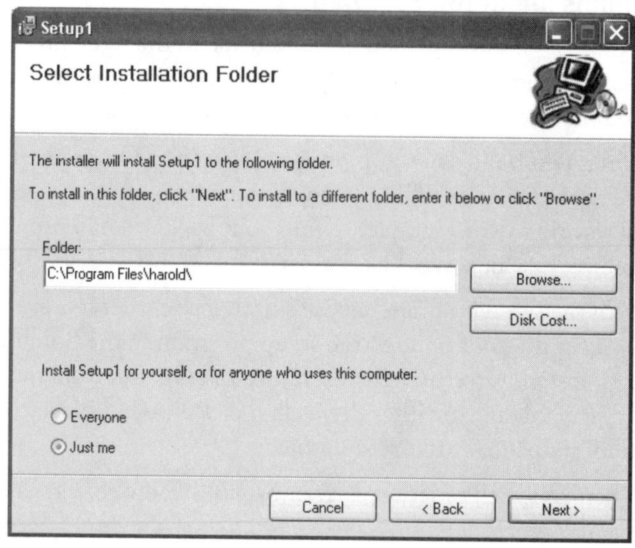

FIGURE 20.9: It's easy to configure many aspects of what the setup program does, such as the changed target folder for the application shown.

NOTE Although you can do almost anything you want using the various editors associated with a Setup project, VB6 programmers may miss the ability to actually modify the source code of a Setup project. Actually, this is not a limitation of VB .NET or Visual Studio .NET; rather, it is a fact of life with the Microsoft Windows Installer. The `.msi` file produced by the Setup project is a database. It is read by a program, `Msiexec.exe`, which processes it for instructions about how to manage the installation. (`Msiexec.exe` is not source-code accessible.)

Using the Setup Wizard to Create a Web Setup Project

As noted earlier in the chapter, the Setup Wizard guides you through the steps for creating a setup and deployment project. Note that this is not one of the Wizards that goes on forever; it is only a few panels.

The steps the Wizard asks you to perform are slightly different, depending if you start the Wizard as an independent project or add it to an existing project. As an example, I'll show you how to run the Setup Wizard as an independent solution to create a Web Setup project.

Running the Setup Wizard

Follow these steps to run the Setup Wizard:

1. With no open solutions or projects in VB .NET, select File ➢ New ➢ Project to open the New Project dialog.

2. Select Setup Wizard, provide a name and location for the project, and click OK. The Setup Project Welcome screen will appear.

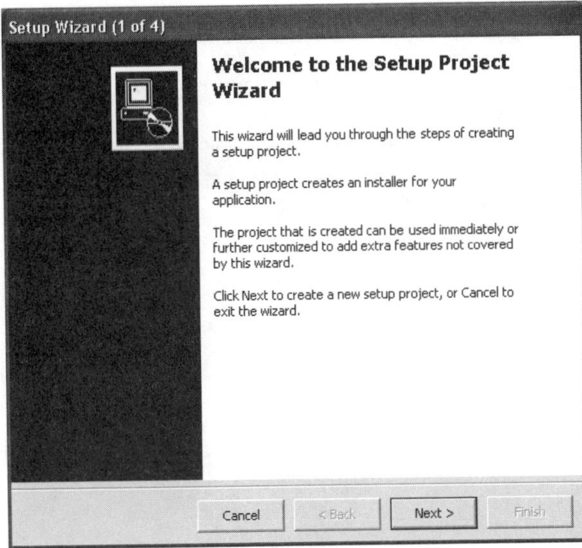

3. There is nothing to do in the Welcome screen, so click Next. In the next panel of the Wizard, choose a setup and deployment project type (see the "Choosing a Setup and Deployment Project Types" section earlier in this chapter). For this example, choose Create a Setup for a Web Application.

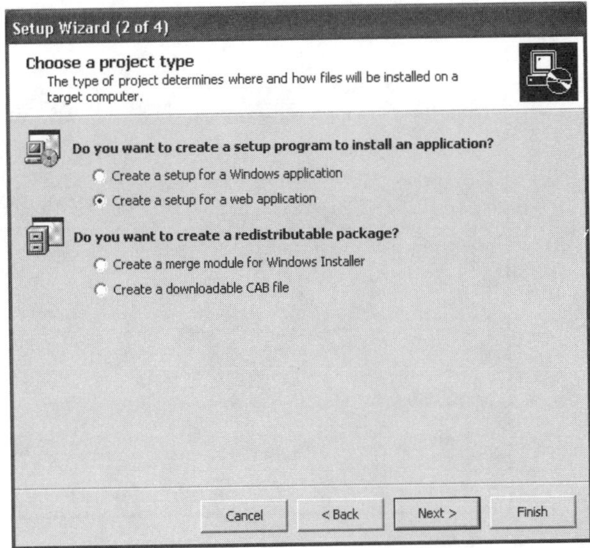

4. Click Next. The next Wizard panel is used to add miscellaneous files, such as HTML, Readme files, or anything that is not a dependency and not part of the project.

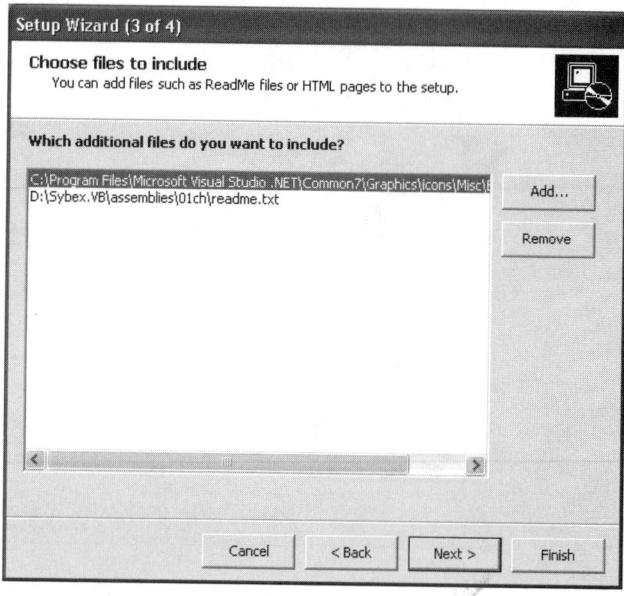

5. Click Next. A summary screen displays the information gathered so far.

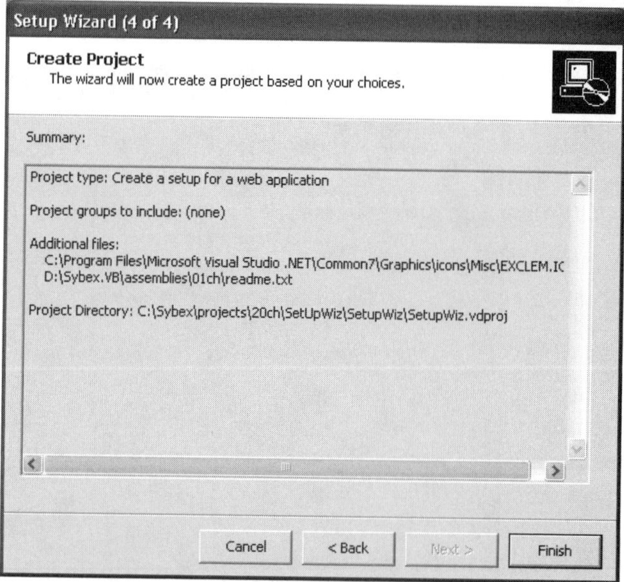

6. Click Finish. A solution containing the Setup project has been created and added to the Solution Explorer.

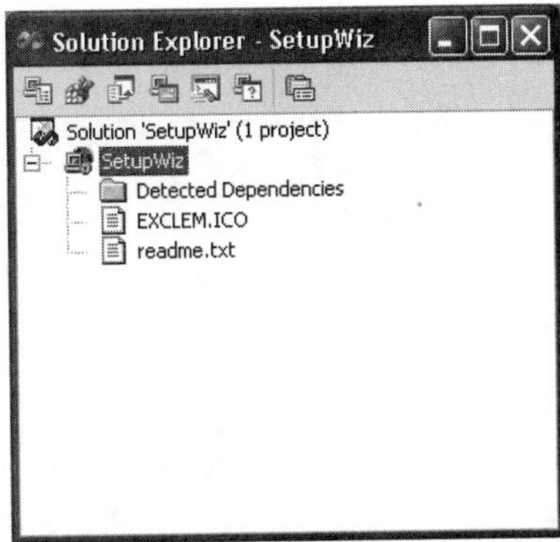

After you've completed the Wizard, the next step is to add an existing project to the solution containing the Web Setup project (choose File ➢ Add Project ➢ Existing Project).

Finishing the Web Setup Project

After you've run the Setup Wizard to create your Web Setup project, you can then add the project output to the Setup project. Select the root node of the Setup project, right-click, and select Add ➢ Project Output. In the Add Project Output dialog, make sure Primary Output is selected, as shown in Figure 20.10, and click OK.

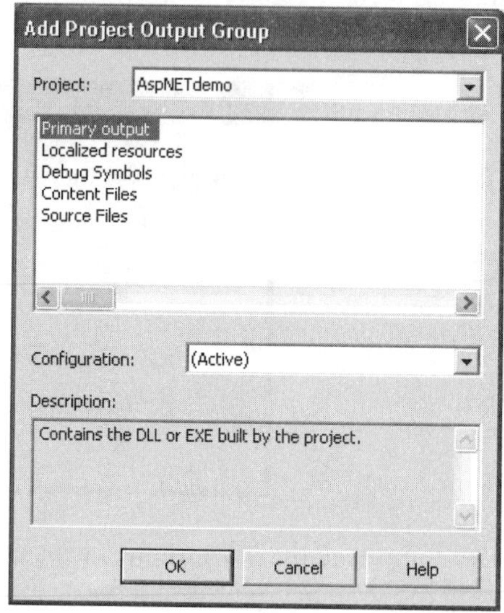

FIGURE 20.10: The Add Project Output Group dialog is used to add the output of the Web Setup project to the solution.

Next, make changes to the Web Setup project settings using the various editors, as described in the "Configuring the Setup Project" section earlier in this chapter.

You can then proceed to build the Web Setup project, as shown in Figure 20.11.

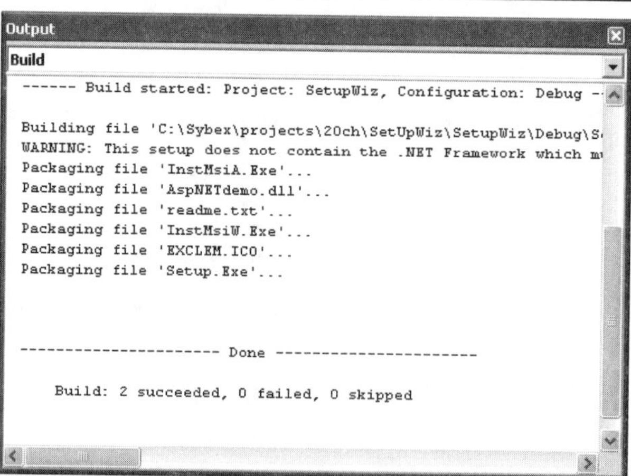

FIGURE 20.11: The Output window shows the results of building the Web Setup project.

Finally, run the installation program. The Setup Wizard will prompt you to select an installation—or virtual—address, as shown in Figure 20.12. The virtual address (and the port designation, which you can also see in Figure 20.12) becomes the portion of the URL for the project following the hostname (and the name of the folder created for the project on the web server).

FIGURE 20.12:
You can select a virtual address for your project.

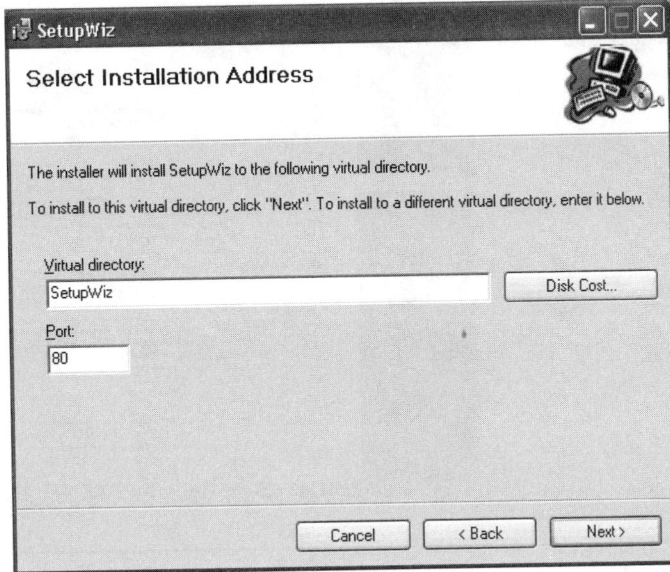

Web Hosting Built into VB .NET

As mentioned earlier in the chapter, VB .NET offers automatic uploading of .NET web projects to web service providers. Most of these service providers provide some sort of free hosting, at least on a trial basis.

To access this automatic upload feature, display the Visual Studio Start page (by selecting Help ➢ Show Start Page). Next, select Web Hosting from the Start menu. A list of Premier and Additional Providers will be displayed, as shown in Figure 20.13.

Prior to uploading a project, you will need to set up an account. Just click one of the Signup links provided by the individual providers. Once you have an account, you can automatically upload your projects to an environment that hosts the .NET Framework by clicking the Upload link and entering your user identification. (The Premier Providers also deploy the .NET Enterprise Servers, including SQL Server.) You will then be able to upload projects or files to a provider such as Unisys, using the interface shown in Figure 20.14.

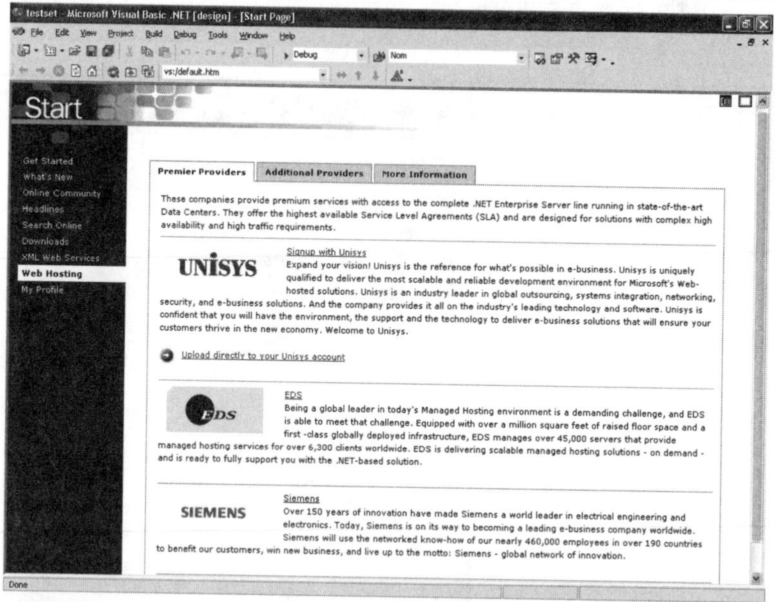

FIGURE 20.13: You can automatically upload your web projects to specified service providers, who generally will supply a free trial account.

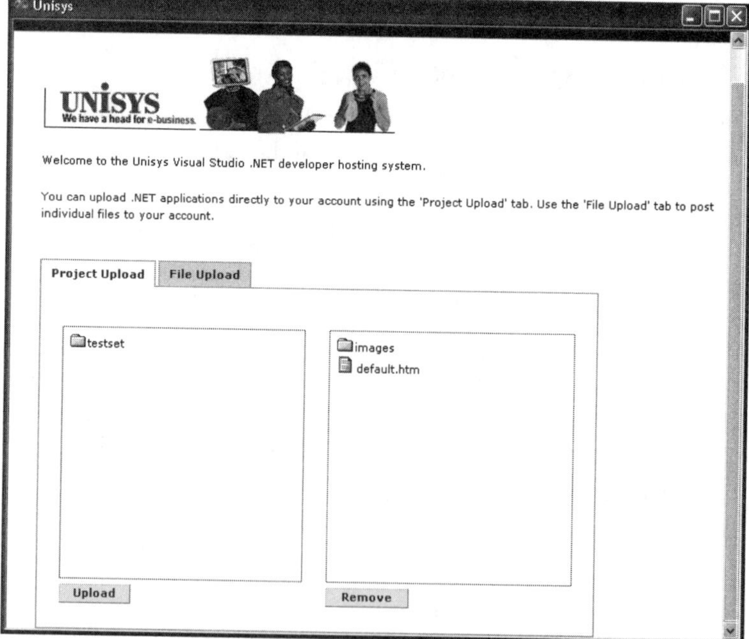

FIGURE 20.14: You can upload projects and files to a service provider such as Unisys from within Visual Studio.

Summary

Whether you like your setups and deployments plain or fancy, the facilities in Visual Studio .NET will help you put them together. In many cases, it's easy and very convenient to simply copy executable files to a system running the .NET Framework—no-touch deployment is certainly a great thing! If you need an installation program, it's not a big deal to use one of the VB .NET setup and deployment projects to conjure up exactly what you need.

Appendix A

Using VB .NET's Help System

No matter how experienced a programmer you are, sometimes you need help understanding a concept or term, or figuring out how a feature works. The auto-completion features of the Code Editor make it less likely that you'll need help with basic language syntax or with knowing the members of an object. But it's still the case that nobody knows everything, and one of the most important skills in an environment as complex as VB .NET is being able to find help when you need it.

Like the Help systems of earlier versions of VB, which I have dubbed "the good, the big, and the ugly," VB .NET's Help system is comprehensive, overwhelming, and not always terribly well organized. It's sufficiently complex to use that you may find yourself referring to the Help on Help topic to understand how the various features work. (To access this topic, choose Help ➢ Help on Help.) Often, the only way to find what you're looking for is to browse through a great many topics. The good news is that one innovative feature, Dynamic Help, can make your life a great deal easier.

This appendix briefly explains the mechanics of how to use the Dynamic Help, Contents, Index, Search, and filtering features of the VB .NET Help system.

Dynamic Help

Dynamic Help is a form of context-sensitive help in which a window provides links to Help topics, depending on the selection in the development environment. To activate Dynamic Help, select Help ➢ Dynamic Help or press Ctrl+F1 on the keyboard. The Dynamic Help window will open.

NOTE Depending on how you have your Visual Studio environment set up, Dynamic Help may appear as a tab in another window, such as the Properties window, rather than in a separate window.

As you can see in Figure A.1, which shows the links in the Dynamic Help window when the MainMenu control is selected in the Toolbox, the Dynamic Help window provides information about whatever is currently active in the environment, which can be very helpful, indeed!

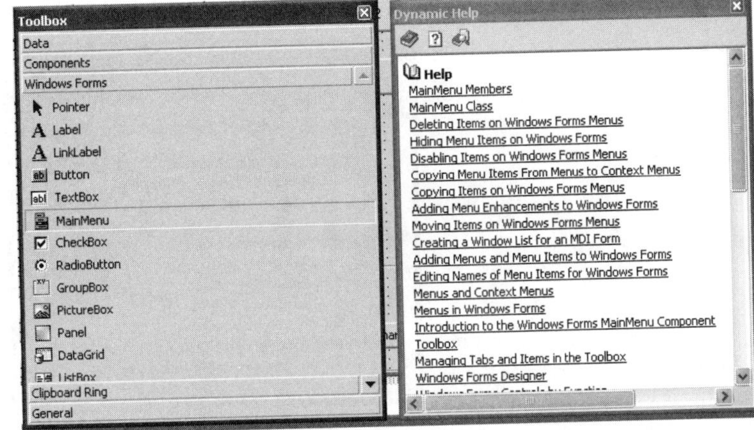

FIGURE A.1: When the MainMenu control is selected, Dynamic Help shows topics related to the MainMenu.

Contents

The Contents window is used to drill down to find information using nodes and links. To open the Contents window, select Help ➢ Contents. The Contents window will open with a few top nodes showing.

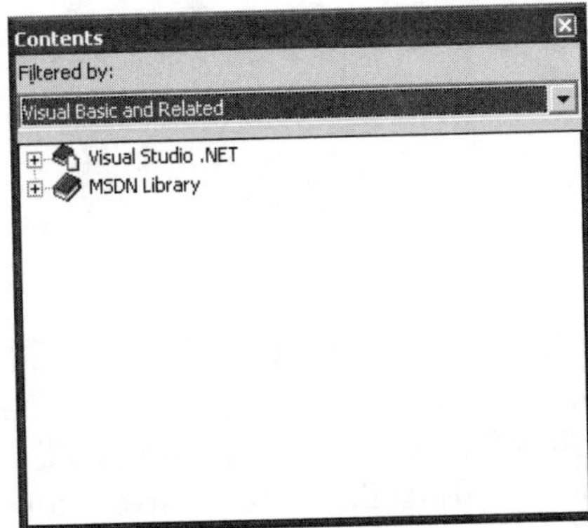

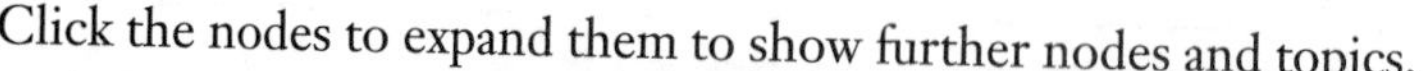

Click the nodes to expand them to show further nodes and topics.

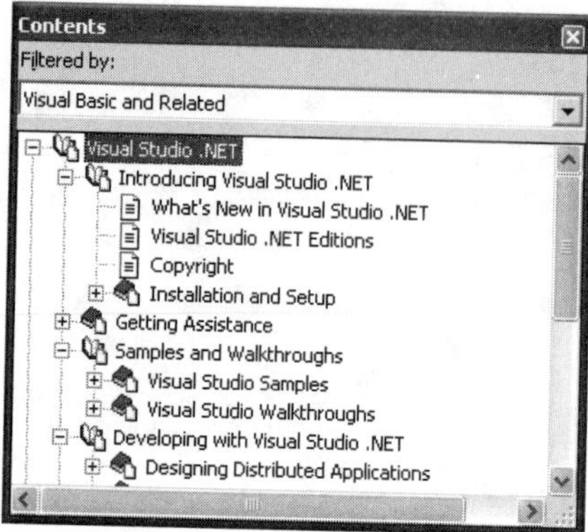

Select a topic to display it. Undoubtedly, it will show further links. Figure A.2 shows an example of the Visual Studio .NET topic page.

FIGURE A.2:

Selecting a topic in the Contents window takes you to the topic's Help page.

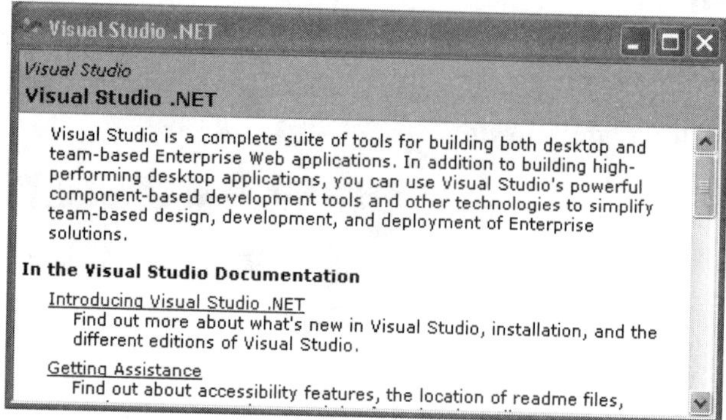

The Contents window, like the Index and Search windows, can be filtered by topic, so that it will show only the information related to the filter. Use the Filtered By drop-down list at the top-left side of the window to choose a filter. You'll most likely want to filter information using the Visual Basic or Visual Basic and Related settings. For more information, see the "Filtering" section later in this appendix.

Index

The Index window allows you to look for specific information. To open the Index window, select Help ➢ Index. With the Index window open, enter the term you are searching for in the Look For box.

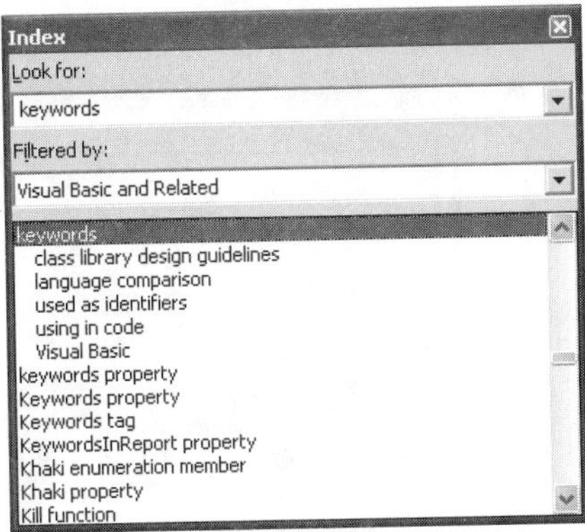

A list of indexed terms, based on the phrase you entered, will appear in the bottom pane of the Index window. If you select a term in the bottom pane, the Index Results window will open, showing all the indexed listings for the term.

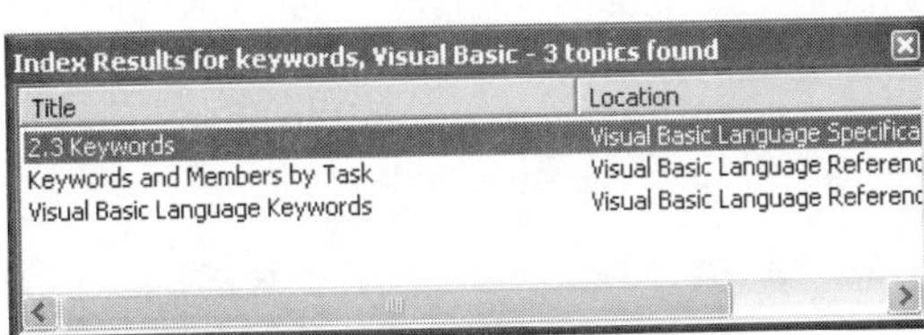

If you double-click a listing in the Index Results window, the topic will open for viewing.

NOTE If there is only one topic indexed for a given search phrase, it will open immediately when you select it in the Index window (rather than opening the Index Results window).

You can open the Index Results window directly once you have already done a search by selecting Help ➢ Index Results.

Search

The Search window works like the Index window, except that it produces more "hits" because it searches within Help documents, not just on the indexed titles.

To open the Search window, select Help ➢ Search. The Search window offers four options:

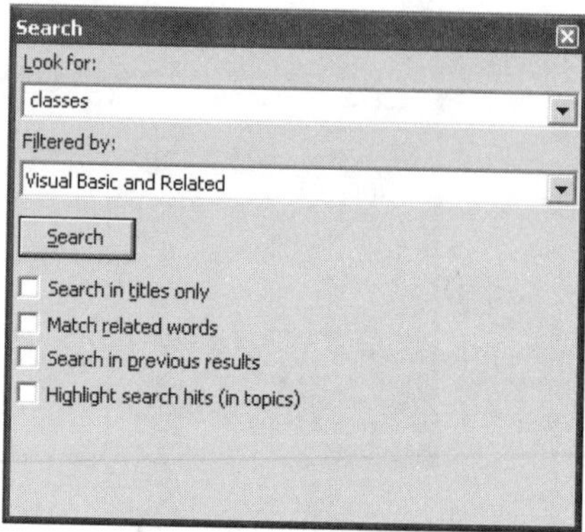

TIP The Search window is the tool I use most frequently to locate information. I find the ability to search through previous results particularly useful.

As opposed to the Index Results window, the Search Results window is likely to show a great many hits—possibly in the hundreds.

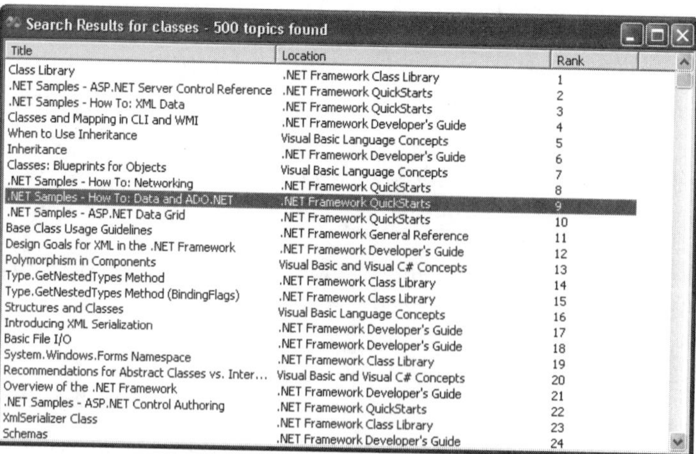

You can open the Search Results window directly once you have already done a search by selecting Help ➢ Search Results.

TIP Many of the topics that result from searches are sections of larger articles. For example, you may see "Caching Versions of a Page" show up in the Search Results window. It's part of a larger topic called "ASP.NET Caching Features," but how would you know? When you have a topic open, you can click the Sync Contents icon in the toolbar (the one that looks like a horizontal, double-headed arrow), and it will show you where the topic fits in the grand scheme of Help information (by displaying the topic's location in the Contents window).

Filtering Help Results

As I noted in the section on the Contents window, Help results can be filtered using the Filtered By drop-down list in the Contents, Index, or Search window.

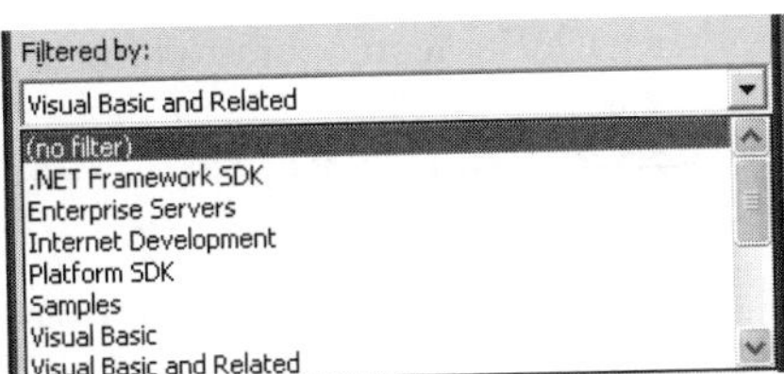

To turn off filtering, select (no filter) in this drop-down list. However, it is likely that you will wish to filter by Visual Basic or Visual Basic and Related, simply to keep your Help searches manageable. (.NET Framework SDK is another very useful filter.)

NOTE You can also set the Help filter on your Start page. To do this, show your Start page by selecting Help ➢ Show Start Page. With the Start page open, select My Profile, and set the Help filter using the drop-down box.

It is an interesting fact that you can customize filters and create new filters using Boolean criteria, as though you were writing the `WHERE` clause of a SQL query (which is likely exactly what you are doing under the covers!).

To open the Edit Help Filters window, select Help ➢ Edit Filters. Using the Edit Help Filters window, you can edit the definition of a current filter or select New from the menu bar to create a new filter. To edit a filter, first select it in the Filter drop-down list. Figure A.3 shows an example of the Edit Help Filters window with the Visual Basic and Related filter selected.

FIGURE A.3:

You can use the Edit Help Filters window to customize Help filters using a Boolean syntax.

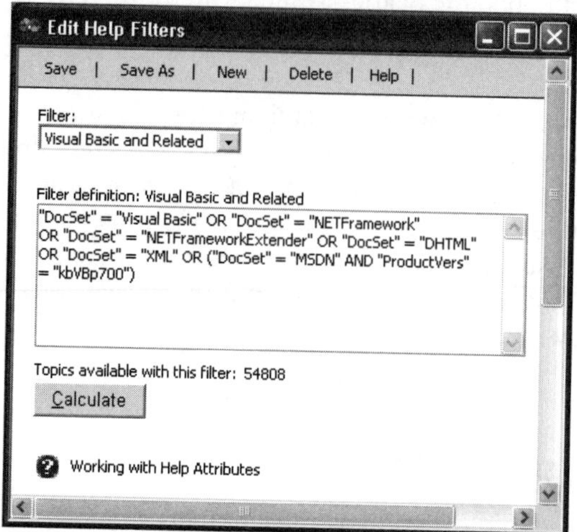

At the bottom of the Edit Help Filters window, you'll find a list of the available attributes that can be used together with Boolean operators to create a filter definition.

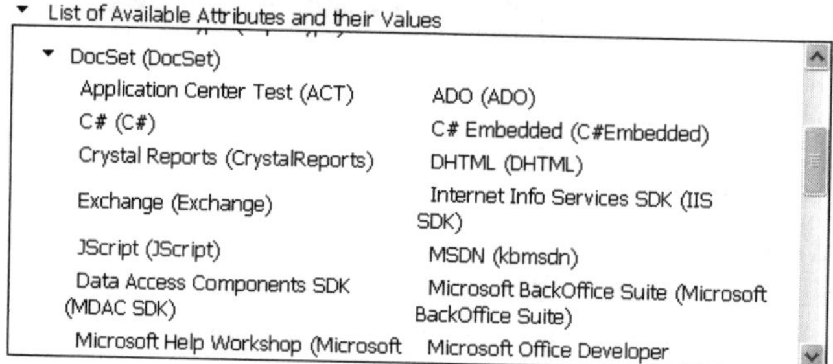

To find out how many topics are included in a given filter, click the Calculate button in the Edit Help Filters window. For example, you may find it relevant to know that the Visual Basic filter has 9,590 topics, and the Visual Basic and Related filter has 54,808 topics. This gives you an idea of the comparative breadth of each topic.

Appendix B

Migrating Applications from VB6 to VB .NET

There are no easy answers to the question of how to convert a VB6 application to a VB .NET application, or even if it's a good idea to attempt to do so. This is a decision that must be made on a case-by-case basis, depending on many factors. You'll want to consider the size of the project, the resources available, and the benefits to be gained. In some cases, it just makes more sense to leave an application in VB6, particularly if many features the application relies on are no longer supported in VB .NET, or the application is unlikely to need further enhancements.

Certainly, a conversion will often be nontrivial, and it might make sense to deploy VB .NET applications, such as ASP.NET web applications, along with legacy applications (such as old-style ASP web applications), rather than attempting to upgrade everything at once. If you do decide to convert a VB6 application, it makes sense to regard the original application as a working prototype, rather than something that will be converted on a line-by-line basis to the new paradigm. You'll likely want to reengineer the application to be more in keeping with VB .NET's object-oriented flavor. (On the other hand, some case studies have found that a migration takes only 10 percent as long as a rewrite.)

A good starting place for considering how to migrate a VB6 application is the "Upgrading from Visual Basic 6.0" Help topic (see Appendix A, "Using VB .NET's Help System"). You should also take a look at Appendix C, "Key Syntax Differences Between VB6 and VB .NET."

Important Unsupported Features

Some features that were important to VB6 (and previous versions of VB) are not supported in VB .NET. If your legacy application relies heavily on these features, it may not be a good candidate for conversion. Important unsupported features include the following:

- OLE Container Control
- Dynamic Data Exchange (DDE)
- DAO or RDO Data Binding (see Chapter 17, "Working with Data and ADO.NET," to learn about the replacement for these technologies)
- VB5 versions of the Windows Common controls and Data-bound Grid control
- DHTML applications
- ActiveX documents
- Property Pages
- User controls
- Web classes

As you can see, many of these unsupported features involve working with OLE (Object Linking and Embedding) and ActiveX or older controls. Part of the point of the .NET Framework is to phase out OLE, ActiveX, and, yes, even COM.

Guidelines for Successful Conversion Projects

It's one thing to convert a small project like many of the examples shown in this book, and it's quite another to convert a deployed, complex application that may include thousands of lines of code written by many different people. To successfully convert a large project, it's important that you follow sound practices. These include the following:

- Create a migration plan.
- Use the native object-oriented programming features of VB .NET in an object-oriented style.
- Don't convert VB6 portions of an application if it doesn't make sense to do so.
- Create a coding-standards document that covers topics such as variable-naming conventions and using constants rather than numerical values.
- Perform rigorous code reviews.
- Take the time to educate all programmers working on a project about .NET (well, maybe that's what this book is for!).
- Run programs at all times with Option Strict and Option Explicit turned on, so that variable declarations, strict typing, and explicit conversions are enforced. (You may want to get the upgraded application working first, and then go this extra step as a second stage.)
- Consider reworking the application architecture to use XML and web services to facilitate interoperability.

The Upgrade Wizard

The easiest way to get a start on converting a VB6 project—and get an idea of how much work is involved in doing the conversion—is to run the Upgrade Wizard.

To start the Upgrade Wizard, open a VB6 project in VB .NET. The Upgrade Wizard starts automatically, as shown in Figure B.1.

FIGURE B.1:

When you open a VB6 project in VB .NET, the Upgrade Wizard starts automatically.

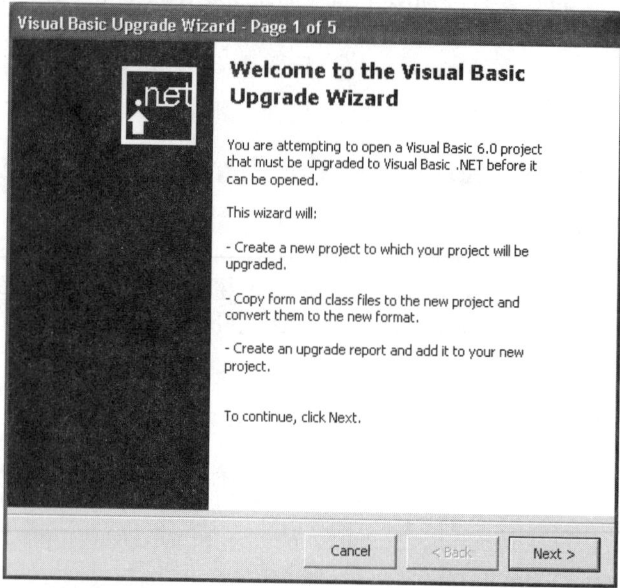

The Wizard creates a new VB .NET project for the conversion and places it in a folder you designate, as shown in Figure B.2.

FIGURE B.2:

The Wizard creates a new VB .NET project structure for the converted application in a location that you designate.

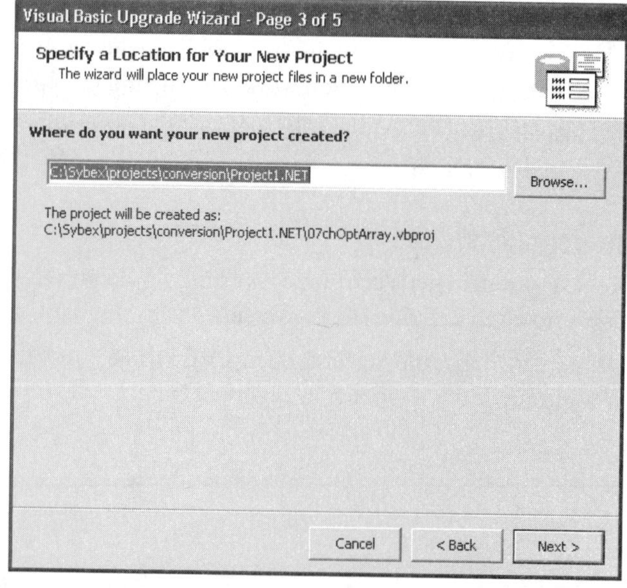

When the Wizard is complete, you'll see items in the Task List related to the conversion.

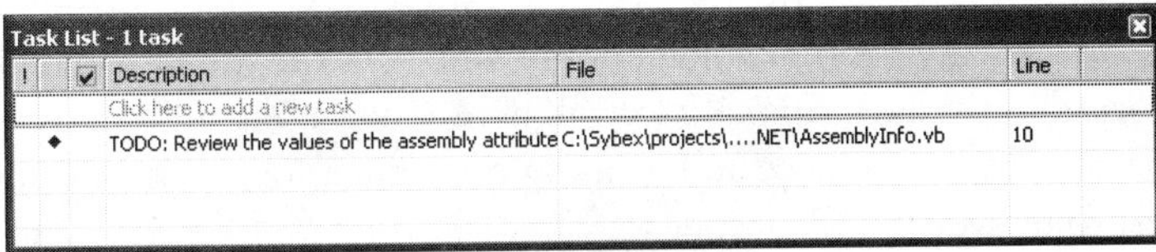

You'll also see an Upgrade Report added to the converted project in the Solution Explorer.

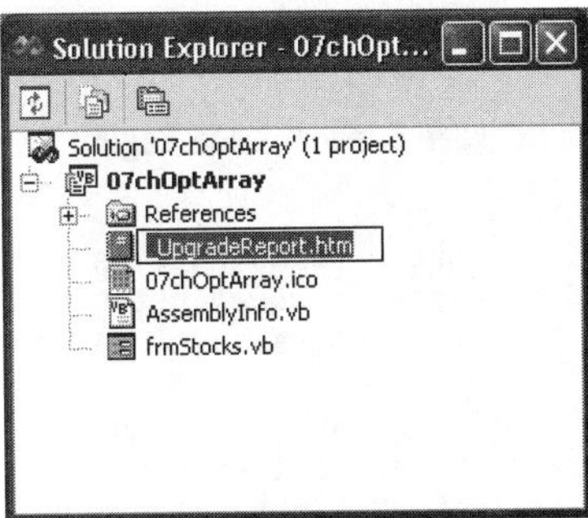

Double-click the Upgrade Report in the Solution Explorer to see details of any errors, warnings, or issues that the Wizard may have encountered. In a small project like the one shown in the examples here, there may not be any problems, as you can see in the Upgrade Report in Figure B.3.

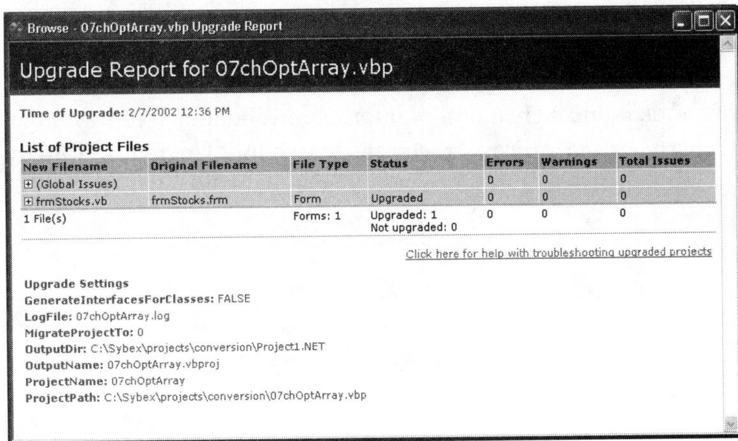

FIGURE B.3:
An Upgrade Report for the converted project is added to the Solution Explorer.

The next step is to review the items in the Task List, and then see if the newly converted project will build. Assuming the program runs without problems—and, actually, the Wizard does a surprisingly good job much of the time—it's time to have a look at the code created by the Wizard. Most likely, the Wizard will have added a reference to the `Microsoft.VisualBasic.Compatability` namespace and be using the compatibility classes, rather than attempting to convert to native VB .NET code.

You should also notice the Upgrade Support code region, which will be added to form modules, as shown in Listing B.1. You'll see that this would not be how you would go about coding a VB .NET form if you were doing it from the ground up.

Listing B.1 The Upgrade Support Code Region

```
#Region "Upgrade Support "
   Private Shared m_vb6FormDefInstance As frmSecurity
   Private Shared m_InitializingDefInstance As Boolean
   Public Shared Property DefInstance() As frmSecurity
      Get
         If m_vb6FormDefInstance Is Nothing _
            OrElse m_vb6FormDefInstance.IsDisposed Then
            m_InitializingDefInstance = True
            m_vb6FormDefInstance = New frmSecurity()
            m_InitializingDefInstance = False
         End If
         DefInstance = m_vb6FormDefInstance
      End Get
      Set
         m_vb6FormDefInstance = Value
      End Set
   End Property
#End Region
```

You'll find a great deal of information about upgrading on the Microsoft website. Go to `http://msdn.microsoft.com` and search for "Upgrading VB6 to VB .NET" for links to the relevant articles.

Appendix C

Key Syntax Differences Between VB6 and VB .NET

There are a great many differences between VB6 and VB .NET. In some ways, the most important changes are conceptual, rather than having to do with syntax or language. To understand these changes, a good starting place is to read this book. Another useful reference is the "Introduction to Visual Basic .NET for Visual Basic Veterans" Help topic and the links within that topic. (See Appendix A, "Using VB .NET's Help System.")

This appendix lists most of the changed programming elements and their replacements in VB .NET (if they exist).

VB6 Programming Element	VB .NET Equivalent
Abs function	Abs method
AscB function	Asc function
As Any keyword phrase	Disable Option Strict or use function overloading
Atn function	Atan method
Calendar property	CurrentCulture property
ChDir statement	ChDir function
ChDrive statement	ChDrive function
Chr$ and ChrB functions	Chr function
Close statement	FileClose function
Cos function	Cos method
Currency data type	Decimal data type
CVDate function	DateValue function
CVError function	Error statement
Date function and Date statement	Now and Today properties
Date$ function	DateString property
Debug.Assert method	Assert and Fail methods
Debug.Print method	Write, WriteIf, WriteLine, and WriteLineIf methods
Deftype statements	Not supported in VB .NET
DeleteSetting statement	DeleteSetting function
DoEvents function	DoEvents method
Empty keyword	Nothing keyword
Eqv operator	= operator
Exp function	Exp method
FileCopy statement	FileCopy function
Get statement	FileGet function
GoSub statement	Not supported in VB .NET
Initialize event	Sub New statement
Imp operator	For Boolean logic, the statement `X = A Imp B` would return true unless A is true and B is false; in VB .NET, this is written as `X = (Not A) or B`

Continued on next page

VB6 Programming Element	VB .NET Equivalent
Input # and Input$ statements; Input$, InputB, and InputB$ functions	Input function
Instancing property	In VB6, you could set the instancing property of a class to `GlobalMultiUse`; with VB .NET, you use static methods to accomplish the same thing
InStrB function	InStr function
IsEmpty function	IsNothing function
IsMissing function	Not supported in VB .NET; all optional arguments must have default values, so it's impossible for them to be "missing"
IsNull function	IsDbNull function
IsObject function	IsReference function
Kill statement	Kill function
LCase$ function	LCase function
Left$, LeftB, and LeftB$ functions	Left function
LenB function	Len function
Let and Set assignment statements	Not needed in VB .NET; the new Set statement is unrelated to the VB6 one
Line Input # statement	LineInput function
Lock statement	Lock and Unlock functions
Log function	Log method
LSet and RSet statements	LSet function, PadRight, and PadLeft functions
LTrim$ function	LTrim function
MidB function	Mid function
MidB statement	Mid statement
MkDir statement	MkDir function
Name statement	Rename function
Now function	Now property
Null keyword	Nothingkeyword
Oct$ function	Oct function
On ... GoSub	Not supported in VB .NET; use Select Case statement
On ... GoTo construction	Not supported in VB .NET; use Select Case statement
Open statement	FileOpen function
Option Base statement	Not supported in VB .NET; all VB .NET arrays are zero based
Option Private Module statement	Not supported in VB .NET; use Module statement
Print # statement	Print and PrintLine functions
Property Get, Property Let, and Property Set statements	VB .NET has a different syntax for property procedures
Put statement	FilePut function
Reset statement	Reset function

Continued on next page

VB6 Programming Element	VB .NET Equivalent
Right$ and RightB functions	Right function
RmDir statement	RmDir function
Round function	Round method
RSet and LSet statements	RSet function
RTrim$ function	RTrim function
SaveSetting statement	SaveSetting function
Scale method	Not supported in VB .NET (VB .NET does not use twips; everything is in pixels)
Set and Let assignment statements	Not needed in VB .NET; the new Set statement is unrelated to the VB6 one
SetAttr statement	SetAttr function
Sgn function	Sign function
Sin function	Sin method
Sqr function	Sqrt function
String function	String constructor
String ($) functions	Not needed in VB .NET
Terminate event	Not supported in VB .NET; use Sub Dispose and Sub Finalize statements
Time function and Time statement	TimeOfDay property; see DateTime structure and Date data type
Time$ function	TimeString property
Timer function	Timer property
Trim$ function	LTrim, RTrim, and Trim functions
Type statement	Structure statement
UCase$ function	UCase function
Unlock statement	Lock and Unlock functions
Variant data type	Object data type
Wend keyword	While...End While statements and End statement
Width # statement	FileWidth function
Write # statement	Write and WriteLine functions

Appendix D

VB .NET Keywords

This appendix lists the VB .NET language keywords, which are reserved, meaning they cannot be used in a program as an identifier. Note that several of these (such as Let and Variant) are reserved, even though they are no longer used in VB.

AddHandler	AddressOf	Alias	And
AndAlso	Ansi	As	Assembly
Auto	Boolean	ByRef	Byte
ByVal	Call	Case	Catch
CBool	CByte	CChar	CDate
CDec	CDbl	Char	CInt
Class	CLng	CObj	Const
CShort	CSng	CStr	CType
Date	Decimal	Declare	Default
Delegate	Dim	DirectCast	Do
Double	Each	Else	ElseIf
End	Enum	Erase	Error
Event	Exit	#ExternalSource	False
Finally	For	Friend	Function
Get	GetType	GoTo	Handles
If	Implements	Imports	In
Inherits	Integer	Interface	Is
Let	Lib	Like	Long
Loop	Me	Mod	Module
MustInherit	MustOverride	MyBase	MyClass
Namespace	New	Next	Not
Nothing	NotInheritable	NotOverridable	Object
On	Option	Optional	Or
OrElse	Overloads	Overridable	Overrides
ParamArray	Preserve	Private	Property
Protected	Public	RaiseEvent	ReadOnly
ReDim	#Region	REM	RemoveHandler
Resume	Return	Select	Set
Shadows	Shared	Short	Single
Static	Step	Stop	String
Structure	Sub	SyncLock	Then
Throw	To	True	Try
TypeOf	Unicode	Until	Variant
When	While	With	WithEvents
WriteOnly	Xor	#Const	#ExternalSource
#If...Then...#Else	#Region		

Appendix E

Selected VB .NET Namespaces and Classes

The .NET Framework is built using libraries of classes that are contained in namespaces. This means that to be an effective VB .NET developer, you must learn all you can about namespaces. The online Help system provides a great deal of information about namespaces and their purpose (the "Class Library" topic is a good starting place; see Appendix A, "Using VB .NET's Help System"). Spending some time with the Object Browser, as explained in Chapter 14, "Using the Object Browser," is also a good way to become familiar with classes and the namespaces that contain them.

Some of the namespaces that are likely to be most important to VB .NET programmers are described in this appendix.

Namespace	Description
Microsoft.VisualBasic	Contains the runtime used with the VB .NET language, as well as classes that support VB .NET compilation and code generation
Microsoft.VisualBasic.Compatability	Contains classes that support backward compatibility with VB6 projects
System	Contains fundamental classes that define types, arrays, strings, events, event handlers, exceptions, interfaces, data-type conversion, mathematics, application environment management, and much more
System.Collections	Includes a set of classes that lets you manage collections of objects, such as lists, queues, arrays, hash tables, and dictionaries
System.Data	Consists mainly of the classes that comprise the ADO.NET architecture
System.Diagnostics	Provides classes used for debugging, tracing, and interacting with system processes, event logs, and performance counters
System.Drawing	Contains classes that provide access to GDI+ basic graphics functionality (namespaces that are hierarchically beneath System.Drawing—including System.Drawing.Drawing2D, and System.Drawing.Text—provide more advanced and specific GDI+ graphics functionality)
System.IO	Contains types and classes used for reading and writing to data streams and files, and general input/output (I/O) functionality
System.Reflection	Contains classes and interfaces that provide type inspection and the ability to dynamically bind objects
System.Text	Contains classes used for character encoding, converting blocks of characters to and from blocks of bytes, and more
System.Text.RegularExpressions	Contains classes that provide access to the .NET Framework regular expression engine
System.Timer	Provides the Timer component (see Chapter 10, "Using Timers, EventLogs, and ServiceControllers")
System.Web	Contains the classes that are used to facilitate browser-server communication and other web-related functionality

Continued on next page

Namespace	Description
System.Web.Services	Contains the classes used to build and consume web services
System.Web.UI	Provides classes and interfaces used in the creation of the user interface of web pages and controls
System.Windows.Forms	Contains the classes for creating a Windows-based user interface
System.XML	Provides classes that support processing XML

Index

Note to the Reader: Throughout this index **boldfaced** page numbers indicate primary discussions of a topic. *Italicized* page numbers indicate illustrations.

SYMBOLS

A

B

C

D

E

F

G

H

I

N

O

P

Q

R

S

T

U

V

W

X

Y

The quotation on the bottom of the front cover is taken from the sixty-fourth chapter of Lao Tzu's Tao Te Ching, *the classic work of Taoist philosophy. This particular verse is from the translation by D. C. Lau (copyright 1963) and communicates the idea that wisdom and maturity have humble origins. The same chapter includes the more well-known verse "a journey of a thousand miles starts from beneath one's feet."*

It is traditionally held that Lao Tzu lived in the fifth century B.C. in China, during the Chou dynasty, but it is unclear whether he was actually a historical figure. It is said that he was a teacher of Confucius. The concepts embodied in the Tao Te Ching *influenced religious thinking in the Far East, including Zen Buddhism in Japan. Many in the West, however, have wrongly understood the* Tao Te Ching *to be primarily a mystical work; in fact, much of the advice in the book is grounded in a practical moral philosophy governing personal conduct.*